RASPUTIN
THE LAST WORD

Edvard Radzinsky

Translated from the Russian by
Judson Rosengrant

Weidenfeld & Nicolson
LONDON

First published in Great Britain in 2000
by Weidenfeld & Nicolson

Published simultaneously
in the United States of America
by Nan A. Talese, an imprint of
Doubleday.

A CIP catalogue record for this book is available
from the British Library.

ISBN 0 297 81975-5

Typeset by Selwood Systems, Midsomer Norton

Set in Bembo

Printed in Great Britain by
Butler & Tanner Ltd, Frome and London

Weidenfeld & Nicolson

The Orion Publishing Group Ltd
Orion House
5 Upper Saint Martin's Lane
London, WC2H 9EA

Dating

The Old Style of reckoning (the Julian calendar) was in use in Russia until February 1918, when the New Style (the Gregorian calendar) was adopted by the omission of thirteen days. Therefore, 1 February (OS) became 14 February (NS). The New Style was already in general use in the rest of Europe. In this book, the dates are Old Style unless otherwise indicated.

Currencies

From 1897, when Russia returned to the Gold Standard, to 1917 the rouble was worth approximately 10 roubles to £1 or 2 roubles to $1.

Language

The author and the translator have wherever possible been true to the language of the period, while aware that a word such as 'Yid' has offensive contemporary connotations.

Letters, diaries and reports quoted have not been modernised. The tsarina Alexandra's letters were written in an idiosyncratic English. The quirkiness of her spelling and grammar has usually been silently corrected.

The city of St Petersburg became Petrograd in 1914. The author and translator have generally followed the colloquial usage and call it Petersburg. There are some characters, however, who refer to it inconsistently and we have followed their usage.

Contents

Illustrations

The corpse of Rasputin[6]
An example of the cartoons published after Rasputin's death[2]

———

Sources
1 Russian State Archive
2 State Historical Archive, St Petersburg
3 Weidenfeld & Nicolson archive
4 Yusupov Palace Museum, St Petersburg
5 Krasnogorsk Archive
6 Museum of Political History, St Petersburg

Cast of Principal Characters

Grigory Efimovich Rasputin (Grishka, Grisha, Our Friend)

The Romanovs

Nicholas II (Nicky, Papa), tsar of Russia, 1894-1917. Son of Alexander III and his Danish wife Marie, married to Alexandra of Hesse-Darmstadt, cousin of King George V.

Alexandra Fyodorovna (Alix, Mama, the Empress), married to Nicholas II, tsarina of Russia, 1894-1917. Youngest daughter of Grand Duke Ludwig of Hesse, granddaughter of Queen Victoria, cousin of Kaiser Wilhelm II.

Tsarevich Alexei (Little One, Sunbeam, Baby), only son of Nicholas and Alexandra, heir to the Russian throne

Grand Duchess Olga Nikolaevna, oldest daughter of Nicholas and Alexandra

Grand Duchess Tatyana Nikolaevna, second daughter of Nicholas and Alexandra

Dowager Empress Marie Fyodorovna (Aunt Minnie), widow of Tsar Alexander III, mother of Nicholas. Daughter of King Christian IX of Denmark

Grand Duke Mikhail Alexandrovich (Misha), younger brother of Nicholas, and briefly his successor as tsar

Grand Duchess Olga Alexandrovna, sister of Nicholas, married (1) Pyotr, Duke of Oldenburg; (2) Nikolai Kulikovsky

Grand Duke Alexander Mikhailovich (Sandro), cousin of Nicholas, married Xenia, father-in-law to Felix Yusopov

Grand Duchess Xenia Alexandrovna, sister of Nicholas, wife of Grand Duke Alexander Mikhailovich (Sandro), mother of Irina

Grand Duke Nikolai Mikhailovich, brother of Sandro, cousin to Nicholas and well-known historian

Grand Duke Pyotr Nikolaevich, cousin of

Nicholas, married to Militsa of Montenegro

Princess Militsa Nikolaevna ('the black princess'), sister of Princess Anastasia (Stana), daughter of Montenegrin king, married to Grand Duke Pyotr

Grand Duke Nikolai Nikolaevich (Nikolasha, N, 'the dread uncle'), brother of Grand Duke Pyotr, uncle to Nicholas, married to Anastasia of Montenegro, and Commander-in-Chief, Russian forces at the start of World War One.

Princess Anastasia (Stana, 'the black princess'), sister of Princess Militsa, daughter of Montenegrin king, married (2) Grand Duke Nikolai Nikolaevich

Grand Duke Konstantin Konstantinovich (KR), celebrated poet, uncle to Nicholas

Grand Duchess Elizaveta Fyodorovna (Ella), sister of the tsarina, wife of Grand Duke Sergei Alexandrovich; later abbess of a convent

Grand Duke Pavel Alexandrovich, uncle to Nicholas, father of Dmitry, married (2) Olga Pistolkors

Princess Olga Valerianovna, married (1) Major General Erik Pistolkors; (2) Grand Duke Pavel Alexandrovich

Grand Duke Dmitry Pavlovich, son of Pavel Alexandrovich by his first marriage, cousin of Nicholas, friend of Felix Yusupov

Prince Felix Yusupov (also Count Sumarokov-Elston), married to Irina, daughter of Grand Duke Alexander Mikhailovich (Sandro), and Grand Duchess Xenia Alexandrovna

Grand Duchess Irina, daughter of Grand Duke Alexander Mikhailovich (Sandro), and Grand Duchess Xenia Alexandrovna. Married to Felix Yusupov

Princess Zinaida Yusupova, mother of Felix and Nikolai Yusupov

Prince Nikolai Yusupov, elder brother of Felix Yusupov

Court and society

Pyotr Badmaev (the cunning Chinaman), Siberian Asian entrepreneur and businessman, society doctor of Tibetan medicine, herbalist, and healer

A. Bogdanovich, contemporary diarist, monarchist, and general's wife, hostess of leading political salon in St Petersburg

Yulia Alexandrovna von Dehn (Lili), senior captain's wife, relative of Anya Vyrubova, confidante of the tsarina, member of Rasputin's circle

Pierre Gilliard, tutor to the royal children

Colonel Dmitry Loman, former officer in Life Guards, court administrator, friend of the Lokhtins, warden of Feodor Cathedral, and follower of Rasputin

Mikhail Novosyolov, member of Ella's circle, assistant professor of Moscow Theological Seminary and editor

Monsieur Philippe (Our Friend, Our First Friend), French magus and alleged healer

Captain Nikolai Pavlovich Sablin (NP), senior captain and master of the royal yacht *Standart*

Sophia Tyutcheva, maid of honour and governess to the royal children, friend of Filippov

Maria Vishnyakova (Mary), nurse to the royal children

Feodosia Voino, doctor's assistant, Anna Vyrubova's maid

Nadezhda Voskoboikinova, widow of a Cossack officer, senior nurse at Tsarskoe Selo infirmary, member of Rasputin's circle

Anya Vyrubova, née Taneeva (Friend, The Friend, Ania, Anushka), lady in waiting to and close friend of the tsarina, sister of Alexandra Pistolkors, member of Rasputin's circle

Akim Zhuk, medical orderly seconded to care for Vyrubova, nurse at Tsarskoe Selo infirmary

The political circle

Pyotr Bark, minister of finance 1914-17

Stephan Beletsky, director of Department of Police

Vladimir Dzhunkovsky, governor of Moscow; deputy minister of internal affairs, head of the political police

Ivan Goremykin, prime minister 1914-16

Alexander Ivanovich Guchkov, Speaker of the Third Duma

Alexei Khvostov ('Fat Belly', 'The Tail'), right-wing anti-Semite, minister for internal affairs 1915-16

Vladimir Kokovtsev, senator and finance minister; prime minister 1911-14

Colonel Mikhail Komissarov (Our Colonel), police officer and head of Rasputin's bodyguard

A. A. Makarov, minister of internal affairs, later minister of justice

Vasily Maklakov, member of Constitutional Democrat Party, minister of internal affairs

Maurice Paléologue, French ambassador

Alexander Protopopov (General Kalinin), Deputy Speaker of the Duma, then minister of internal affairs 1916-17

V. M. Purishkevich, anti-Semite monarchist and member of the Duma

Mikhail Rodzyanko, Speaker of the Third and Fourth Dumas

Prince Scherbatov, liberal, minister of internal affairs

P. A. Stolypin, prime minister 1906-11; assassinated Kiev, 1911

Boris Sturmer ('Old Chap'), prime minister

Vladimir Sukhomlinov, minister for war

Count Sergei Witte, finance minister, prime minister 1905-6

The ecclesiastics

Alexis, disgraced bishop of Tobolsk, head of 1912 Tobolsk Consistory investigation, father of Leonid Molchanov, Khlyst sympathiser

Feofan, Alexandra's confessor, church hierarch, mystic and ascetic, inspector and rector of the St Petersburg Theological Seminary; later bishop of Poltava

Hermogen, bishop of Saratov, head of Tobolsk eparchy

Iliodor ('the Russian Savonarola'), anti-Semitic missionary preacher, monk and priest

Father Ioann of Kronstadt, healer and archpriest of Kronstadt Cathedral

Father Isidor, monk, later prior of Tobolsk Monastery and bishop

Mitya Kozelsky (the Nasal-Voiced), seer

Father Makary, anchorite, Rasputin's 'spiritual father', swineherd at Verkhoturye Monastery

Ivan Osipenko, lay brother, secretary to Pitirim

Pitirim, suspected Khlyst, accused of theft of church property, exarch of Georgia, later metropolitan of Petrograd

Vladimir Sabler, Russified German, chief procurator of Synod

Bishop Sergius, rector of the St Petersburg Theological Seminary, author of controversial religious studies, later appointed by Stalin the first Patriarch of All Russia

Serafin of Sarov (1760-1833) Pitirim, hermit, monk and saint, canonised in 1903

Bishop Varnava (Gopher), bishop of Tobolsk lacking higher seminary education

Victor Yatskevich, director of chancery of chief procurator of Synod

Prince Nikolai Zhevakhov, mystic, deputy chief procurator of Synod, minor official of Council of State, member of Rasputin's circle

Rasputin's circle

Prince Mikhail Andronikov, homosexual gossip-monger, minor Synod official, friend of Beletsky

Vladimir Bonch-Bruevich, expert on Russian sectarianism, underground member of Bolsheviks, later founder of the Cheka

Vera Dzhanumova, wife of wealthy merchant

Alexei Filippov, banker, Rasputin's publisher

Maria Golovina (Munya, 'Bird'), chamberlain's daughter, niece of Princess Olga Valerianovna, friend of Felix Yusupov

Alexandra Gushina, widow of a doctor

Baroness Vera Kusova, wife of cavalry captain in a Crimean regiment

Akilina Laptinskaya ('Owl'), former nun and nurse, Rasputin's 'secretary'

Olga Lokhtina, St Petersburg society hostess, wife of a civil engineer with equivalent rank of general

Sheila Lunts, Jewish wife of a barrister, later Protopopov's mistress

Ivan Manasevich-Manuilov, Jewish journalist, spy and double-agent, former official of special commissions for the prime minister, 'secretary' to Rasputin

Zinaida Manshtedt or Manchtet (Zina, 'Dove'), wife of a collegiate secretary

Leonid Molchanov, son of Bishop Alexis, secretary to a district magistrate

Elena Patushinskaya, wife of a Siberian notary, one of Rasputin's 'celestial' wives

Evdokia Pechyorkina (Dunya), Rasputin's live-in servant

Ekaterina Pechyorkina (Katya), niece of Evdokia, Rasputin's live-in servant

Alexandra Pistolkors (Sana), sister of Anya Vyrubova, wife of Alexander Pistolkors, the son of Olga Pistolkors and the step-son of Grand Duke Pavel

Alexander Prugavin, ethnographer, publicist, prominent expert on Russian sectarianism

Matryona Rasputin, Rasputin's elder daughter, engaged to Pankhadze, married to Nikolai Solovyov

Praskovia Rasputin, married to Rasputin

Nikolai Reshetnikov, former notary convicted of forgery and embezzlement, brother of Anna, 'secretary' to Rasputin, later builder and director of Tsarkoe Selo infirmary

Anisia Reshetnikova, widow of a wealthy merchant, mother of Anna and Nikolai

Anna Reshetnikova, daughter of Anisia and brother of Nikolai

Dmitry Rubinstein (Mitya), banker and chairman of board of Franco-Russian Bank

Georgy Sazonov, economist, publicist, magazine publisher and journalist

Maria Sazonova ('Crow'), wife of Georgy Sazonov

Princess Shakhovskaya, aviator and aristocrat

Aron Simanovich, 'secretary' and financial adviser to Rasputin, gambler and loan shark with criminal record

Vera Tregubova, performer of gypsy ballads

Sophia Volynskaya, Jewish wife of the ex-convict and agronomist Volynsky (one of Rasputin's 'secretaries' and financial advisers)

Vera Zhukovskaya, writer, relative of the scientist N. E. Shukovsky

St Petersburg Area

Barents Sea

Kronstadt
Gulf of Finland
St Petersburg
Peterhof
Lake Ladoga
Krasnoe Selo
Tsarskoe Selo
Pavlovsk
Gatchina

Murmansk

Helsingfors (Helsinki)
Vyborg
Gulf of Finland
St Petersburg (Petrograd)
Reval
Vologda
Verkhoturye
Tobolsk
Pskov
Bologoe
Rybinsk
Perm
Motovilikha
Alapaevsk
Pokrovskoe
Riga
Rostov
Pushkino
Udinka
Moscow
Sarov
Ekaterinburg
Tyumen
Orsha
Kazan
Chelyabinsk
Mogilev (Headquarters)
Ufa
Baranovichi
Brasovo
Orel
Simbirsk
Warsaw
Gomel
Przemsyl
Kiev
Dnepr
Kharkov
Don
Volga
Saratov
Lvov
Tsaritsyn
Odessa
Sebastopol
Ai-Todor
Constanta
Livadia
Aral Sea
Black Sea
Caspian Sea
Constantinople
Tiflis

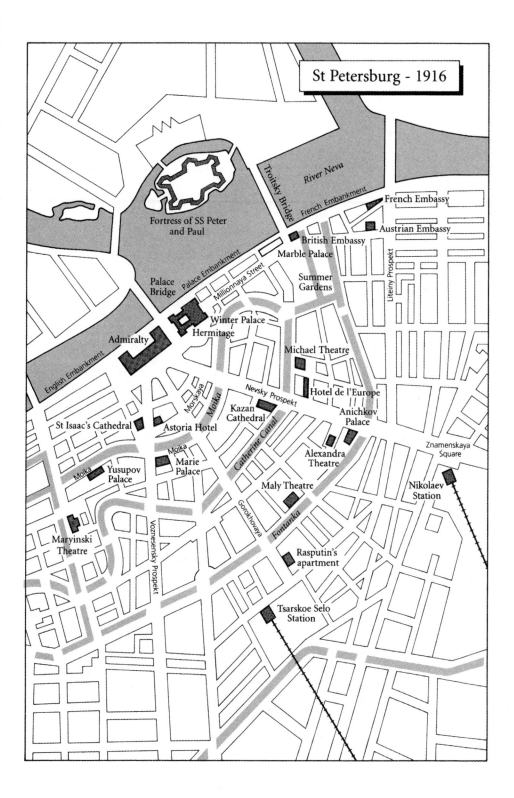

St Petersburg - 1916

Fortress of SS Peter and Paul

River Neva

Troitsky Bridge

French Embankment

French Embassy

Austrian Embassy

British Embassy

Marble Palace

Liteiny Prospekt

Palace Embankment

Summer Gardens

Palace Bridge

Millionnaya Street

Winter Palace

Hermitage

Admiralty

English Embankment

Michael Theatre

Morskaya

Moika

Nevsky Prospekt

Hotel de l'Europe

St Isaac's Cathedral

Kazan Cathedral

Astoria Hotel

Anichkov Palace

Znamenskaya Square

Catherine Canal

Moika

Marie Palace

Alexandra Theatre

Nikolaev Station

Moika

Yusupov Palace

Maly Theatre

Gorokhovaya

Fontanka

Voznesensky Prospekt

Maryinski Theatre

Rasputin's apartment

Tsarskoe Selo Station

THE FAMILIES OF TSAR NICHOLAS II AND HIS WIFE ALEXANDRA

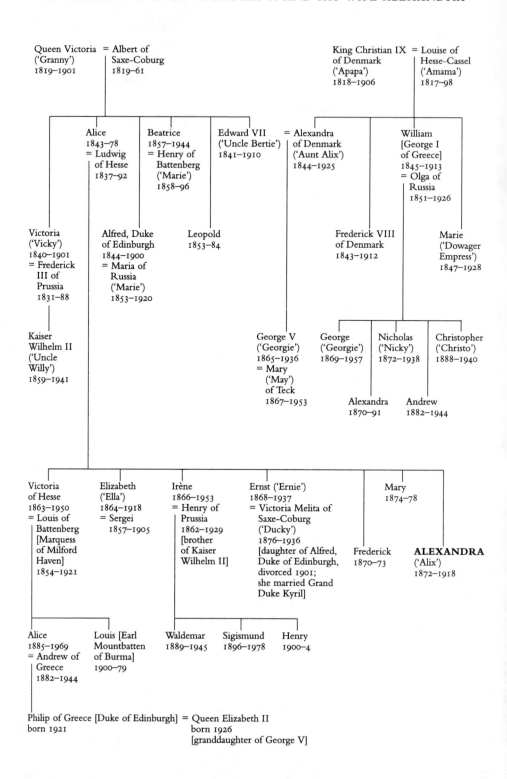

Queen Victoria = Albert of
('Granny')   Saxe-Coburg
1819–1901   1819–61

King Christian IX = Louise of
of Denmark   Hesse-Cassel
('Apapa')   ('Amama')
1818–1906   1817–98

Alice
1843–78
= Ludwig
of Hesse
1837–92

Beatrice
1857–1944
= Henry of
Battenberg
('Marie')
1858–96

Edward VII = Alexandra
('Uncle Bertie')   of Denmark
1841–1910   ('Aunt Alix')
             1844–1925

William
[George I
of Greece]
1845–1913
= Olga of
Russia
1851–1926

Victoria
('Vicky')
1840–1901
= Frederick
III of
Prussia
1831–88

Alfred, Duke
of Edinburgh
1844–1900
= Maria of
Russia
('Marie')
1853–1920

Leopold
1853–84

Frederick VIII
of Denmark
1843–1912

Marie
('Dowager
Empress')
1847–1928

Kaiser
Wilhelm II
('Uncle
Willy')
1859–1941

George V
('Georgie')
1865–1936
= Mary
('May')
of Teck
1867–1953

George
('Georgie')
1869–1957

Nicholas
('Nicky')
1872–1938

Christopher
('Christo')
1888–1940

Alexandra
1870–91

Andrew
1882–1944

Victoria
of Hesse
1863–1950
= Louis of
Battenberg
[Marquess
of Milford
Haven]
1854–1921

Elizabeth
('Ella')
1864–1918
= Sergei
1857–1905

Irène
1866–1953
= Henry of
Prussia
1862–1929
[brother
of Kaiser
Wilhelm II]

Ernst ('Ernie')
1868–1937
= Victoria Melita of
Saxe-Coburg
('Ducky')
1876–1936
[daughter of Alfred,
Duke of Edinburgh,
divorced 1901;
she married Grand
Duke Kyril]

Mary
1874–78

Frederick
1870–73

ALEXANDRA
('Alix')
1872–1918

Alice
1885–1969
= Andrew of
Greece
1882–1944

Louis [Earl
Mountbatten
of Burma]
1900–79

Waldemar
1889–1945

Sigismund
1896–1978

Henry
1900–4

Philip of Greece [Duke of Edinburgh] = Queen Elizabeth II
born 1921   born 1926
                                      [granddaughter of George V]

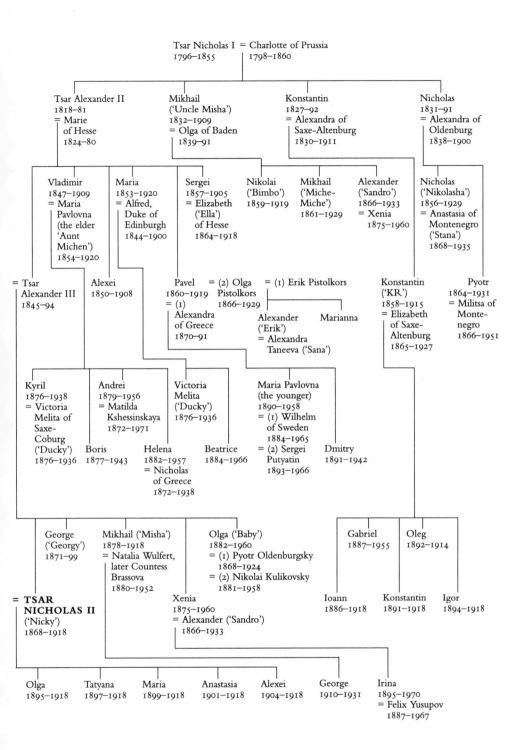

Tsar Nicholas I = Charlotte of Prussia
1796–1855 | 1798–1860

Tsar Alexander II
1818–81
= Marie
of Hesse
1824–80

Mikhail
('Uncle Misha')
1832–1909
= Olga of Baden
1839–91

Konstantin
1827–92
= Alexandra of
Saxe-Altenburg
1830–1911

Nicholas
1831–91
= Alexandra of
Oldenburg
1838–1900

Vladimir
1847–1909
= Maria
Pavlovna
(the elder
'Aunt
Michen')
1854–1920

Maria
1853–1920
= Alfred,
Duke of
Edinburgh
1844–1900

Sergei
1857–1905
= Elizabeth
('Ella')
of Hesse
1864–1918

Nikolai
('Bimbo')
1859–1919

Mikhail
('Miche-
Miche')
1861–1929

Alexander
('Sandro')
1866–1933
= Xenia
1875–1960

Nicholas
('Nikolasha')
1856–1929
= Anastasia of
Montenegro
('Stana')
1868–1935

= Tsar
Alexander III
1845–94

Alexei
1850–1908

Pavel
1860–1919
= (1)
Alexandra
of Greece
1870–91

= (2) Olga
Pistolkors
1866–1929

= (1) Erik Pistolkors

Alexander
('Erik')
= Alexandra
Taneeva ('Sana')

Marianna

Konstantin
('KR')
1858–1915
= Elizabeth
of Saxe-
Altenburg
1865–1927

Pyotr
1864–1931
= Militsa of
Monte-
negro
1866–1951

Kyril
1876–1938
= Victoria
Melita of
Saxe-
Coburg
('Ducky')
1876–1936

Andrei
1879–1956
= Matilda
Kshessinskaya
1872–1971

Boris
1877–1943

Victoria
Melita
('Ducky')
1876–1936

Helena
1882–1957
= Nicholas
of Greece
1872–1938

Beatrice
1884–1966

Maria Pavlovna
(the younger)
1890–1958
= (1) Wilhelm
of Sweden
1884–1965
= (2) Sergei
Putyatin
1893–1966

Dmitry
1891–1942

George
('Georgy')
1871–99

Mikhail ('Misha')
1878–1918
= Natalia Wulfert,
later Countess
Brassova
1880–1952

Olga ('Baby')
1882–1960
= (1) Pyotr Oldenburgsky
1868–1924
= (2) Nikolai Kulikovsky
1881–1958

Gabriel
1887–1955

Oleg
1892–1914

= TSAR
NICHOLAS II
('Nicky')
1868–1918

Xenia
1875–1960
= Alexander ('Sandro')
1866–1933

Ioann
1886–1918

Konstantin
1891–1918

Igor
1894–1918

Olga
1895–1918

Tatyana
1897–1918

Maria
1899–1918

Anastasia
1901–1918

Alexei
1904–1918

George
1910–1931

Irina
1895–1970
= Felix Yusupov
1887–1967

(As a result of marriages some individuals appear more than once)

INTRODUCTION
THE MYSTERY

On 19 December 1916, just before Christmas in the last December of the Romanov empire, a corpse bobbed to the surface of the Malaya Nevka river in Petrograd. Ice-encrusted with a mutilated face. But the most startling thing was its hands. Its bound hands were raised. For there under the icy water that extraordinary individual, although beaten and shot, had still been alive, had still been trying to break free of his fetters. And, as the police would later write in their report, great numbers of people hurried down to the river with flasks, jugs, and buckets. To ladle up the water in which the awful body had just been floating. They wanted to scoop up with the water the deceased's diabolical, improbable strength, of which all Russia had heard.

I had always been afraid to write about him. And not just because it is a subject that somehow smacks of pulp fiction – Rasputin, after all, is one of the most popular myths of twentieth-century mass culture. I had been afraid to write about him because I did not understand him. Even though I had read a great many conscientious books about him. For under the researchers' pens the most important thing had vanished: his mystery. At best, he remained a crude bearded peasant rushing about Petrograd like some Henry Miller character with his phallus steaming.

Nevertheless, everything about him is unstable and mysterious. His face, left behind in numerous photographs, is described in much the same way by those who saw him: the wrinkled, sunburned, weather-beaten face of a middle-aged Russian peasant. A narrow face with a large, irregular nose, thick sensual lips, and a long beard. His hair is parted down the middle and combed across his forehead to conceal (as his daughter would write) an odd little bump reminiscent of a budding horn. His eyes, also described in much the same way by the various witnesses, attract even in the photographs: 'The instantly blazing, magnetic gaze of his light-coloured eyes in which not merely the pupil but the whole eye stares' (Zhukovskaya); 'deep-set unendurable eyes' (Dzhanumova); 'the hypnotic power shining in his exceptional eyes' (Khvostov).

But no sooner do the witnesses depart from the photographs than the mystery begins. Amusingly, they describe him in entirely different ways. I enjoyed writing down the various descriptions left by people: 'tall', 'short', 'neat in a peasant way', 'filthy and sloppy', 'slender', 'stocky with broad shoulders'. The singer Belling, who saw Rasputin many times, writes of his rotten teeth and foul breath. Yet the writer Zhukovskaya, who knew him extremely well, tells us that 'his teeth were perfect and complete down to the very last one, and his breath was absolutely fresh; white teeth for chewing, as strong as a beast's.' 'His mouth was very large, and instead of teeth you saw something like blackened stumps in it,' wrote his secretary, Simanovich. But his admirer Sazonov, who visited Rasputin many times, saw 'strong white teeth'.

He is unstable and oddly changeable. The Grand Duchess Olga, sister of the last tsar, said very accurately of him that 'he is as changeable as a chameleon.' And many who observed him hold the same view. Zhu-kovskaya recalls:

> When you remember that amazing peculiarity of his of changing in an instant . . . sitting there would be a simple, illiterate little peasant, a bit crude, scratching himself, his tongue barely moving and the words slipping clumsily out . . . when suddenly he would turn into an inspired prophet . . . and then another bound of the changeling and his white teeth would be crunching with a savage, bestial voluptuousness, and from behind the heavy curtain of his wrinkles something shamelessly predatory would nod, unrestrained, like a young animal . . . and then just as suddenly instead of an ungirded rowdy, a grizzled Siberian wanderer would be sitting there, someone who for thirty years had been searching the world for God.

But the most mysterious thing for me was the blindness of the royal family. The tsarina Alexandra called Rasputin an 'elder' (starets). Yet how could she, who had read so many books on the Orthodox faith, who knew the works of the famous elders, who had read the lives of those elders – how could she call a peasant wallowing in lechery and drunkenness an 'elder'? Didn't she believe the stories about him? Whom exactly didn't she believe? The courtiers? That's understandable. The police reports? That, too, might be explained. Did she not believe the large Romanov family? Did she not believe the tsar's mother? Did she not believe his brothers? That's harder to explain. But not impossible. But how could she not believe her own sister?

Her beloved and truly saintly older sister to whom she was so close? Maybe she simply did not *want* to believe.

And Nicholas himself? What about him? Why did he agree with his blinded wife? Can it really be that they were just trying to save their ailing son, whom the peasant knew how to treat? And that this was enough for enthusiastic worship or, more accurately, for adoration to take place? For a frightening symbiosis to occur: a highly religious family, the mutually devoted tsar and tsarina, their chaste daughters, and nearby a lewd peasant whose escapades were on everyone's lips? Could the life of their son actually have made them close their eyes to everything? And agree to remain silent about the destruction of the dynasty's prestige, about the inevitable catastrophe of which everyone without exception spoke again and again? And ignore their duty to the country and to the dynasty as sovereigns? In that case we shall understand and pity those good and unhappy parents. But curse the rulers who were responsible for the catastrophe that befell Russia in 1917. And which took not only their own lives and the life of the boy they so cared for and the lives of their daughters, but also the lives of millions of their subjects.

Or was there another, altogether different reason for their astonishing faith in that man? Some entirely different explanation for his actions?

Of course, when his terrible corpse bobbed to the surface at the beginning of the century, it was all very clear. Rasputin was a servant of the Antichrist. So at the time said both Russian believers and non-believers. With the result that eighty years later one still wants to ask oneself, just who after all was Grigory Efimovich Rasputin?

1

THE FILE: SEARCHING FOR DOCUMENTS

The Prison Ball

I supposed that only when I had found the File would I be able to answer those questions. I had long been aware that the File had to exist.

In the 1970s when I was writing my book about Nicholas, I naturally had occasion to look at the papers of the Extraordinary Commission of the Provisional Government.

In March 1917, after Nicholas's abdication and the triumph of the February Revolution, the solitary confinement cells of the Peter and Paul Fortress became crowded. Delivered to that Russian Bastille, where during the tsar's reign political dissidents had been incarcerated, were the people who had put them there – those who not long before had controlled Russia's destiny. The tsarist prime ministers Stürmer and Golitsyn; the minister of internal affairs Protopopov; the head of the infamous Department of Police Beletsky and his replacement Alexis Vasiliev; the aged court minister Count Fredericks; the chairman of the Council of State Schlegovitov; the palace castellan Voeikov; the tsarina's closest friend, Anya Vyrubova; and so forth and so on. In a word, the very highest society. So that the fortress's damp cells, constantly subject to flooding, resembled nothing so much as a brilliant Winter Palace ball.

On 4 March 1917, the Provisional Government formed the Extraordinary Commission of Inquiry for the Investigation of Illegal Acts by Ministers and Other Responsible Persons of the Tsarist Regime. And from the Peter and Paul Fortress the ministers were shunted back and forth for interrogation at the Winter Palace, so familiar to them, where the Extraordinary Commission worked, and where only recently they had appeared in medals and ribbons. Or else the Commission investigators would themselves drive out to conduct their interrogations at the fortress. The transcripts of those interrogations were then deciphered and put into shape. And it was Russia's leading poet, the famous Alexander Blok, who did the putting. He has described in his notebooks the atmosphere of the interrogations and the appearance of the Winter Palace with its empty throne room, 'where all the fabric had been torn from the walls and the throne removed, since the soldiers wanted to break it up'.

The transcripts of the interrogations were then prepared for publication. All Russia was supposed to learn, according the Commission plan, just what had transpired behind the scenes in mysterious Tsarskoe Selo, from which the tsar and tsarina had ruled Russia. On the basis of that information the future first Russian parliament was then meant to decide the fates of the tsar, the tsarina, and the ministers – of those people who had just days before governed Russia.

And one of the main questions concerned the semi-literate Russian peasant Grigory Rasputin.

Section Thirteen

The Commission's executive council and its twenty-seven separate boards of inquiry conducted continuous interrogations of its brilliant prisoners from March 1917 until the Bolshevik coup in October.

A special board of inquiry with the expressive name 'Thirteenth Section' was particularly concerned with 'investigating the activity of the dark forces'. In the political jargon of the day, the 'dark forces' were Rasputin, the tsarina, and those close to them. The 'dark forces', their true influence via Rasputin over the former Tsar Nicholas II in the area of state governance: that was the substance of the Thirteenth Section's work.

The head of the Thirteenth Section was a certain F. P. Simpson, a former head of the Kharkov Provincial Appellate Court. The interrogations themselves were conducted by several investigators: two people with the same last name, Vladimir and Tikhon Rudnev, and Grigory Girchich. They, too, had been reassigned to the Commission from provincial courts. As a kind of guarantee that they would have no links to the capital's former governing clique now under investigation.

And then came the October 1917 coup. The Bolsheviks who seized power put an end to the Provisional Government. Those who the day before had been ministers in that government were sent to the very same cells in the Peter and Paul Fortress. Where not without humour they were greeted by the tsarist ministers whom they had only recently imprisoned in the same place. The Bolsheviks also put an end to the work of the Extraordinary Commission.

But in 1927 the Bolsheviks decided to publish part of the interrogations of the most important tsarist ministers, for the tenth anniversary of their revolution. The publication was supposed to be ideological; that is, it was supposed to demonstrate the 'senescence' of a tsarist regime controlled by the ignorant, debauched peasant Grigory Rasputin.

By that time, Alexander Blok, who worked on the stenographs, had died. The publication of the transcripts was supervised by one of the Extraordinary Commission's most celebrated members, P. Schyogolev, who had agreed to collaborate with the Bolsheviks.

Before the revolution Schyogolev had been editor of the magazine *Times Past*. A publication 'of wholly revolutionary temper', it had been shut down several times by the tsarist authorities. Leo Tolstoy said that 'if I had been young, I would have taken a revolver in each hand after reading *Times Past*.' For his magazine's sake he endured a cell in the Peter and Paul Fortress, where he himself would eventually interrogate the tsarist ministers who had imprisoned him. But after the Bolsheviks came to power, the once incorruptible Schyogolev changed completely. He became part of the Bolshevik regime. Evil tongues maintained that his apartment contained a collection of documents and furniture from the Winter Palace.

Seven little volumes entitled *Proceedings of the Extraordinary Commission of Inquiry* were all that Schyogolev published from the immense quantity of material produced by the interrogations. And those pitiful volumes were for many years the chief documentary basis for all the books written about Rasputin.

It was only four decades later – in 1964 – that another sensational document about Rasputin was added to those volumes drawn from the Extraordinary Commission's legacy. And it was after the appearance of that document that my search for the File began.

The Missing File

In 1964 the journal *Issues of History* published a sensational number that at the time was eagerly read not only by historians. Printed in it for the first time was the 'Resolution of the Investigator F. Simpson of the Extraordinary Commission Regarding the Activity of Rasputin and his Close Associates and their Influence over Nicholas II in the Area of State Governance', a document that until then had been held in a secret repository of the archive of the October Revolution.

The 'Resolution' was a summary of the Thirteenth Section's efforts to clarify Rasputin's role.

I read the issue later when I was starting work on my book about Nicholas II. And the 'Resolution' made a stunning impression on me. In his conclusion Simpson quoted extensively from the testimony of people belonging to Rasputin's most intimate circle: his publisher Filippov; his friend Sazonov, in whose apartment Rasputin had lived and with whose wife he had enjoyed the most intimate relationship; the famous Maria Golovina, a true worshipper of Rasputin who became an involuntary cause of his death; the Petersburg cocottes with whom Rasputin shared tender bonds; and the admirers who fell under his hypnotic influence.

Naturally, I at once started looking for that testimony in the *Proceedings* published by Schyogolev. And naturally I failed to find it there. For it was the testimony of people who had liked Rasputin. Their point of view was absolutely unacceptable to Schyogolev. And naturally he did not include what they had to say.

The quotations that Simpson had taken from the testimony for citation in his report actually changed things very little. For Simpson was trying very hard in his 'Resolution' to defend the same point of view advanced by Schyogolev in his publication.

The 'Resolution' sketched the same picture of a crude, debauched peasant rendered senseless by drunkenness and licentiousness who ruled both the royal family and those corrupt ministers who had agreed to serve him as the favourite.

Was it the whole truth of the testimony obtained by the Thirteenth Section? I had good reason to doubt it. For by then I already knew of the deep dissension within the Commission itself. One of the Thirteenth Section's principal investigators, Vladimir Rudnev, had even resigned in protest. After emigration, he wrote of his reasons: 'In August 1917, I submitted a request to be released from my duties in view of the attempts of the President of the Commission, Muravyov, to incite me to patently biased actions.'

And I resolved to attempt something very difficult for the times: to go to the archive myself and read the testimony that Simpson had quoted in such a biased fashion.

I won't recount the efforts that I made to assemble all the official papers required for the right to acquaint myself with the Extraordinary Commission's documents. Or how worthless those papers actually proved to be. Or how the only thing that did help was my status as a fashionable dramatist, as the author of plays whose productions were nearly impossible to get into at the time, and as the screenwriter of a film that was then enjoying immense success. Suffice it to say that I obtained access to the Extraordinary Commission archive.

How astonished I was to find there none of the testimony cited by Simpson! The documents were gone.

It was highly probable that those documents were the most interesting ones. They represented the testimony of people who had seen Rasputin daily. And of people who for some reason had agreed to serve him with devotion. There, perhaps, lay the solution to the riddle; there, perhaps, was hidden the authentic portrait of that mysterious person.

I called the vanished documents the 'File'. And straightaway began my search for the File.

The Writer Grigory Rasputin

I did find Rasputin's own rather pitiful file in the Commission archive.

First were his famous telegrams to the tsar and tsarina. Solicitously preserved by the latter right up to the revolution, they were confiscated by the Extraordinary Commission and widely disseminated in a variety of publications.

I also found certain mysterious and still unpublished telegrams sent from Tsarskoe Selo to Rasputin with the signature 'Darling' (*Dushka*). Those telegrams, which we shall come back to, shed a certain distinctive light on the relationship between Rasputin and the tsarina.

Also preserved in the archive were Rasputin's own works. The strongest and most puzzling of these, the 'Life of an Experienced Wanderer', was not published in his lifetime. But the other three were: 'Great Festivities in Kiev!' (it was during those festivities that the famous prime minister Stolypin was killed), 'Pious Meditations' (a collection of homilies), and 'My Thoughts and Reflections'(an account of Rasputin's trip to Jerusalem).

These particular documents were transcriptions: the semi-literate Rasputin spoke, and someone wrote down what he said. And wrote it down with affection.

After the revolution, Rasputin's published writings were all removed from the public libraries and transferred to closed repositories. It is hard to appreciate the charm of his books in translation. It is a special world, naive and beautiful, resembling the paintings of the Primitivists. His powerful and tender old-Russian speech unfortunately disappears in translation. It needs a poet to translate it well.

I can imagine the fascination experienced by those who listened to that speech, and who saw those piercing lupine eyes and the electric hands with which he would lightly touch his interlocutor while conversing.

Rasputin's Unpublished Diary

And then I found Rasputin's 'diary' in the archive. With the subheading, 'Written at his dictation. Kramer, L P.'

Rasputin's unpublished diary: it was as if all the characters of Schyogolev's *Proceedings of the Extraordinary Commission* had stepped down from its pages. And many of the stories in the diary, as well as the heroes of those stories, tallied with what I had read in the *Proceedings*! And yet . . . And yet the more I read of the diary, the more my enthusiasm waned. All that Bolshevik historical scholarship was trying to prove at the time – the elder's debauchery, the venality of Petersburg high society, the pathetic stupidity of the tsar – was contained in the diary.

Here is Rasputin instructing the tsar, 'pounding his fist', and explaining to the silly autocrat the enigma of the Russian people: 'How are you thinking of teaching the peasant? Through his ass? You want to tear his ass out, but such anger will grow in his head.' 'With tsars', Rasputin explains, 'you have to use the spirit, not reason ... He doesn't understand reason, but he's afraid of the spirit.' And here he is mastering the submissive tsarina: he has resolved to make peace with Germany, and the tsarina is reverently kneeling before him, promising to carry out his wishes. And then, of course, there is his incessant debauchery with the 'rotten aristocracy': 'Mama [the tsarina] drove me to Kusikha's [to the Baroness Kusova's] in Pavlovsk ... The general's wife V. was there, too. The two of them stick to me like flies. She herself sticks to me and is always afraid someone will find out.'

It was obviously all a crude ideological forgery. It was not for nothing that in the subheading 'written at his dictation', someone had pencilled in the phrase, 'as if': 'as if written at his dictation.'

It is not, I think, very hard to identify the forgery's author. For the author (or authors) was already well known for another forgery that at the time had been spectacularly successful with its readers.

The 'Red Count' And The
Spurious Diaries

In 1927, on the tenth anniversary of the fall of the tsar, the magazine *The Past* began the publication of 'Vyrubova's diary'. All Russia was besotted by the diary, which revealed secret and highly intimate details of the disintegration both of the royal family and of the regime that had recently governed the country.

True, rumours very soon began circulating that Vyrubova had had nothing whatever to do with its publication. Named as the authors of the diverting forgery were two well-known people: the publisher of the *Proceedings of the Extraordinary Commission*, P. Schyogolev, and the celebrated writer Count Alexei Tolstoy (the 'Red Count', as he was known in Moscow), an active Bolshevik collaborator.

Schyogolev and Tolstoy had already co-authored a play with very similar ideas: *The Empress's Conspiracy*, about Rasputin's attempt to carry out a palace revolution and install the tsarina as the country's leader. The play was wildly successful. It ran simultaneously in six of the largest theatres in Moscow and Leningrad.

And in 1927, on this tenth anniversary, it had evidently been impossible to carry out a powerful ideological campaign discrediting tsarism without the help of Schyogolev and the 'Red Count'. Nor could the campaign itself have been dispensed with; it was, in a phrase of the day, a 'social imperative'. Schyogolev, as the publisher of the *Proceedings*, obtained the material, whilst the count did the writing. Thus did the spurious Vyrubova 'diary' make its appearance. Its enormous success demanded that the work be continued. Rasputin's 'diary' was intended as a kind of sequel to Vyrubova's. And as in the creation of Vyrubova's 'diary' and *The Empress's Conspiracy*, Schyogolev provided the 'Red Count' with historical details from the published and, mainly, unpublished *Proceedings*. But thanks to the highly gregarious and frequently drunk 'Red Count', the story behind the Vyrubova forgery soon got out. There was no point in even thinking about publishing a second one, and the idea was abandoned. Schyogolev, who apparently had a taste for literary hoaxes, then turned Rasputin's 'diary' over to the archive. But by the 1930s the tsarist theme no longer interested the country. And so the diary was left to gather dust in the Commission archive.

The Unsleeping Eye Of The Police

But probably the most entertaining documents pertaining to Rasputin that I read at that time in the Commission archive were the volumes of reports by the police agents assigned to cover him. Those 'external surveillance' agents were supposed to write a daily account of all Rasputin's movements about the city. They tried to describe the innumerable visitors who came to his apartment. Noted, too, were any of Rasputin's absences from his lodgings, the times he returned, where he went, and whom he met along the way. No public figure received a more detailed description of his life over the course of several years than the semi-literate peasant Grigory Rasputin. But the volumes left in the archive were a mere vestige. Part of the surveillance documentation had perished during the February Revolution when the tsarist secret police department headquarters were burned down, and part was destroyed by the police officials themselves, since they, too, had been among Rasputin's visitors and he among their guests. As the former minister of internal affairs Khvostov testified before the Extraordinary Commission: 'When I retired from the service, Stürmer [the prime minister] took the documents to his office, especially the ones concerning Rasputin . . . [as] the main interest was in him. Everything was burned at once.' But the reports that have survived reveal the wild mosaic of Rasputin's days – the visits to restaurants and Gypsy singers, the meetings with ministers, the risqué scenes in his kitchen to which the agents were privy thanks to a lack of curtains, as well as the jumble of visitors to his apartment: prostitutes, duchesses, bankers, schemers, pious lady admirers, and high-priced cocottes. The police recorded everything: their names, their arrival times, and their departure times the next morning after a night with the peasant.

Another Rasputin 'Diary'

But the missing File of those who knew Rasputin well never left my mind.

After the start of *perestroika* I renewed my inquiries. At the beginning of the 1990s I made a careful search for it in Petersburg. But the only document concerning Rasputin preserved in the State Historical Archive, located in the once luxurious buildings of the former Senate and Synod (where, as we shall see, at one time congregated many who had been appointed to those bodies by the simple peasant himself), was a small school copybook with a portrait of Pushkin and the semi-literate inscription, 'Diry'.

The discovery in the 1990s of that copybook provoked a wave of articles in the world's leading newspapers. Rasputin's 'diary' had been discovered! But in point of fact Rasputin, who like all unlettered peasants adored writing, managed only to jot down a few reflections in his wretched scrawl. He evidently used the term 'diary' because it sounded important, knowing that the tsar and tsarina kept diaries, too.

Finally, in the former Museum of the Revolution in the villa of the ballerina

Mathilde Kschessinska, a lover of the young Nicholas, I saw another recent sensation: the file photographs, discovered in the 1990s, from the inquest conducted after Rasputin's murder. There was a view of the yard of the Yusupov palace across which Rasputin had run one December night in 1916 while trying to save himself from his murderers. And photographs of his corpse after it had been dragged from the river – of his mutilated face and his naked body with the bullet holes. I succeeded in establishing that the report on Rasputin's autopsy had in the 1930s been in the possession of the Academy of Military Medicine. And then suddenly it had vanished. In fact, it was not only the documents that vanished. Soon afterwards a number of research assistants who had seen the autopsy report also disappeared. It was the time of the Stalinist terror. True, I did turn up an official document regarding the exhumation and burning of the elder's body after the revolution. But still, I found no trace whatever of the missing documents produced by the Thirteenth Section, no trace of the File.

The Search For Documentation

At the beginning of the 1990s my book on Nicholas II was published in Russia. Not having found the File, I had been quite circumspect about Rasputin. I am also the host of the popular Russian television programme, *The Enigmas of History*. After the book on Nicholas II, I was inundated with letters requesting that I do a show on Rasputin. And I decided to do two on his death.

I tried to find for the show whatever new information I could in the way of recollections of him. I remembered a manuscript that I had seen in the Archive of Literature and Art when I was still a student. The 'Memoirs of Zhukovskaya' have to this day still not been published in their entirety in the West.

Vera Alexandrovna Zhukovskaya (a relative of the famous scientist N. E. Zhukovsky) was a young writer. But the unrelenting eroticism of her memoirs made me suspect that they were merely a clever invention, that she had never visited Rasputin.

The strong desire to verify their authenticity reminded me once more of the File. As Zhukovskaya herself wrote, it was a certain Alexander Prugavin who had helped her to gain access to the elder. His was a famous name in Rasputin's day; he was one of the most prominent experts on Russian sectarianism. Moreover, Zhukovskaya claimed that she herself had taken Prugavin to see Rasputin! And that Prugavin had written a tale based on her stories about her meetings with Rasputin. So I could easily verify the whole story. Prugavin's testimony about Rasputin had, after all, been cited in Simpson's 'Resolution'. That meant that it, too, was in the File. I had to find the File.

'A Large Pile Of Ashes'

At the time that I was working on the show, I thought of Vyrubova's papers, too. Transcripts of several of her interrogations had been included in the *Proceedings* published by Schyogolev. But there should have been more. For, as the investigator Rudnev had written, the Thirteenth Investigative Section 'gave special scrutiny' to the activity of the tsarina's closest friend and the elder's chief admirer.

After Rasputin's death, Vyrubova resided with the royal family at the Alexander Palace in Tsarskoe Selo. Towards the end of February 1917, when rebellious crowds were already filling the city's streets, the heir apparent and the four grand duchesses came down with the measles. And Vyrubova, having caught the disease from them, lay unconscious. She had been taken ill as the friend of the most powerful woman in Russia and had awoken in a palace not merely besieged but drowning irretrievably in a sea of revolution. The palace was plunged in darkness, the elevator no longer worked, and the tsarina was rushing among her patients. Yet hardly had Vyrubova regained consciousness than she and the tsarina started burning documents. At the end of March Vyrubova was arrested and brought before the Extraordinary Commission.

In her testimony published in the *Proceedings*, Vyrubova had said in reply to the investigator's question as to 'why she had burned a whole series of documents', 'I burned almost nothing. I burned only a few of the empress's last letters, since I didn't want them to fall into the wrong hands.' And I believed her. Perhaps she had in fact hidden the most important documents. After all, had she not kept the tsarina's letters written during the royal family's later incarceration in Tobolsk, despite all of Alix's calls to burn them? And if she had in fact hidden those letters, then was it not also possible that she had taken them with her on the night she fled Red Russia to Finland across the treacherous ice of the Gulf?

One of the few people close to the royal family to escape unharmed, Vyrubova died peacefully in Finland in 1964. In the Helsinki National Archives I was shown Vyrubova's police dossier which included the inter-rogation conducted by the Finnish authorities after she had turned up in a refugee internment camp in the city of Terioki. The Finns fully understood the significance of her testimony. As was stated in the file, 'this internment-camp deposition is to be conveyed to the prime minister and president.'

But Vyrubova had had nothing new to say. Her answers were a scrupulous reiteration of her testimony before the Provisional Government's Extraordinary Commission. In 1923, Vyrubova wrote and published her memoirs. She wanted to use her maiden name of Taneeva to conceal her identity, but her publishers preferred Vyrubova. I found no drafts of the memoirs in her archive.

In Finland she became a nun, although in secret; that is, she was able to live at home rather than in the convent (she was lame in one leg and they took her invalid status into account). I got in touch with the convent where she had secretly taken the veil, but there was nothing there. Vyrubova had lived by herself, seeing almost no one. It even occurred to me that she might have taken a vow of silence of some kind. But it turned out otherwise. Badly in need of money in 1937, she signed a contract with a Finnish publisher for a new edition of the memoirs. But as she was writing, the Second World War began. The First World War had destroyed her empire and her life, and now the Second World War dashed her hopes of obtaining a little money. Memoirs about the Russian tsar and tsarina fighting Germany were not what was called for in a Finland that had become a German ally. Then after the war, when the Soviet NKVD started to make inroads in Finland and émigrés were almost openly deported to the USSR, the tsarina's friend was very probably afraid to remind people of her existence. Only in 1953, the year Stalin died, did she turn the completed book over to the Finnish publisher. But they failed to publish it; apparently they took the view that the manuscript did not add anything to the earlier editions. Then at the beginning of the 1980s, while going through the Finnish publisher's papers after his death, his daughter came upon an envelope containing photographs. On it was written: 'Photos of Anya Vyrubova with her autographs on the reverse'. And she also found the manuscript of Vyrubova's memoirs. The book was published in 1984. The edition passed unnoticed, since there had been nothing new in it.

Reading those memoirs prepared for publication in Finland, I knew with certainty that Vyrubova had taken nothing new out of Russia with her.

Unlike her prudent friend, the tsarina had (fortunately for us) been unable to burn most of her letters in which she expressed her undying love for Nicky. Almost all these letters she exchanged with Nicholas have survived. And endlessly referred to in them is 'Our Friend'. If one must judge Rasputin's relations with the royal family before 1914 chiefly on the basis of the testimony of other witnesses, then from the first day of the war the tsar and tsarina begin to speak of those relations themselves. Although one other source did help me to comment on their letters: Olga, the younger sister of Nicholas II.

The Last Of The Ruling
Family

The rare journalists who visited her in those years found it hard to believe that the owner of the little house hidden away in Canada, the short woman dressed in an old-fashioned black skirt, a torn sweater, and sturdy brown shoes, had once owned palaces and been waited upon by dozens of servants. She survived until 1960 and thus also managed to pass the century's midpoint. Her funeral at the Orthodox Cathedral in Toronto brought together the remnants of the first Russian emigration. Although her tiny rooms did contain some old furniture, the only thing that really recalled the past was the enormous portrait of Alexander III over the fireplace.

Olga, Nicholas's sister, and the youngest daughter of Alexander III, was the last surviving member of his large family. Her memory had been remarkable right up to her death and had amazed the journalist who transcribed her memoirs. And in preparing for the show on Rasputin, I used those memoirs that she had dictated to the insistent journalist – yet another voice from the forever-vanished Winter Palace court.

Rasputin's Resurrection In The
New Russia

But at the time I still had not found the File. On the other hand, the 1990s saw the emergence from oblivion of documents concerning Rasputin in the Tobolsk and Tyumen archives. Located there are the birth registers of the Church of the Mother of God, on the basis of which it has at last become possible to establish the precise date of Rasputin's birth. Contained in the Tyumen archive, as well, are the 'File of the Tobolsk Ecclesiastical Consistory in Regard to Grigory Rasputin's Affiliation with the *Khlysty*', which had been thought lost, and the 'File Regarding the Attempt on Grigory Rasputin's Life'.

I am grateful to both archives, which considerately provided me with photocopies of the precious Rasputin documents in their possession.

Grigory Rasputin has of late begun to enjoy something of a resurrection in Russia, and he has even become an essential part of a revived national or, more accurately, nationalistic ideology. Here in truth is another of history's jests: the man whom Russian monarchists saw as the destroyer of autocracy has become the standard-bearer of the new autocratic ideas.

In fact, the man himself – or, more precisely, his writings – has played no small part in his resurrection. After *perestroika*, his writings again became available, producing a tremendous impression. In a country where ignorance of the Bible was universal, his forgotten Biblical sayings and muscular language of the people were bewitching.

The new interest in Rasputin derives from a justified sense that the image of him created over the last century is little more than a political legend. That the testimony published by Schyogolev in his *Proceedings of the Extraordinary Commission* was essentially the testimony of Rasputin's enemies. And that there are many inconsistencies.

But all that the new research has yielded is a political legend turned on its head. The 'holy devil' Grigory has become the holy elder Grigory. Russian myths about devils and saints – how many there have been this century! Bloody Nicholas II and then Nicholas the saint, the father and teacher Stalin and then the bloody monster Stalin, the saintly Lenin and then the bloody Lenin. The culmination of all the recent research on Rasputin is the nationalists' favourite tale about the evil 'Yid-Masons'. 'It was, in essence, the Masons who created the Rasputin myth, a myth having as its goal the blackening and discrediting of Russia and its spiritual principle' (Oleg Platonov, *Russia's Crown of Thorns*).

History loves to jest. The fact is that before the revolution and immediately after it the nationalists of the time accused Rasputin himself of being, well, an agent of the Masons! And they also maintained that the 'dark forces' of Masonry had decided to exploit his influence over the tsar and tsarina for their own purposes. Rasputin was accused of being a 'Jewish stooge surrounded by Jewish secretaries'. So much more amusing, then, are history's new jests in present-day Russia. The historian N. Koslov has proclaimed Rasputin's a 'ritual' murder. It turns out that Rasputin was murdered by Jews manipulating Masons under their control!

In this way a new myth has emerged about the tsar and the peasant Rasputin as the preservers of the immemorial Russian ideas of Orthodoxy and autocracy, as men who had become the objects of persecution by Masons dreaming of turning Russia towards the West. It has all become so tedious, simplistic, and vulgar.

After all, they can make whatever claims they want. They can dismiss the reports on Rasputin by the tsarist secret police agents as lies. They can declare that Rasputin never got drunk, that he never engaged in lechery. That he was a pure and good Christian who had been slandered by his enemies. For there was no testimony by his friends. The File was still missing. I needed to find it.

The File

While getting ready for my television show on Rasputin's murder, I decided to take a look at the Yusupov family archive.

The archive has been clumsily divided into two parts. The main Yusupov archive is at the Russian State Archive for Ancient Documents (RGADA). The RGADA archive contains the history of the ancient family's incalculable riches. Descendants of Tartar rulers who had entered the service of the Muscovite tsars, the Yusupovs became over the course of three centuries the wealthiest of landholders; Rasputin's future murderer owned thousands of hectares of land. In the nineteenth century the Yusupovs became the greatest of industrialists. In 1914, their income was 1.5 million gold roubles a year. The richest family in Russia.

The lesser part of the Yusupov archive is held at the History Museum. I found in the two repositories both the largely unpublished correspondence of Felix Yusupov (Rasputin's murderer) and his wife, Irina, and letters written to Felix by his mother, the beauty Zinaida, one of Rasputin's chief enemies. The letters reveal how the plot to murder the elder took shape, and they provide a new picture both of the murder itself and of the secret of the relationship between Felix and Maria Golovina, one of Rasputin's admirers.

The Yusupov Palace itself is full of secrets. Strange rooms that are not shown on any plan of the building are being discovered to this day. Secrets and corpses are in fact quite in the Yusupov family tradition. The great-grandmother of Felix Yusupov was one of the most beautiful women in Europe. After the revolution, the Bolsheviks discovered a secret door in her apartment. And behind the door they found a coffin with the decayed body of a man. Her great-grandson Felix told a story about a dangerous revolutionary lover of hers who had been imprisoned in the fortress at Sveaborg and whose escape she had engineered. She had apparently hidden him in her palace until his death.

In 1925, it was noticed that the plaster under the front staircase in the old seventeenth-century Yusupov Palace in Moscow was a different colour from the adjacent walls. Making a hole, investigators revealed a chamber in which they found seven chests. These had apparently been hastily and haphazardly secreted there by the owners as they were fleeing the country. Discovered in this way were Yusupov family silver, diamonds, pearls, and emeralds, as well as other family documents that were subsequently added to the Yusupov archive.

The day I came to see the Yusupov palace for myself was oddly disturbing.

That morning I had been invited to lunch by Prince Michael, Duke of Kent, who was visiting Petersburg at the time. Descended from King George V, that double of Nicholas II, Prince Michael also closely resembles the last Russian tsar. Both in his features and, more importantly, in his eyes: light-coloured eyes with the same tenderly sad expression described in so many memoirs of Nicholas. Following that meeting with the relative with the face of the last tsar, I went to videotape the palace where the man who had undone the tsar had himself been murdered.

Everything had been preserved: I walked down the same staircase from which Grand Duke Dmitry Pavlovich and the other plotters had nervously listened to what was going on in the basement.

I went into the yard by the same door through which the bloodied Rasputin had fled, while trying to save himself. And then I returned to the basement which had been transformed by Felix into an elegant room. Here they had sat just before the murder. Standing there now are two silly wax figures depicting Felix and Rasputin. The door to the basement was shut and I remained alone. I had a strange feeling that I had seen that basement before: the small space, the windows raised just slightly above the ground through which only the legs of passers-by could be seen, the massive walls that blocked out all sound. It was a double of the Ipatiev House basement, where the royal family had been executed.

The night afterwards I returned to Moscow. The next day was the première of *Khovanschina* at the Bolshoi Theatre. I had been invited by my friend Slava Rostropovich who was conducting the opera. I looked at the stage and the costumes from the times of the kingdom of Muscovy, the same costumes in which Nicholas and Alexandra had been so fond of dressing up for their 'historical' balls. It all seemed like a continuation of the day before.

As indeed it was.

After the opera I went to congratulate Rostropovich. And then in the dressing room crammed with people he said to me, 'What a present I've prepared for you! You'll go crazy! You'll simply die! You must come to see me in Paris immediately! I'm holding it there!' He paused, but I already knew what was next. And he said, 'I bought some documents for you at a Sotheby's auction. It's a complete file, an enormous one. And do you know what it's about?' I knew. And he then finished, 'It's about Rasputin. It's the interrogations of the numerous people he knew by the Provisional Government Commission.'

The longest day of my life had ended.

At Rostropovich's apartment in Paris, in his living room draped with Winter Palace curtains emblazoned with the tsarist coat of arms, and containing an easel with a portrait of Nicholas with those same inexpressibly sad lapis eyes by the great portrait painter Valentin Serov, he pulled out an enormous volume. The testimony of Rasputin's publisher Filippov, of Sazonov, and of Maria Golovina. And so on. It was the File, the source of the testimony Simpson had quoted.

The File, the one I had been looking for so long!

A Very Brief Description Of
The File

The standard cover bore the inscription, 'The Extraordinary Commission of Inquiry for the Investigation of Illegal Acts by Ministers and Other Responsible Persons'. Contained within were nearly five hundred pages of documents on the special forms of the Commission with the Commission's stamp. All the interrogation transcripts were signed by the people who had been interrogated. Here were the signatures of Vyrubova, the gendarme (political police) chief Vladimir Dzhunkovsky, Colonel Komissarov, the doctor of Tibetan medicine Badmaev, the minister of internal affairs Khvostov, the head of the Moscow secret police Martynov, and so on. As though the detention cells of the Peter and Paul Fortress of March 1917 had come back to life. And the signatures of the famous interrogators of the Thirteenth Section who had conducted the interrogations: T. and V. Rudnev and G. Girchich.

What reading it was. The File contained the sensational testimony of Bishop Feofan, the famous church hierarch and ascetic through whom, as had often been claimed before the File, Rasputin had gained access to the royal family. The File also contained the testimony of monks from faraway Siberian monasteries and from the Verkhoturye Monastery where the mysterious transformation of Rasputin began. And, finally, it had the testimony so important to me and so desired by me – the testimony of those who had especially valued and liked Rasputin.

A Photograph Brought To Life

There is a famous photograph of Rasputin that has been compulsory in all the biographies of him. In it Rasputin is depicted surrounded by eighteen or so women and a few men. The photograph is mutely entitled, 'Rasputin surrounded by his devotees'.

The testimony from the File now makes it possible for the first time to identify everyone in the photograph. And not merely to identify them. Included in the File is direct testimony about Rasputin by several of the people in the famous photograph. So that in the pages of this book the famous picture will, as it were, come to life, and the people who were able to observe Rasputin almost every day will begin to speak.

The File also turned out to contain the testimony of people without whom it would be hard to write an impartial biography of Rasputin. The first of these is Alexei Frolovich Filippov, 'Rasputin's publisher and sincere admirer', as he is fairly characterized by those adhering to the new 'holy Rasputin' legends. Filippov was not merely an 'admirer' but a fierce defender of Rasputin. In his testimony, the publisher (and, I shall add, rich man and banker) by force of literary habit described everything to the investigator in detail – from Rasputin's psychology and sexual life to his body and even his reproductive organs, which so preoccupied Petersburg society of the day. The File also includes the testimony of Georgy Petrovich Sazonov, another 'ardent admirer of Rasputin', as he is characterized by the elder's new devotees. And it includes the testimony of Rasputin's friend and one of the most mysterious figures in Petersburg, the Asian healer Badmaev, who treated the most important tsarist dignitaries with Tibetan herbs. And, finally, the File includes the testimony of a whole group of ladies suspected of the most intimate of relations with Rasputin: the young Baroness Kusova, the singer Varvarova, the young widow Voskoboinikova, and the cocottes Tregubova and Sheila Lunts.

In addition to all this, there are several extended interrogations of Rasputin's devotees Maria Golovina and Olga Lokhtina, the latter a lioness of Petersburg society whom acquaintance with Rasputin turned into a half-mad holy fool (*yurodivaya*); the tsarina's friend Yulia [Lili] Dehn; and so on. Many of the interrogations were transcribed in the investigators' own handwriting (specimens of which are in the possession of the Archive of the Russian Federation, as are specimens of the handwriting of many of those who were subjected to interrogation and who signed the documents). So it was not very difficult to establish the documents' authenticity.

The File also allowed me to confirm the authenticity of Zhukovskaya's astonishing memoirs. I found the detailed testimony of Alexander Prugavin himself, in which that expert on Russian sectarianism corroborated what Zhukovskaya had written in regard to both her having met Rasputin through Prugavin and Prugavin's visit to Rasputin with her, and to her stories about Rasputin having permitted Prugavin to write his tale. Moreover, in Prugavin's view, it was 'Zhukovskaya's eroticism' that compelled her to try to understand to the fullest the enigmatic doctrine of the 'elder'. So she had in fact known very well what she was writing about.

And, lastly, there is in the File discussion of the man who became first Rasputin's friend and then his enemy, the monk Iliodor, who published abroad a famous book about Rasputin, *A Holy Devil*. That book has often been considered a mere Pasquil undeserving of serious attention. But in the File the Extraordinary Commission puts questions about the book to the people mentioned in it. It turns out that Iliodor was in the main telling the truth. And that he really did have the letters of the empress and her daughters and was quoting accurately from them. And that he also had the diary of Olga Lokhtina. This is confirmed by Lokhtina herself in the File. After acquainting themselves with Iliodor's book, both Lokhtina and Bishop Feofan had only a few private observations to make. So Iliodor should not be discounted as a source.

A House Recovered From Oblivion

After I had already started writing this book, I received the last batch of unpublished documents about Rasputin in the Siberian archives. Among them was an inventory of property belonging to Rasputin made immediately after his murder. Included was a detailed description of the legendary house in Pokrovskoe. I now knew every chair in his house and every glass on his table: the petit-bourgeois 'city décor' of the upstairs rooms where his Petersburg devotees stayed, and the age-old clumsy peasant style that prevailed below.

Now I had seen what he saw. And I had heard his way of speaking, too, which had been left behind in his writings. Now Rasputin was *alive*. I could begin. Would my portrait be a new one? I did not know. But I knew it would be fair. And the warranty of that would be the participation of those who cared about him.

This book is a completion of the investigation of that mysterious person begun by the Provisional Government in 1917. A unique investigation of

Rasputin in which the only testimony permitted is that of people who actually knew him.

But most important is that here will be heard the voices of those whose unpublished testimony is contained in the File.

Once, as I was finishing the book about the last tsar, I impulsively wrote, 'This is a book I shall never finish'. And once more that whole crowd of former acquaintances has rushed back into my life. And once again I have begun to see that same night in my dreams. That finale in a dirty basement of the history of a three-hundred-year-old empire. And the tsar falls onto his back, and two of the girls crouch by the wall covering themselves with their hands to ward off the bullets, and Commander Yurovsky runs into the gunsmoke to finish off the little boy crawling across the floor. Only now in that smoke I see a bearded man. He who did so much to bring that basement scene. And who knew that it would come.

2

THE MYSTERIOUS
WANDERER

The Period Of Legend

The greater half of his life is obscure. In 1917, the investigators of the Extraordinary Commission talked with Grigory Rasputin's fellow villagers in an unsuccessful attempt to establish his early biography. They merely created an ideological version of the tale of the peasant given to drunkenness and thievery from early youth. Nor are the memoirs of his daughter Matryona much help. Written after she had emigrated, they are the fruit of her own imagination and that of the woman journalist who helped her with them.

But in the Commission archive there is an account of that period by Rasputin himself. In 1907 after he had established himself in the royal family, he would often tell stories about his wanderings in Russia; a transcription under the title 'The Life of an Experienced Wanderer' was kept by the tsarina. But we shall keep in mind: he said what his royal admirers wanted to hear was a kind of 'Life of Saint Grigory'. A legend, that is. We can, however, still find traces in it of what is for us the most interesting thing: Rasputin's transformation. The few documents about his past recently discovered in the Siberian archives will serve as a supplement.

The Missing Birth Date

Grigory Efimovich Rasputin was born in the Tyumen district of the province of Tobol in the village of Pokrovskoe, a small settlement situated deep in the Siberian expanse on the banks of the Tura river near a large highway.

Following that highway for many hundreds of versts, coachmen would drive their horses along the banks of the Tura from the Ural mountain town of Verkhoturye, with its Nikolaev Monastery (which Grigory would later become so fond of), through Tyumen, and then on to Tobolsk.

It was along that same highway through Pokrovskoe past Rasputin's house that the royal family would travel to their deaths in Ekaterinburg in the terrible year of 1918.

The birth date of our hero has been a riddle. Even his recent biographers have offered the most diverse dates for his birth, from the 1860s to the 1870s. Soviet encyclopedias give the date 1864–5.

Surviving to this day in Rasputin's native village of Pokrovskoe are the ruins of the Church of the Mother of God, in which he was baptized. And preserved in the Tobolsk archives for the church are a few 'registers', or books in which births, marriages, and deaths were recorded.

In one is an entry for the marriage on 21 January 1862, of the peasant Efim Yakovlevich Rasputin, aged twenty, and the peasant maiden Anna Vasilievna, aged twenty-two.

Anna promptly bore Efim daughters, but they all died as infants. Finally, on 7 August 1867, she gave birth to a boy, Andrei. The boy perished in childhood, too. As with Hitler and Stalin, all the preceding children died. As if God were cautioning about childbearing in that family.

And then 1869. Before 1869 there is no record of Grigory's birth in any of the registers. So he could not have been born before 1869, and the dates in the encyclopedias are wrong. The registers for 1869 and later have disappeared from the archive.

Nevertheless, it has been possible to establish an exact date. A census of the residents of the village of Pokrovskoe was found in the Tyumen archive, and appearing next to the name Grigory Rasputin in the column for the 'year, month, and day of birth according to the register' is the date 10 January 1869, which puts an end to all surmise. It is the day of Saint Grigory, for whom he was named.

Rasputin's own efforts are responsible for the confusion about his birth date. In the 1907 'File of the Tobolsk Consistory', he states that he is forty-two. That is, he adds four years. Seven years later, in 1914 during the investigation of the attempt on his life by Khionia Guseva, he declares, 'My name is Grigory Efimovich Rasputin-Novy, fifty years old.' That is, he adds five years. In the 1911 notebook in which the last tsarina wrote down his sayings, he says of himself, 'I have lived fifty years and am beginning my sixth decade.' That is, he has added eight years!

It is really not very hard to understand that stubborn adding on of years. The tsarina called him 'elder'. The category of elder is a special institution in Russian ecclesiastical life. In the past, monks had been called elders, but usually only if they were anchorites. In the nineteenth century, however, the term was used for those monks who had been marked by a special sign. Monks who through fasting, prayer, and a life pleasing to God deserved to be chosen by Him. God had given them the power to prophesy and to heal. They were spiritual guides and intercessors before God. But at the same time, elders in the popular mind were also people of great age who had experienced much and who because of their age had repudiated everything earthly. In the lexicon of Russian, the word 'elder' also means 'a very old man.'

Thus Rasputin, whom the tsarina called 'elder', was embarrassed by his by no means advanced age. He was in fact younger than the tsar. And so he exaggerated his age, which was an easy thing to do thanks to his wrinkled, prematurely aged peasant face.

The Shameful Name

Rasputin's last name comes from the shameful word *rasputa*. The touching attempts of Western investigators and Rasputin's Russian admirers to derive his name from *rasputitsa* (the spring or autumn period when Russian roads became impassable from the mud) or from *rasputia* (a crossing of two or more roads) merely attest to their poor knowledge of the rules of Russian name derivation.

'The name "Rasputin" comes from the common noun *rasputa* – an immoral, good-for-nothing person (*neputyovyi*)' (V. A. Novikov, *A Dictionary of Russian Last Names*).

A '*rasputa*' is a dissolute (*besputnyi*), good-for-nothing (*neputyovyi*), debauched (*rasputnyi*) person. Sometimes the word served as a first name. In the days of Ivan the Terrible, there lived on the White Sea a peasant named Vasily Kiriyanov who gave his sons the names 'Rasputa' and 'Besputa' (Yu. Fedosyuk, *Russian Last Names*). Neither student of Russian last names mentions any *rasputitsa*. It is in fact the first derivation, *rasputa*, that accounts for the tsar's attempt to change Rasputin's last name, one so dubious for a holy man.

Rasputin grew into a skinny, unattractive youth. Yet even then his eyes possessed a strange hypnotic charm. And there was in him a certain tender dreaminess that astonished his crude peers and appealed to the young women. He was, according to the testimony of his fellow villagers, caught with wenches more than once and beaten for it.

As I was assembling Rasputin's biography bit by bit, I found in a 1912 issue of the *New Times* an article by a well-known journalist M. Menshikov about a conversation he had had with Rasputin. And in it was a truly poetical story told by the 'elder' about his boyhood: 'At the age of fifteen in my village, when the sunshine burned brightly and the birds sang heavenly songs . . . I would dream of God. My soul yearned for what was far away. I dreamed [of God] many times . . . and wept without knowing why or where my tears came from . . . In that way my youth passed. In a kind of contemplation, a kind of sleep. And then, after life had touched me, I ran to a corner and secretly prayed.' The journalist had been so entranced by his conversation that in the diary of the hostess of a celebrated Petersburg salon, the general's wife Bogdanovich, I found this entry: '26 February 1912. Menshikov dined with us . . . He said he had seen Rasputin . . . that he was a believer, sincere, and so on.'

It was with the same poetic language that Rasputin related the main mystery of his transformation in his 'Life'.

The Joy Of Suffering

Among the papers of the Extraordinary Commission is the testimony of Rasputin's fellow villagers about his sinful youth. 'His father would send him for grain and hay to Tyumen, about eighty versts away, and he would come back on foot, walking the whole eighty versts without money, beaten and drunk, and sometimes even without the horses.' Starting in his youth, there lived in that unprepossessing young peasant a dangerous force that found its way out in merrymaking, fist fights, and drunkenness. That great animal force weighed on him like a heavy burden.

'I was dissatisfied,' Rasputin told Menshikov. 'There was much I found no answer to, and I turned to drink.' Drunkenness was the norm for peasants. His father had drunk, as the witnesses interrogated by the Extraordinary Commission testified, although he later took himself in hand. (He even acquired a little income and owned a plot of land. In the winter he found work as a carter and in the summer, like all the peasants of Pokrovskoe, he fished and worked the land and earned money as a stevedore on steamboats and barges.)

But Rasputin was constantly drunk. And now that tender dreaminess for which his peers contemptuously called him Grishka the Fool alternated ever more frequently with fits of violent debauchery and vicious fist fights. So that another fellow villager described to the Extraordinary Commission a violent and insolent Grishka with a wild nature who 'got into fights not merely with outsiders but with his own father'.

'But all the same, I thought in my heart about . . . how people are saved,' Rasputin recounts in his 'Life'. And it was evidently the truth. The pointless life of his fellow villagers – peasant labour from dawn till dusk interrupted only by drunkenness – was that life?

But what was life? He didn't know. And the violent drunkenness continued. There wasn't enough money for debauchery. And then he got into some dangerous business. His fellow villager E. Kartavtsev testified before the Extraordinary Commission:

> I caught Grigory stealing my haystack fence. He had chopped it up and stacked it on his cart and was about to drive away with it. But I caught him and was going to make him take what he'd stolen to the regional administrative office. He wanted to run and came near to hitting me with his axe, but I hit him with a stake so hard the blood started flowing from his nose and mouth . . . At first I thought I'd killed him, but then he started to stir . . . I set out with him to the regional office. He didn't want to go. But I hit him several times in the face with my fist, after which he himself walked to the regional office . . . After that beating he turned kind of strange and stupid.

'I hit him with a stake, the blood flowed' – it was all so ordinary. Savage, bloody fist fights were a common affair in Siberia. Rasputin's build was anything but powerful, but even so, he was, as we shall subsequently have occasion to see more than once, a person of unusual physical strength. So the beating he took from the by no means young Kartavtsev probably made little impression on him. It was no accident that, as Kartavtsev says, he immediately took up his thieving again: 'Soon after the theft of the stakes from me, a pair of horses was stolen from the common pasture. I myself was guarding the horses and saw Rasputin and his comrades ride up to them. But I didn't give it any meaning. Several hours later I discovered the horses were missing.'

His plucky companions rode off to the city to sell the horses. But, according to Kartavtsev, Rasputin for some reason let the horses go and returned home.

No, something did happen to Rasputin in the course of that beating. The simple Kartavtsev's explanation that Rasputin 'turned kind of strange and stupid' is inadequate here. No, he could not have understood Rasputin's dark, complicated nature. When, during the beating, the blow of the stake had seemed in danger of killing him and the blood had started running down his face, Rasputin evidently experienced something. The beaten youth sensed a strange joy in his soul that he would later call 'the joy of abasement', 'the joy of suffering and abuse'. 'Abuse is a joy to the soul,' he would explain several years later to the writer Zhukovskaya. That is why Grishka went so unresistingly to take his punishment at the regional office. And why after the second theft he did not go to town to sell the horses. Maybe it was his moment of rebirth. And his fellow villagers apparently sensed a change in him. It can be no accident that when after the theft of the horses, 'the matter was brought to court of banishing Rasputin and his comrades to eastern Siberia for their vicious behaviour', his comrades were sent away at 'the verdict of society', but Rasputin was released.

It was time for him to marry, time to bring two more working hands into the household. His wife Praskovia (or Paraskeva) Fyodorovna was from the neighbouring village of Dubrovnoye. She was two years older than Rasputin. Wives in the villages were often chosen not for their youth or beauty but for their strength, so they could work hard in the fields and at home.

According to the 1897 census, although twenty-eight, Rasputin had not yet set up his own household and he continued to live with his father's family. The family consisted of its head, Efim Yakovlevich Rasputin, fifty-five; his wife, Anna Vasilievna, also fifty-five; his son Grigory, twenty-eight, and Grigory's wife, Praskovia Fyodorovna, thirty. All were registered as farmers, and all were illiterate.

Praskovia was an exemplary wife. She bore her husband three sons and two daughters. But more important she was a good worker. Working hands were very much needed in the Rasputin household because Grigory himself was often absent visiting holy places. By then his transformation was complete.

'I came to the conclusion that in the life of the simple peasant Rasputin a kind of great and profound experience had occurred that utterly changed his psyche and compelled him to turn to Christ,' the investigator of the Extraordinary Commission T. Rudnev would later write.

The Mystery Begins

'Until I was twenty-eight, I lived, as people say, "in the world"; I was with the world, that is, I loved what was in the world,' Rasputin himself recounted. Twenty-eight was the boundary, the moment when the transformation took place.

Legend has it that Rasputin once worked as a coachman, that he used his own horses to carry people back and forth along the highway. One day he was on his way to Tyumen with Melety Zborovsky, a seminary student who later became a bishop and then the rector of the Tomsk Theological

Seminary. They started talking about God. And the conversation produced a profound change in Rasputin's soul. Or more exactly, it would seem, his soul had long anticipated such a conversation.

It was a conversation about a merciful God who waits for the return of the prodigal son until the very last human breath, so that 'in the eleventh hour it is still not too late to come to Him.' Melety told him the essential words: 'Go and be saved.'

Rasputin wanted a continuation of that conversation. But he failed to get from the typically uneducated village priest in Pokrovskoe what he had received from the future magister of theology. Whereupon he decided to set off on his own in search of spiritual nourishment – the 'angelic bread of the human soul'.

He first went to the monasteries near his village of Pokrovskoe, to the Tyumen and Tobolsk cloisters. His life as a wanderer had begun. He went by foot along the deep river Tura. And, as he wrote in his 'Life', in the course of those wanderings, 'I saw before my eyes the image of the Saviour Himself walking along the shore. Nature taught me to love God and converse with Him.' This primal pagan worship of nature was very important for his subsequent teachings. For his was a God who lives in the trees and resounds in the voices of birds and gazes at the traveller from every blade of grass.

He returned to his village already a different person. It was in fact then, during his wanderings, that he began to comprehend a certain mystical secret.

And now visions began to visit him ever more frequently. Visions and miracles became his reality. And he felt the divine in himself ever more distinctly. 'Once,' he related, 'I spent the night in a room where there was an icon of the Mother of God. And I woke up in the middle of the night and saw that the icon was weeping: "Grigory, I am weeping for the sins of mankind. Go, wander, and cleanse the people of their sins."'

But in Pokrovskoe they did not trust the former merry drunk and fornicator. And at home they laughed at him, too. Once during a prayer when the members of his family were laughing at his piety, 'he stuck his shovel in a pile of grain and set off, just as he was, to visit the holy places.'

The Wanderers Of Vanished 'Holy Rus'

Thus he became a new person. And not only did he stop drinking and smoking; he stopped eating meat and sweets. He became a pilgrim or wanderer (*strannik*).

In times past, wandering had been a vital part of Russian life. Every peasant made a pilgrimage to holy places. As a rule, these were famous monasteries celebrated for their relics of saints and their miracle-working icons. The gentry made pilgrimages, too. They 'wandered' in carriages, whilst the peasants went on foot with knapsacks on their backs. Even the Russian empresses Elizabeth and Catherine the Great made pilgrimages.

At the end of the nineteenth century, however, only isolated individuals took up wandering. Holy Rus was becoming a legend. And now very few 'God's people' abandoned their homesteads to set out on foot to worship at the holy icons and relics. In his 'Life of an Experienced Wanderer', Rasputin tells of spending time in Kiev monasteries, Moscow churches, and Petersburg temples. From his Siberian village he had walked thousands of versts to Kiev and Petersburg along endless Russian roads with a knapsack on his back, begging for alms and a place to sleep. And so he went from village to village, church to church, and monastery to monastery. The peasants in the villages gave him shelter in consideration of his divine task. They saw in wanderers the last heirs of the disappearing God-pleasing days of old. From time to time on a lonely road robbers would attack the defenceless wanderer. And as Rasputin relates in his 'Life', 'I would say to them, it is not mine but God's. Take from me. I give it to you gladly.' And finally on the endless road a village would appear and a little village church. 'The ringing of its bell gladdens the heart.' But instead of joy at finding a temple of God, 'the devil would whisper of the flesh to the tired wanderer, saying, "Take your place in the parvis, gather alms, the road is long, much money is needed, pray they take you in for dinner and feed you better." I had to struggle against such thoughts.'

Satan Nearby

Satan's greatest ruse is to convince us that he does not exist, but for Rasputin Satan was not only a reality, but was always nearby. Satan, he writes, would appear to him 'in the form of a beggar, he would whisper to the weary wanderer tormented by thirst that it is many versts to the next village'. Rasputin would 'make the sign of the cross or begin to sing a hymn of the cherubim . . . and then you would look, and there would be a village'.

A witness who had seen Rasputin after one of his pilgrimages told the Extraordinary Commission that 'he seemed abnormal . . . He sang something and waved and threatened with his hands.' That would forever remain his way – to speak to Satan constantly and to threaten him, calling on God with hymns for aid in his struggle with the devil. 'A cunning enemy', he wants to return to his own power the soul that has been promised to God. 'And people help him in this. Everyone watches the person who seeks salvation as though he were some sort of robber, and all are quick to mock him,' Rasputin writes in his 'Life'.

All this time Rasputin's strange nervous organization was causing him difficulty, especially in the spring.

'Every spring I would not sleep for forty nights,' Rasputin remembers in his 'Life.' 'Thus it had been from the age of fifteen to thirty-eight.' But in the world of miracles, where he now resided, the treatment was simple. One had only in sincere prayer to ask for the help of a favourite saint. And Rasputin would appeal to Saint Simeon of Verkhoturye.

The Mighty Saint

The constant goal of his wanderings all this time was the Nikolaev Monastery in Verkhoturye. This ancient cloister, founded by the Muscovite tsars in the sixteenth century, stood on a hill at the confluence of two small streams. And the devout from all over Siberia came there to pay homage to its relics of the righteous Simeon.

Saint Simeon of Verkhoturye was becoming Rasputin's favourite saint. And it was to him that he linked the emergence of his own mysterious strength.

Simeon of Verkhoturye was born at the very beginning of the seventeenth century and lived nearby on the banks of the same Tura river. A wanderer like Rasputin, he went among the local villages or lived by himself on the banks of the Tura. Rasputin was shown the stone under the spruce where the saint was fond of sitting. Simeon's death the consequence of extraordinary abstinence and fasting in 1642. Half a century later, as is written in the official Life of Saint Simeon, it was 'noticed that his coffin had begun to rise up out of the earth, and that his uncorrupted remains could be seen through the splintered boards.'

And healing began at the holy grave. The first person to be healed at the end of the seventeenth century, according to the Life of Saint Simeon, bore the name Grigory and took 'earth from the coffin, rubbed his limbs with it, and was healed'. For the next two hundred and fifty years pilgrims came from all over Russia to be healed at Saint Simeon's grave. At the beginning of the eighteenth century, Simeon's relics were solemnly transferred to the Nikolaev Monastery in Verkhoturye.

And as Rasputin would write, it was next to his relics that 'Simeon the

Righteous of Verkhoturye healed me of the affliction of insomnia.' Simeon became his patron saint. And until his death Rasputin would visit the monastery and take his mad admirers there.

As we shall see, he would call on Simeon of Verkhoturye for help in his first attempt to reach the royal family. And his first gift to the royal family would be an icon of Saint Simeon. Simeon would as it were accompany him on his spiritual quest. And later, when Rasputin's life took a downward turn, Simeon would follow him to his death.

For when the royal family perished in the summer of 1918, the relics of Saint Simeon would perish too, ejected from the monastery by the Bolsheviks.

It was at the time of his rebirth that Rasputin's prophecies began. As he related it to Zhukovskaya, 'When the Lord visited me . . . I took leave of my senses . . . and I started to run through the village in a frost wearing only my shirt and calling for repentance. And then I fell with a crash by a fence, where I lay for a day . . . Then I awoke . . . and the peasants came running to me from every direction. "You spoke the truth, Grisha," they said. "We should have repented long ago, for tonight half the village has burned down."'

Thus, it was at the start of the new twentieth century that his fame and the rumours of his miracles began. As Feofan, then inspector of the Petersburg Theological Seminary, told it, 'It was given to him to close the heavens, and drought fell upon the earth until he ordered the heavens to open themselves up again.'

But, as we read in the testimony given before the Extraordinary Commission, Rasputin would more and more frequently return from his travels accompanied by 'two or three female wanderers dressed in something like nun's garb.'

The Chapel Under The Stable

It is no coincidence that Saint Serafim of Sarov, one of the last great Russian saints of the nineteenth century, also went about surrounded by young women.

Among Rasputin's first disciples were Evdokia (Dunya) and Ekaterina (Katya) Pechyorkina (not sisters, as they are frequently identified in the

Rasputin biographies, but an aunt and a niece), who lived with him 'earning their bread' as domestics.

Katya, at the time very young, would eventually follow him to Petersburg, where she would become his maid. And it was she who would be fated to see the face of Rasputin's murderer on that December night in 1916.

There were few men in that circle. Just his relative Nikolai Rasputin, and two other fellow villagers, Nikolai Raspopov and Ilya Arsyonov.

In the future inquiry of the Tobolsk Consistory into the charge against Grigory Rasputin of sectarianism, Nikolai Rasputin would testify that 'a chapel was at the time located under the stable.' And as the witnesses of the Extraordinary Commission would testify, 'they gathered in great secrecy in a dugout under the stable, and sang and read the Gospels, the hidden meaning of which Rasputin would explain to them.' But the investigation would learn nothing more of the hidden meaning revealed by Rasputin in that chapel under the stable.

Rasputin did not stay in Pokrovskoe for long, however. He abandoned his disciples and once again set out to visit the monasteries. And his wanderings became ever more rigorous. 'For experience and to test myself,' he said, 'I frequently did not change my undergarments for six months at a time when going from Tobolsk to Kiev, and I would often walk for three days, eating only the slightest amount. On hot days I would impose a fast on myself. I would not drink kvass but would work with the day labourers just as they worked; I would work and then take my repose in prayer.' This is the lofty manner in which Rasputin told the 'tsars' about his transformation in his 'Life'.

But he told them nothing of what was at the heart of his wandering: the dangerous cloisters concealed deep in the remote Siberian forests, their remarkable beliefs, and the unofficial 'Orthodoxy of the people' that had actually formed both the semi-literate Siberian peasant and his mysterious teachings.

He told them nothing of the hidden religious Rus that had existed for hundreds of years alongside the official Church.

Hidden 'Holy Rus'

Distrust of the official church had deep roots in Russia.

Christianity had been adopted in Rus a thousand years before in the tenth century. But paganism did not for that reason disappear. Christian churches in Russia were often built on pagan holy places. The pagan gods that the princes had forced the people to repudiate lived on unseen. The pagan god Volos, for example, whose untrammelled power was manifest, according to pagan beliefs, in the alternating fecundity and destruction of the natural world, was transformed into 'God's servant, Saint Vlasy the Miracle Worker'. The pagan god of thunder, Perun, was supplanted by the prophet Elijah who caused the storms to rumble. And the pagan delight in nature, the pagan worship and deification of nature, remained in the people's souls. The alacrity with which they agreed after the revolution to destroy their own great Orthodox temples at the behest of the Bolsheviks is strikingly similar to the ease with which they smashed and burned their pagan holy places at the order of the princes.

Entire regions lived through that thousand-year period in a blend of paganism and Orthodoxy. And the ancient sorcerers and saintly healers existed side by side, as well: the healers healed, and the sorcerers cast spells or warded them off.

Siberia and the Trans-Volga were the centres of that strange 'Orthodoxy of the people'.

A 'Russian America'

In the seventeenth century, the forests of the Trans-Volga extended without interruption to the far north. Standing along the banks of the Volga's tributaries were occasional hamlets separated from each other by vast tracts of impassable forest. The people who lived in those hamlets were, in a sense, cut off from the rest of the baptized world, and the area's Orthodox Russians resembled in their savage customs the primeval denizens of those places, the wild Cheremis and Votyak trappers. Weddings were celebrated in the forest, their participants at once worshipping the holy saints and trees. 'They lived in the forest, they prayed to stumps, they married standing around a spruce, and devils sang to them,' it was once said of the Trans-Volga's inhabitants.

In the second decade of the seventeenth century, new residents began to appear in those impenetrable thickets. They were the children of the bloody Time of Troubles (1584–1613), which had rolled across the Russian land in insurrections and the collapse of the state. The Time of Troubles had ended with the accession of the Romanov dynasty to the throne. And now in flight from the rage of the new tsars, those involved in the recent mutinies fled to the Trans-Volga and Siberia. The very people who in the Time of Troubles had visited pillaging and bloodshed upon the entire Russian land.

They found refuge in the forested regions from the knout and the gallows. It was a unique 'Russian America'.

A Disastrous Schism In The Russian Church

Later on, in the seventeenth century, new refugees added their numbers to the forests of the Trans-Volga and Siberia. The church reforms under Tsar Alexis Mikhailovich were accompanied by a renovation of the sacred texts and a change in the very mystery of signing the cross. Believers were now required to cross themselves with three fingers instead of two. The new Orthodoxy produced a sea of blood. Many believers declared the 'new books' and the new rites to be a temptation of Satan. They held to the old ways, crossing themselves as before, and reading only the old versions of the sacred texts. And they called themselves 'Old Believers'.

The great schism in church life had begun. The official church harshly chastised the Old Believers. Imprisonment, execution, and mass self-immolation of the adherents of the old beliefs – all of this happened. And the Old Believers now established their holy cloisters beyond the reach of authority in the boundless forests of the Trans-Volga and Siberia.

As industry developed and the forests were logged, the schismatic cloisters in the Trans-Volga also began to retreat beyond the Urals – to the impenetrable forests of Siberia. So that for the entire three-hundred-year history of the Romanov dynasty there existed in Siberia alongside the official Orthodox Church an unofficial but powerful and secret 'church of the people'.

The Tsar Rules The Church

That which Tsar Alexis Mikhailovich had begun by splitting the Russian Church, his son Peter the Great successfully continued. This reformer tsar destroyed the ancient patriarchate and openly mocked the old church rites. He also established, with a so-called chief procurator appointed by the tsar at its head, a Holy Synod which from that day forth would govern church affairs. And although Nicholas's father, Alexander III, was a deeply religious man, the official church still remained subordinate to the tsar and still dragged out the same sorry existence under his reign that it had dragged out previously. Serving as the head of the Holy Synod as its chief procurator was the emperor's favourite, K. Pobedonostsev. He was one of the cleverest people in the country. But, as frequently happens in Russia, his whole mind was directed towards oppression. The least loophole for freedom of thought and speech was subjected to ruthless attack. He would destroy at the root, any law capable of mitigating even slightly the unlimited power of the tsar over the church. As head of the Holy Synod, this profoundly devout man did everything he could to contain the great and infinite world of church life within the framework of ruthless bureaucratization and to force the church hierarchs to recognize one law only: the command of the tsar and the chief procurator.

The official church found itself in a condition of profound lethargy.

Meanwhile, the social cauldron had begun to boil. Not long before he died, Tsar Alexander III had a conversation with one of his trusted advisers, the adjutant general O. Richter. 'I sense that things in Russia are not going as they should,' Nicholas's father had said, and then he asked Richter to speak his mind. 'I have given it a great deal of thought,' Richter answered, 'and I imagine the country in the form of a colossal boiler in which fermentation is taking place, while around the boiler walk people with hammers. And when in the boiler's walls the slightest crack is formed, they immediately seal it up with rivets. But eventually the gases within will force such a crack that it will be impossible to reseal it, and we shall all suffocate!' And, Richter recalled, the sovereign began to moan as if in pain.

The weak official church could no longer offer assistance in the event of catastrophe. The people did not trust it. Those who stood at the crossroads either went with their troubles in the direction of revolution, or turned for help to holy fools and elders or to the sectarians. To the cloisters lost in the forests.

The Elders' Prophecies

Rasputin's life had passed its halfway mark and was already hurtling towards death. His fourth decade had begun, and he was still going from monastery to monastery.

The faces of the holy images in their ancient frames glimmer before their lamps in the dark refectory. In three rows, extending to the windows stand tables, and on either side of them, benches. Here sit not only the monastery brethren but also the lay people visiting the monastery. A place is found for everyone. What a gallery of faces and types! How many passions overcome or repressed! How many instructive stories! He learned to read pitiable human passions in those faces. He saw the great power of a piety that could help to heal incurable diseases. But he also came to know the Siberian sorcerers and healers, who had brought from the heathen past the secrets of their cures and spells. Thousands of faces and encounters, thousands of confessions and conversations into the night.

Under the icon cases are books in old black bindings and a little chalice – a copper cup with a cross on it that serves as a bell during meals. How many times had the wanderer Grigory Rasputin heard its ring signalling the start of a meal. How many times had he gazed with widened eyes at those ordinary-looking monks, the 'elders', whose spiritual feats the monastery had hidden from view.

The great elders, those who had achieved moral perfection and gained a wisdom that was unattainable in the world at large, lived in the monastery like the most ordinary monks. The monastery rules did not permit the display of spiritual riches on the outside, and it protected the spiritual growth of its votaries from worldly temptations. But that which was hidden during the day was recorded by night in a trembling elder's hand. And how happy Grigory was whenever he succeeded in talking to these men. It was from them that he learned his tender, love-filled speech.

In the monasteries he heard about the elders' prophecies regarding the destruction looming over the Romanov realm. Those predictions are now famous as the prophecies of the elders of the Optina Pustyn Monastery and of Serafim of Sarov. But how many other divinations by obscure elders have perished in distant monasteries that were ravaged in the civil war and destroyed by the Bolsheviks? Rasputin brought back from his wanderings that sense of catastrophe hanging over the kingdom.

The 'Russian Dream'

At the very beginning of his wanderings among the ancient cloisters hidden in the wilderness, Grigory also learned about a new spiritual experience that had first enticed and then come to rule over hundreds of people, and that had secretly captivated whole monasteries. They were secret fellowships, powerful in the rabid faith of their membership. Whilst other Christian sects came from the West, the *Khlysty* (Flagellants) and *Skoptsy* (Castrators) were an exclusively Russian phenomenon. They were sects in which fanaticism, lechery, and faith in God were blasphemously joined together as one. Sects that played a major role in the fate of Rasputin and of the empire.

The downtrodden condition of the people, the cruel oppression of the peasants, and the persecution of their ancestors' old ways of worship all gave rise to the age-old 'Russian dream' of the advent of a Redeemer. At first, the dream was of an earthly Redeemer – a just ruler. And self-proclaimed 'tsars' accordingly made continual appearances over a two hundred year span in the seventeenth and eighteenth centuries.

There have been pretenders of the kind in every country. But only in Russia did the phenomenon reach such a scale and enjoy such success. The first great impostor, the fugitive monk Grigory Otrepiev, declared himself the son of Ivan the Terrible and, to Europe's amazement, routed the powerful Tsar Boris Godunov. And himself became the Muscovite tsar. And ruled until he was exposed and killed by the boyars. But as a result, instead of one impostor, there appeared a multitude of them. The people readily joined the forces of those 'tsars', and Russia was for many years embroiled in the great bloody insurrections of the Time of Troubles. More than a hundred such pretenders, each proclaiming himself to be the 'true tsar', were active in Russia during those two centuries. One such, the illiterate peasant Emelyan Pugachyov, assembled an army of several thousand peasants and Cossacks and very nearly put an end to Empress Catherine the Great herself.

Simultaneously active with the earthly tsar-pretenders over the full three-hundred-year reign of the Romanov dynasty were pretenders of the heavenly sort – the 'Christs'.

The Khlysty And Sexual Frenzy

The Khlysty also appeared in Russia in the seventeenth century during the reigns of the first Romanovs. And became powerful. Their history begins simply enough. The sect's founder was a certain Daniil Filippovich, who proclaimed himself the 'Lord of hosts'. As Khlyst tradition describes him, 'This Daniil Filippovich descended from heaven in great glory in a chariot of fire' and remained on earth in the form of man. According to the same legend, 'fifteen years before the advent of the "Lord of hosts" Daniil Filippovich, "God's son" Ivan Suslov was born to a one-hundred-year-old Mother of God.' At the age of thirty, Suslov was summoned by the 'Lord of hosts' Daniil Filippovich, who made him a 'living god'. Thus, both the 'Lord of hosts' and 'his son Christ' had appeared in sinful Rus. Along with a 'Mother of God', who had given birth to the 'Christ'. They had come to defend an aggrieved and impoverished people.

According to Khlyst tradition, the first 'Christ' Ivan Suslov was seized by the boyars, taken to Moscow, and crucified at the Kremlin's Spassky Gate. But he rose from the dead. And they crucified him again, and again he rose. Afterwards, both Daniil Filippovich and Ivan Suslov died, or, more accurately, they returned to heaven, and others became new 'Lords of hosts', 'Christs', and 'Mothers of God'.

The susceptibility of the *Khlyst* 'living Gods' to decay did not trouble their benighted followers in the least. For according to *Khlyst* belief, with the departure from earthly life (or, more properly, the ascent to heaven) of the latest 'Christ', the Holy Spirit was installed in another body. So that during that time many 'Messiahs' lived in the bitter Russian land.

This particular childish mixture of paganism and Orthodoxy was bound to make its appearance in ignorant, ruthlessly oppressed, servile Russia. The *Khlyst* doctrine opened a world of boundless possibilities to the down-trodden peasant. For it taught that every man may become Christ Himself, and every woman the Mother of God. One had only to rid oneself of the sin of the flesh (the Old Testament Adam) and by a life of righteousness and prayer ready one's soul for the descent into it of the Holy Spirit – that is, to nurture Christ in oneself. And become Him. It was the mysticism of an ignorant people in which the Holy Spirit was materially lodged in people's souls. To illiterate peasants, that literalism was joyously clear.

Now every *Khlyst* community (or 'ark', in their terminology) had its own 'Christ' and 'Mother of God'. At first, the people called the sectarians 'Christs'. But the rite of self-scourging, of flagellation, once more deriving from pagan times and outlandishly combined with notions about Christ's flogging, gave the sect the new name of *Khlysty* (meaning 'whips'). Their own name for themselves was 'God's people' and, later on, 'Christ-believers'.

In preparing their souls for the descent of the Holy Spirit, they naturally preached extreme asceticism. But once again in a quite unexpected Russian form: the suppression of lust took place through boundless debauchery.

In some *Khlyst* sects, abstention, the refusal of family sexual life was, during the rite of 'rejoicing' (*radenie*), transformed into 'group sinning' (*svalnyi grekh*) – into promiscuous sexual relations among the sect membership. 'Rejoicing', the principal *Khlyst* rite, derived from the pagan sorcerers and shamans; *Khlyst* 'rejoicing' was merely the latest mixture of paganism and Christianity. It was during 'rejoicing', in the view of the *Khlysty*, that the Holy Spirit descended upon them. And then the members of the sect would try to conceive as many new 'Christs' and 'Mothers of God' as possible. That conceiving took place in a state of frenzy preceded by *Khlyst* dancing.

Khlyst *Dancing*

I was the witness of such 'rejoicing' on the little island of Chechen in the Caspian Sea. Old Believers fled to the island in the seventeenth century.

But by the eighteenth, fugitive *Khlysty* also began to arrive, and they kept alive the ways of their ancient sect over the centuries. As in the past, the rites were absolutely secret, although present-day rigours permit no comparison at all with earlier times. I shall omit to mention the ruses and, mainly, bribery, by which I managed to see what I saw. I did have to swear a terrible oath to 'remain silent for thirty-three years'. But those thirty-three years have passed.

I quote from my notes of 1964:

> In white flaxen shirts worn over naked bodies they went down into the cellar of a peasant lodge. There in the dry cellar they lit candles. They started to sing something sacred in the half-light – as was later explained, a verse from the Easter canon: 'Seeing, we are gladdened, for Christ has risen.' After that a little old man with joyful, light-coloured eyes – the local Christ – began to chant a *Khlyst* prayer in the flickering candlelight. And then with youthful energy he started to 'rejoice', that is, to whirl wildly in place, crossing himself and continually whipping his body. The choir chanted prayers, their voices ever more savagely, ever more fervently and passionately praying, so that some of them were already screaming and sobbing. But at this point the old man stopped his whirling and cried out wildly, 'Brothers! Brothers! I feel it, the Holy Spirit! God is within me!' And he began to prophesy, shouting incoherent sounds mixed into which were the words, 'Oh, Spirit!' 'Oh, God!' 'Oh, Spirit Lord!' After that began the main communal rite of 'rejoicing', or general whirling and dancing.

They believed that the Holy Spirit comes during the whirling and dancing. And that resurrected in their sweat were the drops of His sweat produced in the Garden of Gethsemane. It was presumably after experiencing the physiological effect of that whirling, which acts upon the brain like alcohol, that they called the whirling 'spiritual beer'.

Everything flew. They were no longer whirling people, but flying hair, billowing clothes, cries, and shouts. Their sweat ran in rivulets, and they themselves were swimming in it as if in a bath. The flames of their candles flickered and died out. And everything was in darkness.

And then, intoxicated by their furious whirling, they fell to the floor. And that was the end of it. But apparently only because I was present.

Russian Spiritual Gymnastics

For it is then in some 'arks' that they are united in 'love', in 'group sinning'. But it is only a sin to the uninitiated. They themselves know that they sin to suppress the flesh – so that they will be purified, so that their souls may shine with the brotherly love of a 'Christ', a love liberated by sin from sin and from any carnal intentions. They drive out sin with sin. That is the *Khlyst* revelation.

And it is at that moment that the Holy Spirit descends into their 'pure bodies'.

That is why they teach that if any children are born from that night, they are born not of the flesh but of the Holy Spirit.

Expressed in *Khlyst* doctrine is the dangerous courage of the Russian soul – it is not frightened of sin. For, as the *Khlysty* teach, in the religious person sin is always followed by great suffering, and that suffering leads to a profound repentance. And a great purification of the soul that brings that person closer to God. The continuous alternation of great sin and great repentance is the central idea. Sin – repentance – purification constitute the essential gymnastics of the soul.

And without grasping that *Khlyst* idea of ridding oneself of sin through sin, without grasping, in other words, the concept of 'spiritual gymnastics' and their importance in sin, we shall not understand Rasputin.

The official church recognized the danger of the *Khlysty* and started to fight against them. In Moscow in 1733 seventy-eight people were condemned, their leaders executed, and the rest exiled to remote monasteries. The grave of the sect's founder, Daniil Filippovich, in the Ivanov Monastery was dug up and his remains burned. But that did not stop the Khlyst movement.

The 'First Arrival' Of The Khlysty
At The Palaces

By the beginning of the nineteenth century, not only illiterate peasants but also landowners, clergy, and the highest nobility had become involved in the *Khlyst* heresy. At the start of the century a secret *Khlyst* sect operated in Petersburg at the Mikhailov Castle, the former residence of Emperor Paul I. At its head was a 'Mother of God', the colonel's wife E. F. Tartarinova, née Baroness Buchsgefden. She had, upon marrying, converted from Lutheranism to Orthodoxy. And it was at that moment that she 'felt that the Holy Spirit had entered her'. She sensed that she was a Mother of God and recognized the gift of prophecy in herself. Half-coherent prophetic incantations and frenzied *Khlyst* whirling under the guidance of the baroness were engaged in nightly in the Mikhailov Castle. And the highest Petersburg nobility participated in the rites. Generals, dukes, and important officials like P. Koshelev, the court steward, and Prince A. Golitsyn, the minister of enlightenment and spiritual affairs. It was all clothed in secrecy, and the participants carefully kept that secret safe from the crude hands of the uninitiated.

Tartarinova's sect continued its activity during the whole reign of Alexander I.

But rites that in the beginning had possessed a severely ascetic character gradually degenerated into a wild orgy of unrestrained passion. It was only in 1837, during the reign of Nicholas I, that Tartarinova was arrested and forcibly removed to a convent. The grandees who joined the *Khlysty* were an exception, however. The sect remained above all a peasant movement, a strange 'Orthodoxy of the people'.

The Fanatical Russian Heresies

But the idea of purifying oneself of sin through sin began to raise doubts among some of 'God's people'. And then the dream of victory over lust and lechery, without which one could not become a 'Christ', gave birth to a fanatical new idea.

In the mid-eighteenth century, the sect known as *Skoptsy* or 'Castrators' separated itself from the *Khlysty*. The founder of the new sect, Kondraty Selivanov, began inveighing against the sexual dissoluteness of the *Khlysty* and preaching an absolute asceticism that was achievable only through the 'fiery baptism' of castration. The basis of the new doctrine was a passage in the Gospel according to St Matthew that was understood by the semi-literate peasants as a guide to immediate action.

In Matthew, Christ says in a discussion with his disciples that 'there are eunuchs who have been so from birth, and there are eunuchs who have been made eunuchs by men, and there are eunuchs who have made themselves eunuchs for the sake of the kingdom of heaven. He who is able to receive this, let him receive it' (Matthew 19: 12). And from this came mass acts of fanatical self-mutilation. The awful procedure of male castration by means of a red-hot iron (axes were also used) was accompanied by an even more horrible operation on women: external sexual organs, nipples, and even whole breasts were cut off. A 'supreme degree' of castration was also invented: the removal of the male sexual organ. All these terrible mutilations of the body were performed voluntarily by the members of the sect. The *Skoptsy* were preparing themselves for eternal life. And taking support in the same passage in the Gospel according to St Matthew, they believed in their advantage over ordinary mortals. The songs of the *Skoptsy* during their ceremonies were full of joy and exultation.

And as with the *Khlysty*, the new sect also attracted the attention of the aristocracy. Landowners, officers, and even clergymen voluntarily castrated themselves. Tsar Alexander I himself found time to talk to the father of the *Skoptsy* movement, Selivanov.

And after that royal attention, the idea appeared in *Skoptsy* circles of sending their 'Christs' to assist the tsar – for the salvation of his reign which was drowning in bureaucratic thievery and unbelief. An elaborate plan was drawn up for the transformation of Russia into a land where 'God's people' would hold sway. The main living 'Christ', Selivanov himself, was to take his place alongside the person of the emperor. And it was proposed that each minister would have his own 'Christ' too. The plan was presented to Alexander I in 1803. The idea made him angry. And the plan's author, the Polish nobleman and eunuch Alexei Elensky, was forced to retire to a monastery.

No matter! The time would still come for one of 'God's people' to rule the country.

Secret Wanderings In Secret
'Little Corners'

But the *Skoptsy* did not become a mass sect. As before, the most influential mass sect remained the *Khlysty*.

By the end of the nineteenth century there were powerful *Khlyst* 'arks' in Siberia, in the factories of Perm, for instance. And *Khlyst* sects had spread throughout European Russia, as well. At the second congress of the Russian Social-Democratic Labour Party in 1903, Lenin spoke of a secret *Khlyst* organization that had 'taken control of masses of villages and farms in the central part of Russia and was spreading with ever greater strength'.

There were *Khlyst* communities in Petersburg and its environs, and in Moscow and its suburbs. The famous poet Marina Tsvetaeva recalls in her autobiographical essay 'Kirill's Daughters' how in the town of Tarus, to the astonishment of her childhood imagination, a *Khlyst* 'Christ' and 'Mother of God' would come by their orchard to pick apples. 'Christ has come for apples,' the adults would say.

So established along the route of Rasputin's wanderings at that time, there were 'arks' – enigmatic communities of *Khlyst* 'Christs' and 'Mothers of God'.

Driven underground by the official church, the *Khlysty* worked out rules of behaviour for themselves in the world. 'Ours', 'our own', the *Khlysty* called each other, and they conferred conspiratorial aliases to take the place of their real names. 'Ours' and the aliases – all of this would soon be heard in the royal palace.

Many of the favourite ideas of the *Khlysty* are to be found in Rasputin's 'works'. Above all, excoriation of the official clergy and contempt for the book learning of the church's hierarchs. 'I have had to spend much time among the hierarchs, I have spoken with them at length . . . Their learning remains insignificant, but they listen to your simple words.' 'Learning for the sake of piety is nothing. The letter has confused their minds and bound their feet, and [they] cannot walk in the footsteps of the Saviour.' And, he says, for that reason, they cannot provide needed counsel to those in want of spiritual nourishment. And then Rasputin adds an important phrase: 'At the present time, those who are able to give counsel have all been driven into little corners.'

The *Khlyst* sects 'driven into little corners', those 'arks' and 'flotillas' scattered all over Russia, kept in constant secret communication with each other. And they did so by employing messengers – 'seraphs' or 'flying angels', that is, wanderers who travelled continuously among the arks.

Hidden here, perhaps, is an answer to the riddle of the first half of the restless and forever secret of the life of the experienced wanderer.

It was in 'hidden Rus' among the *Khlysty* that Rasputin first set out on his path to God. There he learned a mystical secret – the ability to foster Christ in himself. He started with that. And it is no accident that even then, in that obscure period of his life, he was the subject of investigation.

The First Accusation

The first ecclesiastical persecution of Rasputin dates back to 1903, when his fame had already begun to spread as far as Petersburg itself. As a 'man of God', he was denounced in the Tobolsk Theological Consistory for his odd behaviour towards women who came to visit him from 'Petersburg itself'. He was also denounced regarding the fact that even in his youth Rasputin 'had brought from his life in the factories of the province of Perm an acquaintance with the teachings of the *Khlyst* heresy'. An investigator was dispatched to Pokrovskoe. But nothing incriminating was found at the time. Yet from then until his death, the tag of *Khlyst* never left him.

3

THE PATH TO
THE PALACE

Conquest Of The Capital

Rasputin began to prepare for his trip to the capital. A place to which his fame had already preceded him. He was still young. But his face was wrinkled by the sun and wind from his endless wanderings. A peasant's face – even at twenty-five it might sometimes already be that of an old man. His endless wanderings had made him an unerring judge of people. Holy Scripture, the teachings of the great pastors, the countless sermons he had listened to had all been absorbed by his tenacious memory. In the *Khlyst* 'arks', where pagan spells against disease were combined with the power of Christian prayer, he had learned to heal. He had grasped his strength. A laying-on of his restless, nervous hands was enough. And diseases would dissipate in those hands.

Rasputin appeared in Petersburg in 1903 on the eve of the first Russian revolution. To destroy both Petersburg and that whole world of the tsars, which in a mere fourteen years would become an Atlantis of irretrievable memory.

> To our proud capital
> He came – God save us!
> He charmed the tsarina
> Of illimitable Rus . . .
>
> Why did the crosses on
> Kazan Cathedral and Saint Isaac's
> Not bend? Why did not they
> Abandon their places?

Nikolai Gumilyov

A Meeting With Stalin's
Patriarch

The legends and conjectures finally come to an end in the capital. Now begins the story of Rasputin that is corroborated by documents and the testimony of witnesses.

As he himself would recount in his 'Life of an Experienced Wanderer', he had set out for Petersburg with a great goal – to solicit money for the building of a church in Pokrovskoe: 'I myself am an illiterate person, and, most important, without means, but in my heart that Temple already stands before my eyes.'

Arriving in the great city, he 'went first of all to the Alexander Nevsky Abbey'. He attended a service of public prayer and then embarked on a desperate plan – 'to go directly to the rector of the Theological Seminary, Bishop Sergius, who lived at the abbey'. If this account is to be believed, the notion was indeed a wild one, given his suspicious appearance – worn-out boots, pauper's coat, tangled beard, and hair combed like a road-house waiter's. Thus has he been described by the monk Iliodor. And now this wretched peasant is on his way to the bishop's apartment and asking the doorman to be kind enough to announce him to Sergius. Rasputin himself describes what happened next. 'The doorman did me the courtesy of a blow on the neck. I fell on my knees before him . . . He understood there was something special in me and announced me to the bishop.' Thus, thanks to his 'specialness', this peasant directly off the street got in to see Bishop Sergius himself. And captivated him at once.

Astounded by his words, Sergius, according to Rasputin, lodged the unknown peasant at the abbey with him. And not only that! 'The bishop,' Rasputin writes, 'introduced me to "highly placed personages".' The 'highly placed personages' included the celebrated ascetic and mystic Feofan, who was received at the royal palace.

So does Rasputin describe his arrival in Petersburg in his 'Life'.

But the period of legend is over. And the File easily demolishes Rasputin's whole invention. For it contains the testimony of the 'highly placed' Feofan about his first meeting with Rasputin.

Feofan was called before the Thirteenth Section of the Extraordinary Commission in 1917. And Feofan, then forty-four years old and bishop of Poltava, testified that 'Grigory Rasputin first came to Petrograd from the city of Kazan in the winter during the Russo-Japanese War with a letter of introduction from the now deceased Chrysanthos, archimandrite of the

Kazan eparchy. Rasputin stayed at the Alexander Nevsky Abbey with Bishop Sergius, the rector of the theological seminary.'

So there was no unfortunate wanderer. By that time, Rasputin's fame had already reached beyond the boundaries of Siberia. And he had many female admirers in Kazan. And the archimandrite of the Kazan eparchy had himself given Rasputin a letter of introduction to Sergius. So he did not have to make humble requests of the doorman. For he had come to Petersburg with a most powerful letter of introduction from one of the church's hierarchs. And for that reason, he was of course received by Bishop Sergius without hindrance.

And it was not by chance that Chrysanthos had given Rasputin that letter to Bishop Sergius. At that time, Sergius's name resounded not only in church circles. The bishop was then at the centre of an event that excited every Russian intellectual.

At the time of Rasputin's arrival, a series of unusual meetings was under way in the capital on the premises of the Geographical Society. Its narrow elongated hall was invariably packed to overflowing. Gathered on the stage and about the hall were people in cassocks and clerical headgear, and the flower of Russian culture. The meetings were the famous Petersburg religious and philosophical colloquia − a desperate attempt to overcome the destructive separation of the official church and the Russian intelligentsia, and to pull the church out of its lethargy.

At the colloquia the participants talked about the dangerous spiritual crisis in the country and the influence of the sects. The intelligentsia bitterly complained that the official church was becoming increasingly associated in society with obscurantism. That the official preachers failed to speak of the prophetic and mystical essence of Christianity. And that they saw in Christianity only an other-worldly ideal and thus had left earthly life out of the account. The intelligentsia called for the official church to turn its face back to the world and to reveal its spiritual treasures.

The colloquia were chaired by Bishop Sergius, a forty-year-old hierarch and author of audacious theological studies, who had recently been appointed head of the theological seminary.

He had, in the heated disputes, been able to find the right tone. He was not the chair nor a hierarch, but merely a Christian who would say, 'Don't argue, be Christians, and then you will achieve everything.' The colloquia came to an end in April 1903 after twenty-two sessions and twenty-two heated debates, cut short by Chief Procurator Pobedonostsev, who banned them.

(Human destinies are amazing. In 1942, during the war, when he decided to re-establish the office, Stalin appointed Sergius the first Patriarch of All Russia.)

Chrysanthos had chosen Rasputin's protector well: the future patriarch was open to new trends. How interesting the Siberian prophet of the people must have seemed then in 1903, at the height of that whole story.

And Rasputin did not betray their expectations. The 'specialness' in the newcomer soon captivated Sergius in truth. And he did in fact introduce Rasputin to 'highly placed personages'.

As Bishop Feofan has testified in the File, 'Once he [Bishop Sergius] invited us to his lodgings for tea, and introduced for the first time to me and several monks and seminarians a recently arrived man of God, Brother Grigory as we called him then. He amazed us all with his psychological perspicacity. His face was pale and his eyes unusually piercing – the look of someone who observed the fasts. And he made a strong impression.'

By then rumours of Rasputin's exceptional gift had reached Petersburg. Which is why the 'highly placed personages' wanted prophecies. And here Rasputin astonished them. 'At the time,' Feofan testified, 'Admiral Rozhdestvensky's squadron had already set sail. We therefore asked Rasputin, "Will its engagement with the Japanese be successful?" Rasputin answered, "I feel in my heart that it will be sunk." And his prediction subsequently came to pass in the battle of Tsushima Strait.'

What was happening here? An intelligent peasant who knew from the inside the whole unhappy weakness of his great country? Or had Rasputin merely heard what was being written then in all the Russian newspapers: that a squadron consisting of antediluvian ships, sailing without any concealment to engage a modern Japanese fleet in battle, was doomed? Or was it given him to comprehend the mysterious?

In any event, when 'Rasputin correctly told the students of the seminary whom he was seeing for the first time that one would be a writer and that another was ill, and then explained to a third that he was a simple soul whose simplicity was being taken advantage of by his friends,' Feofan fully believed in his prophetic gift. 'In conversation Rasputin revealed not book learning but a subtle grasp of spiritual experience obtained through personal knowledge. And a perspicacity that verged on second sight,' Feofan testified in the File.

The 'Black Princesses'

Feofan invited Rasputin to move in with him – to stay at his apartment. Thanks to Feofan, Rasputin soon turned up at one of the most influential Petersburg houses of the day, the palace of Grand Duke Pyotr Nikolaevich, Nicholas II's cousin.

The main figures in the palace of the ailing grand duke were two women, the Montenegrin princesses Militsa and Anastasia.

The thirty-seven-year-old Militsa and her sister Anastasia who was a year younger, came from a family of poor Montenegrin princes. They were the daughters of the Montenegrin king, Nicholas Njegoš. The elder Militsa was married to Grand Duke Pyotr Nikolaevich. And her inseparable sister Anastasia spent her days and nights at Militsa's palace.

Anastasia, or Stana as she was known in the family, was married to the Duke of Leichtenberg and had had children by him. But Militsa's husband's brother, Grand Duke Nikolai Nikolaevich, had become a too frequent guest at her palace. And soon high society gossips began to talk of an affair between Militsa's sister Stana and Grand Duke Nikolai Nikolaevich.

This forty-seven-year-old giant and dashing cavalryman was one of the most colourful figures in the great Romanov family. The 'dread uncle', as he was called in the family, was a favourite of the Guards'. And, at the time, he was very close to the tsar.

But the Montenegrin sisters were even closer to the tsarina. From the day of her arrival in Russia, the tsarina had been faced with the coldness and hostility of the court. And the Montenegrins had known how to surround her with warmth and an almost servile deference.

And the court sensed the threat. A marriage between Anastasia and Nikolai Nikolaevich would create the most influential clan in the Romanov family. A dangerous clan. The court already knew the strength of Alix's influence over the tsar. It also knew how power was aligned within the family of Pyotr and Nikolai Nikolaevich. Pyotr Nikolaevich was spineless and ill, while the 'dread uncle', Nikolai Nikolaevich himself was, as the empress dowager said, 'sick with an incurable disease – he's a fool'. Or, to put it a bit less starkly, he was unbending in a soldierly way. And he repeated the opinions of the Montenegrin princesses. Or, more precisely, those of the elder one, the intelligent and power-loving Militsa.

The black-haired Militsa passed for a great expert on mystical literature. And she took a lively interest in everything marvellous and supernatural. Her sister Stana obediently echoed her. They had not been born in Montenegro, a country of witches and sorcerers, for nothing. The 'black women', the court maliciously called them, alluding to their black hair and 'black' place of origin.

And it was no accident that Feofan had come to Militsa's palace. As he said in his testimony, 'I more than others was interested in life's mystical side.'

The File, from the testimony of Feofan:

> I became acquainted with the personages of the ruling house . . . in my capacity as . . . the inspector of the Petrograd Theological Seminary . . . The Grand Duke and Duchess Pyotr Nikolaevich and Militsa Nikolaevna often visited the seminary and met with me there. I had heard that the personages of the ruling house wished to become better acquainted with me, but, in keeping with my convictions as a monk, I avoided that . . . Then on the Saturday of Holy Week the Grand Duchess Militsa Nikolaevna invited me to come to hear her confession. Not knowing what to do, I turned to Metropolitan Antony, and with his blessing I went to see her. And after that I started frequenting her house.

And soon Feofan began to feel at home there. He and Militsa had things to talk about. 'Grand Duchess Militsa Nikolaevna was very well read . . . and she knew the mystical and ascetic literature regarding the holy fathers and had even published a work of her own, *Selected Passages from the Holy Fathers.*'

From Militsa's palace the path to that of the tsar was a direct one. 'I was invited,' Feofan testified, 'to the home of the former emperor for the first time by Grand Duchess Militsa Nikolaevna.'

So in his conversations with Feofan, the new lodger Father Grigory could easily have understood where the path to the royal family originated. And Rasputin knew that soon 'the gate would swing open' for him, too.

Another Rasputin Riddle

And, really, how could Feofan, then quite delighted with the Siberian peasant, not have shared his delight with Militsa, who was so interested in everything miraculous? 'Visiting the home of Militsa Nikolaevna, I let slip that a man of God named Grigory Rasputin had appeared among us. Militsa Nikolaevna became very interested in my communication, and Rasputin received an invitation to present himself to her.'

After that, it was all in Grigory's hands. And, of course, he was able to astound the grand duchess, too. And now went to her palace by himself.

From Feofan's testimony: 'He had been there without me. And evidently he had attracted her attention, since they not only started inviting him, but Militsa Nikolaevna asked me to provide shelter for Rasputin in my own home whenever he came to Petrograd.'

But then the riddle begins! According to all the biographies of Rasputin, it was Militsa and Feofan who took Rasputin to the royal palace. But Bishop Feofan states in the File that Militsa had nothing to do with it and he adds:

> How Rasputin came to know the family of the former emperor, I have absolutely no idea. And I definitely state that I never took any part in that. My guess is that Rasputin penetrated the royal family by indirect means . . . Rasputin himself never talked about it, despite the fact that he was a rather garrulous person . . . I noticed that Rasputin had a strong desire to get into the house of the former emperor, and that he did so against the will of Grand Duchess Militsa Nikolaevna. Rasputin himself acknowledged to me that he was hiding his acquaintance with the royal family from Militsa Nikolaevna.

It is impossible not to trust the extremely honest Feofan.

4

WAITING FOR RASPUTIN

The Blood And Fear Of The Tsars

The family whose acquaintance Rasputin now made had long been waiting for him. And the mystical sensation of unavoidable catastrophe that possessed Russian society lived in that family, too.

Nicholas had ascended the throne a very young man and could assume that he would live to see the great jubilee – the tercentenary of his dynasty. And thinking of that jubilee, Nicholas, the honorary chairman of the Russian Historical Society and a man very fond of history, could not have helped but ponder certain patterns in the Romanov family's three-hundred-year history. About how short-lived the Romanov tsars were. And about how much blood they had spilled. Peter the Great had sentenced his son Alexis to death for cursing him and his family. Lawful Romanov tsars had been the victims of family coups – the young Tsar Ioann Antonovich and Peter III. Both had been murdered during the reign of Nicholas's enlight-ened great-great-grandmother Catherine the Great. In Nicholas's beloved Tsarskoe Selo, where his own family was in continuous residence, the palace rooms contained furniture from the time of Catherine, and the rooms themselves were redolent of the same fragrances used in her day. Everything was permeated with memories of the great empress during whose reign two lawful tsars had been murdered.

The relay race of family murders lasted the entire eighteenth century. At the very end of the century Catherine's son Paul I was brutally murdered by the conspirators in a plot involving his own son Alexander, the future victor over Napoleon. Moreover, Alexander's own life ended obscurely. Either he actually did die in Taganrog as was officially announced, or, as persistent legend has it, someone else was buried in his grave and Alexander himself went off to become a wanderer in Siberia. And after taking vows and the name Elder Fyodor Kuzmich, he spent the rest of his life as an anchorite atoning for the sins of his family that had sullied an entire century. In any event, Nicholas II's cousin, the well-known historian Grand Duke Nikolai Mikhailovich, not only dared to speak of expiation of the family's sins but believed the legends about Fyodor Kuzmich and even tried to find the pertinent documents in the family's secret archive.

But had the dynasty itself actually not ended with the reign of great-great-grandmother Catherine? In Catherine the Great's memoirs (long held in close secrecy in the royal archives) there is a clear hint that her unhappy son Paul was not the son of Peter III but of one of her lovers. Blood and mysteries. A family that was a mystery even to itself. Such was the past of Nicholas's three-hundred-year-old dynasty. And his capital of Petersburg itself, that mystical city of ghostly white nights that had been built on a marsh with the blood of thousands of workers tormented by brutality and malaria had been cursed by a Romanov. Evdokia, the first wife of Peter the Great, whom he exiled to a convent, had damned his new capital with the terrible cry, 'May you be barren!'

The memory of spilled blood had haunted Nicholas from childhood. He grew up in the palace at Gatchina. In the favourite palace of his great-grandfather, the strangled Paul I. There, as Nicholas's sister Grand Duchess Olga remembered, the servants claimed to have seen the unshriven spirit of the murdered Paul. And Olga and Nicky were afraid and dreamed about seeing the murdered emperor.

But the blood was not merely in the historical past. Blood had already been shed in Nicholas's own lifetime, too, on his very first steps to the throne. He had become heir on the death of his grandfather Alexander II, who had been assassinated by revolutionaries. Blood surrounded him.

The Long-Suffering Job

Nicholas had been taciturn and reserved from early childhood. And possessed from youth by a mystical feeling of predestined unhappiness. He considered the very date of his birth an indication of his terrible future. He was born on the day of the long-suffering Job. The French ambassador Maurice Paléologue quotes a conversation of Nicholas's with Prime Minister Stolypin: "'Do you know the date of my birth?" he asked. "How could I fail to, 6 May." "And what saint's day is that? The long-suffering Job's. I have more than a presentiment. I have a deep certainty that I am doomed to terrible ordeals.'"

There are some lines in the memoirs of the tsar's sister Olga that sound like an echo of this conversation: 'He would frequently embrace me and say, "I was born on the day of the long-suffering Job and am prepared to accept my destiny." And a line from one of the tsarina's letters continues this melancholy theme: 'you were born on the day of the longsuffering Job too, my poor Sweetheart' (4 May 1915).

A feeling of coming destruction haunted his highly-strung wife, as well. Which is why the shy princess from Darmstadt was so tormented, weeping for no reason, when replying to the proposal of the heir to the Russian throne that she become the future Russian tsarina. 'She wept the whole time and from time to time said only, "I cannot,"' Nicholas wrote in his diary.

And as evidence of the justness of their presentiments there was the abundant blood spilled during the principal event of their lives – their coronation, that mystical betrothal with Russia, that transformation of a mere man into a holy tsar. During a public distribution of souvenirs in the coronation's honour on Khodynka Field near Moscow, there had been such a crush of people that the whole of the following night was occupied with carting hundreds of trampled victims from the bloodied field. It is not hard to imagine how that affected a couple so inclined to mysticism.

And then with the start of the new twentieth century their presentiments became a reality. Blood became a part of Russian life. The bombs of Russian terrorists began exploding cruelly and frequently. And his dignitaries perished. In just the first years of the new century the minister of education, the governor-general of Finland, and, one after the other, two ministers of internal affairs died at the hands of terrorists. As if in proof of the fact that now no security branch could save anyone from death. The long-suffering Job's days of sorrow were approaching. His resigned entries after the deaths of the ministers remain in his diary: 'One must endure with humility and steadfastness the trials sent to us by the Lord.' 'It is His holy will.' A calf destined for sacrifice.

But his wife was a person of entirely different character. She would struggle against her fate. And from the very beginning she sought protection from future misfortunes.

In Search Of A Redeemer

It was the idea of her then inseparable friends, the Montenegrin princesses. Born in a poor country where, as Feofan said in the File, 'the aristocracy was much closer to the common people,' the Montenegrins had brought to the palace this idea: that truth, miracle and strength are hidden in the simple folk, in the common people. An alliance must be forged with the people, bypassing the venal officials and the arrogant court. The people and the tsar with no one between them.

Oddly enough, this was an idea that united all Russian intellectuals, even the most radical, who hated the tsars and who were hated by them in turn. All the famous dominant Russian thinkers – Tolstoy, Dostoevsky, Turgenev – even though they frequently quarrelled with and contradicted each other, and all the diverse tendencies of Russian philosophical thought agreed on one idea: that it was only the common people, destitute, illiterate, downtrodden, who possessed a kind of hidden truth. It was only in the gloom of their wretched huts that the true spirit of Christ survived, preserved through their constant suffering. It was to the folk that one should turn to study a wise and Christian life.

And an amusing thing happened: the Russian tsar confessed then to the very same ideas. That shy tsar of short stature and most un-tsarlike appearance who felt awkward at balls and meetings and in the company of courtiers and ministers, where, it seemed to him, they were always comparing him to his dead giant of a father. How much happier he was with the common people in an atmosphere of adoration and worship.

And there emerged this paradox. The tsar started to seek a connection with the simple folk, and they began to appear at the palace one after another – emissaries of the people. They were found by the Montenegrin princesses. Grand Duke Nikolai Nikolaevich told Nicholas of a minor official named Klopov. Klopov was eager to bring the truth of the people to the tsar. He had written endless letters to the grand duke about the embezzlement of public funds in the flour-milling business. And the letters were brought to the tsar by the Montenegrins and read with delight by Alix and Nicky. And the voice of a simple man of the people was heard, and Klopov was summoned to the palace. After a conversation with Klopov, the tsar sent him off with the broadest sort of secret plenary powers to scour Russia and bring back the people's truth about abuses by high officials. But that initial experience of a meeting with a people's emissary ended in confusion. The poor Klopov unfortunately had no understanding of anything except his flour-milling business.

But a beginning had been made. Alix, the daughter of an English princess, and Nicky, the son of a Danish one, were infatuated with the noble idea of unity with the simple Russian people.

At the time Alix had been giving birth to girls – one after another they came into the world, three grand duchesses. But the chief thing, giving birth to a boy who was meant for the divine crown, was something the religious Alix simply could not accomplish. Seeking help she met the

Montenegrins and listened to Militsa's stories about the people of God and the elders to whom God had given a special, great power.

Zhukovskaya wrote that Militsa's face 'with its large oblong black eyes, weary and proud, seemed lifeless, like the face of an old-fashioned portrait. She was somehow unnaturally pale.' Militsa generously revealed to Alix a world of miracles that amazed the granddaughter of the sceptical Queen Victoria. All kinds of things were mixed up in it – Persian literature, the mysteries of Zarathustra, the pagan world of Militsa's native Montenegro in whose forest-covered mountains lived sorcerers to whom it was even given to speak to the dead, and the miracles of the great Orthodox elders from Russia's monasteries. Militsa had created an astonishing synthesis of mutually exclusive elements, united by only one thing – the alluring power of the miracles created in her magical world by the common people, by those who knew nothing of the vainness of the court, of that pitiful Vanity Fair.

The File, from the testimony of Vyrubova: 'Militsa Nikolaevna and Anastasia Nikolaevna, especially the former . . . in the beginning enjoyed great influence over the royal family, and had, so to speak, a mystical influence. Exceptionally well read in mystical literature and having even studied the Persian language in order to acquaint herself with the Persian mystics in the original, [Militsa] was almost considered a prophetess.'

Alix knew how to make friends and, most importantly, she knew how to *believe with all her heart*. Just as her English mother, Alice, so renowned for her admiration, or, more accurately, her adoration, of the German religious philosopher David Strauss, had known how to believe.

Thus began the search for a man of God. One who would pray to God for a son.

An Hour And A Half With An Idiot?

The first to arrive was Mitya, called 'Kozelsky' or sometimes 'the Nasal-voiced' (for his difficulties in pronunciation). Dmitry Oznobishin, whom everybody just called Mitya, was a resident of the little town of Kozelsk. A description of him survives in the files of the security branch: 'He wears his hair long and unbound and goes about barefoot the year round leaning on a staff. He dresses in a cassock of monk style.' After the revolution, journalists poked fun at the tsarina by describing him as an idiot. As a result, Vyrubova tried in her testimony to protect the royal family from the pathetic Mitya. 'I don't think he was ever at the palace,' she lied to the Extraordinary

Commission. On the contrary, Mitya was there, and more than once.

From Nicholas's diary: '14 January 1906. The man of God Dmitry came to see us from Kozelsk near the Optina Pustyn Monastery. He brought with him an image drawn according to a vision he had had. We talked for about an hour and a half.'

And not by accident. Mitya was, in point of fact, an exceptional person. 'His influence on the popular masses is immense – he gives the money he receives from his admirers to the poor. There is a rumour that he has the gift of foreknowledge and clairvoyance,' I read in the files of the Department of Police. And he did have that gift.

As Bishop Feofan testified in the File, 'The "Blessed Mitya" undoubtedly had the gift of clairvoyance, as I was able to convince myself on the basis of my own experience: at our first meeting, he beautifully and precisely outlined the circumstance of my life . . . The course of the war with Japan was exactly predicted . . . by him, in particular the fall of Port Arthur.' But Mitya's prayers were in vain: the tsarina failed to give birth to a boy.

And then Matryona the Barefoot made her appearance. She brought an icon with her. But dressed in rags and shouting barely comprehensible prophecies like some Delphic oracle, the barefoot woman herself vanished from the court just as suddenly as she had appeared. From the testimony of Vyrubova: 'I heard about Matryona the Barefoot . . . she brought the sovereign an icon in Peterhof, but I never saw her.' We'll make a note of that route to the royal palace: bring a miracle-working icon that will assist in the birth of a son.

Such was the world the royal couple were now living in. A world of miracles, holy relics, icons, and miracle-workers. And they seemed ever more out of place in Petersburg, where enlightened society was becoming openly atheistic. It is no accident that Chekhov wrote in a letter to the writer Kuprin, 'I now look with astonishment on any intellectual who is a believer.'

But the royal couple believed that their world continued beyond the limits of the depraved capital somewhere out there among the distant villages scattered across the boundless empire. The World of Holy Rus, of the simple folk who loved God, the tsar, and the church.

And they were waiting for an emissary from that world.

They Had Been Led Astray By
A Legend

But that world, which had duped the West for so long, no longer existed. Its place had been taken by a resentful, impoverished people with an ever-diminishing faith in its clergy. The writer and religious philosopher Sergei Nilus (whose works Nicholas and the tsarina would read during their incarceration) bitterly records in his book *On the Banks of the River of God* the story of a nun of his acquaintance: 'A nun arrived . . . and told me that it is impossible now for nuns to travel by train: there is no abuse, mockery, or oath that Satanic malice will not pour down on their poor heads . . . She has to put on a dark blue skirt so as to pass for a peaceable old woman, since otherwise she would be unable to walk down the aisle for all the cursing of monasteries and those who practise the monastic life.'

'Such is "Holy Rus"!' Nilus exclaims. 'The poor people! Pitiful Russia!' And the elders who lived in the great monasteries spoke of the same thing with the same anguish. In the words of an ascetic also cited by Nilus, 'A Godless, faithless time has come for Orthodox Russia. The Russian has begun to live by the flesh and only the flesh . . . He is an Orthodox Christian in name but no longer in spirit.' It is thus no surprise that after the Bolsheviks came to power, yesterday's 'chosen people' took an eager part in the destruction of churches, the burning of icons, and the outrages against holy relics.

A Dress Rehearsal For The
Coming Of Rasputin

And then the Montenegrin princesses at last found the tsarina a suitable miracle-worker. Militsa, a collector of rumours about supernatural occurrences, had heard about the Parisian miracles of a certain Monsieur Philippe. This miracle-worker was more agreeable to Alix, who had still not forgotten the European world that she had recently abandoned. Nor did his speech tire her out in the way that the barely comprehensible mumbling of Mitya or the incoherent ravings of Matryona the Barefoot had done. 'The royal family met [at Militsa's palace] with the Christian occultist Philippe, who had come from Paris,' Vyrubova testified in the File.

His last name was Nizier-Vachod. He was a native of Lyons, a soothsayer and healer. He proclaimed that it was given to him to speak with the dead and that he lived, as it were, on the borderline between two worlds. Philippe was summoned to Russia. 'A man of about fifty, small, with black hair and a black moustache and a terrible southern French accent. He talked about the fall of religion in France and the West . . . As we were parting, he tried to kiss my hand, and it was only with difficulty that I managed to snatch it away,' wrote Grand Duke Konstantin Konstantinovich in his diary.

Philippe immediately sensed the tsarina's high-strung nature and the terror in her soul. Appreciating her religiousness, he was able to reconcile his world of magic with that of Holy Scripture. For her, he at once became a man of God who had been sent to assist the divine dynasty. He also knew how to satisfy her hunger for miracles. He made generous use of cheap circus-type theatricality and all the tired baggage once employed by the great eighteenth-century adventurers Casanova and Cagliostro. That which the Paris press had made fun of produced an indelible impression in Petersburg. Nicky, overwhelmed by his wife's passionate faith, shared in her delight. The court, however, watched the Parisian magus with derision. The court understood: he was merely the latest plaything devised by the Montenegrins for their royal friend. 'Militsa introduced Philippe to the empress as someone who knows how to heal all diseases, including syphilis,' A. Polovtsev, a respected member of the Council of State, mockingly wrote in his diary. 'And this Philippe . . . has promised her that she will give birth to a son and not a daughter.'

The ironical stories alarmed Nicholas's mother. 'The dowager empress is very angry with Militsa and Stana . . . At her request, the Department of Police used their secret agents in Paris to check into Philippe's past. The report that came back was frightful: the French termed Philippe a crooked adventurer. The Russian agent in Paris sent an ironical article from a French newspaper about a public hypnosis show of Philippe's,' Polovtsev also recorded in his diary.

But as in the future story with Rasputin, this had no effect whatever on Alix. She knew how to believe. She also knew how to be faithful, and she had a will of iron. In fact, Alix had a great many excellent qualities. Only one thing was lacking: an ability to heed the opinions of society. A quality without which it is unfortunately dangerous to occupy the throne, as Marie Antoinette, another beautiful woman just as completely lacking in that ability, might have told her.

Society grumbled. 'Grand Duke Sergei Mikhailovich told me that after the unfavourable report on Philippe arrived from Paris, the emperor gave the order to sack the agent responsible for it in twenty-four hours,' Polovtsev wrote in his diary. The pattern would be repeated in the story of Rasputin – the great Romanov family's antipathy, Alix's blind faith, and incredible gossip all around. Felix Yusupov recalled a story of his father's. Once he was out walking by the sea in the Crimea and encountered Militsa, who was driving somewhere with an acquaintance of hers. He bowed to her, but she didn't respond. Several days later upon seeing her again he asked, 'Why didn't you respond to my greeting?' 'You could not have seen me,' she said, 'since I was with Dr Philippe. When he puts on his hat, he is invisible, and anyone with him is invisible, too.' That's the kind of mocking tale the courtiers were making up at the time.

Or another facetious rumour of the day: Philippe had been lodged in the royal couple's bedroom to cast spells so Alix would give birth to an heir.

The saddest thing (as subsequently in the story of Rasputin) is that these fables came from the courts of the other grand dukes, who resented the favour shown to Nicky's cousins Pyotr and Nikolai Nikolaevich. And in yet another anticipation of the future story of Rasputin, the dowager empress decided to have a serious talk with Nicky. He, of course, promised his mother to get rid of Philippe. And Alix, of course, proved to be the stronger. She pleaded with him not to touch the 'man of God', and everything remained unchanged. Just as we shall see more than once in the story of Rasputin.

And just as they would Rasputin, they called Philippe 'Our Friend'.

At the time she was carrying a child. And joy – she had done it! Our Friend had predicted a boy. And on 5 June 1901, she gave birth to . . . a girl.

From the diary of Nicholas's sister, Grand Duchess Xenia: '5 June . . . What disappointment: a fourth girl!'

But Our Friend explained it all away as the tsarina's lack of faith. And as would happen with Rasputin, the Romanov family tried to replace the magus with somebody worthier. And the Grand Duke Nikolai Mikhailovich even went to see the most famous man in Russia, the disgraced Leo Tolstoy. But Tolstoy could hardly exert any influence on the tsar.

'How Rich Life Is Since We Know Him'

So as not to anger the dowager empress and the family, and to avoid court gossip, Alix and Nicky arranged to see Our Friend in secret. Just as they would later do with Rasputin.

They started meeting him at Militsa and Stana's, running over to the Znamenka Palace after all their obligatory social business was done. From

worldly vanity to the mystical world of the Montenegrins and Our Friend
with its captivating interlacing of life and miracle.

From the tsar's diary for 1901:

'13 July, Peterhof. At 2:30 we went to Znamenka and sat in the garden until
5:00. Our Friend was there with us.'

'19 July. . . . We set off for Znamenka . . . We listened to Our Friend all
evening. We came back at night in the marvellous moonlight.'

'20 July . . . After dinner we went to Znamenka and spent the last evening
with Our Friend. We all prayed together.'

And how much they missed Our Friend when he went back home to
Lyons.

On 27 August Alix wrote to Nicky (in English, as was her custom),
'Saturday evening towards 10.30 – all our thoughts will fly to Lyons then.
How rich life is since we know him and everything seems easier to bear.'
'To bear' meant getting the better of her premonitions and nervousness.
Philippe had done the most important thing: he had relieved Alix of her
constant stress, her hidden terror.

But Philippe's chief accomplishment was that he had carried off the
long-awaited miracle. Nicky and Alix were happy. She was pregnant, and
Philippe had determined that it would be a boy. True, the doctors, after
tedious medical tests, expressed doubt. But what were scientific fools and
their tests next to a man who consorted with heaven? Alix forbade the
doctors to examine her. Her Montenegrin friends and Monsieur Philippe,
now officially certified a Russian doctor of medicine, became her doctors.
All together awaited the birth of the predicted heir. The time of confinement
was drawing near. Nine months had passed. And then, in August 1902, a
shameful thing happened.

From one of Grand Duchess Xenia's letters: 'Imagine the horror of it:
poor Alexandra Fyodorovna turned out not to be pregnant at all . . . Mama
[the dowager empress] found her in a very melancholy state, even though
she speaks like someone resigned to her fate . . . What a blow to her pride
it must be!'

Polovtsev recorded in his diary what the court was saying about the
matter:

30 August 1902 . . . By hypnotizing her, Philippe persuaded her she was
pregnant. Yielding to his assurances, she refused all meetings with her
doctors until the middle of August, when she summoned the obstetrician
Ott, though only to consult with him about her sudden loss of weight. Ott

declared to her that she was not pregnant . . . An extremely muddled announcement about it was published in the *Government Herald*, so that among all classes of the population the most ridiculous rumours have spread, such as, for example, that the empress gave birth to a monster with horns that had to be strangled, and so on. The episode has not, however, shaken the imperial couple's confidence in Philippe, who in their eyes continues to be a superb and inspiring person . . . It would all be funny if it were not so sad.

And the family sounded the alarm. Philippe was becoming a constant and painful topic of conversation in the Romanov family. Just as Rasputin later would.

'He Will Soon Return . . . In The Form Of Another'

Grand Duke Konstantin Konstantinovich, a celebrated poet who wrote under the pseudonym 'KR', wrote in his diary for 24 August 1902, 'Sergei [Grand Duke Sergei Mikhailovich, cousin to Nicholas and a friend of his youth] claims that Their Majesties have fallen into a mystical frame of mind, that they pray with Philippe at Znamenka . . . spend long evenings there, . . . and return home in a rapturous state, as if in ecstasy, with gleaming eyes and shining faces . . . My opinion is that it is more ridiculous than dangerous. The bad thing is that they cover their visits to Znamenka in secrecy.'

25 August: 'Elena, the daughter of the King of Serbia, said that her brother has fallen under Militsa and Philippe's influence. [Her brother] said that Philippe's mission on earth has reached an end . . . that he will die soon, but will return to the circle of his friends in the form of another. What nonsense!! . . . Sergei told me that he is very upset about the emperor and empress's visits to Znamenka.'

6 September: 'I dropped in on Grand Duke Vladimir Alexandrovich . . . He switched to the burning question of Philippe . . . He thinks it is the Grand Duke Nikolai Nikolaevich who is chiefly responsible for their closeness . . . who is the offender in this business . . . And that Philippe's swindles have drawn down universal ridicule and abuse on the imperial couple.'

Now the whole family demanded Philippe's departure, but Alix would prove that she knew how to believe and defend those she believed in.

Ella From The World Of The Kingdom
Of Muscovy

The tsarina calmly endured the attacks of the Romanov family, who did not like her, and she gladly repaid them in kind. But Philippe became the cause of her first disagreement with her beloved sister Ella, Grand Duchess Elizaveta Fyodorovna. The beauty Ella, the empress's older sister, had married Nicholas's uncle. It was in fact at Ella's wedding that Nicky had first seen the fair-haired beauty Alix and fallen in love with her for ever. After their marriages, Alix and Ella were exceptionally close. Ella's husband, Grand Duke Sergei Alexandrovich, was the governor-general of Moscow.

Moscow occupied a special place in the life of Nicholas and Alexandra. Their capital was Petersburg, that city-mirage built on the Finnish marshes under the direction of French and Italian architects, with its avenues of a precision and straightness repugnant to the Russian soul, and its angel atop a column in front of the Winter Palace symbolically prostrating itself before a Catholic cross. It was the capital of Westernism, the embodiment of the new Russian aristocracy's reaching out to Europe. But the symbol of national identity remained Moscow, the ancient capital of the Muscovite tsars and the first Romanovs. The city of countless churches and impossibly tangled streets so amiable to the Russian soul. And sister Ella and her husband were the custodians of that 'Tsargrad'.

It was in Moscow that Nicky and Alix's best-loved legend of the ancient Muscovite tsars of the people came to life, the legend of a kingdom in which not splendid grandees but people of the holy life, elders, and holy fools (a phenomenon of which we shall have much to say), were the tsars' principal advisers.

And when Nicky and Alix began in 1903, in anticipation of the ter-centenary of the Romanov dynasty, to give their celebrated 'historical' balls, the Moscow of the times of the first Romanovs was brought back in the halls of the Winter Palace. The courtiers were clad in the shimmering gold of the boyar dress of the days of the kingdom of Muscovy and Nicholas himself appeared in the garb of his beloved tsar, Alexis Mikhailovich.

And although the religious Ella, who had made the ideas of Orthodoxy her own, could not help but be alarmed by Alix's friendship with the mysticism-crazed Montenegrin princesses, she understood the loneliness of her sister in cold Petersburg and reconciled herself to the friendship. But the appearance of Philippe forced Ella to join forces with the rest of the Romanovs. Ella knew her sister's character. She knew that to attack Philippe directly would be to strengthen his position. And Ella patiently explained to her younger sister that the Russian tsars had no need of foreign wizards. They had patrons in heaven who were far more powerful. Those patrons were (as Simeon the New Theologian had written) the saints who had gone to heaven. There, in the other world, they became the defenders of the tsars and the people. They realized their great purpose both individually and in concert, forming a Guardian Assembly or Golden Chain. And their protection had often been enjoyed by the Muscovite tsars now sleeping their eternal sleep in the Kremlin Cathedral.

This mystical idea made an impression. But on hearing Ella's words repeated by the tsarina, the intelligent Militsa took up the baton. And soon afterwards a conversation took place between Philippe and the tsarina. For the first time he clearly explained to Alix the reason for her failed pregnancy. It had once more been the result of her weakness of faith. No sooner had she started to doubt and called the obstetrician, than the miracle ended. A miracle can occur only in the presence of absolute faith. Only faith is capable of moving the mountain. Alix was still not ready for such faith. Therefore he had been unable to help her. And then, to Alix's joy, Philippe began to speak of the same thing that Ella, who so disliked him, had spoken of: Alix must ask for the aid of a Russian saint. She must ask him to intercede with God for the birth of an heir. And Philippe repeated a name that Alix had already heard from Militsa, and before that from Ella. It was the name of a great saint from Sarov who had not yet been canonized by the dilatory official Church. Serafim of Sarov, an elder who had died in 1833 at the Sarov cloister.

The Royal Saint

Like Rasputin, Prokhor Moshnin (such was the worldly name of Serafim of Sarov) had left home as a wanderer and gone to worship at numerous monasteries. In his native village, Serafim walked about surrounded by virgins – by 'brides of Christ'. As a result, rumours had begun circulating, and there was an inquiry, and the mystery of his holiness became a subject of police investigation.

And then he lived a long time in silence and abstinence, seeking nourishment in the 'word of God', which is 'angelic bread, and by it the soul is nourished'.

Serafim had much to say about the sanctity of royal power. And he often cited the words of King David's commander Abishai: 'If all of us should be killed, then at least you, lord, would live. But if you were no more, then what would become of Israel?' The tsarina also learned of a prophecy written down by Serafim's admirer Motovilov in 1879. In it Serafim foretold their future rule and their names, Tsar Nicholas and Tsarina Alexandra Fyodorovna. He also predicted his own canonization during their reign.

Serafim was declared the royal family's patron. And in spite of the Synod's resistance, Alix forced Nicky to fulfil the prediction: Serafim of Sarov was canonized. And on 16 July 1903, the imperial train arrived at the Arzamas Station, and the entire Romanov family proceeded on foot to Sarov Pustyn and the Diveev Monastery where Serafim of Sarov had lived and prayed. On 18 July 1903, after a solemn mass, the tsar, the clergy, and the grand dukes took outside the coffin containing the holy relics of the Venerated Serafim and carried it around the church. Thus did the tsarina help bring to pass yet another of Serafim's prophecies transcribed by Motovilov: 'What joy there will be! The tsar and all his family will come to us.'

True, there remained another of Serafim's prophecies of which they were then unaware, the one 'about terrible future insurrections that will exceed all imagination . . . about rivers of Russian blood' that would flow during their reign.

The unreal world of miracles and prophecies was increasingly becoming Alix's real world. In Sarov they spent whole evenings by the spring and the rock where Serafim had lifted his voice in prayer. At night she and Nicky would bathe in the waters of the spring, putting their trust in the saint's help and praying for an heir. Her wait had begun. Serafim, now in the golden chain next to the throne of God, would intercede on their behalf, and she would give birth to a son.

She was becoming more and more a tsarina from a Kremlin eyrie of the times of the kingdom of Muscovy.

Adieu To 'Our First Friend'

Soon afterwards Our Friend was required to return to Paris. Nikolai Nikolaevich had evidently found it difficult to tolerate the ostracism to which the Romanov family was subjecting him and the Montenegrin sisters. And he explained to Philippe the necessity of his departure.

In the meantime, Alix's faith had triumphed. All that she had asked for in her prayers to Saint Serafim had come to pass. From her journal: 'The Heir Tsarevich Alexei Nikolaevich was born on Friday 30 July 1904 at 1.15 in the afternoon.' He was named for their favourite tsar, Alexis Mikhailovich Romanov.

So she could once again think that she had not believed in Philippe in vain. Everything was as Our Friend had prophesied. She had given life to a beautiful baby, a grey-eyed fairy-tale prince born to rule and arouse admiration.

Thus ended the dress rehearsal for Rasputin's appearance at the palace. And in the court and among the great Romanov family the conclusion was formulated: poor, kind Nicky lacked will, and Alix ruled in everything. He regarded the world through her eyes.

Philippe did not return. As he had predicted, although rather sooner – in 1905, he departed this world. And once again Alix was convinced that she had been right to believe in him. That is why she never forgot him. Many, many years later, during the war, she would write to her husband, 'our first Friend gave me that Image with the bell to warn me against those, that are not right & it will keep them fr. approaching' (16 June 1915).

And now all that remained was for Philippe to carry out his promise – 'to return in form of another'. How much she needed him in that new form. For the most terrible thing had happened. The long-awaited prince was suffering from a fatal disease inherited from Alix's family: haemophilia. His fragile blood vessels were unable to withstand the pressure of his blood. The same thing that was taking place outside the palace's windows, in fact. The empire's vessels were worn and fragile, too. The autocratic realm was haemorrhaging.

A Bloody Prologue To His Coming

First there was the shameful, bloody war with Japan. Nicholas was pushed into the war. The military explained that land could be quietly occupied in Manchuria, and that little Japan would not dare to retaliate. And if it did, then there would be a small war and a great victory. The war turned into a large war of great defeats. 'It's painful and distressing,' Nicholas wrote in his diary. But that was only the beginning. The boy's disease and next the terrible year of 1905. The defeats in the war. And then another trial was sent, something unprecedented in Russia in the entire three-hundred-year reign of the Romanov dynasty – a revolution.

The terrible year began with bloodshed – with the massacre of a workers' demonstration on its way to the Winter Palace. The tsar and his family were in Tsarskoe Selo, and in their absence, the frightened Vladimir Alexandrovich, Nicholas's uncle, who was in command of the Petersburg garrison, gave the order to shoot. On 9 January, the tsar wrote in his diary, 'A terrible day . . . Many were killed and wounded . . . My God, how painful it is . . . how dreadful.' The revolutionaries answered with terror. In Moscow, less than a month later, Ella's husband, Grand Duke Sergei Alexandrovich, was blown apart by a bomb. And Nicholas was haunted by this vision: the bare-headed Ella covered in blood and crawling on her hands and knees among her husband's remains. And then terrifying days and chaos in the country. A rail strike that cut off Petersburg and Moscow from the interior, and rallies with calls for armed rebellion.

How she waited for the new man of God to arrive. But they remained alone, with only their prayers and their faith in God. And instead of a man of God nearby, there were their constant guests: the new prime minister, Sergei Witte, and Grand Duke Nikolai Nikolaevich.

This was the Montenegrin princesses' finest hour. The 'dread uncle' Grand Duke Nikolai Nikolaevich – would become dictator. At the time, it seemed the only way to put down the revolution. The romance of Stana, the elder princess, with Nikolai Nikolaevich was in full swing. And if he should become a dictator who triumphed over revolution . . . In the imaginings of the elated Montenegrins, there was even the possibility of a crown, which the short, weak Nicholas would himself pass on to the country's saviour. But Nikolai Nikolaevich let them down. Becoming dictator was not something he was prepared to do. The army was far away fighting the Japanese. And to put down the rebellion by force – well, they didn't have the force. And so he collaborated with Prime Minister Sergei Witte to persuade Nicholas to agree to a constitution.

At the time the royal family was staying in Peterhof, cut off from the capital by the railway strike, and at court people were already saying that there was a ship lying offshore on which the royal family was going to flee to England.

The Appearance Of A
Miracle-Worker

It was then that the Montenegrins feverishly sought a Russian miracle-worker. And Militsa brought Feofan to the palace.

From Feofan's testimony in the File: 'The first time I was invited . . . to the former emperor's home, it was for a discussion of church matters. Later on, I was invited both for theological discussions and for "communion" with the emperor's wife, the frequently ill empress Alexandra Fyodorovna.'

But the straightforward ascetic Feofan could not replace the cunning Philippe. And Ioann of Kronstadt was summoned to Militsa's palace ever more frequently. Father Ioann, archpriest of Kronstadt Cathedral, was at the time famous throughout Russia. He had been highly esteemed by Nicholas's father. He was at Alexander III's bedside at the time of his death. And Ioann of Kronstadt's life had touched congregations both inside the church and beyond. He was endowed with a Christian's greatest power: the gift of healing prayer. People who had reached a point of suffering beyond which the power of science was of no avail came to him for help. And he healed them, people of the most varied creeds: Orthodox Christians, Jews, Moslems. The entire 20 December 1883 issue of the *New Times*, that most respectable of Petersburg newspapers, was filled with expressions of gratitude from those he had helped. The grandmother of Father Alexander Mehn, a celebrated Orthodox cleric, was not only healed by him; Ioann predicted that in her Jewish family a grandson would be born who would become an Orthodox priest. He healed Rasputin's future admirer, the young Vyrubova, as well as Zinaida Yusupova, the mother of Rasputin's future murderer.

The Coming Of The Redeemer

But Ioann was too severe, too burdened by his responsibilities to his congregation. And then Militsa decided to introduce to the tsarina and Nicky someone who could not fail to make an impression on them! Someone she had long cultivated for that meeting. Father Grigory, the wanderer from Siberia. Although she apparently had a foreboding about it. So, before introducing him, she made Rasputin swear not to meet with the 'tsars' (as he called Alix and Nicky) on his own. As before, he would have to remain under her auspices. He would become the new Philippe whom Alix and Nicky would meet at her home. 'According to Militsa Nikolaevna, Rasputin promised not to try to meet the royal family by himself,' Feofan testified in the File.

Militsa was sure of the peasant's success. Ever since she had seen those hypnotic eyes! It was no accident that Ioann of Kronstadt had taken a liking to Father Grigory. And Feofan, whom the tsarina held in such regard, revered him, too. And Metropolitan Sergius himself enjoyed talking to him. That was the kind of recommendations he had! And how it had all come together – the prophet, the healer, the man of the people, and the mystical emissary from Holy Rus.

It was the middle of October 1905, the most terrible time in that terrible year. Nicholas decided to sign the manifesto granting the first Russian constitution, thus bringing down the three-hundred-year autocracy of his ancestors. And close by him in those days were the Montenegrins and Nikolasha (Nikolai Nikolaevich).

From the tsar's diary: '17 October . . . We had breakfast with Nikolasha and Stana . . . We sat and talked, waiting for Witte . . . I signed the Proclamation at five. After such a day my head felt heavy, and my thoughts were starting to get muddled. Help us, O Lord. Save Russia and grant her peace.'

'20 October. Nikolasha, Militsa, and Stana dined with us.'

The 21st, 22nd, 23rd, 24th, and 25th were all, according to Nicholas's diary, days when the Montenegrin princesses were visiting. So it was in fact on one of those days that Militsa told Alix about the marvellous Siberian peasant. She was preparing the impressionable Alix, readying her for her gift – a meeting with the prophet of the people. And Militsa had much to talk about. For there were mystical correspondences of the sort the 'black princess' was so fond of. Like Serafim of Sarov, Father Grigory (as everyone now called him, avoiding his unpleasant-sounding last name) had left home and wandered widely. And like Serafim of Sarov, he had gone about his village surrounded by women followers. And as with Serafim, there had been calumniation, and his holiness and mystery had been the subject of an investigation. How Alix's heart must have beat! It all fitted. Philippe had not left them! He had sent them a defender! Just as he had promised, he had come in 'the form of another'! When all around they were being advised to think about the ship that would carry them out of chaos to England and safety.

The first of November arrived. The terrible month of October had finally come to an end. It was their last day in Peterhof, and they were preparing to move back to their beloved Tsarskoe Selo. How Alix had waited for the old month to carry away their misfortunes with it. And how significant it was that on the first day of the new month they were going to see the remarkable peasant at Militsa's.

From Nicholas's diary: '1 November . . . We went to Sergeevka at four. We had tea with Militsa and Stana. We met the man of God Grigory from the province of Tobol . . . In the evening I packed and did a good bit of work, and then I spent the rest of the time with Alix.'

'2 November. We drove . . . to Tsarskoe Selo, arriving at 5.20 . . . It was good to be back in the cosy old rooms.'

5

WITH THE TSARS

The Seduction

Rasputin himself recounted what happened that November evening.

The File, from the testimony of Bishop Feofan: 'I personally heard from Rasputin that he produced an impression on the former empress at their first meeting. The sovereign, however, fell under his influence only after Rasputin had given him something to ponder.'

It had not been very difficult for that expert in human faces to see how much she needed him, how tormented she was by the misfortunes that had befallen them, and how much his words about simple peasants and their loyalty had moved her: the people would not let their tsar down. He later reported that first conversation to Iliodor, who, however primitively, set it forth in his book: 'When revolution raised its head up high, they were very scared . . . and it was "Let us get our things together" . . . But I talked to them a long time, persuading them to spit on all their fears, and rule.' And that made a very great impression on her. It was more complicated with the tsar. The tsar was preoccupied, too busy with the terrible things he had to deal with. And, apparently, he did not really listen to Rasputin. To 'give him something to ponder', it would be necessary for Rasputin to meet him again.

But Militsa, appreciating the impression that he had made on Alix, once again warned the peasant that he must not try to meet with the 'tsars' by himself. Otherwise, it would be the end of him.

'My explanation of her warning that it would be the end of Rasputin was that there were many temptations at court and much envy and intrigue, and that Rasputin, as a simple, undemanding wandering pilgrim, would perish spiritually under such circumstances,' Feofan testified in the File.

But Rasputin had entirely different plans. And living in the apartment of

Feofan, who had such close ties to Militsa, no longer suited him. He needed freedom of action.

The Charming General's Wife

Rasputin in fact already had a number of other places where he could find shelter besides the ascetic Feofan's shabby apartment. His success in Petersburg had been swift. He had done a great deal since his arrival in the city.

The witness E. Kazakova testified before the Extraordinary Commission that at that time she 'saw many important ladies . . . who looked after him and considered him a man of great righteousness, and who cut his nails and sewed them up to attach to their bodices as mementos'. One such lady was the Petersburg lioness and fashionable salon hostess Olga Lokhtina. She was a little over forty but still very good-looking. At the time she had fallen ill. And Rasputin was invited to heal her. Thus they met for the first time just two days after his meeting with the royal family.

Olga Lokhtina was interrogated by the Extraordinary Commission in 1917, and her testimony remains in the File:

> I saw Rasputin for the first time on 3 November 1905. By then I had grown disenchanted with society life, having undergone a spiritual change, and I was, besides, very sick with an intestinal neurasthenia, which tied me to my bed. The only way I could move around was by holding onto the wall . . . The priest Father Medved [at the time one of Rasputin's loyal admirers] took pity on me and brought Rasputin . . . From the moment of Father Grigory's appearance in my home I felt completely restored, and from then on was free of my illness.

So it was into her apartment that Rasputin decided to move.

The File, from the testimony of Feofan: 'He only stayed with me a little while, since I would be off at the seminary for days on end. And it got boring for him . . . and he moved somewhere else, and then took up residence in Petrograd at the home of the government official Vladimir Lokhtin.' Colonel Loman, a friend of the Lokhtins, testified in the File: 'It was an excellent family home. Lokhtina herself was a beautiful woman of fashion and had a really charming little daughter.'

Father Grigory had chosen their home with care. It was a convenient bridgehead for getting to the royal family. Olga Lokhtina's husband was an engineer and actual state councillor (a civil rank corresponding to the military rank of general, which is why Lokhtina is often called 'the general's wife'). Lokhtin was in charge of paved roads in Tsarskoe Selo. And it was there, sequestered in the 'cosy rooms' of the Alexander Palace, that the royal family now spent the better part of their time. The heir's illness, which they had made a state secret, required them to live as virtual recluses in order to protect that secret. But through the Lokhtin family, Rasputin was privy to all the court rumours.

Several years later photographs of Lokhtina would be published in the largest Petersburg newspapers, and journalists would try to understand what had happened to that charming woman. How had it come to pass that a fashionable salon hostess, a Petersburg beauty, had ended up begging for alms in bare feet and outlandish clothing?

The peasant impressed her at once. 'He spoke very interestingly about his life as a wanderer, and during the conversation he hinted at the sins of his listeners and forced their consciences to speak,' Lokhtina testified. He opened to her a realm of Love and Freedom, where the world of money did not exist and where the only life was that of the spirit. Just a few days after meeting him, the Petersburg matron abandoned her home and daughter and set out with the peasant to his house in Pokrovskoe. Lokhtin gladly let her go so that she could make a complete recovery from her illness in the company of the amazing healer. It did not enter his head to be suspicious of her interest in the uncouth, no longer young peasant.

From Lokhtina's testimony in the File: 'At his invitation, I went to visit him in Pokrovskoe, where I stayed from 15 November to 8 December 1905. Travelling with Rasputin was a great pleasure, for he gave life to the spirit. Along the way he predicted the strike and kept saying, "If only we get there first." And as soon as we arrived, it started.' It was not hard to predict strikes in those days, of course. The whole country was in the grip of them. But she was eager for miracles and in Pokrovskoe everything was just as miraculous. She saw a submissive peasant family:

> I liked the style of his life very much. On meeting her husband, his wife fell down at his feet . . . His wife's humility astounded me. When I am right, I yield to no one. And now here was Rasputin's wife yielding in an argument with her husband, even though it was clear that she was in the right and not him. In reply to my . . . astonishment, she said, 'A husband and wife have to live with one heart, sometimes you yield, and sometimes he does' . . . We slept where we could, very often in one room, but we slept little, listening to the spiritual conversations of Father Grigory, who, so to speak, schooled us in nocturnal wakefulness. In the morning, if I got

up early, I would pray with Father Grigory . . . Praying with him tore me from the earth . . . At home we would pass the time chanting psalms and canticles.

But the investigators had some doubt about the innocence of her life in Pokrovskoe. And she responded:

> Yes, he did have the custom of kissing when meeting and even of embracing, but it is only to bad people that bad and dirty thoughts occur . . . It is also quite true that on one of my visits to the village of Pokrovskoe I bathed together with Rasputin and his family, with his wife and two daughters, and in the absence of bad thoughts, it did not seem either strange or indecent to any of us. I was convinced that Rasputin really was an 'elder', both by his healing of me, and by the predictions I had occasion to hear that came true.

Thus did she sweep aside all the suspicions about their sexual relations.

But the truth of Rasputin's relations with Lokhtina, the first of his fierce devotees known to us, is very important. For otherwise we shall not understand either his teachings or his whole subsequent story. Especially since the studies produced by Rasputin's new admirers have claimed that the testimony about his sexual liaisons with his followers was invented by his enemies.

But we shall let a friend speak. And one of Rasputin's closest. Contained in the File is the testimony of his publisher Filippov:

> Once in 1911 at his place on Nikolaev Street I was the unexpected witness of a painful scene. Arriving at Rasputin's early in the morning for tea as was my custom . . . I saw him behind the screen that separated his bed from the rest of the room. He was desperately beating Madame Lokhtina, who was clad in a fantastic get-up consisting of a white dress hung with little ribbons, and who was holding onto his member, while shouting, 'You are God!' I rushed over to him . . . 'What are you doing! You are beating a woman!' Rasputin answered, 'She won't let me alone, the skunk, and demands sin!' And Lokhtina, hiding behind the screen, wailed, 'I am your ewe, and *you are Christ!*' It was only afterwards that I learned that she was Madame Lokhtina, a devotee of Rasputin's, who was having an affair with him . . . She regaled me with so many witty remarks attesting to her great intelligence and good breeding that I was quite amazed by what I had seen.

The other witnesses who met Lokhtina also speak with astonishment of her quick brain and malicious wit. How, then, had the peasant succeeded in forever chaining that brilliant woman to himself? Where did it come from, that fierce passion that would remain with the unhappy general's wife for ever, long after the peasant felt nothing but revulsion for the old woman she became? The answer lies in the principal mystery of that man, of which I shall speak later.

The royal family returned to the capital in December 1905. And Lokhtina was nearby as Rasputin considered the steps that he would take in order to see them again. Feofan was right about that: it was Rasputin himself who initiated the next meeting with the royal family.

Retained in the File is the evidence of another important witness, Colonel Dmitry Loman, who appeared before the Extraordinary Commission in 1917. He had been brought for interrogation at the Winter Palace, where he had only recently occupied a state apartment. Loman had made a brilliant career at court: he had been entrusted with the building of the Feodor Cathedral, much loved by the royal family. As witnesses would testify, he had been given the commission through Rasputin's assistance. When he first met Rasputin, however, he was merely an officer in a Life Guards regiment and a friend of the Lokhtins.

'I knew Rasputin on his first arrival in Petersburg,' Loman testified. 'Rasputin got into the palace the first time in this way: once the sovereign (I pass this along as a rumour) received from a Siberian peasant, from Rasputin, that is, a letter requesting an audience and permission to present him with an icon that for some reason was especially revered. The letter piqued the sovereign's interest.'

The Leap To The Palace

Loman was right. And the corroboration comes from Rasputin himself. For an undated telegram sent by the peasant to the tsar in 1906 has survived. 'Tsar Father, having arrived in this city from Siberia, I would like to bring to you an icon of the Righteous Saint Simeon, the Miracle Worker of Verkhoturye . . . in the faith that the Holy Saint will keep you all the days of your life and aid you in your service for the advantage and happiness of your loyal sons.' The telegram was apparently written by Lokhtina, the devoted general's wife, so much does it differ from the incoherent telegrams with which Rasputin would later inundate the 'tsars'.

And Nicholas did in fact grant the peasant an audience after receiving his telegram. As the tsar would himself later write in a letter to Prime Minister Stolypin which allows us to establish an almost exact date for that truly historic meeting. Historic, for this time the peasant produced such an

impression on the tsar that the highly reserved Nicholas sent his prime
minister a remarkable letter about it.

> 16 October 1906. A few days ago I received a peasant from the Tobol
> province . . . who brought me an icon of Saint Simeon of Verkhoturye . . .
> He made a remarkably strong impression on Her Majesty and on me. And
> instead of five minutes, our conversation lasted well over an hour. He will
> soon be returning to his native region. He has a strong desire to meet you
> and bless your injured daughter with the icon. [Terrorists had blown up the
> prime minister's dacha. He had miraculously survived and had carried his
> injured daughter out of what was left of the building.] I very much hope
> that you will find a moment this week to receive him.

'He made a remarkably strong impression on her Majesty and on me.' He
had thus managed to 'catch' the tsar, as well.

One can imagine what he talked to the 'tsars' about. Saint Simeon of
Verkhoturye had played a great role in the transformation of the dissolute
Grisha into Father Grigory. And, to be sure, it was also a story about finding
God. A story about his wanderings in the name of God and about everything
that lay beyond the reach of those religious people but was still the object
of their dreams. And here Rasputin had no equals. Here he was a poet. They
were the same thoughts he would expound in his 'Life of an Experienced
Wanderer'. And his favourite was, 'Great, great is the peasant in the eyes of
God!' So the peasant was more powerful than all those pitiful urban
intellectuals who had produced sedition and discord. And most important:
the peasant loved his tsars and would not let them down. Just as the Lord
would not. The people and the tsar with no one between! Thus, they heard
then just what they wanted to hear.

And, finally, the peasant asked for something that must have made their
hearts beat faster. He asked for permission to see their boy. He began
speaking of his illness as if he had known about it for a long time. And he
asked for their consent to relieve the child's sufferings with a prayer. It was
for that reason that he had brought the icon of Simeon of Verkhoturye,
whose relics and icon possessed great healing power.

And it is presumably then that they took him to the child. Because it was
afterwards that the tsar wrote his rapturous letter to Stolypin asking him to
allow the peasant to 'bless your injured daughter with the icon'. For in their
eyes, evidently, a miracle had taken place. The kind that Vyrubova would
later recount. And that would take place many times.

In the half-light of Alexei's room illuminated by the lamps in front of
the icons, their 'Little One', their 'Sunbeam', had not been able to fall

asleep, tormented as he was by his latest attack. And the strange peasant went over to his crib. And his huge crooked shadow bent over the boy in prayer. And before their eyes the boy grew calmer and quietly fell asleep. To wake up healthy the next morning. (A miracle! A miracle!)

Was the peasant familiar with mysterious secrets of healing retained in Siberia from pagan times? Or was it hypnotic suggestion? Or did he really sense in himself then a great and inexplicable power of healing? For us, this is a matter of reflection and doubt. But for her, there could have been no doubt after that meeting. He had come to them, the emissary of the people, the man of God whom his precursor, Our First Friend, had foretold. To save the heir and defend his tsars.

And soon after the tsar had done so, the prime minister received the peasant. And Father Grigory went to Stolypin's home with the same wonder-working icon.

From Vyrubova's testimony before the Extraordinary Commission: 'The late Stolypin . . . after the explosion at his dacha, summoned Rasputin to his injured daughter, and he apparently prayed over her and she recovered.'

From that day forth the royal family revered the Siberian saint whom the peasant had told them about. At the tsar's expense, a magnificent pavilion was erected over Saint Simeon's shrine. And the procession of the cross on the day of Saint Simeon's apotheosis was headed by Father Ioann Storozhev. The same Ioann Storozhev, a priest from the city of Ekaterinburg, who two days before their execution in 1918 would celebrate holy communion with them and give them the blessing that would be their last. And after their execution, 'an icon of Saint Simeon of Verkhoturye of small size in a metal frame' would be found in the Ipatiev House, an icon that had once been brought to them by the Siberian peasant.

Rasputin now became indispensable. Now they themselves summoned him to the palace. Although it was a palace in which they were less than free. After the business with Philippe they had grown cautious. And to keep from provoking rumours, they summoned the peasant from Pokrovskoe along with Feofan, a person of official standing who was then rector of the Petersburg Theological Seminary.

From Loman's testimony in the File: 'Aside from his official audience, Rasputin went maybe two or three times . . . with Feofan, but in the very modest role of a lay brother and follower of Feofan.' But Father Grigory asked Feofan not to tell Militsa about those visits. 'Rasputin himself informed me that he was hiding his acquaintance with the royal family from Militsa Nikolaevna,' Feofan testified in the File.

And Militsa, suspecting nothing, continued to sing the peasant's praises.

'9 December. Militsa and Stana dined with us. They talked to us all evening about Grigory,' the tsar recorded in his diary.

The 'Black Woman's' Prediction

But it was impossible to hide the new acquaintance from Militsa for long. Just as it was impossible for the righteous Feofan to lie. Rumours reached the Montenegrins from Tsarskoe Selo. And after Militsa's very first question, Feofan told the truth. The grand duchess was furious with the peasant. She still did not understand then whom she was quarrelling with.

From the File, the testimony of Feofan: 'Rasputin informed me that Militsa had openly declared to him, "You, Grigory, are an underhanded person." Militsa Nikolaevna told me personally of her dissatisfaction with Rasputin's having penetrated the royal family on his own, and mentioned her warning that if he did, it would be the end of him.'

Was it just the powerful Militsa's helpless irritation? Or the intuition of a mystical woman? But what could Militsa do about someone the tsars themselves had summoned? And in any case she did not have time to deal with Rasputin then. For at the end of 1906 the Montenegrins had become the centre of a court scandal.

From the diary of KR: '6 November . . . I learned with horror from my wife that Stana is to be divorced . . . and will marry Nikolasha!!! The permission for the marriage cannot be anything but an indulgence elicited by Nikolasha's closeness to the sovereign . . . It violates the ecclesiastical rule forbidding two brothers to marry two sisters.'

'10 November. Nikolasha declared that he hadn't raised a finger for the wedding . . . that it could not have been managed without the influence of Philippe from beyond.'

Scandals In The Noble Family

It was the latest in a series of scandals in the great Romanov family. Not long before the tsar's uncle, Grand Duke Pavel Alexandrovich, had condescended to appropriate the wife of the adjutant of another grand duke. And had married her, for which he had been exiled from Russia. For according to the laws of the Russian Empire, 'all members of the Imperial Household are deprived of the right of marriage to persons not belonging to a ruling or sovereign House.' And then another scandal threatened the family. The tsar's younger brother Misha had taken it into his head to marry the wife of a Life Guard from his own Blue Cuirassier regiment, the twice-divorced beauty Natalia Wulfert. The dowager empress convinced him with difficulty to give up the wild idea. And then yet another scandal. This time it was Kirill, the son of another uncle, Vladimir. The dashing Guards Quartermaster had broken up the family of Alix's brother, Ernie, duke of Hesse-Darmstadt. Ernie's wife had left him for Kirill. And Nicholas had been forced to punish Kirill. What could he do? Nicholas's father's chastisement of such misbehaviour had been ruthless. Now, as head of the Romanov house, Nicholas was the one who had to do the chastising. And here was this new scandal with the 'dread uncle'. But just what sort of influence must the Montenegrins have had over Alix, if the tsarina, though filled with disgust by those divorces, meekly put up with it all and forced the tsar to put up with it too, despite all the threatening appeals from the dowager empress to punish Nikolai Nikolaevich and restore order in the family.

From the diary of the general's wife A. Bogdanovich for 25 October 1906: 'They say that she [that is, Stana] has incarnated the medium Philippe in herself, that he resides in her, and that she predicts that everything will now be peaceful . . . The tsar and tsarina believe her every word and in expectation of peace are carefree and gay.'

But this time the general's wife and court scandalmongers were wrong. They still did not know about the peasant who at the time had taken up residence in the hearts of the 'tsars' and brought confidence and peace to their souls.

A Special Desire Of His Majesty

While Pyotr and Nikolai Nikolaevich and the Montenegrins were busy straightening out their personal affairs, Rasputin experienced a swift rise in his fortunes. A mere two months after their first meeting, the tsar was personally engaged in changing the unknown peasant's last name.

In that connection, His Majesty had summoned Count Benckendorff, the head of the royal chancery. Alix was upset about the unpleasant-sounding name, so inappropriate to the character of the holy man who had come to them.

Rasputin was asked to write a petition for a name change. And Benckendorff informed the minister of internal affairs: 'In conveying to me this written petition from Rasputin, His Majesty has deigned to express his special desire that the request be respected.'

And on 22 December 1906, the petition of the peasant Rasputin for permission henceforth to call himself 'Rasputin-Novy [New]' was granted.

The monk Iliodor recounts in Rasputin's own words the story that was evidently meant to be the official one: 'No sooner did I appear in the doorway than the heir started clapping his little hands and babbling, "the New one, the New one, the New one!" They were his first words. The tsar then gave the order to call me not by the name Rasputin, but Novy.'

It is in fact possible that there was another subtext in the name, which I shall take up next. However, one way or another, he had for a time been given the right to call himself just 'Novy'.

But life would not permit it. Life would soon return the name 'Rasputin' to him.

The Riddle Of The New Name

With 'Novy's' appearance, a new and secret life began at court. But it was not until a year later that the royal couple decided to reveal the secret of that new life to Nicholas's sister Olga, whose diary records: 'Autumn 1907. Nicky asked if I would like to see a real Russian peasant.' And then she saw what she would later recall in distant Canada: 'Rasputin led [Alexei] to his room, and the three of us followed, and . . . we felt as if we were in church. There was no electricity in Alexei's room, and the only light came from the lamps in front of the icons . . . The child stood next to a giant shadow with its head bent low. He was praying, and the child joined him in his prayer.'

It was then that Olga learned that Rasputin had promised the 'tsars' that their boy would recover from his illness. As Vyrubova testified, 'Rasputin predicted that in time the boy would recover completely . . . that he would outgrow the disease.'

And his faith in their son's recovery gave them peace. Then, too, they saw the failure of the terrible revolution. Only recently revolutionaries had hunted the tsar like game, and the Tsar of All Russia had written to his mother, 'You understand how I feel . . . not having the possibility of driving outside the gates. And this in my own home! . . . I blush writing this to you.' Only yesterday chaos had held sway in the country. And now, just as the peasant had predicted, they had managed to put down the revolution.

A new life was beginning. All as the 'new' person had predicted. Philippe was the former 'Our Friend'. Rasputin became the *new* one – 'Our New Friend'. And that, apparently, was the hidden meaning of his new last name.

Yet Another Historic Meeting

Rasputin continued to visit the Montenegrin princesses during the whole first half of 1907. Militsa's outburst of anger seemed to have subsided. This was all the more necessary since the tsars continued to meet Rasputin occasionally at her home. And she seemed to forgive and to overlook the fact that Rasputin was now a frequent secret guest at the royal palace. As before, she praised the seer to her acquaintances. She already understood: continual glorification of Father Grigory was very pleasing to the tsarina.

It was then at Militsa's palace that another meeting took place that would have great significance for the fate of the empire.

At that time a new friend had appeared at the tsarina's side, the young maid of honour Anya Taneeva. And soon afterwards the court had begun to talk of the ardent friendship between the tsarina and her young maid of honour. And Militsa immediately began inviting the new favourite to visit her. Anya seemed to be a naive young girl who imitated the tsarina to a ludicrous degree. She engaged Militsa in identical conversations on the tsarina's favourite mystical topics. And, naturally, Anya wanted to meet Rasputin. Especially since she was then, at the beginning of 1907, getting ready to wed the naval officer Vyrubov.

The File, from the testimony of Vyrubova:

I first met Rasputin at Militsa Nikolaevna's in 1907 a few days before my wedding . . . Although I had heard that the sovereign and empress were seeing him at her home. The meeting was preceded by reading mystical books in Russian and French that Militsa Nikolaevna had lent me and that proved the existence of people who, thanks to their lives, had been made seers. At the beginning of March 1907 Militsa Nikolaevna invited me to visit, warning me that Rasputin would be there. She received me in the living room alone and started telling me about people who are endowed with a gift from on high, and who possess the gift of seeing into the future. Militsa Nikolaevna talked to me for about an hour on that topic and asked me not to be surprised if she exchanged a triple kiss with Rasputin . . . I was very nervous, more so since she had said, 'Ask of him whatever you wish, he will pray for you. He can ask anything of God' . . . Rasputin and Militsa kissed each other, and then she introduced him to me . . . And I was startled by his piercing eyes, set deep within their sockets . . . I was concerned about my marriage, since I didn't know the groom very well, and I asked if I should get married. Rasputin answered that he recommended I get married, although the marriage would be an unhappy one.

But soon afterwards Rasputin stopped visiting Militsa. And the Montenegrin learned that the peasant had dared to utter disapproving words about her sister's marriage to Nikolai Nikolaevich. And then the tsarina suddenly started visiting her less and less often. And that Militsa never forgave.

Awaiting The Peasant In Pokrovskoe

Rasputin went back home in the autumn of 1907. To Pokrovskoe, accompanied by Olga Lokhtina and three young devotees of his: the unmarried nurse Akilina Laptinskaya, the engineer's widow Khionia Berladskaya, and the wife of a collegiate secretary Zinaida Manshtedt (or Manchtet, as she is called in some sources).

By that time he had bought himself a spacious new house in Pokrovskoe. At home he changed and became talkative. The simple illiterate peasant revived in him, and he boasted to his fellow villagers and showed off the 'little Petersburg ladies' who had come back with him and who revered him. And he gladly told the local clerics about the grand dukes and even about the 'tsars', who asked advice of him – of the Grishka whom only yesterday they had beaten and made such fun of.

But this time a surprise was waiting for Rasputin on his return. He learned that an inspector from the Tobolsk Theological Consistory had come to the village. And the local village priests with whom Rasputin regularly conversed had been called in for questioning by the inspector. And they had been asked about Rasputin. And soon afterwards his new home was searched, and letters from the 'little ladies' were found and taken away. And then the 'little ladies' themselves were called in for questioning. And, finally, he himself was taken in for interrogation.

Thus was a new file opened concerning the frightening but now familiar charge of *Khlyst* activity. Four years earlier he had succeeded in defending himself against the Consistory's investigators. And now they charged him again.

Mikhail Rodzyanko, the Speaker of the State Duma, who subsequently borrowed the file from the Synod, reported that it vanished soon afterwards. But the missing file has recently been found, surfacing from oblivion in the Tobolsk archive.

The Buried Investigation

The file bears the inscription, 'File of the Tobolsk Consistory in the Charge against Grigory Efimovich "Rasputin-Novy"', a Peasant of the Village of Pokrovskoe in the Tyumen District, of Spreading of False *Khlyst*-like Doctrine and of Forming a Society of Followers of His False Doctrine. Opened 6 September 1907.'

It turned out that while Rasputin was away in Petersburg, the bishop of Tobolsk had been provided with information, as is stated in the file, touching on the period of Rasputin's mysterious wanderings. According to 'the information that has been collected and verified, the peasant in name brought from his life in the factories of the province of Perm a knowledge of the teachings of the *Khlyst* heresy and its ringleaders'. Then, 'while residing in Petersburg, he acquired followers for himself, who after Rasputin's return to the village of Pokrovskoe often came to visit him and lived for some time in his home.' That 'the letters of his followers Kh. Berladskaya, O. Lokhtina, and Z. Manchtet tell of Rasputin's peculiar teachings.' That those Petersburg followers of his 'have walked arm in arm with Rasputin, and that he has often embraced, kissed, and fondled them in the sight of all'. And upstairs in the large new house just acquired by Rasputin, 'special prayer meetings take place at night . . . During those meetings he puts on a semi-monastic black cassock and a gold pectoral cross . . . Those meetings sometimes end late, and it is rumoured that in the bathhouse next to Rasputin's former home "group sinning" occurs. Rumours have been circulating among the residents of the village of Pokrovskoe that Rasputin is spreading *Khlyst* doctrine.'

Thus the file began. It is not hard to figure out who in fact was behind it. Militsa, thanks to her power and her long-standing interest in Orthodox mysticism, had solid links to the Synod. And being well acquainted with mystical teaching, she had long understood the astonishing peasant's secret. And it is her irritated voice that is heard in the concluding denunciation, where Rasputin's 'self-importance and Satanic pride' are mentioned, as is the fact that he had dared to assume the guise of 'an extraordinary preceptor, intercessor, counsellor, and solacer', and that he, a man of little education, had presumed 'to speak of his visits to the palaces of grand dukes and other highly placed personages'.

At the inquest, of course, Rasputin himself denied any connection to the *Khlysty*. He also denied going to bathhouses with women. That is, he denied what he would later acknowledge in Petersburg and even tell his acquaintances. And the 'little ladies' stood solidly behind him. Berladskaya, Laptinskaya, and Lokhtina, plus Evdokia and Ekaterina Pechyorkina, the aunt and niece who were in his service, included nothing in their depositions but rapturous affirmations of Father Grigory's lofty morality. In reply to the inspector's question about Rasputin's kisses, Laptinskaya pompously explained to the Tobolsk provincials that 'it is a commonplace phenomenon in intelligentsia circles.' And so on.

But all this proved to be only the beginning. Upon arriving in Pokrovskoe, the inspector of the Tobolsk Theological Seminary, D. Beryozkin, noted in his review of the conduct of the case that the investigation had been carried out by 'persons ill informed about *Khlyst* practice', and that only Rasputin's two-storeyed residence had been searched. 'Even though it is well known that the place of "rejoicing" is never located in residences . . . but is always set up in backyards – in baths, barns, cellars, and even dugouts.' He had in mind the very secret 'chapel under the floor of the stable' in Rasputin's old house. 'The pictures and icons found in the house were not described, even though they are often indicative of the *Khlyst* heresy,' and so on. After that, Antony, the bishop of Tobolsk, issued a decree ordering further inquiry into the matter. And that the inquiry be entrusted to an experienced, antisectarian missionary. Inspector Beryozkin had already prepared himself to conduct the supplementary inquiry.

Rasputin was given a scare. He had in an instant been transformed into a downtrodden peasant without any rights. But the crazy yet shrewd and worldly-wise Lokhtina apparently made an accurate assessment of the situation. She realized that such a vigorous investigation of an obscure peasant could only have been ordered by some very powerful person in the capital. And that it could only be stopped in the capital.

Lokhtina hurried back to Petersburg. And before long the investigation was suspended. Despite the recent order of the bishop. And it became clear to everyone where the source was of the intervention that had buried the bishop's investigation in the bowels of the Synod.

So Militsa had made a fatal blunder. She had decided to exploit the situation in order to put the peasant in his place. She had been certain that an investigation into his *Khlyst* affiliations would compromise him and close his path to the palace. She erred because she could not imagine the extent of his influence over the royal family.

And the intelligent tsarina easily guessed who stood behind the investigation, who had tried to take the 'man of God' away from her.

A Change At The Palace

And soon afterwards, as Feofan relates in the File, 'the good relations between the royal family and Militsa, Anastasia Nikolaevna, and Pyotr and Nikolai Nikolaevich became strained. Rasputin himself mentioned it in passing. From a few sentences of his I concluded that he had very likely instilled in the former emperor the idea that they had too much influence on state affairs and were encroaching on the emperor's independence.'

The peasant had been boasting a little. He wanted to show his strength. But the fact is that the idea was now a new and permanent one of the tsarina's. It had come to her as soon as she ceased to like her former friend. In enmity, too, her nature was a consistent one. She could dislike with equal ardour and fierceness. And Our New Friend immediately grasped 'Mama's' new mood ('Mama' and 'Papa' were what he now called the 'tsars'; father and mother of the Russian land). And he understood his own role: to constantly instill that response of 'Mama's' in 'Papa'. For it was very difficult for Nicky to change his attachments. And, as Vyrubova very correctly testified, 'he continued to trust Grand Duke Nikolai Nikolaevich.'

Yesterday's friends were now referred to in the royal family in the same way that they had been referred to before by ill-wishers in the court – as the 'black women'. And the tsarina's ears were now becoming more receptive to all she had not wanted to hear before.

'From time to time the idea occurred to me that Militsa Nikolaevna had introduced Rasputin to the empress in order later on to make him a tool for the achievement of her own goals,' Vyrubova testified in the File. So Anya spoke simple-heartedly to the tsarina about the things that Alix herself was then thinking. And together they were indignant with the 'black women', who had dared to launch a disgraceful investigation against the 'man of God'. The New Friend gladly explained to Alix where the vile rumours about her were coming from: 'Everything bad that was being said about the empress now originated with Militsa and Anastasia Nikolaevna . . . They said that the empress . . . was psychologically abnormal, that she was seeing too much of Rasputin,' Vyrubova testified in the File. The good Anya reported everything to Alix, forever estranging the 'black women' from the throne. The tsarina never set foot in the 'black women's' house again.

And soon afterward the omniscient general's wife A. Bogdanovich would write in her diary, 'Radtsig [the tsar's valet, N. A. Radtsig] was saying that the relations between the tsar and Grand Duke Nikolai Nikolaevich have completely cooled, just as they have between the tsarina and the grand duke's wife Anastasia Nikolaevna.'

Alix parted with the Montenegrins without regret. For now she was not alone. In Vyrubova she had found a Friend. A true Friend.

The Dangerous Friend

In March 1917 the tsarina's closest friend was brought from her damp jail cell to the Winter Palace and the Extraordinary Commission. The investigation was trying to get her to elucidate palace secrets. And the enigma of Rasputin's influence. Although the greatest enigma of all was Anna Vyrubova herself. Alix's friend.

'Dim . . . Had difficulty passing the examination for home-study teacher . . . Not interested in anything . . . It's hard to understand how she could have had such a relationship with the highly educated, energetic tsarina.' Such was the testimony of numerous witnesses about Vyrubova. She will enter history so described. Even though it is enough to read the transcripts of her own interrogations to sense how brilliantly cunning and dangerously intelligent this woman was.

From the outset she chose the part that she would play in the investigation with remarkable sureness. It was the role of the same naive, simple-hearted, childishly dim-witted Anya that she had played with such success in the royal family.

The secretary of the Commission, the poet Alexander Blok, who was present for her interrogations, would write of her, 'A person who is degraded and in trouble becomes a child. Remember Vyrubova. She lied childishly.'

It was the only possible tactic in her situation – to lie openly in a childish way, thereby demonstrating her weakness, silliness, and total ignorance of what was going on in the palace. It is almost with astonishment that she learns from an investigator that she was regarded a fanatical admirer of Rasputin.

'So you are claiming that your interest in Rasputin was the same as your interest in many other people in your life?' the investigator Girchich asks in exasperation. 'Or did he still have exceptional interest for you?'

'Exceptional? No!' she says very sincerely. And by way of frustrating any follow-up questions, she starts complaining in a womanish way. 'Because, in general, you think it was easy living at court? I was envied . . . Generally speaking, it was hard for an upright person to live there, where there was much envy and slander. I was simple, so for those twelve years, except for misfortune, I saw almost nothing.'

But a new, very important question follows. 'Why did you burn a whole stack of documents?'

'I burned almost nothing,' she lies openly and as if naively, she who filled a fireplace with the ashes of burned papers.

She is accused of having appointed ministers and taken part in political intrigues with Rasputin. And again she is naively astonished: she and Rasputin talked only about religion. She is presented with proof, her correspondence with Rasputin.

'But why are people who have no connection to politics and are interested only in prayer and fasting carrying on a correspondence about political matters?' the investigator asks triumphantly.

She merely sighs and continues as naively as before. 'Everybody came by with all sorts of questions.'

'Well, we could say they came by for a day, a month, a year, but here they came by for many years on end.'

'It was terrible, that's what it was!' she sighs. 'They never left me alone!'

And then, after all this mendacity, another investigator, V. Rudnev, who was conducting the interrogation jointly with Girchich, would write something astonishing: 'Her testimony . . . was imbued with truth and sincerity. Its only deficiency was her extraordinary volubility and stunning capacity for jumping from one thought to another.'

This while she was lying to his face. Why would he write such a thing? Because she truly did understand people. She immediately grasped the difference between the two investigators. And she chose different tactics with each of them. She could only defend herself against Girchich with naivety and foolishness. But Rudnev, that sentimental provincial who so yearned for human nobility, could be turned into her ally. And she accomplished that by showing her unswerving devotion to the fallen royal family, by showing a willingness to lie only for their sake. She gave him an opportunity to make a judgement about her Christian forbearance in prison. True, it was her mother who hastened to tell Rudnev about that forbearance. Rudnev subsequently recalled

her purely Christian forgiveness in regard to those she had been compelled to endure inside the walls of the Peter and Paul Fortress. This was the taunting of the guards, which expressed itself in spitting in her face and removing her clothing and undergarments, along with blows to her face and other parts of her body . . . I should note that I heard about the taunting not from her but from her mother. Vyrubova confirmed it all with a remarkable lack of rancour, explaining that they weren't responsible, for 'they know not what they do.'

It is true, she asked him not to punish those responsible, so as not to make her situation worse. So, without even checking on whether there had in fact been any taunting, Rudnev believed her and transferred her out of the fortress.

But she saved her trump card for the end. The provincial investigator knew about the legend of which all Russia was talking: that Vyrubova had been 'the concubine of the tsar and of Rasputin'. And as if taking care that the good man should know the whole truth about her, she insisted on an evidentiary medical examination. And Rudnev was amazed: Vyrubova was a virgin. Now he believed her unreservedly. And was prepared to shut his eyes to the 'white lies' Vyrubova had spoken to his face. In his summary he wrote: 'She enjoyed no influence whatever at court, nor could she, since there was too great an advantage in quality of intellect and will in the empress in comparison with the limited, weak-willed, but selflessly devoted and ardently affectionate Vyrubova.' Thus wrote Rudnev of the most influential woman in Russia. The poor provincial could not even begin to suspect the exquisite psychological and erotic intrigues engaged in by the woman under his investigation. And he therefore added his voice to the many-voiced chorus of witnesses who spoke unanimously in their inter-rogations of the 'naive and dim-witted' Vyrubova. True, the majority of those witnesses would perish in the revolution, while the 'naive and dim-witted' Vyrubova would survive intact. The tsarina's friend would know how to make good use of the revolutionary writer Gorky and the revo-lutionary leader Trotsky to break out of her cell. Upon regaining her freedom, she would, while hiding out in Petrograd, initiate a cor-respondence with the tsarina and even attempt to free her! And she would succeed as well in organizing her own flight from Bolshevik Russia! That woman, who dismissed and installed ministers and who from time to time even ruled the iron will of the last tsarina, knew how to look like a simple-hearted Russian scatterbrain. That mask of convenience had long since become her face.

Anya's Game

By the time Anya met Rasputin, she was already close to the throne. Her father, Alexander Sergeevich Taneev, a stout little old man who spoke nothing but pleasantries to everyone, performed the duties of director-in-chief of His Imperial Majesty's Own Chancery. It was something of a family post: her grandfather and great-grandfather had occupied it over the reigns of three emperors. On her mother's side, she had even inherited royal genes;

among her ancestors was an illegitimate child of the mad emperor Paul. In
1904 she was presented to the empress and received the royal monogram
and rank of municipal maid of honour. Alix immediately realized that she
had found a Friend. A year later, in 1905, Anya was already accompanying
the empress on the royal yacht, *Polar Star.* 'During the trip, the empress
complained that she had no friends outside the family, and that she felt like
a stranger,' she explained under interrogation.

Anya understood the tsarina at once. The observant Vyrubova would in
her memoirs precisely describe the consistently peremptory personality of
the lonely Alix. But she would be observant only in her book. In life and
at the palace she had chosen a different role, the only possible one, given
the tsarina's personality: 'kind and simple-hearted'. The devoted girl,
hanging on the empress's every word and astonished by her ideas. That is
how Anya made her appearance in the life of the royal family not long
before Rasputin's own arrival in their midst. And very soon, Anya started
turning up in the tsar's diary.

'9 January 1906. Sergei and A. A. Taneeva had breakfast with us'; '4
February. A. A. Taneeva joined us for breakfast.' The young maid of honour
had in the briefest span of time become a character in the tsar's diary and
in all their lives. And had immediately thrust the Montenegrin princesses
out of the tsarina's heart. At the same time, the sage Anya was visiting
Militsa's palace. To study mysticism, for which the tsarina had such a
passion.

In 1907 Anya got married. Or, more accurately, was compelled to marry.
Rumours of far too dangerous a kind had started to circulate about the
close friendship between Anya and the tsarina. The court viewed the
appearance of the new favourite with jealousy.

Filippov, Rasputin's banker and publisher and someone located at the
centre of Petersburg life, testified in the File that 'Vyrubova's friendship
with the empress was explained by some in court spheres as an intimacy
grounded in sexual psychopathology.' And the monarchist A. Bogdanovich,
the wife of the general who served as the warden of Saint Isaac's, the largest
cathedral in Russia, would more than once record in her diary the words
of courtiers about the 'unnatural friendship' of Vyrubova and the tsarina.

In order to put a stop to the rumours, the devoted Anya decided to
sacrifice herself and get married. And she married a modest naval officer,
Lieutenant Alexander Vyrubov, though it is true that he owned a rather
large estate.

From Nicholas's diary for 4 February 1907: 'Anna Taneeva presented her
future husband Vyrubov.' Once a married woman, she could no longer be

a maid of honour, and the court would be pacified. 'The poor empress sobbed like a Moscow merchant's wife giving up her daughter to be married,' Witte mockingly wrote in his memoirs.

And, of course, the tsarina had asked Vyrubova to talk to the seer Rasputin about her marriage. And Anya, who at once grasped what Militsa had failed to grasp – the peasant's role in the palace, set off to Militsa's to make Our Friend's acquaintance. In order to be able to bring back to the palace what Alix wanted to hear: the most rapturous impressions.

In point of fact, Anya's marriage changed neither her life nor her situation.

The File, from the testimony of Vyrubova: 'In 1907 I married Lieutenant Alexander Vasilievich Vyrubov, and when we came back from our honeymoon we rented a dacha, first in Petersburg and then in Tsarskoe Selo' (since that is where the royal family lived). 'My husband was reassigned to the Field Chancery, and in that same year of 1907 we accompanied the royal family to the sea.' Vyrubov had been assigned to the chancery so that the friends would not be parted.

The singer Alexandra Belling saw Vyrubova at the time. 'I met her at a musical evening,' Belling recalled:

> She had just been married and was happy . . . Her husband, a round-faced dark-haired sailor, never left her side, and constantly gazed into her eyes. She laughed continuously and, it appeared, was enjoying life . . . 'That's terribly funny!' she said to me. 'You got married on the ninth, and I on the eleventh.' And she burst into infectious laughter . . . But in spite of her gaiety, affectionate voice, sweet smile, and kind eyes, one did not sense sincerity in her, or anything that might have disposed one to credulity . . . One evening, as I . . . was singing . . . and Vyrubova was sitting with her hands over her face and listening . . . someone came in and announced that Anna Alexandrovna was 'requested'. She became agitated and hurried out. After a few moments she reappeared in the doorway of the living room with a magnificent white boa round her neck, which made her look quite stunning, and with a splendid bouquet of bright red roses, which she handed to me, warmly thanking me and hugging me, and, as if in pain, pressing her forehead to mine.

And so she had it all: a honeymoon and happiness and a husband who gazed into her eyes. But 'after living with her husband for a year and a half', Vyrubova testified before the Extraordinary Commission, 'I was divorced from him, since it turned out he was suffering from mental illness . . . He went to Switzerland for treatment – I forget which city – and then we divorced, so I have not seen him since.'

The investigator Rudnev sympathetically recalled, 'According to Tanee-va's mother, the daughter's husband had proved to be completely impotent, with an extremely perverse sexual psychology that manifested itself in various sadistic episodes in which he inflicted moral suffering on her and evoked a feeling of utter disgust.'

Had Vyrubova's husband really been a complete psychopath who had then disappeared from view into a Swiss clinic? Not at all. Vyrubova's former spouse remarried, and from 1913 to 1917 lived quietly on his estate. He was held in high esteem in his district, and had even been elected district marshal of the nobility in the city of Polotsk. So it is obvious why the courtiers regarded the reasons given for her divorce with great suspicion and returned even more insistently to their earlier theme.

And the general's wife Bogdanovich, the hostess of a monarchist salon, wrote in her diary for 2 February 1908 that Zilloti, an aide to the chief of the naval high command related how struck everyone has been by the young tsarina's strange friendship with her former maid of honour Taneeva, who married Vyrubov . . . When during a trip to the skerries the boat got stuck on a rock, the royal family spent the night on the yacht. The tsar slept alone in a cabin, while the tsarina took Vyrubova to her stateroom and spent the night alone with her in the same bed.'

Basing her account on the word of Dolly Kochubei, née the Duchess of Leichtenberg (and thus a relative of the Romanovs), Bogdanovich sets forth the reason for the divorce as follows: '10 June 1908 . . . An unnatural friendship exists between the tsarina and Taneeva, and . . . Taneeva's husband, Vyrubov, apparently . . . found among her things some letters from the tsarina that led to mournful thoughts.' The general's wife would frequently return to the topic: '6 February 1909. The young tsarina has had a severe attack of neurasthenia . . . which has been attributed to her abnormal friendship with Vyrubova. Something isn't right in Tsarskoe Selo.'

'Something Isn't Right In Tsarskoe Selo'

But how could she have lived with someone who was impotent and a sadist and yet still play at being the happy couple that Belling so vividly describes? Perhaps she really was happy in those years, happy precisely because her husband was impotent and did not touch her. And only when he tried to master himself and, as they put it in the eighteenth century, direct 'an arrow into her quiver', did he seem so terribly 'sadistic and disgusting' to her.

Perhaps that was why the unhappy Lieutenant Vyrubov had turned into a 'psychopath' in that year and a half. And if this is true, and she did reveal an aversion to men, then it is clear why even later that beautiful young woman had no man in her life. For in 1917, a full ten years after her divorce from Vyrubov, she was still a virgin!

Although there would be numerous flirtations in her life; flirtations for the sake of appearance were part of her game.

I have thought a great deal about her relations with the tsarina, and in the last book about Nicholas II, I attempted to explain them. Now it seems to me that I understand them better. At the basis of her relationship with the tsarina lay a hidden feeling, profoundly secret and repressed. And it both drew the unhappy Alix to her and frightened her. And knowing of the tsarina's religiousness and purity, Anya, to hide that feeling, invented a delightful game that in the beginning attached the tsarina to her even more.

The Innermost Secrets Of The Heart

I found astonishing testimony in the File. In 1917 the Extraordinary Commission interrogated one Feodosia Voino, who had worked as Vyrubova's maid. Voino reported that 'Vyrubova was in love with the tsar, but I don't know if it was mutual. She received letters from the tsar, and one such letter was intercepted by the tsarina. And then Vyrubova and the tsarina had a quarrel, which quickly came to an end, however. Vyrubova herself warned me and the housemaid that she had letters from the tsar in her safe, and that if she should suddenly die, the letters were to be returned to the tsar.'

This might seem like an invention, had not the tsarina's own letters survived. During the war, Alix and Nicky, sighing with love, wrote letters to each other that will remain a tale of the most beautiful romance. But there are some mysterious lines in those letters. For example, in one of them Alix adds the following postscript: 'Lovy, you burn her letters so that they should never fall into anybody's hands?' (6 January 1916). And in another: 'if now not firm, we shall be having stories & love-scenes & rows like in the Crimea' (26 January 1915). And in yet another, 'You will see when we return how she will tell you how terribly she suffered without you . . . Be nice & firm . . . she always needs cooling down' (27 October 1914). So, it turns out that 'she' had dared to make scenes and rows and to harass Nicholas with letters! And Alix, not mincing words, brands the woman as 'rude' (27 October), and says there is 'nothing of the loving gentle woman' about her (20 November 1914). And in another letter, she refers to her as 'the Cow' (6 October 1915)!

But almost at the same time Alix writes to her husband, 'Perhaps you will mention in your telegram, that you thank [her] for papers and letter and send messages' (21 November 1914). And in another letter, 'When A[nya] speaks of her loneliness, it makes me angry, she . . . twice a day comes to us – every evening with us four hours' (2 January 1916).

Anya understood how dangerous for the religious tsarina's soul were all the rumours about the ulterior abnormality of her love for Alix. And the intelligent Anya devised this game. A game that reassured the tsarina. The game of her repressed, pure, and unrequited love for Nicky. Thus at the time did pupils of the Institute for Noble Young Ladies, while idolizing an older girlfriend, fall passionately in love with the older girl's chosen young man. But Anya did not permit herself to contend with the empress, she merely allowed herself to make scenes, ridiculous, naive, harmless scenes. The tsar was compelled to soothe the infatuated Anya with letters, while the tsarina did so with compassion. Her role was the harmless 'third party' who added tension to their relationship. And that stoked the fire, the passion, in Nicky and Alix's great love.

Anya was sly, secretive, cunning, and smart, a dangerous woman who had devoted herself to two passions. Witte wrote, 'All the courtiers close to the royal family cater to Anya Vyrubova . . . Anya arranges various favours for them and influences the closeness to the sovereign of one group of political figures or another.'

Her first passion was power. She was the invisible ruler of the most brilliant court in Europe. But her other passion, forever hidden, was *Alix*. And that secret passion was combined with something frightening and carnal that subsequently came unseen into the palace with Rasputin. While in the palace he turned into a holy man, the unseen field of his lust, his unbridled potency, could not have failed to be sensed by the tsarina. And Alix's passionate carnal dreams in her letters to Nicholas were perhaps not expressions of humble conjugal love but rather an ecstatic summons.

In her memoirs Anya Vyrubova writes that after her divorce she 'grew even closer to the royal family', living in Tsarskoe Selo in a little house next to the palace.

From the entry for 7 September 1908 in the diary of the tsar's sister, Grand Duchess Xenia: 'We drove out to see Nicky and Alix . . . Alix was in the garden with Olga, Tatyana, and the constant Vyrubova.'

A Mighty Alliance Between
The Two

It was at that time that Alix was introducing the mysterious elder to everyone close to the royal family.

The File, from the testimony of Captain (First Class) Nikolai Pavlovich Sablin, master of the imperial yacht *Standart* and one of those closest to the tsar and tsarina: 'I think it was in 1908, while sailing on the *Standart* that the empress began preparing me for the fact that she knew Rasputin. She said there are people who have special power as a result of their ascetic way of life, and she announced that there was such a person, namely, Rasputin, and proposed to introduce him to me.'

From the testimony of Vyrubova:

> The next meeting with Rasputin occurred a year later on the train as I was on my way to Tsarskoe Selo. Rasputin was also on his way there with a lady to visit some acquaintances . . . I was very glad to see him and said I would like to talk to him about my unhappy life. Rasputin gave me his address, 'At the Lokhtins' on Grechesky Avenue' . . . I met with Rasputin in Lokhtina's living room . . . Olga Lokhtina was then . . . still a very nice fashionable lady and not marked by the eccentricity that would later develop in her.

I think it was all much simpler: it was the tsarina who wanted the people dearest to her to be friends, and so Anya went off to what was then Rasputin's staff headquarters at the apartment of the general's wife. Lokhtina speaks of this herself in the File: 'I met Vyrubova before I broke with my family. The first time she visited me was to find out when Father Grigory would be coming to Petrograd.'

Anya knew that all who wished to enjoy the tsarina's love had to love the 'man of God' and feel his power. And she felt it at once. It had always been easy for her to assume roles thus Anya straightaway became Rasputin's most faithful admirer. A fanatical admirer.

Thus Rasputin acquired his most rapturous adherent, and Anya had her story, that the perspicacious elder had predicted her unhappy marriage. He had predicted it, but she had failed to listen, and she was punished for it.

Lokhtina subsequently yielded her role as the elder's chief admirer to Anya. She understood that the other woman would be more useful to Father Grigory. As Iliodor put it, 'Lokhtina resigned herself to that change in her destiny.'

In A Darkened Palace Corridor

The royal family found itself alone. The friends of Nicky's childhood, the grand dukes Sergei and Sandro, had long since become estranged from him. Only the poet KR, Grand Duke Konstantin Konstantinovich, and his wife were welcome guests in Tsarskoe Selo. Alix wrote down excerpts from KR's poems in the copybook containing her favourite sayings. Although that copybook would soon turn into a record of the thoughts of the semi-literate peasant Grigory Rasputin. And soon after that only two people would share the isolation of the royal family. Father Grigory and Anya Vyrubova.

With the fall of the Montenegrins, Anya inherited their most important role. Because Alix did not dare to receive the elder openly – rumours had already begun to spread about the strange peasant in the palace – the tsarina could not let it be known that Rasputin was treating her child. The heir's illness was still a secret.

And so the royal family met with Rasputin in Anya's little house in Tsarskoe Selo. Anya's notes to V. Voeikov, the palace castellan, have survived in the archive of the Extraordinary Commission: 'Dear Vl[adimir] Nik[olaevich] . . . The elder arrived at 2:00 p.m., and Their Majesties wish to see him today. They think it would be better at my house.'

From the tsar's diary for 1908: '6 November . . . We dropped in on Anya . . . and saw Grigory and talked with him for a long time.'

'27 December . . . We went to Anya's, where we saw Grigory. Together the three of us consecrated her Christmas tree, which was very pleasant.'

But sometimes it was necessary to escort Father Grigory to the palace to treat the Little One. And again Anya worked out the ritual for the secret delivery of the peasant to the palace.

Our Friend would come as if to visit Maria Vishnyakova, the royal children's nurse. This allowed him to avoid having his name written down in the lobby register, where all visits to the 'tsars' were recorded. Once in the palace, 'he would drop by to see the nurse Maria Vishnyakova, a very nervous individual and at the time an ardent admirer of Rasputin,' as Anya obscurely put it in her testimony, and from there would be escorted to the royal apartments.

How it all took place is related in the File by the maid of honour Sophia Tyutcheva, the granddaughter of the great Russian poet and the royal children's governess:

Once in the winter of 1908, Grand Duchess Tatyana got sick. While her rooms were being aired out, she lay down in Vishnyakova's room, and I and the other grand duchesses were in the classroom . . . Looking back into the darkened corridor, I saw the figure of a peasant in a tight-fitting coat. I realized at once that it was Rasputin. I asked him what he was doing there. He replied that he needed to see Maria Ivanovna Vishnyakova. I pointed out to him that she was busy and that he wasn't supposed to be there. He departed without speaking . . . I went to Vishnyakova, who at the time was putting the heir to bed . . . and told her that Rasputin had been looking for her . . . 'Oh, I'll catch it from Anna Alexandrovna [Vyrubova]!' Vishnyakova said . . . When we saw each other the next day, Vishnyakova said to me, 'I really did catch it from Anna Alexandrovna because of you.' And she explained that Vyrubova had asked her never to speak to me about Rasputin, since I didn't believe in his holiness. The next day Vyrubova was having dinner with me, and out of a feeling of friendship I told her how I felt about Rasputin. To my utter astonishment, Vyrubova suddenly asked, 'But who is this Rasputin?'

Tyutcheva was astonished because she knew Anya's simple-heartedness and naivety. She still did not know how capable the simple-hearted Anya was of dissembling. Nor what depths were hidden in her 'simple soul'.

The Only One

Rasputin understood that the 'black women' hated him and would attempt to use their last formidable weapon against him – Father Ioann of Kronstadt. And he waited and prepared himself. 'Rasputin indicated reservations with unusual skill . . . Rasputin . . . said of Father Ioann of Kronstadt . . . that he was a saint but, like a child, lacked experience and judgment . . . As a result Father Ioann's influence at court began to wane,' Feofan testified in the File.

Father Ioann, the last person who might have blocked Rasputin's influence, died in 1909. Now the peasant was alone, the only one.

From Vyrubova's testimony in the File: 'And the former tsar and tsarina . . . had great respect for the priest Ioann of Kronstadt. And after his death Rasputin took his place. In all the adversities of life, during the frequent illnesses of the heir to the throne, during the aggravation of the tsarina's heart condition, they turned to Rasputin for support, and the former tsar and former tsarina asked for his prayers.'

And then, casting all caution aside, the tsars started receiving him at the palace.

From Nicholas's diary: '4 February 1909 . . . At 6 o'clock the Archimandrite Feofan and Grigory came to see us. He also saw the children.'

'29 February . . . At 2:30 Grigory came to see us, and we received him with all the children. It was so good to hear him with the whole family.'

'29 March (the Day of Christ's Joyful Resurrection). After dinner I went for a walk with Dmitry. There was a frost and a lot of snow.' After his walk with his young cousin and protégé, one of Grigory's future murderers, the tsar learned that Grigory himself had arrived at the palace. 'After tea upstairs in the nursery I sat for a while with Grigory, who had come unexpectedly.'

Nobody could come to see the 'tsars' unexpectedly. Even the Romanov grand dukes had to obtain audiences. But Father Grigory didn't.

'26 April . . . From 6:00 to 7:30 we saw . . . Grigory . . . I also sat with Grigory a little while in the nursery this evening.'

'15 August. I talked with Grigory a long time this evening.'

The rumours about the peasant, that strange heir of the late Philippe, troubled the Romanov family. On 1 January 1910, Xenia wrote in her diary: 'It is so sad, I feel sorry for Nicky, and it makes no sense.' What did not make sense to her was what the brilliantly educated Alix could have had to talk about for hours on end with that semi-literate peasant.

Nicky and Alix could no longer manage without those meetings. And not just because the boy instantly improved in Rasputin's presence. The peasant was so different from the court atmosphere in which they lived, an atmosphere of intrigues, and the terrible backbiting so traditional in courts. He never had anything but good to say about people, even about his enemies. And they liked his stories about his wanderings, too. In them were people unburdened by the usual yokes of rank and money. In them were God and nature: sunshine on a meadow, a night spent sleeping on the ground under an open sky – everything that the tsar, so fond of the simple life, could only dream about.

The publisher Filippov testified in the File: 'In that period of his life Rasputin . . . was short of money, and I had to lend him small sums of twenty to a hundred roubles that he would then pay back whenever he could. Once I asked him, "Are you, in spite of your closeness to the tsarina, really so hard up?" He answered, "She's stingy . . . she gives you a hundred roubles, and when a week later you ask her again, she reminds you, "But I just gave you a hundred."'

The tsarina's frugality, or, more accurately, her stinginess, had become proverbial at court. 'Alix wouldn't give Rasputin money. She gave him silk shirts, sashes, and the gold cross he wore,' recalled Grand Duchess Olga, Nicky's sister.

The 'tsars' would dress up in costumes of the times of the first Romanovs, and Alix wanted to see Rasputin in an expensive 'costume of the people', too. And arriving in Pokrovskoe now, he would happily strut before his fellow villagers in his costume: in silk shirts, patent-leather boots, and crimson waistbands. And in answer to their questions about where that magnificence had come from, he would tell them about the 'tsars', who loved and appreciated Grigory. So they would not forget who the Grishka they had denounced to church investigators had become.

Iliodor recalled:

> Grigory, indicating his satin shirt, said to me, 'This shirt was sewn for me by the empress. And I have other shirts embroidered by her.' I asked him to show them to me. Grigory's wife brought out several shirts. I started to look at them. 'Do you want to take some as a keepsake?' Grigory asked with a smile.
>
> 'Could I have one or two?'
>
> 'Take three!'
>
> And he picked out three shirts for me, a red one, a white tussore one, and another white one of expensive linen with embroidery on the collar and sleeves.

The 1905 revolution was becoming little more than an awful memory. And for Alix, who so wanted to believe in the miracles of Our Friend, Russia had been pacified not by the cruel Prime Minister Stolypin with his gallows and military tribunals but by the marvellous elder with his prayers.

The long-awaited peace had arrived. But if Nicholas at the time had grown mellow, she continued to be visited by neurasthenia and a terror that seemed to have no cause.

'Head and eyes ache and my heart feels weak'; 'Heart bleeds from fear and horror'; 'When head hurts less, I write down the sayings of our Friend, and the time passes more quickly'; 'I am made sick by sad thoughts.' These quotations are from her last letters. But she was tormented in those earlier years, too. She was an unhappy woman, who was aware that her cursed heredity had destroyed her beloved son, and who lived in a state of constant anguish from her terrible premonitions. And only Our Friend was able to relieve her nervous anxiety. With his soothing words of forgiveness and love and of the future divine reward for all her sufferings. And with his remarkable hands that dispelled the constant migraines that drove her mad with pain. The tormented Alix needed him just as much as her doomed son did.

She wrote a letter to Rasputin then. She was trying to write in a simple-hearted way that would be comprehensible to the peasant – to write in his own idiom.

'I am calm in my soul, I am able to rest, only when you, teacher, are sitting next to me, and I am kissing your hands and resting my head on your blessed shoulders. Oh, how easy is it for me then.'

For her to feel safe now, she needed to have constant confirmation of his special power. And that is why the tsarina and her friend Vyrubova would every day try to find miracles, however minor: he had predicted the weather, he had predicted the day of the tsar's return home, and so on. All this has survived in the tsar and tsarina's correspondence. It was then that Rasputin made the astonishing statement that 'as long as I am alive, the dynasty shall live.' This is confirmed in his daughter's memoirs:

'Father himself used to say in Tsarskoe Selo that when he was gone, the court would be gone, too.'

And we find the same thing in a great many of the depositions. 'It has been established,' wrote the investigator Rudnev, 'that he said to the sovereign, "My death will be your death, too."'

The peasant knew: she was not afraid of those words; on the contrary, they soothed her. For he *was* alive, that strong peasant still loved by all. And he had promised to live a very long time. And, after all, why would the Lord who had sent him take him away?

And then in 1910, at the very pinnacle of his success, when he had become the only one, something mysterious started to happen.

The 'Dark Forces'

The sleepy new year of 1910 was marked by very few events capable of holding the attention of Russia's newspapers and inhabitants. However, it was also to introduce some of the key figures in our story.

Convened in Petersburg was the First All-Russian Congress for the Struggle against Drunkenness, that truly 'Russian disease'. Amusing incidents from ancient history were recalled, such as a battle in which the drunken warriors lost their trousers. The government was accused of making money from that abiding Russian calamity. Whereupon the insulted representatives of the Ministry of Finance walked out of the congress. Village priests were charged with 'excessive admiration' for the famous words attributed to Saint Vladimir, the tenth-century Kievan prince who converted Rus to Christianity, that 'drinking is the Russian's joy.' Where-upon the theological delegation walked out, too.

The State Duma was occupied with the latest scandal. The well-known monarchist Nikolai Markov, known as Markov II, had demanded the passing of new decrees against the Jews. 'The Russian people,' Markov announced, 'do not wish to become the slaves of the parasitic Judaic tribe.' Prince Volkonsky, who was presiding, attempted to expunge his words. Markov II was voted out of the Duma for the next fifteen sessions. At another session, another famous monarchist, Purishkevich, reported that the leftist movement in student circles consisted of 'Jews, and over them, the pro-fessors, among whom there are also numerous Jews, and that is why anarchy rules in the universities'.

This announcement produced an uproar, with shouting and abusive language from all quarters. The Speaker of the Duma 'lost control and displayed his utter helplessness'. As a result, he was removed and a new Speaker was elected, Alexander Ivanovich Guchkov, one of the most bril-liant and adventurous people in the Duma. The newspapers enjoyed pub-lishing his biography. There had not been a single debacle at the beginning of the century that this son of a wealthy Moscow merchant had not participated in. He had gone to help defend the Armenians during their slaughter by the Turks, he had participated in the Boer War in Africa, naturally on the Boer side, and during the Russo-Japanese War, he had even been captured by the Japanese. He was well known in the Duma for fist fights during the sessions and for calling out Pavel Milyukov, the head of the Constitutional Democratic Party, the largest in the Duma.

On taking the post of Speaker, he gave a speech in which he spoke for the first time of certain mysterious 'dark forces' that had made themselves known in the highest summits of society.

In Moscow on Khodynka Field, sadly famous for loss of life during the coronation, aviators were conducting flights. The celebrated Sergei Utochkin, known in Russia as the 'hero of the aerial expanse', made several circuits in a biplane. Seated with some difficulty on the little bicycle-style passenger seat behind him was Vladimir Dzhunkovsky, vice-governor of Moscow (and yet another of our future characters). A female aviator also took part in the flights: the dark-haired beauty Princess Shakhovskaya, who would soon become a fanatical devotee of Rasputin's.

On 7 November occurred what was perhaps the only historic event of the year. On that day all Russia was absorbed in mourning. Leo Tolstoy had died at Astapov Station while fleeing his home. Nicholas wrote in an address on Tolstoy's death, 'I sincerely regret the demise of the great writer . . . May the Lord God be merciful in his judgment of him.'

Of the peasant himself there was only vague talk. No one really knew anything, and for that reason he attracted universal attention.

The Khlyst Saviours

People were struck by the mystery of his biography – the transformation of a fallen man, by his rumoured gift of miraculous healing and prophecy, and by the closed world of the royal family in which he was at home. For those on both the left and the right, it was a happy confirmation of a cherished idea: the 'precious talents of the simple Russian'.

Nor was that all. Another reason for his popularity was the rumour of his links to the *Khlysty.*

Once in my youth I was talking to a family friend of ours, the Acmeist poet Sergei Mitrofanovich Gorodetsky, who was then a very old man. In Rasputin's time, Gorodetsky was one of the most popular poets of the day, the author of a celebrated book of verse called *Spring Wheat.* And grinning under his grey moustache, Gorodetsky said something that I have remembered for its paradox: 'Rasputin was attractive and in fashion because he was a *Khlyst.*'

It was only recently, while working on the brilliant period of Russian literature so rightly called the Silver Age, that I came to understand the meaning of that sentence.

It is amazing, but all the celebrated writers of the age had in one way or another become interested in the then mysterious *Khlyst* sect. The celebrated writer and philosopher Vasily Rozanov went to live in a *Khlyst* community and wrote about the *Khlysty* in his *The Apocalyptic Sect.* Two influential minds of the day, the husband and wife team of the novelist Dmitry Merezhkovsky and the poet Zinaida Gippius, lived in a *Khlyst* community in 1902. And they wrote to Alexander Blok, 'Everything we saw there was . . . ineffably beautiful.' And Blok, Russia's foremost poet, and the famous writer Alexei Remizov (as Blok's wife reports in a letter to her mother) 'went to a *Khlyst* meeting together'. Yet another well-known writer, Mikhail Prishvin, wrote in his journal for 1908: '9 November . . . Together with Blok, Remizov, and Sologub [another influential figure!] I visited a *Khlyst* community.' The famous poets Konstantin Balmont and Andrei Bely also wrote about the *Khlysty.* And the best-known peasant poet of the beginning of the century, Nikolai Klyuev, tells, while creating a fashionable biography for himself, of his wanderings with the *Khlysty.* 'Many looked hard for a rapprochement with the *Khlysty,*' wrote Prishvin.

What made them do so was their shared sense of looming apocalypse.

The same sense, in fact, that had impelled the leaders of the intelligentsia to try to find a common language with the official church in the religious philosophical colloquia of 1903. And to try without success. Now it had been decided to try to act through the sects. The intelligentsia believed that it was in the sects, and above all in the most powerful of them, the *Khlysty*, that those who expressed the true religious aspirations of the people were coming together. The *Khlysty*, Prishvin wrote, 'are a subterranean river . . . An immense kingdom of *Khlysty*, elusive and unidentifiable, has emerged . . . within the Orthodox Church itself.' The intelligentsia believed that an alliance between its own spiritual wing and the spiritual wing of the common people – the sects – would be able to stand athwart the coming storm. The sects, as a bridge to the people. Merezhkovsky wrote, 'We need to "reach out to the people" in our own new way . . . There is no doubt that something is happening and beginning to ripen everywhere and in everyone, and we shall go out to meet it. And . . . the crossing over to the people will be easier and more natural through the sectarians.'

The intelligentsia would later mock the royal couple for their faith in a benighted peasant. Yet at the same time and however paradoxically, they dreamed of the same thing. But all this touched only the intelligentsia's leaders. For the ordinary philistine, the *Khlysty* remained religious criminals, the embodiment of secret debauchery.

While Father Grigory was living with the Lokhtins, the general's wife had in essence become his secretary. There in her salon Rasputin won himself ever more new devotees. It was through the Lokhtins that he met Georgy Sazonov, the publisher of progressive economics magazines.

In 1917 Sazonov was, along with other followers of Rasputin, summoned before the Extraordinary Commission. And in the File I found his testimony.

Sazonov, Georgy Petrovich, sixty years old, testified that his family 'were old friends of the Lokhtin family, of the engineer Vladimir Mikhailovich Lokhtin, his wife Olga Vladimirovna, and their daughter Lyudmila . . . Olga Vladimirovna telephoned with the information that Grigory Efimovich Rasputin had asked permission to visit us.'

Thus began their friendship. And Sazonov describes Rasputin as he was in those years: 'He impressed me as a nervous person . . . He could not sit quietly in one place, but fidgeted and moved his hands . . . He spoke jerkily and for the most part incoherently.' But when that fidgety person gazed at his interlocutors, 'a special power shone in his eyes that had an effect on people who were . . . especially susceptible to external influence.'

By this time a circle of crazed female admirers had formed around Rasputin. 'The women who surrounded him treated him with mystical devotion, called him "Father", and kissed his hand.' But the thing that most pleased the deeply religious Sazonov, just as it had his friend Lokhtin, was Rasputin's 'sincere religiousness', something quite rare in those years. 'That religiousness was not feigned, nor was Rasputin posing. Our maid said that whenever [he] happened to spend the night at our house, he prayed instead of sleeping . . . When we stayed at our dacha, the children saw him in the forest deep in prayer . . . Our neighbour, a general's wife who could not hear his name without revulsion, made an effort to follow the children into the forest, and, even though an hour had passed, also saw him deep in prayer.'

In that period (before 1913), Rasputin did not, as Sazonov describes him, partake of alcoholic beverages or eat meat, and he observed all the fasts. 'I might call that period of Rasputin's life,' Sazonov puts it in the File, 'the period when he achieved a certain spiritual loftiness from which he later lapsed.'

And the delighted Sazonov would later invite Rasputin to move into his large, upper-class apartment. As would be entered in the report of the secret surveillance of Rasputin established at that time, 'On his arrival in 1912, he stayed . . . in the apartment of the publisher of the magazine *Russian Economist*, Georgy Petrovich Sazonov, and his wife . . . Rasputin is evidently involved in a love affair with the latter.'

But knowing of Rasputin's sincere religiousness, Sazonov would never have believed it. Just as Olga Lokhtina's husband could not believe it either. For neither Sazonov nor Lokhtin completely understood that mysterious man.

Rasputin continued to keep his relations with the tsar wrapped in enigma. He was cautious. Even his friend Sazonov had little to say except that Rasputin called the empress and emperor 'Mama' and 'Papa', since they were indeed 'mother and father whom the Lord had placed here to watch over and care for the Russian land'. Rasputin had not at that time begun to drink. Sazonov remembered only one 'sensational' story in the File:

'The tsarina evidently regarded him with adoration . . . He related the following fact: he was walking through a Petersburg park and met the tsarina driving in the opposite direction . . . On seeing him, she ordered the horses stopped, rushed over to him, and kissed his hand in the sight of everyone in the park.'

The story made the rounds of the Petersburg salons. And the kissing of Rasputin's hands by the 'tsars' would occupy a large place in the interrogations of the Extraordinary Commission. And in the File two of those who knew Rasputin and the royal family well, Vyrubova and another of the tsarina's friends, Yulia Dehn, would heatedly deny that it had occurred. Most likely they were lying, for they could not explain to the uninitiated that the humbling of pride preached by the peasant was very close to the hearts of both Nicky and Alix. Christ washing the feet of his disciples and the 'tsars' kissing the hand of a peasant – the hand, in Rasputin's words, that 'feeds you all' – was something the religious royal family could easily understand.

The Fashionable Elder

By 1910, however, even more interesting devotees had announced themselves. A certain Vladimir Bonch-Bruevich had made himself a devoted follower of Rasputin. 'Bonch', as he was often called by his friends, was an expert on Russian sectarianism. He had written numerous works on the Old-Believer and other heresies. But it was not that work that would make him famous in Russian history. This modest investigator of heresies was a member of the underground party of Bolsheviks and one of Lenin's closest associates (he would become a leader of Soviet Russia, the man in charge of the affairs of the Council of People's Commissars and a founder of the Cheka, the Bolshevik secret police). The reasons for Bonch-Bruevich's delight in and enormous curiosity about Rasputin are clear. Lenin's address on the sects at the Second Congress of the Russian Social-Democratic Labour Party had been written by Bonch-Bruevich and contained a whole panegyric by the Bolshevik Bonch on the *Khlyst* sect: 'From a political point of view, the *Khlysty* therefore deserve our full attention as passionate haters of everything that issues from the "authorities", that is, from the government . . . I am convinced that through a tactical rapprochement of revolutionaries and the *Khlysty* we can acquire numerous friends.' So when Rasputin began to be persecuted for his *Khlyst* sympathies, Bonch-Bruevich would immediately write with the authority of an expert, 'Rasputin does not belong the *Khlyst* sect!' He was obliged to defend his potential allies.

A Family Close To The Throne

And then in 1910 at the height of enthusiasm for Rasputin, a whole family turned up among his fanatical devotees.

Maria Golovina met Rasputin for the first time in 1910. She was the daughter of the chamberlain's daughter and a 'most pure young woman', as Rasputin's confirmed enemy Prince Felix Yusupov called her. At once she became slavishly devoted to the peasant. The writer Zhukovskaya described 'Munya', as she was called in Rasputin's circle: 'A young-looking girl . . . gazed at me with timid . . . pale blue eyes . . . She seemed, in her light-grey dress and white hat with violets, so small and touching. Boundless devotion and a readiness to subordinate herself completely were evident in her every glance and word.'

Munya's Aunt Olga had been the heroine of the noisiest scandal in the big Romanov family. Olga Valerianovna was over thirty, the wife of Major-General Erik Pistolkors, and the mother of two grown children, when she began her mad love affair with the tsar's uncle, Grand Duke Pavel Alexandrovich. It ended with the grand duke's marrying Olga, for which the tsar relieved him of his duties and banished him abroad. His son from his first marriage, the still-young Dmitry, remained in Russia and had at first lived with the family of Ella and Grand Duke Sergei Alexandrovich; then, after the murder of Sergei, he had been taken in and raised by the royal family. Pavel was pardoned by the tsar in 1905, and returned with his wife to Russia.

So Munya and her mother were relatives of the grand duke. And they soon became relatives of Vyrubova, too. Vyrubova's sister Alexandra (or Sana, as she was called in the family) married Olga's son by her first marriage, Alexander Pistolkors. 'Sana . . . was a very nice looking woman with a little porcelain face, and she produced the charming impression of a spoiled and self-centred child,' the singer Alexandra Belling recalled.

But Rasputin was later to literally split that family in two.

In 1910 however, when Munya Golovina saw him that year for the first time, Rasputin became absolutely essential to her. Munya was at the time on the edge of madness.

In 1917 Munya Golovina was summoned before the Extraordinary Commission for interrogation. I found her testimony in the File.

The Commission had been impatiently awaiting her testimony. Munya was one of those closest to Rasputin. Moreover, there had been a great deal of gossip about her fateful and unrequited love for Rasputin's murderer, Prince Felix Yusupov, who had exploited the unhappy Munya in arranging the peasant's death, a story that would also make its way into the books about Rasputin.

Munya did in fact have a truly fateful love, but it was not at all for Felix Yusupov. However, let Maria speak for herself:

'In 1910 I lost someone I had been very attached to, which had an untoward effect on my nervous system.'

That 'someone' was the tender friend who linked Maria to the richest family in Russia, the Yusupov family.

The Richest Family In Russia

The Yusupov palace stands to this day on the Moika Canal in Petersburg. And within it are the same furniture, the same paintings, and the same mirrors that once held reflections of that family now disappeared into the grave. The Yusupovs were descended from a nephew of the prophet Muhammad. Their ancestors had ruled in Egypt, Damascus, and Antioch. Among their kin were warlords who had served Tamerlane and the Tartar conquerors of ancient Rus; they had then headed splinter factions of the great Tartar horde and ruled within the Crimean, Kazan, and Nogay territories. The Nogay chieftain Khan Yusuf gave the line his name. The fate of his daughter, the beauty Sumbeki is particularly remarkable. The Nogay khans, Sumbeki's husbands, died one after the other, each at the hands of his successor. But she remained queen, marrying in turn each murderer of her preceding husband. It was then that Khan Yusuf, fearing for his sons, sent them to Russia. The Russian tsar Ivan the Terrible received them graciously and granted them the most spacious lands. Their children, who were converted to Christianity in the seventeenth century, were given the title of prince and the name Yusupov. And from that time forth they occupied the most important posts under the Russian sovereigns, and sometimes were particularly close to them. Hanging in the palace of Felix's great-grandfather Nikolai Yusupov, in the portrait gallery with its pictures of his three hundred lovers, was a double portrait. In it were Catherine the Great and Yusupov himself in the form of a completely nude Venus and Apollo.

In the course of that three-hundred-year period the Yusupovs became the richest family in Russia and the royal family often came to visit their estate in the Crimea, which adjoined the tsar's own.

Felix's mother, Zinaida, was one of the most beautiful women of her day. Rejecting numerous proposals, she had married an adjutant of Grand Duke Sergei Alexandrovich, the Horse Guards commander Count Felix Sumarokov-Elston. The Elstons were the descendants of an illegitimate son of the most famous Prussian king, Frederick the Great. And after his marriage to the last of the Yusupov line, Count Sumarokov-Elston was given the right to call himself by the unwieldy title, Prince Yusupov and Count Sumarokov-Elston.

Zinaida and Felix produced two sons: Nikolai, the elder, and Felix, the younger, who would play a fateful role in the destiny of the Russian peasant Rasputin.

A Story Of Love And Death

After the revolution and exiled in Paris, Felix described his life. He began his seductive journey into vice while still a boy. It all began with a story resembling a sinful dream of youth. A certain young couple invited the boy, who looked like a nymphet, to take part in their sexual games. Later, Nikolai, a Petersburg Don Juan, the idol of the family, whom Felix adored and envied, continued the dangerous games with the boy and conceived the idea of dressing him up as a young woman. And started taking 'her' out to participate in Petersburg night life, a life that closely resembled a feast during the plague, where all strove to reach the very bottom, to try out every form of vice and amusement. The debauchery proceeded to the accompaniment of Gypsy choruses in the private rooms of famous restaurants. It was then that the young Felix experienced the joy of wearing women's clothing and delight in the lewd glances of men who were driven wild by the young 'beauty'.

And as an old man he would remember the triumphs of himself as that charming nymphet. Such as the time during a costume ball when the English king, Edward VII, stared intently at 'her' through his lorgnette. And with what delight and terror 'she' fled from admirers in a private room in a Petersburg restaurant, escaping into a severe frost in an open sleigh without 'her' fur coat and dressed only in a diamond-studded gown.

Thus did Felix discover his own nature. 'I have always been exasperated by people's unfairness in regard to those who enter into love affairs of a special kind,' he wrote. 'One may censure those relationships, but not the creatures for whom normal relationships against their nature are impossible.'

And then his amorous brother Nikolai succeeded in seducing yet another Petersburg beauty, the Countess Heiden. But this time, although a Don Juan is not meant to do so, he fell in love with her. Before then Nikolai had been seeking thrills in Paris in a filthy Chinese opium den, where Felix, under his guidance, had also managed to try out new ways of falling to the bottom. But Nikolai had now been transformed by passionate love.

The Countess Marina Heiden was at the time the wife of Count A. Manteifel of the Horse Guards. But once away in Paris, the unhappy woman forgot her husband and her honour and spent her nights at the hotel where Nikolai and Felix were staying. Count Manteifel at first wanted a divorce, but his regimental comrades were of the opinion that the honour of the most prestigious Petersburg regiment had been besmirched. The count was obliged to call Nikolai out.

In the Historical Museum I found the letters of the heroes of this story and the denouement of their tragedy.

'I implore you,' Marina wrote to Felix, 'not to let Nikolai come back to Petersburg now . . . The regiment will instigate a duel, and it will end very badly . . . For God's sake, arrange things so that your brother does not come to Petersburg . . . The evil talk will cease, and by autumn it will all have subsided . . .' But Nikolai returned to Petersburg anyway. All Felix had to do was tell his powerful mother about it, and the duellists would not have been allowed to shoot at each other. But Felix oddly did nothing. It could be that ideas of honour played a role here. Or did they?

There is a certain entry in Felix's memoirs: 'I . . . imagined myself as one of my ancestors, a great Maecenas in the reign of Catherine . . . Reclining on cushions embroidered in gold . . . I ruled among slaves . . . The thought of becoming one of the richest people in Russia intoxicated me.' But as long as his brother was alive, he could not become a 'great Maecenas', for his older brother was the heir. Could it be that he was unconsciously following the example of his Nogay ancestors who had murdered their brothers and fathers in their struggle for power? And that this was why he had not told his mother of the impending duel? But these are merely dreadful conjectures.

The lovers' last letters have survived in the archive. Nikolai wrote his the night before the duel: 'My last thought was the thought of you . . . To our misfortune you and I met and destroyed each other . . . In two hours my seconds will come . . . Farewell, for ever. I love you.'

The duel took place on 22 June 1908. First they shot at thirty paces. Nikolai fired into the air, and his adversary missed. Manteifel demanded that they reduce the distance to fifteen paces. Nikolai again fired into the air, and then the count took aim and shot him.

Nikolai's last letter is still in the Yusupov archive; it was never given to Marina. Also preserved there is Marina's entreaty to Felix. A futile entreaty. 'Felix, I must prostrate myself on his grave . . . I must see his grave and pray over it. You must understand that, Felix, and help me. Arrange it at night somehow, when everyone at your house is asleep! Help me slip into the church, do this for me, do it for your brother.' But he did not do it.

At the time his mother Zinaida Yusupova was confined to her bed with a fever, and would be tormented by episodes of depression for the rest of her life. Felix himself soon afterwards made a tour of his future properties. 'I imagined myself in all seriousness to be a young lord travelling around the country,' he recalled.

The Unbeloved

As it turned out, however, there was one other victim of the duel: a woman who had loved but who had not been loved in return, and who had forever held onto her love for the one who had perished. This was a love that was not only unrequited but not even suspected. And it was Munya's, a love that remained with her the rest of her life. Felix kept in his archive a letter from her, too. She also wanted to prostrate herself on the grave of the one who had been killed: 'I would like to pray once more near him. It is two weeks today since the terrible misfortune, but it continues to grow, not diminish, and it becomes harder to bear with each passing day.'

The fallen Nikolai had linked her to Felix for ever.

'I cherish my spiritual connection with the past so much that I cannot regard you as a stranger . . . Never have I been as clearly conscious as I am now that the joy of life has gone from my life for ever, that nothing will ever bring it back.'

She decided to withdraw into a convent. Her mother was horrified and she was saved by her relative with the 'little porcelain face', Alexandra (Sana) Pistolkors.

The File, from the testimony of Maria Golovina:

The wife of my cousin Alexander Pistolkors was acquainted with the elder Grigory Efimovich Rasputin, who at that time was considered a holy man who could comfort those in distress . . . The first time I saw Father Grigory was only for a few minutes, and he made a splendid impression on me. We talked about my wanting to withdraw from the world into a convent . . . Rasputin observed to me that one may serve God anywhere, and that one should not change one's life so drastically.

And she believed him at once and gave up the idea of the convent.

Ever since the duel, she had been studying spiritualism in an attempt to speak with the one who had been killed.

All that time I . . . was doing experiments in the raising of spirits . . . I was extremely astonished when . . . Father Grigory asked me, 'Why are you doing all this? You know,' he said, 'how anchorites prepare themselves for visitations of the spirit. Yet you want to commune with a spirit in the very midst of social life' . . . He advised me not to occupy myself with that, cautioning me that I could lose my mind. My mother liked Rasputin, too . . . She was grateful to him for having talked me out of going into a convent . . . I saw him several times at the Pistolkorses' over a span of ten to fourteen days . . . At the time Rasputin did not drink wine at all . . . He preached simplicity in life, fought against formality, and tried to persuade people not to judge one another . . . Rasputin never nursed ill feelings against people who had done him injury of one kind or another.

And she decided to introduce the holy man to the person most dear to her after her mother – to Felix. 'The young woman was too pure to understand the baseness of the "holy man",' Felix would write.

And the meeting took place; the first time they saw each other.

'The Golovins' home,' Felix recalled, 'was on the Winter Canal. When I entered the parlour, the mother and daughter were sitting with the solemn expressions of people waiting for the arrival of a wonder-working icon . . . Rasputin came in and tried to embrace me' (although Felix managed to elude him). And then, 'going over to Mlle G[olovina] and her mother, he unceremoniously embraced them and pressed them to his heart . . . He was of medium height, almost slender, and his arms were disproportionately long . . . He appeared to be about forty. Dressed in a tight-fitting coat and wide boots, he looked like a simple peasant. His face, framed by a shaggy beard, was crude – heavy features, long nose, and small limpid grey eyes that peered out from under thick brows.'

Felix already hated him. The rumours of Rasputin's depravity had suddenly begun to spread in every quarter.

The Anti-Semite Leader Who Wasn't

It was then that Rasputin made his first great blunder.

By 1910 a very definite circle had formed around him.

A few words of explanation. In a state where autocracy had existed from its earliest days, there also existed a tacit, covert alliance of the extreme right and the special police services. The extreme right in Russia consisted of a group of high-born but degenerate aristocrats. They hated the emergent capitalism – the power of money that was starting to take the place of their own power, the power of birth. And they hated the Jews, among whom, despite their complete lack of rights, there were already many new people of wealth.

There were, however, even more Jews among the zealous fanatics of revolution. Lack of rights, poverty, and the humiliation of Jewish young people had turned frightened Jewish youths into fearless bomb-throwers and terrorists. Wishing to weaken the radical movement, the right tried to direct the rage of the starving multitudes against the Jews. And with the blessing of the Department of Police, a war of pogroms against the Jews had rolled across the country. The down of torn feather beds, looted homes, murdered old men, raped women and girls – it all happened. But Count Witte, after having become prime minister in 1905 with the tsar's approval, ordered the Department of Police to bring those responsible for the pogroms under control, and the police did so. But one can imagine Witte's surprise when he discovered that the same Department of Police that was supposed to be fighting against the pogroms was secretly distributing notices calling for them! They were being printed by a certain Mikhail Komissarov, a tall, portly thirty-five-year-old colonel, who five years later would become one of the most important figures in the Rasputin story. Komissarov was not an anti-Semite. He was merely an officer engaged in carrying out someone else's secret will. The religious writer Sergei Nilus had just come upon something called *The Protocols of the Elders of Zion* regarding a sinister plot of the Jews and the Masons under their control. According to the *Protocols*, 'Jewry has from ancient times been the tool of theomachy and the devil. International Jewry and the Masons who serve it must bring down the Christian monarchs and found their own Kingdom of Jew-Masons ruled by an Antichrist-king.' The *Protocols* were published at once by the stunned Nilus. At the tsar's order, Stolypin, who succeeded Witte as prime minister in 1906, conducted an investigation. Naturally, the *Protocols* were exposed as a forgery. They had been written by the same Russian secret police, who had taken as their model another forgery produced in the West, the *Testament of Peter the Great*, a secret plan for the Russian occupation of Europe.

The wave of anti-Semitism had not abated after the crushing of the 1905 revolution. Anti-Semitic organizations promoting pogroms such as the Union of the Russian People and the Union of the Archangel Michael, gained strength. In the Duma the monarchists Purishkevich and Markov II continually gave speeches inciting pogroms. The impending tercentenary of the dynasty heated the atmosphere. And Rasputin, that simple peasant so beloved of the tsar, seemed to have been created to stand at the head of the rightist crusade against the Jews and the intelligentsia.

Stalin's Instructor

It was at this moment that Feofan's friend Bishop Hermogen made his appearance in Rasputin's vicinity.

If Feofan was a mystic, ascetic, and anchorite, then his friend Hermogen, the bishop of Saratov, was someone immersed in church politics.

During the 1905 revolution the question had come up of restoring the patriarchate – of convening a church assembly for the election of a patriarch.

The tsar deferred the question to the Most Holy Synod. And the chief procurator of the Synod, Pobedonostsev, immediately rejected it, frightening the tsar with the idea that a church headed by a patriarch would at once cease to be subordinate to the autocrat. But Hermogen believed that the 1905 revolution had demonstrated the weakness of secular authority. And that a second centre within the state was needed, one that would be independent of secular power and that could, in the event of a return of disorder, keep the state from perishing. The patriarchate needed to be re-established in Rus. And Hermogen saw himself at its head.

He bore the name of the great patriarch Hermogen, who had saved Rus and the state during the terrible Time of Troubles, and he believed that it was his own destiny to rescue the country from the looming bloody discord that, despite the suppression of the revolution, the elders in the monasteries were continuing to prophesy.

From the testimony of the herbalist Pyotr Badmaev before the Extraordinary Commission: 'Once while I was visiting Hermogen I saw Mitya [Rasputin's precursor, the 'nasal-voiced' Mitya Kozelsky] making some elaborate movements with his hands. Hermogen smiled. I asked what it meant. One of those present said, "He sees the patriarchal mitre on Hermogen's head."'

Hermogen was a fanatical opponent of freethinkers who, he was convinced, were destroying Holy Rus. He fought for strict interference by the church in the ideological life of the country.

There had been in his struggle against freethinking one very important episode of which Hermogen himself very likely took little notice. As rector of the Tiflis Theological Seminary he had ruthlessly punished the seminarians for freethinking. And in 1899 he expelled one of them, a certain Iosif Dzhugashvili, who would take his place in history under the name Stalin, and who would restore the patriarchate so desired by Hermogen. History likes to smile.

Hermogen subsequently testified, 'I was introduced to Rasputin by Father Feofan,' who 'spoke of him in the most laudatory terms as an outstanding votary'. At the time, Hermogen and Rasputin liked each other very much. Rasputin's contempt for the bloated church hierarchs was close to Hermogen's heart. But the main thing was that Hermogen dreamed with Rasputin's help of inspiring the tsar to restore the patriarchate.

In the meantime, however, Rasputin was supposed to take part in the fierce battle against freethinking that Hermogen was then conducting. And Hermogen introduced him to another exposer of evil, a young monk whose ferocious speeches and denunciations had made him famous as the Russian Savonarola. The monk's name was Iliodor.

The Russian Savonarola

At the age of twenty-two Sergei Trufanov, a sacristan's son, was received into monastic life and given the name Iliodor. In 1905, at the height of the revolution, he graduated from the Petersburg Theological Seminary and he saw Rasputin, who had just arrived in Petersburg, for the first time in the hallways of the seminary, where he was still a seminarian. In February 1908, the twenty-seven-year-old ordained monk Iliodor was assigned to Tsaritsyn as a missionary preacher. In Tsaritsyn he built a large church with a hall for political meetings. It was there that he began his furious preaching before throngs of admirers. Huge, with a large, fleshy face, high cheekbones, and tiny eyes, Iliodor looked more like a Volga brigand than a pious monk. But Hermogen liked that look of warrior-monk. And Iliodor really did carry on ceaseless warfare in his newly built church. He fulminated against the 'Yids and intellectuals' and the 'rich men and bureaucrats who conceal the people's needs from the tsar'. He flayed the hated Russian capitalism. He excoriated Tatischev, the governor, and drove him from office. His supporters stuck leaflets on buildings inscribed with the words, 'Brothers! Do not surrender Russia to the cruel enemy!' and 'Cry out with a hearty cry: Down with the kingdom of Yids! Down with the red banners! Down with the red Yid freedom! Down with red Yid equality and fraternity! Long live Russia's one father, our Orthodox tsar! Our Christian autocrat and tsar!'

When Iliodor and Rasputin made each other's acquaintance in Petersburg, Rasputin was living in the apartment of Olga Lokhtina. And when the elder's new friend came to visit him there, he left the mad general's wife in raptures.

Thenceforth, she would serve them both – Rasputin and Iliodor.

In the File, Lokhtina herself tells of the meeting of the two pastors.

'I met the ordained monk Iliodor in '08 or '09. After his arrival in Petrograd, he stayed with Feofan at the Theological Seminary. At Rasputin's behest, I went to Feofan and invited Iliodor to visit Rasputin, who was then staying with me . . . I very much liked Iliodor's readiness to obey. Father Grigory ordered him to preach a sermon on some topic and he did so unquestioningly.'

Iliodor opened a new life to Rasputin, who although used to a dozen admirers, now saw crowds of fanatics and took pleasure in their wild delight. As Rasputin later recalled, 'he would meet me with crowds of people and preach about me and my life. I lived in harmony with him and shared my impressions with him.' And, one should say, shared his most valuable impressions. In 1909 and 1910 Iliodor visited him in Pokrovskoe. And it was then that Rasputin showed him the shirts that the tsarina had given him. And showed him, too, what he had not shown even Sazonov or Filippov, who were very close to him. He showed the monk his letters from the tsarina and her daughters, the grand duchesses. And Rasputin did so because for some reason he trusted Iliodor.

From Pokrovskoe Rasputin returned with Iliodor to Tsaritsyn. And again they were met by crowds of supporters, and the crowds' delighted cries and bewitching enthusiasm.

Iliodor has related in his book how on the night of 30 December 1910, two thousand people saw Grigory off to Petersburg. 'I informed the people that Grigory Efimovich wanted to build a convent in which he would be the elder, and I asked them to visit him. The people cried, "The Lord save us! We shall go, we shall go with the father! We shall certainly go!" At the station we sang hymns and praised Christ. Grigory started to give a speech from the platform of the railway car about his lofty position, but it was so confused that even I understood nothing.'

Grigory had always spoken in a mysteriously jerky and confused way. Iliodor had so far understood him. Now he did not. For it was then, in 1910, while he was still a guest in Pokrovskoe, that Iliodor reached a critical decision about Rapustin. And as a result, before his return to Tsaritsyn, Iliodor stole from his friend the letters from the tsarina and grand duchesses that Rasputin had so trustingly shown him. Later on, in 1914, Rasputin testified, 'Iliodor visited me four years ago in Pokrovskoe, where he stole an important letter from me.'

The 'important letter' was one from the tsarina not intended for anyone else's eyes.

But at the time Rasputin did not know any of that. Nor did he understand that by appearing together with Iliodor he had become part of a violently anti-semitic Black-Hundreds group and that a new image of him had begun to emerge: a Black-Hundreds peasant and sorcerer in control of the royal family, an image that would help the liberal opposition in its struggle against the regime. But at the time he was merely trying to help his friend Iliodor, whose patience of the authorities had been exhausted. Those in power understood perfectly well that Iliodor's activity would end in pogroms against the Jews and a savage response by the revolutionaries. The air still reeked of bombs and the spectre of the failed 1905 revolution. Stolypin took measures. In January 1911, by decision of the Synod, Iliodor was ordered to be transferred to a squalid monastery in the Tula eparchy.

But Iliodor refused to submit. He locked himself in his church at Tsaritsyn with several thousand people and declared a hunger-strike. And Hermogen supported him, but that did not help Iliodor. The tsar ordered him removed from Tsaritsyn at once. But Iliodor had his friend Rasputin. And he would ultimately return to Tsaritsyn despite the tsar's objection.

As Iliodor himself describes it, when a certain Countess I. merely hinted at dissatisfaction with Iliodor, 'Rasputin interrupted the conversation. He was trembling as if in a fever, and his fingers and lips shook . . . He put his face next to the countess's and, shaking his finger at her, said in his jerky way and in great agitation, "I, Grigory, tell you that he will be in Tsaritsyn! Understand? Don't take so much on yourself – after all, you are merely a woman! A woman!"'

And the tsarina agreed to help Iliodor, for she liked it that the young priest had such respect for Father Grigory. There followed an order to permit the ordained monk Iliodor to return to Tsaritsyn, and in spite of the prime minister and the Synod, he returned. 'Iliodor remained in Tsaritsyn thanks to Rasputin's personal entreaties,' Vyrubova confirmed in her testimony.

Evidently, there was something very important connecting Rasputin and Iliodor. And it was because of that 'something' that there had, for all the difference in their ages, arisen in Rasputin great confidence in and friendship for Iliodor. A much closer friendship than with Feofan, who at the time idolized Rasputin, or with Hermogen, who had grown fond of him. Hermogen himself afterward observed, 'Rasputin . . . treated me with special courtesy. But . . . he preferred to stay with Iliodor in Tsaritsyn.' It was evidently because of that 'something' that Rasputin, who rejected hatred of every kind, tolerated Iliodor's pogrom-inciting speeches and calls for hate. And Olga Lokhtina, who at the time was initiated into the secrets of Rasputin's teachings, would in acknowledgement of the special relationship between Rasputin and Iliodor bow down before them both, calling Rasputin the 'Lord of hosts' and Iliodor 'Christ'.

Mysterious Rumours At The Height Of His Fame

In the meantime, the peasant's new friend Sazonov had been regaling his friends with stories of Rasputin. The journalist M. Menshikov recalled that

in 1910 at the height of his fame Sazonov brought him to see me . . . [He was] youngish-looking of about forty and almost illiterate . . . Some of his utterances were striking in their originality, like the Delphic oracle in a mystical delirium. Something prophetic rang out in those enigmatic words . . . Some of his judgements about hierarchs and high-ranking dignitaries seemed shrewd and accurate to me . . . But then very quickly it started to be heard on every side . . . that he was leading society ladies and young women astray.

Yes, it was then in 1910 that it started to be heard. And heard 'on every side'. Mysteriously 'on every side'.

Those rumours had begun to spread six months earlier. And the first to become concerned was the fanatically devoted Feofan.

In February 1909 Feofan had been promoted to the rank of bishop. He would later take umbrage whenever anyone dared to assert that it was Rasputin who had made him a bishop. 'My candidacy for the bishopric was put forward by the church hierarchs led by Bishop Hermogen. I would never have permitted myself to take advantage of Rasputin's influence . . . I was known personally to the royal family and had four times or so heard confession from the empress and once from the sovereign . . . and I was already the rector of the Petersburg Theological Seminary.' All that is true: Feofan deserved in every way to become a bishop. But the fact that he was also a friend of 'Our Friend' helped, of course. The 'tsars' appreciated Rasputin's friends.

And that is why the tsarina was so surprised when Feofan, Rasputin's devoted admirer, suddenly began, soon after he became a bishop, to doubt the holiness of the man with whom he had not long before been so delighted.

The File, from the testimony of Feofan: 'Rumours began reaching us at the abbey that Rasputin was unrestrained in his treatment of the female sex, that he stroked them with his hand during conversation. All this gave rise to a certain temptation to sin, the more so since in conversation Rasputin would allude to his acquaintance with me and, as it were, hide behind my name.'

And Feofan, whom an unknown someone had informed of the rumours, discussed them with the monks at the abbey. 'After discussing everything, we decided we were monks, whereas he was a married man, and that was the reason why his behaviour had been distinguished by a great lack of restraint and seemed peculiar to us . . . However . . . the rumours about Rasputin started to increase, and it was beginning to be said that he went to the bathhouses with women . . . It is very distressing . . . to suspect of a bad thing.'

There were in the bathhouses of Petersburg so-called 'family rooms'. In which families would bathe. And, obviously, those 'rooms' were not only used by married couples.

It was very hard for the ascetic Feofan to take up the bathhouse question with Grigory, whom he considered a man of the holy life. But Rasputin evidently learned about the rumours at the abbey. And decided to broach the question himself.

From Feofan's testimony:

> An occasion helped . . . Rasputin himself mentioned that he had gone to bathhouses with women. We immediately declared to him that, from the point of view of the holy fathers, that was unacceptable, and he promised us to avoid doing it. We decided not to condemn him for debauchery, for we knew that he was a simple peasant, and we had read that in the Olonets and Novgorod provinces men bathed in the bathhouses together with women, which testified not to immorality but to their patriarchal way of life . . . and to its particular purity, for . . . nothing was allowed. Moreover, it was clear from the Lives of the ancient Byzantine holy fools Saint Simeon and Saint Ioann that both had gone to bathhouses with women on purpose, and had been abused and reviled for it, although they were nonetheless great saints.

Very likely, Rasputin himself had at the time talked about the visits of Saints Simeon and Ioann to bathhouses with women. For he would later frequently use that example. And in alluding to the great saints who had tested themselves by looking at the bodies of women, 'Rasputin, as his own justification, announced that he too wanted to test himself – to see if he had extinguished passion in himself,' Feofan testified in the File.

But Feofan warned him of the danger, 'for it is only the great saints who are able to do it, and he, by acting in that way, was engaging in self-deception and on a dangerous path'.

But the rumours of the peasant's suspicious visits to family bathhouses with society ladies persisted. And soon afterwards they truly were heard 'on every side'.

One of those closest to the royal family, Captain Sablin, heard the rumours, too. And his testimony is also preserved in the File. 'Rumours started to reach me that he was cynical in his treatment of the ladies and was, for example, taking them to the public bathhouses . . . At first I did not believe the rumours. It seemed impossible that any society woman, unless possibly a psychopath, could give herself to such a slovenly peasant.'

But Sablin decided not to talk to the empress about those instances.

> The least distrust, or worse, mockery of him, had a morbid effect on her . . . I explain her blind faith and that of the sovereign by their boundless

love for the heir . . . They had caught hold of the belief that if the heir was
alive, it was due to Rasputin's prayers . . . I would wonder in my reports to
the sovereign whether, in order not to tease society, 'it might not be better
to send Rasputin back to Tobolsk'. But the sovereign, thanks to his character,
would reply evasively or, agreeing, would say, 'Speak to the empress about
it.'

Sablin did not realize that at the time the tsar already had a special justification for Rasputin, and for that reason did not ascribe any importance
to the rumours.

Meanwhile, the rumours had reached the publisher Sazonov.

From the testimony of Sazonov in the File:

After rumours had reached us about Rasputin's going to bathhouses with
ladies, I asked him about it . . . He answered in the affirmative, adding that
'the sovereign knows . . . I don't go with one person but . . . with company,'
and explaining that he regarded pride as the greatest sin. The society misses
undoubtedly were puffed up with pride, and in order to deflate it, it was
necessary to humiliate them by forcing them to go to the bathhouse with a
dirty peasant . . . To me as someone with a deep knowledge of the national
soul, that made sense . . . although I . . . asked Rasputin not to do it any
more. He gave me his word.

Two years later the police would record a visit to a family bathhouse by
Rasputin and Sazonov's wife, and they would go to the bathhouse by
themselves, without any company.

And then to the rumours about the bathhouses were added new ones about
the Tobolsk investigation into Rasputin's having established a *Khlyst* sect in
Siberia. And about his having taken his devotees to the notorious bathhouse
there, as well.

And it was apparently for that reason that Nicholas, to Alix's displeasure,
decided for the time being not to receive Rasputin at the palace. And Alix
asked the peasant not to be angry with them and to pray for them. And he
prayed, but he was angry. Sablin in the File tells of being at Vyrubova's
when Rasputin telephoned her in a futile attempt to gain entry to the
palace. 'And he said from his heart, "They ask me to pray but are afraid to
receive me."'

And then Alix thought of a brilliant move.

The Monks' Journey

In 1917 the investigators of the Extraordinary Commission visited a small, secluded retreat not far from the Verkhoturye Monastery, where an anchorite named Father Makary lived. Makary, an elder well known for his holy life, had since childhood been a swineherd in the monastery's employ. He ate nothing for months, herded his pigs, and stood for hours in prayer in the deep forest. Being illiterate, he knew of Christ only through church services and the prayers he memorized by ear. But Makary was considered to be the spiritual father of Grigory Rasputin. And that was why the monk Makary was interrogated in his half-tumbled-down cell. Interrogating him was not easy, since the monk's speech was confused.

His deposition remains in the File. The sixty-year-old monk Makary testified that 'I came to know the elder G. E. Rasputin twelve years ago when I was still the monastery swineherd. At the time Rasputin had come to our monastery to pray and to make my acquaintance . . . I told him about the sorrows and misfortunes of my life, and he bade me pray to God.' After that, Makary took monastic vows and began to live as an anchorite.

'Rasputin apparently spoke to the former tsar about me, for money came to the monastery from the tsar for the construction of cells for me . . . Besides that, money was sent for me to travel to Petersburg . . . and I then went to Tsarskoe Selo, where I talked to the tsar and his family about our monastery and my life in it. I did not see any kind of bad actions by Rasputin and the others who came to us with him.'

And that was all they were able to extract from him about Rasputin.

The monk had indeed also been summoned to Tsarskoe Selo in the summer of 1909, but not at all to tell the tsars about his life in the monastery.

'23 June. After tea, Feofan, Grigory, and Makary came to see us,' Nicholas recorded in his diary.

It was then that Alix told the three of them about her idea. Knowing of Feofan's doubts about Rasputin, she had devised the plan of getting Feofan together with Makary, who had such respect for Rasputin. So that they and Rasputin could go back to Our Friend's home together. She believed that the trip would renew Feofan's friendship with Father Grigory and dispel all his doubts. And that Feofan would then use his authority to put an end to the growing rumours, which were already beginning to scare her.

Feofan at the time was unwell. But the tsarina's request was law. 'I took myself in hand and in the second half of June 1909 set off with Rasputin and the monk of the Verkhoturye Monastery Makary, whom Rasputin called and acknowledged to be his "elder",' Feofan testified in the File.

And then he described their trip in its entirety. First, they went to the monastery at Verkhoturye, Rasputin's favourite. But even before they got there, Rasputin astonished Feofan. 'Rasputin started to behave without constraint. It had been my view that he had begun wearing expensive shirts for the royal court's sake. But he wore the same kind of shirt in the railway car, spilling food on it and then putting on another one that was just as expensive.' Rasputin had obviously decided to show Feofan how many favours the tsarina had done for him. But just as clearly Feofan was ready to regard everything with suspicion.

And the farther they went, the more suspicious he became. The ascetic Feofan was amazed when 'as we were approaching the Verkhoturye Monastery, and, as is the custom with pilgrims, keeping the fast so we could prostrate ourselves before the relics, Rasputin ordered himself something to eat and then cracked nuts.' Rasputin, now aware of his power, no longer felt the need to dissimulate. His God was a joyful one. And he allowed himself to kick off the fetters of ecclesiastical regulation.

Feofan was offended by everything: 'Rasputin assured us that he revered Simeon of Verkhoturye. However, when the service in the monastery began, he went off somewhere to town.' Rasputin's two-storey house grated on Feofan, too. How different it was from Feofan's own dwelling, which he had turned into a monastic cell, and from his idea of what the house should be like of the person he only recently had held in such esteem.

We can imagine the arrangement of Rasputin's house quite accurately using the inventory of his property made after his death. On the ground floor where he lived with his family, it was the usual arrangement of a peasant lodge. But, to make up for that, upstairs the once indigent peasant had attempted to arrange everything city fashion and thus suitable for the 'little ladies' and other guests from Petersburg. There he put Feofan, as well. And the monk took indignant note of the piano, and the gramophone that Rasputin so liked to dance to, and the claret-red plush armchairs, and the sofa and the desk. A chandelier was suspended from the ceiling, and placed around the room were several bentwood 'Viennese' chairs, then in fashion. And there were two wide beds with soft springy mattresses and a divan. Two weight-clocks in ebony cabinets chimed majestically, and there was a wall clock and another cabinet clock. The monk was particularly outraged by the 'large soft carpet covering the entire floor'.

Rasputin also introduced Feofan to his followers – Arsyonov, Raspopov, and another Rasputin – 'my brothers in the life of the spirit'. But, as the monk observed, 'although they sang very harmoniously . . . they still made an unpleasant impression, generally speaking.' Feofan, a mystic of broad education who was well acquainted with heresies, sensed something dangerous in that singing.

Apparently he tried to talk about it with Makary.

'The monk Makary . . . is, for me, a mystery. Much of what he says is incomprehensible, but from time to time he will say things that illuminate all life.'

But although capable of 'illuminating all life', Makary this time replied with 'something incomprehensible'.

After thinking over all he had seen, Feofan concluded that Rasputin did not 'occupy the highest level of spiritual life'. And on his return trip to Petersburg Feofan 'stopped at the Sarov Monastery and asked God's help in correctly answering the question of who and what Rasputin was. I returned to Petersburg convinced that Rasputin . . . was on a false path.'

On his return, he conferred with his friend the Archimandrite Benjamin about what he had seen on the trip. They then summoned Rasputin to the abbey.

'When after that Rasputin came to see us, we, to his surprise, denounced him for his arrogant pride, for holding himself in higher regard than was seemly, and for being in a state of "spiritual temptation".'

The Dangerous State Of 'Spiritual Temptation'

This was a terrible charge.

I had a conversation at the Trinity-Saint Sergius Abbey with the monk Father Isaiah about the state of 'spiritual temptation'. He told me: 'A special spiritual loftiness is required to prophesy and heal. When it is lacking, the gift becomes a dangerous one, and the person becomes a sorcerer and falls into the state of "spiritual temptation". He is now tempted by the devil, and it is by the power of the Antichrist that he performs his miracles.'

'Arrogant pride', 'holding himself in higher regard than was seemly', and 'spiritual temptation' – Feofan and Benjamin were, oddly enough, repeating everything that Militsa had once warned Rasputin about! It was the voice of the 'black woman' that was in Feofan and Benjamin's arguments.

'We proclaimed to him that we were for the last time demanding that he change his ways, and that if he himself did not do so, we would sever relations with him, make an open declaration of everything, and inform the tsar.'

Rasputin certainly had not expected to hear that from Feofan. 'He was completely taken aback and started crying, and instead of trying to justify himself admitted that he had made mistakes. And he agreed to our demand that he withdraw from the world and place himself under my guidance.'

It was a safe enough promise. The peasant knew that the tsarina would never allow him to carry it out. For not only the boy, but she herself would wither away without him. Feofan lived in another world altogether. He had merely asked Rasputin, and the latter had promised, 'to tell no one about our meeting with him'. 'Rejoicing in our success, we conducted a prayer service . . . But, as it turned out, he then went to Tsarskoe Selo and recounted everything there in a light that was favourable to him but not to us,' Feofan recalled in the File.

A Disputation With The Tsarina

But there was 'someone' who felt that what had happened was not enough. And that 'someone' expected a great deal more from Feofan, and had evidently been informing him of new rumours.

From Feofan's testimony in the File: 'After a while rumours reached me that Rasputin had resumed his former way of life and was undertaking something against us . . . I decided to resort to a final measure – to denounce him openly and to communicate everything to the former emperor. It was not, however, the emperor who received me but his wife in the presence of the maid of honour Vyrubova.'

Vyrubova's presence in the room with the tsarina made everything clear to him. The naive Feofan had been left open to 'a cunning manoeuvre: Rasputin had brought Vyrubova into play . . . and Vyrubova would out of gratitude have to support Rasputin.'

So that the bishop knew even as he was beginning his monologue that he was doomed. But duty above all else. Just as in ancient times when pastors had suffered for the truth before the tsars, Feofan too was ready to suffer.

> I spoke for about an hour and demonstrated that Rasputin was in a state of 'spiritual temptation' . . . The former empress grew agitated and objected, citing theological works . . . I destroyed all her arguments, but she . . . reiterated them: 'It is all falsehood and slander' . . . I concluded the conversation by saying that I could no longer have anything to do with Rasputin . . . I think Rasputin, as a cunning person, explained to the royal family that my speaking against him was because I envied his closeness to the Family . . . that I wanted to push him out of the way.

Poor Feofan did not understand that it was not Rasputin, but Alix herself who had reached that conclusion.

From Feofan's testimony: 'After my conversation with the empress, Rasputin came to see me as if nothing had happened, having apparently decided that the empress's displeasure had intimidated me . . . However, I told him in no uncertain terms, "Go away, you are a fraud."'

The bishop did not understand the peasant, either. Grigory did not like conflict. He was ready to humiliate himself, if only to be reconciled to the kind, naive Feofan: 'Rasputin fell on his knees before me and asked my forgiveness . . . But again I told him, "Go away, you have violated a promise given before God." Rasputin left, and I did not see him again.'

A Reprisal

Feofan continued to act. He received at that time a 'Confession' of a repentant devotee of Rasputin's. Or, more likely, it was given to him by that same 'someone'. And after reading it, the honest Feofan understood with horror that Rasputin was 'a wolf in sheep's clothing', that he was, as Feofan testifies in the File, merely a 'sectarian of the *Khlyst* type', who 'taught his followers not to reveal his secrets even to their confessors. For if there is allegedly no sin in what those sectarians do, then their confessors need not be made aware of it.'

And Feofan decided to show the confession to the 'tsars'. 'Availing myself of that written confession, I wrote the former emperor a second letter . . . in which I declared that Rasputin not only was in a state of spiritual temptation but was also a criminal in the religious and moral sense . . . In the moral sense because, as it followed from the 'confession', Father Grigory had seduced his victims.' But no answer to Feofan's request for an audience was forthcoming.

From Feofan's testimony: 'I sensed that they did not want to hear me out and understand . . . It all depressed me so much that I became quite ill − it turned out I had a palsy of the facial nerve.'

Rasputin could now celebrate: 'Mama' could be certain − the face of the elder Feofan, of the one who had moved against him, had been punished by heaven itself with the stamp of palsy. And the unhappy bishop departed to recover in the Crimea, still without an answer. He received it in November 1910 and was transferred out of Petersburg to the place he had been accustomed to going for treatment − the Crimea, where he became bishop of Taurida.

But he was an indomitable Russian pastor. And he would not give up. Now Feofan inundated his friend Bishop Hermogen with letters. He had decided to enlist in the battle one of the most vociferous and influential members of the Most Holy Synod.

Hermogen understood: a break with Rasputin would mean the end of his dream of a patriarchate.

From Feofan's testimony in the File: 'When Rasputin's bad actions began to come to light, Hermogen vacillated for a long time, not knowing what attitude to take. But I . . . wrote him a letter indicating that he should make his relationship to Rasputin clear. For if I had to speak out against Rasputin, then it would be against him, too.'

From Hermogen's testimony: 'At the beginning of 1910 I received a letter from Bishop Feofan . . . The bishop set forth a number of facts discrediting Rasputin as someone who was leading a dissolute life. The letter, along with my own personal observations, served as the occasion for an abrupt change in my relations with Rasputin.'

Those 'personal observations' most likely assumed their final shape in Petersburg, where Hermogen had come for a meeting of the Most Holy Synod. It is possible that 'someone' had a talk with Hermogen. And explained to him that so long as Rasputin remained at court, Hermogen's much-desired assembly for the reinstitution of the patriarchate would not take place. For Rasputin was speaking out against it.

That, too, is in the book by Hermogen's favourite, Iliodor: 'The "elder" . . . said: "And it would be good without an Assembly; there is God's anointed sovereign, and that is enough; God rules his heart – what need is there for an Assembly besides!"'

And then Iliodor, too, got ready to speak out together with Hermogen.

Apparently, Iliodor had, in 1910, already obtained proof of just how powerful Rasputin's enemies were. And he decided not merely to betray his friend Grigory but to join the ranks of his enemies with a great trophy. That, in fact, was why in Pokrovskoe he had stolen the letters of the young grand duchesses and, more to the point, the letter of the tsarina herself. A letter that would, he believed, prove the tsarina's fall into sin. Which would mean a scandal and divorce. And then they who had moved against Rasputin would be at the summit of church power!

But in the meantime Iliodor exploited Rasputin's trust and friendship as much as he could. Using money collected by Rasputin, he even equipped a vessel for carrying pilgrims on a trip down the Volga, draping the vessel with his favourite slogans against Jews and revolutionaries. And he waited.

And when Hermogen spoke out against the 'elder', Iliodor understood: the time had come.

And then during a sermon in his church Iliodor indicated to his flock that he had been mistaken about Rasputin, that he was a 'wolf in sheep's clothing'.

War had been declared.

A Ravished Nurse?

Meanwhile in Tsarskoe Selo itself, a new blow was struck against Rasputin.

From Tsarskoe Selo crept rumours that the *Khlyst*, as everyone in Petersburg had suddenly started calling him, had been visiting the royal nursery, and that he had raped Vishnyakova, the heir's nurse.

On 3 June 1910 the general's wife Bogdanovich recorded in her diary that the tsarina 'is incensed with those who have been saying that [Rasputin] is a scoundrel and so on. Tyutcheva and the senior nanny Vishnyakova have therefore been placed on leave for two months.'

If the maid of honour Sophia Tyutcheva was well known at court as a fierce opponent of the elder, the information about the royal nurse Mary (as Maria Vishnyakova was called at court) came as a complete surprise. After all, it was by visiting Mary that Rasputin had been gaining entry to the palace in the first place. And she had been assigned that role for a reason. Mary was regarded as one of Rasputin's most devoted admirers.

A letter from Rasputin to Mary about the rearing of the heir has remained in the archives.

'12 November 1907. Show him little examples of Divine edification, [and] in all his children's toys, seek edification.' After which follow words bearing witness to their more than friendly relations. 'I have not found pride in you, but have found a deep regard for me in your soul. And you saw and understood me from the first. I would like very much for us to see each other again.'

From the testimony of Vyrubova: 'In the beginning, the tsarevich's nurse . . . deeply admired Rasputin and visited him in Pokrovskoe.'

But now 'vague whisperings' were beginning to spread at court.

The File, from the testimony of Colonel Loman: 'That Rasputin had violated the honour of Vishnyakova was something of which there were only 'vague whisperings'; no definite charges were brought forward against Rasputin.'

According to the whispers, in that same year of 1910 Mary had gone on a three-week holiday to Pokrovskoe with Rasputin and his devotees. At night, Rasputin had crept into her room and violated her.

Simultaneously with those rumours Sophia Tyutcheva spoke out against Rasputin.

She declared the unacceptability of Rasputin's visits to the palace nursery. Her declaration was immediately accompanied by awful rumours to the effect that the peasant had been undressing the grand duchesses at night.

From the testimony of Vyrubova: 'Probably he did happen to pass through the nursery, but there was not a word of truth to the rumours going about that he undressed the grand duchesses. Those rumours were spread by the maid of honour Sophia Tyutcheva.'

Tyutcheva, age forty-seven, was summoned before the Extraordinary Commission in 1917. And I found her testimony in the File.

Naturally she had nothing to say about Rasputin's undressing the grand duchesses. The rumours hadn't originated with her. The people behind them were a bit more powerful.

But Rasputin had in fact come to see the royal children and had conversed with them and had on occasion touched them. When he was healing them. And that is all. Tyutcheva, however, was speaking out against any visit at all by the peasant to the children's wing, since she 'considered him a dangerous person with an absolutely clear tendency toward the *Khlyst* sect'.

She also spoke about Mary – about the royal children's nurse, Vishnyakova.

Feofan's Rage

Tyutcheva testified in the File:

> Once on entering the children's wing, I came upon a terrible commotion. Vishnyakova told me with tears in her eyes that she . . . and the other devotees had participated in rites of 'rejoicing'. That what she had accepted as a command of the Holy Spirit had turned out to be simple debauchery . . . I understood from her account that Feofan, who was her confessor . . . had in his humility sent them to Rasputin, whom he considered to be one of God's elders. Rasputin forced them to do whatever he needed, passing himself off as someone acting at the command of the Holy Spirit . . . At the same time he warned them not to tell Feofan, covering it up in sophistry: Feofan was a simpleton and would not understand such secrets and would condemn them, thereby passing judgement on the Holy Spirit and committing a mortal sin.

And that too was immediately communicated to Feofan by 'someone'. And it shocked him and elicited a new flash of indignant rage. He realized that he himself had sent Vishnyakova and those like her to Rasputin and thus had corrupted their souls. That is why he had demanded that Hermogen speak out at once against his former friend Father Grigory, whom he now simply called Rasputin. That is why he composed a new epistle to the tsar and implored Tyutcheva 'to convey the letter to the sovereign'. 'I answered that in view of the fact that my repugnance for Rasputin was known at court, I did not consider it possible to carry out such an errand,' Tyutcheva testified in the File.

And after her refusal, Feofan apparently conceived of a desperate plan: to wait for the royal family's arrival in the Crimea and in a sermon expose to everyone that 'wolf in sheep's clothing'.

Meanwhile, as Tyutcheva testified, 'Vishnyakova went to the tsarina. But the tsarina said she did not believe rumours and . . . forbade her to talk about it.'

The same day a footman in a cap with feathers (that medieval post had been retained at court) came to her and 'conveyed the sovereign's order that she appear in his study at 6:30 p.m.'.

And Tyutcheva gives an account in the File of her evening conversation with the sovereign:

' "You have guessed why I summoned you. What is going on in the nursery?" I told him. "So you too do not believe in Rasputin's holiness?" I answered in the negative.'

And that reticent man could no longer restrain himself. He told her what he had not told anyone. Usually, when cutting off attacks on Rasputin, he had drily alluded to the fact that their relations with Rasputin were their own personal affair, their personal life. But here for the first time he blurted out, 'But what will you say if I tell you that I have lived all these years only thanks to his prayers?' And 'he began saying that he did not believe any of the stories, that the impure always sticks to the pure, and that he did not understand what had suddenly happened to Feofan, who had always been so fond of Rasputin. During this he pointed to a letter from Feofan on his desk' (so it did get through, after all).

'You, your majesty, are too pure of heart and do not see what filth surrounds you.' I said that it filled me with fear that such a person could be near the grand duchesses.

'Am I then the enemy of my own children?' the sovereign objected.

He asked me never to mention Rasputin's name in conversation. In order for that to take place, I asked the sovereign to arrange things so that Rasputin would never appear in the children's wing. Before that the tsarina had told me that after six I was free, as if hinting that she did not wish me to visit the children after that hour. After my conversation with the sovereign, I went to the nursery whenever I wished. But the distance between the family and me continued to grow.

The Mary Riddle

The most remarkable thing about Tyutcheva's testimony is that she did not dare tell the tsar the story about Vishnyakova. Because she did not dare insult him with that filth? Or perhaps because there was in fact no story to tell, just 'vague whisperings'? Even though stories about Vishnyakova's rape are to be found in many memoirs. But how many other legends about Rasputin have also survived?

And for this reason the present-day creators of legends about 'holy Grigory' have glibly declared the story of the rape to be nothing more than a fabrication.

But Vishnyakova's testimony has also turned up in the File! So the nurse Mary may now tell her story herself.

Summoned before the Extraordinary Commission in 1917, Mary testified, 'I, Maria Ivanovna Vishnyakova, of the Russian Orthodox faith, reside at the Winter Palace, the Castellan Entrance.' And she proceeds to relate her autobiography. An intriguing autobiography, in my view, one highly reminiscent of the typical story of the illegitimate child of a distinguished father.

As a child, she was given to a peasant family to be raised, and then, at someone's expense, she attended courses to train for work as a nurse. When she finished her training, the unknown student from a peasant family was immediately taken into the household of the Duke of Leichtenberg. Very soon afterwards, just before the birth of Grand Duchess Tatyana Nikolaevna, she was invited to become a nurse for the royal family. She was only twenty-four at the time. One after another the royal children were born and grew up. And, finally, she became the nurse of the heir. So her whole life was spent in the palace. And even after the scandal with Rasputin, when Alix dismissed her and she had ceased to be the royal children's nurse, for some reason they still did not dare to banish her from the palace.

When the events in her story took place, she was thirty-six years old. And, as was always the case with royal nurses, that well-groomed, blonde, beautiful woman had no personal life of her own. She became an old maid.

In her interrogation, Mary remained faithful to her former employers and testified that

the former sovereign and empress were exemplary spouses in their love for each other and their children . . . [The tsarina] spent the whole day in the circle of her children, not allowing them to be either fed or bathed without her. Until they were three or four months old, she breast-fed them herself, although together with a wet-nurse, since the tsarina did not have enough milk . . . The empress herself taught the children English and Russian and their prayers, with the help of the nurses and Princess Orbeliani.

And then Mary finally turned to her own story.

Once in the spring of 1910 the empress suggested I visit the Verkhoturye Monastery in the Tobolsk province for three weeks, with the idea of returning in May for a trip to the skerries with the royal family. I readily agreed, since I am fond of monasteries. Zinaida Manshtedt, whom I had met in Tsarskoe Selo at the home of friends of mine and liked very much, was supposed to take part in the trip . . . And, according to the empress, Rasputin and Lokhtina were also expected to go . . . I met all the people who were going when I arrived at the Nikolaev Station.

We stayed at Verkhoturye Monastery for two or three days, and then set off to visit Rasputin at his home in the village of Pokrovskoe. Rasputin had a two-storey house, large, and quite well furnished, like that of an official of middle rank. Rasputin's wife lived on the ground floor with her dependants, and we were lodged upstairs in different rooms. Rasputin behaved decently in relation to me for several days, and then one night he appeared in my room, started kissing me, and after reducing me to hysterics, deprived me of my virginity. On the way back Rasputin left me alone. But waking up by accident in the middle of the night, I noticed that he and Zina Manshtedt were lying in the same berth. Upon our return to Petrograd, I reported everything to the empress, and I also told Bishop Feofan in a private meeting with him. The empress did not give any heed to my words and said that everything Rasputin does is holy. From that time forth I did not see Rasputin, and in 1913 I was dismissed from my duties as nurse. I was also reprimanded for frequenting the Right Reverend Feofan.

And the last words, or more precisely, the virtual scream, with which her testimony ends explode from the dry transcript of the interrogation: 'I cannot testify any more. I implore you to end the interrogation, since I do not have the strength to speak any more about my unhappiness . . . and consider it my right not to go into the details!'

The tsar's sister, Grand Duchess Olga, recalls, 'When the rumours reached

Nicky that [Rasputin] had raped the nurse, he immediately ordered an investigation. They caught the young woman in bed with a Cossack of the Imperial Guard.' Thus, evidently, was the tsar's sister informed. Thus did Alix defend the peasant.

Grand Duchess Olga, however, would soon have an opportunity to learn something new about Father Grigory, and this time from her own personal experience.

The Peasant's Caress

It happened in Vyrubova's house. Rasputin already felt quite at home in Tsarskoe Selo. And all the secrets of the great Romanov family were now known to him. He knew that Olga's husband, the Duke of Oldenburg, was a homosexual.

And the peasant drew his own unique conclusion.

On the evening in question, Alix and Nicky had come to Anya's little house for a meeting with Father Grigory. Olga had been invited, too. 'Rasputin . . . it seemed, was very glad to see me again,' the grand duchess recalled, 'and when our hostess and Nicky and Alix left the parlour for a few moments, Rasputin came over to me and, after putting an arm around my shoulders, started stroking my hand. I immediately moved away from him without saying a word.' Her husband to whom she related the story 'said with a sombre face that I should avoid Rasputin in the future. For the first and only time I knew that my husband was right.'

The Transformation Of The General's Wife

It was also in 1910 that Lokhtina's husband suddenly 'regained his sight' and presented his wife with the ultimatum that she no longer tolerate Rasputin's presence in their home. In reply he heard, 'He is holy. You are banishing grace.' Her husband stopped giving her money. But yesterday's magnificent spendthrift now needed nothing more than a black dress and a white peasant kerchief for her head.

It was then that Rasputin told the 'tsars' about the former society lady who had traded the vanity of vanities for a new life. And the tsarina naturally took an interest in her. Thus giving rise to a paradox. Lokhtina's former status was the wife of a state councillor – was there any way that could have opened the door for her of the least accessible palace in Europe? Yet her rank as faithful follower of a semi-literate peasant accomplished that very miracle.

We shall find reference to this in the evidence of her second idol, the monk Iliodor: 'She . . . abandoned society and occupied herself exclusively with visiting the empress at the palace . . . and interpreting for the tsars the "wise apothegms" and prophecies of "Father" Grigory.'

And she not only interpreted them. This woman, who combined, as may happen in Rus, a shrewd mind with absolute madness, came up with the idea of transcribing Rasputin's thoughts and publishing them.

As she testified in the File, 'Father Grigory wrote down his spiritual thoughts in a little notebook . . . I transcribed what he had written down . . . and a pamphlet was published [his 'Pious Meditations', 1911]. I revised neither the substance of his notes, nor the thoughts expounded in them. My work came down to correcting his grammar; but Father Grigory's thoughts I did not improve.' However, he sometimes did write things down in his monstrous scrawl, but the semi-literate Rasputin could not write for long. So her main work, evidently, was to transcribe his spoken homilies. This was difficult, for his speech, by all accounts, was incoherent, the larger part of his influence coming from his eyes and hands. The hypnotic effect of his eyes and his glancing caresses. But she understood what he failed to express in words.

It was apparently with her that the tsarina studied the difficult art of writing down the elder's words.

In the middle of 1910, when Lokhtina's husband finally told her, 'Either . . . or . . .' she made her choice. 'From 1910 on I was completely estranged from my family, who demanded that I leave Father Grigory and didn't want me to live with them any more.' In short, she was driven from her home, and that part of the family's property belonging to her was taken away. So this hostess of a Petersburg salon abandoned her beloved daughter and left home with a knapsack on her back. She set off for Tsaritsyn to visit Iliodor (or 'Christ' as she called him), the main friend of Rasputin (or the 'Lord of hosts' as she called him). And on the way, the general's wife begged for alms.

What an interesting year 1910 turned out to be. At the height of the peasant's fame, an attack against him gradually took shape and then increased in strength. And it proceeded along a broad front: Hermogen, Feofan, Lokhtina's expulsion from her home, and the stories of Tyutcheva and Vishnyakova.

And, finally, the newspapers. For it was in 1910 that the newspaper campaign was unleashed. Rasputin became the main character of newspaper articles. The largest newspapers took pleasure in printing articles about the 'semi-literate and depraved peasant-*Khlyst*' who was enjoying great popularity in 'certain court circles'. Articles about him always produced a sensation, and the reading public rushed after them. The anti-government Constitutional Democrat newspaper *Speech* published a whole series of articles.

And finally in 1910 a powerful newspaper salvo was fired from Moscow as well – from the camp of Grand Duchess Elizaveta Fyodorovna. A member of the grand duchess's circle, Mikhail Novosyolov, an assistant professor at the Moscow Theological Seminary and editor of *The Religious-Philosophical Library*, published a whole series of sensational articles: 'Grigory Rasputin's Past Life', 'Grigory Rasputin, the Itinerant Spiritual Artiste', and 'Another Thing about Grigory Rasputin'. Published along with these articles was the confession of a certain maiden whom Rasputin had seduced, and reference was also made to the investigations of the Tobolsk Consistory, which had accused him of *Khlyst* involvement.

In 1910 Rasputin's name had begun to acquire a wicked meaning. It was turning into a punning synonym for 'debaucher'.

The Peasant And Europe

That all those events coincided was no accident. And the reason for it was the peasant himself. Or, more accurately, his new role. For in the period 1909–10 extremely powerful and influential people had begun to talk about the unthinkable: Father Grigory was not only treating the heir, and not only praying with the 'tsars', he had also begun to interfere in high political affairs. The semi-literate peasant had presumed to decide the destiny of Europe.

In October 1908 the telegraph brought to Russia the news that Austria-Hungary had unceremoniously annexed the Balkan protectorate of Bosnia and Herzegovina, where a large number of Orthodox Serbs lived. A powerful movement to defend its 'fellow Slavs' was begun in Russia, which considered itself the leader of the Orthodox world.

The beginning of 1909 saw a barrage of articles in the newspapers, and there were noisy demonstrations. Society demanded war to defend Russia's 'fellow Slavs', and the members of the Duma gave speeches about Russia's historical obligation to watch over its Balkan brothers who 'are united with

Russia by a common faith and common blood'. A well-attended pan-Slavic congress, including members of the Duma, gathered in Prague.

Worried, too, were the Orthodox Balkans, who feared that Bosnia and Herzegovina were the first step in a German expansion, a German march to the East. Serbia and Montenegro protested. And the ruler of Montenegro, the father of the Montenegrin princesses, joined those clamouring for war and pleaded for decisive interference by Russia. He was supported by his powerful son-in-law, Grand Duke Nikolai Nikolaevich, the 'chief military man' in the Romanov family. The Russian General Staff, who were eager to avenge Russia's humiliation in the war with Japan, also wanted war, as did the young Russian bourgeoisie, who were intoxicated by the mirage of seizing new spheres of influence and the dream of capturing the Straits. The party of war that took shape was a motley one.

But it could not be a local war with Austria-Hungary. Germany had no intention of remaining aloof. And on 8 (21 OS) March 1909, Germany presented Russia with an ultimatum: recognize the annexation of Bosnia and Herzegovina or accept the invasion of Serbia by the Austrian army under German protection. The start of the world war had become a possibility. But older, more experienced people who understood the weakness of the poorly equipped Russian army were afraid of war.

As the general's wife Bogdanovich wrote in her diary for 13 March, 'God forbid we go to war . . . We'll have another revolution, if we do.' Stolypin also understood the danger of war. After the difficult pacification of the country, he was unwilling to take the risk. He dreamed 'of twenty years of peace for Russia' after the shocks of the 1905 revolution and the war with Japan.

And Alix, too, was mortally afraid of war. She had not forgotten the recent revolution that had followed the war with Japan. And she knew: in the event of a war with Germany, her brother and her small dukedom of Darmstadt would become her enemies.

But the tsar vacillated, and listened with pleasure to the bellicose speeches of the 'dread uncle'. And the reason was not merely that 'the sovereign to his final hour passionately loved Nikolai Nikolaevich', as Vyrubova put it. It was simply that Nicky was a true Romanov and adored everything military. Like all his ancestors, he had been given a military education and had received his training in the celebrated Preobrazhensky regiment. He kept until his death his Guards' habit of pacing his room 'with his right shoulder thrust forward'. As Count Nikolai Panin had put it back in the eighteenth century, 'Until the day a crippled tsar is born, we shall wait in vain for a change in views.' Nicholas wanted to be in harmony with society, the beloved society he loved. So deep in his heart the tsar wanted war.

And then came Father Grigory's turn. He knew how to read Alix's secret desires. He knew his role, and he performed it. Rasputin spoke out decisively against the war. As was appropriate for a man of God, he predicted, indeed forewarned of, defeats and revolution. And the tsarina, later remembering those predictions of his, would write to the tsar on 1 November 1915, 'Our Friend was always against this war, saying the Balkans were not worth the world to fight about.'

She was grateful to Rasputin, and happy, for it had turned out that her own wishes were remarkably consistent with the commands of Father Grigory and heaven.

And so, Stolypin, the tsarina, and finally heaven (Father Grigory) were all against it. And the tsar faltered. And soon afterwards the Council of Ministers acceded to the annexation of Bosnia and Herzegovina. Society and the press gave vent to rage and revilement. Tsushima Strait, the greatest defeat in the recent war with Japan, was recalled. The phrase 'diplomatic Tsushima' became a common newspaper term for the decision.

Even the most perceptive people believed at the time that the tsar's refusal to fight had been dictated by Rasputin's wishes.

In the File, Rasputin's publisher Filippov cites a famous interview with Count Witte, one of most intelligent politicians of Nicholas's reign: 'Count Witte . . . acknowledged that "there is no doubt we are obliged to the influence of Rasputin that war did not flare up in the Balkans."'

So in 1909 the Montenegrin princesses and Grand Duke Nikolai Niko-laevich had a right to be indignant. It was not enough that Rasputin had hounded them out of the royal palace; now the semi-literate peasant had had the audacity to interfere in high political affairs. He had not given aid to the Orthodox in the Balkans; he had not come to the assistance of their own Montenegro.

The powerful minister Stolypin was also indignant with Rasputin. The newspaper articles against the peasant in the palace had undermined the prestige of the royal family, and resulted in dangerous rumours. And now the prime minister had himself been exposed to humiliation many times.

From the diary of A. Bogdanovich: 'About three weeks ago Stolypin came with his report and had to wait about half an hour. Because the tsar was at his wife's, in whose bedroom the "Blessed One" was sitting.' And it was with the peasant and not with Stolypin that they had decided the fate of war in the Balkans. And Stolypin learned one other piece of news that could not have failed to disturb him. It turned out that his political rival, the former prime minister Count Witte, had established contact with Rasputin. And a meeting had already taken place; Father Grigory had visited Count Witte.

'I said to him then, "Listen, why have you come to see me personally? If they find out about it, they'll say you're having dealings with a dangerous man." Rasputin presented some very original and interesting views to me in the conversation,' Witte later recalled. And that meeting of the peasant with the liberal Witte, who in 1905 had forced the tsar to grant a constitution, produced panic among the monarchists.

From Bogdanovich's diary: 'The fact that the Blessed One has been singing the same tune as Witte constitutes a grave danger . . . Witte wants to return to power.'

Stolypin learned that the semi-literate peasant had not only been seeing Witte, but he had also been involved in the preparation of the highest appointments and had arranged for a look at a candidate for the post of chief procurator of the Most Holy Synod.

And indeed Rasputin had. Alix wanted to strengthen her position in the Synod. She was afraid that her enemies would use the Synod to charge Our Friend with *Khlyst* views. And she decided to place at the head of the Synod someone who would be loyal to the elder. It was then that the candidacy was first proposed of the Russified German Vladimir Sabler for the position of chief procurator. Alix then suggested a remarkable new method of appointment to a post: the man of God would have to examine the candidate. Considering Our Friend's special relationship with heaven, it was logical for him to meet the future head of the Church's governing body. A meeting was arranged, and Rasputin convinced himself of Sabler's subservience to 'Papa' and 'Mama'. And Sabler, a man with a non-Russian name, was, to everyone's amazement, subsequently placed at the head of the Most Holy Synod.

The Prime Minister Versus The Peasant

Stolypin must have appreciated the significance of his wait in the tsar's reception room. It was not just a humiliation, it was a signal: a kind of secret prime minister was attending the tsar.

By then the great prime minister-reformer had grown weak. It is usually the fate of reformers in Russia. Afterwards, when one of the monarchist leaders, the highly intelligent Vasily Shulgin, was asked whom Stolypin had hindered, he tersely replied, 'Everyone.'

'Everyone.' He was hated by the left, for he had more than a few times ruthlessly suppressed their opposition in the Duma, once uttering the immortal words, 'You, gentlemen, require great upheavals, whereas I require a great Russia.' He was hated by the right, for his reforms promised the victory of Russian capitalism: Moscow, the ancient 'Tsargrad', was fated to become a Manchester. His contempt for the anti-Semites of the Union of the Russian People provoked the hatred of 'rightist' pastors like Iliodor and Hermogen. And there was one other powerful figure who was stirring up dissatisfaction with him: Grand Duke Nikolai Nikolaevich, for Stolypin had categorically opposed Russia's participation in the Balkan conflict. Nevertheless, Stolypin was supported by the tsar, for Stolypin threatened the tsar with social catastrophe and famine if he did not carry out his reforms. Moreover, his enormous height and booming voice reassuringly reminded Nicky of his giant father and instilled him with confidence.

But Stolypin made a fatal move. A move that might at first have seemed quite auspicious and even to promise a return of his popularity: he spoke out against Rasputin. The prime minister started talking about the situation in society surrounding the 'elder'.

Nicholas deflected the conversation. And asked the prime minister to meet Rasputin himself. The tsar remembered the impression that Rasputin had made on Stolypin just a few years before.

Stolypin later described that second meeting to a future Speaker of the Duma, Mikhail Rodzyanko. From the first moment the giant prime minister had clearly sensed 'the great power of hypnosis that was in that person and that produced a very strong impression that, although repellent, was still moral'. But the moral impression was evidently so strong that the prime minister, after 'overcoming' it, began shouting at Rasputin, calling him a *Khlyst* and a sectarian, and threatening him with exile on the basis of the 'appropriate law in regard to sectarians'.

That was a blunder. And as the future would show, a fatal one for the prime minister. Rasputin had a right to feel insulted. And serene. He knew that the Tobolsk Theological Consistory had failed to obtain any concrete proof of his *Khlyst* connections. And the tsar knew it, too, for he had in that year of general persecution of Our Friend acquainted himself with the case.

Who Was Behind It?

So by 1910 everyone had gradually become opposed to Rasputin: the left, for whom he had only recently come to personify the alliance of Iliodor and the anti-Semites; the right and the monarchists, whom he threatened with the return of Witte; Nikolai Nikolaevich and the party of war; the court, which hated the peasant favourite; the ecclesiastics, who were certain he was a *Khlyst*; the prime minister Stolypin; the tsarina's sister Ella – they were all sick of him.

The first, of course, to take action was the most offended and most passionate of them all, the 'black princess'. Feofan was a close friend of Militsa's. And, of course, she was the mysterious 'someone' who had opened the bishop's eyes, and had acquainted him with the Tobolsk investigation and the confessions of ladies whom Rasputin had 'violated'.

Sister Ella also went into action. The abbess of the Martha and Mary Cloister had already grasped that the second Our Friend was far more dangerous than the first. And the speaking out of Sophia Tyutcheva had been no accident, since she had, besides her own strong Moscow ties (the famous Tyutchev estate outside the city and a house within it), a close friendship with Ella. And the richest family in Russia, the Yusupovs, was also very close to Ella. Thus, in Moscow a front of those hostile to Rasputin had already taken form – what Alix would call the 'Moscow clique'. And it was Ella who had helped Feofan obtain the appointment in the Crimea when he was exiled from the capital. She realized that the indomitable Feofan would continue his denunciations during the royal family's trips to their Crimean palace at Livadia.

And Prime Minister Stolypin also continued his offensive against the peasant. The Department of Police was put on the case. In the autumn of 1910 the prime minister gave the order for external surveillance of Rasputin's movements. It was his idea to place on the tsar's desk the secret agents' reports and to convince him, finally, of the profligacy of the 'holy peasant'.

As it is stated in the papers of the Department of Police, 'surveillance of the well-known elder G. E. Rasputin was instituted on the order of the Chairman of the Council of Ministers Stolypin in October 1910.'

Alix responded immediately. As stated in the same Department of Police documents, Rasputin 'was observed for several days only. After which the surveillance was terminated.' The tsar rescinded the order. He could not explain to his prime minister that the facts which the latter had intended to bring to his attention meant nothing to him. And that it was given neither to Stolypin nor to his agents to understand Father Grigory's behaviour. Or, more accurately, the mystery of that behaviour. A mystery that the 'tsars' had come to grasp.

The Peasant's Gift To The Tsarina

Finally 1911 arrived. In order to quiet the mounting wave of criticism, it was again necessary for the royal family to stop summoning the peasant to the palace, and to meet with him in secret at Anya's.

Nicholas's diary for 12 February: 'We went to Anya's, where we had a long talk with Grigory.'

But everybody in the court knew. 'This peasant Rasputin . . . does not come to the palace, but he does visit Vyrubova in Tsarskoe [Selo], and the tsarina frequently drops in on Vyrubova. Everyone continues to castigate Vyrubova behind her back and to curry favour to her face . . . All these lords are afraid of one thing only, holding onto their warm little places, although they care little for Russia,' Bogdanovich wrote in her diary.

And it was then in February 1911, that Alix started keeping a special notebook.

After the royal family's execution, Yurovsky, their murderer, took some royal documents from the Ipatiev House. Among them was a notebook that the tsarina had brought with her to their last home. And that dark blue notebook has to the present day been held in a Moscow archive. Located in the notebook next to the tsarina's calligraphic inscription is Rasputin's own preposterous scrawl: 'A gift to my warm-hearted Mama. G. Rasputin. 3 February 1911.'

The gift was his sayings, which he had dictated during their meetings at Anya's house, and which the tsarina had then diligently copied out in the notebook in her own elegant hand. Lokhtina had taught her a great deal, and now the tsarina herself knew how to translate those fragmented Delphic conjurations of his into normal speech.

The majority of the teachings written down by the tsarina concerned the unjust persecution of the righteous. And the value of that persecution for the soul. 'Lord, how my enemies have multiplied! Many are they who have risen up against me!' 'In persecution is Thy path. Thou hast revealed the cross of joy to us.' She would a few years later in the Ipatiev House be able to repeat 'In persecution is Thy path' and 'Grant us forbearance and silence the mouths of our enemies.' And again, like an incantation, 'My soul, seek joy in persecution . . . heaven awaits those who are banished for the truth.'

And more and more it seemed to her that she was witnessing scenes from the Gospels with her own eyes, that she was witnessing the defamation of a prophet. She would save him! She would stand up to his enemies! She knew how to fight!

The Road To Jerusalem

Maria Vishnyakova and the maid of honour Sophia Tyutcheva, despite Nicky's goodwill, were dismissed from their posts. The nursery once more became Alix's fief alone. So that she could once again bring Our Friend to the nursery in the evenings. So that he could without interference heal her poor son and help her daughters, too, whenever they were ill.

It was perhaps then that Grigory grasped the astonishing law that the more severely his persecutors attacked him, the harsher would be the tsarina's reply. And the more quickly they would disappear from the palace. And the stronger would be his position.

But she saw that Nicky was nervous. For all this time his mother and the whole large Romanov family had been troubled. As Konstantin Konstantinovich wrote in his diary, the dowager empress 'is in despair that they continue to receive the holy fool Grisha'.

Our Friend needed to absent himself from Petersburg for a time. But to send him to Pokrovskoe now would mean to yield to them, to his enemies. Alix was incapable of yielding. And it was decided that Rasputin would, as befitted a man of God, go on a pilgrimage. To see the places most holy to any Christian. As a reward for everything that he had done for the royal family. For all the persecution he had suffered.

And Rasputin set off for Jerusalem with a group of Russian pilgrims.

6

THE EMPRESS'S
ALTER EGO

The Mysterious Co-Author

From Nicholas's diary, 4 June 1911: 'After dinner we had the pleasure of seeing Grigory just after . . . his return from Jerusalem.'

We can easily imagine the story he told the 'tsars' about his pilgrimage.

His impressions of his journey to Jerusalem were published later that year under the title, 'My Thoughts and Reflections'. As the publisher Filippov testified in the File, 'The pamphlet was published by me . . . I didn't correct or smooth out Rasputin's aphorisms, but conveyed them verbatim.'

This does not mean, however, that Rasputin wrote them that way. He could not have written such a quantity of text. He would in the future scribble out his famous memos to the ministers, those few words, at great effort in a monstrous scrawl. So what Filippov published 'verbatim' was a text in Rasputin's own words that had been transcribed by someone else. But before we clarify who that was, let us listen to the peasant's rapturous voice.

> The sea comforts without any effort. When you rise in the morning, the waves speak, and lap, and gladden your heart. And the sun shines upon the sea, as if coming up ever so quietly, and at the same time a person's soul forgets everything . . . and gazes at the brilliance of the sun. The sea wakens you from your sleep of cares, and much is thought all by itself. O God, grant us spiritual peace. At sea, illness is temporary, but ashore it is forever – such a wave. At sea, sickness is seen by everyone, but ashore it is unknown to any – a demon confuses the soul. Conscience is a wave, but whatever waves there may be at sea, they will die away, while conscience will be calmed only by a good cause.

And the peasant's impossible dream came to pass: he saw His city and His tomb.

'What shall I say of the moment when I approached the tomb of Christ
. . . And such a feeling I had in myself that I was ready to treat everyone
with affection, and such a love for people that everyone seemed holy,
because Love does not see any defects in people. There, at the tomb, you
see all people with a spiritual heart.'

But he knows: the rest is silence, the rest is Mystery, and mouths must
be closed to preserve the great moment of the encounter with the Lord's
Tomb.

'O God, what can I say of the Tomb! I shall say only what was in my
heart: "Lord, resurrect me Thyself from the depths of sin."' One should
imagine that nervous person's magnetic eyes filling with tears as he told it
all to the 'tsars', because, as a true actor, he *saw* what he was saying.

O, what an impression Golgotha produces! From that place the Mother of
God looked at the heights of Golgotha and wept while the Lord was
crucified upon the cross. As you gaze at the place where the Mother of
God stood, your tears begin to flow, whether by your will or no, and you
see before you how it was. O God, what a feat took place! And they took
down the body and placed it below. What sadness is here, and what a
weeping at the place where the body lay! O God, O God, what was the
reason for it? O God, we shall sin no more: save us with Thy suffering.

And they, who had never ever been to the Holy Land, would see it through
his eyes. And a few years later, as they were preparing for their own
Golgotha, they would remember those stories of his.

And so, the semi-literate Rasputin could not have written so much. And
Lokhtina says not a word about working on the book. And, anyway, the
didactic text she transcribed is too different from this inspired one. And
how much does this text resemble the remarkable 'Life of an Experienced
Wanderer'. Rasputin would seem to have had the same co-author in both
texts. Someone capable of putting the hypnotic force of his words down
on paper. Filippov gives a hint of the co-author's identity. He testified in
the File that 'the proofs were corrected by the empress.'

Of course! The proofs were corrected by the same person who had
written down the words. Only the tsarina with her brilliant literary gift
(read her letters!) could have conveyed what Rasputin told them in just that
way. Although she did not work alone, I think. But with her inseparable
Friend, who adored writing, too. For the tsarina, that work was contact
with the mystical, with what was hidden. For the Friend, it was something
that bound her ever more tightly to Alix.

The Great Minister's Fall

But even after his return, Our Friend was unable to live in peace.

The newspaper articles continued. One can imagine what that semi-literate peasant felt upon seeing himself vilified in the *newspapers*. And once again he dictated to 'Mama' for the notebook his teachings about those who had suffered for the truth.

Alix was furious. And at the end of 1910 the tsar had written Stolypin a brusque note demanding that he put a end to the newspaper campaign against Rasputin. But Stolypin simply ignored the note and the vilification of Rasputin in the press continued. The prime minister was in fact mounting a resolute attack of his own. Even though his attempt at organizing official surveillance of Rasputin had been countermanded, his agents were still at work. Information was still being collected.

And at the beginning of autumn 1911 the prime minister set off to see the tsar with his report.

There is in the File very important testimony by Sazonov about the episode:

His struggle with Stolypin was very interesting, as I shall relate from what Rasputin himself told me. Stolypin demanded that the tsar have Rasputin sent away. He brought along for his report Rasputin's file from the Department of Police and communicated everything known to him of a compromising character . . . including that he, Rasputin, had been going to the bathhouses with women, to the great temptation of society. To which the tsar had answered, 'I know, and he preaches Holy Scripture there' . . . And after the report, he ordered Stolypin to clear out and tossed the report itself in the fireplace . . . That is why a month before Stolypin's murder I knew . . . his fate was sealed. Compare that with little things like the fact that Stolypin was not assigned more or less decent and comfortable quarters for the Kiev festivities, that he wasn't given an automobile, and so on.

Stolypin was deposed not by the Duma, and not by the rightists or the leftists. That mightiest of prime ministers was brought down by his attack on the peasant.

And Stolypin began to 'die a political death'. Now Alix conducted a ruthless campaign against the enemy of Our Friend. And soon afterwards Rasputin spoke or, more accurately, gave voice to her thought. 'Rasputin said of Stolypin . . . that he had seized too much power,' Vyrubova testified.

The peasant knew: the weak tsar did not forgive accusations of weakness. The dread prime minister was still carrying out his duties when a rumour began circulating that he would be reassigned as governor-general of the

Caucasus. As his constant rival Count Witte enjoyed noting in his memoirs.

It was then that Rasputin engaged his friend Sazonov in a conversation that stunned the journalist and publisher. And soon afterwards a remarkable expedition – the peasant and his friend Sazonov – set out for Nizhny Novgorod.

Ten Days Before The Murder

The post of minister of internal affairs was a key one in the government. And the prime minister usually tried to obtain the post for himself. As one of the tsarist ministers would later put it, 'A prime minister without that post is like a cat without his balls.' That is why Prime Minister Stolypin was also minister of internal affairs.

And what must have been the amazement of Rasputin's friend Sazonov when the peasant told him that he had received a new assignment from the 'tsars' – to find another minister of internal affairs to replace Stolypin! And Rasputin suggested to the quite startled Sazonov that he think about who the best person for the position might be. And Sazonov, overcoming his fear and amazement, evidently did think about it. Because the candidacy that was soon afterwards discussed in Tsarskoe Selo was that of the Nizhny Novgorod governor Alexei Khvostov, whose father was a close friend of Sazonov's. Thus the expedition to Nizhny Novgorod.

The evidence remains in the File.

From the testimony of Sazonov: 'Rasputin, carrying out the sovereign's commission, went to Nizhny, where at the time Khvostov was governor. I went with Rasputin at his request as an old friend of Khvostov's father's.'

Alexei Nikolaevich Khvostov was very tall and very stout (Rasputin would later on give him the nickname 'Fat Belly') and still young, just thirty-nine. He was the nephew of the tsarist minister of justice, Nikolai Khvostov, had come from a family of wealthy landowners, and was known for his extreme right-wing views.

But Khvostov met the visitors in a most unexpected way.

From Sazonov's testimony: 'He greeted me, as an old family friend, with courtesy, but he received Rasputin very coolly and was clearly surprised by our visit. He did not even invite us . . . to stay for dinner. We saw him between trains.'

Khvostov describes the event more vividly in the File:

Ten days before Stolypin's murder, Georgy Petrovich Sazonov, an old acquaintance of my father's, came to visit me along with Grigory Rasputin, whom I had never seen before, in Nizhny Novgorod, where I was governor

. . . Sazonov, clearly not wanting to disturb our conversation, remained in the parlour. Rasputin was with me in my study. Rasputin spoke of his closeness to the tsar . . . and of having been sent by the tsar to 'look into my soul', and he finished by offering me the post of minister of internal affairs.

Khvostov naturally told him that 'the position is already occupied'.

'Rasputin answered, however, that Stolypin would nonetheless be leaving . . . It all seemed so strange and peculiar to me that I attributed no significance to Rasputin's conversation with me and spoke to him in a half-facetious tone. And he left angry. I didn't invite him to dine and refused to introduce him to my family, even though he asked me to.'

It would be surprising if it had not seemed strange to Khvostov. The prime minister and minister of internal affairs was the mighty Stolypin. And suddenly that strange pair arrives: Sazonov, an acquaintance of his father's and merely one publisher among many, and an uncouth, semi-literate peasant about whom incredible rumours have been circulating. And they start talking to him in all seriousness about the removal of Stolypin himself! Khvostov, like many another 'serious person', was unaware at the time of the peasant's actual position at court. And he could not believe that the tsar would entrust the fate of that all-powerful post to that pair. It all looked absolutely fantastic to him. And beginning to suspect that it was just some court game, Khvostov preferred to politely show the strange emissaries the door. Although he did ask police agents to follow them. After which Khvostov 'received from the local office a copy of a telegram that Rasputin had sent to Vyrubova that read approximately, "Though God rests easy with him, that is not enough for it."' And deciding that it was indeed a court intrigue of the tsarina's Friend, Khvostov let it go at that. But what must have been his astonishment, if not horror, when ten days later Stolypin was murdered. And how sinister Rasputin's words that 'Stolypin will none-theless be leaving' must have seemed to him then.

The Prime Minister's Mysterious Death

From the diary of KR: '3 September . . . We were horrified to learn that the day before yesterday in Kiev . . . Stolypin was wounded by several revolver shots.'

Stolypin was killed thanks to several very odd blunders by the secret police.

A monument to Nicholas's grandfather Tsar Alexander II, the serfs' emancipator, was to be unveiled in Kiev on the occasion of the fiftieth anniversary of the abolition of serfdom. The tsar came for the festivities, along with the grand dukes and Prime Minister Stolypin. And on the eve of the festivities, a certain Dmitry Bogrov appeared at the local offices of the security branch. He was a revolutionary terrorist who had been recruited by the royal security service but who had not had any contact with it for several years. And now Bogrov suddenly turned up with information that an attempt on Stolypin's life was in the offing. The attempt was evidently going to take place in the Kiev Opera Theatre at the gala performance. And Kurlov the chief of the gendarme corps (political police), Spiridovich the head of palace security, and Kulyabko the chief of the Kiev security office, were all of a sudden strangely trusting. They did not even arrange for surveillance of Bogrov. And not only did they let him into the theatre, they let him in with a revolver!

The tsar left his box seat for the second intermission. Stolypin was standing by a wall with his back to the orchestra and was talking to the court minister Fredericks. He was approached by a young man whose coat-tails stood out among the endless bureaucratic and military uniforms. It was Bogrov. He calmly drew his revolver and shot twice. Stolypin managed to turn towards the empty royal box and bless it with a sign of the cross.

He was carried out to the lobby. Two days later he died.

With their previous experience of murders in which the right-wing and the secret police had, by the hands of agents-provocateurs, culled unwanted tsarist officials, the Duma immediately started speaking of provocation. The monarchist Shulgin made a speech directly accusing the secret police: 'We have in recent times had a whole series of analogous killings of Russian dignitaries with the collusion of officials of the political police . . . Stolypin, who, according to Prince Meschersky, had said that "a secret police agent will kill me" . . . perished at the hand of a police agent with the collaboration of the highest security officials.'

A Senate investigation into the actions of Kurlov and Spiridovich was about to begin. But someone apparently got nervous about it. Pressure was applied to the tsar, and at his command the case was closed.

Rasputin And The Assassination

Rasputin was in Kiev on the day of the murder. He later wrote a virtual ode about the Kiev festivities. But his bombastic eulogy was hardly noticed by anyone. Then the news quickly began to spread of his meeting with Khvostov on the eve of the murder and his prediction of the prime minister's imminent departure. There was even a rumour that Rasputin had directly foretold Stolypin's impending death. And in his book Iliodor quotes words allegedly belonging to Rasputin: 'You see, I foretold Stolypin's death seven days before it happened.'

This is what people were beginning to talk about in Petersburg parlours. So that Rasputin's name was at once connected to Stolypin's murder. The rumours apparently made a strong impression on Sazonov, too. He was frightened that Rasputin, and hence he himself, would be drawn into a dangerous game. Stolypin's murder showed how such games ended. 'I started to distance myself from him when I saw that he was beginning to acquire influence over supreme questions of government,' Sazonov testified in the File.

The Extraordinary Commission took a special interest in the rumours that Rasputin had somehow been linked to Stolypin's death. And in that regard they interrogated the future head of Rasputin's own bodyguard, Colonel Komissarov. But they found no evidence.

Had Rasputin really predicted not only Stolypin's departure (an easy thing for him to do, since he knew the intentions of Tsarskoe Selo) but also his death? If he really had predicted his death, he need not have been a prophet to do so. It could have been connected to the appearance nearby of one of the most mysterious personalities of the day, Pyotr Badmaev, the doctor of Tibetan medicine.

A Very 'Cunning Chinaman'

The sixty-year-old Badmaev bore the titles of actual state councillor and doctor of Tibetan medicine. He was a Buryat from a distinguished family of Asiatic descent who grew up on the Siberian steppe, where he had roamed with the family's enormous herds. At the time his brother had a flourishing Tibetan pharmacy in Petersburg and practised Tibetan medicine. And Badmaev set off for Petersburg, too. There he converted to Orthodoxy and acquired an important godfather: he was baptized by Tsar Alexander III.

Badmaev testified before the Extraordinary Commission: 'I completed the course of study at the Academy of Military Medicine . . . but by my own choice did not take a degree, so as to have the right to practise according to the principles of Tibetan medicine. And then I started practising in the highest circles of society.' He treated all illnesses – neurasthenia, pulmonary diseases, venereal diseases – by means of Tibetan herbs, but his chief claim was in restoring masculine potency.

The monarchist Purishkevich subsequently quoted some words about Badmaev that supposedly came from Rasputin: 'He has two infusions: you drink a little glass of one, and your cock gets hard; but there's still the other: you drink a really tiny glass of it, and it makes you good-natured and kind of stupid, and you don't care about anything.' And in Petersburg they believed in that.

Afterwards the rumour would circulate that Rasputin had drugged the tsar with those herbs of Badmaev's in order to make him 'good-natured and kind of stupid'.

In any case, Badmaev treated high society: the former Prime Minister Witte; the metropolitans of Kiev and Moscow; Alexander Protopopov, the Deputy Speaker of the State Duma; and so on. The 'cunning Chinaman', Rasputin would call Badmaev. For in addition to medicine, Badmaev had another absorbing occupation: he was an entrepreneur, a businessman.

He dreamed of Russia's capture of Mongolia and Tibet. And he showered the royal chancery with endless projects. He founded a trading company, Badmaev & Ko (his trading partner), leased land from the Tartars and Mongols, established a huge livestock-breeding farm, and bought numerous camels. He dreamed the farm would become a bridgehead for penetrating first Mongolia and then Tibet. He petitioned the tsar for subsidies to support his grandiose plans, but to no avail. In the end he was ruined and had to liquidate his farm. But he had information, passed down from generation to generation in his Buryat family, about Trans-Baikal gold. And in 1909 he founded the First Trans-Baikal Mining and Industrial Association for the exploitation of gold deposits. But Stolypin, to Badmaev's great displeasure, had remained cool about these dealings. Badmaev then got one of his secret patients involved in his business – Grand Duke Boris Vladimirovich. But after the episode of Kirill's marriage, the sons of Vladimir were unpopular in the royal family. And again state subsidies were not forthcoming. Badmaev needed a lot of money and he attempted to put right his relations with Tsarskoe Selo by himself. And, as he testifies in the File, he sent 'herbal medicine' for treatment of the heir. But the powders 'were returned with thanks'. He had been shown the door.

There was only one person left who could help him – Rasputin. And Badmaev made his first steps towards closer relations with Grigory.

One of Badmaev's patients at the time was Lieutenant General Kurlov, chief of the gendarme corps and the person most suspected of engineering Stolypin's murder. And if the assassination really was arranged, then the 'cunning Chinaman' might have received from his grateful patient a hint of the impending demise of Stolypin, so disliked by Badmaev. And then, in striking up an acquaintance with Rasputin, that master of intrigue could, as evidence of his potential, have brought that information to Rasputin, that hint about the end of Stolypin. Who, as everyone knew, was a mortal enemy of Father Grigory.

And Rasputin could have predicted to the tsarina, with her constant craving for his predictions, that the disliked prime minister would soon perish. As divine retribution.

The Paradox Of The Dead Man

Stolypin's death is a watershed in Rasputin's biography.

Before it, Rasputin was a secret, the subject of obscure rumours and vague newspaper articles. And 'serious people' simply dismissed as cock-and-bull the stories about the enormous influence at court of some peasant. The governor of Moscow Vladimir Dzhunkovsky, for example. His sister Evdokia was a maid of honour and a friend of Tyutcheva's, and she hated Rasputin. Naturally, she told her brother about the situation at court, but he did not believe her. Especially since, with the rank of aide-de-camp, he himself visited the capital for duty at court, was invited to tea with the sovereign, and met the courtiers. As he wrote in his memoirs, 'I considered all those rumours to be the invention of the newspapers and ascribed no meaning to them . . . I was indignant whenever his name was linked to those of the sovereign and the empress.'

But with Stolypin's murder, Dzhunkovsky started to take an interest in Rasputin's activities. So the assassination of Stolypin, of the person who had been defeated by the obscure peasant, compelled 'serious people' to take a closer look at that peasant.

The senator Vladimir Nikolaevich Kokovtsev, from an old gentry family, was made the new prime minister. Not a brilliant man but hard-working and honest. 'And that is all,' as Dzhunkovsky wrote of him.

'Stolypin died in order to cede his position to you,' Alix told him, meaning, 'to you as someone who is presumably able to listen to the voice of the man of God and not persecute him'.

It seemed that the most serious threat to Grigory had passed with Stolypin's death. But Alix would soon grasp a paradox. The death of the mighty prime minister had proved not a deliverance but exactly the opposite. When he died something irreparable happened: fear passed out of the aristocratic system. And without fear it could not work. No, it was not for nothing that the dying Stolypin had made the sign of the cross at the royal box. The weak Nicholas and the pitiful ministers were now left one-to-one against the Duma. And the peasant, whom it had already become fashionable to hate, was defenceless in the absence of fear. The murdered prime minister had taken vengeance from beyond the grave.

The first to be emboldened by Stolypin's absence were the hierarchs.

The Prophets' Brawl

Feofan was remote from the world and capable only of writing vain appeals to the tsar or asking his friends to expose Rasputin, but Hermogen knew how to act. Upon arriving in Petersburg for a meeting of the Synod, he understood that the time had come to put an end to Rasputin. The pitiful Kokovtsev did not scare him. And Sabler, the chief procurator of the Synod, compromised by rumours of his link to Rasputin, did not scare him either.

Well understanding who was in charge in the royal family, Hermogen knew there was no point in appealing to the tsar. He therefore decided to break Grigory himself – to denounce him and force him to leave the court voluntarily. And if Grigory did not agree, then Iliodor had prepared a lampoon called 'Grishka'. The letters that Iliodor had stolen from Rasputin were quoted, including a letter from the tsarina, a secret weapon that made both Iliodor and Hermogen confident that it was all over with yesterday's friend.

And then came 16 December, the day of denunciation.

The participants had all gathered by eleven o'clock ahead of Rasputin's arrival. To Hermogen's quarters at the Yaroslav Monastery had come Mitya Kozelsky, in whom the tsarina had put such faith before Rasputin. Mitya was tall and scrawny with a withered arm and dressed in shabby but clean peasant clothes. Ivan Rodyonov was there, too, a publicist with close ties to the Union of the Russian People and an admirer of Iliodor's who had helped him write the 'Grishka' lampoon. Iliodor himself, whom Rasputin continued to regard as his friend, was to bring Grigory to them at eleven.

Iliodor had gone to get the elder: 'Rasputin greeted me very affectionately. I invited him to come with me to Hermogen's . . . "He's expecting you." And he said to me, "Well, go on and take me, then . . . as soon as you can, I want to see him."' They got in a cab and set off. It is amazing, but that intuitive person sensed nothing. Just as he would later sense nothing when he was taken to be killed. Evidently, he had complete faith in Iliodor. And that faith had turned off his wild beast's senses. His exposed nerve endings went to sleep and he became an ordinary simple-hearted peasant. Along the way Grigory talked with naive awe about the opulence of the tsar's new palace in Livadia. And about how 'Papa himself showed me around the palace . . . and then we came out onto a porch and gazed at the sky for a long time.' Finally, they arrived. The players in the drama were eager to begin. As Rasputin and Iliodor were taking off their coats in the hallway, Iliodor sarcastically said to Rodyonov, 'Take a look at his elder's rags, Ivan Alexandrovich!' Rodyonov said, 'Oh-ho! The hat's worth at least three hundred roubles, and the fur coat would cost around two thousand here. Truly ascetic apparel!' Only then did Rasputin grasp that something was amiss. But it was too late.

Iliodor wrote:

> The historic moment had arrived. Hermogen, I, and all the witnesses had gathered in the front room. The 'elder' sat down on the large sofa. Mitya, limping and waving his withered arm, paced back and forth near Grigory . . . All were silent . . . And then something . . . happened that was improbable, ridiculous, but at the same time terrifying. Mitya cried out savagely, 'Ah, ah, ah, you are a Godless person, you have done wrong to many mamas! You have offended many nurses! You are sleeping with the tsarina! You are a scoundrel!' and he began to grab at the 'elder'. Rasputin started to back toward the doorway. But Mitya, poking him in the chest with his finger, started yelling even louder and more insistently, 'You are sleeping with the tsarina! You are an Antichrist!' And then Hermogen, who was dressed in his bishop's robes, took his cross in his hand and said, 'Grigory, come over here!' Rasputin, his whole body trembling, approached the table, pale, hunched over, and frightened.

And then came the finale, as described by Iliodor.

> Hermogen took hold of the head of the 'elder' with his left hand, with his right started beating him on the head with the cross and shouting in a terrifying voice, 'Devil! I forbid you in God's name to touch the female sex. Brigand! I forbid you to enter the royal household and to have anything to do with the tsarina! As a mother brings forth the child in the cradle, so the holy Church through its prayers, blessings, and heroic feats has nursed that great and sacred thing of the people, the autocratic rule of the tsars. And now you, scum, are destroying it, you are smashing our holy vessels, the bearers of autocratic power . . . Fear God, fear His life-giving cross!'

And then Rodyonov, unsheathing the sabre he had brought with him, led the utterly flummoxed Rasputin over to the cross. And they demanded that he swear to leave the palace. And Rasputin swore. The planned performance had come to a successful end. As a pitiful little peasant of the kind he had once been in Pokrovskoe, Rasputin emerged, or, more accurately, ran from the bishop's quarters. And was glad that he had done so in one piece and unharmed. Since he believed that the nobleman Rodyonov was quite capable of hacking him to death with his sabre. A constant peasant fear.

His oath on the cross had meant nothing, of course. He had his own relations with God that were unattainable to those well-fed princes of the church. And his God could forgive an oath on the cross that had been torn from him in terror at the threat of being killed. But he himself could not forgive his friend's treachery. After all, he knew that Iliodor had betrayed not only him. But Hermogen, too. Because there was a secret thing that Iliodor had concealed from Hermogen and Feofan. Something that bound him tightly to Rasputin. And Iliodor's treachery and the bishop's violence impelled the enraged Rasputin to send a telegram to 'Mama' at once.

'Upon leaving the Yaroslav Monastery . . . Rasputin went to a telegraph office and sent the tsars a telegram . . . ,' Iliodor wrote, 'that was full of incredible slander . . . He wrote that Hermogen and I had allegedly wanted to take his life, to strangle him, in Hermogen's quarters.' There was no particular slander here: they had threatened him with a sabre and struck him on the head with a bronze cross.

Thus 16 December came to a close, a special day in the life of that mystical person.

On the same day five years later he would be killed.

One can imagine Alix's astonishment and fury when she received his telegram and later learned the details from Anya about how yesterday's friends had attempted to take his life and deprive her and the heir of the help of the man of God.

Meanwhile, Hermogen pressed on. He gave a thundering speech against the *Khlysty* at a meeting of the Synod. First, he assailed Russian literature – all those works by the fashionable writers of the day describing *Khlyst* practices. The *Khlyst* theme had by then also found its way into vulgar literature, where the writers Artsybashev and Kamensky had described scenes of *Khlyst* 'rejoicing' and 'group sinning'. And Hermogen denounced the temptation posed by those writings, too. Then, finally, he turned to his main point, a denunciation of Grigory Rasputin, 'charging him with *Khlyst* tendencies'. The Synod listened to him in fear. The hierarchs could guess how furious the tsarina would be. So it was only a minority who dared to support him. The majority, however, followed the chief procurator in expressing its dissatisfaction with the pastor's interference in 'things that were not of his concern'.

But Hermogen did not relent. More than that, he even dared to say in private conversation that Grigory had committed adultery with the tsarina.

And she found out about it all from Vyrubova. For her now, Hermogen and Iliodor were simply liars who for personal advantage had pretended to be friends and admirers of Father Grigory. And who had dared to accuse him, a friend of the royal family – Our Friend. And, most monstrous of all, they had dared, knowing her, to accuse her, as well! One may guess what she said to Nicky! And one may imagine his rage, the rage of the tsar!

Another Prediction Of The Death Of The Tsars

And the thunder crashed.

The File, from the testimony of Victor Yatskevich, director of the chancery of the chief procurator of the Most Holy Synod: 'During the Yuletide meeting [an unprecedented event in the life of the Synod] Hermogen received an order to return to his eparchy. He did not obey the order and, as I heard, asked by telegram for an audience with the tsar, indicating that he had an important matter to discuss, but was turned down.'

That is how Iliodor describes it, too. He came to Petersburg to assist Hermogen. The monk wrote the telegram to the tsar at Hermogen's dictation in the latter's quarters at the Yaroslav Monastery.

> Hermogen was sitting next to me, and bitterly, bitterly sobbing, and I painstakingly wrote out, 'Tsar Father! I have devoted my whole life to the service of the Church and the Throne. I have served zealously, sparing no effort. The sun of my life has long passed midday and my hair has turned white. And now in my declining years, like a criminal, I am being driven out of the capital in disgrace by you, the Sovereign. I am ready to go wherever it may please you, but before I do, grant me an audience, and I will reveal a secret to you.'

A prompt reply to the telegram was received from Nicholas through the Synod: the tsar had no wish to know any secret. 'Upon reading the answer, Hermogen started crying. And then he suddenly said, "They will kill the tsar, they will kill the tsar, they will surely kill him."'

Unlike the majority of such predictions, these words of Hermogen's were published before the 1917 revolution, before the royal family perished.

Hoping to avoid a scandal, Sabler tried to moderate the tsar's rage. But, as he sadly informed Prime Minister Kokovtsev, the sympathies of Tsarskoe Selo were with Rasputin, on whom, in the tsar's words, 'they had fallen like robbers in the forest after first drawing their victim into a trap.'

The denouement arrived. The Synod officially retired Hermogen *in absentia* to residence at the Zhirovets Monastery. The monk Iliodor was ordered into exile at Florischev Pustyn near the town of Gorbatov and forbidden to show himself in Tsaritsyn and Petersburg.

And then an unprecedented thing happened. Hermogen and Iliodor refused to budge from Petersburg. In open defiance of the tsar. Moreover, they dared to begin speaking publicly. The mutinous pastors agreed to newspaper interviews, where they vilified Rasputin, the Synod, and Chief Procurator Sabler.

It was then that Iliodor brought his main, secret weapon into play.

The Secret Weapon

And soon afterwards Vyrubova received from Grigory's former friend a warning about the possible onset of a war: 'Sister in Christ! How long, then, will you stand by Grigory? . . . If you do not abandon him, a tremendous scandal shall break out all over Russia. And then what a calamity there will be! Heed me. Fear God. Repent. Iliodor.'

Vyrubova already knew what scandal the monk's epistle was referring to. She had already heard about it: Iliodor had promised to publish a lampoon against Father Grigory which would include letters to Rasputin from the tsarina and the grand duchesses.

Vyrubova invited Iliodor to come and see her.

Iliodor arrived at Anya's little house in Tsarskoe Selo. Waiting for him there was the entire little circle of the elder's admirers: Vyrubova herself, her sister Sana, and her sister's husband Alexander Pistolkors. The monk has described in his book the danger he felt. In the drawing room sat 'Pistolkors . . . brave and cruel . . . [who], according to him, had during the [1905] revolution hanged by his own hands eighty-five Latvians in the Baltic region'. True, the monk does not also describe himself, a huge fellow with fists the size of large stones. The conversation was opened by Pistolkors. 'Father Iliodor! What is this scandal you are threatening in your letter to Anyushka? And who is it that intends to make that scandal? Is it not you? It can be done; after all, the French revolution came about when the queen was slanderously accused of stealing some diamonds.'

Pistolkors was alluding to 1785 and the famous matter of the 'queen's necklace'. An episode in which there had also figured letters from a queen – forged letters from Marie Antoinette. Pistolkors meant to say that the letters that Iliodor was threatening to publish were also fabricated. And he was reminding the monk how a similar falsehood had ended in France. It had destroyed the reputation of Marie Antoinette and brought the revolution closer, and with it the death of the queen, as well as of many who had originally conspired in the affair.

But this time the queen's letters were genuine.

The conversation failed to produce the desired result. Iliodor had apparently gone in the hope that Vyrubova would ask for the letters and that he could then trade them for his and Hermogen's right to remain in their former places. But Vyrubova could not have proposed such a thing, even if she had wanted to, since the tsarina would not have allowed her to yield to blackmail. And after hearing the monk out, Vyrubova remained silent. And that silence was a threatening one. Iliodor understood: there would be no trade. But he was not frightened. For behind him stood powerful people.

Meanwhile, the letters to Rasputin from the tsarina and the grand duchesses were being disseminated throughout Petersburg.

Only from the File has it at last become clear to whom the tsarina was obliged for that dissemination.

The Tibetan Physician Again

The File, the testimony of Badmaev: 'I treated the holy fool Mitya Kozelsky for a pulmonary catarrh for about two years . . . Mitya impressed me as an intelligent religious peasant.'

When the scandal broke, Badmaev, that dangerous man, immediately grasped how much might be derived from the situation. And at the height of the scandal he made friends through Mitya with Iliodor and Hermogen.

At the time Hermogen and Iliodor had still made no move to leave the capital. Alix was in a rage. The minister of internal affairs was ordered to convey the obstreperous pastors to their places of exile under a political police escort. But the minister, A. A. Makarov, realized that this should not be attempted. The pastors' arrest would immediately turn them into heroes in the eyes of society. And the approaching session of the Duma already promised a great scandal. But Alix did not want to think about society. She wanted justice. As Marie Antoinette had once wanted it.

Badmaev understood that his hour had come to rescue the hapless minister Makarov. And to spare Grigory future shocks. And everyone would be grateful to him.

It was then that Iliodor suddenly vanished. To the joy and relief of the minister of internal affairs. Now the monk could be searched for and reports about the search be sent to the tsarina.

What really happened was that Badmaev had suggested to Iliodor that he hide out at his dacha. And, as Badmaev testified in the File, 'Iliodor came to me at night.' At the same time Badmaev 'provided Hermogen with a medical document certifying that he was suffering from an intestinal catarrh and that he would unavoidably have to remain in Petersburg for a while'. Both rebellious pastors now had complete faith in Badmaev. And he succeeded in reading what Petersburg had been whispering about.

From Badmaev's testimony in the File: 'Hermogen read me a manuscript of Iliodor's called "Grishka".' And he added the following: 'On the basis of letters from the tsarina personally given to Iliodor by Rasputin, they were convinced that Rasputin was sleeping with the tsarina.'

And Badmaev went into action.

The 'cunning Chinaman' laid out the whole intrigue in the File. First he approached the government and offered to save the situation. He promised to persuade Iliodor and Hermogen 'to set off for their places of exile without excesses'. And at the same time he extracted a promise from Minister of Internal Affairs Makarov 'that Hermogen's departure into exile would take place in dignity, without guards, in a special car'. Makarov, pleased, agreed at once. 'And I took Hermogen to the station in my own motor car,' Badmaev testified in the File. After which a grateful Hermogen wrote to Iliodor, 'Go to Florischev Pustyn, and pay attention to what Pyotr Alexeevich tells you – he won't do anything bad to you.' And Iliodor, for whom Badmaev had arranged a separate compartment, also agreed to go into exile quietly, to Makarov's delight. The government was now in Badmaev's debt.

But he wanted the tsarina in his debt, too. And before Iliodor's departure, Badmaev asked him for the originals of the tsarina's and grand duchesses' letters. As he explained to Iliodor, 'I intend to petition for your return from exile, and I ask you to forward the original letters to me . . . so that I may be convinced of the justice of your words' (that is regarding the tsarina's relations with Rasputin). 'Iliodor agreed, and told me to send someone to Florischev Pustyn to get them.' And two weeks later Badmaev's messenger arrived. But apparently having changed his mind, Iliodor 'substituted copies' in full view of the messenger.

But even though Badmaev did not have the originals, he did have Iliodor's manuscript and copies of the tsarina's and grand duchesses' letters. He could now make his play.

At the time Badmaev had also begun to make friends with Rasputin. Since there was now a pretext: he had done him a great service by sending both his mutinous enemies into exile. But he would have to be very cautious about meeting Rasputin. For he had discovered something new from his patients: security agents were now following Rasputin relentlessly.

A Chronicle Of His Life

It had come to pass at the beginning of 1912. What Stolypin had been unsuccessful in doing was done by the new minister of internal affairs, Makarov. 'A second surveillance of Rasputin was established at the order of Minister of Internal Affairs Makarov on 23 January 1912.'

The tsar had been forced to go along with it. After Rasputin's experience with Hermogen and Iliodor, it really had become necessary to protect him. And they explained to the peasant that his enemies might simply lie in wait for him, and beat, maim or even kill him! That was why they were guarding him. 'Thrash, maim, and kill' were things the peasant understood very well.

Rasputin was given the code name 'Russian' in the agents' reports, thus underlining his image as a simple *Russian* peasant, an image so dear to the 'tsars'' hearts.

Thus was begun a remarkable chronicle of his life. Now we shall know everything about him. Literally every step of his is reflected in the reports of the external surveillance agents who hurried after him.

The Department of Police summarized the daily reports of its agents. 'On this visit to Petersburg, he is living on Kiroch Street in the apartment occupied by the publisher of the magazine *The Russian Economist*, Georgy Petrovich Sazonov, and his wife, Maria Alexandrovna, with whom Rasputin is apparently involved in amorous relations.' He had only to emerge from his building and agents would doggedly follow the unprepossessing bearded fellow in the peasant coat. '24 January 1912. The Russian (who lives at 12 Kiroch Street) went to the store at 10:15,' an agent reported. 'After four or five minutes he emerged carrying what appeared to be a bottle of wine. Then he set off in the direction of the Moika quay . . . At 4:00 p.m. the surveillance was transferred to the second shift.' And that shift followed him no less doggedly.

'There is an almost daily visit by Rasputin to the apartment of the Golovins, Munya and her mother,' an agent reports. He usually arrived at the Golovins' between two and three o'clock. Zinaida Manshtedt and Yulia Dehn would at that time gather there, as well. 'He spent the entire afternoon in the company of the named women.'

The Golovins' home was typical of the old Petersburg impoverished aristocracy.

'I liked to visit that rather dark, mysterious old home. I liked the coolness of its large rooms and its prim, old-fashioned furniture,' Zhukovskaya recalled. 'Munya . . . in her unvarying grey knitted cardigan. Light-coloured locks from her carelessly done hair fell onto her prominent forehead. As always, she greeted me with a welcoming smile . . . Her attitude towards Rasputin was not worship before holiness but a kind of blind faith.' She asked herself, 'How could a prim family like the Golovins, raised according to the strict rules of an earlier narrow morality, not merely reconcile themselves to Rasputin's unbridled behaviour but even pretend not to notice, or in fact not notice, anything of what went on around him?' And as the grand dukes also asked themselves, thinking about the royal family.

The Devotees In The Police Reports

Day after day the police recorded his life. And described the people in his circle. We have already come across a number of them. For example, Zinaida Manshtedt (or Manchtet), thirty-nine, the wife of a collegiate secretary. Five years earlier, in 1907, she had stayed in Rasputin's house in Pokrovskoe and had been interrogated by the Tobolsk Theological Consistory. Three years later, in 1910, this little blonde would go to Pokrovskoe with the royal nurse, Vishnyakova, who would see her on the train 'lying with the elder in her undergarments'.

But 'Yulia Alexandrovna von Dehn, the wife of Senior Captain Karl von Dehn', as she is identified by the police, had only recently made Rasputin's acquaintance. This very pretty young woman, a distant relative of Vyrubova's, had now become the second close friend of the tsarina, who called her Lili. Lili's husband was against her meeting the elder. But to become friends with the tsarina and not make the acquaintance of Our Friend was, of course, impossible. And when her son became ill, Lili called Rasputin.

In 1917 Lili was summoned before the Extraordinary Commission, where she gave the testimony that has survived in the File:

He arrived together with Lokhtina . . . His eyes were striking. Not only was their gaze penetrating but their placement was unusual: they were set deep within their sockets and their whites were somehow raised. The first thing I experienced when he came in was fear . . . It passed as soon as he started to talk to me in a very simple way. I took him to the nursery where my ailing son was asleep. Rasputin prayed over the sleeping child and then started shaking him, trying to wake him up. I got scared, since . . . I was afraid that the appearance of someone unknown might startle him. But, to my amazement, he . . . woke up saying 'uncle' and reached out to Rasputin. Rasputin held him in his arms a rather long time, and petted and stroked him, and talked to him the way one talks to children, and then laid him back down on the bed . . . The day after his visit the boy started to get better. That made an impression on me . . . I started going to see him two or three times a week, either at his place or at the Golovins' or Sazonovs'.

Frequently glimpsed in the agents' summaries for 1912 is the 'peasant woman from the Mogilyov Province, Gorodets District, Akilina Nikitichna Laptinskaya', one of the principal characters in Rasputin's story.

This very stout but still young high-bosomed woman had in 1907 stayed in Pokrovskoe along with the other 'ladies', and had been investigated by the Tobolsk Theological Consistory along with Lokhtina and Manshtedt. Akilina Laptinskaya testified at the time that she had been introduced to Rasputin at Olga Lokhtina's in 1905. And that as a nurse she had helped Lokhtina in what was then a time of illness.

But Rasputin had most probably known her even earlier.

Maria Golovina testifies in the File that 'Akilina Nikitichna Laptinskaya . . . used to live at the Verkhoturye Monastery . . . but then after some unpleasantness there she left to take part in the Japanese war as a nurse.' The Verkhoturye Monastery was a special monastery in Rasputin's life, the place where his transformation began. And most probably this woman, whom he trusted completely and almost blindly, entered his life during one of his visits to the monastery. And in the period when Rasputin was subject to drunkenness, Akilina would help him tame his flesh. And through the uncurtained windows of the kitchen the police agents would observe curious scenes involving the corpulent Akilina and Rasputin.

In 1912 Akilina left her former occupation of sister of mercy and entered service as a housekeeper in a private home. As it is stated in a Department of Police account, she served 'as housekeeper in the home of Nikolai Shepovalnikov, a medical doctor and the headmaster of a private preparatory school'. She was by then already becoming one of the main figures in Rasputin's circle. In the hierarchy of Rasputin's devotees, Laptinskaya was a close second to Vyrubova, Rasputin having begun to avoid the crazy and now ageing Lokhtina.

Akilina would soon embark on an extraordinary career.

'He would go on drives around the city in the Golovins' brougham or in motor taxis or, less often, in horse cabs hired by his devotees. He would appear all day long with one of the mentioned women (with Yu. Dehn, Z. Manchtet, or A. Laptinskaya . . . or with Maria Golovina or Sazonova),' the agents reported. But, finally, when he was left alone . . .

A Secret, Mysterious Life

From the testimony of the external surveillance agents: 'He rarely appeared outside alone . . . Whenever that happened, he would go off to a street where there were prostitutes, select one of them, and go to a hotel or a bathhouse.'

'Passing time with highly placed ladies has not ended his visits to prostitutes.'

'He hired a prostitute . . . on Haymarket Square.'

'He visited Anokhina's apartment with a woman . . . Anokhina, Feodosia rents her apartment for brief encounters.'

'Rasputin, walking down various streets, would accost women with vile suggestions, which the women would respond to with threats and sometimes would even spit on him.'

'He went to the Nevsky, hired the prostitute Petrova, and went to a bathhouse with her.'

Bathhouses very often figure in this unending pursuit of the female body. The baths in Pokrovskoe to which he had taken the 'little ladies', the baths in Petersburg to which he now took the 'little ladies' and prostitutes.

'The Russian visited the . . . family baths with Sazonov's wife (forty-three).'

'He visited the family baths on Konyushenny with a prostitute hired near Politseisky Bridge.'

'He went with the prostitute Anna Petrova to the same place.'

Sometimes Rasputin would hire prostitutes several times in the course of a single day. This indefatigability was scrupulously emphasized by the agents: 'he visited the baths *twice* with an unidentified prostitute.'

'From the prostitutes Botvinina and Kozlova . . . he went to the Golovins', left there around two o'clock, and *again* hired a prostitute and went to the baths with her.'

Noted along with this is the strange haste of his visits to the prostitutes. 'He was at the Ivanovsk Monastery with Zinaida Manchtet, the wife of a collegiate secretary, and then he went to Goncharnaya, met a prostitute, and went with her to a hotel, where he stayed for twenty minutes.'

On another occasion, again after seeing Zinaida Manshtedt, where he spent an hour and a half, 'the Russian, with an unknown woman, possibly a prostitute, visited the house [the address is given], and came out again twenty minutes later.'

'Maria Sazonova remained with him for two hours . . . after which he hired a prostitute and went with her to her apartment, from which he soon emerged again.'

Such were the features of that rather strange sex life led by Rasputin as caught by the *external* surveillance agents.

Only once did the tireless agents succeed in establishing just what went on *inside*, that is, behind the doors of the apartments of the daughters of joy. And the result was most mysterious. After approaching a prostitute, 'Rasputin bought her two bottles of beer, but did not drink himself . . . asked her to undress, looked at her body, and left.'

We shall take note of that agent's testimony.

And another observation, also useful for subsequent reflection: 'The Russian, while walking alone, talks to himself and waves his arms and slaps himself on the body, thereby attracting the attention of passers-by.'

He conducted that strange conversation with himself after leaving each prostitute.

'A Truth Beyond Our Comprehension'

Maria Golovina had been corresponding all these years with her 'beloved brother' Felix Yusupov. Felix was then living in England at Oxford University, where the young Anglophile was receiving his education. Although, as Yusupov himself accurately put it, 'studying was never my strength'. He spent much of his time at Oxford amusing himself. He found brilliant company in such Oxford students of the day as the future regent of Yugoslavia, Prince Karageorgievich, King Manuel of Portugal, a Greek prince, and various other titled young gentlemen. And that merry company read in amazement in the English newspapers about the scabrous adventures of the 'medieval elder' so beloved of the Russian court.

So Golovina soon received a mocking letter from Felix in which he recalled their meeting with Rasputin and wondered why the newspapers were all devoting so much attention to holy Grigory's indecent behaviour.

Felix kept Maria's enigmatic and lofty reply in his archive.

14 February 1912. In whatever century people who reveal another life have appeared, they have always been hunted down and persecuted, like all who have followed in Christ's footsteps. You know and have seen him too little

to understand his personality and the power that rules him, but I have known him for two years now and am certain that he bears God's Cross and suffers for a truth beyond our comprehension. And if you have any familiarity with occultism, then you know that everything great is hidden beneath a kind of shell that for the profane closes the way to the truth.

In this way did she try to give him an inkling of a truth that was comprehensible only to initiates.

At the time rumours were circulating in society about the young Prince Yusupov's imminent return in connection with an impending and brilliant marriage. And Maria was beginning to dream of a meeting between her 'brother Felix' and Father Grigory.

The Magnificent Couple

The Crimea. The last powerful Tartar khanate had held dominion there, and then the divine peninsula had been ruled by the Yusupovs' ancestors. Now along the sea there stretched a band of golden sand. And above the sea stood the royal family's white palace of Livadia and the palaces of the grand dukes and the Crimean palace of the Yusupov family.

All through 1911 and the beginning of 1912 Felix had been receiving letters in Oxford from his mother, who had remained in the (for her) therapeutic climate of the Crimea. The 'neighbours' (as the royal family is referred to in those letters) had not forgotten the Yusupovs.

'31 May 1911. Our neighbours have moved back to Petersburg. On the day of their departure I received a touching letter and a bouquet of lilies in farewell.'

And on her name-day Felix's mother received an unexpected gift from the 'neighbours'.

'14 October 1911. Suddenly Alexei [a servant] ceremoniously enters and announces, "The Sovereign Emperor!" I thought my guests were going to have conniptions . . . I was terribly touched by that attention and had not expected such a present on my name-day . . . The empress continues to feel unwell and does not go out.'

Yes, Alix had not come to see her. And the reason was not illness. Rather it was Zinaida Yusupova's close friendship with Elizaveta Fyodorovna and her attitude toward Our Friend.

But the tsar, grand duchesses and Alexei did come to see her. And not just once. And Zinaida joyfully wrote about it to Felix. For those visits were proof that what had been planned would soon take place. This was a wedding that would make the Yusupovs relatives of the royal family. Irina, the daughter of Grand Duke Alexander Mikhailovich (Sandro), and the tsar's sister Xenia, had fallen in love with Felix. And Zinaida had in her son's absence made great efforts to bring the brilliant marriage about.

Zinaida, as Sandro wrote in his memoirs, 'was the mad passion of my early youth'. And he had not forgotten how 'his heart had ached' a mere nine years before at the 'historical' balls, when dressed in a golden boyar's kirtle he had danced 'all the dances' with the beauty. And Zinaida was aware of her power over Sandro.

'15 November. I am going to tea at Ai-Tudor [Sandro's estate],' Zinaida wrote. 'Irina was astonishingly beautiful.' (A valuable compliment coming from her.) '[Her parents] asked about you, when you would be graduating from Oxford.'

This was a summons. And Felix got ready to return to Russia.

The 'Cunning Chinaman's' Intrigue

And so, warned by his patient Kurlov of the surveillance of the peasant, Badmaev tried not to 'shine' in the police reports. He met Rasputin at that time at the apartments of third parties. This was not difficult, since Badmaev doctored all of Petersburg.

'He produced a good impression on me of an intelligent, though rather simple peasant,' Badmaev testified in the File. 'That barely literate peasant had a good knowledge of Holy Scripture.'

'Intelligent and interesting.'

'A simple peasant, uneducated, but understands things better than the educated do.'

In this delighted way did Badmaev speak of Rasputin. But later, after he and Badmaev had become close friends, Rasputin would announce with a grin, 'The Chinaman could deceive even the devil himself.'

It was then, at the start of his friendship with Rasputin, that Badmaev passed on to the Duma Iliodor's anti-Rasputin pamphlet 'Grishka'.

The Mystery Of The Tsarina's Letter

Printed in 'Grishka', which would later serve as the basis of Iliodor's famous book *A Holy Devil*, were the letters he had purloined from Rasputin, the letters from the tsarina and the grand duchesses. If the letters from the grand duchesses were of no particular interest, the letter from Alix was explosive.

'My beloved and unforgettable teacher, saviour, and mentor,' the letter began.

How wearisome it is for me without you . . . I am calm in my soul, I am able to rest, only when you, teacher, are sitting next to me, and I am kissing your hands and resting my head on your blessed shoulders. Oh, how easy is it for me then. I wish only one thing then: to fall asleep, to fall asleep forever on your shoulders, in your embrace. Oh, what happiness it is even to feel your presence near me. Where are you? Where have you flown? It is so hard, and what anguish there is in my heart . . . Only do not, my beloved mentor, tell Anya about my sufferings without you. Anya is kind, she is good, she loves me, but do not reveal my sorrow to her. Will you soon be back by my side? Come back soon. I wait for you and am in torment without you. I entreat your holy blessing and kiss your blessed hands. She who loves you for ever, M[ama].

The letter has been little used by historians; they have not believed in it. And Badmaev, the man who had passed Iliodor's 'Grishka' to the Duma, did not himself have the original. So perhaps there was no letter from the tsarina, after all?

But the original was soon found. The police, according to an Extraordinary Commission inquiry, tracked down a certain Madame Karbovich, one of Iliodor's followers, with whom he had left the letters for safe keeping. A search of her premises was conducted by officers of the Department of Police, and the originals of the tsarina's and grand duchesses' letters were confiscated.

And, as Kokovtsev writes in his memoirs, 'Makarov gave me the letters to read . . . There was a comparatively long one from the empress, which had been reproduced with complete accuracy in the copy distributed by Guchkov' [Speaker of the Duma].

Prime Minister Kokovtsev recalled that Makarov 'did not know what to do with it, and indicated his intention of passing it on to the sovereign . . . I objected that by doing so he would place the sovereign in an awkward position and acquire in the empress an implacable enemy . . . I recommended that he hand the letters over to the empress directly.'

But Makarov apparently also misinterpreted the contents of the letter. And believed that if the tsar read such a letter, it would be the end of the tsarina. And, as Kokovtsev recalled, Makarov handed the envelope containing the letters to the sovereign. As Makarov himself told Kokovtsev, the sovereign 'turned pale, removed the empress's letter from the envelope, glanced at her handwriting, and said, "Yes, the letter is genuine," and then opening a desk drawer, he flung the letter into it in an abrupt and for him uncustomary manner'.

'Your dismissal is assured,' Kokovtsev told Makarov after his story.

Vyrubova confirms all this in her testimony, too: 'The minister of internal affairs personally brought the originals of the letters to the sovereign. I myself saw the letters brought by Makarov and can affirm that they were originals and not copies.'

And in the File, Vyrubova adds that Minister of Internal Affairs Makarov 'provoked the tsarina's rage by not giving the Rasputin letter to her'.

In fact, the tsarina herself certified the authenticity of her letter. On 17 September 1915, she wrote to the tsar about her enemies that 'they are no better than Makarov, who showed outsiders my letter to Our Friend.'

The tsar could not have failed to understand Makarov's ulterior motive in giving the letters to him. And the tsarina should have been furious with him. Makarov ought to have destroyed the letters. And announced to all the scoundrels who were interfering in the personal life of their family that there were no letters, that they simply did not exist. But Makarov had done none of that.

All the same, just how had her letter reached Guchkov? Was it really true, as Alix believed, that it had come from Makarov, that he had shown it to 'outsiders'?

Of course the minister was not at fault, as the File proves.

Once the tsar had been given the letters, there was nothing at all that Badmaev could count on in the way of gratitude from Alix. Realizing that none would be forthcoming, the 'cunning Chinaman' decided to obtain the gratitude of her enemies.

From Badmaev's testimony in the File: 'After reading the copies of the letters, I was convinced that they contained no evidence whatever that the tsarina was sleeping with Rasputin.'

As an experienced doctor, he readily grasped that it was merely a letter by a woman who, tormented by the illness of her son and by terrible foreboding, was pleading for release from her sufferings. And that this was her 'sorrow'. And that only Rasputin was capable of relieving her attacks of acute neurasthenia. At the same time, she had been trying to write in a way that would be meaningful to the elder – to write in his own lofty, love-filled idiom.

But as Prime Minister Kokovtsev justly observed after reading the letter, 'the separate parts and expressions in the tsarina's letter that were essentially a manifestation of her mystical tendencies provided a pretext for the most disgraceful gossip.' So Badmaev understood perfectly well how her enemies would read the letter. And how grateful they would be to him for the opportunity.

And he decided to render the Duma an unforgettable service. He secretly acquainted Protopopov, the Deputy Speaker of the State Duma, with Iliodor's manuscript.

From Badmaev's testimony in the File: 'Protopopov asked me for permission to familiarize Guchkov and Rodzyanko with it. He pledged not to use it but violated his pledge.'

And then, as Kokovtsev recalled, 'they started distributing around the city hectographic copies of four or five letters to Rasputin, one from Empress Alexandra Fyodorovna and the others from the grand duchesses.'

Thus did Guchkov exploit the letter. One can imagine his astonishment and rage upon reading Iliodor's lampoon and the tsarina's letter. Stolypin's murder, Iliodor's manuscript, and the newspaper articles about the influence of the semi-literate peasant *Khlyst* were, for him, all interwoven in a single picture of the collapse of power.

The easily enraged Guchkov was seething. It was then that he learned of other new evidence against Rasputin that overshadowed everything that had gone before. It was in Mikhail Novosyolov's latest denunciatory article.

In it Novosyolov branded Rasputin in the imprecatory style of the ancient Orthodox pastors. 'Indignant words involuntarily burst from the breasts of Orthodox Russian people in regard to . . . the vile corrupter of human souls and bodies, Grigory Rasputin.' And he asked the Most Holy Synod how long they were going to tolerate that 'sex maniac . . . *Khlyst* . . . and charlatan . . . and the criminal comedy that has victimized many whose letters were in his hands.'

As a supplement to the article, Novosyolov sent Guchkov a disturbing pamphlet called 'Rasputin and Mystical Debauchery'. Reprinted in it were Novosyolov's own 1910 articles against Rasputin and something named 'The Confession of N'. Everyone who knew Rasputin could easily recognize in the confession's anonymous author the unfortunate Berladskaya, who not so very long ago had told church investigators in a Tobolsk inquiry how Rasputin had sustained her spiritually, how he had literally saved her life after her husband's suicide. Now she was telling an entirely different story.

Mystical Debauchery

Berladskaya's tragedy began, as she stated in the 'Confession', when she learned that her husband was deceiving her. She left him along with the children and 'initiated a divorce proceeding'. Her husband committed suicide. She blamed herself for his death and no longer wished to live. 'An acquaintance offered in conversation to introduce me to a certain "peasant who can soothe the soul and speak of what is hidden".'

Rasputin was able to soothe her and help her out of her stupor, and he introduced her to his disciples, who strengthened her 'conviction of his holiness'. 'I tried to submit in everything, and when my heart rose up with its "Don't" and "I don't want to," or the onus was on me to "do penances" and my heart was not wholly in it, I would fight it, insisting that it was beyond my understanding, that it was all new, and that his words were a sacred law and not for me to argue with.' And then his caressing began. 'Sometimes his caresses oppressed me – the constant hugging and kissing and wish to kiss on the lips. I saw it more as a test of forbearance and was glad when it was over.'

It all happened after they set out for Pokrovskoe with her small son.

> We were on our way, Grigory, one nurse, and my son and I. In the evening after everyone had retired (O Lord, what must You hear!), he climbed down from his berth and lay down beside me and began stroking me hard and kissing me and saying the most tender words and asking, 'Will you marry me?' I replied, 'If necessary.' I was completely in his power and believed that my soul would be saved only through him, however that might be expressed. I regarded it all – the kisses, the words, the passionate glances – as a test of the purity of my love for him, and I recalled the words of one of his disciples about a troubling test, a very grave one. Lord, help me! Suddenly he suggested that we tempt ourselves in sinful love . . . I was certain he was testing me, and was himself pure. (O Lord, help me to write everything.) He forced me to ready myself . . . and began to perform what is possible for a husband . . . threatening violence over me, fondling me, kissing me, and so on . . . forcing me to lie still without resisting. O holy Lord and Master!

Following this she sets out Rasputin's remarkable views on 'sin', which he tried to explain to her. I shall omit those views for the time being, returning to them when we at last move on to the chief mystery, his teaching.

After receiving the article and pamphlet, Guchkov played them like a musical score. Novosyolov's article was published in the newspaper the *Voice of Moscow.* And since Prime Minister Kokovtsev and Minister Makarov had already had occasion to listen to displeased speeches from the tsar in regard to Rasputin, the newspaper and the copies of the pamphlet later found during a police search were confiscated at once.

Guchkov could now take action.

Rebellion In The Duma

Just as Guchkov had anticipated when he heard about the confiscation of the publications exposing the peasant-favourite's debauchery, the entire Duma exploded. And then, to the deputies' delight, Guchkov introduced a resolution of 'urgent inquiry to the government in respect to the unlawfulness of its demand that the press publish no articles about Rasputin'.

The resolution was passed by an unprecedented majority (one vote against). Rasputin had thus united for the first time the mutually hostile right and left. Moreover, the proscribed article was quoted in full in the Duma's resolution! And the tsar now had to accept in the form of a Duma resolution of inquiry the most terrible accusations against someone loved by his family.

What must Alix's view of the publication have been? It was the second account by one of Rasputin's faithful followers of the sinful exploits of the 'Man of God'. First Vishnyakova, and now Berladskaya. Could she really fail to believe it as she had done the first time? Or did she know something that gave her an entirely different explanation for what had taken place?

And so, Novosyolov's compilation was confiscated. But as so often happens in Russia, both the holographic copies of the manuscript and the surviving printed copies were sold out in both capitals. And, as Rodzyanko later recalled, they went for fabulous sums.

After Guchkov's resolution of inquiry, a veritable flood of newspaper publications about the elder commenced. As a form of protest 'against the unlawful stifling of the press', newspapers all over Russia joined in describing the adventures of Our Friend, often making them up. The censor confiscated the issues, the publishers happily paid the fines, readers chased down the confiscated newspapers, and circulation grew.

Rasputin's name had become a common noun.

From the diary of Grand Duchess Xenia for 25 January: 'How will it all end? It's terrible!'

From the diary of the general's wife Bogdanovich: '18 February 1912.

There has been no more shameful time. Russia is now ruled not by the tsar but by that rascal Rasputin . . . Rasputin has been complaining that the press has been attacking him and that he is ready to go, but that "his people" need him here.' By 'his people' he meant the royal family.

'22 February. All Petersburg is in a state about the way this Rasputin is carrying on in Tsarskoe Selo. He can, sad to say, do whatever he wants with the tsarina!!!!'

'Don't Make It Too Painful For Him'

Mikhail Rodzyanko, the newly-elected Speaker of the State Duma, believed that Guchkov's resolution of inquiry had left the supreme authority no choice but to resolve the Rasputin matter. And he had in advance started preparing his report to the tsar.

But he first had to talk to the dowager empress. She was horrified by what she had read in the newspapers. And she summoned Rodzyanko.

He was led into the old empress's little study. She immediately asked about Guchkov's resolution. In his memoirs Rodzyanko describes explaining to her that the resolution was supposed to 'put minds at ease', 'since the talk about Rasputin had gone too far in society'. But the widow of Alexander III had already grasped that Rasputin was the awful instrument by which they had decided to topple the monarchy. As Kerensky later put it, 'without Rasputin there would have been no Lenin.'

And Rodzyanko told her all about Rasputin's debaucheries. She listened without a word. And then, as they were parting, she suddenly said, 'I have heard that you mean to speak to the sovereign about this. Don't do that. He is too pure of heart to believe in evil.'

She knew her son's character. If he was pressured, he would become extremely stubborn. And would remember that he was the autocrat. He who could no longer be any such thing. For Stolypin, the last person able to protect her son from all those mad talkers, was gone. And, on parting with Rodzyanko, she begged that fat man who understood her son so poorly, 'Don't make it too painful for him.'

On 13 February, the dowager empress summoned Prime Minister Kokovtsev for a visit.

'The conversation, which lasted an hour and a half, was completely given over to Rasputin,' Kokovtsev wrote in his memoirs.

After that she went to see Nicky and Alix.

From Nicholas's diary: '15 February. Mama came for tea; we had a conversation with her about Grigory.'

Xenia's diary for 16 February: 'Mama is so pleased that she said everything . . . Alix defended Rasputin, saying he was a remarkable man and Mama should meet him . . . Mama merely advised them to let him go now while the Duma was still waiting for an answer . . . Alix declared that it was wrong to yield . . . But that they were still very grateful to Mama for having spoken so frankly. And she even kissed Mama's hand.'

So Nicky's mother could repeat to herself what she had said two days earlier to Prime Minister Kokovtsev: 'My unhappy daughter-in-law is incapable of realizing that she is bringing about her own downfall and that of the dynasty . . . She deeply believes in the holiness of that dubious individual.'

But the tsar did follow his mother's advice. As was his custom whenever a scandal flared up around Rasputin, he decided it would be better for Father Grigory to go back to Pokrovskoe for a while.

'18 Feb. 1912. He departed from the Nikolaev Station,' the secret agents recorded. 'Winter Woman, Bird, Summer Woman, Dove, and Owl accompanied him to the station, along with some fifteen other unidentified people of both sexes.'

All of Rasputin's permanent devotees had now been given nicknames of their own in the agents' reports. And they had been conferred with a policeman's sense of the picturesque. Akilina Laptinskaya (thirty-two) was named 'Owl' for her staid, thrifty quality. Pretty little Zina Manshtedt, who still looked like a girl despite her thirty-seven years, was called 'Dove'. Mother Golovina (fifty-two) was called 'Winter Woman', since she was no longer young and lived on the Winter Canal. Her daughter Munya with her clear eyes was 'Bird', and Sazonov's dark-haired, dark-eyed wife was 'Crow'. But Vyrubova, thanks to her closeness to the 'personages', was spared a cognomen.

The agents followed Rasputin onto the train and reported that 'On the 22nd he arrived in Tyumen and was met by his wife and daughter, who were very glad to see him.'

The peasant wrote to the 'tsars' from Pokrovskoe about Guchkov's resolution. The letter to Tsarskoe Selo is preserved in Lokhtina's diary. 'Dearest Papa and Mama! Now the accursed demon gains strength. And the Duma serves him; there are a lot of lutioners [revolutionaries] and Yids in it. What do they care? They'd just as soon see the end of God's anointed and down with him. And Guchkov, their lord . . . slanders and makes a discord with his resolutions. Papa, the Duma is yours, whatever you want to do, do it. Nobody needs these resolutions of inquiry.'

A Report By The Fattest Man
In Russia

On 28 February, 'armed with documents', that is, with Novosyolov's pamphlet, the 'fat man Rodzyanko' (as he was known in Tsarskoe Selo) set off with his report to the tsar. The Speaker of the Duma began by touching on the perpetually bad administration of the Caucasus. And then he at last turned to the main issue. Rodzyanko brought to the tsar's attention the 'universal indignation accompanying the discovery that Rasputin is a *Khlyst*.'

'What makes you think he is a *Khlyst*?' the tsar asked.

Rodzyanko declared that the police had determined that he went to bathhouses with women.

'Well, what of it? That is accepted among the common people.'

And then Rodzyanko started talking about Novosyolov's pamphlet, about the Tobolsk investigation, about the letters and confessions of Rasputin's victims, about the general's wife L. whom Rasputin had driven mad, about the 'rejoicings' that had taken place in Sazonov's apartment where Rasputin was staying, and, finally, about the baneful influence Rasputin might have on the soul of the heir.

'Have you read Stolypin's report?' the tsar asked him.

'No, I know about it, but I have not read it.'

'I rejected it,' the tsar said.

It seemed to the naive Rodzyanko that the tsar regretted having done so. He did not understand that the tsar was trying to say that Rodzyanko was not telling him anything new, that he had heard it all before. The tsar could only snort to himself. He knew there had been no 'rejoicings' whatever at Sazonov's apartment, that the general's wife L. was Lokhtina, who only seemed to be mad because she had left the world of vanity behind and chosen a new life, and that there was no firm evidence in the Tobolsk file that Rasputin was a *Khlyst*.

And the tsar suggested to Rodzyanko that he obtain the Tobolsk file from the Synod and study it. Rodzyanko was happy: it seemed to him that he had won. After which the tsar presented him to the heir. Rodzyanko playfully introduced himself to the boy as 'the largest, fattest man in Russia'. And the boy, 'that remarkably sweet child', told him how he was collecting money for charitable causes, how 'he had stood all day with a cup and had collected a whole fifty roubles'.

The fat man decided he had been shown the child as a mark of the highest trust.

But the tsar had really shown him the heir so that he would understand that the boy's soul was pure. Because Our Friend had taught him to love and serve his neighbours.

Rodzyanko enthusiastically got started on his inquiry the very next day. 'I had been instructed to obtain the file from the Most Holy Synod, to examine it, and then to report my opinion of Rasputin. Damansky, the deputy chief procurator, brought me the file.'

Damansky, a pitiful Synod clerk and son of a Siberian clergyman, had become Rasputin's friend and been another of his opponents at the Synod. Rasputin had stayed with him at his home, so Sabler was forced to take on Damansky as deputy chief-procurator.

So Alix immediately learned from Damansky that Rodzyanko had been given the Tobolsk file. And it worried her. There was no direct evidence whatever, but she understood how Rasputin's enemies could use the indirect kind.

And as Rodzyanko recalled, Damansky

telephoned me the next day and asked me to receive him. As soon as he arrived he announced, 'I've come to ask you to give me back the secret file on Rasputin.'

'Is it by imperial order?'

'No, but a very highly placed person makes this request. The empress.'

'Please convey to the empress that she is as much a servant of the tsar, her husband, as I am.'

'Your excellency, I have brought with me the religious instructor of the emperor's children.'

This turned out to be the archpriest Vasiliev. He started telling me, 'You have no idea what an excellent person Rasputin is . . .' I flew into a rage. 'You have come here to praise a debauched scoundrel and *Khlyst*! Get out of my office!'

But the Duma's resolution of inquiry had only been the start of Guchkov's game. And on 9 March 1912, an incisive continuation followed. When the matter of the Synod's budget came up, Guchkov rose to his feet. He gave the celebrated speech against Rasputin with which any account of the dynasty's fall ought to begin.

The Clock Of Revolution Had Begun
To Tick

He spoke of the tragedy that had befallen the country. 'At its centre is an enigmatic, tragicomic figure, a kind of ghost or relic of age-old ignorance.'

Stolypin, the rock that had shored up the dynasty, was no more. And that is why that speech rang out, and with it Guchkov's audacious question, one that would have been inconceivable a year earlier when Stolypin was still alive: 'By what avenues has this man achieved his central position? By having seized such influence that even the supreme bearers of state and church power bow down before it! . . . Just think who is lording it at the summit!'

The tsar was in a fury; he had been denigrated in relation to Alix. As Guchkov later told the Extraordinary Commission, 'It was conveyed to me by one of the ministers that the emperor had declared, "Hanging Guchkov would not be good enough!" I replied, "My life belongs to my sovereign, but my conscience does not, and I shall continue to struggle."'

And then Badmaev, as the File makes clear, deftly made a play to the other side. In case the source of Guchkov's information came to light in Tsarskoe Selo.

From Badmaev's testimony: 'I sent a telegram to Rodzyanko: "What are you gentlemen in the Duma doing? Can one actually rely on the evidence of the aggrieved Iliodor?" Rodzyanko answered that he himself was troubled, and that Guchkov had given his speech impromptu, without warning anyone.'

Rodzyanko was troubled because now the tsar's pride had been wounded, had been insulted. Now it would be impossible to talk to him about Rasputin at all.

After Guchkov's speech, Felix's mother, Zinaida Yusupova, tried at the request of her friend Ella – the Grand Duchess Elizaveta Fyodorovna – to talk to the tsarina about Rasputin. Her 'Crimean estate neighbour' retorted that 'Guchkov and Rodzyanko ought to be hanged.'

Rodzyanko had by then finished preparing his report for the tsar on the Tobolsk file, wherein, naturally, he triumphantly stated that Rasputin's guilt was proved. The tsar returned to Prime Minister Kokovtsev Rodzyanko's request for an audience with the instruction, 'The Duma's behaviour is deeply disgraceful. I do not wish to receive Rodzyanko.' As he was leaving for the south, the tsar told Kokovtsev, 'I am simply suffocating in this atmosphere of gossip, falsehood, and malice. I shall try to postpone my return from the Crimea as long as possible.'

Ahead was his train and the white palace in Livadia.

From Bogdanovich's diary for 14 March: 'The entire royal family is leaving for the Crimea tomorrow, and Rasputin is to go with them. It is sad to write what sort of taste the tsarina must have if she tolerates that *Khlyst*.'

The empress walked across the railway platform without saying goodbye to those who had come to see off the royal family. The tsar was sombre. He was very tired of the whole story.

Rasputin had in fact been summoned from Pokrovskoe to the Crimea. But Alix had not done this herself. Her Friend had sent Rasputin a telegram in code without a signature. Alix had proved to them that the Russian tsarina's will was greater than the dishonest judgments of society.

A Blessing On Madness

Prior to his summons, the peasant had been living the slow life of the village in Pokrovskoe. But that life was destroyed by the arrival of the insane general's wife. Lokhtina had walked to Pokrovskoe barefoot, living on alms. The former Petersburg arbiter of fashion was frightfully dressed in a strange shapeless white garment hung with ribbons and little icons. Followed by the villagers' astonished gazes, she walked through the village, shouting 'Christ is risen!' Even though Easter was still a good way off.

The story of her 'madness' had survived in the File.

The previous year, 1911, Lokhtina, driven out of her family, had gone to Tsaritsyn.

From the testimony of Maria Golovina:

She returned barefoot from Tsaritsyn dressed in a white nun's habit. It was then that I made the acquaintance of Iliodor, who expressed the view that Lokhtina had reached such lofty heights in her spiritual life that she could be blessed as a holy fool (that is, as someone who feigns madness in Christ's name). Iliodor even wanted in that regard to conduct a prayer service in our home to bless Lokhtina as a holy fool. But my mother was categorically opposed to it. Nevertheless, Lokhtina, on hearing that opinion of Iliodor's, abruptly changed her behaviour and started to act like a holy fool . . . They not only stopped letting her into her apartment in Petersburg but also onto her own estate in the Kazan province that she had conveyed to her daughter as a gift . . . She lived exclusively by alms.

Now Lokhtina lived like some Russian King Lear in a skirt. The newspapers wrote a great deal about Rasputin's having driven the unhappy general's wife out of her mind. As Golovina later testified, 'Lokhtina's behaviour raised the fear that she might hurt Father Grigory.' And Rasputin forbade her to act like a holy fool. Lokhtina obeyed him. But Father Grigory's main struggle was with her constant shouting that 'Christ is risen.' But she continued to shout it. He became so angry about the shout that it was as if he were afraid of something. And he would mercilessly beat her for it.

Yet during all this the mad general's wife continued to retain a kind of strange power over the peasant. And not only over him, but also over Vyrubova and even over the 'tsars', to whom she would occasionally dare to send sharp or even wrathful telegrams. Moreover, Munya Golovina would respectfully kiss her hand.

It was at the beginning of March 1912 that Lokhtina came to visit Rasputin in his beloved Pokrovskoe. After again driving Rasputin into a rage with her customary 'Christ is risen,' she presented herself to him at his lodge. But this time the cruellest of blows was waiting for the general's wife in Pokrovskoe. She learned of something irreparable – the rupture between Iliodor and Rasputin. 'Christ' and the 'Lord of hosts' had become enemies. Her universe was destroyed. 'Lokhtina, who worshipped both Iliodor and Rasputin, tried to reconcile them, but she failed to do so, and it had a grave effect on her mental balance,' Munya testified in the File. It was on this visit that she became a victim of the break between them.

Rasputin's Angry Wife?

It happened in the middle of the day. The bizarre episode played itself out in front of Rasputin's astonished fellow villagers. They saw his wife drag the 'Petersburg lady' by the hair through the gate of the Rasputin house out onto the street. And right there on the street start beating the former Petersburg lioness.

And the beaten general's wife trudged down the street away from Rasputin's lodge.

It is from this episode that the famous legends about Rasputin's jealous wife derive, a wife who pulled ladies from her husband's bed and dragged them by the hair from her home. And that is how the simple villagers, who were not initiated into the secret world that began behind the gates of the Rasputin home, would have had to report it to the newspaper people.

An early photograph of Rasputin, probably at the family home in Pokrovskoe. Even out of focus he is immediately recognisable. The narrow face with a 'large, irregular nose, thick sensual lips, and a long beard'; the hair, as his daughter would write, was always 'parted down the middle and combed across his forehead to conceal an odd little bump reminiscent of a budding horn.'

A page from Rasputin's 'Diry', which was his semi-literate way of spelling 'Diary'. 'Our hero, who like all semi-literate peasants adored writing' – although he barely knew how to hold a pen – 'had managed only to note down a few reflections in his wretched scrawl. He had evidently used the term "diary" for its important sound, knowing that the tsar and tsarina kept diaries, too.'

Rasputin at Pokrovskoe: his wife Praskovia bore him three sons and two daughters, but 'more important was that she was a good worker. Working hands were very much needed in the Rasputin household, because Grigory himself was often absent visiting holy places.'

In this group, also at Pokrovskoe, the women's clothes suggest they are local. The woman to his left is probably his mother, Anna; the man on the second left his father, Efim.

The Rasputin home in Pokrovskoe. On the ground floor where he lived with his family, 'it was the usual arrangement of a peasant lodge'. But upstairs the once indigent peasant had attempted to arrange everything 'city fashion.' There was a piano, to which the visiting monk Feofan 'took indignant note of' as well as the gramophone that Rasputin 'so liked to dance to, and the claret-red plush armchairs, and the sofa and the desk. A chandelier was suspended from the ceiling, and placed around the room were several bentwood "Viennese" chairs, then in fashion. And there were two wide beds with soft springy mattresses and a divan. Two weight-clocks in ebony cabinets chimed majestically, and there was a wall clock and another cabinet clock. The monk was particularly outraged by the "large soft carpet covering the entire floor.".'

Father Ioann, archpriest
of the Kronstadt Cathedral,
was famous throughout Russia
for the gift of healing prayer.
He healed Rasputin's future
admirer, the young Anya
Vyrubova, as well as Zinaida
Yusupova, the mother of
Rasputin's future murderer.

The youthful Rasputin with the monks Iliodor (left), and
Hermogen, who was a fanatical opponent of the freethinking
that he was convinced was destroying Holy Rus. It was
Hermogen, who fought for strict interference by the church
in the ideological life of the country, who demanded the
excommunication of Tolstoy. At the time, Hermogen and
Rasputin liked each other. Rasputin's contempt for the
bloated church hierarchs was close to Hermogen's heart.

Hermogen introduced Rasputin to another exposer of evil,
a young monk whose ferocious speeches and denunciations
had made him famous as the Russian Savonarola. Iliodor,
ten years Rasputin's junior, was huge with a large, fleshy face,
high cheekbones, and tiny eyes, and looked more like a Volga
brigand than a pious monk.

Iliodor opened a new life to Rasputin, who had been used
to a dozen admirers, but now he saw crowds of fanatics and
took pleasure in their wild delight. As Rasputin later recalled,
'Iliodor would meet me with crowds of people and preach
about me and my life. I lived in harmony with him and
shared my impressions with him. . . .' In 1910, while he
was Rasputin's guest in Pokrovskoe, he stole from his friend
the letters from the tsarina and grand duchesses that Rasputin
had so trustingly shown him.

The 'important letter' was one from the tsarina not intended
for anyone else's eyes.

A rare photograph of Rasputin with Alix, her daughters, the heir Alexei and their nurse, Maria Vishnyakova. In 1908, when Alexei was not yet four, Rasputin's visits were usually in secret, arriving at Tsarskoe Selo as if to visit Maria Vishnyakova. This allowed him 'to avoid having his name written down in the lobby register, where all visits to the tsars were recorded. Once in the palace, he would drop by to see the nurse Maria Vishnyakova, a very nervous individual and at the time an ardent admirer of Rasputin. And then from the nurse's he would be escorted to the royal apartments.'

In St Petersburg in 1906 the tsar and tsarina, with a phalanx of grand dukes a few steps behind, walk to a sitting of the Duma.

On another state occasion, also in St Petersburg, the sovereign, on a horse with a golden coat, is escorted by the grand dukes also on horseback, and the tsarina with the dowager empress in a calash.

Sergei Witte, perhaps the most influential politician of Nicholas's reign, although he was only intermittently a minister and prime minister (1905–6). The tsarina hated him for creating the 1905 constitution that limited the tsar's powers and the future powers of her son – that had 'robbed the Little One' of his legacy. And however useful the brilliant prime minister might have been, she had never been able nor did she wish to overcome her feelings.

The monarchist Purishkevich, whose bald head and pointed moustache were as well-known throughout Russian from newspaper portraits as his right-wing views, was Rasputin's implacable enemy and in November 1916, 'heavily breathing, with a thundering voice', he spoke publicly of 'the tsar's ministers who have been turned into marionettes, marionettes whose threads have been taken firmly in hand by Rasputin and the Empress Alexandra'.

Alexander Guchkov, son of a wealthy Moscow merchant and one of the most brilliant and adventurous people in the Duma, had helped defend the Armenians during their slaughter by the Turks, had supported the Boers in Africa, and during the Russo-Japanese War, had been captured by the Japanese. He was well-known in the Duma for fist-fights during the sessions. On taking the post of Speaker in 1905, he spoke for the first time of certain mysterious 'dark forces' in the highest summits of society. Seven years later he distributed a private letter from the tsarina to Rasputin, which in the opinion of many was proof that the peasant was sleeping with the tsarina.

P. S. Stolypin, Prime Minister in 1909 was 'hated by the left, for he had more than a few times ruthlessly suppressed their opposition in the Duma, once uttering the immortal words, "You, gentlemen, require great upheavals, whereas I require a great Russia." He had categorically opposed Russia's participation in the Balkan conflict. He was hated by the right, for his reforms promised the victory of Russian capitalism: Moscow, the ancient 'Tsargrad,' was fated to become a Manchester. But Stolypin made a fatal move. A move that might at first have seemed quite auspicious and to even promise a return of popularity: he spoke out against Rasputin. He was, however, assassinated in 1911, in Kiev.

Four photographs of Rasputin taken between 1900 and 1916. His eyes attract, even in photographs, as witnesses testify: 'the instantly blazing, magnetic gaze of his light-coloured eyes in which not merely the pupil but the whole eye stares', 'the hypnotic power shining in his exceptional eyes', 'deep-set, unendurable eyes'. The number of fingers used to cross himself was important: 'Believers' used three fingers instead of two.

That version was also believed by the investigator of the Extraordinary Commission, with his biased interrogation of Lokhtina about her fight with Rasputin's wife 'out of jealousy'.

And in the File, Olga Lokhtina explained to the naive investigator that 'as far as jealousy is concerned, Rasputin's wife really was jealous of me (if it may be called jealousy) but not in regard to her husband but to Iliodor, whom I revered . . . As for a fight, there was one,' Lokhtina acknowledged and then explained.

Cast Out Of Heaven

Once when Rasputin and his family were visiting the home of a fellow villager, I dropped by the other person's lodge, and discovering there the great poverty of the hosts, started pleading with Father Grigory to give me a cow. I should say that when I get an idea into my head . . . I don't give up until what I have what I want. This took place in the presence of some recently arrived visitor, and I reproached Rasputin's wife for her stinginess [not Rasputin himself but his wife; he was above ordinary life and could only be asked about the eternal] . . . After Rasputin's visitor left, she started accusing me of denouncing her in front of an outsider, and grabbed me by the hair . . . and struck me.

But the simple investigator was disinclined to believe her. He did not understand that the special relations between Rasputin's wife and his devotees precluded jealousy.

Those relations are in fact described in the testimony given before the Extraordinary Commission by the government official B. Alexeev, one of Rasputin's devotees. During a visit by Alexeev and his wife to Pokrovskoe, the two wives were walking through the house. And they came upon a risqué scene involving Father Grigory. Alexeev's wife 'gasped and turned away. And then Rasputin's wife explained, "Each must bear his cross, and that is his."' So that Lokhtina was telling the truth: jealousy had no place here. But she too had failed to grasp the reason for the behaviour of Rasputin's wife. A Russian peasant woman could not, of course, give away a cow. And an accusation of stinginess in that regard would have seemed merely ridiculous to her. She beat Lokhtina for quite a different reason. The idea that Lokhtina herself subsequently recounted to the investigator, that she had 'decided to remain true to both of them, to both Rasputin and to Iliodor', apparently frightened Rasputin. He must have been concerned that the crafty Iliodor was using the mad general's wife as a spy. She needed to be got out of Pokrovskoe. And that is why it was necessary for Rasputin's wife to find a pretext to fight with Lokhtina, in order to drive her out of the Rasputin home. And that is what she did.

After the quarrel with Rasputin's wife, Lokhtina 'went from them to Florischev Pustyn', the monastery to which Iliodor had been exiled. 'I was not allowed to see Iliodor, and all I could do was shout in his vestibule that I had come . . . Then they sent me away, and a report was filed that I had been suffering from an attack of madness.'

But she would not submit. She was not accepted at home. The paths to Rasputin and Iliodor had been closed. So she decided to find a place at least a little closer to her former heaven. She decided to live near the monk Makary, the spiritual father of the 'Lord of hosts', at Rasputin's favourite monastery. 'I went to Verkhoturye to see Father Makary . . . The elder's cell was undergoing repair, and I was placed in a small storage room, across the door of which the elder put a board with a rock leaning against it. I was fed once a day, receiving whatever food was left over from Father Makary.'

But the monks did not understand her impulse and demanded the woman's departure from their male cloister. However when Lokhtina had decided on something, it was impossible to change her mind. Then 'the police came and presented a writ requiring me to leave. I replied that I would not do so voluntarily . . . But I had to go, since the monks . . . attacked [Father Makary] and beat him. I sent a telegram to the sovereign about it: "I ask you to defend Father Makary . . . whom you do not know."' And the sovereign defended him. The monks were punished, and the cell of Rasputin's spiritual father was quickly repaired. And a small addition was made to Makary's cell so that the mad general's wife could live near him.

But the investigator was apparently dissatisfied with Lokhtina's story. He still did not believe the innocent reasons for her fight with the peasant's wife. And he kept returning to her relations with Rasputin. But she was evasive and obscure about those relations, as was appropriate with people uninitiated into the teaching of the 'Lord of hosts': 'Passions were remote from me whenever I was near Father Grigory.' And she added, 'a poor tree may not yield good fruit. And if that is true, then how do you explain that Rasputin's devotees, both men and women, abandoned luxury and a life contrary to the Gospels and never again returned to their former paths? I speak of the true devotees who followed his precepts.'

His true devotees were those who followed his precepts, or, more accurately, who practised his teachings. Only they understood the meaning of what went on in his house.

A Summer With The Tsars

After receiving the telegram from Vyrubova, summoning him to Livadia, Our Friend left Pokrovskoe at once.

From the agents' report: '10 March. Rasputin boarded a train returning to Petersburg.' And from Petersburg he set off after the 'tsars' to the Crimea.

The tsar's sisters, Olga and Xenia, had left for the Crimea along with his immediate family. During the trip the two grand duchesses started talking about Rasputin.

'10 March. On the train Olga told us about a conversation she had had with [Alix]. She had for the first time told her that the poor little one had that awful disease, and that she herself was sick because of it and would never completely get over it . . . Of Grigory, she said how could she not believe in him when she saw how the little one got better whenever he was near him or praying for him,' Xenia wrote in her diary. And she added, 'My goodness, how terrible it all is and how one pities them!'

When Rasputin arrived in the Crimea, Alix declared that 'she had not known anything about it.' But as Xenia wrote in her diary, 'she was pleased and is reported to have said, "He can always tell when I need him."' And, as usual, Nicky had to resign himself.

Rasputin stayed in Yalta, from where he was driven to Livadia by car. He was brought to the palace in secret, without being entered in the lobby register. But whenever the royal car passed through the city, and the peasant with the unkempt beard gazed pompously through its open window, the whole city knew: he was being taken to the tsarina. And the palace guard who allowed the royal car to pass through the gate also saw who was being taken to the palace. All the more so, since Our Friend proudly stuck his head out the window, not wishing to hide.

All this time the newspapers had been blaring about Rasputin. Only the sinking of the *Titanic* in April 1912, and the drowning of the great vessel's unlucky passengers in icy water beneath a clear, star-filled sky, managed to push aside for a little while news of the peasant in the palace. But in May 1912 the names of the participants in the Rasputin story once again began to flash across the front pages.

In May 1912 Iliodor resigned his holy orders as a sign of protest. On 8 May 1912, he submitted to the Synod the request (although it was more like an ultimatum), that it bring 'Rasputin to trial for the terrible crimes he has committed on religious grounds, or divest me of my holy orders. I cannot be reconciled to the fact that the Synod, the bearer of the grace of the Holy Spirit, is sheltering a 'holy devil' who has cursed Christ's Church . . . I will not be reconciled to the profanation of what belongs to the Lord!'

And again the papers were full of noise about Rasputin.

It was then that a manuscript Rasputin had once prepared with Lokhtina was published by his friend Damansky, the deputy chief procurator. And Alix could once more read in it an abundance of words about unjust persecution, the lasting fate of the righteous. 'I endure terrible smears. It is awful what they write. O God! grant me patience and close up the mouths of mine enemies! . . . Comfort Thy own, O God! Grant me Thy example.' He repeated all this to the tsarina, and asked her permission to leave the Crimea and go home. But he knew that she would not let him. And she did not let him. He could rest easy.

At the beginning of May he returned to Petersburg.

'Rasputin has again appeared on the stage,' Bogdanovich recorded in her diary.

That same month Rasputin went to Moscow. At the Nikolaev Station the agents recorded those people who came to see him off, the same people who usually did: 'Owl' (Laptinskaya), 'Winter Woman' and her daughter (the Golovins), and 'Crow' (Sazonova).

The following encounter took place on the train.

'You Want To Be A Governor? I Can Do That'

When a couple of weeks later a pointed article in his defence suddenly appeared amid the sea of anti-Rasputin articles, it produced a sensation.

The author of the article, Alexey Filippov, was rich, had his own banking house, and edited a successful newspaper. He had besides a well-deserved reputation as a liberal: he had spent a year in the Peter and Paul Fortress for impermissible words about the authorities. Thereby fulfilling the sardonic words of a fashionable poet: 'Here's what: stand for the truth and you'll end up sitting for it.' Filippov was a friend of the maid of honour Sophia Tyutcheva, who had suffered because of Rasputin, and he therefore regarded the latter with repugnance. At least until that day in May when they met each other on the train.

In 1917 Alexey Frolovich Filippov, aged forty-eight, was summoned before the Extraordinary Commission. And in the File, he related:

In 1912 I went to the Trinity-St Sergius Abbey [a famous monastery near

Moscow]. As . . . I was taking my seat on the train I noticed in the car a peasant of striking appearance dressed in a tight-fitting coat, a man with mystical eyes set deep in sockets whose orbits were surrounded by brown spots. He was accompanied by . . . a plump woman in black (who turned out to be his secretary Akilina Laptinskaya) . . . He was examining with childishly naive affection an immense new leather purse that had obviously just been given him by someone. I asked him, 'Where did you get the purse?' With that question began my acquaintance with Rasputin . . . Some sense told me that my new acquaintance was a sectarian, that he belonged to the *Khlyst* sect. He spoke picturesquely in aphorisms on the most varied topics . . . and I was especially struck by his deep faith in the Russian people and by his thoughtful rather than subservient attitude towards autocratic power. He stood for the unity of the tsar and the people without an intermediary bureaucracy . . . I was particularly sympathetic to him since I had recently . . . been sentenced to a year in the Fortress for daring to point out to a representative of the supreme authority that he did not understand the essence of autocracy . . . I therefore involuntarily blurted out, 'If only someone like you could reach the tsar . . .' He then went out into the corridor after discreetly beckoning me to follow, and said, 'Don't tell anyone . . . but I'm the Rasputin they've been cursing in the newspapers.'

The conversation continued.

His interest in [church] art prompted me to propose our going to Moscow together. He agreed to it with a youthful eagerness uncharacteristic of his age . . . Rasputin was not met by anyone in Moscow, and he went to stay with Nikolai Ivanovich Reshetnikov, a former notary who later became his secretary. But he turned up on time the same day at the Kremlin church hostel. He listened with unusual attention to my hour-long lectures on, for example, the cathedral of Basil the Blessed . . . We spent two days in Moscow, filling our time with visiting churches. During that time Rasputin and I became friends, and on returning to Petersburg where I edited the newspaper *Smoke of the Fatherland*, I started to visit him . . . We saw each other every day then, and I was struck that Rasputin occupied a wretched little room not at all corresponding to the idea of him . . . as the powerful favourite of the imperial family . . . Rasputin himself did not drink wine and he discouraged others . . . Delighted by my arguments on the theme of governing the state, he exclaimed, 'You want to be a governor? I can do that.' He lived simply and even humbly, and spoke sparingly and reluctantly of the court and his relationships there. In answer to a question I asked him once about whether the empress really did not give him anything, he said, 'She's stingy . . . terribly stingy.' Rasputin was at the time hard up, as was apparent from the twenty-five kopeks he would take from me for cab fare, and the twenty-five roubles he once sent for when he was short for a trip to Siberia, although later on he would fling hundreds and even thousands . . . every day to whatever chance acquaintances happened to ask him.

It was at that time that Rasputin introduced Filippov to Vyrubova, and although Filippov witnessed scenes in which Anya expressed her usual naive admiration for the peasant, he apparently understood something: 'Vyrubova impressed me as a woman whose attitude towards Rasputin was one of enthusiasm . . . but who was using him as a way of exerting a certain influence over the empress.'

And in response to Rasputin, Filippov introduced him to his own friends.

Soon afterwards at the editorial office of *Smoke of the Fatherland* I happened on a conversation between the paper's publisher, Alexander Lvovich Garyazin, and . . . the legal counsel of the Maritime Ministry, Ivan Bazhenov, who was repeating the words of some courtier about Rasputin's sexual outrages with the empress and saying there ought to be a conspiracy to kill 'that dog'. I objected that I had just made his acquaintance and had been utterly charmed by him, and I shared my impressions . . . I suggested to Garyazin that he take Rasputin for a drive somewhere in his automobile.

Garyazin, who owned his own car, something very rare in those days, readily agreed to meet with the scandalous and enigmatic celebrity. 'Rasputin rejected . . . the idea of visiting a museum, finding that pictures were rubbish . . . and much inferior to life . . . Garyazin suggested a visit to the Foundling Hospital, and, to his utter amazement, Rasputin agreed.' At the hospital Rasputin

was transformed . . . He picked up each child, tested its weight, and asked it what it was eating. In the automobile he said 'it would be a good idea to bring country girls there from all over Russia. They would learn how to bear healthy children and keep their infants strong' . . . Impressions he conveyed to the empress, who unexpectedly came to the Foundling Hospital, made a quick survey of it, and busied herself with ideas for organizing an institute for the protection of motherhood . . . I took advantage of a convenient opportunity and included an article in *Smoke of the Fatherland* defending Rasputin, an article that provoked equal astonishment both on the left and the right among those in the press who had been persecuting him. [The article, 'Childhood and Sin', appeared in *Smoke of the Fatherland* on 16 May 1912.]

Rasputin was wildly delighted with the fact that I was the only one who had dared to defend him in print at a time of the greatest persecution of him and of Guchkov's speeches against him in the Duma . . . He carried out all my requests and wishes at once and unquestioningly, and more often than not came to me for advice and let me in on the intimate details of whatever it was he was going through . . . Although he never said one word about any intimate relations whatever not only with the empress, whom he always characterized as the 'smart one', but with any other woman, as well.

How much does this image fail to resemble that of the awful lust-driven peasant who at the very same time was stalking the streets of Petersburg in pursuit of women! Just who was that peasant? A cunning changeling? A sexual psychopath? Or is it that despite my having written so many pages, I still do not know him any better than I did before? And am still only on the way to his secret?

A Dandy With 'Mistakes In Grammar'

In the summer of 1912 exciting news spread through society.

'7 June 1912. Olga Nikolaevna was betrothed last night to Dmitry Pavlovich,' the general's wife Bogdanovich wrote in her diary.

Dmitry was the tsar's favourite. His letters to Nicholas have survived, the scoffing letters of a rake. A duellist and hard drinker, tall and well built like most of the Romanovs, a favourite of the Guards – he had everything that Nicky lacked. Despite the return of his father from exile in 1905, Dmitry had continued to live with the royal family. But Alix did not like him. For the youth did not hide his disdain for the peasant.

And she looked forward to the marriage of her daughter and Dmitry with dread. It was then that another rake arrived in Petersburg from England, one who, fortunately for Alix, changed everything – Felix Yusupov.

As Felix later recalled, he and Dmitry saw a lot of each other in the course of 1912–13. 'He was then living with the royal family at the Alexander Palace, but we spent . . . all our free time together.' Felix, who was several years older than the handsome Dmitry, completely captivated the grand duke. In place of the reclusive, monotonous life of the Alexander Palace with its grand duchesses and the empress eternally fussing over the unfortunate boy, Felix revealed another world to him. He did what his own older brother had done for him: he introduced Dmitry to the feverish life of nocturnal Petersburg. Now at night a car waited for the two playboys. 'Almost every night we drove to Petersburg and carried on a merry life in restaurants, night cafés, and among Gypsies. We invited performers to dine with us in private rooms. And often Pavlova would join us.' But it was not only the famous ballet star Anna Pavlova who joined them. Felix's unconventional tastes, which he writes about himself in his memoirs, also attracted to the private rooms male ballet dancers who shared those tastes.

The royal family was horrified. 'Their Majesties, knowing of my scandalous adventures, looked askance at our friendship,' Felix recalled. Or, to put it more accurately, knowing of Felix's homosexual propensities, which at the time were punishable by imperial law, the tsars regarded Dmitry's passionate attachment to Felix with fear.

Olga's future husband was forbidden to see Felix. 'The secret police were keeping an eye on that now,' Felix recalled.

The centenary of the Battle of Borodino, the site near Moscow which saw the onset of the destruction of Napoleon's *grande armée*, was celebrated in August 1912. Reaching all the way up Tver Street from Moscow's Brest Station were ceremonial lines of soldiers and behind them crowds of people. The bells of the city's innumerable churches kept ringing. To cries of 'Hurrah', the tsar, Alix, the heir, and Olga took their places in the first barouche. Dmitry sat in the last calash. All eyes sought the fiancé of the tsar's eldest daughter.

But Felix proved to be stronger. Stronger than both the royal prohibitions and the happiness of becoming the husband of the tsar's daughter. The encounters with Felix continued. Rumour had a simple explanation: Dmitry was bisexual. And Dmitry, the future lover of the celebrated Coco Chanel, was then madly infatuated with Felix. In the idiom of the salons of the day, it was called 'making mistakes in grammar'. Dmitry preferred to move out of the Alexander Palace. Now he was lodged in his own house in Petersburg, and Felix helped him to furnish it in the luxury for which his own home, the Yusupov palace on the Moika Canal, was celebrated. With precious furniture and paintings.

And so, Dmitry had made his choice. Now with a clear conscience Alix could, or, more accurately, was compelled to, break off Olga's engagement. Dmitry had compromised himself by his scandalous friendship. But this time, too, Nicholas remained loyal to his affections. He continued to have a soft spot for Dmitry. He chose to regard the rumours with caution. And the peasant understood what was required of him. And he did not let his benefactress down. Rasputin predicted that Dmitry would from his debauched life soon contract a skin disease. So at his request Alix ordered the girls 'to wash their hands with a special solution after any meetings and handshaking with the grand duke'.

Had The Prince Been Slapped?

It was then that another meeting may have taken place between Rasputin and Felix, although the latter does not mention it. The meeting is overgrown with legend. The actress Vera Leonidovna Yureneva told me about it: Felix, infuriated by Rasputin's meddling in Dmitry's betrothal, repeated what he had successfully carried off many times before. He dressed up as a young woman and appeared before Rasputin. When the latter made his usual advances, the 'bad boy' started laughing at him and insulting him. For which he was slapped.

For me, however, there is one thing in the legend that rings false. Why didn't Felix shoot him on the spot? Shooting the debauched peasant after he had dared to raise his hand against the prince would have been welcomed by everyone! True, the situation itself was perhaps not the best one. And for that reason it may have been necessary to do nothing.

The rumours of a slap had in fact seemed quite fantastic to me, until I found in the File the remarkable testimony of the tsarina's friend Yulia Dehn.

'In regard to Prince Felix Felixovich Yusupov . . . that effeminate and elegantly dressed young man visited Rasputin both before my acquaintance with him and during the year of that acquaintance [1911–12] . . . I know that during some argument between the prince and Rasputin, who did not care for the prince's behaviour, Rasputin had struck him, after which the prince stopped visiting him.'

She speaks about it as a known fact. Even though Yusupov was in Petersburg at the time and might easily have refuted her words if they had been an invention.

Rasputin's Exoneration

The tsar had not received Rodzyanko, and the charges that Rasputin was a *Khlyst* continued unabated. But then what unexpected joy for the tsarina! God had intervened for the elder. The truth had won out: Alexis, the new bishop of Tobolsk, had conducted a new investigation. And the Tobolsk Theological Consistory had reached a new Decision.

The Right Reverend Alexis, Bishop of Tobolsk . . . has thoroughly examined the evidence in the file on Grigory Novy. Travelling through the Tobolsk district . . . he stopped in the village of Pokrovskoe and there engaged in a lengthy discussion with the peasant Grigory Novy about the objects of his faith and aspirations, and talked about him with people who knew him well ... From all of the above-indicated, the Right Reverend Alexis has derived the impression that the case against the peasant Grigory Rasputin-Novy of belonging to the *Khlyst* sect was instituted without sufficient basis, and for his own part he considers the peasant Grigory Novy to be an Orthodox Christian and a person of great intelligence and spiritual aptitude who is seeking the truth of Christ and who can, when the opportunity arises, provide good counsel to anyone who may need it.

On the basis of Bishop Alexis's report 'in regard to new information', the Consistory decreed in an act dated 29 November 1912, that 'The case of the peasant Grigory Rasputin-Novy of the village of Pokrovskoe is hereby suspended and considered closed.'

After reading the Decision, the tsar asked that copies be immediately distributed to the Synod, the ministers, and the Duma. So that the fat man Rodzyanko might be appeased.

The reasons for the appearance of the Decision, which is contained in the Tobolsk archive, had been a mystery to me. And then in the File I found the testimony of the son of Bishop Alexis of Tobolsk, testimony that made the whole story clear.

Parting The Curtain Of Exoneration

In 1917 Leonid Alexeevich Molchanov, the son of the late Bishop Alexis, was called before the Extraordinary Commission.

He had met Rasputin in 1912. At the time he was secretary to the chief magistrate of the Pskov District Court and was twenty-three years old. His father had been transferred that year from Pskov to Tobolsk, and he had gone to visit him during his vacation: 'On 7 July I set out by steamboat from Tyumen to Tobolsk ... When it became clear that Rasputin would be taking the same boat, the news produced something of a sensation in the crowd.' And although 'after the newspaper articles . . . my attitude towards him was one of opposition', Molchanov still wanted to meet him.

'I spent the entire day with him until the Pokrovskoe landing, where he had to get off . . . Rasputin said that much falsehood was being written about him, that Hermogen and Iliodor, instead of performing their pastoral duties, had taken up politics, and that the sovereign did not care for those "synodians" who, instead of performing their pastoral duties, only cared about splendid clothing and ribbons and medals, and who turned up in

Tsarskoe Selo in the capacity of dignitaries rather than pastors.' After hearing Rasputin's stories about his persecution, Molchanov immediately responded with the story of his father's own persecution by the members of the Synod. It turned out that his father had once been the bishop of Taurida. And, as his son explained, Bishop Alexis had been slandered. With the purpose of removing him from the Crimea, 'so that the pulpit could be cleared for Feofan, who was being forced out of Petrograd'. And to do that, the 'synodians' had sent Alexis deep into Siberia to distant Tobolsk. 'Rasputin began to feel sorry for my father . . . [and] announced that as soon the opportunity presented itself, he would tell "Papa" and "Mama" about it.'

The story would naturally have interested Rasputin. But when he learned what it was that Molchanov's father had been 'slandered' with, the story obviously interested him even more.

Victor Yatskevich, the director of the chancery of the chief procurator of the Most Holy Synod, speaks about it in the File. It turns out that Alexis lost his southern pulpit not at all because of Feofan but because of the young teacher Elizaveta Kosheva. With whom the hierarch had had a liaison. At first he had been transferred to Pskov. But located in the Pskov eparchy, as Yatskevich testified, 'was the notoriously heretical Vorontsov Monastery, which had become a nest of the Ioannite sect'. These were the devotees of Ioann of Kronstadt. They worshipped Ioann as an earthly incarnation of Christ. And they had their own 'Mother of God', too: Porfiria Kiselyova. 'Thus,' Yatskevich explains, 'they were an ordinary sect of the *Khlyst* type.' And not only did Alexis not move against them; he even began to give their 'ark' his protection. For which he was transferred even farther away, to Tobolsk.

Cold Tobolsk, however, was very hard on the bishop. As his son related to Rasputin, Alexis suffered from nephritis, and cold regions had a severe effect on him. But that provincial bishop had no friends in the Synod to help him with a move to the south. So Rasputin understood that sitting in Tobolsk, which governed his own native village, was the bishop he needed. Aggrieved, without connections, badly in need of support, and, above all, a protector of the *Khlysty*.

And by 10 July, Molchanov's father 'received a telegram from the village of Pokrovskoe in which Rasputin asked for his blessing and permission to visit him in Tobolsk. Rasputin remained as his guest for three days.' And soon afterwards followed Alexis's first incentive. The provincial bishop was summoned to Tsarskoe Selo to Anya's little house. Which at court was mockingly called the 'parvis of power'. Just as mendicants in a church parvis ask for money, so there people solicited high offices.

The File, from the testimony of Molchanov: 'My father made Vyrubova's acquaintance and . . . conducted a night service and mass at the Feodor Cathedral . . . after which he took breakfast at Vyrubova's . . . At breakfast a telegram was sent to the yacht [that is, to the royal family] . . . and a gracious reply was received.'

So in the autumn the bishop prepared a grateful response. The investigation of the Tobolsk Theological Consistory regarding Rasputin's affiliation with the *Khlyst* sect was closed.

A Miracle, A Miracle!

In the autumn of 1912 Rasputin performed one of his true miracles: he saved the life of the heir. And even his enemies would be forced to acknowledge it.

The tragedy began in early October at Spala, the tsar's hunting castle in the Belovezh forest reserve. Something taking place in one of the inner rooms of the castle was kept secret from everyone. Even Alexei's tutor, Pierre Gilliard, had no idea where his pupil had disappeared to. And then, the scene famously described by Gilliard in his memoirs took place. During a ball, Gilliard had left the hall by an interior corridor and found himself before a door beyond which desperate moaning could be heard. And then at the other end of the corridor he saw Alix running towards him, holding up her gown to keep from tripping over it. She had evidently been summoned at the height of the ball: the boy was suffering a new attack of intolerable pain. In her agitation she did not even notice Gilliard.

From Nicholas's diary for 5 October: 'We celebrated a joyless name-day today. Poor Alexei has been suffering from secondary haemorrhages for several days now.'

The swelling was followed by blood poisoning. The doctors were already preparing Alix for the inevitable end. It was time to make an announcement of the heir's illness.

From the diary of KR: '9 October. A bulletin has appeared about the illness of the Tsarevich. He is the sovereign's only son! May God preserve him!'

The year before, Alexei's kidneys had haemorrhaged. But, as Xenia recorded in her diary, 'They sent for Grigory. Everything ended with his arrival.'

This time Rasputin was far away. But Alix believed: his prayers were stronger than any distance.

From the testimony of Vyrubova: 'And then Rasputin was sent a telegram with the request that he pray, and Rasputin replied with a soothing telegram that the heir would live. "God has seen your tears and heeded your prayers . . . Your son will live."'

And when Alix, with a face tormented by sleepless nights, triumphantly showed the telegram to the doctors, they merely nodded their heads in sorrow. But they noted with astonishment that even though the boy was still dying, she immediately became calm. Such was her faith in Rasputin's power! And the doctors must have thought that the Middle Ages had finally returned to the palace. But the heir did recover! It seemed to her then that she had seen a Biblical miracle with her very own eyes! By prayer alone without even coming to Spala, he had saved her son.

On 21 October the court minister Fredericks announced from Spala that 'The most critical and grave period of his Imperial Highness's illness has . . . passed.'

'Was that really not enough to gain the parents' love,' Vyrubova recalled. And on Rasputin's arrival in Petersburg, the 'tsars' again heard something encouraging.

From the testimony of Vyrubova: 'The doctors said the heir's haemorrhaging was hereditary, and he would never get over it in view of the delicacy of his vessels. Rasputin reassured them, declaring that he would outgrow it.'

How could she not have deified him after that! This is the right word: she had already made him a God. As we shall see later on, it was a very convenient one for her.

The rumours that the heir might die forced Nicky's brother Mikhail to take action. In the event of Alexei's death, he would become the heir. He knew that the family would in that case never permit him to marry the former cavalry captain's wife, Natalia Wulfert. But the ash-blonde hair and velvety eyes of the most elegant woman in Petersburg had conquered him, and so Misha wasted no time.

On 31 October the dowager empress received a letter from Cannes. 'My dear Mama . . . How difficult and painful it is for me to cause you distress . . . but two weeks ago I married Natalia Sergeevna . . . I would never, perhaps, have made the decision to do so, had it not been for the illness of little Alexei.' For the family of Alexander III, the future of the throne now lay only with the sick boy.

And that future was now in the hands of the strange miracle-worker.

Rasputin's Merry Life

At the time the strange deity was continuing to lead an amazing life. And the agents were continuing to submit their reports to the Department of Police: '3 December 1912. He visited the editorial offices of the religious newspapers *The Bell* and *The Voice of Truth* with Lyubov and Maria Golovina . . . After which he took a prostitute on Nevsky and went to a hotel with her.'

'9 January 1913. He wanted to visit the family baths with Sazonova, but they were closed. He parted with her and took a prostitute.'

'10 January . . . He approached a prostitute.'

'12 January. After visiting the Golovins, he took a prostitute.'

The same clear-cut alternation: from the prim household of the Golovins to a prostitute; then after a meeting with Vyrubova, a visit to the baths with one of his initiated devotees; then during a break, a prostitute; and in the evening sometimes even an automobile to Tsarskoe Selo!

But that pursuit of the body had now become habitual to him. Now for some reason he was not at all afraid of reports to the 'tsars'. 'If on his first visits he exhibited a certain caution before his encounters with prostitutes, glancing behind and going down back streets, then on his most recent visit those encounters have taken place quite openly,' the external surveillance report summarized.

But then that subject in the tight-fitting peasant coat and unkempt beard who was given to darting down dubious streets and 'running into' the apartments of prostitutes had, in society's view, *once again* presumed to meddle in international affairs.

Earlier that winter Rasputin had taken one more step towards his death.

Who Was The Peacemaker?

After the murder of Stolypin, an uncompromising opponent of Russian participation in wars, the Montenegrins' father, King Nikola of Montenegro, felt more confident. And he took action. A secret alliance against Turkey was concluded among the Orthodox states of Serbia, Montenegro, Greece, and Bulgaria. The moment they had chosen was opportune: Turkish political life was in chaos.

And on the night of 26 September 1912 (9 October NS) the Winter Palace heard the sensational news that Montenegrin troops had occupied the Turkish fortress at Scutari in Albania. The tsar understood how that impudent disruption of the status quo in the Balkans would ignite an explosion of indignation among the great powers. The minister of foreign affairs was instructed to persuade Montenegro to end its occupation of the fortress. But the Montenegrins' father knew of the bellicose mood in Petersburg and of the support of Grand Duke Nikolai, the 'dread uncle', and he callously continued the siege of Scutari.

And then more threatening news came from the dangerous Balkans. On 5 (18 NS) October Serbia and Bulgaria entered the war against Turkey, followed by Greece the day after. And the Turkish army sustained defeat after defeat. News of the successes of the Balkan alliance – of their brothers in the faith – against the Turkish Moslems gave rise to an outpouring of joyous nationalism in Russia. There were continual demonstrations in Petersburg bearing the slogan, 'A Cross for Holy Sophia', a reference to the great Byzantine cathedral turned into a mosque in Istanbul. The old idea of pan-Slavism was abroad again, the idea of a great federation of Orthodox Slavic states with Russia at its head, and everyone was again caught up in the old dream of the Russian tsars: of taking Constantinople back by force from Turkey – Constantinople, the ancient capital of Byzantium, from which Rus had adopted its Christian faith.

The response was immediate. The Austrians and Germans threatened war.

And again the Balkan boiler was about to blow up the whole world.

On 10 and 29 November and on 5 December 1912, the Council of Ministers met in Petersburg. And the situation of a few years before was repeated. Russian society wanted to fight: the demands for military assistance to its 'Balkan brothers' were unanimous, and the registering of volunteers began. Even Rasputin's friend Filippov was for war at the time. And there was no Stolypin powerful enough to overcome public opinion (or, more accurately, public insanity). War was again at the very threshold. And once again it would be a world war. The Austrian fleet and the ships of the great powers had already blockaded the Montenegrin coast. General mobilization was anticipated in Russia. Speaker of the State Duma Rodzyanko counselled the tsar to fight.

And then the tsar suddenly demonstrated character: he resolutely moved against public opinion. He demanded that the minister of foreign affairs put pressure on Montenegro. And on 21 April 1913 the Montenegrin king, after many hours of persuasion, consented to withdraw from Scutari in return for monetary indemnification. And the Russian foreign minister, Sergei Sazonov, announced with relief, 'King Nikola was going to set the world on fire to cook his own little omelette.' This was in reply to the constant reproaches that Russia had once again betrayed its Balkan brothers.

And then a rumour raced through Petersburg. It was Rasputin's wish that had stood behind the tsar's decisiveness! It was he who once again had prevented the 'tsars' from defending their fellow Slavs.

And it was true.

The File, from the testimony of Filippov:

> In 1912–13, at the very height of the resolution of the Balkan question when we were on the verge of war with Austria, Rasputin, in response to my urgent demand that Russia vigorously go to war against the Germans in defence of Slavdom, observed that the Germans were a power, while the little brothers were just swine for whose sake not a single Russian was worth losing . . . Rasputin found that we would not be ready to fight the Germans . . . until we had regained our strength from the shock of the war with Japan.

From Vyrubova's testimony: 'Rasputin was adamantly opposed to any war whatsoever. He was against Russian interference in the Balkan war.'

From the testimony of Badmaev in the File: Rasputin 'told me that he had asked the tsar not to fight in the Balkan war at a time when all the press was clamouring for Russia to take part, and he succeeded in convincing the tsar not to fight.'

And so the unbelievable had occurred: a semi-literate peasant had defeated all the parties and forced the tsar to act in contempt of public opinion! And he had done so alone!

Thus said the court and all Petersburg. From the very beginning Rasputin had had a clear realization of his main task at court – to grasp what the 'smart one', that infinitely strong-willed woman, wanted in the innermost reaches of her soul. And to give expression to it as his own prediction, as knowledge from God. He knew very well how horrified she was by even the thought of war with Germany. And he managed once more to give voice to her secret wishes. And once more he frightened the tsar with apocalyptic predictions of what would happen in the event of war. And she accepted those predictions with relief as God's command given utterance by the man of God. And took his side. And the tsar was forced to submit.

However, that is not my assumption. Gilliard, the tutor of the royal children and someone who had lived with the family for many years and who understood Alexandra Fyodorovna very well, wrote of Rasputin in his memoirs: 'His prophetic words most often merely confirmed the hidden wishes of the empress herself. She herself did not suspect that she had induced them, that she was their 'inspirer'. Her personal wishes, passing through Rasputin, acquired in her eyes the force and authority of revelation.'

But that was not understood in society. And once again it was believed that the semi-literate, debauched peasant had cancelled a just war. And Nikolai Nikolaevich, who had for the second time suffered defeat in the Balkan story, would never forgive that. The unbending 'dread uncle' also believed that the peasant was guilty of Russia's humiliation.

And in the File, Konstantin Chikhachev, the deputy chief of the Saratov Judicial Chamber, relates to the investigator some words he heard from Rasputin himself: '[Nikolai Nikolaevich] used to be terribly fond of me . . . We were friends right up until the Balkan war. He wanted the Russians to enter the war. Whereas I did not, and spoke against it. He has been angry with me ever since.'

Thus, the pan-European butchery was postponed. Thus, the grand duke and the other hawks fully believed that as long as the peasant was in the palace, there would be no war. But they knew that he was in the palace for the long term, and that he would not give up his place.

So only one solution remained: to remove him for good.

The Dangerous Dzhunkovsky

It had come at last: 1913, the festive year of the dynasty's tercentenary.

At the very end of 1912, Minister of Internal Affairs Makarov fell, just as Prime Minister Kokovtsev had predicted to him. He was sent into retirement in early 1913, on the eve of the jubilee celebrations. The new minister of internal affairs, Vasily Maklakov, was chosen from among the provincial governors. He was a distant relative of Count Leo Tolstoy and the relative of a well-known liberal and Constitutional Democrat. But unlike his relatives, he was a monarchist, and during his term as governor he had become famous for expelling Jews from his province. He was just past forty. And in view of his youth, Vladimir Dzhunkovsky, the governor of Moscow and a former associate of Ella's husband, the murdered Grand Duke Sergei, was appointed his deputy.

All the secret police forces were concentrated in Dzhunkovsky's hands: he became chief of the gendarme corps, and the Department of Police was subject to him, as well. He also had complete responsibility for arranging the security of the royal family during the jubilee celebrations.

In 1917, during his interrogation by the Extraordinary Commission, Dzhunkovsky testified that he had been known to the tsar for a long time: 'ever since I was a young officer, inasmuch as I had served in the Preobrazhensky regiment, first battalion'. The same place Nicholas, then the heir, had received his own military training. For Nicholas, so fond of everything military, that meant a great deal. The tsar had met Dzhunkovsky during the latter's duty assignments at the Winter Palace and was thus acquainted with his monarchist views. The tsar was also pleased with the old Guards officer's magnificent bearing. The external appearance of the new chief of gendarmes was truly fearsome. The poet Alexander Blok described Dzhunkovsky as possessing an 'imposing face, sharply pointed moustaches, and a beetle brow'. Moreover, the formidable Dzhunkovsky was a man of the world and knew how to entertain. He could, whenever invited to breakfast, amuse the royal children with his very fine bird calls.

But for now, Dzhunkovsky readied the capital for the celebrations. Later on, after the death of the tsar and the end of the monarchy, he would describe it all in his memoirs.

Great Celebrations With The Peasant

The sacred day arrived. Three hundred years before, the Muscovite Assembly of the Land had elected as tsar the boyar Mikhail Romanov. And on the morning of 21 February 1913, bells began ringing all over Russia. And processions of the cross with lighted candles were conducted around all its churches.

At 8:00 a.m. Petersburg was awakened by the cannon of the Peter and Paul Fortress. Dzhunkovsky began his drive around the city early in the morning. The streets were already filled with people. An especially large crowd had gathered next to Kazan Cathedral, where the royal family would appear. At noon a deafening 'hurrah' was heard from the troops stretched out in a chain from the Winter Palace to the cathedral. And a squadron-strong military escort in crimson Circassian coats came into view, and after them the tsar and the heir in an open calash, and then a coach carrying the two empresses with giant Cossacks on its footboards, and then another coach with the grand duchesses.

A festive prayer service began in Kazan Cathedral. And those invited, the leading people of the empire, saw the hated peasant inside the cathedral. It would have been impossible not to: he stood among the most distinguished guests.

The File, from the testimony of Yatskevich, director of the chancery of the chief procurator of the Synod: 'During the service . . . I saw a peasant next to the senators. I was told it was Rasputin.'

The peasant was striking for the magnificence of his 'national dress'. 'He was luxuriously clad in a dark raspberry silk peasant shirt, high patent-leather boots, wide black trousers, and a black peasant's coat,' recalled Rodzyanko, who had been astonished to observe Rasputin standing in front of the members of the State Duma. And the Speaker of the Duma was seething. The huge, corpulent Rodzyanko strode over to Rasputin and ordered him to leave the cathedral at once. 'If you do not leave, I shall order the ushers to carry you out,' he recalled having said. And the peasant was afraid of a scandal. And he moved toward the doorway, saying, 'O Lord! Forgive him his sin.' Rodzyanko triumphantly escorted him to the doorway of the cathedral, where a Cossack gave Rasputin his fur coat and put him in a car. It is not difficult to imagine what Alix felt when she learned that Rasputin had been ejected from the cathedral, a place to which he had been summoned by the House of Romanov.

And then, in May, the centre of celebrations shifted to Kostroma, where three hundred years before the young boyar Mikhail Romanov had lived at the Ipatiev Monastery. And from which he had been called to take his place as tsar. It was to the Ipatiev Monastery (where the dynasty began) that the royal family went, a mere four years before their arrival at the Ipatiev House in Ekaterinburg (where the dynasty ended). The day before, an aide told Dzhunkovsky, who had come on ahead, that Rasputin was in town. And that he had been asking for a ticket to the Kostroma ceremonies. Dzhunkovsky happily ordered the aide to turn him down.

On 19 May crowds of people lined the banks of the Volga, and to a thunderous salute of cannon, the ringing of church bells and chants of 'God save the tsar', the royal flotilla docked at a special royal landing place near the Ipatiev Monastery.

From the landing, the royal family proceeded to the ancient Cathedral of the Assumption. And Dzhunkovsky entered the cathedral after them. What was Dzhunkovsky's astonishment when next to the cathedral altar he saw . . . Rasputin, who, as it turned out, 'had been escorted there . . . at the empress's orders'.

Dzhunkovsky had occasion to be amazed the next day, too, when in Kostroma the foundation of a monument to the Romanov dynasty was to be laid.

The colourful gold and pink brocade of the choristers, the ancient vestments of the clergy, the military tunics, the swallow-tailed coats, the sovereign in the uniform of his own Erivan regiment, which had been founded by the first Romanov, the tunics of the grand dukes. And nearby the same Rasputin in a silk peasant shirt and wide pants. Before the laying of the monument, a prayer service had been conducted in the cathedral. And the peasant had been present for that, too!

Here it was Yatskevich who was indignant. 'During the Kostroma ceremonies on the day the monument was to be laid, Rasputin followed close behind the royal family as it came out of the cathedral, and I was once more astonished and indignant that Rasputin had been let into the cathedral, where the only others present were the royal family and Chief Procurator Sabler!'

And then, a few days later, the celebrations passed to Moscow, the ancient capital. And again there were lines of troops and a sea of people and a ringing of bells. The sovereign on a horse with a golden coat escorted by the grand dukes also on horseback, the empress and the heir in a calash, the grand duchesses in barouches, and Ella and the tsar's daughters in another barouche.

From Xenia's diary for 24 May 1913: 'Everything went splendidly, thank God. At the [Kremlin's main] Spassky Gate all dismounted and filed in a procession of the cross into the Cathedral of the Archangel.' Nicky lit an icon lamp over the tomb of Mikhail Fyodorovich, and that lamp, fashioned of gold, in the shape of the hat of the twelfth-century Kievan prince Vladimir Monomakh, the ancient crown of the Muscovite tsars, burned over the tomb of the first Romanov. 'Rasputin stood by the entrance, and everyone saw him but me . . . There was such displeasure and protest among the clergymen,' Xenia wrote in her diary.

'All that left its residue in me,' Dzhunkovsky recalled. He did not realize that he had blundered badly. Alix now no longer trusted Dzhunkovsky and was afraid of his agents. And on 12 June 1913, Maklakov, the new minister of internal affairs, gave the order 'to suspend the surveillance of Rasputin and to recall the agents now located in the province of Tobolsk'. The police were forbidden to follow him.

For a short time the peasant was without his regular chroniclers.

The 'Moscow Clique'

Elizaveta Fyodorovna was not misled by the popular rejoicing of those days of celebration. She knew that the dynasty had been dealt a terrible blow by the disgrace of the Russo-Japanese War and the revolution of 1905–7. And what a danger was now therefore presented by the unknown peasant, about whose debauchery all the papers were trumpeting.

From the testimony of Grand Duchess Elizaveta Fyodorovna before the Extraordinary Commission: 'When rumours started to reach me that Rasputin was conducting himself in his private life in a way that was quite different from his conduct at the imperial palace, I warned my sister about it. But she did not believe the rumours and considered them slander of the kind that always haunts people devoted to holy life.'

The circle of Rasputin's enemies that had gathered around Ella – the 'Moscow clique', as Alix called it – became ever more active. And Zinaida Yusupova, now one of the circle's most intransigent members, at that time started to visit her Moscow palaces more often. Ella was a frequent guest at Arkhangelskoe, the renowned Yusupov estate near Moscow, which yielded nothing in luxury to the Romanov palaces. 'To see the two of them together is satisfaction itself. They are both so impossibly fine,' recollected the journalist D. Reginin.

'The grand duchess [Elizaveta Fyodorovna] will be staying with us at Arkhangelskoe,' Zinaida more than once wrote to her son Felix in the summer of 1912.

The alliance with Ella suited Zinaida very well in the period immediately following the jubilee celebrations. For it was then, just as Zinaida's long pre-nuptial negotiations with Irina's parents – Sandro and the tsar's sister Xenia – were at last drawing to a close, that Grand Duke Dmitry obtruded himself.

The Battle Of The Princes

Dmitry, on learning about the wedding preparations, had suddenly fallen in love with Irina! In love with the future bride of Felix, his closest friend, whom he idolized! And for the sake of whom he had ruined his own marriage to the daughter of the tsar. And he had not just fallen in love with Irina. He wanted to marry her himself.

It was hard for Petersburg to believe that story. According to the actress Vera Leonidovna Yureneva, things looked much more complicated to society.

'It was, to be blunt, Dmitry Pavlovich's way of taking revenge. The grand duke had learned that Felix, for whose sake he had sacrificed his own marriage to the monarch's daughter, was now calmly undertaking to wed the tsar's niece. And that was the end of their relationship. Dmitry was in a rage. And he started courting Irina himself. He had, quite simply, decided to wreck that alliance.'

There is, however, a quite different possibility of the most ordinary sort. Dmitry at the time liked both the gentlemen and the ladies. The young man could simply have fallen in love with the frail beauty. But one way or another, Dmitry did ask Irina for her hand.

And the Romanov family was split in its sympathies. Zinaida described the situation in a letter to Felix.

28 May 1913. My dear boy. [Irina's] parents have explained their position
. . . Her mother does not deny that the grandmother [the dowager empress
Maria Fyodorovna] is for Dmitry. But she says that she herself would have
nothing against [you] if Irina will hear of no one else. We parted very
touchingly . . . What I am also afraid of is what will happen to your
relationship with Dmitry, since I am certain of his duplicity. He is doing
everything he can to arouse Irina's interest and is always by her side . . . I
am frightened of him and the fatal military tunic. It is quite terrifying.

Her eldest son had been shot by an officer in military tunic because of love.

But Felix was unconcerned. He knew his strength.

'It was for Grand Duchess Irina to choose between us. We made a tacit
decision to do and say nothing that might influence her choice,' Felix
recalled. 'She answered that she had decided to marry me, and that no one
could make her change her decision. Dmitry reconciled himself to her
choice. But it had an effect on our relations. The shadow the marriage had
cast on our friendship could never be dispelled.'

Yet not only did Dmitry acquiesce; he even helped Felix. For it was then
that Irina's parents obtained certain information about their future son-in-
law that thoroughly frightened them. Alexander Mikhailovich heard about
it in Paris and wrote to his wife, Xenia: '9 November 1913. I have been
greatly disheartened all this time by rumours about Felix's reputation . . .
Do not be too quick to announce the wedding . . . If we hear these things
again, we shall cancel the wedding.'

But Felix sped at once to Xenia's palace. And prevailed! And Dmitry
lent corroborating support. Dmitry nobly stood up in defence of his friend.

'12 November . . . I knew they were talking about old stories,' Zinaida
wrote to Felix from Moscow. 'Dmitry Pavlovich's behaviour is most laud-
able. I never expected help from that quarter . . . But I look at his
interference a little differently than you do. I do not think he is beyond
reproach, and by acting in a comradely way was merely protecting himself.'

True, there did remain the question of who had taken the trouble to
furnish the information to Irina's family. Had the tsarina herself made that
effort so that her husband's sister would know everything about the person
she was admitting into the great Romanov family? She certainly was capable
of passionate dislike when it came to the enemies of the man of God. So
that Dmitry, as a bystander, was obliged to invent an altogether different
explanation for Felix's 'mistakes in grammar'. And in doing so he had, as
Zinaida Yusupova very correctly observed, merely been protecting himself.

But the episode healed the rift between Rasputin's murderers and brought
them together again.

In that difficult time Zinaida's friend Grand Duchess Elizaveta Fyodorovna had been on Felix's side. And now, while getting ready for his marriage after deciding to change his life, the 'bad boy' confessed everything to Ella. 'When I revealed to her what . . . she had not known about my private life, she heard me out and said, "I know more about you than you realize . . . He who is capable of evil may do much good once he has chosen the right path."' She, who had been the wife of the homosexual Grand Duke Sergei, could understand and love her 'little Felix'.

'Allow Me To Get Rid Of Rasputin'

In the autumn of 1913 Rasputin was once again living in Yalta from which, as in the previous year, he was driven to Livadia and the royal palace.

At this time a certain R. G. Mollov was the examining magistrate of the Odessa Judicial Chamber. As magistrate he lived for an extended period in Yalta, and his testimony has remained in the File. It was during that period in 1913 that the mayor of the city, a General Dumbadze, expressed a complaint to the magistrate. 'Dumbadze said that a court automobile was frequently sent for Rasputin to take him back to Livadia. Dumbadze had reported to the emperor that the population of Yalta was quite stirred up against Rasputin. The emperor replied that he had the right to live as he wished and to receive whomever he wished, and asked others not to interfere in his family affairs.'

And then Dumbadze decided to rescue the family's prestige on his own. He sent a telegram to Petersburg to the director of the Department of Police, Stepan Beletsky, offering to 'kill Rasputin on one of his boat trips to Yalta'. The simple Dumbadze did not realize how many eyes would read the telegram before it landed on Beletsky's desk. So Beletsky had to hurry. As he himself testified, 'I sent a telegram marked "personal" to Maklakov,' the minister of internal affairs. With the result that Rasputin's next boat trip 'took place without complications'.

'Our Own' Capture Georgia

This time Rasputin had come to the Crimea with obligations to fulfil.

The exarch of Georgia had died in August 1913. And Rasputin was now finally able to keep his promise of showing his gratitude to Bishop Alexis of Tobolsk.

The File, from the testimony of Molchanov: 'In the autumn of 1913

Rasputin . . . was going back and forth to Livadia, and he promised to do what he could to get my father transferred to the south. My father's wishes were no more ambitious than any city in the south, but then the exarch of Georgia suddenly died . . . I went to see Rasputin off . . . and asked about appointing my father to be exarch of Georgia.' And Rasputin 'definitely promised to ask the tsars'.

Well, of course! To get his own exarch of Georgia in the Synod. It was the fourth most important pulpit in Russia. And the peasant made an effort. It was complicated. A compromised bishop! But she trusted Our Friend. Trusted him, as a man of God, to be the main authority in church matters – to the horror of Chief Procurator Sabler of the Holy Synod.

As Sabler testified, when he came to Livadia to make his report to the tsar, 'Nicholas said, "But all your candidates have fallen through, and the choice has come down to Bishop Alexis of Tobolsk" . . . I permitted myself to object firmly, declaring that he did not have the necessary moral qualities, that he was living with the teacher Elizaveta Kosheva, who went everywhere with him and would follow him to Tiflis and compromise him . . . But the appointment went through.'

The disgraced bishop from the back of beyond was made exarch of Georgia with a promotion to the rank of archbishop. One of 'our own', as the tsarina called the friends of Our Friend, stood at the head of the Georgian Church.

Feofan's Prophecy

That summer Feofan was no longer in the Crimea. Having obtained the Crimean pulpit through Ella, he had the previous summer been exiled from the Crimea to Astrakhan, which was destroying his health. To Ella's indignation, he was even forbidden to come to the Crimea for medical treatment whenever the royal family was there.

On his departure from the Crimea, the indomitable but naive Feofan had told everything he knew about Rasputin to the latter's friend Damansky, the deputy chief procurator.

As Feofan testified in the File, he concluded the conversation with a prediction: 'Rasputin is a vessel of the devil, and the time shall come when the Lord will chastise him and those who protect him.' After which he crossed himself and left.

At the time Damansky must have smiled. But a year later, when he learned that he had cancer, he remembered Feofan's prediction.

In Astrakhan Feofan contracted malaria and a lung disease. Ella was still able to help to some degree by having him transferred to the Ukraine to live out his days as the bishop of Poltava. And Ella continued to anger her sister by arguing to Alix that it was inhuman to forbid Feofan to seek treatment in the Crimea, that Feofan was her confessor and had done her no harm, and that just as it was their own private affair to love Rasputin, so it was Feofan's not to. But Alix was afraid of Feofan's character, afraid that he would get through to the sovereign.

And Rasputin helped her − he looked for an offence of Feofan's that would forever bar him from the Crimea.

A Veiled Lady In The Crimean Night

This amazing story has remained in the File.

In 1917 an investigator of the Extraordinary Commission travelled to Yalta, where the widow of a local priest, Olga Apollonovna Popova, sixty years old, lay completely paralysed, as she had done for several years. And she gave her testimony.

> I have been acquainted with Bishop Feofan for six years. He usually came to see me as an invalid about twice a year . . . He never said anything either about Grigory Rasputin or about his life in Petersburg . . . Grigory Rasputin I did not know at all. The first time Rasputin came to me was on 13 October 1913, around midday. Rasputin engaged in a discussion of my life − of my illness and poverty . . . Then he said straight out, 'If you want, you can have a thousand roubles tomorrow, leave this apartment, and see your children happy. We won't have a long conversation about it,' Rasputin said, 'but is it known to you that Feofan has been saying that he had sexual relations with the empress?' He expressed it all in vulgar language. 'If it is known to you, don't conceal it, don't conceal it, and the thousand roubles is yours.'
>
> I objected that nothing of the sort was known to me nor could be. Rasputin got very angry . . . and ran around the room wringing his hands. And he tried again to persuade me to slander the bishop. I was so outraged, I spat in his face. Rasputin moved away towards the door and said, 'You and your children shall remember me!' Then he changed his tone. He repeated several times, 'No one has ever dared to talk to me so insolently . . . I know you will think better of it and take back your words. You will take them back, you will, you will,' he repeated and gazed at me intently . . . Apparently, my reproof had begun to have an effect. He moved his chair very close and said, 'Well, I will come with *her* today, if you'll permit it.' I

understood him to mean the empress. 'You will tell the truth when she is here, you will change your mind . . . You think about it, your children will be happy, and your son's road will be easy . . .' Rasputin evidently realized that he had been pressuring a sick old woman. The thought occurred to me to tell everything to the empress . . . Rasputin said they would come around midnight.

An automobile drove up to our apartment after twelve. When my son opened the door, Rasputin came in accompanied by a tall woman in a black dress with a thick veil covering her face. She sat down next to me, asked about my illness, checked my pulse, and looked at the bedsores on my back. Then Rasputin came over to the bed, touched the empress's shoulder, and said, 'Well, will you tell the truth to her?' I answered that I told the truth to everyone, all the more since I did not have long to live.

After Rasputin moved off to the side, the empress said, 'Tell me, did he [Feofan] talk to you about having relations with that person?'

'That is a complete lie, a foul lie! He never said any such thing and nor could have. I believe the Lord will punish whoever has cast such aspersions on him.'

Rasputin then said something to the empress, but I could not make out the words. Rasputin started whirling around the room and saying 'She's afraid! She's afraid!'

I answered, 'I am not afraid! I will not take your thousand, and I will not sell the bishop!'

Rasputin again tried to persuade me to tell the truth, adding, 'Your children won't get anything for this.' Just as she was about to leave, the empress leaned over to me and said, 'So you are saying it did not happen?'

'It did not and it could not have. He offered me a thousand roubles if I would agree to slander the bishop.'

And the empress asked again, 'So this is your final word?'

I again answered, 'Nothing was said nor could have been said!'

The empress sat nervously and kept taking her glove on and off, while Rasputin repeated, 'She's afraid! She's afraid!' Then Rasputin took her by the arm and, after giving me a spiteful look, walked out of the room.

What is the significance of this scene? That he was so certain of the infiniteness of his influence that he would allow himself to lie shamelessly in her presence? Or was it that he had simply realized that it was her dream to drive Feofan out of the Crimea for good. And he knew that she required a pretext. He had merely read her will and carried out her secret wish.

Subsequently, the tsarina wrote Olga Popova a letter.

From Popova's testimony in the File: 'Soon afterwards I received a letter written in a fine woman's hand with no signature . . . It was suggested in the letter that I think better of it and tell the truth.'

The royal family's next-to-last meeting with their beloved Livadia was coming to an end. And the Ipatiev night was drawing closer.

A Portrait Of The 'Holy Family'
In 1913

That Petersburg winter Rasputin finally settled down in his own apartment for the first time. Before that he had lived with the Lokhtins and the Sazonovs on charity. And then he had rented his own wretched little corners. The addresses of the 'Russian' have survived in the files of the Department of Police: 37 Liteiny Avenue, 70 Nikolaev Street.

'On Nikolaev Street Rasputin occupied a room in an apartment. In the room were a simple bed and a painted wooden buffet table,' Molchanov recounts in the File.

But this time his daughters came to him from Pokrovskoe. The peasant had decided to give them a Petersburg education. Let them become 'little ladies'. Besides, he was tired of not having his own home, of hanging around bathhouses and the squalid apartments of prostitutes. And so Akilina Laptinskaya took matters in hand.

And in October 1913 after his return to Petersburg from Yalta, Rasputin moved into his first separate apartment: at 3 English Avenue in a building belonging to Alexei Porfirievich Veretennikov. The apartment had been given to Rasputin for a very modest sum by yet another failure attempting to take advantage of his influence. Veretennikov was a major general who had been forced into retirement and who dreamed of returning to the service.

Both Rasputin's daughters, whom he had enrolled in a private preparatory school, were now living in the apartment. In 1990, after I published *The Last Tsar*, my book about the royal family, a ninety-year-old woman named Anna Popova called me. We talked on the phone with the help of her granddaughter. She said that she had attended the Steblin-Kamensky private preparatory school with Rasputin's daughter Matryona.

She told of going with Matryona to English Avenue to ask Rasputin for a charitable contribution. And with what frozen fear she had 'gazed at the sorcerer'. And how he had taken out his wallet, rummaged in it a long time, and finally given them a bank note. 'He gave very little,' Popova recalled.

He was poor at the time. 'The apartment of four or five rooms was badly and uncomfortably furnished. In one room lived Laptinskaya, who in the absence of a maid put out the samovar and cooked fish soup, while his two daughters shared another room whenever they came home from the Steblin-Kamensky *pension*,' Molchanov described the apartment in the File. But, even so, it was the first dwelling of his own to which he could invite all his devotees. Laptinskaya could at last quit her work as a housekeeper and move in with him. Now she proudly called herself his 'secretary'. The secretary of an illiterate peasant. And to help her, Katya Pechyorkina came from Pokrovskoe to work as a cook and maid.

Descriptions of Rasputin and his daughters have survived from that time.

'A wild Siberian strength shone from their broad, pallid faces with their enormous bright-coloured lips . . . And their powerful bodies smelling of sweat burst their modest little children's dresses made of thin cashmere.' Varvara was thirteen and Matryona was already sixteen. Matryona had 'a broad white face with a blunt chin . . . and a low forehead suspended above sullen grey eyes . . . She would impatiently shake her head, flipping her low-cut bangs away from her eyes . . . She would pass the tip of her tongue over her broad, bright-red lips in a kind of predatory, animal movement,' Zhukovskaya recalled.

And in the File, Molchanov spoke of Rasputin in 1913: 'His speech was fragmented and not altogether coherent. He kept his eyes on the person he was talking to, and there was a kind of strength in his eyes . . . His movements were characteristic of a neurasthenic: he hopped jerkily about and his hands were always touching something.'

He continued to stun his admirers with his knowledge of people, or, more accurately, their hidden thoughts. 'In that period Rasputin, in addition to his nervousness, manifested an exceptional perspicacity,' Filippov testified in the File. 'In the presence of my wife and sister-in-law . . . he noticed on the basis of elusive signs of some kind that my sister-in-law and I were drawn to each other. And after taking her off to the side, he explained to her that my feelings for her would lead to my divorcing my wife, which is in fact what happened.'

The first time he met Filippov's acquaintance, the famous professor of jurisprudence Ozerov, Rasputin discerned 'an absence of spiritual tran-quillity in him as a result of the fact that he cared only about money'. When Filippov explained to Rasputin that Ozerov was a respected member of the Council of State, the peasant said, 'He's just a state nobody.' 'It was a brilliant characterization of Ozerov,' Filippov added.

It was at this time that Rasputin made the acquaintance of the old woman Guschina. Her husband had just died, and life had become a burden for her. Her testimony remains in the File.

Guschina, Alexandra Georgievna, seventy-three years old, widow of a doctor: 'Each time at church I would come upon a man dressed in a peasant coat praying very zealously. His manner of prayer was peculiar: he would immediately kneel and lean on his fingers in a strange sort of way . . . Many people would come to him with greetings and requests to pray for them.' She was told that the man was Rasputin.

'Once he came up to me after mass and asked, "Why are you so downcast?" I told him about my misfortunes, and he said, "It is sinful to be downcast. You should pray to God."'

And he invited her to visit him. And the old woman came to English Avenue. There she found her way into one of the most famous photographs of the Rasputin circle, a photograph that has adorned endless books about him. Actually, that comes later.

A Cry Of Pain

The newspaper harassment continued throughout 1913. Rasputin grew accustomed to reading interviews that he had never given, after which the press would ridicule him.

And his friend Filippov tried once again to defend him in the newspaper Smoke of the Fatherland: 'A whole literature has been created about the elder . . . a pile of articles regarding his extraordinary and even inexplicable influence in the highest spheres . . . Rasputin is an ordinary Russian peasant of inspired intelligence . . . who mainly has not severed his ties to the common people and who therefore finds his strength in them.' And Filippov mocked the journalists who 'publish rumours that Rasputin could have removed such pillars as Hermogen and Feofan'. So even his close friend Filippov did not know the extent of the peasant's influence in Tsarskoe Selo.

But sometimes Our Friend yielded to the journalists and himself gave interviews. To Alix's dismay, for they were often more dangerous than the ones the journalists made up for him.

Under Filippov's influence the idea had occurred to Rasputin of putting out his own newspaper.

'I thought of starting up the most real, just newspaper of the people. The money will be given to me – people who believe have been found – I will bring good people together, and I will cross myself and say, "Bless us, O Lord," and strike the bell,' he announced in an interview in the Petersburg Courier.

But Alix evidently put that idea to rest. She realized that he would drown in the business. He would drown in the distraction. She needed him for herself, for the boy, and for conversations about the soul.

At the time the journalists were trying to learn about Rasputin's role in the decision not to participate in the Balkan war. And he answered, 'In general, it does not make sense to fight: to take each other's lives, violate the testament of Christ, and prematurely kill your own soul. Let the Germans and the Turks kill each other – it's their bad luck and blindness, but we, lovingly and quietly looking to ourselves, will become higher than the rest.' And he was again reviled for betraying fellow Slavs. And again Alix instructed Vyrubova to talk to the elder about avoiding journalists.

But they kept calling him. And he shouted into the receiver, 'What do they want from me? Do they really not want to understand that I am a little fly, and that I don't need anything from anybody? Do they really have nothing else to write about besides me? I do not trouble anybody. And I could not trouble anybody since I do not have the strength. They discuss every step, they mix everything up. Leave me alone. Let me live.'

And this monologue instantly found its way into the papers along with derisive commentary.

And they called again. And again he shouted into the receiver and hung up.

> I tell you, I am a little fly and there's no use in concerning yourself with me. There are bigger things to talk about, but for you it's always one and the same: Rasputin, Rasputin. Be silent. Enough writing. You shall answer to God! He alone sees everything. He alone understands. And judges. Write, if you have to. I shall say nothing more. I have taken it all to heart. Now I am burned out. I don't care any more. Let everybody write. Let them add to the din. Such, it appears, is my fate. I've endured everything. I'm not afraid of anything. Go ahead and write. How much will they worm out of you? I tell you, I don't care. Goodbye.

And they published that monologue, too. What was to be done? He was the hero of the day.

The ambiguity of his situation in relation to the 'tsars' had manifested itself in the story of Prime Minister Kokovtsev and the former prime minister Count Witte.

Did The Peasant Sink A Second Prime Minister, Too?

After Kokovtsev's appointment as prime minister in 1911, Alix had released a 'trial balloon'. She sent Rasputin to 'examine his soul'.

As Kokovtsev subsequently recalled, 'I was startled to receive a letter from Rasputin literally containing the following: "I am planning to leave for good, and would like to meet you in order to exchange thoughts . . . say when."' And Kokovtsev agreed to meet him. An almost comical scene ensued. Rasputin entered and sat down without saying a word. His silence continued. He gazed at the prime minister. 'His eyes, set deep in their sockets, close to each other, small, and of steel-grey colour, were fixed on me, and Rasputin did not take them off me for a long time, as if he was thinking of producing some sort of hypnotic influence on me or was simply studying me.' But the peasant suddenly muttered, 'Should I leave or not, then? I no longer have an existence, and they are weaving whatever they want about me!'

Here the prime minister, according to Alix's plan, was supposed to say how he would defend Rasputin. But Kokovtsev said, 'Yes, of course, you will be doing a good thing if you leave . . . You must understand that this is not your place here, that you are injuring the sovereign by going to the palace . . . and giving ammunition to anybody you like for the most improbable inventions and conclusions.'

In reply Kokovtsev heard, 'All right, I am bad, I shall go. Let them manage without me.' Rasputin was again silent for a long time, and then he got up from his place and said only, 'Well, so we have made each other's acquaintance, then. Goodbye.'

And when Rasputin told her about Kokovtsev's suggestion that he 'leave', Alix no longer liked the prime minister. For the meeting with Rasputin had not just been a meeting with the man of God. It had above all been a trial to test Kokovtsev's readiness to submit to her opinions, his readiness to join the camp of her friends, to become one of 'ours'.

The tsarina complained to Nicky. And the sovereign asked the new prime minister to render an account of his meeting with the peasant.

When I had finished my account, the sovereign asked me, 'You did not tell him that we would send him away, if he did not leave of his own accord?' Upon receiving my answer that . . . I had no reason to threaten Rasputin with exile, since he had said that he had long wished to leave, the sovereign told me that he was glad to hear it. And that he 'would be quite pained if anyone were uneasy because of us.' Then the sovereign asked, 'What sort of impression did that peasant make on you?' I replied that I had been left with a most unpleasant impression, that it had seemed to me . . . that standing before me was a typical Siberian tramp.

Kokovtsev later formulated it even more candidly for the Extraordinary Commission: 'I served eleven years in the Central Prison Administration . . . and saw all the convict prisons, and . . . among the Siberian vagrants of unknown ancestry, as many Rasputins as you like. Men who, while making the sign of the cross, could take you by the throat and strangle you with the same smile on their faces.'

And Rasputin understood: it was time to move against Kokovtsev. 'Mama' no longer wanted the prime minister.

From Filippov's testimony in the File: 'The actual removal of Kokovtsev took place under pressure, highly skilful and persistent pressure, applied by Rasputin, who had the peculiar knack of characterizing a hated person with a single phrase or epithet that left its mark in the midst of a discussion of quite extraneous topics, a knack that had an extraordinarily magical effect on weak and haughty natures like the sovereign's.'

And although Kokovtsev had put the government's finances in order and a period of genuine stability had begun, he was sent into retirement in January 1914 as a member of the Council of State, where he was rewarded, like Witte before him, with the title of count.

It would seem that the fall of Kokovtsev should have brought about a return to the political stage of the highly intelligent Count Witte, who was so well disposed to Rasputin and who 'sang his tune', as Bogdanovich put it.

Appointing Witte, the favourite of the progressive parties and of industrial capital, would seemingly have solved all the problems. On the one hand, he was attractive to society, and on the other, he had enough intelligence and authority to seal the mouths of the elder's enemies. And Witte knew that the quick-witted Rasputin understood all this and would support him. But like many people, Witte did not grasp the true situation: Rasputin could be influential only in those instances where the tsarina had not come to her own conclusion. In the other instances he was obliged to play her game: to give expression to Alix's opinions by means of his own premonitions, predictions, and wishes.

In regard to Witte, Alix's opinion was firm. She hated him. For he was the creator of the constitution that in 1905 had limited the powers of the tsar and the future powers of her son – that had 'robbed the Little One' of his legacy. And however useful the brilliant prime minister might have been, she had never been able, nor did she wish, to overcome her feelings. Just as Marie Antoinette had been unable to overcome her own aversion both to Lafayette and Mirabeau, however useful they might have proved and however they might have tried to save her.

And Rasputin understood all this and did not even hint at his regard for Witte.

But where Alix did not have an opinion, there Rasputin's kingdom began. Here a nearly forgotten eighteenth-century practice came back into its own: that of acting through the 'tsars'' favourite. And if Rasputin could not bring about Witte's reappointment, he could still influence the appointment of the new finance minister, a position to which Alexandra Fyodorovna was perfectly indifferent.

It was then that bankers started to gather around Rasputin. And they introduced him to Pyotr Bark. Bark was a child of the young Russian capitalism. He had left the Ministry of Finance as a forty-three-year-old senior official to become the managing director of the Volga-Kama Bank, where he made good use of his old government connections. And then he left the bank and returned to active government service, becoming under Kokovtsev the deputy minister of commerce and industry. Knowing of the situation surrounding the prime minister, Bark and, most importantly, the bankers who supported him, launched a campaign to take control of the Ministry of Finance. As Filippov testified in the File, 'The fall of Kokovtsev, an extremely cautious politician in matters of finance who had evinced exceptional firmness and independence regarding the banks, was advantageous to the bankers.'

In January 1914 Ivan Goremykin became prime minister – a seventy-five-year-old whom Rasputin addressed as 'Elder', using the archaic vocative form. With Goremykin began Russia's classic policy of counter-reform, in this case a rejection of Stolypin's changes. Discussed in that connection were candidates for the new minister of finance. And Rasputin suddenly started talking about Bark's good soul and abilities. When the empress passed on Father Grigory's thoughts on Bark, the tsar could only wonder at Rasputin's importunity regarding a subject of which he had so little grasp. The only explanation was inspiration from on high. And Bark was appointed minister of finance. It was the first time that a state rather than a church appointment had come about at Rasputin's prompting. Of course, what had taken place was not merely the appointment of a new minister of finance but a revolution, one which Rasputin did not understand. He only knew that money was now being managed by one of 'ours'. In fact, it was the end of the policy conducted by Stolypin and continued by Kokovtsev. A minister of finance had been appointed who was the protégé of the mighty banks. Those banks would now through their minister of finance begin running the finances of the quasi-feudal state. Filippov, who was himself a banker and knew the machinations of banking from the inside, provided an explanation in the File.

'Bark . . . gave the banks promissory notes . . . [which] began the widespread subsidization of private banks with state funds, allegedly in support of industrial enterprises . . . The funds were then used by the banking chiefs to purchase stock certificates and speculate on their fall, which would prove especially dangerous in the initial period of the war.'

But Goremykin had neither the strength nor the ability to return Russia to the mute tranquillity of the times of Alexander III. However he enjoyed the most 'obedient' relations with Alix, received the man of God, and carefully read the interminable memos that Father Grigory sent him along with petitioners. 'Dear Elder of God, listen to them, assist them if you can, with apologies, Grigory.'

Rasputin's friend Filippov testifies in the File how the drunken Rasputin once called the elderly Goremykin at his apartment to pass on the latest petition. Goremykin apologized for not being able to receive Rasputin, since his wife was gravely ill, and Rasputin, slurring his speech, assured him 'the old woman will soon recover.' And the old woman did.

The Shadow of Marie Antoinette

The last peaceful year of their empire came to an end with a betrothal in the large Romanov family.

Zinaida's relations with the royal family had become ever more strained. Rasputin stood between them. And in November 1913 Zinaida wrote to her son about a dinner at the Livadia Palace.

> I was seated at the royal table, and during the dances I was called to sit next to the hostess, who congratulated me and spoke a great deal about the two of you. In spite of her conspicuous courtesy, the conversation was dry, and it was clear how far I was from being in her good graces. [The tsar] got off with smiles and handshaking, but didn't say a word. The fat one [Vyrubova] acts as if she enjoys all the rights of a fifth daughter . . . The black sisters [the Montenegrin princesses] walk about like people stricken with the

plague. None of the courtiers will even go up to them, seeing that the hosts ignore them completely.

It was Felix Yusupov's turn to visit his future relatives. The tsar liked to play tennis. There is even a film strip, like a message from a vanished Atlantis: Nicholas on his tennis court. On 11 November, Nicholas wrote in his diary about playing tennis with his niece's future husband. And added the sentence, 'He's the best player in Russia; there's something to be learned from him.' (That obviously non-military Adonis had to have at least some good points!)

And on 22 December 1913, Xenia recorded in her diary the mother's customary entry on a daughter's betrothal: 'God grant them happiness in love. I cannot believe that Irina is getting married!'

Since Zinaida's relations with the tsarina were strained, the wedding took place on what was for Alix 'enemy territory' – the Anichkov Palace of the dowager empress. The couple were married in the palace church. On 9 February 1914 Nicky entered in his diary, 'Alix and I and the children went to the Anichkov in the city for Irina's wedding to Felix Yusupov. Everything went well. There were lots of people.'

A royal escort and two automobiles brought Felix's new relatives, Nicky, Alix, and the girls, from Tsarskoe Selo.

Irina arrived at the palace ahead of the groom. The beauty wore a gown of white satin embroidered in silver with a long train. A rock crystal tiara with diamonds supported a lace veil. An alarming detail: the tiara had once belonged to Marie Antoinette.

The groom, resplendent in a black *redingote* with gold-stitched collar and lapels, was at the time stuck in a palace lift. It was an old one that worked intermittently. So it was soon possible to see the entire imperial family, including the emperor, making desperate attempts to free the groom from his accidental prison. While the kind Nicky and the girls tried to help, Alix silently looked on.

A few months remained before the start of world war. And exactly three years until the fall of the empire in February 1917.

The Place of Tragedy is Ready!

Felix's parents relinquished to him the left side of the ground floor of their palace on the Moika Canal. As he has described it in his memoirs, 'I installed a separate entrance and made the necessary changes. On the right were the main rooms, including the ballroom with its columns of yellow marble and arcades in the back looking out onto the winter garden, and the living room with its sapphire-coloured wallpaper and its paintings and Gobelin tapestries . . . All in the style of Louis XVI.'

All in the style of the king whose head was chopped off by revolution.

'To the right of the lobby I built temporary quarters for the times I would come to Petersburg by myself. One of the doors opened onto a hidden stairway leading down into the basement . . . I wanted to build in that part of the basement a Renaissance-style salon. The work had barely been completed when revolution broke out, and we never used that living space into which we had put so much effort.'

A crafty description. Felix did use the living space. He managed to build the 'Renaissance-style' dining room in which he would murder Rasputin.

Zinaida and the tsarina did not talk to each other during the wedding.

Alix had devised the terms 'ours' for those who liked the elder, and 'not ours' for those who did not. The latter included Elizaveta Fyodorovna's entire circle, the Moscow aristocracy, the great Romanov family, Petersburg high society, the Duma, Grand Duke Nikolai Nikolaevich, the military aristocracy who surrounded the bellicose grand duke, and the peasant's former allies, the monarchist right. 'Not ours' included just about everyone. And arrayed against them all were Alix, her Friend, and Nicky. Three valiant musketeers.

7

TEA WITH RASPUTIN:
THE PEASANT'S SALON

The Inquisitive 'Satanist'

At the beginning of 1914 one of the most influential salons in Petersburg took shape at the apartment of the peasant from Pokrovskoe. The various descriptions of that salon resemble Akutagawa's *Rashomon*. Absolutely contradictory descriptions of everything that happened there. For it was necessary to be among the initiated to see everything in its true light. The salon, like everything else in Rasputin's life, held its mystery.

On 5 August 1917, the celebrated student of sectarianism, Alexander Stepanovich Prugavin, was interrogated by the Extraordinary Commission. The sixty-six-year-old scholar testified, 'Having studied religious, and especially mystical, movements among the Russian people my whole life, I was naturally . . . interested in Rasputin's personality, too.'

In the winter of 1914 a beautiful young woman came to see Prugavin. Introducing herself as a novice writer whose work had appeared under the pseudonym Zhukovskaya, she said that her name was Vera, and that she was 'interested in religious and mystical movements' and wanted to penetrate Rasputin's inner circle. Vera Zhukovskaya relates in her memoirs how Prugavin 'looked at me in distress . . . and began asking me to give up my intention of making Rasputin's acquaintance, since the consequences of that acquaintance would be harmful to me . . . I repeated that I had made a firm decision and even asked him to obtain Rasputin's address and telephone number for me.'

Vera Zhukovskaya was a child of that time 'on the eve of apocalypse'. Like Prince Yusupov and many other young people of the day, she was completely absorbed in the search for unknown sensations. She had already experienced a great deal, including cocaine. And 'in Paris her search for religious revelation had,' as Prugavin testified, 'gone so far as Satanism and participation in black masses.' And, as she herself wrote, she had 'visited the secret meetings of the *Khlysty.*'

Rasputin's rather frightening notoriety gave her no rest.

'I have done everything to warn you, and now I wash my hands of it,' Prugavin told her then. And the next day he gave her Rasputin's address and telephone number.

As Prugavin testified in the File, Zhukovskaya not only visited Rasputin, she once even took Prugavin himself to see him.

So everything that will now be set forth is the testimony of a witness who was well acquainted with the 'elder'.

'Rasputin lived at 3 English Avenue. His telephone was 64646,' recalled Zhukovskaya. 'I didn't tarry and called him at once . . . I happened to make the call at a rare moment when Rasputin's phone was free. I heard a rather raspy voice say, "Well, who's there? I'm listening." My voice slightly trembling, I asked, "Father Grigory? This is a young lady speaking. I've heard a great deal about you. I'm not from here, and I would very much like to meet you."'

In less than an hour she was entering the doorway of

an enormous grey building . . . Standing nearby in the lobby were a stuffed wolf and a bear . . . against the background of a decadent-style window on whose sill a bush of pink heather had begun to wither . . . The lift stopped at the very top . . . At my ring, the door was opened by a short plump woman in a white kerchief [this was Akilina Laptinskaya]. Her widely spaced grey eyes gazed unwelcomingly. 'Do you have an appointment? Come in . . .' A door on the other side of the vestibule opened, and Rasputin quickly emerged, moving as if sideways and shuffling his feet. Stocky with unusually broad shoulders, he was dressed in a lilac silk shirt with a crimson waistband, striped English trousers, and two-tone high-top shoes . . . Dark, wrinkled skin . . . His hair, carelessly parted in the middle and quite long . . . and his beard were of an almost uniformly dark reddish-brown colour. Coming right up to me, he took my hand and bowed. I saw a broad, pock-marked nose . . . and then he gazed at me with small, light-coloured eyes set deep in his wrinkles. On the right one was a little yellow excrescence . . . A kind of unpleasant feral power emanated from them. They gazed intently with infrequent blinking, and that motionless, magnetic stare was disconcerting. 'Take her to my room,' Rasputin said in an undertone, indicating me.

She was taken to a narrow room with a single window 'through the vestibule past a closed door behind which restrained voices could be heard'. It was there, in the apartment's largest room, that his 'salon' of admirers gathered, and it was their voices she heard.

> Left alone, I looked around. Next to the wall by the door was a bed covered with a multicoloured silk patchwork quilt on top of fluffed-up pillows, and beside the bed there was a washstand . . . Near the washstand by the window was a writing desk. In the very centre of the desk was a large gold pocket watch with the state coat of arms on its cover . . . There was no icon in the corner, but on the windowsill there was a large photograph of the altar of St Isaac's Cathedral, and hanging from the photograph a handful of different coloured ribbons. And by analogy I remembered a little peasant cabin belonging to 'God's people' [the *Khlysty*] on the outskirts of Kiev: there had been no icon in the corner there either, but standing on a windowsill was an image of the Saviour with ribbons hanging from it . . . Pulling up a chair, he sat down across from me, placing my legs between his knees.

It was with the woman's legs pressed between his knees that the seduction began (as we shall hear from many witnesses). Or, more accurately, a monologue on the religious basis of sin.

> 'Don't you believe the priests. They're foolish. They don't know the whole mystery. Sin is given so that we may repent, and repentance brings joy to the soul and strength to the body, understand? O, you are my dear, my honey bee . . . Sin should be understood . . . Without sin there is no life, because there is no repentance, and if there is no repentance, there is no joy . . . You want me to show you what sin is? Wait a while till next week, then come to me after taking communion, when there will be heaven in your soul. Then I will show you what sin is . . .' Someone terrifying and ruthless was gazing at me from the depths of those almost hidden pupils. And then his eyes opened wide, the wrinkles were smoothed out, and after giving me a tender glance, he quietly asked, 'Why are you looking at me like that, little bee?' and bending down, he kissed me with cold monastic exultation.

And then she left. Evidently a bit disappointed by his affectionate yet indifferent parting words: 'Only see that you come back soon.'

The Salon Assembles

And then . . . We shall take her word for it that 'nothing happened' later. Rasputin merely introduced her to his 'salon'. And she wrote it all down in detail.

There were about ten ladies in all. At the far end of the table was a young man in a morning coat, frowning and, apparently, troubled by something. Next to him, leaning against the back of her chair, sat a very young pregnant lady in a let-out blouse. Her large blue eyes gazed tenderly at Rasputin. These were the Pistolkorses, husband and wife, as I later learned in talking to them. But in all the subsequent years of my acquaintance with them, I never saw Pistolkors himself at Rasputin's again, only Sana. Next to Sana sat Lyubov Vasilievna Golovina, and I liked her pale, sere face very much. She acted as if she were the hostess, serving everyone and keeping the general conversation going.

She saw Vyrubova, too.

I looked at her with curiosity: a tall, stout blonde who was dressed too simply, somehow, and even tastelessly. Her face was ugly with a bright crimson sensual mouth and large blue eyes that gleamed unnaturally. Her face constantly changed. It was somehow evasive, duplicitous, deceptive, and a mysterious voluptuousness and a kind of unquenchable anxiety alternated in it with an almost ascetic severity. I have never seen another face like it in my life, and I must say that it produced an indelible impression.

Sitting next to her was Munya Golovina . . . who gazed at me with timid, blinking, pale blue eyes . . . The rest of the ladies were of no consequence, and all somehow of one face.

The Little Dandy

Another lady, too, has described Rasputin's devotees. Like Zhukovskaya and many others, she had been subjected to the seduction rite. She had listened to and transcribed the same hypnotic whisper that 'there is no sin in this. That is something that people have made up. Look at the wild animals. Do they know anything of sin? There is wisdom in simplicity. Do not shrivel your own heart.'

She, too, had heard strange assurances from Father Grigory's permanent devotees. The very pure Munya would tell her something mysterious: 'He makes everything holy.' And on behalf of them all, Munya would ask her not to torment him . . . and to yield to him, 'for with him there is no sin'.

'Little Dandy', Rasputin eloquently called her. Vera Dzhanumova was the young woman's name, and it is mentioned more than once in the police agents' reports. 'Rasputin sent a telegram to Dzhanumova: "Pampered treasure, I am firmly with you in spirit. Kisses."' Or, 'He took Dzhanumova . . . out to the Donon.'

Vera Dzhanumova, the wife of a wealthy Moscow merchant, would after emigrating from Russia publish her memoirs, in which she, too, would describe Rasputin's salon.

He sat at the table surrounded by his admirers. Everything was mixed up together at that table – chinchilla, silk, and dark homespun, diamonds of the first water and slender egret feathers for the hair, the white kerchiefs of sisters of mercy and the scarves of old women – and all of it was described by the astonished 'Little Dandy'. 'The doorbell would bring a basket of roses and a dozen embroidered silk shirts of various hues, [or] a heavy peasant's coat with a brocade lining of astonishing work.' The tidy Akilina Laptinskaya would gather it all up and carry it off to the other rooms. The tea drinking would begin. A table set for tea with sweets for the guests. Rasputin did not eat sweets, as the witnesses have testified. 'He never ate sweets,' his secretary Simanovich recalled. And his daughter Matryona would mention the same thing in her book of memoirs. Let us remember that, and remember it well: he did not eat sweets.

Before 1913 he did not drink wine and condemned those who did.

From the testimony of Lokhtina: 'Father Grigory did not use to drink at all.' And Sazonov also declares, 'In that period . . . he did not drink anything.' And if wine did turn up on his table, then there was just a little and of the sweet variety. He had become used to sweet wines in the monasteries during his wanderings.

And the ladies would keep arriving. Whenever the bell rang, Munya would run into the hall to open the front door, and that daughter of the maid of honour to two empresses and the relative of a grand duke would help the new arrivals to remove their overshoes. For he had taught them humility.

Then Princess Shakhovskaya arrived. 'The princess, who had abandoned her husband and children to follow Rasputin continually for four years, was a woman of striking beauty and dark eyes,' Dzhanumova recalls. That beauty was one of the first Russian woman aviators and she had even walked away from a crash.

And all those who came began with the ritual of hand-kissing.

From Alexandra Guschina's testimony in the File: 'I would drop by to visit him only in the afternoons . . . I saw many ladies, [who] all treated him with extreme deference and kissed his hand.'

Then the salon sat down to tea. Zhukovskaya recalls:

On one corner of the table an enormous brightly polished samovar was boiling . . . [but] what had been put out was very odd: right on the tablecloth next to sumptuous tortes and magnificent crystal bowls with fruit

were little piles of peppermint gingersnaps and heaps of large crude rolls.
The jam had been served in smeared jars, and lying next to a luxurious dish
of sturgeon in aspic were large slices of black bread . . . In a deep bowl in
front of Rasputin were twenty or so boiled eggs and a bottle of Cahors. All
extended their hands to him and their eyes gleamed: 'Father, an egg!'
Rasputin took a whole handful of eggs and started presenting them to the
ladies, placing an egg in each extended palm . . . Vyrubova got up and went
over to Rasputin, where she gave him two pickles on a piece of bread.
Rasputin crossed himself and then started eating, biting off by turns first
some bread, then some pickle. He always ate with his hands, even fish, and
after wiping his greasy fingers a little between bites, he petted the women
sitting next to him while uttering his 'teachings' . . . And then . . . a tall
girl in a gymnasium frock came in. Everyone's hands were extended to her
in greeting: 'Mara, Marochka!' It was a very curious thing to see all those
princesses and countesses kissing Rasputin's daughter, and one even . . .
kissed her hands.

Faces Out Of Oblivion

But what is most astonishing is that the File will now give us the chance to
see many of those who sat around Rasputin's table with our own eyes.

Two photographs were taken of the 'salon' at approximately that time.

And both of them survived the war and the revolution. The first and
most popular is probably in all the books about Rasputin. It was taken in
the same main room described by Zhukovskaya, where Rasputin's salon
used to gather round the table for tea. Visible in the background is an open
doorway leading to the hall and the next room, the 'special room'.

Rasputin is sitting on a chair in the centre. He is wearing a light peasant
blouse girded at the waist with a cord, a polished boot gleams, his beard
and hair are carefully combed, since he has just come from mass, and his
left hand is pressed against his breast. But you only notice that afterwards,
for the dazzling gaze of his eyes draws you in, pushing everything into the
background and becoming the centre of the picture. Next to him is the
already plundered table, the table after tea with a dish and a pile of left-over
rolls and little bagels. And around Rasputin and by him and behind him
and along the wall and in front of the doorway to the other room crowd
the same ten or so women and a few men. And peering from next to the
doorway is the telephone that was used to call him from Tsarskoe Selo
about the sick boy.

The second picture is also popular, but it contains fewer people than the first one. Rasputin is sitting at the same table set for tea. He is dressed in black. And again his eyes gleam in the same way. This time he is surrounded by seven ladies and a girl in a then fashionable sailor's blouse sitting decorously around the table, their faces turned towards the photographer. Some of them were also in the first picture. The only young man in the picture stands next to the closed glass door. That very pleasant young man in a moustache was in the first photograph, too.

Both pictures are usually accompanied by the mute inscription, 'Rasputin surrounded by his admirers,' although sometimes, it is true, there is a line to the effect that 'Vyrubova is in the second row.' All the other people in both photographs have remained anonymous, their names having slid into oblivion.

But in the File I found their names! It turns out that the investigators of the Extraordinary Commission had identified them.

The File, from the testimony of Vyrubova on the two photographs: 'That one and the other group analogous to it were photographed by chance – I don't remember on whose initiative – on one of those Sundays when Rasputin liked to have his close friends gather round his table for tea after mass.'

And she identified those 'close friends', 'the visitors of the first period': 'Golovina, Dehn, my sister Pistolkors, and the highly dubious baptized Yids, the Volynskys'. And also Molchanov.

Yes, the pleasant young man in both photographs is Leonid Alexeevich Molchanov, whose testimony I have already cited many times – the son of Bishop Alexei who became exarch of Georgia, thanks to Rasputin.

And summoned before the investigators, Leonid Molchanov himself identified each person in the first photograph in detail. And that polite young man's memory had retained not merely their last names but also their first names and patronymics. Clearly these people constituted Rasputin's permanent circle.

Thus, that photograph taken in 1914 on the eve of a terrible war came to life. And it turned out to include not only many familiar people, those already glimpsed more than once in these pages, but also those belonging to Rasputin's future.

From Molchanov's testimony in the File: 'Two group photographs were taken in that apartment of Rasputin's on English Avenue and later widely disseminated.' And then he turned to the first picture with all the people.

'In the last row from left to right are Alexandra Pistolkors and her husband.'

They are standing against the wall – a stout, well-groomed, tall young gentleman, and next to him, his wife Sana with her childlike little porcelain face and her great belly (she was pregnant, as Zhukovskaya mentioned). We shall recall once more that Alexandra Pistolkors, née Taneeva, was Vyrubova's younger sister, and that her husband, Alexander Erikovich Pistolkors, was the son of Munya Golovina's Aunt Olga, who had made a scandalous marriage to Grand Duke Pavel. Alexander Erikovich, a former Life Guards officer famous for his cruelty in the suppression of the 1905 revolution, was now retired with a modest post in the state chancery.

Next to the Pistolkorses a young man with a moustache strains to make his face stand out from the others. This is in fact Molchanov himself.

From Molchanov's testimony: 'After the Pistolkorses comes me, and then Prince Zhevakhov, brought by his colleague Pistolkors.'

The short moustached prince stands by the doorway, although he is barely visible behind the women's heads and hats. Yet Prince Nikolai Zhevakhov, a mystic who had taken many trips to monasteries, and who collected apocalyptic visions and reported on them to the tsarina, would become a true devotee of the 'elder'. And Rasputin would later take that into account. In September 1916 this young man who had previously occupied an extremely minor post, would with Rasputin's help be appointed deputy chief procurator of the Most Holy Synod.

Next to the prince, Molchanov identified two rank-and-file characters, Ervin Khristoforovich Gill, the husband of a pretty devotee of Rasputin's, and Nina Dmitrievna Yakhimovich, a tall, broad-shouldered lady and one of his truly uncomplaining devotees. And then Molchanov named two figures of greater significance: Olga Vasilievna Loman and her daughter Nadezhda. This was the family of Dmitry Loman, who as has already been mentioned was the builder and warden of the 'tsars'' favourite Feodor Cathedral in Tsarskoe Selo. A former faithful devotee of Rasputin's, Loman had in 1913 begun making overtures to Rasputin's enemy Grand Duchess Elizaveta Fyodorovna, after which 'Vyrubova had announced to ours' that 'we should be more guarded' with him.

From Loman's testimony: 'From that time on I began to notice a cold attitude toward me . . . and I was afraid I would be sent away from the palace for good . . . and suffer for it.'

The resourceful colonel therefore tried to re-establish relations with Rasputin. His wife, an ugly middle-aged lady with a mean face, and their young daughter were now frequent visitors at Rasputin's salon.

The young woman with the hard, cold face standing to the right of Olga Loman and her daughter is another very important figure from Rasputin's future life. She is Anna Ivanovna Reshetnikova, the daughter of the very rich and very old Moscow merchant's wife Anisia Reshetnikova, with whom Rasputin often stayed in Moscow. Anna's brother would become one of the most trusted people around Rasputin. The brother did not have the best of pasts.

From Filippov's testimony: 'The former notary Reshetnikov, who had been convicted of forgery and embezzlement, had been pardoned thanks to Rasputin.'

Reshetnikov would very soon start collecting money from Rasputin's visitors, and his sister Anna would play a special role in the scandal involving Rasputin at the Yar, a restaurant in Moscow. (See Chapter Ten.)

'In the second row is Sophia Volynskaya.' She, too, is a person from Rasputin's future, of the second stage of his life, which would begin that same year, 1914.

From Filippov's testimony in the File: 'Volynskaya, a beautiful, not very young Jew . . . the wife of the agronomist Volynsky . . . was a fateful person for Rasputin in the sense of his shift from charity to the cruel exploitation of his clients with the help of that same Volynskaya. Her husband [who had also been tried] . . . was pardoned, and out of gratitude had made himself something like a financial adviser and instigator of several profitable ventures for Rasputin.'

So he had managed to release Reshetnikov and Volynsky, two of his future 'secretaries', from punishment. That was part of his teaching, too. It was not for nothing that the tsarina wrote down in her notebook his words, 'Never fear to release prisoners, to restore sinners to a life of righteousness . . . Prisoners . . . become through their sufferings in the eyes of God – nobler than we.'

True, rumour had it that the beautiful Jew Volynskaya had visited the 'special room', where she had paid with her flesh for Rasputin's efforts on her husband's behalf. But it was merely a rumour.

From Molchanov's testimony: 'Next comes Vyrubova' (Vyrubova herself, with her large fleshy moon-like face, had been forced to stand by the hated 'Yid').

Next to Vyrubova are two acquaintances of ours whose testimony from the File has already been cited. The old woman in mourning is Alexandra Guschina, the inconsolable widow who met Rasputin during prayer. The good-looking woman beside her in the fashionable bonnet with the plume is Yulia Dehn, after Vyrubova the tsarina's closest friend.

And, finally, there is one other noteworthy character in the row – the rough, short old peasant man with the shaggy hair and beard, a kind of minor pagan god, a Russian Pan. And Molchanov identifies him, too. He is 'Rasputin's father'.

'In the first row are Zina Timofeeva, Maria Golovina, Maria Gill, Rasputin, and Madame Kleist, in regard to whom I was told that she was a dilettante actress and dancer,' Molchanov continues in his survey.

These young devotees – Zina Timofeeva, Olga Kleist, and Maria Gill – had passed through the 'special room' and had thus been rewarded with seats in Rasputin's front row. But they would soon share the fate of those 'who flashed by and vanished'. The only one who would stay any length of time was Maria Gill: 'the twenty-six-year-old captain's wife' is among the visitors after 1914 mentioned by the agents who watched Rasputin.

And among these ephemeral devotees she sits, too – Maria Golovina, the famous Munya, as Rasputin himself called her. With a calm and unattractive face, growing old, 'a most pure young woman', as Felix Yusupov described her. She has remained unruffled amid all the madness taking place around the elder. For she has been initiated and knows all the secrets of the elder's teaching.

And finally the last character in the photograph. She sits right on the floor, a heavy-set woman with the wide, stubborn peasant face, and thus her heavy peasant legs and bottom are out of view. From Molchanov's testimony: 'At Rasputin's feet is Akilina Laptinskaya.' She, too, was one of the keepers of Rasputin's secrets.

The Jealous Man And The
Fat Secretary

Akilina, Rasputin's 'secretary', had already inaugurated the second stage in his life. It was at the beginning of 1914 that she began to take money from his supplicants. 'Laptinskaya, being a person of exceptional intelligence and perseverance, was guided exclusively by mercenary considerations: various people made presents to her of specific sums on the occasion of Rasputin's arrival or for Rasputin. And Rasputin threw her out a couple of times or so for taking bribes and on suspicion of stealing sums in the thousands,' Filippov testified.

But by the beginning of 1914 Rasputin had not only got used to her greed and given up on it; he had come to appreciate just how convenient it was. Now he would not have to borrow money and wait for handouts from the stingy tsarina. Now Laptinskaya would hand money over to him. And he himself could be generous, do good works, and give money to the men and women who asked for it. The fat Akilina, of course, had never been afraid of his rages. She was not only his 'secretary'. Like other simple people, Rasputin liked an abundance of flesh.

And he was jealous of her!

In the File Filippov recalls an episode relating to 1915 when the former nurse Akilina started working on the hospital train organized by the empress.

> I happened to run into Akilina Laptinskaya before her departure for the front. I stopped by to see her in her car and gave her a box of candy. Rasputin found out about it . . . and started berating me furiously and at length for 'leading his sweetheart astray whom he had long kept for himself as the apple of his eye'. For a long time I could not understand what he was talking about. It turned out the 'sweetheart' was Laptinskaya, a woman . . . of inordinate corpulence . . . The 'sweetheart', who had often visited me, was forbidden to see me.

Rasputin, that pursuer of women, struck Filippov as pathologically jealous. For example, one of his true worshippers, a certain Elena Patushinskaya, the wife of a modest notary in Yaluturovsk, had come to visit him in March 1914. Noted many times in Pokrovskoe by the external surveillance agents, she had dropped out of sight in Petersburg. This is what Filippov says about her in his testimony:

'I remember Patushinskaya, the wife of a notary from Siberia and a pretty woman, who lived with him for several months on two separate occasions, although never showing herself, since Rasputin was not only physically but also Platonically jealous. For example, he did not like it when people said, "Oh, what a good-looking woman" in reference to "his women".'

So the pretty Patushinskaya, hidden in the apartment's depths, did not get into the photograph.

From Molchanov's testimony: 'That group was photographed by the photographer Kristinin completely by chance at the wish of one of those present.'

Regarding the other photograph, he testified: 'Not long before that or soon afterward he also photographed another group similar to the first . . . As far I remember, besides Rasputin that group included Madame Golovina, Madame Gill, Dehn, a woman who had come from Siberia with some request for Rasputin, an old woman from Vasiliev Island, and Rasputin's elder daughter Matryona.'

The two photographs, taken before the terrible July of 1914 and the beginning of the world war, sum up, as it were, the first period of Rasputin's life.

Molchanov's testimony is completely confirmed by the testimony in the File of one other figure who appears in both photographs – Munya Golovina.

The small cardboard photograph shown to me in which I am depicted in
the first row as the second person from the left also depicts those who had
gathered at Father Grigory's apartment on English Avenue. Shown besides
me and Father Grigory are Zina Timofeeva, Maria Sergeevna Gill . . . Olga
Kleist, [and], at Rasputin's feet, Akilina Laptinskaya . . . In the second row
are Alexandra Alexandrovna and Alexander Erikovich Pistolkors, Sofia
Leontievna Volynskaya, Anya Vyrubova, Alexandra Georgievna Guschina,
a doctor's widow, and Rasputin's father, now passed away.

And Munya conscientiously lists the same names.

Ladies Outside The Frame:
The Mysterious Priestess

But the person who may have been the salon's most important and mysterious visitor remained outside the frame. She was absent when the pictures
were taken. Olga Lokhtina was then living at Father Makary's cloister. And
she returned to the capital, to the 'Lord of hosts', only occasionally. Her
appearances at Rasputin's home are described in much the same way by all
the eyewitnesses.

From Zhukovskaya's memoirs:

A loud noise was heard in the vestibule. I turned toward the partly open
door where something unbelievably bright, wide, and developing . . . was
already fluttering on the threshold . . . In an absurdly high, resounding
voice it sang out hysterically, 'Chri-i-i-st is Ri-i-sen!!!' Then the something
rushed past me . . . and flopped down between Rasputin's chair and mine
. . . After rushing in, Lokhtina embraced his head from behind and started
kissing him wildly, yelling in a broken voice choking with emotion, 'Dear
little one, blessed vessel, little bearded one . . .' Desperately fighting her off,
Rasputin yelled, half-suffocated, 'Unhand me, Satan!' When he had at last
released his neck from her grasp, he threw her with all his might into a
corner . . . Breathing heavily, Lokhtina made her way over to the couch . . .
[and] roundly cried out, 'But you are still mi-i-ne! And I kno-o-w you lo-
o-ve me-e!'

'I loath you, you scum!' Rasputin quickly and decisively retorted. 'But I
will kiss you again.'

Immediately running over to Rasputin, Lokhtina grabbed him by the
head . . . Rasputin struck her so hard that she was hurled against the wall,
but . . . again she started yelling ecstatically, 'Go ahead, beat me, beat me,
beat me!' And bending her head, she tried to kiss the place on her breast

where Rasputin had hit her . . . She recalled a kind of strange priestess, relentless in her rage and adoration.

Filippov, of course, has already described a similar scene of battery.

But after the battery Zhukovskaya saw an altogether mysterious rite. Suddenly Vyrubova went over to Lokhtina, kneeled down in front of her, kissed her hand, and then returned to her place. 'You have guessed, at last!' Lokhtina said very calmly. And then she said, 'Is there a reason I am not seeing my novice? Promptly, now! Kneel, and my hand, my hand!'

And Munya, keeling before Lokhtina, kissed her hand.

And it was no invention. For Munya Golovina even had occasion to explain her strange reverence for Lokhtina to an investigator in the File.

From Golovina's testimony: In 1913, as a form of protest against the attacks on Lokhtina, I started calling myself her novice and served her whenever she came to Petersburg . . . I wanted thereby to take the place of her beloved daughter, and I proposed to Lokhtina that it would be easier for her if she transferred her love, even if it was to some outsider.' That was all that she was able to explain to the investigator.

But the question still remains: why did Vyrubova, a rather cold, calculating person, also bow down before Lokhtina? And why in the File do the witnesses speak of the insolent telegrams sent by the general's wife to Tsarskoe Selo that were nonetheless tolerated by the tsarina herself? And why did the tsar's daughters correspond with her?

'She left letters and papers at the Napoikins' apartment [where she lived] . . . I made copies of the letters to her from the grand duchesses Olga, Tatyana, and Maria,' Prugavin testified in the File. And by no means did Rasputin always beat her. Sometimes he even conversed with her for a long time. And she behaved severely with his devotees, like someone older. That in fact is how another witness, the singer Belling, has described the mysterious general's wife:

A woman came in . . . dressed in a white homespun dress of old-fashioned cut with the white headgear of an Orthodox nun on her head . . . Hanging from her neck were numerous little books with crosses – twelve copies of the Gospels . . . She . . . whispered something to Rasputin, and whenever someone spoke loudly, she looked angrily in that person's direction, and then could no longer restrain herself and said, 'Here at the father's, as in a temple, you should behave with grandeur.'

'Leave them alone, let them enjoy themselves,' Rasputin said.

'One should have joy in one's heart but humility on the outside,' she sternly reproved him.

And Prugavin, the student of sects, was probably right when in the File he slightly parted the curtain concealing the strange general's wife: 'I would not be prepared to say that she was mentally ill merely because she maintained that Grigory was the "Lord of hosts" and Iliodor, "Christ", since I would in that case also have to acknowledge the mental illness of the *Khlysty*, in whose mysticism one finds the assertion of such incarnations regarding one or another teacher.'

So the question remains: just who was the strange general's wife?

Yet Another Mysterious Lady

There is yet another of Rasputin's admirers who was not in the photograph. Even though her name is often glimpsed in the reports of the security agents: 'On 27 August at 10:55 Vera Illarionovna, the Baroness Kusova, arrived to see him . . . The baroness spent the night at his place.'

'The Baroness Kusova left his place at 07:30 on 28 August.'

'The striking brunette Baroness K.,' as Dzhanumova describes her.

'Kusova regularly frequented Rasputin's salon; she was regularly in attendance there. She had various kinds of business there, various deals,' a witness testified before the Extraordinary Commission. Which means she was one of the practical ladies with the mercantile ideas who traded her 'body'?

Vera Kusova herself says something similar, in any case.

The File, from the testimony of Baroness Vera Illarionovna Kusova, twenty-seven years old:

> I made Grigory Rasputin's acquaintance in 1913 . . . My husband was serving in the Crimean regiment, whose patron was the empress . . . The royal family was then living in the Crimea. I wanted to make better arrangements for my husband. With that purpose but also out of curiosity I once approached Rasputin at the shore . . . After introducing myself to him, I stated my request. Rasputin promised to help me. In July I went to Petersburg for about two weeks and visited Rasputin with the purpose of asking him again about an arrangement for someone who was very close to me, and also with the purpose of asking him for spiritual support in relation to a misfortune that had befallen me . . . It turned out, however, that he was unable to give me any spiritual solace, since I saw that he spoke commonplaces to those who came to him for advice. Nevertheless, I continued to visit Rasputin in order to meet with people there who were interesting or necessary to me . . . I did not view Rasputin as a holy person.

And then the investigator presented Kusova with a certain telegram for her to explain. 'There was much that was revealed to him,' she suddenly said, 'and that is why I wrote to Laptinskaya in 1916, "Oh, if only Father Grigory, who would somehow help from there, too [that is, from beyond the grave], would teach me."'

So when Rasputin was already dead and she could no longer meet people at his home 'who were necessary' to her, she not only continued to communicate with Akilina but even asked for Grigory's help from beyond the grave. For, it turned out, 'Much was revealed to him.' Even though she had just declared that 'he was unable to give any spiritual solace.'

Perhaps, like Vyrubova, she was by no means telling the Commission everything.

All the more so, since in Lokhtina's testimony in the File we learn something quite different about Kusova: 'At our first meeting . . . she related . . . that her life was in fact not good . . . Later I happened to hear that her husband drank heavily, and that she suffered because of it. She related that once while drunk he had ridden a horse into her bedroom.' Yes, the baroness was, above all, an unhappy woman in need of comfort. And more. In the same testimony given by Lokhtina there is a most interesting fact. It turns out that the baroness, like Lokhtina herself, greeted those around her with 'Christ is risen,' even though it was not Easter.

A Sermon And A Dance

And all during tea Rasputin spoke without stopping. And while he talked he would from time to time nervously break off a piece of bread and throw it down on the tablecloth, or crumble the rolls with his stubby fingers. But they did not see that. They were listening to him and attending to his sermon.

From Guschina's testimony: 'Rasputin impressed me as a holy man. He spoke of God and the soul.'

Prince Zhevakhov (the same one who is in the photograph) recalled the first time he heard Rasputin preach. His colleague Pistolkors had taken him to a Petersburg apartment on Vasiliev Island filled with the curious. And he never forget Rasputin's inspired speech.

'How is brutalized man with his beast's habits to begin living a life that is pleasing to God?' Rasputin said. 'How is he to climb up out of the pit of sin? How is he to find the path that leads from our cesspool into fresh air and the light of God? There is such a path. And I shall show it to you.

Salvation is in God . . . And you shall see God only, and only when you see nothing else around you. Because everything around you, all that you do, and even the room in which you sit, conceals God from you. What then must you do to see God?' he asked with a sort of nervous intensity in the hush that had fallen. 'After a church service in which you spend time in prayer, go outside the city on a Sunday or a holiday to some clean field. And walk, walk, until behind you see not the black cloud from factory chimneys that hangs over Petersburg but the blue of the horizon. Stand then and think about yourself. How small and insignificant you will seem to yourself then, and the whole capital – what an anthill it will have turned into in your mental gaze . . . And then what will become of your pride, your self-esteem, your consciousness of power? And you will lift up your eyes to heaven . . . and you will feel with all your heart, with all your soul, that you are one with the Lord, our Father, and that He is the only one who needs your soul. That He alone will stand up for you . . . and help you. And will find for you such compassion . . . That will be your first step along the path to God. This time, you may not go any further along that path. Return to the world, resume your former activity, but hold on to what you have brought back like the apple of your eye. It is God you have brought back with you. And preserve Him and let everything you do in the world now pass through Him . . . Only then will any earthly affair be transformed into the work of God. For it is as the Saviour has said, "the Kingdom of God is within us." Find God, and live in him and with him.'

'What a reverent hush there was in the room!' Zhevakhov recalled. Even though Rasputin had said nothing new. But a sort of nervous power emanating from him had hypnotized his listeners. So that one may easily imagine what silence, what reverence there was whenever he spoke at the table to those who were devoted to him. And often he would suddenly break off what he was saying, and the resonant voice that Dzhanumova found so astonishing would command, 'Write!'

He had become used to it. He would give someone a pencil, and she would transcribe his words. He often repeated his teachings. He knew how important it was to repeat things to his 'fools' (as he called his devotees in one of his telegrams – 'fools' because they were educated and did not understand simple things). And he dictated ways to keep Love in one's soul through all calamities and revilement. But above all he spoke about Love for the Creator to those unhappy women, those widows and women who had been divorced or cast off by their husbands, or who no longer enjoyed their love. Abandoned and offended women constituted the absolute major-ity in his salon.

'Creator! Teach me to love. Then shall all my wounds received in love be as nothing and my sufferings become pleasing to me.' And the words sounded like the Song of Songs: 'God, I am Thine, and Thou art mine. Do not deprive me of Thy love!' This transcription was made by the tsarina.

When they were spellbound by his teaching, when the faces of his 'fools' shone, he instructed them to sing hymns. And all together the Petersburg ladies sang the old hymns. Along with the peasant.

Guschina, Vyrubova, and Golovina have talked about those hymns. 'Akilina in a high beautiful soprano voice started to sing and the others joined in . . . Rasputin's pleasant deep voice resonated like an accompaniment, setting off and playing up the women's voices. I had never heard such spiritual singing before. It was beautiful and sad. Then they started to chant Psalms,' Dzhanumova recalled.

And he schooled the royal family in the same thing. As witnesses would testify, they often sang hymns together in their house arrest after the revolution. And at the moment of greatest enthusiasm, of almost general exaltation, Rasputin would suddenly leap to his feet and demand music. And then his famous, somehow desperate dancing would begin. Filippov recalled:

There was in his dancing something *Khlyst*-like. . . . He danced assiduously and at length, with special nervous, frenzied movements, leaping and from time to time shouting 'Oh!' the way someone would cry out upon being lowered into icy water . . . He danced fifteen minutes to an hour without ceasing . . . inspired to the point of a kind of ecstasy or frenzy . . . He said that all religious people must be good dancers, and in that connection mentioned King David, who had danced down an entire road in front of a temple.

But sometimes at the height of the festivities the telephone would ring, reducing his entire salon to holy awe. And Akilina's solemn voice would inform Rasputin that there was a call 'from Tsarskoe Selo!'

And then the guests would begin to leave. And parting with Rasputin was a ritual, too.

'They started to disperse,' Dzhanumova recalled, 'and kissed the father's hand, and he embraced each one and kissed her on the lips . . . 'Some rusks, father,' the ladies asked. He handed out burned rusks to them all, which they wrapped up in their scented handkerchiefs . . . and put away in their handbags . . . and then they whispered to the maid, asking for the father's dirty linen . . . And with his sweat, if possible.' And under the intelligent Akilina's stern gaze, the ladies would collect the peasant's dirty linen. And Munya would help those who were leaving to put on their boots.

From the testimony of Molchanov: 'They would try to say goodbye to
him in private, for which they would step into the hallway. I shall note this
strange behaviour on the part of Vyrubova: once after saying goodbye to
Rasputin in the hallway, she came back into the room for some reason, but
on doing so refused to shake my hand goodbye, announcing that she had
already said good-bye to the father and would not be saying any more
goodbyes.' It was so nice to take away with oneself the warmth of the holy
hand that brought happiness.

Finale Of The First Period: The Mystery Remains

We have come as far as 1914, carefully following the track of Rasputin's
biography.

I have tried to tell everything in detail, and have patiently cited the
testimony of both his friends and his enemies. But the two questions posed
at the beginning remain. Just who was he really? And what was he for the
royal family?

One thing is clear, however: Rasputin was no calculating Tartuffe who
made fools of people with pious sermonizing. Tartuffe's was a European
personality. Rasputin's is mysteriously Asiatic and a good deal more complicated, and his secret a good deal stranger.

I have quoted Rasputin's thoughts at length. Were they searchings,
appeals to God, moments of lucidity, insights? I can now answer that they
were all those things.

But the prostitutes, the endless 'little ladies', the devotee-'fools', who
visited the 'special room' and, becoming half-mad, mixed up religion with
lust? And I can answer that yes, they too existed.

Yet at the same time Sazonov, Molchanov, and Filippov all speak in the
File of this period of Rasputin's life as a 'spiritual' one: 'A period in
Rasputin's life that I may call a period in which he attained a certain
spiritual loftiness from which he later slid' (Sazonov), 'in that period
Rasputin drank little, and the whole period of his life bore the stamp of
modesty' (Molchanov), 'being poetically dreamy in the first period of
1911–13' (Filippov).

Did they not know about his secret life? But Filippov knew a lot.
Then why do they speak of his spirituality? And, finally, the royal family:
yes, Rasputin preached love, was disinterested, told the 'tsars' about things
they did not know – about the work and everyday life of the common
people, about the joys of the wanderer at one with nature and God – and

he relieved the tsarina's attacks of nervousness, and instilled confidence in the tsar. And he saved their son.

But the unending articles in the newspapers, the police descriptions of his pursuit of prostitutes, the inquiries by the Duma with quotations from the evidence of his victims, the story of the royal children's nurse. All this reached the tsar and tsarina. On every side. Both prime ministers, Stolypin and Kokovtsev, the maids of honour at court, the tsarina's beloved sister Ella and the other members of the Romanov family all the way to the Grand Duke Nikolai Nikolaevich (in whom, by the way, the tsar continued have so much trust that he appointed him commander-in-chief in the war), the tsarina's confessor Feofan – all these people told the tsar and tsarina about Rasputin's debauchery. But they did not believe it!

Did not believe it? Or did they know something that explained his behaviour? Something that was beyond the ken of all those shallow accusers?

8

GAMES OF
THE FLESH

The Mystery Of His Teachings

To venture an answer to all these questions, I shall first have to return to
the attempt to explain Rasputin's teachings.

Zhukovskaya says of Rasputin:

> I first heard of him in Kiev. At the time I had just graduated from preparatory
> school and, thanks to a chance acquaintance, was visiting the secret meetings
> of God's people, as they called themselves (much later I learned that they
> are also the ones called the *Khlysty*). And it was there on the outskirts of
> the city during the usual evening tea with raisins, the favourite beverage of
> 'God's people', that Kuzma Ivanych, as our host was called, suddenly started
> talking about the elder Grigory Rasputin . . . Narrowing his bright eyes (all
> the *Khlysty* have utterly special eyes: they burn with a sort of liquid,
> iridescent light, and sometimes the gleam becomes perfectly unbearable),
> he . . . said with reluctance, 'He was one of our brethren, but we have since
> disavowed him: he has buried the spirit in the flesh.'

None of the most prominent experts in Russian sectarianism then doubted
that Rasputin was a *Khlyst*. Alexander Prugavin, who devoted his whole
life to study of the sects, and who as a Socialist-Revolutionary greatly
respected the *Khlysty* and saw in them an 'Orthodoxy of the peasantry',
collected the stories of people who had visited Rasputin, proving thereby
that Rasputin was a *Khlyst* who, through his escapades, had distorted and
compromised the *Khlyst* idea. The theologian Novosyolov, the head chaplain of the army and the navy Georgy Shavelsky, the celebrated philosopher
Sergei Bulgakov, the archbishop Antony Volynsky, and the bishops Hermogen and Feofan – all both left and right – maintained that Rasputin
was a *Khlyst*. And, finally, his friend Filippov testifies in the File that 'Some

sense told me that [he] was a *Khlyst* . . . that he belonged to the *Khlyst* sect.'

Rasputin evidently did start out as an ordinary *Khlyst*. It is no coincidence that from the very start (in their investigations of 1903 and 1907) the Tobolsk Theological Consistory twice concerned itself with his *Khlyst* affiliation. And if the second investigation may be attributed to harassment by the Montenegrin princesses and Grand Duke Nikolai Nikolaevich, then to whose influence is the first investigation to be ascribed? And although the second investigation was broadly conceived, the poor training of the Tobolsk investigators in sectarian questions wrecked it (as Inspector Beryozkin admitted in the file). In the interrogation of Rasputin's adherents, the investigators were overmatched by their fanatical faith in his holiness. Nonetheless, one of those adherents, Khionia Berladskaya, subsequently wrote a 'Confession', as we have seen, with testimony about the lechery that she and Father Grigory were engaging in at the time. And Rasputin himself, who categorically rejected the dangerous accusations that he went to bathhouses with women, would soon afterwards in Petersburg be saying quite the opposite. So he had lied during the investigation, as had his followers, since they did not wish or were unable to explain to clergy of the official church the mystical secrets their remarkable teacher had revealed to them.

The Secret Of His Friendship With Iliodor

But evidence of Rasputin's closeness to the *Khlysty* is not only to be found in the story of the Tobolsk inquiries; it is also provided by Rasputin's sworn enemy the monk Iliodor. And not by his writing, but by his behaviour after he resigned from holy orders. Retained in the Tobolsk archive is the testimony of those of Iliodor's votaries who followed him to the farm where the monk resided after his defrocking. Iliodor had built a new house there, which he symptomatically called 'New Galilee' ('New Israel' was a *Khlyst* community outside Petersburg). And he began to preach his own remarkable new doctrine.

That doctrine has been set forth by his admirer Sinitsyn: 'Christ was crucified, Iliodor states, but it was not he who was resurrected but the eternal truth that he preached and that Iliodor now preaches.' And Iliodor 'will create a new religion and, thanks to that religion, the whole life of people will be changed'. And so that it would be clear that he was the founder of a new religion and therefore a new Christ, Iliodor began to wear a white robe like that worn by Jesus. And 'he blessed those who came to visit him as Jesus did, by laying his hand on the head of the one he was blessing . . . And he openly called himself the "King of Galilee".' And so in 'New Galilee' with its new 'King of Galilee', another *Khlyst* 'ark' was formed. Iliodor no longer dissimulated. He proved to be quite simply a *Khlyst*. And that secret *Khlyst* affiliation of his (which proved a very unpleasant surprise for Hermogen and Feofan) apparently also explains why Rasputin formed such a close friendship with and had such a remarkable trust in the ill-fated monk.

A Khlyst *Encounter In Tsarskoe Selo*

Even more interesting is the testimony of the famous poet and sectarian Nikolai Klyuev.

'They called me a Rasputin,' Klyuev wrote in an 1918 poem. Klyuev's destiny began, as he himself said, when 'an elder who had come from Afon' (a *Khlyst* sect had been crushed at the Afon Monastery) said that 'I myself . . . ought to become a Christ.' And the elder introduced Klyuev to the 'brethren'. And Klyuev's wandering began. 'The Dove-brethren [as the *Skoptsy* were called] . . . brought me virtually to the ends of Russia to the province of Samara. I lived there for two years as King David in a large Golden Ark of white dove-Christs, and then with various people of secret identity, I walked all over Russia.' They became so enamoured of the *Khlyst* poet Klyuev in Petersburg that he was called to Tsarskoe Selo. He was brought to the tsarina at the Alexander Palace, where, as he recalled, 'on a wooden stage covered with velvet brocade in a cold hall of the Tsarskoe Selo palace I stood before a row of golden chairs dressed in crude peasant boots, an alumnus of the barn and an emissary of the bear.' And then he had a conversation with Rasputin.

'We had not seen each other for seventeen years, and now God had brought us to press our lips together . . . We kissed . . . as if we had only parted the day before . . . and a conversation took place . . . I tried to speak to Rasputin in the secret language of the soul about the birth of Christ in man . . . He answered irrelevantly and finally admitted that he had become a strict follower of Orthodoxy . . . Upon leaving, I did not kiss Rasputin again but bowed to him in monastery style.'

Most likely Rasputin, the friend of the tsars, simply did not want to and could not acknowledge his former acquaintance. Especially since his own teaching, although created 'on the basis of orthodox *Khlyst* doctrine', had moved a good distance beyond it, as Prugavin correctly observed. Rasputin had created his own personal teaching.

An Imperceptible Halo

'An Orthodoxy of the people', a present-day priest has described Rasputin's teaching to me. A naive Orthodoxy of the people that began with great holiness and ended in great sin.

But first a few words about the *Khlyst* Resurrection of Christ in man. For that resurrection to take place, it is necessary to suppress the flesh and sin. That is, in order to achieve a transformation of the soul, one must first mortify the Old Testament Adam in oneself – the man of sin. And to do that, it is necessary to reject everything worldly: honour and glory, love of oneself, even shame. And to care about one thing alone: God's will. Only then will everything worldly in you pass away and the voice of God be heard. This in fact is the mystical *Khlyst* Resurrection, when in you there is no longer 'yours' but only the mind and thought of God. And then the Holy Spirit will come to dwell in you, and your mysterious transformation into a new Christ will occur. But that path to 'God in oneself' is long and painful.

From Zhukovskaya's memoirs: 'Munya gave an especially good account of how Grigory Efimovich mortified his flesh . . . how in the heat of the day he stood for hours in a swamp, placing himself at the mercy of mosquitoes and midges. Now he can permit himself anything: the one who has subdued his own flesh need fear no temptation!'

And after his wanderings, when he sensed the ability in himself to heal and even to prophesy, he came to believe that God was in him.

There is an echo of this in the File in Filippov's testimony about Rasputin's diet. It turns out that it was not merely a diet but also a path to the 'divine in oneself'. 'Rasputin did not merely avoid eating meat . . . He ate fish, as Christ and the apostles had done. And by apostolic rule, he ate with his hands . . . breaking his bread and never slicing it . . . Moreover, he found that meat blackens man, whereas fish lightens him. Therefore, both from the apostles and from those people who eat fish there always emanate beams of light like a halo, albeit an imperceptible one.'

He saw himself as having just such an 'imperceptible halo', and so did his devotees.

His Mission

But at the same time, Rasputin apparently suffered bitterly. His ferocious temperament would not allow him to defeat lechery completely, to forget about woman's flesh. And it was evidently then that he began to reflect: if, despite all his great spiritual feats, the hunger for the flesh still remained, then it was probably there for a reason, and some purpose was hidden in it. For he had not experienced the torment of the flesh without reflection. It had been a kind of sign. And gradually he came to realize that it was his mission. He who had achieved great perfection was obliged to heal others as well of the torments of the flesh, of the Old Testament Adam within. And above all to heal them – women, those weak divine creatures, those vessels of sin in whose very nature was concealed the devil-pleasing thirst for lechery. Of course, as we shall see, he could heal men, as well. But to undertake his mission, he had to continue his discipline and become truly impassive. As impassive as the saints. Thus did he begin to create his doctrine.

The Naked Rasputin

It was indeed in Rasputin's relations with women that the naive, rather frightening mysticism of the doctrine discovered by the ignorant peasant was hidden. As is clear from the File, those relations greatly worried his friend and publisher Filippov. And that apparently is why Filippov tried to talk to Rasputin about them. But Rasputin was evasive. For Filippov, an ordinary man living in the external world, could not understand him. 'He would even . . . quickly and facetiously attempt to change the subject whenever someone started in on a more or less ribald theme.' Nevertheless, Filippov was once quite startled by his supposedly modest friend.

> Once when he was staying with me, Rasputin, unbeknownst to me, went into the kitchen where at the time my maid, a very pretty Ukrainian, was working. Re-emerging, he said, 'What a little stinker you've got there!'
> 'How's that?' I asked.
> 'Why, she spit in my face!'
> It turned out Rasputin had dragged her into a room and started fondling her, and she had slapped him.

Yet at the same time Filippov witnessed the adoration by the aristocratic beauties of that peasant who had been rejected by a maidservant. He saw how Lokhtina, who had broken her life for his sake, sought his caresses. And again Filippov tried to find an explanation for it and discuss it. And again Rasputin avoided all explanation.

Then Filippov apparently embarked on an investigation of his own. He frequently went to bathhouses with Rasputin. And there he carefully examined the naked Rasputin. 'I had an opportunity to observe the physical peculiarities of his body, since we bathed together at the bathhouse on Cossack Lane. Externally Rasputin was exceptionally clean: he often changed his linen, went to the baths, and never smelled bad.' But in the bathhouses of the rich where they bathed, Rasputin remained a peasant who trusted no one. 'He did not when he bathed check in the small neck cross given to him by the empress but stuffed it in the toe of his boot with a sock.'

But clearly the main thing that interested Filippov was Rasputin's naked body. He sought the reason there for Rasputin's success, the secret of the sexual legend of which all Petersburg was gossiping. But he found nothing supernatural.

'His body was exceptionally firm, not flabby, and ruddy and well proportioned, without the paunch and flaccid muscles usual at that age . . . and without the darkening of the pigment of the sexual organs, which at a certain age have a dark or brown hue.' Those were the only 'physical peculiarities' that he remarked. Nothing unusual, no enormous sexual organ of the sort already created or soon afterwards to be created by legend. A neat, clean peasant with a young-looking body, and that is all.

And it was apparently then that the disappointed Filippov resorted to interrogating any ladies who could help in his researches about his friend. He informed the investigator of the Extraordinary Commission, who evidently was also quite exercised about it all, of the surprising results of his interrogation of Rasputin's women. 'According to the comments of Ptashinskaya, who told Annenkova (Anchits) about it, as well as of the other women who made personal statements to me about it, Rasputin did not seem very interested in physical relations.'

And so the ladies did not experience any supernatural amorous ecstasies. But there was still a part of Rasputin's life in that 'holy period' that apparently was hidden from Sazonov and Filippov. Rasputin's friend Filippov would have been quite astonished to learn that his strange humble friend had all that time been engaging in mad pursuit of streetwalkers. That there had been endless encounters with prostitutes, forays with them into apartments and bathhouses, all of it recorded by the amazed police agents. True, there was in those reports one basis for caution. There was no testimony from the ladies of the pavement whom Rasputin had visited. It was apparently for that reason that the Extraordinary Commission decided to trace Rasputin's prostitutes. Retained in the File are the names of those they tried to summon for interrogation before the Commission. In vain.

They had all slipped away in the gathering chaos. But the question remains: had the agents not in fact tried to interrogate Rasputin's prostitutes before the revolution? Or had their testimony merely perished in the destruction of the documents on Rasputin about which I have already written and will still write? Most likely, they were destroyed. But rarely is everything destroyed. And one deposition did survive! And a very valuable one.

One of the agents had written 'how it turned out on clarification that after approaching the first prostitute, Rasputin bought her two bottles of beer, but did not drink himself . . . asked her to undress, looked at her body, and left'. That testimony stunned me. Because I had once heard something like it before, many years before. I had heard it but had not understood.

The Prostitute 'Peach'

At the beginning of the 1970s I travelled quite often to the Lenfilm studios in Leningrad. They were making the film *A Day of Sunshine and Rain*, for which I had written the screenplay. At the time they were shooting a scene involving a non-speaking part, that of a 'Petersburg old woman', as the type was called – a relic of the tsarist empire. They brought in several old Leningrad woman for screen tests. And one of them was ugly, the witch Baba Yaga incarnate. In reply to a nasty remark by the director in that regard, the assistant who had recruited the old women said with dignity, 'You don't like her? Well, Grishka Rasputin liked her a lot in his day.' Even so, she did not get the part. But I, as any young writer should have been, was burning to talk to her. I recall tracking her down in the studio cloakroom and inviting her to the studio commissary. She ate the entire meal in silence, I recollect. And only when she had finished did she begin to speak. 'If it's about Grishka, I'm sick and tired of talking about it . . . There wasn't anything between us. After all, Grishka was impotent.' I remember my delight!

So began our conversation, of which an entry in my journal remains.

She said that it happened in 1914 before the war. She had been turned out of her house – she tediously related the plot, similar to that of the story of Katyusha Maslova in Tolstoy's *Resurrection*, about how she had entered service as a maid in a house on Ligovsky Avenue, how she had been seduced by the master's son, and how she had ended up on the streets of Petersburg. She was seventeen at the time. Once she was picked by a peasant in a tight-fitting coat. He immediately promised her such good money that she began to wonder where a peasant would get such a sum – maybe he had killed somebody. But as if reading her thoughts, he said to her, 'Little fool! Don't you know who I am? I'm Grigory Efimovich Rasputin.' He took her to the same cheap hotel where they all took her and ordered her to undress. He sat down across from her. And sat and watched in silence. His face suddenly turned very, very pale, as if all the blood had left it. She even got scared. Then he gave her the money and left. On his way out he said, 'Your kidneys are bad.' He took her to the same hotel another time. And even lay down with her but did not touch her. And she was a 'real peach'. Which is what everybody called her. She saw him again, but he picked others. She was glad, since she was afraid of him – it was as if he was crazy – she was afraid he would stab her. Such things had happened. He said something else to her that first time, but she was not paying attention, since 'it was cold in the room – it was winter – and I was sitting naked and all hunched up.' In 1940 she had a kidney removed.

A Solution To The Riddle of Rasputin?

And Filippov recalls in the File a remarkable conversation he had with Rasputin.

> I . . . heard Rasputin's explanation of his attitude toward women: he found little spirituality and 'glow' in them . . . At the same time, one must always 'become more refined', and even in his relations with women he did not so much use them physically as feel refined feelings from proximity to women, and that, Rasputin added, 'is something womenfolk do not understand . . . The saints would undress harlots, and look at them, and become more refined in their feelings, but would not allow any intimacy . . .' And Rasputin himself believed that by refining one's nerves and experiencing the highest Platonic states, one could raise one's body into the air in spite of its weight . . . And he explained Christ's ascension and walking on water as examples of that ability of the soul, and said that Christ himself had not avoided Martha and Mary but was their desired guest.

This is an almost verbatim repetition of what the police agent wrote, that Rasputin had 'asked her to undress, looked at her body, and left'. And of what the old prostitute 'Peach' related. And so, to refine one's nerves was to master one's flesh, and to delight in mastery of the flesh, of the Old Testament Adam. And from that delight came the ability to walk on water and to raise oneself into the air. The ability to 'be Christ'.

But what about those he slept with? The endless 'little ladies'?

His enemy the monk Iliodor, in testimony based on Rasputin's own words, speaks of 'refining', as well, although in a diametrically opposed way.

A strong will gave him the possibility of abruptly turning away from the life of the rake to feats of fasting and prayer. First by those feats, and then by extreme sexual debauchery, he refined his flesh and took his nerves to the highest degree of oscillation . . . In general, this may be achieved by feats, sexual depravity, or, finally, as the result of any debilitating disease, of consumption, for example. In all these instances, people are very nervous, impressionable, feel deeply, and can penetrate the soul of another, read the thoughts of strangers, and even predict the future.

There is a difference here, and a similarity. Both here and there Rasputin is a peculiar kind of vampire. There, he drank the mysterious energy of victory over the sin concealed in the female body. And here, that energy is engendered in accepting sin from the female body. These are not two different stages, as Iliodor thought. They are the two paths that Rasputin discovered. And along which he travelled simultaneously.

The Struggle With The Devil

In the beginning Rasputin had achieved his goal and become impassive. And when he told Iliodor that he had spend a night without passion with two young women, he was telling the truth. It was an exercise. To temper himself, Rasputin went around Petersburg setting himself exercises in impassivity like the ancient saints: he picked up prostitutes and looked at the naked bodies of 'harlots'. But, apparently, it often happened that he felt something quite different in himself, that unhappy 'saint'. And thus, as the agent wrote, upon leaving the prostitutes, 'the Russian, while walking alone, talks to himself and waves his arms and slaps himself on the body, thereby attracting the attention of passers-by.'

Let us not forget that for Rasputin the devil was real. And if the devil appeared to Dostoevsky's character in a state of delirium, then for Rasputin the devil walked with him stride for stride. And it was his argument with the devil after his visits to the prostitutes that the agent had observed.

The 'Saint' Draws The Spirit Of
Darkness Unto Himself

But alongside Rasputin's exercises with harlots were the real 'little ladies', his 'fools' – Lokhtina, Berladskaya, Manshtedt, the Baroness Kusova, and so on. They were supposed to come to his aid whenever the wicked devil ceased to obey. And instead of impassivity, he would feel a lust that took away his strength and did not allow pure thoughts to exist.

It was evidently at this time that it occurred to Rasputin to perfect a certain experience of the great elders that he had heard about in the monasteries. An expert on monastic life, the mystic Sergei Nilus, has written of the 'visible devil', who appeared in the dreams of the elders Abbot Manuil and Abbot Feodosy. Neither Manuil nor Feodosy thought of ridding themselves of the uncanny. Rather, they found a place for the demon within their 'egos', so that there took place in them both a clash between demonism and the spirit of Christ dwelling in their souls, and a victory over demonism.

The peasant decided to proceed in the same way. He resolved to take unto himself the devil of female lechery that so tempted him. And to deal it the final blow in his own body. The devil residing in the 'little ladies' would now belong to him. And he was already summoning his devotees to come to him, as to a physician, to rid themselves of the lechery living within them. And as evidence in the Tobolsk archive makes clear, in 1913 a priest named Yurievsky, attempting to resume the investigation of the Theological Consistory into the matter of Rasputin's *Khlyst* affiliation, described from the words of witnesses 'the magical rites that Father Grigory performed in his bathhouse with his followers . . . First he would pray, after which the phrase "demon of lechery, get thee hence" would be repeated three times. And then Rasputin would perform the sexual act with the woman. The power of copulation was such that the woman no longer felt her usual state of lustfulness. She felt as if all lewdness had left her.'

No, it was not the power of copulation here; it was the power of the terrible faith of his devotees that this semi-literate hypnotist-sectarian, who devoutly believed in his destiny and who had infected them with that belief, was a saint. It was the ecstasy of union with a 'saint' that was the source of their happy disembodiment. As in the *Khlyst* 'arks' (which Rasputin had previously experienced) where they piously believed that it was through 'group sinning' that they would rid themselves of the demon of lechery. (Yurievsky presented the results of his investigation to Bishop Alexis of Tobolsk, Molchanov's father, and the bishop naturally threw it in the fire and ordered the priest to drop the matter.) And Beletsky, the chief of the

Department of Police, testified before the Extraordinary Commission that Rasputin 'explained to his neophytes in my presence that it was by absorbing into his own membrane the sins he was struggling against . . . by absorbing filth and vice into himself, that a person achieved the transformation of his soul washed clean by his sins'. Or, more accurately, washed clean not by his sins but by the constant repenting of sin. For repentance involved great torment and suffering and prayer. And it seemed to him that he had through his own prayer obtained forgiveness, and that his soul had again been made pure. These were the depths into which the unhappy semi-literate mystic had resolved to plunge. And they were what his wife had in mind when, after catching him with a 'little lady' in one of his regular 'exorcisms of the demon', she said, 'Each must bear his cross, and that is his.' And they were the reason that he would say to Zhukovskaya, 'Without sin there is no life, because there is no repentance, and if there is no repentance, there is no joy.'

That 'holy eroticism' gradually developed his sensuousness to its full extent. Now he could sense sin in a woman at once. And then she was given no quarter – he went after her. As he had Filippov's pretty servant. And as he had Zhukovskaya. And the more sinful her thoughts, the more she stimulated him 'to take sin into himself, to rid himself of the demon'. His desire as a measure of her impurity. That was what he had been talking to Berladskaya about after he slept with her. And in giving herself to him, Berladskaya, as she wrote, believed 'that he was a saint, and that he was now busying himself so loathsomely only for my benefit and purification, and so I felt terribly sorry for him, and there arose a feeling of gratitude'. And he believed it too.

It was in fact about this that Lokhtina was speaking when she confirmed in the File some words of hers published by Iliodor: 'For a saint, everything is holy. That Father Grigory was like everyone else, then? People make it a sin, but he by that self-same sin only sanctified you and brought down upon you the grace of God.'

'For A Saint, Everything Is Holy'

Nevertheless, Rasputin suffered in that first 'holy period'. He felt that lust had not been conquered, but that it had conquered him. Thus came into being the Rasputin condition that recalls Dostoevsky – continuous suffering from a consciousness of one's own sinfulness, continuous appeals to God with prayer and repentance.

And thus was manifested Rasputin's fearsome Russian talent for inner righteousness while enclosed in a membrane of continuous sin.

Where suffering from repentance transforms sin into Love.

Love was the chief thing for him. Love everywhere overflowing. The pagan Love of nature, of trees, grass, and rivers. Christian Love in the family. Only Love was holy. And therefore if a married woman loved her husband, she was for Rasputin untouchable. But whatever was not love was a lie. As Lili Dehn testifies in the File, 'he . . . demanded purity in family relations.' Once he ran into her and her father on the street, and deciding that her father was her lover, he 'made a huge scene, promising to tell my husband that I had been out walking with a man'. That is why for him the tsarina's great love for the tsar was sacred.

But if a woman did not love her husband and remained in the marriage, she was sinful. Rasputin was against love's being subordinated to the laws of marriage. It was for him something terrible that came from the official church. Everything that was not true love was to him criminal and subject to change. For him, Grand Duchess Elizaveta Fyodorovna's remaining faithful to her homosexual husband was repellent. And like all the *Khlysty*, he considered it a duty to replace non-love in a marriage with a new spiritual and physical union, 'like one dove with another'. That is why upon learning that the tsar's sister Olga was living in a marriage of 'non-love' with a homosexual, he tried to embrace her, to infect her with love. He believed that the women whom he had rewarded with Love or had liberated from lechery would be linked to him for ever by invisible bonds.

'You know,' he explained to Zhukovskaya, 'there is this path from earth to heaven. If I love someone seriously, I keep it, that path, in my mind and know by it whether she is going off the track . . . Because I have removed all sins from her, she goes pure with me, but if she has gone off the track, then the sin is mine and not hers.' And Filippov, in describing Rasputin's ridiculous jealousy in regard to Laptinskaya and the rest, had not understood. Rasputin was not jealous. He bore a responsibility for them and was afraid that someone might corrupt them. For he sincerely believed that in sleeping with them, he had rid them of sin. And that without him, they would engage in sin. That is why, as Lili Dehn testified, he required of his admirers that they 'visit him almost daily'.

A Second Transformation

But was the experience of the holy zealots who had exhausted themselves with asceticism and fasting suitable for yesterday's sinner? After all, the hillock of righteousness he had clambered up with such difficulty as a youth was so small. So the devil, once let into his soul, remained there. And the terrifying experience of exorcising lechery turned into mere lechery. Ceaseless lechery that for him became a narcotic. Thus had his experiments ended. Such a transformation of the soul was called a 'state of spiritual temptation'. And after a certain point, as we shall see, he would for that very reason come to hate *them* – the 'little ladies' who had given themselves to him. And who had thereby allowed the devil to become established in his soul. For it was no longer simply the satisfaction of lust, but that 'refining of the nerves' that gave him his mysterious dark strength.

And his salon gradually became an ordinary sect. At whose head stood a ruler, Rasputin. And by his side the consecrated Lokhtina. Who was not afraid to 'spread the word' to the whole world, calling Iliodor 'Christ' and Rasputin the 'Lord of hosts'. But in order not to do them injury, she pretended to be a holy fool. With holy fools it was all just talk.

Yurodstvo (holy folly) was Rasputin's second secret. For in the concept of *yurodstvo* there was for Alix also an explanation of Our Friend's peculiar actions. Familiarity with the concept also allowed the tsars to disregard the reports of his debauchery.

The Tsars And The Madmen

From the diary of KR: 'They continue to receive the holy fool Grisha.' The File, from the testimony of Andrei Zeyer, 'who was in charge of assigning the royal family's carriages': 'Rasputin visited the palace frequently, it seems to me . . . The first time I saw him was at church . . . Colonel Loman kissed him. When I asked him who he was, Loman evasively replied that he was a holy fool.'

Alix, of course, called Rasputin 'elder' merely as a matter of convention, emphasizing thereby that Our Friend had been chosen by divinity. Elders were individuals, usually monks in monasteries, who lived in isolated places and engaged in fasting and prayer. As someone well versed in mystical literature, the tsarina knew perfectly well that in addition to elders, there were in Russia other remarkable and truly 'divine' people. Those who had committed themselves to the feat of *yurodstvo* – the holy fools.

Holy fools are a Russian phenomenon. At the basis of the feat of *yurodstvo* lie the words of the Apostle Paul's First Letter to the Corinthians that 'We are fools for Christ's sake' (4:10), 'for the wisdom of this world is folly with God' (3:19), and of the Evangelist Mark that 'if any man would come after me, let him deny himself and take up his cross and follow me' (8:34). The holy fools rejected in Christ's name the life of ordinary people and agreed to simulate madness in order, as He had done, to endure suffering and revilement voluntarily. And thus to partake of His suffering, His persecution. 'Sinners beat them, but the wise heeded their words,' it was said of holy fools in the days of the kingdom of Muscovy.

And in contrast to sinners who are eager to call themselves holy, the holy fools were holy men who called themselves sinners. In order to endure constant abuse from the world. The Englishman Giles Fletcher, who visited Muscovy at the end of the sixteenth century, described those strange people. 'They use to go stark naked, save a clout around their middle, with their haire hanging long, and wildely about their shoulders, and many of them with an iron coller, or chaine about their neckes, or middes, even in the very extremity of winter.' Yet in Muscovy the voice of the holy fool was taken as the voice of God. When holy fools wished to eat, they could enter any shop and take whatever they liked, and the owner was glad. And the most beautiful cathedral in Moscow was erected next to the Kremlin and dedicated to the holy fool Basil the Blessed.

The cruel Muscovite tsars held in awe and feared the holy fools, whom they called 'blessed'. Ivan the Terrible, one of the bloodiest Russian tsars, had accused the cities of Novgorod and Pskov of treachery. Novgorod was surrounded by the tsar's troops, its inhabitants were burned at the stake, infants were tied to their mothers and thrown with them into the river Volkhov, and the tsar's warriors went out in boats and with their pikes finished off those who swam to the surface. And then the tsar set off for Pskov in order to destroy its inhabitants. The bells were rung in Pskov and wives parted with their husbands. But when he entered the city, the first thing the omnipotent tsar did was to bow down before the holy fool Nikolai. It was Lent. The holy fool, who went about clad in heavy chains on his naked body, silently extended a piece of raw meat to the tsar in response to his greeting. 'I am a Christian and do not eat meat during Lent,' the tsar said. 'You do worse, you devour human flesh, forgetting both the fast and God,' the holy fool answered. And the omnipotent tsar meekly departed with his troops without harming Pskov. Such was the power of the holy fools. Their counterfeit madness concealed behind a mask of foolishness both simple holiness and wisdom. Their behaviour itself was a mockery of the conventions and vices of the world, of that which the world itself hid from view. The very nakedness of the holy fools was a stripping bare of a world that thought about adorning the body but that did not think about the soul. By their violation of social decorum the holy fools rent the veil covering man's secret vices.

Lust was a cardinal sin. And the holy fools badgered women, thus making obvious what people preferred to conceal and make secret. Which is why the behaviour of the holy fools sometimes displayed the sexual dissoluteness that was so carefully concealed by society. Which is why they could copulate right on the street. As G. Shavelsky, the head chaplain of the imperial army and navy, wrote, 'On the tsarina's desk was the book *Sainted Holy Fools of the Russian Church*, with her marginal notes next to the passages where the sexual dissoluteness of the holy fools was discussed.'

So she had grasped Rasputin's secret, or so she believed.

The holy fool renounced all blessings, and not just worldly ones but also those of the spirit – honours, glory, even the respect and affection of one's neighbours. More than that, he challenged those blessings and enticements to battle, acting not in human fashion but in a distorted (*urodskii*) way (hence the etymology of 'holy fool': *yurodivyi* or *urodivyi*).

Alix could have understood the secrets of the holy fools' behaviour from the example of the ancient Byzantine holy fool Simeon, who bore the same name as the saint of Verkhoturye. And Feofan, too, initially sought in Simeon's Life an explanation for Rasputin's actions.

The holy fool Saint Simeon 'intentionally went to bathhouses with women, for which he was abused and insulted'.

It is indeed in the 'Life of the Holy Fool Simeon,' published in *Monthly Readings*, that the tsarina could have found what to her would have seemed like a solution to the riddle of Rasputin's numerous shocking and even horrifying actions.

'People could not completely recognize his holiness, since he hid it from them,' it is written in the Life of Simeon. 'For *yurodstvo* is that feat whereby a person who is filled with true Christian wisdom reveals himself through his profound humility, through his mad external actions.' Simeon, however, frequently revealed himself as sexually crazed. For example, 'when the wife of an innkeeper was asleep by herself in her room and her husband was selling wine, Simeon came to her and started to remove his clothing, pretending that he wanted to lie with her. She started screaming, and the innkeeper came running, and his wife said to him, "He wants to rape me." And the husband savagely beat the elder. But Simeon found happiness in enduring the abuse.'

And again:

There were two bathhouses in the town, one for men, and the other for women. Simeon went to the women's bathhouse. They shouted at him, 'Stop, holy fool, do not go in there, that is the women's bathhouse.' But Simeon said, 'There is hot and cold water there, and there is hot and cold water here; there is nothing else in particular, neither here nor there.' With these words he entered the bathhouse naked and sat down among the women. They at once fell on him, beat him, and drove him out. Afterward the deacon asked the saint, 'Father how did your flesh feel when, naked, you went in among naked women?' The elder replied, 'It is all the same, I was among them like a tree among trees, not sensing that I had a body . . . but all my thoughts were directed to God's work.' Being impassive, he went in to the women, and just as in ancient times the bush on Sinai remained unconsumed by the fire, so did he from being touched by women . . . And those who spread lies against him at once fell ill for it. And only he could heal them with his kiss.

And Alix saw that Bishop Feofan, who had dared to rise against Rasputin and had not understood his holiness, had also fallen ill. Reading the story of the holy fool Saint Simeon, it must have seemed to the tsarina that she was reading Our Friend's own story. So that the tsars could have recalled the holy fools and Saint Simeon when they were told the horrors about Rasputin and the bathhouses and the prostitutes. And they would know until the day of their death: they had met a truly saintly holy fool as if resurrected from the days of the Muscovite kingdom of the first Romanovs. And who had called down upon himself, as befitted a holy fool in view of his meekness, the abuse and persecution of the unseeing. In that is the explanation of the sentence spoken by the tsar in reply to Stolypin's charge that Rasputin was going to the bathhouses with women: 'I know, and he preaches Holy Scripture there.'

The Sect

Was Vyrubova initiated into Rasputin's *Khlyst* fellowship? Unlike Lokhtina, probably not. Vyrubova believed, as did the tsarina, that he was a holy fool. Or, more precisely, she tried to believe it but she never ceased to have her suspicions. And it is for that reason that Vyrubova continued all that time to be interested in *Khlyst* teachings. She was apparently looking for anything that might disprove what was being said in the papers – anything that would please the tsarina. It was for Vyrubova, in fact, that the future Bolshevik leader Bonch-Bruevich compiled his vindication of Rasputin.

Another strange text was found in the search of Vyrubova's little house, one entitled 'Secrets of the *Khlysty*'.

Vyrubova testifies in the File that 'When the indications that Rasputin was a *Khlyst* appeared in the newspapers, I turned to an acquaintance of mine, Gofshtetter, who wrote for the *New Times*, asking him to explain to me just what that was. And Gofshtetter then gave me the page presented to me during my interrogation by the Extraordinary Commission containing an explanation of the essence of the religious views of the *Khlysty*.'

Gofshtetter had sent her a remarkable text, and it is unlikely that she showed it to the tsarina. 'The fawning kiss of the spiritual father's hands, the sensation of heavenly grace from his touch alone, and, on the spiritual father's part, the constant display of his superhuman possibilities and, with the help of that display and hypnosis, the suppression of personal will and freedom of thought in his followers and their constant half-hysterical ecstasy – all are features of the sect.'

What did she think – that intelligent, enigmatic woman who, almost daily, had observed everything that took place in Rasputin's salon – as she read that piece of paper that described it all so exactly?

The Sensational Telegrams

Thus, without understanding it themselves, Rasputin's devotees became a sect. With its law of deification of the teacher and its secrecy. Apparently, only his 'initiated' devotees, Lokhtina, Laptinskaya, Kusova, and Munya Golovina, knew the main secret of the 'Christ' Grigory. The others knew only that it was given to him to prophesy and to deliver them, sinful women that they were, from the demon of lewdness, to make them 'as unclouded as a piece of glass'. But all of them together guarded the secrets entrusted to them. And Feofan, who talked to Rasputin's victims – Vishnyakova, Berladskaya – testifies in the File that 'Rasputin was able to instil in his followers that they must not confess to the sin of adultery, since that would only confuse their confessors, who would not understand it.' During that whole time only a handful broke the compact. For there was the feeling that they constantly felt in his presence and without which there could have been no sect. Lili Dehn speaks of the feeling in the File. It was a feeling of fear. Fear of the power he had convinced them of so many times. And without him, without his power, without his miracles, they could not live. Without him they were like blind people without a guide. No sooner had he set off for Pokrovskoe than 'his fools' would shower him with telegrams. Dozens of those telegrams have survived in the Extraordinary Commission archive (file Nos. 7094–710).

'24 July 1913. I am very sick. I implore you to help. Sana.'

'13 April, 1916. I returned gloomily sick at heart. I beg for help. Sana.'

'In our circle Alexandra Pistolkors was called Sana,' Golovina testifies. The one with the porcelain face, Vyrubova's younger sister.

And she, the older sister, sent them, too. Vyrubova's telegrams with requests for help have a place of honour.

'26 November 1914. They write that father is weak, pray. Should we worry, he comes today with a report . . . Anya.'

And there are the telegrams sent by Vyrubova from the royal yacht *Standart*.

'We live quietly and a little miserably. I often remember. Anya.'

Most often she writes at the request of 'Mama' – the tsarina. For, as Vyrubova testified in her interrogations, after the episode of the theft of Alix's letter by Iliodor, the tsarina herself 'wrote no letters to Rasputin whatever'.

I was just about to leave off reading all those identically insane telegrams, when four coming one after another made me sit up. They were sensational!

'Love And Kisses – Darling'

Attached to pages 253–5 and page 258 (I cite the page numbers on purpose) of the archive were four telegrams, all with the same signature: 'Love and kisses – Darling.' I quote them here in full.

'25 October 1914. From Petrograd for Novy. I have returned for three days. I am tired but glad I have been able to hold up. I have faith my strength [will increase] through your prayers. Love and kisses – Darling.'

'7 December 1914. From Petrograd for Novy. Today I shall be back in eight days. I sacrifice my husband and my heart to you. Pray and bless. Love and kisses – Darling.'

'9 April 1916. Pokrovskoe from Tsarskoe Selo for Novy. I am with you with all my heart, all my thoughts. Pray for me and Nicholas on the bright day. Love and kisses – Darling.'

'2 December 1916. Pokrovskoe from Tsarskoe Selo for Novy. You have not written anything. I have missed you terribly. Come soon. Pray for Nicholas. Kisses – Darling.'

Who Was She?

The author of the last two telegrams from Tsarskoe Selo leaves no doubt. Concealed beneath the signature 'Darling' is the empress. So Vyrubova's entire testimony turns out to be a lie. Alix continued to write to the peasant as before! And she wrote, apparently, despite her promise to the tsar. Only instead of 'Mama' she now signed herself 'Darling'. The tsarina's authorship is evident in both the sender's address (Tsarskoe Selo) and the main content. The telegram sent on 9 April 1916 ('Pray for me and Nicholas on the bright day') refers to 8 April, a day Nicky and Alix noted their whole life, the day they were engaged at Coburg Castle. And the other telegram sent from Tsarskoe Selo in which 'Darling' asks Rasputin to pray for Nicholas naturally also belongs to Alix. But then what must have been the extent of her attachment! 'I am with you with all my heart, all my thoughts,' 'I have missed you terribly.' This was the Tsarina of All Russia talking to a peasant.

But there are the other two telegrams with the same signature, 'Love and kisses – Darling.' And even though the first of them does not mention Nicholas at all, it does contain the sentence, 'I sacrifice my husband and my heart to you'!

In combination with the other telegrams and the letter published by Iliodor, it sounds terrible. Almost shocking.

Only afterwards did I realize that it was unlikely that the unhappy tsarina had had anything to do with the 'terrible telegram'. In the first place, it had been sent not from Tsarskoe Selo but from Petrograd. As regards 'Darling', it was Rasputin's favourite word. He called Zhukovskaya and the singer Belling 'Darling' as well. For him, all his devotees were 'Darlings' and the tsarina was unaware that she was a 'Darling' too. Because they were all equals as far as the democratic peasant was concerned.

So the first two telegrams sent from Petrograd most probably belonged to one of the numerous 'Darlings' with whom Rasputin engaged in the 'exorcism of lechery'.

But at the time of the Extraordinary Commission's investigation someone had stitched the four telegrams together, presumably in preparation for publication. And most likely on purpose. The combination 'I am with you with all my heart and all my thoughts – I have missed you terribly – I sacrifice my husband and my heart to you' promised an explosion. But for some reason it was never published.

9

FIRST BLOOD

'He Was Exhausted'

At the end of 1913 and the beginning of 1914 Rasputin was evidently starting to experience a spiritual and physical crisis. The monotonous flitting by of 'fools', the passing file of their naked bodies, had become habitual. It was not 'refining' his nerves. And the constant presence of the demon had completely worn him out. 'He was exhausted with respect to inner content; from . . . mellow spiritual poise he entered a period of doubt and painful disillusionment with everything, especially the meaning of life,' Filippov testified in the File.

It was then that he began to fear that he would lose his power. As Stepan Beletsky, the head of the Department of Police, testified, 'At the end of 1913 the Department of Police intercepted the letter of a hypnotist from whom Rasputin was taking lessons.'

And it was no myth. An external surveillance agent scrupulously reported, '1 February 1914. According to information in our possession, Grigory Rasputin, residing at 3 English Avenue, has been taking hypnotism lessons from a certain Gerasim Papandato (nicknamed the "Musician"), approximately twenty-five years old, swarthy of face, moustache, double-breasted uniform jacket.'

And now Rasputin more and more often refused to come when he was called upon to heal sick children, saying, 'It may be that God will take him now to save him from future sins.' He required stimulants. Sober, he felt horror. Something was coming. It was inevitable. It was on its way. It was then that he started to drink.

The Atmosphere Of War

From the beginning of 1914, people predicted there would be a war. And pasted into the tsar's diary for 1913 are some unusual photographs: the tsarina, the heir, and a grand duchess all dressed in the uniforms of the regiments they commanded. A martial mood had taken hold of Europe. People had not fought a bloody war in a long time. A whole century had passed since the Napoleonic wars had held the entire continent in their grip. The only wars had been regional. Mankind had forgotten the blood and the stench of thousands of rotting bodies. And the tsar, who had just come back from Germany, sensed that its emperor, the martial 'Uncle Willy', was no longer opposed to going to war. And France, which was eager to avenge the humiliation of its crushing defeat in the recent conflict with Prussia, wanted the same thing. Moreover, Nicholas himself kept returning to the old dream of taking back Constantinople, the capital of ancient Byzantium, from the Turks and hoisting the Orthodox cross there. And of seizing control of the Straits, thereby turning the Black Sea into an internal Russian sea. An excellent gift for the just-begun fourth century of his dynasty: a Russia that reunited the Orthodox world on the ruins of a defeated Ottoman Empire!

And once again he listened with approval to the warlike dreams of Grand Duke Nikolai Nikolaevich. And felt with joy the popularity of his own mood. The young Russian bourgeoisie wanted war, and so did the old aristocracy.

The only problem was Alix. Nicky knew her panicky fear of war. And he knew her premonitions. And although he had written down in his diary, '31 December. Bless Russia and all of us, O Lord, with peace and tranquillity,' she felt that he had done so for her sake. What he really wanted was war. She was a German, and she would not dare to speak against a war with the Germans. And once again Our Friend was the only person who could save them from war, as he had done so before. Nicky would give in whenever Father Grigory started prophesying. It was therefore essential to her that Our Friend hurry back to Petersburg again [from his last visit home].

A Calamity

And Rasputin set out from Pokrovskoe. In Moscow he stayed, as ever, with Anisia Reshetnikova. Rasputin and her daughter Anna were inseparable the whole visit. She accompanied him to restaurants and paid for him. From Moscow, Rasputin was supposed to go on to the Crimea for the spring sunshine. And wait there for the royal family's arrival. But the royal family had decided to remain in Petersburg for a while. Rasputin was summoned to the capital. His father, Efim Rasputin, and Anna Reshetnikova came with him.

It was then that the photograph which also included his father and Anna Reshetnikova was taken of Rasputin in the circle of his men and women admirers.

Once in Petersburg Rasputin did not let Alix down. On a visit to Tsarskoe Selo, he began his usual discussions with the tsar, threatening future cataclysms, and so on. But they elicited a surprising reaction. Not only did the tsar not want to hear him, he even hinted to the peasant that for the sake of social calm it would not be a bad thing for him to stay in Pokrovskoe for the time being.

From Molchanov's testimony in the File: 'In March 1914 I dropped in to see Rasputin and found him quite distraught. "Well, it is a calamity, my fellow," he said to me. "All of a sudden I have to go to my village of Pokrovskoe for good." Since Vyrubova and Pistolkors seemed preoccupied about something at the time, I decided that for some reason they were dissatisfied with Rasputin in Tsarskoe Selo.'

Rasputin was an awful celebrity. The papers scrupulously illuminated his every move. On 22 March, 'Rasputin left for Tyumen with his father,' the *New Times* wrote. His father proceeded to Pokrovskoe, while Rasputin remained in Tyumen. On 28 March the newspaper's correspondent saw him 'at the home of a Mr Stryapchikh' (a Tyumen friend of Rasputin's with whom he usually stayed, and in care of whom his devotees' telegrams were often addressed). 'He drank tea on the sofa in the company of two young ladies, one a magnificent brunette, and the other older but still retaining traces of her former beauty.' And the next day, 'behind his own horses, he left in the cool of the morning for Pokrovskoe, where he would spend Holy Week.' Following the same highway along which he and his father had once carted passengers and goods for half-kopek pieces, Rasputin drove his horses dressed in a magnificent gentleman's fur coat and expensive beaver cap. The highway had not yet turned to mud, since it was still the season of Siberian morning frosts. Space, liberty, a place where one could breathe easily.

On The Eve Of Catastrophe

At the time, the situation in the country was highly auspicious. The tercentenary celebrations had strengthened the dynasty's prestige, the economy was booming, and the autocracy again seemed unshakeable. True, that strange genius, the young poets' poet Velimir Khlebnikov, had in a miscellany of the modernist literary group 'Union of Youth' listed the dates of the ends of the great empires. Concluding the list was his prophesy for Russia, the date for the fall of the Romanov Empire: 1917. But hardly anyone besides the authors of the obscure publication was likely to have read it at the time.

Yesterday's feeling of apocalypse now seemed odd. The revolutionaries had been banished or were dragging out a pitiful existence abroad. Lenin gloomily announced to his cohorts that his generation would not see revolution. The coming victorious war with its promise of new markets reconciled the young bourgeoisie to the autocracy. Probably the only thing the great Romanov family and the people in power were worried about was the peasant, who remained 'the last revolutionary in Russia', the last banner of opposition. And he remained, it was seriously thought, the chief obstacle to the start of the future victorious war. And Grand Duke Nikolai Nikolaevich continued his attacks on the elder in his conversations with the tsar. Alix understood the situation: they needed to get Nicky to Livadia quickly.

The Last Spring In Beautiful Livadia

The royal family set off for the Crimea at the end of April. Nicky had, as always, resisted for a while. But Alix had won. Rasputin was not staying in Pokrovskoe 'for good'. The papers were already reporting that he had left for the Crimea, for Yalta.

The Livadia palace was deserted. Grand Duke Dmitry, the tsar's former favourite, was no longer received. The tsar's brother Mikhail was in exile abroad. And the tsarina's devout sister and Rasputin's sworn enemy, Grand Duchess Elizaveta Fyodorovna, was not visiting Livadia any more, either. Only 'ours' were there: Vyrubova, Lili Dehn, and Rasputin. As usual, he was driven in secret from his Yalta hotel to the Livadia palace.

And as usual, Yalta thrived on the gossip about his secret visits. The last spring in the Livadia palace was drawing to an end. Neither the royal family nor Rasputin would ever see it again.

'Rasputin proposes to return to Petersburg in May,' the *Russian Word* wrote. And in fact he did go to Petersburg, but, as usual, he stopped along the way in Moscow. 'Grigory Rasputin arrived in Moscow on 13 May 1914, and, as is his custom, stayed with Anisia Ivanovna Reshetnikova. Rasputin denied rumours that he intends to retire to a monastery, and that he had clashed with Dzhunkovsky,' the paper wrote.

After Dzhunkovsky's lack of success in establishing official surveillance of Rasputin, the head of the gendarmes was lying low, and there had been no further clashes. But Rasputin knew that he was still being followed, clandestinely. But there was no point in complaining now: the tsar was no longer with him. The tsar meant to go to war.

And Rasputin felt out of place in Petersburg. He wanted to leave. As if he had had a presentiment of something, he himself wanted to get out of that dangerous city. But with war in the offing, Alix was afraid to let him go for very long. He was her last hope. Those anticipating the war understood that. The semi-literate peasant was once more at the centre of world events.

But summer came, a deceptive political vacation. And Alix put her trust in the summer lull and let him go back to Pokrovskoe for the season. As the papers reported, 'Rasputin is leaving for Pokrovskoe, where he will remain until August, when he will return to Petersburg again.' And in the meantime, the papers rushed to conduct interviews with that human sensation.

In the light of the looming events, a journalist from the *New Times* asked Rasputin, 'Are you aware of what Count Witte has been saying about your good efforts to intercede against those who have been calling for war?'

'The national dignity must be protected, but sabre rattling is unbecoming. I have always said that,' the peasant replied. The newspaper immediately published this with a very clear hint to its readers: during the Balkan events, questions of war and peace had been given up to the authority of the semi-literate peasant. And that had ended with Russia's humiliation and the betrayal of the Slavic peoples. Can we really allow that to happen this time?

How many times had Alix forbidden him to speak to journalists! On 30 May the *Saint Petersburg Courier* reported that Rasputin had 'appealed to the police with a request to guard his apartment against the visits of newspaper reporters, who were annoying him, at the same time changing his telephone number'. And then he finally broke away from the capital. He left the city and fled to Pokrovskoe, where it happened all over again.

Two Bloody Events Strangely
Coincide

Rasputin left Petersburg together with his faithful admirers Golovina and
Vyrubova. They arrived in Tyumen on 8 June. And then they proceeded
along his favourite route from Tyumen to the Verkhoturye Monastery with
its relics of Saint Simeon. And then, after saying goodbye to Vyrubova and
Golovina (his admirers were returning to Petersburg), Rasputin drove his
horses on to Pokrovskoe. With the journalists now following on his heels
instead of agents. Although it is possible that some of them were performing
the role of agent, too.

He did not succeed in living quietly in Pokrovskoe for long.

Two events occurred in the last days of June. Although externally incom-
mensurate, each had an influence on the fate of whole peoples, on the
future deaths of millions, and on the map of the entire globe. One is well-
known: on 28 June 1914 (NS), in Sarajevo, the Serbian nationalist student
Gavrilo Princip assassinated Archduke Franz Ferdinand, heir to the throne
of Austria-Hungary. Which meant the inevitable explosion of the 'Balkan
boiler'. The war parties in Russia, Germany, and Austria-Hungary were
exultant. 'Well, now we shall settle accounts with Serbia!' said Count
Berchtold, the Austro-Hungarian foreign minister. But it was clear that
Russia would not allow Serbia to be stifled. On 22 July the tsar's emissary,
Count I. L. Tatischev, reported that Kaiser Wilhelm had decided to support
Austria-Hungary. World war was becoming a reality.

Alix decided to bring back the peasant to the capital, although she
realized that Nicky would be obstinate. But as she was trying to persuade
Nicky, the telegraph brought news to Petersburg that put an end to her
efforts: in distant Pokrovskoe an unknown woman had walked up to
Rasputin and stuck a knife in his stomach. The one person who apparently
could have stopped Russia's intervention, and consequently world war, fell
to a knife.

Could Rasputin really have stopped the war? Much would later be said
about that. His future acquaintance the singer Belling recounted in her
memoirs how once during dinner he said, 'If not for the damned evil-doer
woman that cut up my intestines, there would be no war . . . While my
intestines were healing, the Germans started fighting!'

As Rasputin's friend Sazonov testifies in the File, 'Rasputin himself confirmed to me: if he had been in Petrograd, there would have been no war.'

The peasant had the right to say that, since he knew that it was not he who was the main actor in the matter but *she*. All he had to do was play his part – come to Petersburg and prophesy against the war. So that on the basis of his prophecies the tsarina would have the right to break the tsar's will.

But the court and society believed that *he* was the one. As Guchkov testified, 'Rasputin's attitude towards the war was negative. An Italian correspondent asked him before it began whether or not there would be a war. He answered, "Yes, they are starting one. But God willing, there will be no war, and I will see about it."'

The Murderer's Account

It had happened as Rasputin was coming back from church. He was almost home. Someone was waiting for him by his gate. It was a young woman. She asked for alms, and as Rasputin was giving her money, she pulled out a knife and stabbed him. The woman, a certain Khionia Guseva from Tsaritsyn, was seized. All the Russian papers gave front-page coverage to the event.

Preserved in the Tambov archive are the three volumes of the investigation into 'the attempt on the life of the peasant . . . Grigory Efimovich Rasputin'. Khionia Guseva herself provided testimony: 'On 29 June (NS) after the mid-day meal I saw . . . Grigory Rasputin coming . . . I had a dagger in a sheath under my skirt . . . and I pulled it out through a slit in my blouse. I stabbed him once in the stomach with the dagger. After which Rasputin ran away from me while I rushed after him . . . in order to inflict a fatal blow.'

They ran past houses and petrified crowds. A small woman brandishing a dagger, and Rasputin pressing his shirt against his wound. But she failed to stab him a second time. 'He picked up a shaft on the ground and hit me on the head with it, at once knocking me down . . . It was afternoon and people came running from all directions and said, "Let's kill her," and picked up the shaft. I quickly got to my feet and said to the crowd, "Hand me over to a constable. Don't kill me." They tied my hands and took me to the regional office, and on the way they . . . kicked me, but they didn't beat me.'

The young woman had a terrifying face with a nose ravaged as if by syphilis. But Khionia explained, 'I am only a girl and never had children nor suffered from syphilis . . . I was spoiled by medicines, which ruined my nose when I was thirteen.'

When he learned that Khionia was from Tsaritsyn, Rasputin came to and declared that the attack had been a fatal greeting from the Tsaritsyn monk Iliodor. But Guseva denied that Iliodor had had anything to do with it. She explained her action as her own decision after reading about Rasputin in the newspapers: 'I consider Grigory Efimovich Rasputin a false prophet and even an Antichrist . . . I decided to kill Rasputin in imitation of the holy prophet who stabbed four hundred false prophets with a knife.'

Rasputin lay between life and death for several days. All his admirers and the royal family sent him telegrams with best wishes for his recovery. Guseva's interrogation was already under way. 'During her interrogation,' the *New Times* reported, 'Guseva expressed regret at not having killed the elder. Khionia Guseva is a hatter by profession . . . She made Rasputin's acquaintance in 1910 when he visited the Balashev monastery hostel in Tsaritsyn, where Khionia's friend, the nun Xenia, lived.' The newspapers were fascinated by the romantic possibilities. One version had it that Rasputin had seduced Guseva when she was young and beautiful. Another speculated that Rasputin had corrupted the young beauty Xenia as a minor during a rite of 'rejoicing', and that Guseva was taking revenge on her behalf. And although it soon became clear that the alluded-to Xenia had only seen Rasputin from a distance and was by no means young, no one bothered to refute anything. Readers wanted the 'Rasputin story'.

Sent To A Madhouse

No sooner did he improve than the correspondents broke into his ward in the hospital at Tyumen. His misfortune temporarily reconciled at least a part of the press to him. And as a result the tone of some of the newspapers became almost sympathetic for a while. The *Stock Exchange News* wrote, 'He sat worn out by ill-health in a hospital smock and recounted his experiences . . . The wider public is unacquainted with his thoughts, which he records in a notebook almost every day.' And the correspondent offered a quotation: 'It is a great thing to be present in the final hour of the sick. You receive two rewards: you are visiting a sick person, and at the same time everything earthly seems like an illusion to you and a trap of the demon.'

Guseva was sent to a Tomsk hospital for the insane. It was the only possible way of avoiding a scandalous trial that might have brought about yet another wave of hatred against Rasputin.

N. Veryovkin, deputy minister of justice at the time, testified during his interrogation before the Extraordinary Commission, 'Guseva had been recognized insane . . . but the woman shouted, "I am in my right mind and I remember clearly: I meant to stab him with a knife."' She was placed in a psychiatric hospital. Her relatives later applied for her release on the grounds that she had recovered. But the minister of justice issued instructions that her 'release must not take place before any danger that the patient may present to those around her is completely eliminated'. So Guseva was destined to rot in the hospital until she was liberated by the revolution.

The attempt on Rasputin's life was a shock for the unhappy general's wife. At the time she had been visiting Iliodor at his farm. The *Saint Petersburg Courier* reported that 'Lokhtina, upon learning of the attempted murder of Rasputin, ran to Iliodor's house and shouted, "The day of judgment has come. Repent before it is too late."' She spent half a day banging on the door and shouting before Iliodor's votaries finally conveyed 'Christ's' command that she clear out. She was afraid to go to Pokrovskoe; she was a pariah for Rasputin's admirers, too. 'The year that Guseva made her attempt on Rasputin's life, all his admirers had turned away from Lokhtina because of her closeness to Iliodor . . . Lokhtina continued to believe that Iliodor was not involved. Rasputin, however, had no doubt of it,' Maria Golovina testified.

The Attempt Explained

Rasputin would not stop talking about his Tsaritsyn enemy. The correspondent for the newspaper *Kama-Volga Speech* conducted an interview with him: 'The Tsaritsyn woman, she . . . admired Iliodor. The woman, she would go for anything, as long as it was somebody else's idea. Iliodor egged her on, she wasn't acting on her own. She was just the hammer striking, but the anvil belonged to somebody else.'

And in his book *A Holy Devil*, Iliodor actually did confirm that he knew Guseva. 'I know Khionia Guseva well. She is my spiritual daughter . . . Until the age of eighteen, she had a very beautiful face, and then she became deformed: her nose fell away. Her own explanation is that she prayed to God to take away her beauty. And he took it. It was simply that during a pilgrimage to the holy places she had slept in flophouses in the big cities and had been infected by the foul disease syphilis and turned into a freak.' But Iliodor categorically denied any part in the attempted murder: 'I have been unjustly accused by Rasputin of sending a murderer to him.'

Rasputin, however, handed over to the inquest a letter that had been sent to him in Pokrovskoe three days after the dagger attack: 'I, and not you, Grigory, have emerged the victor in this struggle! Your hypnosis has been dispersed, like smoke in the sun. I say that in spite of everything, you shall die! I am your avenger! The prisoner.'

'I think the letter was written by Iliodor himself,' Rasputin testified. The investigators attached the letter to the File. But unlike the investigators of 1914, we do not have to do our digging among scraps of evidence or rely on conjecture.

In the New York Public Library I read a most rare book given to the library by the daughter of the Russian general Denikin (who commanded the White Army during the civil war). The book was called *Martha of Stalingrad*, and its author was Iliodor. He wrote it after his emigration to America and published it in Russian. And in the book Iliodor says that it was he who decided to take Rasputin's life. At his 'New Galilee', he gathered his flock by the banks of the river. Around four hundred people came. 'The congregation chose the three most beautiful young women . . . Those three beauties,' Iliodor writes, 'were supposed to lure Rasputin and kill him.' But Khionia Guseva, who was present, said, 'Why ruin beautiful women whose lives are ahead of them? I am a wretched woman and of no use to anyone . . . I alone shall bring about his execution. Father, give me your blessing to stab him as the ancient prophet stabbed the false prophets.'

Iliodor gave her his blessing for the murder.

And so Iliodor did stand behind Guseva's dagger. But was he alone?

Who Was Involved In The Attempt?

It is not a very difficult question to answer. Because by 2 July Iliodor was already on his way out of the country. As he himself wrote, 'I abandoned my homeland and, after dressing in women's clothing, escaped over the border. On 19 July 1914, I crossed the river near the town of Tornio, four kilometres above the customs house and the border-guard post.' But Iliodor failed to mention the most interesting part. As witnesses would testify, 'Iliodor fled from his home by automobile.'

But where could the poor priest have found an automobile? By what route was the monk taken to Tornio? Who hired and paid for the guide who knew where the border-guard post was and could successfully take Iliodor over the border to Finland? Beletsky would recount in his testimony how he later tried to gain Rasputin's confidence by informing him of a fact of which Rasputin had been unaware – that Iliodor's wife had been permitted to take the monk's dangerous archive out of the country with her!

She was let out 'despite dispatches and even several telegrams to the Department of Police in Dzhunkovsky's name from the chief of the Saratov Gendarme Directorate and the Saratov district governor indicating the time of Iliodor's wife's departure and requesting that she be detained and searched. But permission was granted [by Dzhunkovsky] only after she had left and successfully crossed the border.'

The same Dzhunkovsky who was head of the gendarmes and the head of the secret police. A close friend of Ella's and Grand Duke Nikolai Nikolaevich's. So it had been no accident.

On 1 July, immediately after the attempt on his life, Rasputin was placed under police surveillance for his own protection.

Some highly interesting testimony given by Dzhunkovsky before the Extraordinary Commission remains.

'I instituted dual surveillance of Rasputin. I received daily reports about Rasputin's whereabouts, how long he spent at each location, and with whom . . . The surveillance was established . . . just before the attempt on his life.'

But the official surveillance was established after the attempt on Rasputin's life. It was the unofficial surveillance that was under way before the attempt.

Grigory Novy

Rasputin was caught in a web. 'It was Iliodor's idea to kill me.' How long could he have believed that? Could the intelligent peasant really have failed to heed Beletsky's story about how 'important people' had catered to Iliodor? Of course not! So that he would very soon have grasped the inevitability of his own downfall. And that of the naive, unhappy couple surrounded by a family who did not like them, a hostile court, and a crazed society clamouring for war.

And he would now ever more frequently drown his premonitions and terror in wine. He had reached a final turning point in his life. He had long abstained from wine. For he knew himself. He tells an investigator in the Tobolsk file that he 'gave up wine about ten years ago; I have a foul character when I'm drunk'. That 'foul character' was the aroused beast, the insanity and extremity of the debauch. There is a wind that perpetually bursts from beyond the Urals and rushes across the limitless Russian plain. And likewise in the Russian soul there beats and rages a boundless and dangerous force. And woe if it should break free. Now he would drink in earnest, in black earnest. Now he needed money, and huge amounts of it. Now he would have to overlook his secretary Laptinskaya's extortion of money from his supplicants. Yes, it would be a kind of payment for his work; after all, he had been torn from peasant labour at the pleasure of the 'tsars'. The 'tsars' did not pay him. At least let their subjects give him money so that the poor peasant could carouse to his heart's content. Could at last go on a spree! So that all those gentlemen would have something to remember him by! To remember the peasant Grishka! The name he had been given by the 'tsar's proved prophetic: after the dagger blow he became both Rasputin and Novy [New].

War

Alix watched the animated joy of the war preparations with horror. While there at the other end of the world in Siberia her half-alive 'alter ego' lay tied to his bed.

The text of the ultimatum to Serbia had been approved by Austria-Hungary on 6 July. But its presentation in Belgrade was postponed until 10 July to coincide with the departure from Petersburg of President Poincaré of France, who had been visiting Russia. So the president and the tsar would not be able to come to an immediate agreement on joint action. Poincaré had arrived in Russia on 7 July for an official three-day visit. The signing of a secret *accord intime* formally acknowledged the military obligations imposed on both sides by the Franco-Russian alliance.

At a dinner in honour of the French president, Stana, that 'black woman', joyfully cried out, 'We shall have war before the end of the month . . . [and] our armies will unite in Berlin.' At manoeuvres under a glowering sky, the tsar and president had earlier watched the mighty Russian army with delight. And during the manoeuvres Alix had almost fainted. At the dinner honouring the French president, as the amazed French ambassador, Palé-ologue, would record, 'She continually bit her lips, and her feverish breathing made the diamond-studded netting covering her breast sparkle . . . the poor woman was evidently struggling with an attack of hysteria.'

An hour after Poincaré's departure from Petersburg, the Austro-Hungarian envoy in Belgrade handed the Serbian government the ultimatum. Serbia immediately appealed to Russia for protection. On 12 July the Council of Ministers under the chairmanship of the tsar promulgated a 'Resolution Regarding the Period of War Preparation'. That evening the members of the General Staff committee were informed of the tsar's decision 'to support Serbia, even if to do so it should be necessary to announce a mobilization and undertake military action, although not until Austrian troops have crossed the Serbian frontier'.

France prepared for war along with Russia. Germany and Austria-Hungary had already begun preparations two weeks before. At the same time, England placed its navy in a state of combat readiness. Feverish diplomatic talks were in progress, but they could no longer change anything. Mad Europe was disposed to fight.

Meanwhile, Alix's agitated telegrams had been flying first to Tyumen and then to Pokrovskoe, where the wounded Rasputin had been moved.

'12 July 1914. Urgent Tyumen. For Novy from Peterhof. A grave moment. They are threatening war.'

'16 July 1914. Bad news. Terrible times. Pray for him. I have no strength left to struggle with the others.'

She kept pleading for help. And once again the peasant did not let her down. Although half-alive, he picked up his clumsy pen.

On 16 July a 'Ukase Regarding a Declaration of General Mobilization' was signed. Nikolai Nikolaevich was jubilant. The whole bellicose Romanov family rejoiced. But it was then, evidently, that the tsar received the telegram from Pokrovskoe that Alix had been so keenly anticipating.

A Prophecy

Rasputin had most likely sent several such telegrams. But with its fearful prediction, this was the most terrifying.

From Badmaev's testimony: 'And at the time of the war, he . . . sent a telegram about the same thing [not to fight], but they did not listen to him.'

From Vyrubova's testimony in the File: 'And then after the order for mobilization was given before the start of the present war, he sent the sovereign a telegram from the village of Pokrovskoe with a request to make some arrangement so there would be no war.'

As is clear from the records of the external surveillance of Rasputin after the war had already begun, 'On 20 July 1915, while in the village of Pokrovskoe, Rasputin said to agent Terekhov, "Last year when I was lying in the hospital, I asked the sovereign not to go to war, and in that regard sent the sovereign about twenty telegrams, including a very serious one."'

A photocopy of that 'serious' telegram from Rasputin to the tsar was published in Paris in 1968 in *La révolution russe*.

A threatening cloud hangs over Russia: misfortune, much woe, no ray of hope, a sea of tears immeasurable, and of blood? What shall I say? There are no words: an indescribable horror. I know that all want war from you, and the loyal [wish it] without realizing that it is for the sake of destruction. God's punishment is a grievous one when the path is taken away. You are the tsar, the father of the nation. Do not permit the mad to triumph and destroy themselves and the nation. Everything drowns in great bloodshed. Grigory.

It is amusing, but there was another perspicacious person who also foresaw it – Vladimir Ilyich Lenin. He believed that 'war between Austria and Russia would be a very useful thing for revolution' throughout Eastern Europe.

And the unbelievable occurred. After that telegram of Rasputin's, the tsar's telegram ordering the mobilization which was awaited by his allies and the whole world was cancelled. In the evening, when everything in the telegraph office had been made ready for the sending of the telegrams containing the ukase on general mobilization, a telephone call was received from the tsar rescinding the order. The ministers and the General Staff were thrown into a panic. It was decided to declare the rescission of the ukase 'a misunderstanding, a mistake, that would soon been corrected'. Sergei Sazonov, the minister of foreign affairs, and Yanushkevich, the military chief of staff, conferred about whom to dispatch to the tsar to persuade him to rectify his 'mistake'. But Nicholas was receiving no one.

Only Grand Duke Nikolai Nikolaevich managed to get an audience. The 'dread uncle' succeeded in convincing the tsar of that which the tsar so wanted to be convinced. At three o'clock in the afternoon, Nicholas received Foreign Minister Sazonov and in the presence of his personal representative to the court of Kaiser Wilhelm, Count I. L. Tatischev, gave his consent for a general mobilization. Sazonov immediately telephoned Chief of Staff Yanushkevich to inform him of the decision, concluding with the sentence, 'You may now break your telephone.' He feared both the tsar and Rasputin.

At 5:30 p.m. on 17 July (30 NS), the telegrams regarding the general mobilization of the army and navy were sent out.

Germany ordered the Russian government to suspend by 12:00 noon on 19 July (1 August NS) 'all operations threatening Austria and Germany', that is, to halt the mobilization. Germany declared war on Russia the evening of the day that the ultimatum expired.

'On 2 August [NS] the German ambassador, Count Friedrich Pourtalès, handed the declaration of war to Sazonov with tears in his eyes. At 2:00 p.m. a solemn mass was conducted at the Winter Palace. And a public declaration of war was also made there. I saw only gladness on people's faces. The tsarina and tsar came out to the thousands who filled the square, and the crowd fell to its knees. She, however, seemed so agitated that she covered her face with her hands, and from the convulsive movement of her shoulders, one could surmise that she was crying,' Vasiliev, the last director of the Department of Police, wrote in his memoirs.

'20 July [2 August NS]. Germany has declared war on us, pray, they are in despair,' Alix said in a telegram sent to Pokrovskoe.

At the time the whole country was reading this announcement from the tsar:

> We declare to our loyal subjects that Russia, in keeping with its historical obligations, and being of one faith and blood with the Slavic peoples, has never regarded their fate with indifference. The fraternal feelings of the Russian people for Slavs have been aroused with particular force and complete unanimity in recent days, when Austria-Hungary, treating the acquiescent and peace-loving reply of the Serbian government with contempt, and spurning the well-intended mediation of Russia, presented demands to Serbia that were clearly unacceptable to a sovereign state. Austria-Hungary has rashly resorted to armed attack, beginning a bombardment of defenceless Belgrade . . . In this terrible hour of trial, may our internal quarrels be forgotten, and may the bond of unity between the tsar and people grow ever stronger.

Thus did the tsar write in his proclamation, 'given on this twentieth day of July in the twenty-first year of our reign', regarding Russia's entry into the war.

Nicholas appointed the 'dread uncle' commander-in-chief – the army's favourite, the six-and-a-half-foot tall Grand Duke Nikolai Nikolaevich, the peasant Grigory Rasputin's main enemy.

There was nothing to do but submit. The joyful fervour regarding the future spilling of blood was universal.

Alix, too, had to conform to it – in a new telegram.

'21 July. Nicholas asks you to bless his cousin as he goes to war. The mood here is cheerful.'

Meanwhile, the 'dread uncle', having become commander-in-chief, at once moved to deal with the peasant. Dispatches about Rasputin's 'serious telegram' had been sent by Dzhunkovsky to the commander-in-chief. And the grand duke decided to have a serious talk with the tsar about the peasant who had dared to frighten the Tsar of All Russia with talk of defeat. According to the testimony of the same agent Terekhov, 'Rasputin said that they allegedly wanted to hand him over for trial because of that telegram . . . but that the sovereign . . . had answered, "These are our family affairs; they are not a matter for trial."'

The grand duke had been put in his place.

Lying in his bed, the wounded Rasputin could only watch the world straining for war.

On 4 August (NS) England declared war on Germany. On 23 May 1915, Italy sided with the Entente. On 27 August 1916, Rumania allied itself with the Entente. On 6 April 1917, the United States entered the war. The First World War had begun.

10

THE NEW RASPUTIN

The Return

August 1914 was drawing to a close when he finally made it to the capital. Now he lived in a new apartment on Gorokhovaya Street.

From Filippov's testimony in the File: 'Vyrubova transferred Rasputin to a building on Gorokhovaya convenient for meeting anyone coming to the city from the Tsarskoe Selo station.'

Agents loitered in the building's courtyard. After the attempt on his life he was again being guarded, and the police chronicle of his life had resumed. The 'Dark One' – such was the disparaging nickname given to him by Dzhunkovsky's people.

The first to visit were his old acquaintances: 'Molchanov visited the Dark One on 21–3 and 29 August' (from the external surveillance log).

Molchanov testified in the File:

I did not see him until the end of August 1914, when, after recovering from the attempt on his life, he returned to Petrograd . . . He walked around hunched over in a gown, since his wound was still bandaged and he wasn't allowed to wear his normal clothing. His mood was noticeably depressed. He told me about the attempt, how some 'stinker' had wounded him, how he had run away pressing his shirt against the wound, how they had operated on him in Pokrovskoe using stearin candles for light, and how amazed the doctor had been that he hadn't died.

He was still suffering from lingering horror and pain. And it was hard for him to stand up straight. But after throwing a coat over his hospital gown, Anya took him to see the tsarina. 'On 25 August the Dark One went with Vyrubova to Tsarskoe Selo' (from the external surveillance log).

How Alix had waited for him. The Russian offensive in East Prussia had misfired, and General Samsonov's army had perished in the Masurian Lakes. By the beginning of September, the entire Russian army had been pushed out of eastern Prussia. The horrors of war. And, continuing to hope that it would somehow be possible to stop the slaughter that had already begun, she wrote to Nicky on 25 September: 'This miserable war, when will it ever end. William [Kaiser Wilhelm], I feel sure must at times pass through hideous moments of despair when he grasps that it was he . . . wh. began the war & is dragging his country into ruin . . . It makes my heart bleed when I think how hard Papa & Ernie struggled to bring our little country to its present state of prosperity in every sense.'

She was already imagining the destruction of her little principality. 'This miserable war, when will it ever end.'

But the tsar did not heed her prayer. For despite the defeat of Samsonov's army, Russian troops in the south-west had been operating with rare success, smashing the Austro-Hungarian army and occupying Galicia and its ancient capital of Lvov. It was the second time the tsar had come to believe that a war could strengthen his regime. The first time had been the war with Japan, which ended in the 1905 revolution.

The Prophecies Change

And Rasputin understood at once: he could not for the time being come out against the war. Everyone was in a happy fervour. 'We shall sign a peace only in Berlin!' was the universal refrain. 'They have all lost their minds,' the poet Zinaida Gippius wrote.

The German representatives were put to flight. A touching atmosphere of unity in the government and the Duma membership prevailed at the Duma session. And Alix had to talk constantly about carrying the war to a victorious conclusion; even she was weary of not joining in the universal refrain. Our Friend lent her his support. At the time, Vyrubova testified, Rasputin 'indicated it was imperative to carry on to victory. He said not a word about a separate peace.'

Yet while forecasting victory, he did not forget to add what she so wanted to hear. 'Rasputin predicted the war would be very hard on Russia and involve enormous losses,' Vyrubova testified.

'They are taking him to Tsarskoe Selo,' the agents noted once again. It was too risky to bring him in. And he disappeared into Anya's little house.

And then a calash would drive out from the Alexander Palace with the tsarina. And sometimes the children would come with her. The calash would stop at Anya's house, the only place Alix could meet with Our Friend. She did not dare bring him to the Alexander Palace. The tsar did not want to annoy the 'dread uncle'. Our Friend's visits to the palace could occur only as a last resort when the heir was ill. She ordered that his visits not be recorded in the palace register, that chronicle of court life. But thanks to eternal Russian carelessness, entries regarding his visits did find their way into the register. On 17 October 1914, 'Rasputin was received by Her Majesty at 08:30.' On 23 April 1916 at 09:20 and on 5 September at 09:45 'Rasputin was deigned to be received.' Just three times, but how many more did he actually come to aid 'Sunbeam' (as she called her son)?

A Peculiar Occurrence

Rasputin's health gradually returned and with it his enthusiasm for life. According to the external surveillance agents, after his return, the pretty brunette Baroness Kusova visited him daily at his home (from 22 August to 29 August). And in Tsarskoe Selo, he not only met the tsarina and Anya. As the agents reported, residing there in the palace of Grand Duke Pavel Alexandrovich were Sana and her husband Alexander Pistolkors. But Olga, Alexander's mother and the grand duke's wife, despised Rasputin. And Sana and Erik were thus obliged to meet him at Anya's house.

But from 7 October, the good-looking Sana with her porcelain face became a continual guest at the peasant's home on Gorokhovaya Street. The agents made no note of her husband's presence. And Rasputin had been visited by his old friend Filippov on 26 August. Life was getting back on track. Or, more accurately, getting on a new track. For immediately after his return he started drinking heavily. And he would be drunk even in the afternoon. '5 October, 6:30 p.m.,' a security agent punctiliously recorded, he 'got in a droshky drunk and dozed in the cab along the way.' A constable on the corner, 'taking him for a drunk, was about to send him to the precinct', when an agent explained to him that it was Rasputin.

Alix's New Roles

Alix's confidence started to return the day that Rasputin arrived in the capital.

God's envoy had defeated death, and she had to see that as auspicious. Now she was strong. Now he was with her. He remained with her even in her letters to Nicky, in that almost daily conversation with the tsar.

For the first time in their lives, Alix and Nicky were forced to remain apart for long periods. The tsar was continually at the front at General Staff Headquarters. How much she feared Nicky's association with the 'dread uncle' and his entire circle. All of them despised Our Friend. And were very likely passing on various kinds of filth to the credulous tsar. That is why, inundating him with letters, she would constantly remind him about Our Friend. The historian Pokrovsky calculates that in 1914–15, merely the first year and a half of their correspondence, Rasputin is mentioned more than a hundred and fifty times.

From her letters. '19 Sept. 1914 . . . You, I know, not withstanding all you will have to do, will still miss yr. little family & precious agoo wee one [the heir]. He will quickly get better now that our Friend has seen him & that will be a relief to you.'

As soon as Nicky returned to Tsarskoe Selo, she organized a meeting between them.

'20 Sept. . . . Our Friend . . . was so glad to have seen you yesterday . . . Gr[igory] loves you jealously and can't hear N[ikolai Nikolaevich] playing a part.'

Now when meeting Our Friend at Anya's, Alix observed the rule she had worked out with Nicky that there should be no witnesses to those meetings. That, apparently, is the reason why she wrote to Nicky: '23 Sept . . . Ania was offended I did not go to her, but she had lots of guests, & our Friend for three hours.'

But the very next day, '24 Sept . . . flew for a half an hour with Olga to Anias house, as our Friend spent the afternoon with her & wanted to see me. He asked after you . . . may God give you courage, strength, & patience, – faith you have more than ever and it is this wh. keeps you up . . . And our Friend helps you carry yr. heavy cross and great responsibilities.'

'24 Oct. . . . Our Friend intends leaving for home about the 5-th & wishes to come to us this evening.'

But she did not want to let him go without his meeting Nicky, who would soon be returning to Petrograd. She wanted him to instil in the tsar new and essential ideas that had occurred to her at the beginning of that terrible war.

'25 Oct. . . . Our Friend came for an hour in the evening; he will await yr return and then go off for a little home . . . It seems Lavrinovsky [the governor of Taurida] is ruining everything – sending off good Tartars to Turkey . . . and our Friend wishes me quickly to speak to Maklakov [the minister of internal affairs], as he says one must not waste time until your return.'

So now Our Friend was advising what that enormously wilful, imperious nature had long dreamed of – to undertake herself the government of the state during Nicky's absence!

Nicky returned to Tsarskoe Selo at the end of October. The peasant was waiting for him. The return was a happy one. Pushing back the Austro-Hungarian forces, the Russian army had already reached the German border. True, it meant the opening of a second front: on 29 October Turkey had entered the war on Germany's side.

From Nicholas's diary: 'I have been in a furious mood in regard to the Germans and Turks. Only . . . under the influence of a calming conversation with Grigory has my soul regained its poise.' After the daily horror of making momentous decisions, how much was he in need of Our Friend with his essential words about God's Love for the dynasty, and about a novel but easily grasped idea: now that the tsar was at the front, the empress would have to be the 'sovereign's eye'. She would have to take a greater interest in state affairs.

Following that, Our Friend could quietly go back to Pokrovskoe. And after him the tsar, too, returned to the army in the field – first to the troops in the rear, then by train to the Caucasus and the army on the new Turkish front. Our Friend's task now was to keep sending encouragement via incoherent telegrams about future victory.

Which he did punctually. 'Angels in the ranks of our warriors, the salvation of the steadfast heroes with delight and victory,' Our Friend cryptically wrote to Nicky in one telegram.

But at that time a new idea had taken possession of Alix. And for a while it even pushed aside her avidness for state responsibilities.

Thousands of wounded and maimed were being brought from the front. And the tsarina gave herself up to the cause of mercy with all the strength of her boundless energy. She organized her own hospital train and set up a hospital in Tsarskoe Selo in the great palace. She and the grand duchesses became sisters of mercy. It was fully consistent with her religiosity. And Our Friend immediately responded in kind.

On 21 November 1914, Alix wrote to Nicky, 'This is the wire I just received from our Friend: "When you comfort the wounded God makes His name famous through your gentleness and glorious work." So touching & must give me strength to get over my shyness.'

The 'elder' sensed that the tsarina was trying to come out of her voluntary seclusion in Tsarskoe Selo. She had decided to become a 'sister of mercy for Russia'. It was something she needed to do in order to silence the vile whispers that continued to haunt her about being 'a German'. And how hard it was for her, that shy woman who was ashamed even of her English accent that for some reason was regarded as 'German' in Russia. Together with her daughters, she was now hard at work in the hospitals.

'27 Oct. 1914 . . . We are going to another hospital now directly . . . We shall go as sisters (our Friend likes us to) & to-morrow also.'

'28 Nov. 1914 . . . At times I feel I can't any more & fill myself with heart-drops & and it goes again – & our Friend wishes me besides to go, & so I must swallow my shyness.'

Surrounded by the hostility of the court, she yearned for love. And there it was – the love of the wounded, the love of the simple people! Her dream had come true.

On a hospital tour, she came to Voronezh and met up with the tsar. So they could go to Moscow together. There in the ancient capital they were supposed to take part in church services, as she had dreamed of doing and as 'Grigory had requested'.

They were met by the din of Moscow's innumerable church bells, solemn prayers, and the joy of the common people.

From Moscow Alix went back to her beloved Tsarskoe Selo, while Nicky returned to the Headquarters she hated so much and the 'dread uncle'. Rasputin was in Pokrovskoe at the time, and she called for him.

'14 Dec. 1914 . . . Our Friend arrives to-morrow and says we shall have better news from the war.' Now he was coming. And nature itself rejoiced in the arrival of the man of God.

'15 Dec. . . . Bright sunny day, He must have arrived, A[nya] has gone to meet him.'

As soon as he arrived he heard the phone ring – it was 'Mama'.

'16 Dec. . . . I spoke a second to Gr[igory] by telephone, sends: "Fortitude of spirit, – will soon come to you, will discuss everything."'

Matters at the front had grown more complicated, but Our Friend told her what she wanted to hear. '17 Dec . . . This morning our Friend told her [Anya] by telephone that He is a little more quiet about the news.'

But at the same time she did not forget to carry on her jealous struggle against the commander-in-chief through the words of Our Friend.

'22 Jan. 1915 . . . Ania . . . begs me to tell you what she forget giving over to you yesterday fr. our Friend, that you must be sure not once to mention the name of the commander in Chief, in your manifest – it must solely come fr. you to the people.'

As would become clear, the commander-in-chief knew about those letters of hers.

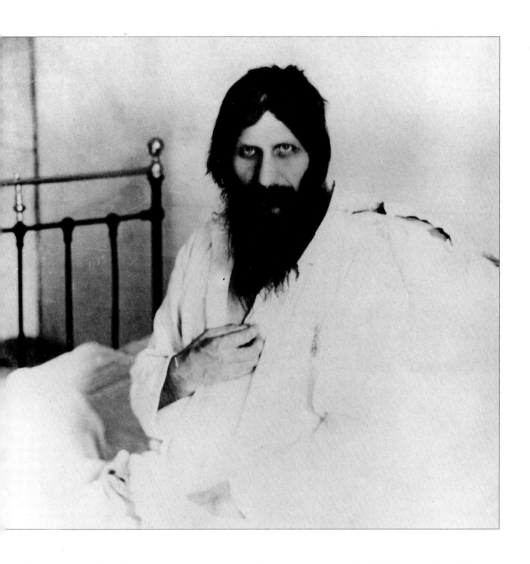

Rasputin wearing a hospital smock recovering from an attempt on his life. The assailant, Khionia Guseva, later testified: ' "I had a dagger in a sheath under my skirt ... and I pulled it out through a slit in my blouse. I stabbed him once in the stomach with the dagger after which Rasputin ran away from me while I rushed after him ... in order to inflict a fatal blow." They ran past houses and the petrified crowd. A small woman brandishing a dagger, and Rasputin pressing his shirt against his wound. But she failed to stab him a second time. "He picked up a shaft on the ground and hit me on the head with it, at once knocking me down. . . . It was afternoon and people came running from all directions and said, 'Let's kill her,' and picked up the shaft. I quickly got to my feet and said to the crowd, "Hand me over to a constable. Don't kill me. They tied my hands and took me to the regional office, and on the way they ... kicked me, but they didn't beat me."

'She explained her action as her own decision after reading about Rasputin in the newspapers: "I consider Grigory Efimovich Rasputin a false prophet and even an Antichrist. . . . I decided to kill Rasputin in imitation of the holy prophet who stabbed four hundred false prophets with a knife."

'Rasputin lay between life and death for several days. All his admirers and the Royal Family together sent him telegrams with best wishes for his recovery.'

Anya Vyrubova, who became the tsarina's companion, was 'sly, secretive, cunning, and smart. A dangerous woman.' Sergei Witte, sometime prime minister, wrote, 'All the courtiers close to the royal family cater to Anya Vyrubova. . . . Anya arranges various favours for them and influences the closeness to the sovereign of one group of political figures or another.'

Anya Vyrubova was a second mother to the grand duchesses:
Olga, Tatyana, Maria and Anastasia.

Nicholas and Anya Vyrubova
on the beach at Livadia in the
Crimea. 'The last powerful
Tartar khanate had been there,
and then the divine peninsula
had come to be ruled by the
ancestors of Felix Yusupov.
Now along the sea there
stretched a band of golden
sand. And above the sea stood
the royal family's white palace
of Livadia and the palaces of the
grand dukes and the Crimean
palace of the Yusupov family.'

Anya Vyrubova with the tsarina.
'Everyone continues to castigate
Vyrubova behind her back and
to curry favour to her face. . . .
All these lords are afraid of one
thing only, holding onto their
warm little places, although they
care little for Russia', wrote one
courtier in her diary.

Two group photographs were taken in March 1914 in Rasputin's St Petersburg apartment and later widely disseminated. For the first time it is possible to identify most of those shown.

Above: 'Alexandra (Sana) Pistolkors and her husband Alexander are standing against the wall – a stout, well-groomed, tall young gentleman, and next to him, his wife with her childlike little porcelain face and her great belly (she was pregnant). Next, the young man with a moustache who strains to lift his face above the others is in fact, Leonid Molchanov, who identified those shown to the Extraordinary Inquiry in 1917. Still in the back row, and barely visible, is Prince Zhevakhov, brought by his colleague Pistolkors, and who would, thanks to his devotion to Rasputin be rewarded in September 1916 with the appointment of deputy chief procurator of the Most Holy Synod.

'Next two rank-and-file characters, Ervin Khristoforovich Gill, the husband of a pretty devotee of Rasputin's, and Nina Dmitrievna Yakhimovich, a tall, broad-shouldered lady and one of his truly uncomplaining devotees. And then Molchanov named two figures of greater significance: Olga Vasilievna Loman and her daughter Nadezhda. This was the family of Dmitry Loman, who has been mentioned many times by us as the builder and warden of the tsars' favourite Feodor Cathedral in Tsarskoe Selo. The young woman with the hard, cold face standing to the right of Olga Loman and her daughter is another very important figure from Rasputin's

future life. She is Anna Ivanovna Reshetnikova, the daughter of the very rich and very old Moscow merchant's wife Anisia Reshetnikova, with whom Rasputin often stayed in Moscow.

'In the second row is Sophia Volynskaya, a beautiful, not very young Jew . . . the wife of the agronomist Volynsky . . . Next comes Anya Vyrubova, with her large fleshy moon-like face, and next to her the old woman in mourning is Alexandra Guschina, the inconsolable widow who met Rasputin during prayer. The good-looking woman beside her in the fashionable bonnet with the plume is Yulia (Lili) Dehn, after Vyrubova the tsarina's closest friend.

'And, finally – the rough, short old peasant man with the shaggy hair and beard, a kind of minor of pagan god, a Russian Pan, is none other than Rasputin's father.

'In the first row are devotees Zina Timofeeva, Maria Golovina, Maria Gill on Rasputin's right, with Olga Kleist, and sitting on the floor a heavy-set woman with the wide, stubborn peasant face, Akilina Laptinskaya. She too was one of the keepers of Rasputin's secrets.'

In the other photograph Molchanov stands with his back to the door. To the Extraordinary Commission he recalled that besides Rasputin the group included 'Madame Golovina, Madame Gill, Dehn, a woman who had come from Siberia with some request for Rasputin, an old woman from Vasiliev Island, and Rasputin's older daughter Matryona.'

Mikhail Rodzyanko, Speaker of the Duma, who introduced himself to the eight year old tsarevich as 'the largest, fattest man in Russia.'

Maurice Paleologue, the influential French ambassador in St Petersburg, whose gossipy diaries remain an important source as to what court and society were saying about Rasputin immediately before and during the first world war.

The full list of this St Petersburg police gathering is no longer available, but number 3 is Stephan Beletsky, director of the Department of Police, and next to him (third from right) is Vladimir Dzhunkovsky, the chief of gendarmes, who controlled the political police. 'He could amuse the royal children with his very fine bird calls.'

Cartoons mocking Rasputin's position were widely distributed. In addition to the tsar and tsarina, Anya Vyrubova (left) looks up lovingly.

Nicholas with the German Kaiser Wilhelm, a first cousin of the tsarina. 'From the beginning of 1914, everyone simultaneously started predicting there would be a war. And the tsar, who had just come back from Germany, sensed that its emperor, the martial "Uncle Willy," was no longer opposed to going to war.'

Another Attempt On His Life?

Right before Christmas Our Friend was involved in a strange incident.

'Around Christmas . . . I read in the *Stock Exchange News* that an automobile had run into . . . his droshky,' Molchanov testified.

Automobiles rarely collided with droshkies in those days. A remarkable incident for the times. Simultaneously the newspaper persecution resumed. Now he was reminded of all his efforts for peace. 'Grigory Rasputin is a most evil enemy of the holy church of Christ . . . During the struggle for liberation of the Balkan countries . . . only an enemy of the Orthodox Church could have advised Russian diplomacy to regard the frenzied brutality of the Turks with equanimity . . . It is not for Russia's good that she has been sent such detractors of Orthodoxy, such soulless false prophets,' the magazine *Reactions to Life* wrote in December 1914.

So he had been warned: do not presume to stick your nose into political affairs. But it was impossible to step aside; the tsarina needed prophecies and required them of him.

As a result, he was now constantly drunk. Endless drinking bouts and mad revelry, if only to suppress his fear. And more and more, after he had got drunk, he would break into a wild dance reminiscent of *Khlyst* 'spiritual beer'. His health had returned, and along with it an intimidating animal strength and stamina.

And now he was a wild habitué of private restaurant rooms.

The most detailed description in the File of Rasputin's drunkenness is to be found in Filippov's testimony. Filippov himself was not unacquainted with that 'Russian disease'. And in describing the awfulness of Rasputin's drinking at the time, that observer and participant could not hide his admiration for those 'aesthetic orgies'.

In 1914, after he had fallen into a period of wildness and orgies, Rasputin once sat at my place from 12:00 noon till 12:00 midnight, during which he drank a great deal, sang, danced, and talked to the audience that had gathered there. Then, after driving several people to Gorokhovaya Street, he continued drinking sweet wine with them until 4:00 a.m. When the church bells started ringing (this was just before Lent), he expressed a wish to go to prime, and . . . took himself to church and stood through the entire service until 8:00 a.m., and then on returning home, received some eighty people as if nothing had happened. At the same time, he drank in a remarkable way, without any of the brutishness so typical of the drunken Russian peasant . . . I often wondered how he kept his head clean, since it always had some kind of oil on it, and how it was that after every kind of drinking bout and other excess he did not sweat . . . By the way, he never suffered from the vomiting that usually follows a drinking bout. Nor do I recall any external indecency in his clothing, unbuttoned trousers, for example, even though in 1915 he called on me daily, sometimes even twice a day, and his drinking bouts reached . . . such dimensions that my apartment was turned into a virtual bar room.

Drunkenness To The Rescue?

But then the business took a serious turn. On one of his binges, he was beaten up. During another, he boasted and talked about his meetings with the 'tsars'. It seemed to his friend Filippov that Rasputin was perishing right before his eyes. He was especially frightened by Rasputin's drunken conversations about the royal family. And Filippov decided to have a talk with Vyrubova.

'At the end of 1914 and the beginning of 1915 Rasputin . . . drank especially hard and was involved in sprees at the Bear and other restaurants where he even dared to parade his influence with the Lofty Personages. I wrote a letter to Vyrubova in which I described the concrete escapades of Rasputin's at the Bear that had ended in his being beaten, and I insisted that decisive measures be taken to influence Rasputin.' But, as Filippov testified, rather than taking measures, Vyrubova immediately told Grigory about the dangerous complaints of his friend. After which Rasputin himself appeared and 'engaged in stormy remonstrations'. He said that 'no Vyrubova, and in fact no one at all, could influence his behaviour, and that even if he should take off his boot and make Vyrubova kiss his foot, she would do so.' The enraged Filippov went to Vyrubova for an explanation, and she replied with a sigh, 'You are speaking of the fact that I told him the contents of your letter about him, but that is the only time and he is the only person; before him I am powerless.'

The intelligent Vyrubova did not try to explain a paradox that Filippov would not have understood. Father Grigory's enemies would come to understand it only afterwards, when it was too late. Prince Yusupov would formulate it: every scandal around Rasputin served only to strengthen his position.

It was the tsarina's trap. She was at the time informed ever more often about Father Grigory's drunkenness. But every report of his indecencies provoked the tsarina's stormy anger with those who reported them. She could not explain to those normal people living in the ordinary world what she herself knew – the mystical secret of his madness, his *yurodstvo*. Could idle people really grasp the actions of those vanished saints of ancient Rus? That humble need to endure abuse? And now she acknowledged her cross: to defend him from those people. To protect the man of God and keep him by the throne. Each episode of mad drunkenness accompanied by its chorus of denunciations forced her to attack his enemies. And to make short work of them cruelly and without explanation. And in order to avoid explaining to those people who understood nothing, she devised her own version of what she was told. Now, whenever she was shown the agents' reports about Rasputin's drunken feats, she indignantly ordered the police to track down the contemptible person who had dared to impersonate Father Grigory. The peasant appreciated the advantages of the situation. Each drunken scandal helped him lure his enemies out into the open where they could be annihilated. So he could tipple without a thought.

But from time to time at the height of his drunkenness, a call would come from Tsarskoe Selo, and he would be advised that Alexei was in a bad way. And mysteriously sobering up, so that even the smell of alcohol on him dissipated, he would set off in the car that had been sent for him to save the boy. At the palace he was the same as before: clean, affectionate but not servile, independent, and sometimes even menacing, as befitted a prophet.

The Noose Is Tightened

It was then after a long interval that Zhukovskaya appeared at his new apartment on Gorokhovaya Street. As she recounted in her memoirs:

> After crossing beneath a dark archway into a courtyard poured with asphalt, I approached a reddish-brown three-storey building whose front door opened towards me by itself. A very courteous doorman explained to me in anticipation of my inquiry that Rasputin lived on the second floor, and that the door to his apartment was covered with crimson cloth. While the doorman was removing my boots, I gazed suspiciously at a certain personage ... sitting in the corner next to a little iron stove: he would look at everyone entering with excessive attention and then assume a profoundly indifferent expression. Personages of the same sort were now on the floors leading to his apartment, as well as next to the building.

In his new residence on Gorokhovaya Street Rasputin was under tireless surveillance – or rather, guard – for his own protection, naturally. And so that the tsarina would not put an end to the surveillance, she was from time to time shown 'intercepted letters with threats to kill Rasputin'.

A Department of Police summary has survived:

> External surveillance was established of the Dark One, residing at 64 Gorokhovaya Street. At first it yielded no results, since he was too cautious and moreover surrounded by devotees who would try to take him away. Such remained the case until a letter (anonymous) with a threat to kill Rasputin was received. In response to it, the security Branch offered to assign two agents, Terekhov and Svistunov, to guard Rasputin. He accepted the offer. The agents guarding Rasputin also executed the Department of Police requirement of identifying the parties who were visiting him. Having complete confidence in the agents, Rasputin often took them with him, which made the work easier. On his trips to Pokrovskoe or Moscow, he was accompanied by the same agents who reported to the Department of Police . . . twice a week by letter.

A Palace Coup?

Rasputin had known since the jubilee celebrations how Dzhunkovsky regarded him. And he had known since Stolypin's time that the agents were not so much protecting him as spying on him. But he could not now refuse the guard. Take it away, and there would be no obstacle to his being shot down on the street like a dog. There was a war going on and Petrograd was packed with armed people. So an assassination attempt could be pinned on just about anyone. And the last episode, the automobile collision, had demonstrated that his enemies were active. But he had already begun to grasp that he would not have long to live as the captive of his enemies' surveillance. Waiting for his own guard to do him in. But there was a way to be saved! Remove his enemies! Chase them away, toss them out on their backs. Dzhunkovsky, all of them! A palace coup and the coming to power of 'ours'. And he knew that it would come about, that it would happen. Because he already understood: it was exactly what 'Mama' was dreaming about. So enough of drowning his fear in drunkenness. The time to take action had come. All the more so since at the end of 1914 and the beginning of 1915 a team of bold, dangerous people had clustered around him.

The Team Of Rascals

They were the ones Filippov would honour as 'rascals and speculators', but whom Rasputin called his 'secretaries'. And their appearance on the scene was no coincidence. Money had drawn them together. The enormous amounts of it that were now whirling around the modest apartment on Gorokhovaya Street.

At the time a mighty weapon had fallen into Rasputin's hands – the petitions of citizens. Entrepreneurs, military officers, civilian officials, poor Russian people, and wealthy Jews who although they had made themselves rich were still without rights – all dreamed of circumventing the monstrous machine of Russian bureaucracy. And Our Friend was able to provide a means. Bypassing the interminable bureaucratic obstacles, their petitions went directly from the peasant's hands to the summits of power, to the ministers, and even the 'tsars'. He gave the petitioners his semi-literate notes of recommendation to the ministers, notes he termed 'petranudge' ('patronage'). And behind each other's backs the ministers endeavoured to fulfil the favourite's request! And now his ante-room was crammed with petitioners.

Zhukovskaya has described it: 'The "waiting room", an empty room with a couple of chairs,' was 'full of the most diverse visitors, beginning with a general in all his decorations and ending with some unprepossessing person in a provincial dark-blue knee-length coat who was strongly reminiscent of some village innkeeper.'

The File, Molchanov's testimony: 'A great number of petitioners turned up at Rasputin's . . . Rasputin would usually run into the other room, take a pile of papers, and then in his scrawl write a note to the ministers or other people with power . . . Rasputin's requests were passed on to the tsars through Vyrubova.'

'Vyrubova and I often called on Rasputin in Petrograd. The evening always ended with Vyrubova's getting a stack of various petitions from Rasputin and taking them back home with her and then to the palace,' Vyrubova's maid Feodosia Voino testified in the File. And Rasputin himself gave petitions to the tsarina at Anya's little house. 'In the last years Rasputin . . . started to bring pocketfuls of petitions. The former tsar did not like it at all . . . I warned Rasputin about that attitude towards his petitioning, but Rasputin paid no attention,' Vyrubova testified. The tsar had to tolerate it. Because Alix valued those petitions. They went with the image of Rasputin created by her, that of the disinterested peasant. And a few years before, it had been the truth.

But everything had changed. His new life of fantastic drinking bouts and binges with Gypsies demanded immense expenditure. And he not only spent the money, he was generous about giving it away.

He would now take the money himself, but more often his 'secretaries' would find rich petitioners for him. His retinue of 'secretaries' was a distinctive way of collecting tribute from his petitioners. The huge amounts of money that the peasant was spending staggered the imagination of his acquaintance Molchanov. Alhough he 'did not put the question of where Rasputin was getting that kind of money, thinking it had been given to him in Tsarskoe Selo', Molchanov testified in the File.

The 'Secretaries'

He liked his situation very much, that semi-literate peasant, who now had secretaries just as the important officials did.

The intelligent Akilina Laptinskaya, who remained devoted to him to her grave (literally, as we shall see), remained his chief attendant and principal secretary. And she kept an eye on the other secretaries, lest their hands get too sticky. But the sharp secretaries did not succeed in obtaining tribute from every petitioner. Poor people could as before reach Rasputin for nothing merely by coming up to him on the street and asking for a meeting. That was 'God's business'. The tsarina was touched by Anya's stories about his help of the poor. And it was easy for attractive young ladies to get to Rasputin, too – all they had to do was find out his phone number. And use it as Zhukovskaya had done to call him up. An appropriate answer to his question 'How old are you and are you beautiful?' would open the door of his home on Gorokhovaya Street.

But men of means, to say nothing of the rich, gained access to Rasputin through his secretaries.

From Filippov's testimony: 'His secretaries, male and female, asked for and received enormous sums, of which only a third actually reached Rasputin's hands. The other tens of thousands remained in those of Simanovich, Volynsky, Dobrovolsky, and, towards the end, Reshetnikov.'

The 'secretaries' of the first phase were two scoundrels he had rescued from prison, Volynsky and Dobrovolsky.

But soon afterwards a third secretary appeared, the Jew Simanovich.

From Vyrubova's testimony: 'At Rasputin's I encountered the disagreeable Yid Simanovich and Dobrovolsky, also an exceptionally disagreeable and low type. For me, it was clear those gentlemen were intermediaries between Rasputin and his petitioners and were organizing some sort of business. Dobrovolsky's wife, a heavily made-up and dubious personage, was on friendly terms with Rasputin's daughters.'

The 'secretary' Simanovich subsequently related that 'Rasputin accumulated a large amount of capital' by extorting his petitioners. But that was a lie. He accumulated nothing and left nothing behind. The money, as it were, burned in his hands: he either squandered it or gave it away. Only a little, for essentials, he sent to Pokrovskoe to his poor household. He no longer needed money for living expenses in Petrograd. Those around him paid for everything. His apartment was paid for out of the resources of the 'tsars', and his immense restaurant bills and the endless drinking bouts at his apartment were defrayed by his devotees and petitioners. But even so, whenever he learned that his secretaries had been cheating him, he would be overcome by a peasant rage. 'The Dobrovolsky couple had great influence – he was a former inspector of public schools in the Tsarskoe Selo district. But when it was proved that they had not been giving all the money to Rasputin, after stormy explanations, they lost their influence,' Beletsky, the director of the Department of Police, subsequently testified. The Dobrovolskys' intrigues were exposed by the third secretary, Simanovich. At the time Rasputin, a former friend of the savage anti-Semite Iliodor and of members of the anti-Semitic Union of the Russian People, was in the process of making the Jew Simanovich chief among the people he trusted. Simanovich would become a member of the distinctive 'Brain Trust' that was then taking shape on Gorokhovaya Street.

'To The Best Of Jews'

Thus did Rasputin write on the photograph of himself he gave to Simanovich. A security agent has provided a description:

> Aron Simanovich, a merchant of the First Guild, forty-one years old (born in 1873), four children . . . He is a 'merchant' in name only; he is not involved in business of any kind, although he does gamble at various clubs. He goes to Rasputin's almost every day . . . An extremely harmful person and a great intriguer capable of any kind of chicanery or speculation. There have been instances of bringing to Rasputin persons of the female sex of easy virtue by the look of it, and of furnishing wine.

(After the introduction of the dry law in 1914, wine had to be 'furnished'.) Rasputin and Simanovich had met several years before in Kiev, where the latter owned a jewellery shop. Even then he had a record with the criminal investigation division as a club gambler and loan shark. He lent money at high rates of interest to the golden youth who visited the clubs. After his move to Petersburg and the fall of Dobrovolsky, Simanovich became the peasant's chief financial adviser and the supplier of the most profitable petitioners.

In the beginning Simanovich freed Jews from military service through

Rasputin. For a consideration, naturally. But in 1915 the business got more serious. When the defeats in the war started to mount, the favourite Russian explanation for all failures at once came into being. It was not the third-rate generals nor the profiteers who were bilking millions in the supply of weapons and outfitting, who were at fault, but spies. Spies – the 'internal Germans' who would not permit defeat of the external variety. In keeping with the traditional anti-Semitism, the Jews had been declared spies from the start. At the order of the commander-in-chief, several Jews were hanged in Dvinsk for espionage. (It would later emerge that innocent men had been hanged.) The ruthless eviction of Jews who kept the Jewish faith, including rich entrepreneurs, had begun in Petrograd. Simanovich kept them in Petrograd through Rasputin.

Rasputin liked Simanovich. He liked his dignity in the presence of the powerful Anya. He liked it that he truly loved his disenfranchised people and stubbornly tried through Rasputin to change the royal family's attitude towards Jews. And he liked it that that rascal, though taking in enormous sums from rich Jews, disinterestedly helped the poorer members of his tribe. He liked Simanovich's delight in the scale of his binges and Simanovich's almost awed admiration for his mysterious power. For Simanovich, who loved his children, never forgot the miracle that he believed Rasputin had worked with his son, who had been ill with the then incurable disease called Saint Vitus's dance.

A Ten-Minute Miracle

'I brought in my ailing son, sat him down on a chair in the bedroom, and left the apartment. My son came home an hour later. He was healed and happy, and the disease did not recur again.' It is one of the few stories about Rasputin in Simanovich's memoirs that is not the fruit of his lush imagination.

In 1917 the Extraordinary Commission decided to verify the talk about the miracle. Simanovich's son was called before the Commission. And retained in the File is the remarkable testimony of Ioann Simanovich, a twenty-year-old student of Jewish faith.

> From 1909 to 1910 I began to show symptoms of the nervous disease called Saint Vitus's dance. I had at the onset of the disease gone to doctors, particularly since on one occasion I was forced to lie in bed because my whole left side was paralysed . . . Among the doctors who treated me I can name Professor Rosenbach and Dr Rubinko, who lived in Petrograd . . . In 1915 Rasputin heard about my disease from my father and suggested

bringing me to his apartment. After remaining alone in the room with me, Rasputin sat me on a chair and, taking his place opposite me, peered intently into my eyes and started stroking my head with his hand. At the time I experienced a special kind of state. The session lasted ten minutes, I think. After which Rasputin said to me as we were parting, 'It's all right, it will pass!' And, really, I can now attest that after that meeting with Rasputin, the attacks were no longer repeated with me. Although more than two years have passed since that session . . . I ascribe the healing exclusively to Rasputin, since the medical remedies merely alleviated the form of the attacks but did not eliminate their manifestation. Whereas after the visit to Rasputin the attacks ceased.

What must the tsarina and his own devotees have felt upon learning that Our Friend, like Christ, had exorcised the demon from someone by his mere touch. So Simanovich, to the extent he was capable of it, was devoted to him. Beletsky later testified how Simanovich had led Rasputin 'away from suspicious acquaintances', and with the help of money, had 'restricted his dangerous revelry to private rooms'.

The 'Brain Trust'

But the essential point was that Simanovich connected Rasputin with the Jewish bankers. And connected him with the richest of them, the famous 'Mitya' – Dmitry Lvovich Rubinstein. This Jew and businessman, in a country of official anti-Semitism and mongrel capitalism, had achieved a stunning success. A merchant of the first guild, he had become a banker and chairman of the board of the Franco-Russian Bank. With a doctorate in law, he knew how to exploit the numerous gaps in the semi-feudal legal code. He understood the importance of the press. And when the pro-government and very respectable newspaper *New Times* was traded as a joint-stock company, he tried to acquire a controlling share, which his competitors declared an 'attempt by international Jewry to take possession of the Russian press'. And the son of the deceased owner of the paper, the famous Alexei Suvorin, mounted a distinctive protest. To attract the attention of the government, he shot several times through a window during a stockholders' meeting. Mitya was not allowed to buy the *New Times*. Rubinstein fully understood the shakiness of his situation in those years of patriotic fervour. And it was then that the idea occurred to him of achieving the impossible – of receiving through Rasputin the civil rank of actual state councillor (corresponding to the military rank of general), while still remaining an Orthodox Jew. For that, the peasant summoned Loman, the builder of the Feodor Cathedral, to the apartment on Gorokhovaya Street.

'Rubinstein had decided to make a donation for the construction of houses next to the Feodor Cathedral in exchange for the rank of actual state councillor. I declined the offer, for, as a Jew, he could not receive that rank,' Loman testified in the File. But Rubinstein continued to entreat Rasputin. He needed to show everyone that he enjoyed the royal family's special favour in order to demonstrate the soundness of his financial empire. And he pressured the peasant, believing in his omnipotence with the tsarina. Rubinstein, like everyone else, did not realize that Rasputin could only do what the tsarina herself wanted. But the peasant did try. 'Rasputin told me that Rubinstein had asked him to obtain the rank of actual state councillor for him, and I believe he did ask the sovereign and empress about it, although I . . . know that he was turned down on it,' Vyrubova testified. But in a great many other difficult matters that the Jewish banker was daily faced with, Rasputin was able to help. 'I saw that fat little Jew a couple of times at parties at Rasputin's . . . He didn't drink or enjoy himself and kept leading Rasputin off into the study and talking to him about something. Coming out of the study he would usually say, "Now don't forget to tell Anushka," and Rasputin would answer, "All right, I'll do it."' (The File, from the testimony of the singer Varvarova.)

Rasputin's secure position seemed to the banker to be a guarantee of the soundness of his own situation. And the banker Rubinstein, who had an excellent grasp of the political state of affairs, became one of Our Friend's faithful advisers, a participant in the 'Brain Trust on Gorokhovaya Street'.

But after the appearance of Jews in his circle, Rasputin had to justify himself before Lokhtina and the other old admirers who had been with him since the days of the Black-Hundred Iliodor, and before his friends in the Union of the Russian People.

The File, from the testimony of Lokhtina: 'Regarding Rasputin's attitude towards the Jews . . . I can only pass on the words of Father Grigory: "I distract them so they won't make a lot of trouble for Russia."'

Another devoted client of Rasputin's and member of the 'Brain Trust' was Rubinstein's business competitor, Ignaty Porfirievich Manus, a banker and stockbroker, and the chairman of the board of a transportation and insurance company. He was Orthodox, and Rasputin, naturally for a large sum of money, obtained the rank of actual state councillor for him. At the same time, the peasant found enjoyment in goading the two bankers, who were competitors and hated each other, into a contest to cater to him. The dry law in force during the war required Rubinstein to spend exorbitant amounts to obtain the wine that Rasputin and his guests consumed in incredible amounts. The two bankers were also obliged to vie with each other in regard to the amount of money they passed on to the peasant. And the latter, like a pump, sucked up huge sums without a trace, sometimes without any accounting, distributing those sums at once to his acquaintances and drinking companions.

The File, from the testimony of Varvarova: 'Rasputin would say to me, "I received 10,000 from Rubinstein today, so we shall have a fine binge."'

1914 Was Coming To An End

Christmas worship was under way in the Moscow cathedrals. Surviving in the diary of the celebrated writer Ivan Bunin is a description of a service on Ordynka Street at the Martha and Mary Cloister, whose abbess was Grand Duchess Elizaveta Fyodorovna.

They would not allow Bunin into the church, mysteriously explaining to him that the grand duchess was with the visiting Grand Duke Dmitry Pavlovich. And the writer, standing outside, listened through the temple's open doors to the mournful and emotionally charged singing of its virginal choir. And then out of the church floated icons and banners carried by virginal hands with the tall, thin-faced grand duchess in front dressed in white with a cross sewn in gold on the brow of her headgear and a large candle in her hand, and behind her a file of singing sisters with candle flames held close to their faces.

At the time, the circle of those who hated the elder was drawing ever closer around Elizaveta Fyodorovna. And her protégé, Grand Duke Dmitry Pavlovich, who so hated Rasputin, was now a frequent guest in Moscow, alongside the Yusupovs and the commander-in-chief. Holiness, political power, and money had joined together.

Total Surveillance

The offensive against the peasant continued. Dzhunkovsky took another step which frightened the tsarina again. As stated in the police summary:

> We have received additional intelligence about an assassination attempt, the order has been given to take more thorough measures. For which we have started assigning him a guard of 5–6 people and an automobile and driver. They have been working in two shifts – eleven people in all. The allocation of posts: one in the apartment or by the door to the stairs, one in the lobby in a doorman's uniform, one for communication between the internal and

external surveillance, and a driver by the gate with the motor. In the event
of a trip, one of the agents will go with him.

Those who were behind Dzhunkovsky wanted to know Our Friend's every
move. Now at any hour of the day or night he would be followed by
an agent – an all-seeing eye – who would in his reports compile an
uninterrupted twenty-four-hour chronicle of Rasputin's life. Of his
drunken life.

And evidently both the peasant himself and the people who surrounded
him understood the need to hurry. 'Ours' must come to power.

A Very Dangerous Prince

It was then that another very popular figure of the day, a personality known
to 'all Petrograd', Prince Mikhail Andronikov, became a frequent guest at
Rasputin's apartment.

Having established a relationship with Rasputin, the prince immediately
found his way into the police reports. Here is one characterization of him:

> Andronikov, Mikhail Mikhailovich, thirty-nine years old, attended the
> Corps des Pages. From a family of old Georgian aristocracy, an official in
> the Department of Internal Affairs, released from service for non-attendance
> at same. In 1914 appointed an official for special commissions attached to
> the chief procurator of the Most Holy Synod.

The prince was a typical figure both for Russia and for that insane time.
Although he did not occupy any particular office, he was a very important
personage. He had quit the tedious office work of the Ministry of Internal
Affairs, but, malicious tongues asserted, he still maintained close contact
with the most important structure of the ministry, the office of special
services. And he was a personal friend of Stepan Beletsky, the former chief
of the Department of Police. At the time in question, the prince was
registered as working for the Synod, although he was rarely seen there. But
that modest Synod official was nonetheless received by all the ministers.
And although regarded with scorn, he was received at the best Petersburg
salons. All were afraid of the prince's tongue. For that busy but dangerous
bee worked tirelessly all day long spreading rumours and gossip throughout
Petersburg's working places and salons.

The already cited member of the Council of State Polovtsev recalled:

> I have known the prince for a long time . . . He spent almost all his time
> visiting ministers and highly placed personages . . . He found out things from
> them and himself passed on rumours and facts from court and administrative

circles . . . People received him in order to stay abreast of court and bureaucratic intrigues, and in order to set needed rumours in motion through him . . . And on the other hand they feared him – they knew he was well received everywhere and could with his loose tongue do harm to anyone who was unpleasant to him . . . It would be ridiculous to call him a conservative or a liberal. His opinions about people in power depended on his relationship to them: if they received him, he praised them; if they avoided him, he belittled and hated them.

He intrigued all day long. He hoodwinked and manipulated. Polovtsev wrote:

> Andronikov himself cheerfully told me, 'As soon as some X is appointed director of some such department, I send him the following letter, "At last the sun of truth has begun to shine on Russia. The mad government, which has been leading us to ruin, has finally realized that the destinies of departments must be placed in noble hands. God preserve us on our difficult path." And then this X, who has never heard of me, starts calling me up and is ready to receive me on whatever grounds I require.' Secret papers were transmitted by couriers. He would bribe them to show him the envelopes they were carrying. And without even opening them, he had an excellent understanding of their contents. For example, decorations were usually distributed on 1 January. And he would hurry to congratulate those receiving the decorations before the letters themselves arrived. And the highly placed receivers of the decorations would be thinking in awe, 'What influence this prince must enjoy in the highest spheres!'

There was, for all those abilities of his, a certain circumstance that impeded the prince's career: his homosexual propensities and the dark rumours about his apartment. The prince rented, as the police recorded, 'a large furnished seven-room apartment'. The apartment's centrepiece was his legendary bedroom. 'Behind a special screen in that bedroom,' wrote V. Rudnev, the Extraordinary Commission investigator who interrogated him, 'there was a sort of chapel with a large crucifix, a lectern, a crown of thorns, a row of icons, and the complete vestments of a priest.'

'Although I never happened to see him praying there,' his valet, Pyotr Kilter, testified, 'the prince received among the icons and the crown of thorns extremely young guests . . . Throngs of people visited the prince, for the most part cadets, schoolboys, young officers, all of them very good-looking people . . . They all came as if to their own homes – they drank, they ate, they spent the night, and two to a bed, moreover. Andronikov conducted himself suspiciously, disappearing into the bathroom with one of the young people.'

The Gossips

'The prince detested women,' his friend Beletsky testified, 'and he was visited by only one, the middle-aged Natalia Chervinskaya.' The reason for the close friendship between the prince and Chervinskaya was simple. They were united in their hatred of the war minister, Vladimir Sukhomlinov. Chervinskaya hated the sixty-two-year-old minister for deserting her sister and marrying a younger woman. Andronikov at the time had been very close to Sukhomlinov. But hoping to get even closer to the powerful minister, Andronikov now informed Sukhomlinov of several of his new young wife's escapades. Information that had, of course, been provided to the prince by Chervinskaya. After which Sukhomlinov unceremoniously threw the faithful prince out. So Andronikov had come to hate him, too. The prince's hatred was dangerous. It was rancorous and vindictive. And it united him with Chervinskaya.

Grand Duke Nikolai Nikolaevich hated Sukhomlinov, too, for the minister had spoken out in favour of limiting the grand duke's influence in the army. Nikolai Nikolaevich's hostility, however, was also a reason for a certain security in the old minister's position. For anyone the grand duke was against was automatically liked by the tsarina. But in 1915 the military failures had begun to mount, with, naturally, an increase in the criticism of the war minister, on whom they tried to heap all the sins. And it became clear to Andronikov that a favourable moment was at hand for attacking Sukhomlinov. Moreover, Chervinskaya, the 'walking rumour' as she was called in parlours, had informed Andronikov of an important new circumstance: it turned out that Sukhomlinov had also managed to offend Rasputin. As Andronikov testified, 'Rasputin had the habit of pestering the ministers with his notes . . . Sukhomlinov did not receive him at all and, in general, was ill disposed towards him.' So the prince's plan was a simple one: Rasputin would have to make the tsarina end her support of the war minister. And Andronikov decided to befriend Rasputin.

The Alliance Of The Prince And
The Peasant

That decision was why immediately after Rasputin's return to Petersburg after the attack by Guseva, the agents noted that a certain middle-aged woman was becoming a constant guest at Rasputin's apartment. And they identified her at once.

As the agents reported, every day at the end of August 1914 'Chervinskaya, Natalia Illarionovna, age forty-eight' appeared at Rasputin's. Andronikov's closest friend was preparing the ground for the prince's arrival. And soon afterwards the friend himself appeared at Rasputin's apartment on Gorokhovaya Street. As the prince would later state in his testimony, 'I went to see him when he was still indisposed after his wounding and return to Petrograd.'

The prince, however, did not hide from the investigators his reason for making friends with Rasputin. 'I realized I would have to utilize Rasputin to bring certain actions of Sukhomlinov to the attention of Tsarskoe Selo.'

But after he got closer to Rasputin, Andronikov must have appraised the situation differently. He saw the peasant's covert trips to Tsarskoe Selo with his pockets full of petitions. He saw the 'waiting room' filled with rich petitioners. So he must have realized that the Sukhomlinov story was a pitiful bagatelle in comparison with the possibilities being revealed at the building on Gorokhovaya Street. The prince was constantly in need of money. He had a modest position as a Synod official. But he had to maintain a huge apartment and a number of young men and to continue to visit the most expensive restaurants, in keeping with his place in society, and so on. And he wanted a hand in that business of recruiting rich petitioners.

But at the time the peasant and his 'Brain Trust' needed the prince for an entirely different purpose. Andronikov was acquainted with the most influential people. Through him it would be possible to 'take a look' at 'our' candidates for the most important posts in the government. When the prince realized what Rasputin wanted from him, he must have been delighted. His dream had come true – a pitiful intriguer and diligent spreader of rumours, he now found himself at the centre of great politics! He would appoint ministers and unseat them. Because he would govern by means of that peasant. Yes, the peasant was cunning. But he was, after all, merely a semi-literate peasant.

Andronikov evidently then suggested to Rasputin that they start with the main thing, finding the next chief of the Department of Police. And that is why at the beginning of 1915 a remarkable meeting took place – Rasputin's visit to the apartment of one of Andronikov's closest friends, Stepan Beletsky.

The Return Of A Master Of Provocation

After the February Revolution, Stepan Petrovich Beletsky took the stand before the Extraordinary Commission, and the poet Alexander Blok, whose job was to transcribe and edit the interrogations, gives a description of him in his notebooks: 'A soft voice, grey hair, and snub-nosed . . . and bleary eyes constantly shining.'

At the time of Andronikov's visit, Beletsky was a bit over forty, around the same age as Andronikov. But unlike Andronikov, he already stood high on the bureaucratic ladder. From 1912 he had performed the sinister duties of director of the Department of Police. Years that had been marked by provocation on the part of the secret police. Under Beletsky, there had been massive infiltration of the revolutionary movement by *agents provocateurs*; it was under him that Stolypin had mysteriously been murdered; it was under him that the anti-Semitic case had been organized against the obscure Jew Mendel Beilis, who was falsely charged in 1913 with the 'ritual murder' of a Ukrainian youth. So Stepan Petrovich had become an adept of his department's most exquisite intrigues. It was now already a year, however, since he had been deprived of his powerful post and sent into retirement as a senator. But the highly intelligent Stepan Petrovich, still at the height of his powers, was naturally eager to resume his career. He frequented influential conservative salons, where he made Andronikov's acquaintance and then became close friends with him. As Blok recorded in his notebooks, Beletsky related how he 'had been warned not to spend so much time at Andronikov's'.

But he visited him often. And happily participated in the new intrigue.

According to the data of the external surveillance agents, Rasputin 'on 30 January 1915 visited the former director of the Department of Police Beletsky'.

Beletsky was presumably promised his former post. Now they had to look for 'our' minister of internal affairs, as well. For Beletsky himself already knew that he would not be suitable for the post of minister. As he later testified, 'The tsar was cool towards me.' So the main question of finding 'our' minister still had to be decided.

The Lady In Charge

Andronikov believed in the peasant's omnipotence. Like everyone else in society, he did not appreciate the true situation. The palace coup that the peasant was preparing would have to come about because it was what the tsarina herself wanted. As soon as the war started and Nicky was swallowed up by it at Headquarters, she had made a decision to help him – to take part in the government of the country. Indeed, how could she not take part in it, if the ministers were everlastingly 'doing the wrong thing' and God's envoy was standing beside her and continually conveying His commands to her. Commands that so happily coincided with what she herself wanted.

Rasputin, of course, had had numerous opportunities to see what happened when they did not coincide. And he had occasion to see it again at the very beginning of 1915.

The Great Prime Minister's Last Wish

It was in January 1915 that Rasputin was visited by a lady in a veil. Unlike Zhukovskaya, she apparently did not understand just who the person sitting in the booth was. And the security branch agent sitting there clarified who the mysterious visitor was and submitted his report: 'The Countess Witte visited the Dark One on 8 and 25 January, both times wearing a thick veil. On 25 January she asked the doorman to escort her by the back stairway and gave him a three-rouble tip.'

Yes, it was the great former prime minister's wife. Witte was dying at the time (he would be dead in February) and he had just finished a long letter to the tsar. After enumerating in the letter the great acts of Nicholas's reign that had been accomplished with his own participation (the constitution, for example), the old man asked the favour of the title of count for his beloved grandson. So it is clear with what purpose Countess Witte was visiting Rasputin, about whom Count Witte had spoken so warmly.

And Rasputin, of course, carried out her request and asked Alix about a last favour for the count. The tsar was supposed to be coming back from Headquarters, and would be able to grant the dying Witte that boon in plenty of time. But Alix, who hated the former prime minister, was deaf to Our Friend's request. And the peasant was forced to realize that it was hopeless. So Witte's beloved grandson did not become a count. And when the tsar returned, Rasputin did not ask him about it. He knew his place: one might go against the tsar, but never the tsarina.

A Fatal Friend

The initial look at Beletsky had yielded excellent results. The dignitary was eager to go back to his previous post and truly understood the obligations that he would have to assume in return. The first of 'ours' had been found.

Rasputin's next step should have been to inform Anya, the messenger between Our Friend and 'Mama'.

But there was no one to inform. The main communications link had been knocked out. At the very beginning of the new year, fate had dealt a cruel blow to their plans.

On 10 January 1915, Rasputin celebrated his name-day and birthday. On that day, after a long absence, he was visited by his old acquaintance, the young Molchanov. And when Rasputin chided Molchanov for having 'forgotten him', the latter was not inclined to explain the remarkable reason for his disappearance. Although he did explain it in the File.

'At the beginning of 1914, I received disturbing news about my father's health . . . and on 20 May my father passed away.' After his father died, Molchanov stopped coming to Rasputin's: 'After my father's death a feeling of apathy visited me. Moreover, reviewing the past of all the people who had linked their destinies to Rasputin – Iliodor, Hermogen, [and] Damansky who through Rasputin had made a brilliant career and then had fallen ill with an incurable disease – I came to the perhaps superstitious conviction that Rasputin's hand was a heavy one.' He could also have included his father, who had obtained his post through Rasputin. And also Anya, Rasputin's main devotee, who, while Rasputin was merrily and drunkenly celebrating his name-day, was lying unconscious. For on 2 January 1915, there had been a railway accident, which delayed the change in power for several months.

Resurrection From The Dead

'I had left the empress,' Vyrubova remembered, 'and set off for the city . . . by train. I had taken a seat in a first-class car, the first behind the locomotive. There were many people in the car. We had not gone but six versts to Petrograd, when a terrifying crash was heard. I felt myself tumbling head over heels somewhere and then I hit the ground. When I came to, everywhere around me was silence and darkness. Then I heard the moans of the injured and dying who had been crushed under the wrecked cars. I myself could neither move nor cry out: a huge railway sleeper lay on my head.'

She was pulled from under the train wreckage and placed nearby right on the snow. 'Two hours later Princess Orlova and Princess Gedroits appeared. They came over to me. Gedroits felt the broken bone under my eye and said to Orlova, "She's dying," and left.'

The two maids of honour may have been glad: they thought the Friend was gone.

'Only at 10:00 p.m. at the insistence of General Resin [the commander of the regiment that guarded the palace], who had arrived from Tsarskoe Selo, was I transferred to a warm shelter by some kind student-orderlies.' And then she saw the tsarina.

> I remember being carried through a crowd in Tsarskoe [Selo], and I saw the empress and all the grand duchesses in tears. I was carried to an ambulance and the empress jumped into it and, after sitting on the floor, held my head on her knees, and I whispered to her that I was dying . . . A priest came and administered the last rites. After which I heard them whispering to come say goodbye, that I would not survive till morning . . . The sovereign took my hand and said I had strength in my hand . . . I remember Rasputin coming in and saying to the others, 'She will live but remain a cripple.' I suffered inhuman torment day and night for six weeks.

From Nicholas's diary for 2 January 1915: 'I learned . . . there had been a train collision . . . Poor Anya along with a number of others was severely injured . . . and brought to the palace infirmary. I went down there at 11:00. Her relatives had come with her. Grigory arrived later.'

From Andronikov's testimony before the Extraordinary Commission: 'When he arrived, the entire royal family was standing by the injured Vyrubova. Vyrubova was absolutely hopeless . . . He started making some gestures and saying, "Anushka, listen to me." And she, who had not responded to anyone, suddenly opened her eyes.'

So, the tsarina once again saw the occurrence of a miracle.

But was it really a miracle? We have already said that Vyrubova's position suddenly became more complicated in 1913–14. The game of being in love had led to an unexpected flash of jealousy on the part of the tsarina. And with a sense of Anya's personality, we may wonder if that iron lady hovering between life and death was not acting out a scene. So that the tsarina would see what she had so dreamed of seeing – the Friend saved by the man of God! And that salvation would seem to the tsarina to be a mystical sign, a miracle requiring a renewal of their friendship.

'That This Accident Should Be Profitable . . .'

Thus wrote Alix. Although the first thing she imagined was how Nicky would have to visit the Friend at her little house. And it irritated her.

Alix to Nicky: '26 Jan. 1915 . . . Longs to go over to her house . . . but lovy, fr. the very first you must then tell her that you cannot then come so

often . . . because if now not firm, we shall be having stories & love-
scenes & rows like in the Crimea . . . You keep fr. the first all in its limits
as you did now – so as that this accident should be profitable & with
peaceful results . . . I have heaps of petitions our Friend brought here for
you.'

The File, from the testimony of Feodosia Voino, thirty-six years old, the
doctor's assistant who became Anya's maid:

> I started working for Vyrubova after her accident on the train. That was at
> the end of January 1915. Vyrubova was then still in a very serious condition
> and could not have managed without outside help . . . A medical orderly
> started work after I did, when Vyrubova was able to move around. In the
> daytime I worked in the hospital near Vyrubova, and at night I went to her
> on my own and gave her massages and performed all the medical chores.
> When she was unable to get up, the tsarina and the children came to see
> her quite often, but the tsar rarely did.

The File, from the testimony of the medical orderly, Akim Zhuk, forty-
nine years old, from the combined Tsarskoe Selo regiment, seconded to
the infirmary for performance of the duties of medical orderly: 'By order
of the doctors who were treating Vyrubova, I started visiting her . . . It was
necessary to sit Vyrubova up to change her dressings. I have great physical
strength and Vyrubova was a heavy woman.'

Alix to Nicky: '27 Jan. 1915 . . . Ania gets on alright . . . Only speaks
again of getting into her house. I foresee my life then! . . . I find her
stomach & legs colossal (& most unappetising) – her face is rosy, but the
cheeks less fat & shades under her eyes. She has lots of guests; but dear me –
how far away she has slipped from me since her hideous behaviour, especially
autumn, winter, spring of 1914 . . . cannot be at my ease with her as before.'

'5 April 1915 . . . Ania has been wheeled by [Z]huk . . . to-morrow she
wants to come to me! Oh dear, & I was so glad that for a long time we
should not have her in the house, I am selfish . . . & want you to myself at
last, and this means she is preparing to invade upon us often when you
return.'

The Return 'To Their Own
Circles'

The peasant had not abandoned the crippled Friend. As before, he made
appointments to meet the tsars at Anya's little house. He worked hard. He

had to restore their former friendship. And he knew that he would. Alix was too lonely without Anya.

From Zhuk's testimony: 'Rasputin in fact visited Vyrubova very often . . . Usually the entire royal family visited Vyrubova on such days – the tsar, the tsarina, the children, and Rasputin.'

And of course Our Friend won in the end. He revived their relationship. And it was not long before the great jealousy was forgotten and the great friendship was restored. And once more Alix and the Friend were inundating each other with letters, and once again they could not see enough of each other.

After the revolution, they would have to burn those letters, filling the fireplaces of two rooms with cinders. For the letters now ceased to be personal. Soon after their reconciliation the tsarina and her Friend took up the government of the country. The palace coup that they meant to carry out with Rasputin had begun.

The File, from Zhuk's testimony:

> When Vyrubova was unable to walk, the tsarina came to see her quite often . . . And later the tsarina came to see her quite often, and they continued to write to each other. The correspondence was so frequent that I had sometimes barely managed to bring Vyrubova back to her rooms from the royal chambers in the evening when letters from the tsarina would start to arrive. And it happened two or three times that they managed to exchange letters while Vyrubova was getting ready to go to bed . . . She drove to the palace every day from 3:00 till 5:00 p.m., and then in the evening from 9:30 until 12:00 or 1:00.

That's the kind of enthusiasm Alix had brought to the cause.

But there was a 'taboo' that the Friend now scrupulously observed. 'She would not go to the tsarina's in the evening . . . on the days the sovereign was back from Headquarters.' She was permitted to see him only the day before he left for the front. 'Vyrubova was usually invited to the palace for dinner at the time of the tsar's departure.'

Maybe There Had Been No Debauchery After All?

The revelry on Gorokhovaya Street continued unabated for the whole month of February 1915 and most of March. During that time Rasputin gave the external surveillance agents generous material.

'12 February. Rasputin and an unidentified woman were followed to

Prince Andronikov's. He returned at 4:30 a.m. in the company of six drunken men with a guitar. They sang and danced until 6:00.'

'10 March. Seven or eight men and women arrived around 1:00 a.m. They sang songs and stomped and shouted, and then went somewhere unknown with Rasputin.'

'11 March. Rasputin was followed to No. 8 Pushkin Street to the prostitute Tregubova's.'

From an agent's report: 'Tregubova, Vera Ievlevna, twenty-six years old, a baptized Jew. A woman of easy virtue who trades exclusively in acquainting rich people with Rasputin, for the most part Jews who want to put their commercial affairs in order. She once said that she makes up to 300 roubles a month. Visits Rasputin almost daily.'

In 1917 the Extraordinary Commission interrogated Vera Tregubova. And contained in the File is her testimony, which completely contradicts the agent's characterization of her. In her testimony, Vera Tregubova declared that she was in fact a graduate of the Conservatory. And had inadvertently made Rasputin's acquaintance 'at the apartment of Lieutenant-General Dubelt's elderly widow, Alexandra Ivanovna'. Living there were two other women, 'a kind of landowner, who looked to be about fifty-five and was terribly fat . . . [and] Dubelt's . . . sister, Lydia Ivanovna Kondyrev'. And at that time, 'around 10:00 p.m. a man in a tight-fitting khaki coat and boots dropped by. I guessed it was Rasputin, whose portrait I had seen before . . . Calling him by first name and patronymic, the hostess Dubelt started telling Rasputin what a good thing it would be to get me a place as a singer on the imperial stage, that it was in general hard for me as a Jew to find any position. To which Rasputin answered, "I have many Jewish acquaintances, they're all right, good people."'

Towards the end of the evening the drunk Rasputin started making advances, according to Tregubova. 'I'll do anything you want, only come to my home. Come tonight at 12:00 midnight.'

'Why should I come to you? I don't sell my body,' Tregubova proudly replied. 'During this Rasputin was holding me by the hands and pawing me.'

To call a respectable singer who was seeing Rasputin for the first time a prostitute 'who visits Rasputin daily'! Tregubova's testimony raises doubts about the other external surveillance reports. Maybe all those reports about drinking bouts and debauchery had been made at the order of Rasputin's enemies? Maybe nothing of the sort ever happened?

But unfortunately for Tregubova, Kondyreva also testified.

Lydia Ivanovna Kondyreva, seventy-eight, the widow of an actual state councillor, stated that it was all 'quite the other way around':

I was living at the home of my sister, A. I. Dubelt, when one evening at the end of 1914 a beautiful young lady came by, obviously someone of her acquaintance, who had brought Rasputin along with her, although before that my sister had been completely unacquainted with him. The young lady introduced Rasputin, announcing that he 'wanted to visit you this evening'. Also in the apartment was Sofia Dmitrievna Oznobishina from Kazan, a beautiful, well-preserved woman of fifty-five and the widow of my cousin, who had held the rank of chamberlain. Rasputin was offered tea. The young lady who brought him enjoyed, in my opinion, friendly relations with Rasputin, calling him first Grigory Efimovich, then 'Father' and using the familiar form of address. Rasputin remained silent for the most part, and then taking advantage of a few moments alone with Oznobishina, he started stroking her hand, and patting her on the cheek, and calling her to him. Oznobishina regarded these attentions with humour and laughed out loud . . . He departed with the young lady . . . I asked my sister Dubelt about the beautiful young lady who had brought Rasputin. She told me that Vera Tregubova apparently did not have any regular employment and spent all her time with Rasputin. She had at one time lived at Albertini's, a lady who rented furnished rooms through whom she had insinuated herself into my sister's confidence.

So the agents were performing their duties honourably and may be trusted. All the more so, since Tregubova will herself continue to be an extremely active character in the external surveillance reports. For example, '26 May. Rasputin came home drunk in Manus's motor with Tregubova and was passionately kissing her.'

All this time Dzhunkovsky had been sending the agents' evidence on to Headquarters, where Nikolai Nikolaevich showed it to the tsar. And on coming back to Tsarskoe Selo, the tsar told Alix about it, provoking her fury. 'My enemy', she was already calling Dzhunkovsky.

So far they were just reports of drinking bouts of the kind the 'tsars' had heard about many times. What was needed was something that would stand out.

'25 March. Rasputin has left for Moscow,' the agents reported.

It was on that trip to Moscow that the delighted Dzhunkovsky, who had no idea where the dangerous peasant was leading him, got what he was looking for. In Moscow at the Gypsy restaurant, the Yar, a scandal took place that gave impetus to a sequence of events that would in some measure affect the history of Russia.

Gypsy Moscow

After arriving in Moscow, Rasputin continued to booze. And the principal locus of that boisterous revelry was the distinctive, now almost vanished world of Gypsy Moscow.

Petrovsky Park is still in Moscow, but living around it then were the great Gypsy artistes who sang and danced at the famous Moscow restaurants, the Yar and the Strelna. These were Rasputin's favourites. The winter garden spread out under a dome, with its palm trees, cactuses, and artificial grottoes. And the obliging waiters hurrying to the tables along paths extending from the grottoes.

The star attraction of the restaurant programme was the Gypsy ensemble the Lebedevs. The Gypsies performed three times a night for all the customers. And then the ensemble was invited into the private dining rooms. In each private room was a large table in front of which the ensemble arranged itself. The guests made requests and paid generously for each number. The soloists were frequently invited to sit down at the table. But the Gypsies did not drink while they were working, and the guests understood that. If a Gypsy woman was invited into a private room, her mother or sister would accompany her. She could not go into a private room alone. True, there were incidents in which blood was spilled. Once as the ensemble was leaving, a drunken officer tried to detain a pretty dancer in his private room. But her father ordered her to leave, and the drunken officer shot him.

The main revels, however, continued even after hours. Not infrequently after 1:00 a.m., when the restaurant closed, its habitués would follow the Lebedevs home to their 'Gypsy camp'.

Ivan Ivanovich Rom-Lebedev was one of the last of the celebrated clan that had been the pride of Moscow in Rasputin's day. I knew that tall handsome old man. He lived into his eighties and was a playwright and founder of the Moscow Gypsy Theatre. Here is what he told me in his reminiscences about the nocturnal revels at their 'camp'.

After entering the home, the guests would seat themselves around a table and waiters would fill their goblets. And the ensemble would start with the traditional song:

> For Friendly Conversation,
> Around the banquet table,

> In the custom of our fathers,
> We sing this song to you.

On such nights, Rom-Lebedev recalled, 'Although a boy I did not sleep. I eagerly listened to what was going on in the guest hall. Leo Tolstoy's sons would come . . . Grand Duke Dmitry Pavlovich came more than once.' But Rom-Lebedev would remember what happened in March 1915 for the rest of his life.

He was awakened by noise and realized that some guests had arrived. And he went out into the corridor. Usually the waiters would put candies in his hand as they ran by him. But this time they raced past, severe and full of concentration. There were gendarmes standing in the corridor by the doorway to the guest hall. Someone very important had come. From the hall burst the song:

> Grigory Efimovich is a jolly good fellow!
> He has deigned to favour the Gypsies at last!

It was the boy's habit to press his eye to the keyhole. He saw the whole ensemble by the balcony door. His father was standing in front. His mother was sitting along the side. At the centre of the table was a peasant dressed in an embroidered Russian peasant shirt. Someone handed him a goblet of champagne, and the ensemble began to chant, 'Bottoms up, bottoms up.' After which a Gypsy dance began. And then the boy's grandmother went over to the peasant and, bowing at the waist, invited him to dance. And he started dancing, squatting slightly in front of the grandmother and slapping his hands against the tops of his boots. It was all clapping, crying 'oh' and leaping. The revels came to an end just before morning.

It was during his March trip to Moscow that a scandalous event centring on Rasputin occurred in a private room of the famous Yar restaurant during a performance by a Gypsy ensemble. And in 1917 the investigators of the Extraordinary Commission interrogated those who might be able to shed light on the tangled circumstances of the story.

An Orgy At The Yar

The File, from Dzhunkovsky's testimony: 'In March 1915 the Moscow mayor, Adrianov, informed me that a certain Grigory Rasputin had behaved disgracefully in the Moscow restaurant Yar – that he had pulled down his trousers and exposed his reproductive organ, at the same time boasting that the shirt he was wearing was sewn by the empress. I . . . gave orders to proceed with the case as prescribed by law.'

Dzhunkovsky also instructed the head of the Moscow security branch, Martynov, to conduct an investigation and report back to him.

From the File, the testimony of A. P. Martynov:

> I immediately summoned Lt. Colonel Semyonov, at the time the super-intendent . . . of the district in which the restaurant Yar was located. Semyonov informed me that he had been present at the restaurant Yar the evening that Rasputin had caroused. The latter had come to the Yar with a small party . . . taken a private room, invited singers, and organized a drinking bout. I don't remember all the details, since it happened over two years ago, but at the time I reported in detail to the Department of Police on the basis of Semyonov's account.

From Dzhunkovsky's testimony before the Extraordinary Commission:

> Martynov reported that on 26 March around 11:00 p.m. G. Rasputin . . . arrived at the restaurant with Anisia Ivanovna Reshetnikova, the widow of a respected citizen, Nikolai Nikitich Soedov, a contributor to Moscow and Petrograd newspapers, and an unidentified young woman. The whole party was already tipsy. After taking possession of the room, the arrivals summoned by telephone the editor and publisher of the Moscow newspaper *The Season's News*, the titled citizen Semyon Kugulsky . . . Evidently, the group had been able to drink wine there, too, since an even drunker Rasputin was dancing the 'Russian' and then he began to speak frankly to the girl singers in this manner, 'This cloak was given to me by the "old woman", she sewed it.'
>
> After doing the 'Russian' [Rasputin said], 'Oh, what would "she herself"' say if she saw me now?' Rasputin's subsequent behaviour assumed the disgraceful character of a kind of sexual psychopathology. He evidently exposed his sexual organ and in that condition continued his conversation with the girl singers, presenting a few of them with hand-written notes on the order of 'Love unselfishly' . . . In reply to the comment of the leader of the ensemble about the indecency of such behaviour in the presence of women, Rasputin retorted that he always behaved that way with women, and remained seated in the same condition. Rasputin gave a few of the girl singers ten to fifteen roubles each, taking the money from his young companion, who afterwards paid all the other expenses at the Yar. They parted company around 2:00 p.m.

Dzhunkovsky exultantly set about preparing a report for the tsar, and accordingly asked Martynov to clarify what might have brought that ill-mixed party together. He was apparently puzzled by the immediate inclusion at the revel of the two journalists, since he knew how Rasputin avoided journalists. And Martynov provided a new report with 'supplementary information obtained by secret means':

> The nobleman Nikolai Soedov, who occupies himself with quasi-literary work, has long moved in the circle of middle-level Moscow businessmen who are not squeamish about the occasional business deal of dubious honesty. His literary work is limited to participation in the vulgar press . . . When he was in Petrograd, he turned up at Rasputin's as a representative of the press. During Rasputin's trip to Moscow, he presented himself to him and set about implementing through Rasputin a plan he had devised for the supply of military underwear in large sizes. He had apparently succeeded in interesting Rasputin in the business in Petrograd and had promised him a certain percentage from it. The binge itself was of a type common in Moscow business circles as a way of 'moistening' a proposed deal . . . Since Soedov had earlier offered . . . the newspaper owner Kugulsky a share in the deal, Kugulsky had in expectation of future benefits provided the money for the carousal . . . The news of Rasputin's arrival and his noisy conduct attracted attention in the restaurant, and the restaurant's owner, Sudakov, hoping to avoid unpleasantness, assured everyone that it wasn't really Rasputin but someone else. When this reached Rasputin, he started proving he was the real thing in the most cynical way by dropping hints about his close connection to the most lofty personages . . . As for supplying underwear, the deal fell through.

The description of Rasputin's 'sexual psychopathology' is highly suspicious. We shall recall the testimony of Filippov, who was present at Rasputin's revels, and who said of Rasputin's unusual cleanliness during his drinking bouts, 'Nor do I recall any external indecency in his clothing, unbuttoned trousers, for example, even though in 1915 he called on me daily.' And, in fact, there are no other descriptions in the agents' reports of such 'psychopathology'.

And the presence of the two unscrupulous journalists and the odd ease with which their business deal fell through put one even more on one's guard.

What Really Happened?

What probably happened was this. One of those carousing with Rasputin, as we have seen, was a certain Soedov, a shady individual who provided information to the vulgar press. And who, as Martynov, the head of the Moscow security branch, wrote, 'did not fail in his articles . . . to refer to the actions of the Moscow administration in the most laudatory terms'. He was, in other words, most likely a paid informer of the security branch, a not uncommon thing among petty journalists of the day. And he had obviously been given the assignment of drawing Rasputin into a scandal. Soedov had promised Rasputin a profitable contract. Rasputin had agreed to it. And then Soedov had suggested celebrating everything at the expense of his other partner in the future business, the editor of a trashy newspaper. Now there were two witnesses who were writers and who could scatter around Moscow whatever they wished. And then the usual Rasputin spree with his favourite *Khlyst* dancing, a Gypsy ensemble, the throwing around of money taken from Kugulsky and Soedov, and the boozy bragging about the shirts sewn by 'Mama'. A spree that on the orders of the resourceful Dzhunkovsky had been turned into a description of an orgy that included derogation of the royal family and the display of Rasputin's sexual organ.

And in fact Beletsky himself would recall that 'Rasputin talked about the offence done to him by Dzhunkovsky's complaint about his conduct in Moscow. He admitted in good-natured fashion that there had been a sin, but in exactly what he did not say. I took him to mean the intoxication.'

All the rest about Rasputin's 'sexual psychopathology', etc., appears to have been invented. And soon afterwards all Moscow was full of rumours. But Dzhunkovsky was for some reason in no hurry to inform the tsar about the scandal. He was evidently concerned about the alacrity with which Rasputin had accepted Soedov's and Kugulsky's invitation. He was asking himself the question that we are asking. Could that intelligent and canny peasant really not have understood how dangerous a jaunt with those dubious journalists might be? And for that reason Dzhunkovsky delayed: he sensed some kind of dirty trick. That is why it was only three months later, when Rasputin was himself away from Petrograd, that he was willing to risk informing the tsar about the scandal.

A Solution To The Yar Puzzle?

Rasputin, however, could only have been laughing then. After all, he had seen the rule verified more than once that whoever moved against him would be deprived of power. And he was therefore afraid of nothing. Certainly not of any reports! So the action of the gendarme chief was, in a paradoxical way, welcomed by the peasant. For it meant the end of an enemy. The enemy was cunning, but he was even more cunning.

If you consider that Rasputin understood all this, then the scandal at the Yar looks like a deliberate provocation on the part of the peasant himself. And it is the reason why he was so ready for a spree with the two agent-journalists. All the more so since he had prepared a great surprise during that spree. One that would soon explode every one of Dzhunkovsky's accusations. It is in fact here that a key to Rasputin's personality may be found, a personality remarkable for its combining of the uncombinable. He is simple-hearted, naive, lives on suspicions, and the next moment he is careful, crafty and wary in a characteristically peasant way. And the main thing is that he is able to learn. And what teachers he had! At the time, Rasputin's team already included true masters of intrigue: first Simanovich, and then (already several rungs higher) an intriguer of Petersburg-class, Prince Andronikov. And then, shortly before the Yar incident, a world-class intriguer took his place by Rasputin's side, the great adventurer Manasevich-Manuilov. He was known as the 'Russian Rocambole', after the spy and adventurer hero of Ponson du Terrail's then famous series of novels.

A Russian James Bond?

Ivan Fyodorovich Manasevich-Manuilov began his life in a quite remarkable fashion. The son of a poor Jew named Manasevich, he was adopted by the rich Russian merchant Manuilov, who left him an enormous estate. He could receive the money, however, only on his thirty-fifth birthday. But the young Manasevich was not inclined to wait. He left the provinces, came to Petersburg, and, after converting to Lutheranism, lived merrily in the capital – drinking, gambling, and borrowing from loan sharks against his inheritance. At the time, the young Jew was, to society's amazement, protected by one of the most influential monarchist ideologues, Prince Vladimir Meschersky. Taking the prince's homosexual orientation into account, the gossips drew glib conclusions about the reasons for the anti-Semite Meschersky's peculiar attachment to the young Jew. Manasevich's career proceeded apace. He secretly began to collaborate with the security branch, performing the most diverse tasks. For example, he purloined from the hotel room of Count Witte's secretary documents that were compromising to the great prime minister. And handed them over to then Minister of Internal Affairs Vyacheslav Plehve, who detested Witte. Soon afterwards with Meschersky's help, Manasevich, a Jew by birth and a

Lutheran by faith, was sent to the Vatican as a defender of the rights of Orthodox Christians.

In 1917 he was required to answer the questions of the Extraordinary Commission.

'Besides your official functions at the Vatican, what other functions did you have?'

'Observation of Catholic propaganda.'

'Of the Pope's influence in Russia? How did you keep track of the advancement of Catholicism?'

'I had agents working for me.'

'That is, you were an agency head?'

Manasevich had all that time been employed in intelligence. During the Russo-Japanese War he had managed to penetrate the Japanese embassy in The Hague, where he obtained diplomatic codes. As he testified before the Extraordinary Commission, 'In the shortest time I had acquired the codes of the following states: America, China, Bulgaria, and Rumania.' But in 1905 his espionage colleagues proved that the information provided by Manasevich had often been invented, and that he had misappropriated for his own use the monies that had been allocated for his agents. And so Manasevich retired and began working as a contributor to the large newspapers. He stayed afloat. He was accustomed to double and even triple games. He entered into secret dealings with the famous Vladimir Burtsev, a revolutionary and a tracer of police provocateurs. And at the same time he continued his work with the Department of Police. A fabulous sum was later named for the mass of documents he sold to Burtsev. Manasevich's inheritance had long since been consumed by his debts to loan sharks, yet he continued to spend. He gambled at the card table and on the stock market. In 1910 the Department of Police decided to search his apartment. But of course they found nothing. He continued his tangled labours: he worked for the newspapers, for the intelligence bureau (or rather the intelligence bureaus of several countries simultaneously), for the secret police, and for the revolutionaries. And everywhere he received money. 'Loathsome, short, clean-shaven,' as Blok, who was present for his interrogations, described him.

In 1915 his fortunes changed again. Until then the journalist Manasevich-Manuilov had spoken out bitterly against Rasputin in the *New Times*. Rasputin had even complained that Manasevich had 'harassed him with a camera'. In 1915, secretly at first, Manasevich began to play the part of a newly converted admirer of the elder. And soon afterwards, to universal amazement, he became a close friend of Rasputin's.

That former Saul turned Apostle Paul naturally seemed useful to Rasputin. All the more so, since, like Rasputin himself, he was very fond of restaurants and sprees. Thus, a master of intrigue and provocation found his way to Gorokhovaya Street. And had joined Rasputin's 'Brain Trust.'

The Mysterious Reshetnikova

As Dzhunkovsky was ordering an investigation of the scandal at the Yar, a merry and drunken Rasputin was on his way out of Moscow. That trip, as it happens, was described in detail by an eyewitness. And contained in the description are the atmosphere and mood that possessed Rasputin at the time.

The File, from the testimony of Konstantin Yakovlevich Chikhachev, forty-eight, deputy chief of the Saratov Judicial Chamber.

> At the beginning of 1915, while serving as the deputy prosecutor of the Saratov Judicial Chamber, I was travelling on business from Moscow to Petrograd. And at the Nikolaev Station I saw a crowd of people standing around a man whose picture had been published in the newspapers many times. Rasputin was taking the same train [he returned from Moscow in March, so Chikhachev is in fact describing the finale of the drunken trip] . . . Several ladies with flowers and candy were seeing him off. He was dressed in a coat made from sable fur . . . a beaver hat, an embroidered coloured silk shirt girded with a silk waistband with tassels, and high patent leather boots [his sharp eyes registered everything] . . . A tall, lean man of forty with pale eyes, a long beard, and long hair. He joked with the ladies, nervously rubbed his hands together, fidgeted in place, and shook his shoulders – he was tipsy. The people on the platform had recognized Rasputin and were watching his behaviour with curiosity [yesterday's impoverished peasant had long since become a superstar].
>   I entered the same second-class Compagnie Internationale sleeping car in which a small compartment had already been prepared for Rasputin . . . Travelling in the same car were the Khotimskys, husband and wife. He was an official for special commissions of the Department of State Properties, and she was the niece of Witte's wife. She decided to make Rasputin's acquaintance and went into his compartment, introduced herself, and introduced us. Rasputin invited us all to join him in his compartment.

And then almost at once one of them 'unceremoniously asked, "Listen, Grigory, where on earth did you get drunk?"

"At Reshetnikova's. You saw her, the one that was seeing me off. My devotee.'"

The same name – Anisia Ivanovna Reshetnikova – was listed in the police report along with those of the other people who had been carousing with Rasputin. And in the scandal at the Yar it was in fact that name that would play a very nasty trick on the powerful chief of the gendarme corps.

Rasputin Vivant

But let us return to the car, where in the now departed train the conversation transcribed by Chikhachev was already under way. At first the visitors to his compartment talked to Rasputin in a facetious way, like gentry with an intoxicated peasant.

> 'Perhaps you would like something more to drink?'
>
> 'Sure, but they haven't got any wine here, have they?' It turned out the Khotimskys had brought back several bottles of red wine from the Crimea. We uncorked one and asked the conductor for glasses, and Rasputin's tongue was loosened. He readily answered all our questions, and the conversation proceeded unconstrainedly, frequently even with enthusiasm, as if he were among old friends. He gave the impression of being a completely spontaneous person who said whatever he thought. He replied to several questions by saying he didn't understand them. No hypocrisy, no posing, no trying to seem more intelligent or better than he really was . . . He often interlarded his speech with expressions like 'see?' and he often used uncensored swear words, while gesticulating, rubbing his hands, or picking his nose.

And then his fellow travellers turned to the topics then of greatest concern to ordinary Russians.

> Rasputin spoke reluctantly about the tsar and tsarina, but at various points he said, 'He is simple, but God gives to him for his simplicity. No one has taken Constantinople, but it is possible that he will do so.' And he also said, 'They are all trying to persuade the tsar to become commander-in-chief. The sovereign wanted to, but I have been speaking against it. Can the tsar really be in command? He will be asked about everyone who is killed. But the tsar wanted to. He even turned pale when I started speaking against it.'

An astonishing observation! Does it mean that even at the beginning of 1915 the 'tsar wanted to become the commander-in-chief'? And that the peasant understood he should not? And it is no invention. Those words of Rasputin's are a remarkable complement to an entry in the diary of Grand

Duke Nikolai Mikhailovich at the very start of the war: '29 August 1914. The choice of Nikolai Nikolaevich as commander-in-chief has obviously already been recognized a failure, but it is also recognized that it is still not the time for him to take the reins of the complex running of the army himself. But when they beat us and we retreat, it will then be possible to try it! It's unlikely I'm very far from the truth! We'll wait and see.'

Words that would turn out to be prophetic, as we shall soon see.

(One thing, however, is clear: Rasputin already knew then that the days of his enemy Nikolai Nikolaevich were numbered. Because the tsar wanted to take his place. Although at the time the tsarina was apparently against it. She was afraid that the tsar would then get tangled up in the war.)

Rasputin's guests continued to question him avidly about the tsars. He 'was very approving of the fact that the tsarina was looking after the wounded. "She will at least find out how the people suffer." In reply to a question about whether it was the tsarina who had given him his magnificent fur coat, he said no, it was a gift from his devotee Reshetnikova, and that the tsarina had given him another less good that he didn't wear.'

Reshetnikova's name had come up once again. She was apparently very rich, if her fur coat was more costly than the tsarina's gift and had impressed even those wealthy people.

After the 'tsars', they moved on to another topic of concern.

Rasputin did not conceal that he liked women. He said that they are good, but they all deceive. He regarded court and aristocratic women with contempt. 'The fools! They themselves come crawling to me. One came to me to ask for a boon. She should have said right out what she needed.' In reply to the question why he enjoyed so much success with women, was it that he hypnotized them, he said in vexation, 'I myself am a simple man and don't deal in hypnotism and don't understand what it means.'

And then a third question of concern:

Rasputin was reluctant to talk about the war, alluding to the fact that, in general, one should not fight. In reply to the question when the war would end, he expressed the thought, 'When they take Constantinople, that will be the end of it,' or else took refuge in generalizations like, 'People in general will stop having wars when little boys stop having fist fights.'

And then they looked around his compartment.

'In reply to the question who paid for the compartment, he said it was probably his devotee Reshetnikova who had done it. In the compartment lay boxes of candy, which he shared but did not touch, expressing himself vulgarly that he didn't eat that "scum"!'

And all that time Rasputin was not alone. 'They' were nearby and controlled the peasant's every move. The experienced Chikhachev noticed 'them' at once. 'The compartment next to Rasputin's was occupied by some gentleman . . . Who kept his door ajar, so he could listen to what was being said. He was evidently a police agent.' On parting with Rasputin, Khotimskaya said that she was 'exceptionally pleased to have met such a famous person, and that as soon as she got home she would without fail call all her friends on the telephone. But Rasputin cut that half-gibe short with the doleful observation that "Nothing good will come of it. They'll curse you on the very first call."'

Showing through Chikhachev's account is the usual Rasputin story: the slightly drunk peasant, beginning humbly, gradually bewitches everyone in the compartment. And they are already hanging on his words, the words of someone from the, for them, inaccessible world of the 'tsars'.

And Rasputin sensed that he had bewitched them. And he began his usual seduction and recruiting of a new feminine heart. 'Rasputin began courting Khotimskaya. He sat down beside her and admired her voice when she started singing him ballads and revue tunes. His didn't take his eyes off her, he rubbed his hands in delight, and expressed his pleasure with unusual expansiveness . . . According to Khotimskaya, when they were left alone together, he suggested she come to his compartment during the night.' And Chikhachev was convinced that it was the truth. 'In fact, after we had all separated and I later than the others was walking down the corridor of the car and accidentally touched the handle of Rasputin's compartment instead of my own, he, apparently expecting Khotimskaya to join him, jumped up and at once opened the door to the compartment with the joyful exclamation, "Come on in! Come on in!"'

Evenings With Rasputin

On 30 March, according to the agents, 'Rasputin returned from Moscow.'

From the external surveillance log: '30 March 1915. Returning from Moscow he sent telegrams to Moscow.'

'To Princess Tenisheva. I rejoice for the discovery, I grieve for the wait, I kiss my own dear one.'

'Kozitsky Lane for Dzhanumova. Pampered treasure, I am firmly with you in spirit. Kisses.'

This was in memory of 'refining nerves' in Moscow. The nerve refining continued in Petrograd.

From the external surveillance log: '3 April. He brought to his apartment some woman who spent the night with him.'

He maintained the whirl of diversion in Petrograd. He happily accepted a variety of invitations. And the agents in their cabs had a hard time keeping up with him. 'He was followed to someone's apartment,' the external surveillance agents wrote. The railway acquaintance continued. And described in Chikhachev's testimony is a visit by Rasputin to Khotimskaya's apartment.

He was fashionable, mysterious, frightening. And Khotimskaya planned to go 'to a party where Rasputin would be present'. The company was recherché: the well-known writer Breshko-Breshkovsky; Lezhin, a professor at the Conservatory, and his wife, a well-known singer; and Chikhachev himself.

'Rasputin arrived in time for dinner in a new silk shirt, and was at first shy but then became more lively, especially after he sat down at the table and had a glass of red wine.'

And of course 'at the request of those present', he told the story that had recently preoccupied all of Russia, that of Guseva's attempt on his life.

> She came up to me, asked for a three-rouble note, I got out my purse and was rummaging in it. While I was rummaging, she stabbed me in the stomach with a big knife. I started running, and she ran after me with the knife, the stupid woman. I yelled, 'Drop it, bitch!' But she didn't drop it. Then I picked up a birch stake, and I am thinking, 'At what point do I split open her head?' Then I felt sorry, and hit her pretty lightly on the shoulder. She fell down, and people grabbed her by the arms – they wanted to tear her apart. I stood up for her, and then my strength failed me and I fell down.

And then the mocking conclusion of the story, which must have affected those well-nourished women: 'If only a pretty one had stabbed me; that one was a noseless stinker.'

He was able to address every topic easily and naturally.

'Why do you quarrel with Hermogen and Iliodor?'

'I was their friend, so long as I went along with their wishes . . . They asked me to stand up for them, I stood up; they asked for money, I got it for them. When I started contradicting them, I became a bad person . . . Hermogen wanted to be patriarch. Where does he get off! The patriarch should be a pure man of prayer; he is the only one, like the sun.'

The drunker he got, the more frightening his naturalness became. More accurately, it was his game: drunk, he could put them in their pitiful place. 'When the host asked him a question several times . . . while Rasputin was enthusiastically discussing something with someone else, Rasputin at first impatiently waved him away, and then he shouted at him, "Why don't you go to . . .'" And they heard 'impossible, crude peasant swearing, so that the ladies present ran out of the room in embarrassment'. But at the same time that naturalness captivated those ladies and gentlemen.

'He differed from many in his spontaneity, and did not try to seem better than he was . . . He came close in his whole demeanour to the type of the "sainted holy fool".' So Chikhachev realized the role Father Grigory was playing. Even if he did not realize that it *was* a role.

Rasputin made one other noteworthy visit soon after his return to the capital, a visit that is reflected in several works by fashionable literary people of the day for the fact that appearing along with Rasputin at the soirée in question was the Russian James Bond, Manasevich-Manuilov.

From the agents' reports: '9 April. At 9:45 Rasputin . . . arrived at Alexei Frolovich Filippov's at 18 Sadovy Street . . . He was left there till 2:00 a.m. It was noted that some kind of meeting or spree was going on.'

'Bond' Gathers The Celebrities

That remarkable soirée is described in the File by the host himself, Filippov. True, it was in sum a fairly deplorable one for him. But everything in its place.

Several days before the soirée a series of mysterious phone calls were placed to the apartments of several famous Petrograd literary people. Among these was a certain Teffi. That name was known to all reading Russia at the time. It was the pseudonym of the famous humorist Nadezhda Lokhvitskaya. She was already past forty then, but yesterday's *femme fatale* was still very pretty. Many years later after she had emigrated, she remembered that phone call in her little sketch, 'Rasputin'. 'A Petersburg thaw marked by neurasthenia . . . Rozanov called and talked disconnectedly about some invitation. "I can't tell you anything over the phone." He simply did not dare to say anything concrete.'

The writer Vasily Rozanov was a dominant mind of his time. Unlike the now forgotten Teffi, Rozanov's works are even today seminal works for Russian intellectuals. Once in love with the writings of Dostoevsky, Rozanov, then twenty-four, married Apollinaria Suslova, Dostoevsky's tormenting mistress and prototype of the heroines of his novels, who was twice Rozanov's age. And Rozanov himself, a mystic who had visited the *Khlysty* and was morbidly interested in the secrets of *Khlyst* 'rejoicing', was himself not unlike a Dostoevsky character. So his passionate interest in the invitation is understandable, although its enigma would be clarified for Teffi only when another well-known writer of the day, the journalist Alexander Izmailov, came by to see her.

'You actually didn't understand whom he was talking about?' Izmailov asked. 'You really don't know whom one can't talk about over the telephone? About Rasputin!' For it 'was enough to mention his name for the police to listen in'. That's who the semi-literate Father Grigory was then!

Izmailov explained it all to her:

There's a publisher named F. in Petersburg whom Rasputin visits quite a bit . . . He's a friend of his . . . And M–ch, who is well known in literary circles, also goes there. This same M[anasevich] suggested that F[ilippov] invite some of the writers who would be interested in taking a look at Rasputin . . . The group won't be large, but the list has been put together carefully . . . so there won't be any unpleasant stories afterwards . . . M[anasevich] ran by this morning to show me the list of the people who've been invited.

And even though they were all quite terrified of getting into a 'story' (an acquaintance of Izmailov's, a prominent public figure, had been photographed in Rasputin's company and 'regarded himself as discredited for ever'), their interest in Rasputin intensified. For 'all Petersburg' was talking about him. Several days earlier Teffi had dined with friends. And in the dining room on the mirror above the fireplace was the sign, 'No talking about Rasputin'. As a result, Teffi had talked all evening 'about Rasputin with a certain maid of honour named E.'. The maid of honour said that the first time she saw Rasputin, he said to her, 'You shall come to me!' And she 'felt her heart beat'. And had not to that day forgotten his peremptory tone. 'As if my fate was an open book to him,' the maid of honour recalled with horror.

So Manasevich had worked it all out correctly. Around 10:00 p.m. the invited famous writers (who, by the way, were contributors to the largest newspapers) gathered at Filippov's apartment.

The File, from Filippov's testimony: 'I decided . . . to arrange a reception with ten or so journalists who were interested in Rasputin – representatives of the most diverse tendencies: Rozanov from the *New Times*, Teffi from the *Russian Word*, Izmailov from the *Stock Exchange News*, and so on.'

For Filippov, the soirée planned by Manasevich appeared to be a no-lose situation. He had many times observed how privately acquainting Rasputin with ill-wishers invariably ended in victory for the peasant. And so it happened this time! 'Rasputin charmed everyone present, even those who had been predisposed against him,' Filippov testified. And he who had witnessed those seductive sessions many times described Rasputin's usual strategy.

Rasputin did not join in the conversation immediately but as was his custom carefully studied those present, and only then began with well-aimed retorts, for the most part in the form of aphorisms. Particularly effective were his replies to the well-known religious mysticism of Rozanov and Teffi . . . In the middle of dinner, finally dissolving under the influence of the wine, Rasputin offered to give an impromptu talk on what love is . . . Rasputin was dressed in a white silk shirt girded at the waist . . . with a small cord, and he improvised standing up in a slight sing-song with his eyes gazing upwards. At the same time, the picturesqueness of his expressions . . . close to the style of the 'Song of Songs' was such that Teffi started to write them down, and she kept that fragment with Rasputin's autograph as a memento. Rasputin was informal with Teffi, as if divining her ageing but still passionate nature.

And Teffi described that evening, too. 'There were about six people in the smoke-filled room . . . Manasevich stood by the doorway . . . as did a couple of others . . . Rasputin was . . . quite tall, dry, sinewy, with a face as if extruded into his long fleshy nose, and . . . sharp, close-set eyes . . . His eyes gleamed so brightly it was impossible to make out their colour.'

'The host and I have arranged it,' Rozanov informed Teffi, 'you are to sit next to him . . . he's fond of ladies. Don't fail to touch on erotic topics, draw him out, he'll be interesting there.'

Teffi sat in the corner to Rasputin's right, with Rozanov and Izmailov to his left.

Teffi has described 'Rasputin's informality', or more accurately, his customary advances.

Rasputin drank a lot. 'Why aren't you drinking anything? Drink something, God will forgive you,' and urging me, he rapidly touched my shoulder like a hypnotist. 'You have sad eyes, *he* torments you a lot . . . Oh, but we are all fond of women's tears. I know all about it. What's that ring on your finger? Stick it quietly under the table, I'll blow on it and warm it up. Why did you take it off yourself? I would have done it for you.' But I knew perfectly well [what was going on] and took it off myself. 'When you come to see me, I'll tell you a great deal you didn't know.' And again he rapidly and furtively touched my shoulder.

Next was a recitation of Rasputin's poetry. 'That turned out to be a poem in prose in the style of the "Song of Songs" . . . I remember the phrase, "Beautiful are her lofty peaks. But my love is higher and more beautiful than they, for love is God."'

After which the peasant gave the famous writer his autograph. 'He licked the pencil for a long time. He wrote in an uncouth scrawl, "God is love, you love, God forgives, Grigory." And then the host anxiously came over to Rasputin. "A phone call from Tsarskoe!"' And Teffi was astonished to realize that those in Tsarskoe Selo had known where he was! While Rasputin was gone, Rozanov started giving Teffi instructions. 'The main thing is to get him to talk about his *Khlyst* "rejoicings".'

That is what they had all come for. Rozanov, like all those present and like Rasputin's friend Filippov, knew that the peasant belonged to the secret sect. And they were looking forward to that story, but . . . 'But Rasputin did not return to the table. The host said he had been urgently called to Tsarskoe Selo.'

The Solution Of The Intrigue

The scandal burst the very next day. It turned out that the alarm had been sounded in Tsarskoe Selo regarding the soirée. And the next day Filippov was stunned to find his apartment searched.

The File, from Filippov's testimony:

> Colonel Ivanov, who was carrying out the duties of the head of the security branch, told me in confidence in response to my indignation that the person at fault in it was Rasputin, who had alleged that during his presence the literary people had been copying down what he was saying . . . Intelligence had also reached their agents that I had at my disposal documents compromising to the empress, and that Rasputin was going to be murdered at my apartment.

At the same time a scared Izmailov ran to Teffi and told her that "F[ilippov] came by today and said that he . . . had been interrogated as to just which literary people had dined at his place, and what Rasputin had said there. They threatened to banish him from Petrograd. But the most offensive and amazing thing was that Filippov saw on the interrogator's desk the same sheet in Manasevich's handwriting. We need to be very careful. Even if they don't interrogate us, they will certainly follow us.'

Yes, it was Manasevich! Having decided to take his place by Rasputin, he had carried out a purge of the team surrounding Father Grigory. Simanovich, who took care of finances, knew his place. But Filippov, who played the role of counsellor and who really did have immense influence on Rasputin, apparently worried him. And 'Bond', in the finest traditions of the Department of Police, had engaged in his customary duplicitous game. He himself had suggested that Filippov organize a literary soirée, and he himself had told Tsarskoe Selo about the soirée, attributing the initiative to Filippov. And he had passed on to the security branch 'the same sheet' – the list of literary invitees. The list had frightened Alix. All the people on it were well-known 'leftist writers'. Which is why there had been a call from Tsarskoe Selo interrupting the meeting. And Manasevich had, of course, provided the information about the 'documents compromising to the empress' that were supposedly in Filippov's apartment. And at the same time, he had told Rasputin about the malign intentions of the literary people, who had been recording the conversation in order to ridicule him. Even though they had agreed not to 'write anything down'. Manasevich could be pretty confident here. He had no doubt that they would break their promise and write.

And one of the soirée's participants, the well-known writer Anatoly Kamensky, did in fact finish a play about Rasputin.

'An echo of that evening . . . was Anatoly Kamensky's play . . . which encountered extraordinary difficulties with the censorship in Yavorskaya's staging . . . The literary people present at the soirée had given me their word not to publish comments about the meeting, which is why . . . Rasputin attacked the production of Kamensky's play so fiercely . . . The latter had, in Rasputin's words, "violated his oath",' Filippov testified in the File.

In a yellowed 1915 issue of the newspaper *Footlights and Life* I found a report about the play and an event that had caused an uproar in Petrograd. 'A production of A. Kamensky's *Maybe Tomorrow* was set for 8 December 1915, in Petrograd at the Yarovskaya Theatre. At 8:00 p.m., when the theatre was already crowded with people, the management announced that the performance could not take place: it had been officially forbidden.' The play was, of course, allowed once Kamensky had revised it and turned its hero, the Russian peasant Rasputin, into a Swede!

After that episode, the frightened Filippov began to distance himself from Rasputin. And Rasputin himself began to mistrust Filippov. Now Manasevich-Manuilov became his adviser and the chief member of his team. And Manasevich-Manuilov was already anticipating the governmental changes that promised so much.

But everything in fact turned out quite differently.

11

A PYRRHIC
VICTORY

'He Curiously Enough Said
The Same As Me'

The war continued. And at the same time another war was going on – the one between Alix and the commander-in-chief (Nikolasha or N., as she variously called Nikolai Nikolaevich in her letters).

'4 April 1915 . . . Though Nikolasha is so highly placed, yet you are above him. The same thing shocked our Friend, as me too, that Nikolasha words his telegrams, answers to governors, etc. in your style – his ought to be more simple and humble.'

In April the tsar and the commander-in-chief were supposed to inspect the troops stationed in conquered Galicia and Poland. At court a rumour persisted that the Grand Duke Nikolai Nikolaevich had decided to become king of Galicia and Poland. Alix was scared that during their trip the 'dread uncle' would incline Nicky to agree to it. And Our Friend at once expressed the view that the tsar should not make the journey. Or if he did, that he should go by himself.

6 April 1915 . . . But the idea of L[vov] and P[eremyshl] already now, makes me anxious, is it not too soon, as all the spirits are not much for Russia – in the country, yes, but not at L[ithuania] I fear. – Well, I shall ask our Friend to quite particularly pray for you there – but, forgive my saying so – it's not for N. to accompany you – you must be the chief one, the first time you go . . . really don't take him, as the hate against him must be great there – & to see you alone will rejoice those hearts that go out to you in love . . . Au fond, our Friend wld. have found it better you had gone after the war to the conquered country, I only just mention this like that.

7 April 1915 . . . How interesting all you are going to do. When A[nya] told Him in secret, because I want His special prayers for you, he curiously

enough said the same as me; that on the whole it [the trip] does not please
Him 'God will help . . . but better after the war.' – Does not like N. going
with you, finds everywhere better alone – & to this end I fully agree. Well
now all is settled, I hope it will be a success . . . God bless & guard this
voyage of yours.

But the tsar did make the trip with the commander-in-chief. Nicholas did
not know then that the Germans were preparing a decisive counterattack,
and that he would never see those cities again.

But Our Friend was now not only performing the duties of the tsarina's
wise parrot. A metamorphosis had gradually taken place. From a diviner of
her desires, from a conventional character in her letters by whom she
entreated her husband, he had imperceptibly begun to turn into a true
adviser. The seer produced in her imagination had gradually acquired reality.
The peasant was becoming autonomous. He had begun to dictate his own
thoughts to her. His peasant mind prompted decisions that derived from
his favourite populist idea of 'living by one's conscience', an idea whose
simplicity of realization was for her a source of delighted wonder.

'10 April 1915 . . . Gr[igory] is rather disturbed about the "meat" stories,
the merchants won't lessen the price tho' the government wished it, &
there has been a sort of meatstrike one says. One of the ministers he
thought, ought to send for a few of the chief merchants & explain it to
them, that it is wrong at such a grave moment, during war to heighten the
pri[c]es, & make them feel ashamed of themselves.'

And the merchants were summoned and suitably shamed. But for some
reason they failed to heed those calls to their consciences, and the prices
continued to rise.

The First Wizard In
The Court

It was at this time that Rasputin also started to make droll recommendations
to the tsars. 'Finds, you ought to order fabricks [factories] to make Ammunition, simply you to give the order even choose wh. fabrick, if they show
you the list of them . . . Be more autocratic my very own Sweetheart, show
your mind' (14 June 1915).

It's funny, but Rasputin suggested measures that are quite reminiscent of
the Bolshevik empire of Stalin's times. Who during the Second World War
had with an iron hand converted all the factories to meet the needs of the
front. Rasputin would propose the same thing: '29 August 1915 . . . But

Friend finds more fabrics ought to make ammunitions, where goodies are made too.'

And the tsar would try to implement it all! Compulsory alienation of foodstuffs from the peasants and landowners would be introduced, along with nationalization and militarization of the factories – all that Rasputin called for would be done. Or, more precisely, would be started, since it would be completed by the Bolsheviks. For some of the measures instituted during the period of War Communism after the revolution, had in fact been proposed in advance of Lenin by the Russian peasant Grigory Rasputin. And had been implemented by the last tsar.

Not long before his death, the peasant started to talk to the tsarina about raising 'the wages to all poor officials all over the country' in order to strengthen the machinery of the state in a time of troubles. And his idea of how to obtain the money for this sounds funny on the lips of the Russian tsarina: 'there is always money had fr. some capitals,' Alix would write to her husband on 25 September 1916. That is, simply seize the money from the rich.

And that age-old peasant dream would also be implemented by the Bolsheviks. So it was no accident that Bonch-Bruevich, Lenin's future close friend and comrade-at-arms and a founder of the bloody Cheka, had in his articles been so delighted with the 'intelligent, talented peasant'. Just as it was no accident that in his article on Rasputin, that founding father of the Bolshevist state described a remarkable scene. In order to test 'his gift for knowing people', Bonch-Bruevich had decided to show Rasputin a certain portrait dear to himself. Upon seeing the portrait, Bonch-Bruevich wrote:

> Rasputin became agitated. 'Who is that? Tell me, who is that?' He rushed straight over to the large wall portrait in which the proud, intelligent face of an old man was limned.
>
> 'Well, he's something! My goodness! He's a Samson, my friend, a real Samson, yes sir! Introduce me to him! We'll go see him right now! That's somebody the people should follow in regiments!' And Rasputin hurriedly turned on the nearby electric light, wanting to get a better look at the face of that stunning old man. I explained to him that it was Karl Marx.

'That's somebody the people should follow in regiments,' Rasputin had predicted in that article published in the newspaper *Day* on 1 June 1914, on the eve of a war that would destroy the empire of his tsars and become the pretext for a Marxist state.

The Meetings At Anya's

Alix and Anya's great friendship had by then definitely recovered. '14 April 1915 . . . Poor Ania has got again flebitis [sic] in her right leg & strong pain . . . poor girl, she now really is good & takes all patiently . . . Yesterday morning for the first time she walked alone on her crutches to the dining room without being held.'

By the end of April the Friend was already going everywhere on her crutches. And it would have been absurd to be jealous of a flabby, disgracefully fat cripple. After visiting her infirmary in the morning, Anya would now spend the rest of the day at the palace, just as in times past.

And Our Friend, who had saved Anya and her friendship with Alix, was present for their conversations, sometimes visibly but more often invisibly.

The File, from the testimony of Maria Belyaeva, Vyrubova's twenty-year-old maid.

'In May 1915 . . . Vyrubova would get up between nine and ten, drive to her infirmary where she would remain until one or two in the afternoon, then drive to the tsarina's at the palace and remain there until five o'clock . . . Sometimes she would have dinner with the tsarina or would go out. But after dinner she would every time go off to the tsarina's, where she would remain until twelve o'clock.'

The Friend and the tsarina were inseparable, including on the rare evenings that Anya spent at home. For if she was home, it meant that Our Friend was at her house. And, it follows, that Alix was there, too.

'15 April 1915 . . . Temp. 37.2 again yesterday evening, but . . . am feeling decidedly stronger, so will go to Ania this afternoon & meet our Friend there, who wishes to see me,' Alix wrote to Nicky.

'16 April 1915 . . . Our Friend was not long at Ania's yesterday, but very dear. Asked lots about you.'

The Secret Letter

An event occurred at that time that produced a wave of rumours in Petrograd and great concern among the Allies. Maria Vasilchikova had come from Germany. She was a maid of honour of the tsarina, the daughter of the director of the famous Hermitage, and the owner of a large estate near Vienna, where she had been caught by the war. The Germans had refused her permission to return to Russia. But then her mother died. And under the warranty of Alix's brother Ernie, duke of Hesse-Darmstadt, she was allowed to leave Germany for three weeks. In the event that she did not return, the Germans would appropriate her estate. Ernie had interceded for her, since she had, to her misfortune, agreed to convey a letter from him to the empress.

But at the time, the epidemic of spy-mania was in full swing. And the poor Vasilchikova was doomed. Vyrubova testified before the Extraordinary Commission:

> The empress was informed of her arrival by Elizaveta Fyodorovna, who refused to receive her . . . After her arrival in Petrograd Vasilchikova sent me a letter in Tsarskoe Selo with a request to receive her. But at the order of the former empress, I replied with a refusal. Since at court she was suspected of spying, she was expelled from Petrograd and her maid of honour insignia was taken away from her . . . As to how she [the tsarina] regarded the possibility of concluding a separate peace with Germany, I definitively state that I never heard any such discussion of the possibility or the desirability of a separate peace either from the former sovereign or from the former empress. On the contrary, they both supported the war till the end . . . For the three years of the war, she did not write or read anything in German. She loved her brother, the duke of Hesse, very much, but for three years she did not receive any news from him at all.

She had lied again. She knew that Vasilchikova had conveyed a letter to Alix from her brother.

Alix to Nicky: '17 April 1915 . . . I had a long, dear letter fr. Erni [sic] . . . He longs for a way out of this dilemma, that someone ought to begin to make a bridge for discussion. So he had an idea of quite privately sending a man of confidence to Stockholm, who should meet a gentleman sent by you . . . So he sent a gentleman to be there on the 28th . . . So I at once wrote an answer . . . & sent it the gentleman . . . he better not wait – & that tho' one longs for peace, the time has not yet come. – I wanted to get all done before you return, as I know it would be unpleasant for you.'

Although Ernie's letter had been a personal one, Nicholas decided he would be honest about it, and passed it on to the Ministry of Foreign Affairs. As a sign that he had not been a party to any peace proposals. That was a mistake. For the rumours immediately started to spread.

'In Russia everything is secret but nothing is hidden.' And the terrible, tenacious rumour was born that the tsarina was a spy who was corresponding with the Germans and giving them military secrets. A rumour that for the country at large would become an explanation for the catastrophe at the front.

From Vyrubova's testimony: 'She [the tsarina] heard on more than one occasion from nurses and the wounded in the infirmaries that she, as a German, was suspected of spying by the people and the army.'

Although if anyone is to be suspected of divulging military secrets, it should probably be brother Ernie. His offer to begin peace negotiations strangely coincided with the secret preparation of a German counter-offensive. It was as if he were warning Alix: hurry! And soon after the rejection of Ernie's offer, a powerful German offensive began in the second half of April. And a painful Russian retreat.

'7 May 1915 . . . Went to A[nya] till 5, saw our Friend there – thinks much of you, prays, we sat and talked together, – and still God will help. It's horrid not being with you at a time so full of heartache & anxiety.'

The rumours of treachery were naturally also linked to the hated elder. People started saying there were German spies in the circle of the constantly drunk Rasputin. And she heard that too in her infirmary.

She was tormented by the knowledge of how the commander-in-chief would use those vile rumours at Headquarters. Which is why in almost every letter to the tsar at Headquarters, she persisted in writing about Our Friend. And never failed to write his name with a capital letter, like that of a saint.

'14 June 1915 . . . I send you a stick (fish holding a bird), wh. was sent to Him fr. New Athos to give to you – he used it first & now sends it to you as a blessing – if you can sometimes use it, wld. be nice & to have it in yr. compartment near the one Mr. Ph[ilippe] touched, is nice too.' Thus did Our two Friends meet in Nicky's compartment.

Against the background of the Russian army's defeats, the rumours about secret negotiations with the Germans had alarmed the Allies. In the same letter of 14 June Alix wrote:

> Paul came to tea & remained 1 & 3/4 hours, he was very nice & spoke honestly & simply, meaning well, not wishing to meddle with what does not concern him . . . Paleolog [the French ambassador Maurice Paléologue] dined with him a few days ago & then they had a long private talk & the latter tried to find out from him, very cleverly, whether he knew if you had any ideas about forming a separate peace with Germany, as he heard such things spoken about here, & as tho' in France one had got wind of it . . . Paul answered that he was convinced it was not true . . . I said you were not dreaming of peace & knew it would mean revolution here & therefore the Germans are trying to egg it on.

No, Nicky was not thinking of betraying his allies, and had every intention of prosecuting the war to the end. The heavy losses, however, had forced him to consider calling up new conscripts in order to continue fighting. The call-up would have to send Rasputin's only son into the army. 'Says you will save your reign by not calling out the 2nd class now,' Alix wrote in her letter of 14 June.

It was not only that Rasputin feared for his son. The peasant had gladdened her with information about the changed mood in the villages – that a new harvest of blood might bring on a revolution much more quickly than a separate peace. That is why, after writing the obligatory words about carrying the war to a victorious conclusion, she asked Nicky not to draft new conscripts, thereby covertly calling on him to think about ending the war.

Alix was at the time being openly spied upon. In her letter of 14 June she wrote that 'Mary Vassiltchikov [the Princess Vasilchikova, of the same last name as Ernie's unfortunate courier] & family live in the green corner house & fr. her window she watches like a cat all the people, that go in & out of our house . . . [She] told C[ounte]ss Fred[ericks] that she saw Gr[igory] driving in – (odious). So to punish her, we went to A[nya] this evening by a round about way.'

Princess Vasilchikova was expelled from the capital. But rumours about the tsarina's sneaking out of her own palace for meetings with the peasant had reached Headquarters. And Headquarters was given a scare. First the appearance of Ernie's letter, and now the peasant, who had not long before warned of defeat and who detested the war. How great his influence had become if it made the tsarina forget her royal majesty and quit her own palace! And, finally, there were rumours that the peasant had been poisoning the tsarina against the commander-in-chief.

And the commander-in-chief decided to take the initiative.

Rasputin's Merry Days

Dzhunkovsky had apparently been ordered to hurry up his report to the tsar. New information was being continously sent on from the agents to the chief of the gendarme corps.

26 April. Around 10:00 p.m. some unknown men and women began to gather along with the banker Rubinstein at Rasputin's. At 11:00 guitar playing was heard. This continued until 2:00 a.m.

27 April. Rasputin was summoned to Tsarskoe Selo, but since he hadn't had much sleep, Volynsky and the Baroness Kusova advised him not to go

looking like that. Between themselves they were of the view that 'our elder has grown spoiled.' They advised him to go back to bed for another two hours.

30 April. He brought a prostitute home with him.

2 June. He came home completely drunk at 10:00 p.m. Instead of going up to his apartment, he sent the porter for the masseuse Utkina, who lived in the same building. But it turned out she wasn't home. Then he himself went to apartment 31 in the same building to the dressmaker Katya's. Apparently she wouldn't let him in, since soon afterwards he returned to the stairway and started making advances on the porter, asking her for a kiss. Freeing herself, she called his apartment, and the maid took him away.

But Dzhunkovsky's chief blow was to be his report about the scandal at the Yar.

The Sacrificial List Is Open

Meanwhile, the brutal defeats continued. In May and June the Russian army withdrew from Galicia, Poland, and a part of the Baltic territories. By June Lvov, the ancient capital of Galicia, had been surrendered. The Germans had taken charge of the palace of the Austrian Hapsburgs.

'12 June 1915 . . . William will now be sleeping in old Fr[anz] J[osef]'s bed wh. you occupied one night – I don't like that, it's humiliating, – but that one can bear . . . I hope to see our Friend a moment in the morning at Anias . . . that will do me good.'

The defeats at the front forced the commander-in-chief to continue more actively a favourite practice of Russian rulers: finding the people guilty of the failure. The best candidate for punishment was the war minister, Sukhomlinov. Not only was he disliked by the grand duke; the Duma also hated him for his devotion to the 'tsars'. And the old minister was not merely held responsible for the shortage of cannon, shells, bullets, and uniforms; he was also a focus of the popular campaign of spy-hunting.

First, Sergei Myasoedov, the counter-intelligence chief and a man close to Sukhomlinov, was on the basis of a suspect denunciation charged with spying and executed. After which the shadow fell on the minister.

Prince Andronikov and Chervinskaya started hurrying among the salons. 'I was sure Sukhomlinov was surrounded by a whole group of spies,' Andronikov later explained to the Extraordinary Commission. Something similar was repeated by both the Duma opposition and the grand dukes. Andronikov used Rasputin, too. His voice was added to the popular chorus, and he threw his own stone at the minister. Manasevich egged him on: for once, Rasputin stood with everyone else. And the tsar yielded to the commander-in-chief's demands and in June handed over Sukhomlinov. The old minister was removed from office, arrested, and sent to the Peter and Paul Fortress. The peasant did not fully understand what had happened. The innocent Sukhomlinov, accused of state treason, was the tsar's first important sacrifice to public opinion and to the commander-in-chief. After it, new sacrifices would surely follow. But if the peasant did not grasp the implications, the tsarina did.

On 24 June she wrote to Nicky, 'Now others can think that public opinion is enough to clear out our Friend.'

'Our Friend's Enemies Are Ours'

The sad situation at the front demanded new decisions that would unite society. The commander-in-chief spoke constantly to the tsar about this. And persuaded the tsar to take a popular step – to nominate new ministers who would force the Duma to support the government. He explained that 'a person with the German last name of Sabler cannot be chief procurator of the Most Holy Synod at a time of national hatred of Germans! Moreover, he is hated by the Duma.' Nicholas knew that the Duma hated Sabler for his loyalty to Our Friend. But he understood that in everything else the commander-in-chief was right. It was decided to appoint Alexander Samarin, from an old aristocratic family and the head of the nobility in patriarchal Moscow, as the new chief procurator. The tsar agreed as well to changing the minister of internal affairs. It was decided to remove the Rasputin loyalist Maklakov. And to nominate the liberal Prince Scherbatov from a distinguished noble family – he was respected by both the opposition and the court. General Alexei Polivanov, who had once been close to Guchkov and was now close to the commander-in-chief, and who would also have to be approved by the Duma, was nominated minister of war.

But there was also a trap here. When the future ministers were summoned to Headquarters, they declared that they could not work productively so long as Grigory Rasputin remained in Petrograd.

The File, from the testimony of R. G. Mollov, appointed deputy minister of internal affairs under Scherbatov: 'When I was offered the post of Deputy Minister of internal affairs, I immediately asked Prince Scherbatov, "What is the situation with Rasputin?" Scherbatov reassured me by saying that when he had accepted the post of minister of internal affairs, the sovereign had given him and the new chief procurator, Samarin, his word that Rasputin would never return from Siberia.'

The File, from the testimony of Yatskevich: 'Samarin . . . set the condition of "the removal of all extraneous influences from church life". The sovereign gave him a polite but evasive answer.' That is the truth: the most well-bred of monarchs was polite with them. And nothing more. And Prince Scherbatov had fobbed off the wished-for as the actual. Tsars do not make promises to their subjects. Nicholas was merely availing himself of an oft-tried device: sending the peasant home for a while.

Nicholas returned to Tsarskoe Selo at the beginning of June. He told Alix nothing about the new ministers. Especially since the decision had not yet been made. But it was not for nothing that Rasputin had as allies Andronikov and Manasevich, both of whom had worked for the Synod. First Our Friend, and then Alix and the Friend, learned that Sabler was to be removed. They decided to ask Nicky to leave Sabler in place until Our Friend could find a suitable candidate.

Nicky was not inclined to explain to her that a candidate had already been found. Instead he talked to her about how summer was coming on. And how Grigory usually went home. And how in order to reduce the number of silly rumours about him, it would be a good thing for him to go back to Pokrovskoe now. So that in the autumn, when the situation at the front was better, he could come back. 'The empress told me that it really was necessary for Rasputin to leave, and she added that the sovereign wished it, too,' Yulia Dehn testified in the File.

Before leaving for Headquarters, the tsar summoned Sabler. But he did not have the resolve to tell him. The File, from the testimony of Yatskevich:

> Sabler . . . was received by the sovereign with his latest report and, as always, treated affectionately . . . In answer to his question as to when he should give his next one, the sovereign said, 'I shall write to you, I shall write.' And then the conversation was broken off, since the heir had come into the study, as he always seemed to do whenever it was necessary to show someone the door. Sabler happily returned to his dacha, and around 8:00 received a note about his retirement: the sovereign wrote 'that circumstances obliged him', etc.

Thus was Samarin appointed. And the tsar had not been impolite.

The Wanderer Collects His
Knapsack

Petrograd was soon afterwards filled with rumours of Grishka's departure. And Manasevich and Andronikov expected that Rasputin would rush to the tsarina. But the peasant, to their astonishment, very calmly got ready to leave. More than that, he talked about how happy he was that he had at last been given permission to leave the capital. And he repeated something he had often told his devotees and that Zhukovskaya had written down:

> What a joy is freedom. In the daytime you would chop down trees, and what trees we have! They have never seen the like here. And at night you would build a bonfire on the snow and we would all dance around it . . . you would throw off your shirt and go about naked in the frost, but the frost was no match for you! Here in your cities it's just a heap of storm clouds, and not life! . . . The only reason I keep my strength is because I know that as soon as there's some kind of commotion, then my knapsack's on my back and my stick's in my hand and I'm off.

Neither Manasevich nor Andronikov grasped that departure was in fact his strongest action. That they could not manage without him – not Alix, not the tsar, not the boy. And that they would always call him back. They would live in triviality for a while but they would call him back. They would give in.

Rasputin learned of the changes in the government on the day of his departure. It had turned out amusingly: one thing had been prepared, and something altogether different had resulted. He called Vyrubova to tell her. Anya limped off to the tsarina in horror. Now the peasant could rest easy. For he knew that 'Mama' would not leave the tsar in peace.

On the evening of 15 June Rasputin set out for the village of Pokrovskoe.

The Tsarina's Attack

Alix by then was already writing her first letter. She would now overwhelm Nicky with desperate letters. And in them He would demand, advise, and prophesy – Our Friend, who had no suspicion he was doing any such thing.

> 15 June 1915 . . . Town is so full of gossip, as tho' all the ministers were being changed . . . & our Friend, to whom A[nya] went to bid goodbye, was most anxious to know what was true. (As though also Samarin instead

of Sabler . . . certainly Samarin wld. go against our Friend . . . – he is so terribly Moscovite & narrowminded.) Well, A[nya] answered that I knew nothing. He gave over this message for you, that you are to pay less attention to what people will say to you, not let yourself be influenced by them but use yr. own instinct . . . He regrets you did not speak to Him more about all you think & were intending to do & speak about with yr. ministers & the changes you were thinking of making. He prays so hard for you and Russia & can help more when you speak to Him frankly. – I suffer hideously being away from you. 20 years we shared all together, & now grave things are passing, I do not know your thoughts nor decisions, & it's such pain.

Nicky tried to assuage her anger, and wrote that everyone spoke of Samarin 'as a pure and devout man', etc. But she was implacable. '16 June. Just received yr. precious letter . . . Yes, Lovy, about Samarin I am much more than sad, simply in despair, just one of Ella's not good, very bigoted clique [this about her beloved sister!] . . . now we shall have stories against our Friend beginning & all will go badly . . . that means Ella's influence & worries fr. morn to night, & he against us, once against Gr[igory] . . . My heart feels like lead.'

And she let loose on poor Nicky an impassioned monologue:

16 June . . . I always remember what our Friend says & how often we do not enough heed His words. He was so much against yr. going to the Headquarters, because people get round you there & make you do things, wh. would have been better not done – here the atmosphere in your own house is a healthier one & you would see things more rightly – if only you would come back quicker . . . you see, I have absolutely no faith in N – know him to be far fr. clever & having gone against a Man of God's, his work can't be blessed, nor his advice be good . . . When Gr[igory] heard in town yesterday before He left, that Samarin was named . . . – He was in utter despair . . . now the Moscou set will be like a spider's net around us, our Friend's enemies are ours, & Schtcherbatov will make one with them, I feel sure. I beg your pardon for writing all this, but I am so wretched ever since I heard it & can't get calm – I see now why Gr[igory] did not wish you to go there – here I might have helped you. People are afraid of my influence . . . because they know I have a strong will & sooner see through them & help you being firm. I should have left nothing untried to dissuade you, had you been here . . . & you would have remembered our Friend's words. When He says not to do a thing & one does not listen, one sees one's fault always afterwards . . .

I entreat you, at the first talk with S[amarin] & when you see him, to speak very firmly . . . for Russia's sake – Russia will not be blessed if her Sovereign lets a man of God's sent to help him – be persecuted, I am sure.

Tell him severely . . . that you forbid any intrigues against our Friend or talks about Him . . . otherwise you will not keep him . . .

Do not laugh at me, if you know the tears I have cried to-day . . .

Our first Friend [Philippe] gave me that Image with the bell to warn me against those, that are not right & it will keep them fr. approaching, I shall feel it & thus guard you from them – Even the family feel this & therefore try & get at you alone.

And then she gave explicit expression to her desire to participate in the government. 'It's none of my doing, God wishes your poor wify to be your help, Gr[igory] always says so & Mr. Ph[ilippe] too – & I might warn you in time if I knew things.'

She would now write the same thing endlessly. The drip erodes the stone. Until it breaks it.

Abraham Does Not Wish To Sacrifice His Son

Rasputin arrived in Tyumen on 19 June. But from there, too, the agents continued to supply Dzhunkovsky with information about all Our Friend's movements. 'In Tyumen the Dark One stayed at the monastery with his friend the monastery prior, Martemian' (an ordained monk who through Rasputin's efforts had just recently been appointed abbot of the Tobolsk Monastery). After dinner, according to Martemian, the 'Dark One' 'drank two fourths [sic.] of the monastery's wine by himself'. Rasputin arrived in Pokrovskoe on 21 June escorted by the agents Terekhov and Svistunov, who followed him everywhere and who were for the most part lodged at his house, where they read him books and newspapers.

In Tyumen Rasputin had learned definitely that his only son was being drafted into the army. He had sent a desperate telegram to Anya, in which he had written of Abraham, who had been threatened with the loss of his son Isaac. Alix immediately wrote to Nicky: '20 June . . . Beloved one . . . his only son ought not to be taken . . . will you say, please.'

But Nicky said nothing. It seemed to her that this, too, was another machination of the commander-in-chief, who had taken control of Nicky's will.

25 June 1915 . . . I loathe yr. being at the Headquarters and many others too . . . Ah my Nicky, things are not as they ought to be, & therefore N.

keeps you near, to have a hold over you with his . . . bad counsels . . .
Remember our Friend begged you not to remain long . . . I here, incapable
of helping, have rarely gone through such a time of wretchedness – feeling &
realising things are not done as they should be, – & helpless to be of use –
it's bitterly hard; & . . . Nikolasha knows my will, & fears my influence
(guided by Grigory) upon you; its all so clear.

The day before she had written, 'Sweetheart needs pushing always & to be
reminded that he is the Emperor & can do whatsoever pleases him – you
never profit of this – you must show you have a way & will of yr. own, &
are not lead by N. & his staff, who direct yr. movements.'

She knew how awful this last sentence was for him. And of course she
had hit the mark.

The Disastrous Report

On 5 June 1915, the report of Colonel Martynov, the head of the Moscow
security branch, regarding the scandal in March at the Yar was at last
delivered to Dzhunkovsky's desk. And now, with Rasputin far away from
the capital, Dzhunkovsky and the commander-in-chief decided the time
had come.

The circumstances were propitious. Dzhunkovsky had been summoned
to the tsar to report on the disorders that had been taking place in Moscow.
As the French ambassador Paléologue wrote, 'On the famous Red Square
. . . a mob cursed the royal persons, demanding that the empress be sent to
a nunnery, the emperor abdicate the throne in favour of Grand Duke
Nikolai Nikolaevich, and Rasputin be hanged.'

Once he had given an account of the disorders, Dzhunkovsky planned
to turn to Rasputin. And, after explaining that 'the conduct of this man
has facilitated negative feelings in society', to show the tsar the reports of
the scandal at the Yar, as well as all the material on Father Grigory gathered
by the external surveillance agents over the preceding year.

From Dzhunkovsky's testimony: 'The sovereign received me at 10:00 p.m.'
Everything had gone as planned. After giving his account of the Moscow
events, Dzhunkovsky had turned to Rasputin.

> The sovereign . . . listened very attentively, but did not utter a single word
> during my report. Then he extended his hand and asked, 'Is it written out?'
> I removed the memorandum from the folder, the sovereign took it, opened
> his desk, and put the memorandum inside. Then I told the sovereign that

in view of the seriousness of the issue, and of the fact that I considered Rasputin's actions extremely dangerous and had to suppose that he could become a tool of any organization bent on destroying Russia, I said I would ask the sovereign's permission to continue my investigation of Rasputin's activities and to report on them to him. [This was naturally an innuendo that there were German spies in Rasputin's circle, a favourite topic of the day.] In reply the sovereign said, 'I not only grant my permission, I even request that you do that. But, please, so that only you and I will see the reports – let them remain between ourselves.' I thanked the sovereign very much for his confidence in me. The sovereign kept me for another half an hour or hour, while we talked about various matters, and then he let me go. It must have been around 12:30 a.m. when I left the sovereign . . . The memorandum I had left with him contained the most detailed description of what had taken place at the Yar, and everything that had happened there was, moreover, described in the most candid way – that it had not been the first instance, that it was all a kind of crescendo and had cast an unattractive shadow, and that I therefore considered it my duty as a loyal subject to report it, believing that it posed a threat to the dynasty.

The day after Dzhunkovsky's report, the tsar received the commander-in-chief.

In the tsar's unbearably stuffy sun-baked railway car, the 'dread uncle' yelled once again in his commander's voice what Dzhunkovsky had said – the drinking bouts at the Yar, and the fact that all the military secrets entrusted to the tsarina were becoming known to a drunken, debauched peasant, around whom suspicious individuals had been gathering, some of them German agents, for sure. The grand duke suggested deciding the question without delay 'within the Family' by bringing Alexandra Fyodorovna to Headquarters away from Vyrubova and Rasputin's circle, and showing her Dzhunkovsky's report. The sovereign expressed no objection. And the grand duke would afterwards be certain that the tsar had agreed. That was a mistake.

The grand duke had merely confirmed for the tsar what Alix had written about him: subjects do not understand the modesty of tsars. And the commander-in-chief, accustomed to the tsar's diffidence at Headquarters regarding tactical matters, forgot himself. That was his first irreparable blunder. There had been another: talking about Rasputin. Nikolai Niko-laevich and Dzhunkovsky had not said anything new. It was the same thing that society people had said about the behaviour of holy fools. And as for German spies, the tsar knew they were accusing everyone, even poor Alix.

In short, he now wanted only one thing: to leave those people who grasped nothing and return to Tsarskoe Selo.

The day after his report to the tsar, an exultant Dzhunkovsky told Grand Duke Dmitry about his gracious reception by the tsar, and gave him a copy of the 'candid memorandum'. And that was yet another blunder of the crudest variety, for the tsar had requested that all reports 'remain between ourselves'. And of course no sooner did Dmitry get back to Petrograd than he started telling his father and the other members of the great Romanov family about what had happened, along with the happy news of the tsar's anger and the certain end of the nefarious peasant. However his father, Pavel, knew the tsar too well to doubt how that 'anger' would end. And since at the time he was trying to secure the title of princess for his wife, Olga, he preferred to remain in Alix's good graces.

So he warned her about the rumours.

And Alix wrote to Nicky:

22 June . . . my enemy Dzhunkovsky . . . has shown that vile, filthy paper (against our Friend) to Dmitri who repeated all to Paul & he to Alia. Such a sin, & as tho' you had said to him, that you have had enough of these dirty stories & wish him to be severely punished.

You see how he turns your words & orders round – the slanderers were to be punished & not he – & that at the Headquarters one wants him to be got rid of (this I believe) – ah, it's so vile . . .

If we let our Friend be persecuted we & our country shall suffer for it . . .

Ah my Love, when at last will you thump with her hand upon the table & scream at Dzhunkovsky & others when they act wrongly – one does not fear you – . . . they must be frightened of you.

'Rumours reached me of some scandal in Moscow connected with Rasputin's name,' Vyrubova subsequently testified. 'I ascribed no significance to those rumours.'

The Bomb Explodes

In fact, as soon as the sovereign returned from Headquarters with the report of Rasputin's spree at the Yar, the Friend had taken a vigorous part in exposing the liars who were slandering the elder. She was presumably aware of the dirty trick that had been prepared for his persecutors either by the sly elder himself or by the skilled provocateur Manasevich.

It was stated in Dzhunkovsky's report and Martynov's memorandum that

Rasputin had gone to the Yar 'with Anisia Ivanovna Reshetnikova, the widow of a respected citizen'.

And Vyrubova at once triumphantly announced that Rasputin did indeed know well the said Anisia Ivanovna Reshetnikova. But that Anisia Ivanovna not only could not have been drinking with them, she could not even have gone with them to the Yar! From Vyrubova's testimony: 'I sometimes . . . dropped by for tea at . . . Anisia Reshetnikova's, an old woman of ninety who never left her house except to go to church, a typical Moscow merchant's wife who had endless tea and little things to eat at her house along with constant visits from the clergy. Grigory Efimovich Rasputin always stayed at her home.'

The old woman's home with its old-fashioned furniture, dusky icons, and dependants in dark kerchiefs, was located on Devichy Field. And Rasputin had stopped there often on his visits to Moscow.

From Vyrubova's testimony: 'I regard it as absolutely impossible that such an old woman could have been drinking with Rasputin at the Yar, since she could not even move from one chair to another without help.'

Vyrubova lied very effectively. She knew perfectly well that Rasputin really had been at the Yar with a Reshetnikova. Anisia Ivanovna's unmarried daughter. Who had the same initials and patronymic as her mother: Anna Ivanovna Reshetnikova. And who had evidently been identified to the police by her mother's first name.

It was the same Anna Ivanovna Reshetnikova who had been represented in the famous photograph of Rasputin 'surrounded by his devotees', who had seen the tipsy Rasputin off to Moscow in March, and who had, in his words, made him the gift of a 'thousand-rouble fur coat'. Vyrubova was very well acquainted with Anna Ivanovna and knew she had participated in all of Father Grigory's escapades, just as she was perfectly well acquainted with Reshetnikova's brother, Nikolai Ivanovich. That Reshetnikov, who had formerly served as one of Rasputin's 'secretaries', had by then become the builder and director of her infirmary.

This was the bomb that, in the eyes of the 'tsars' (who so wanted to believe the elder had been slandered), would ultimately destroy the entire Yar investigation.

When Nicky returned from Headquarters, Alix was in a virtual delirium of anxiety. She begged not to be shut up a nunnery – to at least be allowed to see her husband and the Little One. One may imagine the tsar's fury upon seeing what she had been driven to. But, as usual, he concealed his emotions behind a mask of silence and imperturbable courtesy. When he heard the story about Reshetnikova, the tsar presumably came to the conclusion that Dzhunkovsky, like everyone else, had out of hatred of the peasant presented him with a lie. And he must have been very disappointed. He had trusted the former Preobrazhensky Guards officer. And soon afterwards, Dzhunkovsky, as he himself recalled, 'sensed a change'. Now 'it was very hard for me to operate. I ran into an invisible but very powerful rebuff.'

A Torrent of Telegrams

While passions blazed, Rasputin was in Pokrovskoe leading his now customary life, and one that Dzhunkovsky's agents continued to describe just as conscientiously as before.

> 24 June. In his own home . . . he played the gramophone, danced, sang along disconnectedly, and related how he had released three hundred Baptists from punishment. They had promised a thousand each, but only gave a total of five thousand.
>
> 26 June. Some woman came to see Rasputin's neighbour Natalia and asked questions about Rasputin, who, as soon as he heard about it, immediately sent the peasant constable to look for her, although he didn't find her. Rasputin was very scared and remembered women he had been acquainted with in Tsaritsyn.

On 27 June the agents recorded a telegram from Vyrubova. After which they noted that the 'Dark One has been receiving a mass of telegrams and sending numerous letters', but 'has not been handing them over for posting'.

Now he knew all about it. Soon he could start to get ready. He had not been mistaken: those pitiful wolves had broken their teeth on him. Excitement. Nerve refining.

> 11 July. The officer's wife Patushinskaya arrived. The Shady One went outside . . . and took hold of her by the lower part of her torso . . . He was very gay and had been drinking wine.
>
> 13 July. After bathing he went to see the wife of the sexton Ermolai. . . . He goes to her almost daily for intimate purposes . . . Patushinskaya went to Yaluturovsk, summoned by her husband. On leaving she voluptuously kissed the Dark One on the lips, nose, beard, and hands.

The agents precisely described it all to Dzhunkovsky. But their descriptions were no longer needed.

The Happy Author's Arrival

Alix had by then discovered a pretext for Our Friend's return. Surviving in the files of the Department of Police is an advertisement clipped from the newspaper *Evening Times* for 24 July 1915: 'Just from the printer: Grigory Rasputin's "Thoughts and Reflections". Copies limited. The publisher, A. F. Filippov, is the managing director of a banking house, the editor and publisher of a variety of stock-exchange newspapers, and a well-known admirer of Rasputin.'

After distancing himself from the dangerous elder, Filippov had brought some earlier business to a conclusion. From Filippov's testimony: 'Rasputin's pamphlet "My Thoughts and Meditations" was published by me with an introduction written by me. The picture of Rasputin was taken in Siberia after he was wounded by Guseva and was still half-forgotten. The pamphlet was published at Vyrubova's insistence. The proofs were corrected by the empress.'

Thus, a pretext had been found: the happy author needed to come back for the new publication. Our Friend was essential to her in those decisive days of the palace coup.

From the surveillance log summaries: 'Rasputin left for Petrograd on 28 July. He arrived in Petrograd on 31 July.' And the very same day a car took Grigory to chasten his enemies. On 31 July and 1 August, according to the external surveillance log, 'the Dark One visited Tsarskoe Selo.'

A Trial In Tsarskoe Selo

The meeting in Tsarskoe Selo on 'what is to be done' lasted two days. The matter under discussion was the commander-in chief. Alix indicted the grand duke. Cited were the appeals made during the recent disorders in Moscow. Alix was sure that they had been the grand duke's own doing. She recalled all that she had written about in her letters: the grand duke was behaving like an autocrat. And then the time came for the prophet to have his say in court.

He played his part. Rasputin asserted what she was so eager to hear. And afterwards (on 10 September 1915) she would write to Nicky, 'our Friend read their cards in time, and came to save you by entreating you to clear out Nikolasha and take over the Command yourself.'

As befitted a prophet, Rasputin had foretold and forewarned. 'If the tsar had not taken N. N.'s place, he would have been thrown off the throne,'

Lili Dehn said later, citing words presumed to have come from the tsarina. But the words had not been the tsarina's.

On 9 December 1916, Alix would write to Nicholas, 'Our Friend says "that . . . if he (you) had not taken the place of Nikolai Nikolaievitch, he would now be thrown off the throne."'

Yes, on that fateful day Rasputin had demanded that the tsar remove the grand duke and become commander-in-chief himself, lest there be a coup d'état. Once again, he had echoed her desires. Did the tsar believe that the 'dread uncle's' intent had been malicious? I don't think so. But he liked the idea that the sovereign was obliged in times of defeat to assume responsibility for the war. He could no longer resist the temptation that had held him in its grip since the war began. He wanted to be commander-in-chief.

The File, from the testimony of Prince Scherbatov: 'Rasputin had come to Petrograd for three days just before the dismissal of Grand Duke Nikolai Nikolaevich, so that I saw him once at the Tsarskoe Selo train station.'

The 'tsars' did not want Our Friend linked to the impending decision that would be certain to shock the country and enrage the opposition. The peasant therefore had to go back home. And wait there while the tsar's decision was announced in his absence.

In the meantime all that had been decided was held in the strictest secrecy.

The previous commander-in-chief was finished. Thus had Rasputin once again tested the rule: it was enough for them to speak out against him to bring about their downfall.

The Drunken Boat

Rasputin left once more for Pokrovskoe on 5 August. As the agents wrote, Vyrubova and Pistolkors 'brought him to the station in their own motor, but they didn't get out of the motor themselves'. He was seen off by Princess Shakovskaya, the Baroness Kusova, and other admirers. His 'fools' already knew that he would be coming back soon.

He was in a tense, animated state. En route, he nearly seduced a lady travelling on the train, and the whole episode was carefully described by Dzhunkovsky's agent ('it is apparent from everything that the subject has hypnosis,' the agent reported). The peasant was enjoying himself – let them write it down. He knew that the reports no longer meant anything to Dzhunkovsky. And he could not help bragging. The agents reported, 'Rasputin came to the car where the security agents Terekhov and Svistunov were sitting . . . and started talking to them about the war – that the war was not going well for us, and that there would soon be great changes in Petrograd . . . In conclusion, Rasputin said that he had been to the tsar's twice, and that he had offered him a separate railway car for the trip . . . but Rasputin had allegedly refused.'

Of course the tsar had offered it – the peasant had spoken such desired words!

He continued his scandalous merry-making on the way to Pokrovskoe – he was celebrating his victory. The agents reported:

> On 9 August at 11:00 he boarded the steamboat, where he took a separate cabin, and set out for Pokrovskoe. He emerged drunk from his cabin about an hour later and went to see the soldiers of the local escort detachment, who were travelling on the same steamboat. Giving them twenty-five roubles, he made them sing songs . . . He withdrew to his cabin . . . When he came back he gave the soldiers one hundred roubles . . . the singing grew louder, and Rasputin joined in. The singing continued until 1:00, and [then] he took the soldiers to second class, meaning to treat them to dinner. But the captain would not allow the lower ranks to be present. He then ordered them dinner, paid for it, and sang again. Then he started arguing with the passengers, ran into the steamboat waiter, and calling him a crook, said that he had stolen three thousand roubles from him. After the captain told him that on their arrival a police report would be filled out, he withdrew to his cabin. Resting his head on a little table by the open window, he muttered something to himself for a long time, while the public 'admired' him. Rasputin fell from the table to the floor and lay on the floor the rest of the way to the village of Pokrovskoe.

At 8:00 p.m. the agents and two deckhands carried Rasputin ashore, where the four heaved the dead drunk peasant into a wagon, which took him home. The captain filled out a police report at public insistence.

On August 10, the agents reported: 'Rasputin, ah-ing in amazement that he had got drunk so quickly – he had only had three bottles of wine, added, "Oh-oh, dear fellow, it didn't turn out so good!" The Tobolsk governor, Stankevich, who hated Rasputin, immediately exchanged letters with Petrograd, and after receiving Dzhunkovsky's happy consent, at once proceeded with the case. To his own ruin.'

'The case was supposed to be heard at the district court and Tsarskoe Selo was very agitated about it,' Beletsky recalled. But Rasputin wasn't worried. When he heard that the governor meant to hold him in custody for three months for drunkenness and harassment of the other passengers, Rasputin, according to the agents' reports, 'merely spat and said, "What is the governor to me!"'

He was right. The poor governor was unfamiliar with Rasputin's law: it was enough to attack him, for . . . So Stankevich had assured his own future dismissal. In Tsarskoe Selo Our Friend would explain, not without mockery, that 'I was not drunk . . . I was treating the new draftees out of patriotic considerations.'

'Where Are We Heading, Where Are We Heading?'

Society had been agitated the whole of August. At the beginning of the month sensational rumours had begun spreading in the circles close to the throne, rumours they were afraid to credit. And then a strange letter was received by Felix and Irina Yusupov in the Crimea.

The war had caught the Yusupovs in Germany in 1914. They had miraculously escaped arrest by the Germans and had managed to take the last train leaving for Russia. Since then, a happy event had occurred in the life of the young Yusupovs: the beauty Irina had given birth to a daughter. Irina and the infant were both frequently ill. And taking refuge from the terrible Petrograd climate, Irina and her daughter had been living in the Crimea at Ai-Tudor, Irina's father's estate. In August 1915, Felix joined them there from Petrograd, where he had been in military training.

It was then that Felix's mother, Zinaida Yusupova, sent her son from Petrograd via a trusted messenger an enigmatic letter that proved highly disturbing to him.

'9 August . . . In general, it is all vile and especially in the sphere of the Validols. The "Book" has tremendous influence, and in a few days it will manifest itself in the area of a great change . . . I do not yet dare write about this and am not even supposed to know, but in my opinion it will all be disastrous. If you haven't, then Irina has probably guessed what I'm talking about. I'm tired out from writing such a complicated letter . . . the Validol instead of Bonheur.'

The letter was written in code, and the mother, not trusting the quickness of her son, was relying on the intelligent Irina. I think she easily decoded it. We too shall attempt her work of the remote past.

'Validol' derives from the word *vali*, which is what rulers were called by the Ottoman Turks – an Egyptian pasha, a Moldavian overlord. It was

Zinaida's name for the tsar and the royal family. The 'Book' was Rasputin, who was always quoting from the good book. 'Bonheur' ('Luck') was Nikolai Nikolaevich, since that was what he had been called at court during the previously lucky days of the war.

And so, on 9 August she had informed her son that 'In general it is all vile and especially in the royal family. Rasputin has tremendous influence, and in a few days it will manifest itself in the area of a great change. I do not yet dare write about this and am not even supposed to know, but in my opinion it will all be disastrous . . . The tsar instead of Nikolai Nikolaevich.' It's always the same: 'In Russia everything is secret but nothing is hidden.' The court already knew everything.

The news of the removal of the grand duke as commander-in-chief, who was so popular with the army, produced universal shock. And like Zinaida, everyone believed that Rasputin was behind it.

From the testimony of Prince Scherbatov:

> The decision to make himself commander-in-chief (even though he had been saying for two weeks that such a thing was out of the question) was explained as the influence of the empress and Rasputin. But I think that he, being a weak-willed person, was always afraid of anyone with too great a role, whether Stolypin, or the Grand Duke Nikolai Nikolaevich. We did not suppose that the tsar had any tactical or strategic abilities, or that he would introduce anything useful in the military sense. But that he would introduce into Headquarters those negative qualities the court always introduces into the military milieu. Furthermore, his presence at Headquarters made proper government of the country technically impossible. If the ministers were going back and forth to Headquarters, even if just once a week, that would each week deprive any government of more than two days.

He was right about that. After the tsar's departure for Headquarters, the government of the country would gradually be transferred to her hands. Her dream had become a reality.

And it began. Dzhunkovsky recalled that he had already grasped his fate on 10 August 'from what Rasputin told my agent in Pokrovskoe. He said, "Well, your Dzhunkovsky," and whistled. And on 16 August there was a note from the sovereign saying I was to leave.' By the middle of August the newspapers were already full of rumours that 'a reshuffling at the very highest ranks' was in the offing.

Nicholas left for Headquarters near the end of August to inform the 'dread uncle' of his removal. How afraid Alix was that he would change his mind, and how she prayed that he would not!

> 22 Aug. 1915 . . . God anointed you at your coronation, he placed you where you stand & you have done your duty . . .
>
> All is for the good, as our Friend says, the worst is over . . . shall wire to Friend to-night . . . – & He will particularly think of you . . .
>
> The meeting with N. won't be agreeable – you did trust him & now you know, what months ago our Friend said, that he was acting wrongly towards you & your country & wife . . .
>
> God is with you & our Friend for you – all is well – & later all will thank you for having saved your country . . . The left are furious because all slips through their hands & their cards are clear to us & the game they wished to use Nikolasha for.

Just before his departure, Alix gave Nicky a little comb that had belonged to Grigory. '23 Aug. 1915 . . . Remember to comb your hair before all difficult talks & decisions, the little comb will bring its help.'

But the dowager empress ('Aunt Minnie', as she was called in the great Romanov family) understood it all. She had no illusions about the peasant's role.

From the diary of Grand Duke Andrei Vladimirovich:

> 24 August . . . In the afternoon I went to see Aunt Minnie . . . Found her in a despondent state . . . She believes the removal of Nikolai Nikolaevich will lead to inevitable ruin. She kept asking, 'Where are we heading? Where are we heading? It is not Nicky, not he . . . He is sweet, honest, and kind. It is she. She alone is responsible for all that is happening . . .' She also added that it reminds her of the times of Emperor Paul, who in his last year started sending away all the people who were devoted to him, and our great-grandfather's sad end haunts her in all this horror.

From Aunt Minnie's diary: '21 August . . . All my words have been to no avail . . . There is no room in my brain for all this.'

On 25 August Nicky informed Alix from Headquarters of the most difficult conversation of his life.

> Thanks be to God, it's all over. And here I am with this new responsibility on my shoulders, but let God's will be done! . . . The whole morning of that memorable day, 23 August . . . I prayed a great deal and endlessly reread your first letter. The closer the moment of our meeting, the more did peace

reign in my soul. N. came in with a warm, cheerful smile and simply asked when I would order him to leave. I answered in the same style that he could remain another two days. Then we talked about matters pertaining to the military operations, about some of the generals, and so on, and that was it.

Just as they had meant to send Grigory's enemy Stolypin off to serve as governor- general of the Caucasus, now the tsar was sending another of the peasant's deposed enemies there.

But the tsarina would battle with Nikolai Nikolaevich until the end, until the very revolution itself. Soon afterwards (on 15 September 1915) she would write, 'I find he is taking far too big a suite . . . I very much dread they will try to continue making messes.'

'Ours' Take Action

And so, Rasputin was living in Pokrovskoe, waiting for the completion of the palace coup. And it truly was a coup. The commander-in-chief had fallen. And along with him the highly important minister of internal affairs and the head of the Department of Police had been removed from their posts. And, according to Alix's plan (although the tsar did not know it yet), Chief Procurator Samarin of the Holy Synod was also to fall.

The peasant proposed 'our' candidates to her for minister of internal affairs and chief of the Department of Police. Everything that had been thought out on Gorokhovaya Street at the beginning of the year was now coming to pass. And those who were bringing it to pass were the new rulers: the tsarina and the Friend and their absent chief assistant, our Friend. Or, more precisely, his man, Prince Andronikov, with whom Rasputin had discussed everything during the three days he was in the capital. Immediately after Grigory's departure, the 'dubious prince' was received by Vyrubova.

The File, from Vyrubova's testimony: 'I met [the prince] not long before he brought Khvostov to see me . . . He was a scented person of servile behaviour and dyed facial hair who always brought a mass of rumours, flowers, and candy.' But then he brought Khvostov, the future minister of internal affairs, to her for a look.

From Alix's letter to Nicky of 29 August: 'Beloved, A[nya] just saw Andr[onikov] & Khvostov & the latter made her an excellent impression.'

After which Andronikov, that shady 'scented and dyed' personage, passed on a list of candidates for the head of the church to the tsarina herself!

From Alix's letter to Nicky of 7 September: 'Well, Dear, here are a list of names, very little indeed, who might replace Samarin. Ania got them through Andronikov.'

The tsarina wanted people who were loyal. But she was afraid that Nicky would err. He had erred so many times before: Stolypin, Kokovtsev, Dzhunkovsky, and so on. And now she had decided to take care of the ministers herself. But how not to err? Very simple. Follow the rule reiterated many times in her letters: only he should be a minister who believed in and was devoted to the man of God. For that would automatically mean devotion to and faith in 'Mama', since the wishes of the 'man of God' always coincided with her own. Such must the ministers be now! But since she and Anya did not know any such people, the novice stateswomen sagely decided to rely on Grigory. And Grigory, although leaving the capital, had sent the 'scented and dyed' Andronikov to help them.

But what kind of candidates had Andronikov presented in Grigory's name? The first was Beletsky, whom they had intended as early as the beginning of the year to make the head of the Department of Police. But there was a certain difficulty with the minister of internal affairs. Andronikov had proposed Rasputin's old acquaintance Alexei Khvostov, the same young Nizhny Novgorod governor Rasputin and Sazonov had visited on the eve of Stolypin's murder.

The Road To Power,
1915-Style

In the four years since that visit, Khvostov had left the post of governor, retired from the service, and been elected to the Duma. He had, however, remained just as jolly, fat, and ruddy-cheeked as before. In the Duma, he had become the leader of a rightist faction whose members proudly wore on their lapels the pin of the anti-Semitic organization Union of the Russian People. His anti-Semitic speeches had been very well received in Tsarskoe Selo. As Khvostov later explained to the investigators of the Extraordinary Commission, 'I took up German espionage and German domination. That question interested me to the highest degree.' It would have been hard to find a better candidate – a man of the Duma yet a leader of the right and an indomitable foe of German espionage, which, in view of the rumours circulating around Rasputin and the tsarina, was no small matter. And, finally, Khvostov was a Russian, which was highly important, given the unfortunate predominance of German last names at court.

Andronikov knew Khvostov well, as of course he did more or less all important people. And he knew that Khvostov would accept any conditions to ascend Olympus with such speed. And after his conversation with Khvostov, it seemed that Andronikov was able to persuade Rasputin of it, too. For the peasant remembered the reception that Khvostov had given him. But Andronikov apparently convinced him that the old haughty Khvostov no longer existed. There was a new Khvostov, who understood that in order to be minister, he would have to serve Our Friend.

Rasputin's wavering was decisively overcome by the prince's proposal to appoint Beletsky, whom Rasputin had already met and of whose loyalty he was assured, under Khvostov. Beletsky would take responsibility for the Department of Police away from Khvostov and, it follows, responsibility for Rasputin's security along with it. So the candidacy was a superb one. And after meeting Vyrubova, Khvostov proceeded to the tsarina. 'The empress received me graciously and hinted . . . that, although I was not without fault as far as Rasputin was concerned, she was sure that my eyes had been opened . . . and she would not stand in the way of my nomination, providing Rasputin's security remained with Beletsky.'

While Anya and the tsarina were talking over future nominations with Andronikov, a dangerous event occurred in the Duma.

The Peasant Unites The Haters

Society and the Duma were full of rumours leaking from the palace. The removal of the grand duke had created a new reality. There was a new commander-in-chief who was considered incapable of heading the army, and there was Prime Minister Goremykin, an old man completely under the tsarina's thumb who was considered incapable of heading the government. And there were persistent rumours about impending nominations that, in the tsar's absence, would become the prerogative of the tsarina. That threatened the creation of a cabinet of 'dark forces'. One that would, it was believed, operate with the prime minister's responsibilities assigned to the semi-literate peasant. Who was about to return to the capital.

On 25 August 1915, the Progressive Bloc was formed in the Duma. The struggle against the 'dark forces' had accomplished the impossible. It had united all those extremely disparate and at times mutually hostile people. It comprised 300 deputies out of a possible 442. The Bloc was supposed to remove the 'dark forces' (Rasputin and the tsarina) from power without repercussions, and lead the country to the creation of a truly constitutional monarchy. And to that end to secure the retirement from the government of Goremykin and the creation of 'a government of confidence' that would be answerable to the Duma. The Bloc's slogan was: 'The masses remain calm – the Duma speaks for them.'

At the same time, Guchkov was preparing in the Duma a resolution of inquiry regarding Rasputin's scandal at the Yar. It was then that Khvostov demonstrated that his recommendation by Our Friend's envoy had not been in vain. 'Khvostov said that . . . a resolution of inquiry was being prepared in the Duma. They had asked Khvostov for his signature, but he refused and observed that if the question were raised, the amnesty [the tsar's amnesty for convicts was then being considered] would not be granted. They thought it over . . . and rejected the resolution,' Vyrubova testified. On 30 August 1915, Alix wrote to Nicky, 'Guchkov ought to be got rid of, only how is the question, war-time – is there nothing one could hook on to have him shut up . . . but it's loathsome to see his game, his speeches & underhand work . . . [They] say he [Rasputin] lives at T[sarskoe] S[elo], as before they said we had Ernie here.'

The most preposterous rumours were abroad in the capital, while Our Friend remained as before in Pokrovskoe awaiting the promised changes. All that time he fought for his son's release from the draft. He realized that his pitiful, weak-minded son would perish at the front. And he sent his wife Praskovia to Petrograd to entreat the tsars to leave his son at home. And he sent pleading telegrams and petitions. And in her next letter Alix again asked Nicky, 'Can you not find out when his province is called up & let know at once? Does it concern His son? Please, answer as quickly as you can.' On 30 August she repeated her request. 'I enclose a petition from our Friend, you write your decision upon it, I think it certainly might be done.'

But again the Tsar remained silent. And again she asked him. '1 Sept. 1915 . . . Our Friend is in despair his boy has to go to war, – the only boy, who looks after all when he is away.'

And again Nicky said nothing. He could not explain to her that while he might change ministers, he was unable to leave the peasant's son at home. It would be a provocation to the family and to society. While focusing on the struggle for 'ours', Alix had somehow failed to remember that not long before Grand Duke Konstantin Konstantinovich's son Oleg, just a boy, had been killed. And his father had been unable to endure his grief – the grand duke had been throttled by an attack of angina pectoris. And there were other young grand dukes at the front. How could he then excuse the peasant's son from service! But, as always, she stubbornly kept trying to get her way. '11 Sept. 1915 . . . I understand the boy had to be called in, but he might have got him to a train as sanitary [medical orderly] or anything . . . an only son . . . One longs to help without harming Father or Son.'

Although Rasputin's son would eventually be drafted, she would be able to secure him a place as a medical orderly – on her own hospital train.

Indignant discussion continued in the Duma about the impending appointment of ministers pleasing to the peasant, and about the fact that Prime Minister Goremykin was travelling back and forth with reports to the tsarina.

On 6 September Zinaida Yusupova wrote to her son in the Crimea in her amusing code, 'The general mood is one of disgust. The "Fur Coat in Mothballs" [the old man Goremykin] continues to travel back and forth to the Valida [the empress]. She is simply triumphant!'

The opposition continued its attacks. This time the news was from Moscow, the seat of the anti-Rasputin opposition. Vladimir Gurko, a respected man of right-wing convictions with the high rank of chamberlain who was also a member of the Council of State, took a public stand. And a phrase spoken by Gurko soon spread throughout Russia: 'We desire strong authorities . . . meaning . . . authorities with a whip [khlyst] and not under a Whip [Khlyst].'

'A slandering pun, directed against you & our Friend, God punish them for this,' Alix wrote to the tsar on 8 September.

'The Ministers Are Rotten'

The peasant understood: he who had saved their son so many times had been unable to protect his own. His son had been drafted into the army. And it was then that Rasputin took to drink once and for all. And the beast, the 'Dark One', the fearsome peasant fully awoke in him.

An agent reported:

5 September. The Dark One was visiting his brother. His father went there, too, and started cursing him in the foulest language. The Dark One, enraged, leapt up from the table, pushed his father out the door, knocked him to the ground, and started hitting him with his fists. His father yelled, 'Don't hit me, you scoundrel!' And they had to be pulled apart by force. One of his father's eyes was so badly pummelled it had swollen shut. As he left, the old man started cursing the Dark One even more, threatening to tell everyone that he [Grigory] didn't know anything except how to hold Dunya [the maid Dunya Pechyorkina] by her soft parts. After which, the Dark One had to be kept from attacking his father again.

The agents enjoyed reading him the newspapers, which were just as interested in him as before. And he was apparently also tormented by visions. He sensed that there, far away in Petrograd, the inevitable was looming.

'6 September,' the agents recorded, 'Rasputin said, "My soul is full of grief. It has even made me deaf . . . Two hours I feel all right in my soul, but five hours are bad . . . and bad because of what is going on in the country, and because what the damned papers write about me greatly annoys me. I'll have to take them to court."'

While Rasputin was carousing in Pokrovskoe, the tsarina was tirelessly pleading for Khvostov's nomination as minister. And our Friend's predictions were once more brought into play.

'7 Sept. 1915 . . . one needs an energetic man who knows people in every place, & a Russian name.'

'9 Sept. 1915 . . . Clean out all, give Goremykin new ministers to work with & God will bless you & their work . . . My image of yesterday, of 1911 with the bell has indeed helped me to "feel" the people . . . And the bell would ring if they came with bad intentions & wld. keep them fr. approaching me . . . And you my love, try to heed what I say, it's not my wisdom, but a certain instinct given by God beyond myself so as to be your help.'

The tsar wavered; he was still unaccustomed to her direct participation in affairs. She was tense. All her indomitable energy had been directed to help him. And it made her angry that he did not understand that.

'10 Sept. 1915 . . . Please speak seriously about Khvostov as Minister of the Interior to Goremykin am sure he is the man for the moment, as fears nobody and is devoted to you.'

But appointing a new minister of internal affairs was only the beginning.

On 11 September she was already demanding the head of Chief Procurator Samarin. 'Now they [the Duma] have betted that you cannot send Samarin away – & you will . . . At once my love, clear him out & Stcherbatov [the minister of internal affairs] too . . . Please take Khvostov in his place . . . Take a slip of paper & note down what to talk over [with Prime Minister Goremykin]. . . . 1) Samarin . . . Samarin is stupid insolent fellow.' She would now write directly and insistently about Khvostov. And she would not relent until he yielded.

12 September: 'The ministers are rotten.'

14 September: 'People get angry I mix in – but it's my duty to help you. Even in that I am found fault with, sweet Ministers and society . . . Such is the unedifying world.'

Sometimes she wrote two letters a day. She was sure their enemies at Headquarters would not let Nicky carry out these wise decisions. It was not for nothing that a foe of the man of God – Nicholas's young cousin Dmitry – was at Headquarters.

13 September: 'Why don't you send him back to his regiment? . . . It does not look well, no Granddukes are out [at the front], only Boris from time to time, the poor Constantins boys always ill.'

She could fight, and in combat she was ruthless. Her daughter's former fiancé who had been raised in her family, was to be sent to the front closer to death for having dared to go against the elder.

And all that time Our Friend had been with them. He had not forgotten to send the needed telegrams. On 8 September she wrote:

'About the war news our Friend writes (add it to yr. list of telegrams) . . . "Don't fear it will not be worse than it was, faith and the banner will favour us."'

On 9 September she wrote: 'Did you copy out his telegr. for yourself on the extra sheet? If not, here it is again: "Do not fall when in trouble God will glorify by his appearance."'

Such were the seer's predictions one and a half years before the revolution. Rasputin had also sent a badly needed telegram requesting the nomination of the God-pleasing Khvostov.

Ahead lay a meeting at Headquarters of the Council of Ministers at which Alix expected that the appointment of Khvostov would at last be announced. And she asked Nicky to turn for help to Our invisibly present Friend.

'15 Sept. 1915 . . . Remember to keep the Image in yr. hand again & several times to comb yr. hair with His comb before the sitting of the ministers. Oh, how I shall think of you & pray for you more than ever then, Beloved One.'

They were worried in Petrograd. The deputy internal affairs minister, G. R. Mollov, had received reliable information from one of his agents that Khvostov had been summoned to Tsarskoe Selo by the empress and given hope of an appointment to the post of minister of internal affairs. 'I informed Prince Scherbatov,' Mollov later recalled, 'that it appeared that his and my days at our occupations were numbered . . . Scherbatov . . . did not agree, and said that he had recently returned from Headquarters, where he had been graciously received by the sovereign.' The Sabler story was being repeated.

On 15 September an agitated Colonel Globachyov, chief of the Petrograd security branch, arrived at the Ministry of Internal Affairs. 'Globachyov presented me with a telegram from one of the agents assigned to Rasputin. In the telegram it was mentioned that Rasputin had received a letter from Vyrubova with approximately the following contents: "Sana [a diminutive form of 'Alexandra' – that is, Alix] is feeling sad and is eager to see you in about ten days time. Bless." It was mentioned in the same telegram that Rasputin meant to come to Petrograd soon afterwards,' Mollov testified in the File. Putting the two events together, Mollov clearly understood what lay in store.

Alix at the time was continuing to shower the tsar with letters. She could not stop. Her energetic temperament would not permit her. On 17 September she sent him two complete letters.

'17 Sept. . . . Only wire a word to quiet me. If no ministers yet changed – simply wire "no changes yet," & if you are thinking about Khvostov say "I remember the tail" [*khvost* in Russian].'

But Alix knew that if he hadn't already decided without her, she would prevail on his return. And she entreated Nicky to 'come & quickly make the changes . . . Khvostov hopes that in 2, 3 months one can put all into order with cleverness & decision . . . how infinitely do I long to help you & be of real use . . . Some are afraid I am meddling in state affairs (the ministers) & others look upon me as the one to help as you are not here (Andronikov, Khvostov).'

So Andronikov, the 'shady prince', had become a good soul.

'Really, my Treasure, I think he is the man & our Fr. hinted to A[nya] in his wire . . . Khvostov has refreshed me . . . I yearned to see a "man" at last – & here I saw & heard him . . . Nobody is any the wiser I saw him,' Alix reassured Nicky.

But he continued to waver. He still could not get used to her new role. And he failed to announce the new appointments at the Council of Ministers meeting at Headquarters.

She pressed on. '18 September . . . I am bothering you with this talk, but I should like to convince you . . . that this (very fat young man of much experience) is the one you would approve of & that old woman who writes to you I should say too.'

The Friend had during that time been tirelessly sounding out the new candidates.

20 Sept. 1915 . . . I send you . . . a summary of her [Anya's] talk with Beletzky – that does indeed seem a man who could be most useful to the minister of the Interior, as he knows everything . . . Andronnikov gave Ania his word of honour, that nobody shall know, that Khvostov comes to Ania

(she sees him in her house, not in the palace) or Beletzky, so that her & my name will remain out of this . . . Our Friend's wife came, Ania saw her − so sad & says he suffers awfully through calumnies & vile things one writes about him − high time to stop all that − Khvostov & Beletzky are men to do that.

Praskovia had been unable to protect her son. She took leave of the capital, saying that she had to return to Pokrovskoe, 'because Grigory's life was threatened with danger'. And in fact he had, as the agents reported, received the following typewritten letter: 'Grigory! Our Fatherland is being destroyed, they want to conclude a shameful peace . . . We, the delegates, beseech you to do something so that the ministers will be answerable to the people. And if you do not do that, we shall kill you, there will be no mercy. The lot has fallen to us ten.'

It was devoutly believed in society that everything happening at the top had been inspired by the semi-literate peasant, who had taken control of the tsarina's will.

The Scandalous Pastors

Simultaneously with the struggle for new, obedient ministers, Alix was involved, and no less energetically, in the struggle for an obedient church.

There was a logic in this. The church was a state institution strictly controlled by the tsars through the Synod. Moreover, ideas about the Anglican Church, which was dependent on the will of the monarch, lay in the subconscious of that 'English' princess. Of that last 'English' princess, I should add, to struggle for the unlimited autocracy of the times of the indomitable medieval kings.

And on 11 September 1915, she wrote to Nicholas, demanding he replace Samarin, the chief procurator of the Synod. 'You are the head & protector of the Church & he tries to undermine you in the eyes of the Church. At once my Love, clear him out.' She wanted to rid the Synod of those bishops who would not submit: 'you must set yr. broom working & clear out all the dirt that has accumulated at the Synod.'

Unfortunately, however, she had little idea of who was needed to replace them. And the peasant − the man of God next to the throne − had once again to provide the candidates. Who, if not he, should dictate the appointment of church hierarchs? Naturally after discussing it with her. And here Rasputin remained her alter ego.

Before Alix got involved in running the church, Rasputin had had few church allies among the 'highly placed'. For the majority of the latter, he remained a suspicious, ignorant peasant and covert sectarian. For Rasputin himself, the official church was the bishops in their medals, something remote from and hostile to him. He held them in contempt and had a peasant's fear of them. But gradually that fear passed. His royal devotee's acceptance of his holiness had inspired him with confidence. She was indignant at their presumptuous failure to acknowledge someone who was such a great authority for the 'tsars'. So that recognition of Rasputin was becoming synonymous with loyalty here, as well. And from about 1912 Alix began to see that high appointments were given to those who revered Our Friend. Thenceforth, his (meaning her) support began moving clergymen into high posts. And now even in the first Russian capital, Mother Moscow, sat someone who venerated Father Grigory, the eighty-year-old Makary. He, too, was from the Siberian hinterland, where he had graduated from Rasputin's local Tobolsk Theological Seminary.

Another influential member of the Synod was the exarch of Georgia. As already related, Molchanov's father, a disgraced bishop who had been censured for his liaison with a young teacher, had been appointed exarch of Georgia in spite of the Synod. It was then that Rasputin's practice began of recommending culpable pastors for high church positions. Above all, those accused of homosexuality, a serious offence from the point of view of both the Russian legal code of the day and the church. Because their situation made them utterly dependent on him. And also because it was connected with the mystical idea of the unity of the male and female principles in the *Khlyst* conception of Christ. And the *Khlyst* Rasputin, who believed that the Holy Spirit had descended on him, apparently sensed that unity in himself – he was above gender. Hence, not only his very civil attitude towards homosexuality but apparently even his possibility of treating lust, and not merely in women but also in men. Perhaps it is here that an explanation is to be found for Rasputin's extremely close relationship with Iliodor (in the past) and Felix Yusupov (in the future).

But one way or another, after Bishop Alexis died in 1914, Pitirim, a homosexual suspected of *Khlyst* connections whose candidacy had been advanced by Rasputin and, it follows, the tsarina, became exarch of the Caucasus.

The File, from the testimony of Yatskevich:

Pitirim is one of the most infamous names in our church. While bishop of the Tula eparchy, which was actually run by his lay brother Karnitsky, with whom the bishop had a liaison condemned by the church and the law, he had stolen the riches of the bishop's sacristy, which became clear after his transfer to the Kursk eparchy. His young lay brother ran the bishop and the eparchy in Kursk, as well. It was then in fact . . . that he began openly protecting . . . a society of monks in the Bogodukhov Monastery who had been exposed as *Khlysty*. As a result, he was removed from Kursk. He then became bishop of Saratov, where he found himself another young lay brother, a certain Osipenko, who took the place of the previous one.

That was the sort of person Rasputin had put forward to be exarch of Georgia. And the sovereign (meaning the tsarina) would subsequently cross out all the Synod's candidates for exarch and write in 'Pitirim'.

It was at that time, as well, that another homosexual devoted to Rasputin turned up in his vicinity – Father Isidor. The clergyman Isidor Kolokolov, as the same Yatskevich testified in the File, 'had been accused of sodomy with a lay brother Flavion, and for it had been appointed an ordinary monk at one of the monasteries. Isidor frequented Rasputin's home and soon afterwards became . . . the prior of one of the monasteries in Tobolsk, where he took his lay brother . . . even though the Synod had documentary proof of their cohabitation.'

Isidor became one of those closest to Rasputin. He would be received by the tsarina more than once and mentioned in her letters. 'Spent a lovely evening with our Friend and Isidor,' she would write to the tsar (3 November 1916).

And, finally, there was Varnava, another bishop promoted by Rasputin and a most unusual figure.

Varnava, a priest from the little town of Golutvina, lacked a higher seminary education. But he had acquired enormous influence with the local population and the Moscow merchants thanks to his lively, accessible discourse. And Rasputin had noted him at once. He personified, as it were, what Our Friend had been telling the tsars about the pastors of the people: 'although not schooled but believing; for from the schooled there is no sense to be had, as almost all are non-believers.' Alix understood that this double of Our Friend was ready to serve. And at the sovereign's personal wish (meaning, once again, the empress's), Varnava had been appointed bishop of Kargopol. Even though the appointment of a man without a higher seminary education had provoked a storm in the Synod.

After Molchanov's father, Bishop Alexis, became exarch of Georgia, Varnava was appointed bishop of Tobolsk. Rasputin should indeed have taken an interest in the spiritual authorities of the Tobolsk eparchy, inasmuch as his own village of Pokrovskoe was under their jurisdiction. Neither he nor the tsarina had forgotten how much trouble the Tobolsk Theological Consistory investigation had caused.

Alix was pleased. She wanted pastors who venerated Our Friend to be everywhere. Varnava immediately enjoyed special status. Not asking the Synod's permission, as he was supposed to, Varnava would vacate his eparchy and come to Petrograd by special dispensation of Tsarskoe Selo. The tsar rewarded him with a medal, to the Synod's indignation. He corresponded with the tsarina, not forgetting to inform her of solacing miracles and auspices.

'Our dear empress . . . during the procession round the church in Barabinskoe, a cross suddenly appeared in the sky and was visible to everyone for about fifteen minutes, and since the holy church sings 'The cross is the authority of the tsars, the confirmation of the faithful,' I gladden you with this vision,' the bishop telegraphed her.

Varnava knew that in view of the Synod's hatred of him, he was completely dependent on Rasputin. Although in his soul, according to the testimony of Manasevich who knew both of them intimately, 'Varnava hated Rasputin after he started drinking . . . for the sake of Tsarskoe Selo, he forgave him a great deal.' Rasputin sensed that, and when Varnava's visits to the capital started to drag on, a drunken call would follow to Varnava: 'Isn't it enough? You came here by car, now please go on back home on your own two legs. There's no taking it easy here.'

So the tsarina wouldn't learn to believe in Varnava in earnest, Our Friend, who assigned nicknames to everyone, called the Tobolsk bishop 'The Gopher'. 'For a certain duplicity,' Vyrubova would explain. A duplicity, I shall add, that Our Friend sensed in relation to himself. Rasputin's nicknames were immediately adopted by the tsarina. Fond of mysteries and codes since childhood, she used them in her correspondence with her husband and with Anya. So Varnava, thanks to Rasputin's light touch, now became 'The Gopher' in her correspondence and conversations.

The Tsarina As Patriarch

In August 1915 the tsarina decided to take control of the Synod. To do that she needed to depose Chief Procurator Samarin, the favourite of Ella and the Moscow clique. Rasputin was delighted to take part from Pokrovskoe. He knew very well how to go about it. The scheme was the same as before. Entice Samarin into a scandal, force him to attack Rasputin and 'ours'. And that would compel the tsar to make a decision.

Rasputin now frequently went to Tobolsk to meet Varnava. There in Varnava's spacious cell in the Tobolsk Monastery a script was worked out that would be sure to produce a scandal in the Synod. And a basis for the scandal was found. Buried in the Tobolsk Monastery was the former metropolitan of all Siberia, Ioann Maximovich, who had died two hundred years before. In the commemoration of his bicentennial, the Synod intended to canonize him. And Rasputin agreed with Varnava that this ceremony could not wait. That Varnava would solemnly glorify Ioann's relics before his official canonization by the Synod. It was a direct challenge to the Synod, and it wasn't difficult to imagine Samarin's anger. But first Nicholas needed to be drawn into the story. Varnava sent a telegram to the tsar in Petrograd. From Vyrubova's testimony: 'Varnava petitioned the tsar by telegram for permission to chant Ioann's laudation. The sovereign answered by telegram: "You may chant his laudation but you may not open his relics."' The game was then played out. Varnava, as if misunderstanding the tsar, both eulogized Ioann and opened his relics. Samarin at once summoned Varnava to the capital and prepared to punish the wilful bishop. At the same time he wanted to know what Rasputin's part in the whole story had been. And a struggle began whose outcome was foreordained.

Alix immediately wrote to her husband: '29 August 1915 . . . Samarin intends getting rid of him [Bishop Varnava], because we like him & he is good to Gr[igory] – we must clear out S[amarin]: & the sooner the better he won't be quiet till he gets me & our Friend & A[nya] in a mess – it's so wicked.' And she would now write constantly to Nicky about it until he removed the detested Samarin.

Meanwhile, Varnava had been summoned by the Synod and had appeared in Petrograd. '7 Sept. 1915 . . . Samarin wishes Varnava to go & tell you all against Grigory . . . You see, he . . . only persecutes our Friend, i. e. goes straight against us both,' Alix wrote to Nicky. Rasputin had for her long become a synonym for them.

'9 Sept. 1915 . . . I saw poor Varnava to-day my dear, it's abominable how Samarin behaved to him . . . such cross-examination as is unheard of & spoke so meanly about Grigory using vile words in speaking of Him . . . vicious about the salutation that you have no right to allow such a thing – upon wh. Varnava answered him soundly & said you were the chief protector of the Church, & Samarin impertinently said you were its servant.'

That was enough.

Victory, Victory!

On 26 September 1915, Samarin was relieved of his duties as chief procurator.

On 26 September 1915, after Prince Scherbatov had made his report, the sovereign informed him of his dismissal as director of the Ministry of Internal Affairs.

On 26 September Khvostov became director of the Ministry of Internal Affairs. On 28 September Beletsky was appointed head of the Department of Police and Khvostov's deputy.

Alexander Volzhin was appointed chief procurator to replace the dismissed Samarin. A lazy sybarite, he was a baron from an old noble family, and, it seemed to Alix, hardly capable of holding his own views. But the main thing was that he was a distant relation of Khvostov. That, for her, was proof enough of his future devotion. For when she believed in someone, she believed recklessly.

The palace coup had been carried through. The most important Ministry of Internal Affairs, the secret police, and the leadership of the church had all passed under the control of 'ours'. It was a victory. Alix's victory.

Less than a year and a half remained before the revolution.

And Rasputin had left Pokrovskoe. On 28 September the agents reported, 'Grigory Efimovich Rasputin arrived in Petrograd.'

He arrived a completely different man. All who saw him would notice it.

As the singer Belling described him, 'When Rasputin entered the parlour, I gasped. What regal bearing . . . how much personal dignity in his bows and how delicately he shook hands – a completely new man.'

There was great self-importance in the peasant now. The commander-in-chief himself had been defeated. And all his foes had been swept away by 'Mama'. All had learned of his power. And his son had been promised a place in the tsarina's infirmary instead of at the front. He was victorious everywhere.

The File, from the testimony of Molchanov: 'He was in an exceptionally joyful state of mind as a result of the fact that the grand duke had been removed, and Samarin and Scherbatov dismissed, and Khvostov, of whom Rasputin said that he was a good person and close to him, appointed in their place.'

The Good People's Plan

What Rasputin did not realize was that while he was on his way back from Pokrovskoe, the 'good person close to him' was already discussing with two other 'good people' a plan to turn him into an obedient marionette.

From Beletsky's testimony: 'Immediately after the release of the ukase about Khvostov and then about me, information regarding Rasputin's departure from Pokrovskoe was passed on . . . And an arrangement was worked out among Andronikov, Khvostov, and myself regarding our relations with Rasputin.'

But none of those who took part in 'working out the arrangement' understood anything about the peasant or his situation. As Beletsky would relate during his interrogation in 1917, they had not comprehended 'the true dimensions of that colossal figure'. For the two bureaucrats and the fatuous Andronikov, Rasputin remained a semi-literate peasant, a picturesque folly of the royal couple, who were bound to him by their son's illness. And in their deliberations, Beletsky, Khvostov, and Andronikov quite simply decided to exploit the dark peasant for their own very broad purposes. The arrangement that they had worked out was uncomplicated: to start giving Rasputin money for his drinking bouts, thereby simply making him their paid agent. And then through him to exert pressure on Tsarskoe Selo in the required direction. At the same time, all three had each devised secret plans that were concealed from the others in the hope of carrying them out with Rasputin's assistance. Plans that would set all three against one another and then destroy them. For they did not grasp that they were dealing not with a peasant but with the alter ego of the Russian tsarina.

The Gentlemen Humiliated

As soon as Rasputin arrived in Petrograd, 'a dinner was arranged the very next day at Andronikov's apartment, and our meeting with him took place,' Beletsky recalled. And like the singer Belling, they were stunned. 'Not only I, who at the time had not yet studied him sufficiently, and Khvostov, who had not seen him for a long period of time, but even Andronikov and Chervinskaya were struck by a certain change in him: there was greater aplomb in him and confidence in himself. From his very first words Rasputin gave us to understand that he was a bit dissatisfied with the fact that our appointments had taken place in his absence, and he emphasized this to the prince, considering him at fault.'

They had not understood his taunts. We have seen Alix's letters. Rasputin was up to date the whole time with the intrigue to appoint Khvostov and Beletsky. He was simply playing with them now, forcing the proud bureaucrats to humiliate and justify themselves.

And justify themselves they did. Andronikov, according to Beletsky, 'quite skilfully countered the reproach . . . by expressing . . . gratitude for supporting our appointments. He gave Rasputin to understand that . . . we especially appreciated it, and . . . that his advice and support at the palace had immediately put us on the right track and saved us from mistakes.'

After that, the prince 'at once invited us to the table, and began to regale him in earnest, showing special attention and respect for him'. How the shrewd peasant must have laughed at those gentlemen. He had immediately put them in their places.

After which he continued to scoff. During the dinner, they learned to their amazement, as Beletsky would write, that 'Rasputin, as it turned out, had been aware of our appointments, and had not had anything against us.' And no sooner had they calmed down, and no sooner 'had he congratulated us . . . wishing us success in our duties', than he suddenly started reproaching Khvostov with the fact 'that when he had come to see him in Nizhny Novgorod, Khvostov had not even given him anything to eat, whereas at the time he, Rasputin, had had only three roubles in his pocket'.

Thereby giving the proud Khvostov a chance to humble himself, too. And so he did. 'Khvostov answered that he hadn't known . . . and that Rasputin should have said something at once about his material circumstances, and that, of course, that would not happen now . . . And he added that Rasputin could now rest easy about his security.' Manasevich-Manuilov, who was present for the affair, added a poignant detail of his own: when the fish soup was served, Khvostov told Rasputin 'that he would not eat until the latter had given his blessing, and after he had given it, Khvostov kissed his hand'.

It was then Beletsky's turn to abase himself. 'Rasputin had already reproached me at that point for the former spying on him, and he informed me that the tsar himself had told him about it.' And the new director of the Department of Police justified himself and feebly reminded Rasputin that 'on the other hand, there had been no attempts on his life under me, since I had also kept an eye on Iliodor, who had devised the attempt on his life under General Dzhunkovsky.' Beletsky believed that he had deftly 'turned his attention to Dzhunkovsky and distracted Rasputin from talking about me'.

Not at all. Throwing them from the fire into cold water, the peasant had overwhelmed them and he realized that they were ready to serve. And he became apparently quite well disposed towards them. Then he went after Dzhunkovsky. 'Recalling the insult Dzhunkovsky had done to him with the complaint about his behaviour in Moscow, he angrily ended with the words, "I shall not forgive him for that."' Continuing to frighten the two bureaucrats with his fury, he 'railed against Samarin' and forced them to betray the 'worthiest person' in their circle.

'None of us defended Samarin; quite the contrary,' Beletsky gloomily recalled. Finally, they made their grand gesture. Andronikov 'called Rasputin into his study' and handed him fifteen hundred roubles.

How naive they were, to attempt with a pitiful fifteen hundred roubles to buy someone through whose hands hundreds of thousands were passing at the time! And he took them in again: 'he visibly showed his satisfaction.' After which he received tribute from Khvostov and Beletsky, as well. 'We had decided to do it in secret from the prince . . . and when we were alone with him, we personally gave him three thousand in an envelope for his favourable disposition towards us. He crumpled up the envelope and stuck it in his pocket and left after giving everyone a kiss.' He carelessly crumpled three thousand roubles, showing that for him it was small change. In 1917, after he had come to understand everything, Beletsky would sadly write in his deposition, 'Not knowing the peculiarities of his nature, we tried to buy his confidence with crumbs.' At the time, however, they came to the happy conclusion that they had bought the peasant off.

The peasant, however, continued to put them through their paces. He knew that Khvostov and Beletsky had not only concealed their acquaintance with him from the Duma; they had also hidden it from their friends and even from their wives. And a torrent of phone calls rained down on their apartments. Rasputin informed them of the petitions of people whom he was protecting and demanded their assistance. And when, in self-defence, they stopped coming to the phone themselves, he would, to their horror, talk about the petitions with their wives. And he would not only talk. Beletsky recalled how Rasputin first sent to his wife some 'lady with a request to find work for her, and then, two days later, another four sisters of mercy with petitions from the provinces'. And soon afterwards Beletsky's wife 'demanded that she be spared both lady petitioners with letters from Rasputin and his telephone conversations'. And Khvostov and Beletsky humbly pleaded with Andronikov to take on himself the task of daily dealings with the bothersome peasant. And 'in defence of family life and our position', Andronikov agreed.

The prince was now supposed to 'pass on . . . any petitions originating with Rasputin, and receive any petitioners sent by him'. Moreover, 'it was proposed that we put our own person in Rasputin's apartment in order to know his interior life in its details and gradually remove any undesirable elements.' There was a noble purpose: to separate the elder from these elements. And a not so noble one: to attach their own person to the elder.

At first, their 'own person' – that is, an informer for Khvostov and Beletsky – was Andronikov's friend Chervinskaya. 'After initiating Madame Chervinskaya into our plan and obtaining her consent, Khvostov and I became convinced . . . that Rasputin really was close to her [and] valued her advice and heeded her opinion . . . in view of which Vyrubova would be kindly disposed towards her.'

They understood Vyrubova no better than they had understood Rasputin. That highly intelligent woman (whom they regarded as dim-witted) instantly understood everything.

From Vyrubova's testimony: 'Chervinskaya came to see me just once. She made a strange and unpleasant impression on me, as if she had come in order to worm something out of me.' Vyrubova stopped receiving her after that.

Khvostov and Beletsky then explained to Rasputin that their 'wives were unwell', so they 'could receive neither him nor his petitioners at home. But he should send them all to Prince Andronikov and view his home as he would' their own. They now invited Rasputin to dinners at the prince's, 'in order to have an opportunity to influence him without being shy about it'.

Those leaders of the country's chief ministry and of the secret police who were supposed to know everything still did not know the main thing. The person they were so pitifully trying to buy off and whom they had so dangerously humiliated, was a member of the secret cabinet that, for all intents and purposes, was at the time governing both the country and themselves!

The Ladies' Cabinet Of
Ministers

The File, from the testimony of Mollov, the deputy minister of internal affairs: 'About two days after the dismissal of Scherbatov and the appointment of Khvostov, Rasputin arrived in Petrograd and, as Colonel Globachyov reported to me, started going to Tsarskoe Selo every day by automobile.'

The peasant had all that time been regularly visiting the tsarina and her Friend. In Tsarskoe Selo, Rasputin returned as it were to his former activities. As before, he was the chief doctor. For example, on 9 October 1915, Alix wrote to her husband, 'Our Friend is with her [Anya], & we shall probably go there in the evening – he puts her out by saying she will probably never really walk again.' And on 2 November 1915, she wrote, 'I am only rather anxious at Baby's arm, so asked our Friend to think about it.'

But that was not his main worry now. And it was not what their daily deliberations were concerned about, either. After the fall of the former ministers, a new 'cabinet of three' was actively at work in Tsarskoe Selo: the peasant and Anya, with the tsarina, as prime minister, at its head.

That whole year before the revolution Alix burned with incredible energy. On the eve of the revolution that had toppled the French throne, Marie Antoinette had turned into a similar dynamo of energy and had ruled the ministers. A war with Austria was under way at the time, and Marie Antoinette, the daughter of an Austrian empress, was called an 'Austrian' and a 'spy'. And now a war with Germany was under way, and Alix, the daughter of a German duke, was being called a spy and a 'German'.

That is why she liked it so much that Khvostov, that fighter of German spies, was now working at her side. That is why she dreamed of going to Headquarters with her daughters to see her husband and Baby. She wanted to show herself to the troops and dispel the vile rumours. And Our Friend set about his main task: to demand what she desired.

On 9 October 1915, she wrote to the tsar, 'our Friend always wanted me also to see troops, since last year till now he speaks of it – that it would also bring them luck . . . We arrive 15th morning at 9 . . . What intense joy to meet again, I do miss you both so dreadfully!'

She showed herself to the troops, and then, full of memories of the love of the people, she returned to Tsarskoe Selo to govern. She was careful to see that only 'our' ministers appeared in the newly renovated government. And when Nicky nominated Alexander Fyodorovich Trepov, whom she did not want, to be minister of transport, Our Friend, who did not even know Trepov, was at once 'grieved'. 'He does not know Trepov,' she wrote to the tsar on 1 November, 'many [meaning, she herself and consequently Anya] are against him as being a very weak and not energetic man. Our Friend is very grieved at his nomination . . . and he is sad you did not ask his advice. I too regret the nomination . . . he is not a sympathetic man – I know him rather well.'

Even now after the removal of the 'dread uncle', she continued to fear the tsar's long absences – his life at Headquarters – far away from her. Since he had started taking the Heir to Headquarters, loneliness and homesickness no longer tormented him so sharply. And she suddenly began to worry that the trips would disrupt the heir's studies. And it at once became clear that Our Friend no longer approved of the trips, either. So she was right when she wrote to Nicky on 4 September 1916: 'I fully trust in our Friend's wisdom . . . He sees far ahead & therefore his judgement can be relied upon'.

The Ruler Of Fogs

Our Friend, however, was not only required to heal and to forecast needed ministers. He was also constantly called upon to anticipate and avert her attacks of nerves. And to guard the alliance of the tsarina and her Friend.

When Alix and the girls went to Headquarters, Anya had naturally wanted to go with them; Alix didn't like to be separated from her Friend. But Alix's nerves were on edge. And on 6 October she would with her former irritation write to the tsar, 'I am sending you a very fat letter from the Cow, the lovesick creature could not wait any longer, she must pour out her love otherwise she bursts.' And Father Grigory, whose sense of the tsarina was unerring, did not want complications in the cabinet.

And so his immediate prescription was for Anya to stay at home. '10 Oct. 1915 . . . A[nya] is very put out He won't let her go anywhere . . . He finds it necessary to remain on here to watch how things are going.'

But Anya's being 'put out' was merely part of the game. She had achieved her main purpose. Her dream had come true – she was a fully-fledged member of the shadow cabinet that governed Russia. She entered her role so deeply that the power-loving Alix sometimes had to put her in her place. '3 Nov. 1915 . . . The tail [Khvostov] & Beletzky dine at Ania's – a pity, I find, as though she wanted to play a political part. O she is so proud & sure of herself, not prudent enough . . . our Friend always wishes her to live only for us & such things,' Alix wrote to the tsar.

Again Our subtle Friend had perceptively wanted the same thing the tsarina had.

In his *Reign of Emperor Nicholas II,* the historian S. Oldenburg has carefully counted the number of times the tsar went against Grigory. He disregarded Grigory's advice in 1915 when he visited Galicia and convened the Duma in April. And when he did not convene the Duma in November 1915, did not end the Kovel offensive in 1916, and did not at Rasputin's suggestion nominate Tatischev as minister of finance, Valuev as minister of transportation, or General Ivanov as minister of war. All the other decisions you have read about in this book and will have occasion to read about many more times. In his interrogation of Olga Lokhtina, the investigator asked her to respond to the same question – to recall the times when Father Grigory had not been heeded in Tsarskoe Selo. The File, from Lokhtina's testimony: 'Last time, I could not recall when Father Grigory's advice was not followed in Tsarskoe Selo . . . but now I do. They didn't listen to Father Grigory in regard to Count Ignatiev [the minister of education], who had been dismissed against Father Grigory's instructions.' That, however, was the only time she could remember.

The tsar took action a great many times on the basis of Rasputin's predictions or 'instructions', as the tsarina called them. Only they should hardly be called Rasputin's. In the majority of cases they were her 'instructions'. And the tsar understood that very well.

This does not mean that she was dissembling. No, she believed absolutely that Our Friend had links to heaven. And for that reason, let me repeat, it made her glad whenever her intentions perfectly coincided with his instructions. Although of course she did sometimes cross the line and for the good of the cause inform the tsar of her own wishes as if they were Our Friend's.

But on the other hand, in those areas where she had little understanding, the peasant was fully independent. And here she expected from him decisions inspired by God. And that, above all, concerned the war. In that area his help was all-encompassing.

'22 Dec. 1915 . . . Our Friend is always praying & thinking of the war – He says we are to tell him at once if there is anything particular – so she [Anya] did about the fogg, & He scolded for not having said it at once – says no more foggs will disturb.'

But the ruler of fogs was required not only to pray constantly but also to propose strategic ideas.

An 'Unconscious Spy'?

The army at the time was becoming increasingly restive.

There is no question that German agents had been spreading rumours about the drunken peasant to whom the debauched German tsarina was telling military secrets, which the peasant and the scoundrels surrounding him were selling to German intelligence. And those rumours had demoralized an army already dejected by defeat.

That question – was the tsarina telling the peasant military secrets? – tormented and fascinated the opposition at court. Not only was Alix openly spied on at court (as Princess Vasilchikova had done). Her letters also started to disappear, apparently with the courtiers' help. On 20 September 1915, she informed the tsar, '[Beletsky] feels sure that my long lost letter . . . to Ania . . . is in Orlov's hands.'

Prince Vladimir Orlov ('fat Orlov'), a lieutenant-general, was in command of the royal campaign chancery. It has not been possible to clarify the matter of the letter, but soon after the appointment of Nikolai Nikolaevich as governor-general of the Caucasus, the obese giant Orlov, who resembled the Porthos of Dumas's novel, was requested to join the 'dread uncle' there.

But even those who were not part of the opposition considered Rasputin an 'unconscious spy', who might blurt out military secrets to the rascals surrounding him. And here we shall have to find an answer to that most important question: did Rasputin know about the military operations being planned?

'No,' Vyrubova decisively answers. 'There was in the sovereign's study a secret map, [but] the study was always locked. And not even the children were allowed in that study. The sovereign never talked about military matters with his family.'

Vyrubova, however, was perfectly aware that Our Friend knew all the secrets even without the secret map. And she was also aware who had passed the most secret plans on to him.

From Alix's letters:

'3 Nov. 1915 . . . He [Khvostov] brought yr. secret marcheroute . . . to me & I won't say a word about it except to our Friend to guard you everywhere.'

'8 Nov. 1915 . . . Sweet Angel, long to ask you heaps about yr. plans concerning Roumania, our Friend is so anxious to know.'

'8 Nov. 1915 . . . He wanders about and wonders what you settled at the Headquarters, finds you need lots of troops there so as not be cut off from behind.'

What was to be done? Alix had little understanding of military matters, which is why she put her trust in heaven and the 'man of God'. So, the peasant did know the plans. And it is entirely possible that he became an 'unconscious spy'. For Manasevich, who was so fond of double games, and the banker Rubinstein, who would be accused of espionage, were a dangerous circle for someone possessing such secrets.

Those secrets, which alarmed so many, brought him closer to death.

A Vision

Our Friend had in truth changed greatly on his return. From his relations with then Prime Minister Goremykin, Minister Khvostov, and the other 'powerful of this world', the commonsensical peasant had learned only contempt. He knew he could do better. And now that the tsarina had undertaken to govern the country, he of course understood: his decisions would be more rational. And ever more frequently he began to express his own views.

'4 Oct. 1915 . . . Yesterday we saw Gregory at Ania's . . . He begged me to tell you, that it is not at all clear about the stamp [paper] money, the simple people cannot understand.'

It was then that the peasant seriously remarked to Filippov, 'that if he should be invited to be minister of agriculture, Russia would then be "piled high with millet and wheat"'.

A dangerous, mysterious visionary force suddenly revived in him. And his rolling eyes and wheeze and the deathly pale white face during those visions have been described by witnesses. And sometimes the visions were remarkable.

On 10 October 1915, Alix wrote to Nicky:

> another subject worries him very much and he spoke scarcely about anything else for two hours. It is this that you must give an order that waggons with flour, butter and sugar should be obliged to pass. He saw the whole thing in the night like a vision, all the towns, railway lines etc. it's difficult to give over fr. his words, but he says it is very serious . . . He wishes me to speak to you about this all very earnestly, severely even . . . He would propose 3 days no other trains should go except these with flour, butter and sugar – it's even more necessary than meat or ammunition just now . . . if passenger trains only very few would be allowed and instead of all 4 classes these days hang on waggons with flour or butter fr. Siberia . . . the discontentment will be intense if the things don't move. People will scream and say it's impossible . . . but it's necessary and . . . essential.

Of course, the intelligent peasant could have understood even without visions that both Galicia and Poland were strewn with Russian corpses. And if a famine should be added to the constant blood-letting! The capital was unused to food shortages. An empty belly would be its undoing.

One way or another, everything would happen just as he said. It was in fact with a food shortage in the capital that the empire started to collapse in February 1917.

But despite Alix's pressure, the tsar was unable to follow the peasant's advice, for there was no one to organize it all. The new minister of internal affairs, Khvostov, who had been entrusted with the task, was at the time occupied with quite another matter.

The Peasant Breaks His
Fetters

The next session of the State Duma was approaching. 'With dangerous speeches,' Beletsky wrote, 'in which Rasputin's vastly increased influence might be touched on.' And Rasputin learned that to avoid doing battle with the Duma over him, Beletsky and Khvostov had come up with a 'salutary idea'. The two officials, who had been appointed through his efforts, had decided to remove him, the one who directed the decisions of the tsars, from Petrograd. As Beletsky testified, they had the idea of arranging 'a long trip to the monasteries for Rasputin, so that when the Duma opened, he would be away from the capital'.

And Beletsky added a remarkable sentence: 'I already knew from previous experience that speaking out against Rasputin in the Duma only increased his influence, given the peculiar personalities of the most august personages.' So that finally he, too, understood.

And fearing that speeches against him would strengthen the peasant, they decided to 'convince the most exalted personages that such a trip to the holy places would be useful not only for the purpose of conciliating the Duma, but also for dispelling all the unjust talk about Rasputin's life, and bearing witness to the religious impulses of his nature in a time of war'.

Summoned to accompany Rasputin on his trip to the monasteries were his friends Bishop Varnava, Martemian, now abbot of the Tobolsk Monastery, and Archimandrite Augustin. 'I remember Varnava's arrival in Petrograd with Archimandrite Augustin and Abbot Martemian, two dreadful monks . . . Augustin wore a silk cassock and was perfumed and pomaded (Varnava called him "my nestling"), while Martemian was twice as fat as the fat man Khvostov. Both monks . . . produced an impression of complete mediocrity,' Vyrubova related.

In order to predispose the monks, on their arrival they were given, as if in reimbursement for their expenses, fifteen hundred roubles apiece from a secret fund, while Abbot Martemian received an additional two thousand roubles over and above. 'We decided not to stint any money on the trip,' Beletsky testified. The monks were being bribed to keep track of Rasputin.

The officials had failed to realize that Rasputin's goodwill was far more important to the monks than money. And of course the monks told everything to Our Friend. So Rasputin presumably had a good laugh while recommending that they take the police money.

Rasputin had in fact decided to see what advantage he himself could extract from the situation. He pretended that he had agreed to go. But in return he asked Khvostov to speed up the removal of an enemy of his, Governor Stankevich of Tobolsk.

From Khvostov's testimony: 'I agreed and received the sovereign's consent. At the same time, the sovereign noted, "I already have a candidate for Tobolsk, a good friend of mine." And lifting up his blotting pad, he pulled out a note on which the name Orlovsky-Taneevsky was written in the empress's hand. Only later did I learn that he was Rasputin's candidate.' Indeed he was: 'Orlovsky is the name our Friend wld. like as gov., he is the president of the Exchequer chamber at Perm,' Alix wrote to Nicky as early as 25 August.

So even here Khvostov had, without realizing it, been carrying out Rasputin's orders.

And then before Rasputin's scheduled departure a festive dinner took place. At the dinner Rasputin continued to play the fool: he shared some heartfelt memories. 'Rasputin told how still unknown to anyone he had wandered among the monasteries . . . and how he had been to Jerusalem . . . and, by bribing the custodian, had been present at an Easter service,' Beletsky testified.

After dinner Martemian asked for a supply of Madeira, because 'Rasputin was an immoderate drinker.' He was 'provided with Madeira from the stores of the Department of Police'. After which Rasputin did not mention the trip again! So one can imagine how merrily Rasputin and his monk friends drank the police wine. It was only then that Beletsky realized that Rasputin had simply been fooling them.

Of course! Why would a member of the tsarina's cabinet want to leave the capital? But Rasputin did not forgive them their double-dealing. While continuing to make fun of the 'Tail' or 'Fat Belly' (as he now called the minister in Tsarskoe Selo), Rasputin suddenly forgot their request that petitions be passed on to them through Andronikov. And he again started flooding Khvostov with them. He sent dozens of people to him at his home and at the ministry. This time it was Khvostov's wife who rebelled. At the same time Beletsky was also experiencing a boom in petitions, to his horror. It was as if the peasant had broken his fetters. Something had to be done quickly. Both officials were also worried about Prince Andronikov. And not only because he had failed to deal with Rasputin. The impudent Andronikov had been exploiting the situation and coming to them with requests on behalf of his own clients. Besides that, he had been involving Khvostov and Beletsky in dubious intrigues. For example, he got them into a fight for his apartment, the place where they were accustomed to meeting Rasputin. Petrograd at the time was crowded with refugees from the territories lost in the war. A great many of those people wanted to rent apartments. And Countess Tolstaya, who owned the building in which Andronikov lived, asked the prince to vacate his apartment: she did not care for Rasputin's visits. Andronikov demanded help. And they did the unbelievable. In order to protect the apartment as a place for meetings with Rasputin, Khvostov pushed through a new bill to protect renters during the period of the war. The prince could now stay in his apartment. But Tolstaya dragged him through the courts and eventually won her case. The court's hatred of Rasputin overcame the law and decided the case in her favour.

The End Of The Triumvirate

Both Khvostov and Beletsky decided to get rid of the importunate prince. Beletsky, who was an expert in provocation, adroitly took matters in hand. They knew that Andronikov, who was constantly in need of money, was taking large amounts of it from petitioners to arrange for Rasputin's protection. And they also knew that the prince had frequently appropriated from the peasant the amounts due to him. And Beletsky told Rasputin about it.

After which another 'fish soup dinner' took place at Andronikov's apartment. And to the delight of both officials, a glowering Rasputin went into the prince's study with him and started shouting at him, 'and was not shy in his expressions'.

At the same time it was conveyed to Vyrubova by Beletsky and Khvostov that she might keep in mind 'certain peculiarities' of the prince and see him less often. And Vyrubova began receiving Andronikov less frequently. The prince fretted and brought her candies from the best confectioners and fruits and flowers as soon as they appeared in Petrograd. But 'she asked him not to bring her anything in the future, since it was unpleasant for her.'

And then they dealt their final blow. Beletsky had learned from his agents in the Department of Police that Andronikov, who was also used to operating on two fronts, had sent the dowager empress a copy of the picture taken in 1914 by the photographer Kristinin of 'Rasputin surrounded by his admirers'. As we shall recall, the picture included Vyrubova. Beletsky immediately told her about it. The Friend was enraged and 'demanded an explanation from the prince'. The frightened prince said that 'in sending the picture, he had been moved by the best of feelings for Rasputin, and had wanted Marie Fyodorovna [the dowager empress] to see what worthy people surrounded the elder.'

Andronikov was banished from Anya's home. And Rasputin suggested 'meeting somewhere other than at the prince's'.

Khvostov and Beletsky had thus forced Andronikov out of the game. Now only the two of them remained.

The Gentleman Colonel

They replaced Andronikov with someone more reliable. Someone who would, according to their plan, take on all the dirty work himself. And not only relieve them of Rasputin's petitions, but, most importantly, obtain needed information from Rasputin.

The thirty-six-year-old Colonel Mikhail Komissarov had already been employed in special services for twelve years. He had, as we have seen, taken part in the scandalous story of the covert printing by the Department of Police of notices calling for pogroms against the Jews. Despite the wrath of the then Prime Minister Witte, someone had appreciated Komissarov's zeal. First he had headed the secret department for the surveillance of foreign embassies and military agents. Then he was chief of the Warsaw gendarme directorate. When Warsaw was surrendered to the Germans, the colonel, left with nothing to do, had returned to Petrograd. And Beletsky suggested him to Khvostov for Rasputin's security detail. Khvostov agreed. He did not know that Colonel Komissarov was connected to Beletsky not only by his former work but also by a close friendship. Khvostov did not realize that Beletsky had placed his own man with Rasputin.

For by then Beletsky had plans of his own. The intelligent Beletsky, unlike the fanfaron Khvostov, had finally come to appreciate Rasputin. He realized that any opposition towards him would mean the end of a career. And it was apparently then that he made a move truly worthy of the chief of the secret police. He decided to provoke Khvostov into a battle with Rasputin so that Khvostov would break his own neck. And free up the coveted position of minister.

12

THE BATTLE OF THE INTRIGUERS

Agents, Agents, Agents

Called before the Extraordinary Commission in 1917, Mikhail Komissarov related how the intrigue unfolded. The colonel had been assigned to Rasputin partly as a servant, partly as a guard, and partly as an informer. But he wasn't required to wear his uniform, which he did not wish to sully. The colonel wore mufti, which soothed his pride. In addition, Khvostov spared no money, giving him a car, a driver and the command of a detail of five experienced agents. Thus did Komissarov's undercover surveillance of Rasputin begin.

The official surveillance of Rasputin by agents of General Globachyov's Petrograd security branch continued, however. As before, a security agent sat on the stairs by the door to Rasputin's apartment, with two agents downstairs and more outside, along with a security branch automobile. Rasputin did not let the security branch agents into his apartment, and as before took pleasure in eluding them, whether by car or carriage. The peasant's attitude towards Komissarov and his agents was entirely different. The intuitive Rasputin knew that Beletsky was with him, and that Beletsky was ready to serve. Moreover, Rasputin and Komissarov had known each other before. As Komissarov testified in the File, 'I first met Rasputin at Badmaev's apartment,' which the valiant colonel 'had been visiting as a patient'. Komissarov quickly became friends with the peasant's daughters and Laptinskaya. They were flattered by the imposing gentleman of lofty rank who virtually waited on Grigory Efimovich. 'Our colonel', as they often referred to him, had been accepted as a member of the household. Beletsky was quite right when he told Vyrubova and the Tsarina that Komissarov would be able to assure Rasputin's complete safety.

Komissarov set up a security system for Rasputin that was perhaps comparable only to the royal family's. The colonel replaced all the custodians and doormen of the building on Gorokhovaya Street with agents. And in addition to the special driver and car, he kept agents disguised as express carriage drivers on continuous call by the building. And in short order everyone close to Rasputin was identified and information about them was compiled. Simultaneously, all of Rasputin's 'incoming mail was subject to perlustration'.

The Colonel's Difficult Assignment

'The detectives under my command reported on Rasputin every evening. And I passed on everything "interesting" to Khvostov in writing and to Beletsky orally. . . I saw the latter either at the office or at his home, which I visited fairly often as a friend,' Komissarov testified.

So Khvostov received from the colonel only the information that Beletsky wanted him to receive. Soon afterwards, the security branch agents were also placed under Komissarov's command. Their chief, General Globachyov, was ordered not to obstruct Komissarov's work, to collect information for him, and to assist him in every way possible. And the main thing – never to record in the security branch agents' summaries the visits made by Komissarov and his agents to Rasputin's apartment. Komissarov now gave Rasputin cash, and always with the same noble purpose – so that he would stop taking money from petitioners and compromising 'higher circles'. 'Five or six times over a period of five months, I gave him at Khvostov and Beletsky's orders a thousand or fifteen hundred roubles,' Komissarov testified. For someone of Rasputin's appetites, those large sums for the day were but a drop in the bucket. But Rasputin took the money. He turned no one down.

On holidays, the solicitous Komissarov gave his charge gifts in the name of Beletsky and Khvostov. 'Once I bought . . . a case with a silver teapot, a gold watch with a chain, and two bracelets.' But Rasputin, to the colonel's amazement, 'carelessly gathered up those expensive items . . . without even looking at what had been sent him.' Although he would occasionally respond by sending gifts of his own to Khvostov (or the 'Tail' or 'Fat Belly', as he now invariably called him, provoking the minister's impotent rage). Thus, as Komissarov testified, he once sent the minister 'a wooden box inscribed, "To the Tail", which Khvostov hurled to the floor in a rage'. And Rasputin also 'sent him letters through me . . . What he wrote I do not know, but on reading them Khvostov would almost every time swear in desperation and toss the letters away.' So the peasant made fun of him whenever he had the chance. Yet even as he was accepting money from Beletsky and Khvostov, Father Grigory was still calmly taking it from the petitioners, as well. 'The agents reported to me,' Komissarov testified, 'that . . . even on the stairway the petitioners openly talked about how much Rasputin would have to be given.'

The tasks assigned to the gentleman colonel by his two chiefs began to diverge more and more. Rasputin continued to drink heavily. Komissarov's job, as ordered by Beletsky, was to see that the peasant did not go to Tsarskoe Selo drunk. But his other job, as ordered by Khvostov, was to see that Rasputin did go there drunk. And reveal himself in Tsarskoe Selo for what he was. But Komissarov was soon astonished to realize that Rasputin's condition did not in fact depend on anyone else. 'No matter how drunk Rasputin was, as soon as he received a call informing him that Vyrubova would be arriving in twenty minutes, he would at once turn completely sober. Whether he drank something or just got himself under control, I am unable to clarify . . . Or, whenever we took a drunken Rasputin to Tsarskoe Selo by train, he would be completely sober by the time we arrived . . . He did know how to sober up.'

Komissarov's most important task, however, was to find out from Rasputin the news from Tsarskoe Selo. 'All the conversations with Vyrubova usually took place at 10:00 a.m. So that Rasputin, wherever he was, would return by that time to take the call from Tsarskoe at 10:00,' Komissarov testified. And 'our colonel' would also arrive by that time to gather information from Tsarskoe. All the more, since the peasant was still sober in the morning. And Rasputin gave him the news from Tsarskoe, or, more accurately, told him what he wanted him to know. The most important information was conveyed directly to the minister and the chief of the Department of Police directly at the special apartment that Komissarov had rented for their clandestine meetings with Rasputin.

The Secret Dinners On
Italian Street

The building still stands in Petersburg. 'I rented an apartment on Italian Street. It was in a corner building. An apartment was taken on the first floor,' Komissarov testified. The apartment was furnished, and an agent and his family were moved into it. The day before Rasputin was supposed to arrive, the agent would order a luxurious dinner for several people from a restaurant, and then he and his family would vacate the secret apartment.

The dinner naturally consisted of fish, but 'wines and champagne were also served in great quantities.' In order to loosen the tippling peasant's tongue.

'Once or twice', the colonel too was invited for dinner. He testified in the File that 'during dinner Rasputin passed on what was being said in Tsarskoe Selo, mainly by Vyrubova and the empress.'

At first, Rasputin used the formal mode of address with both officials. He 'tried to conduct the conversation in the spirit of his "Meditations" and drank cautiously. But Komissarov . . . poured him a glass and said, "Grigory, drop the divinity. Better drink up and try talking a bit more simply." From then on he was no longer shy with us and used the familiar mode of address . . . and even invited us to go to the Gypsies,' Beletsky testified. Thus did Rasputin continue to make fun of the agents. Komissarov enjoyed recounting humorous little scenes to his hosts, such as Grigory and he 'deciding on matters of state and the requisite changes in the cabinet'. With Khvostov's help, those stories of Komissarov's sped through Petersburg. But Beletsky took no part in that. Apparently he could not get over the thought that the cunning peasant had merely been making fun of Komissarov, of himself and of Khvostov. It made matters worse that Rasputin would not, despite all Komissarov's efforts, let him near the financial matters that so interested both Beletsky and Khvostov.

The Riddle Of Rasputin's Money

That question was also of great interest to the Extraordinary Commission. The only thing that Komissarov could distinctly relate was that 'Rasputin initiated no one into his financial affairs. He himself kept a close eye on safeguarding his interests and never forgave anyone who tried to cheat him out of money. He would denounce them in "special terms" [that is, curse them roundly]!' Beletsky and Khvostov were by no means merely curious about Rasputin's money. Both officials understood, as did the Extraordinary Commission after them, that the truly enormous sums provided by the rich petitioners and bankers could scarcely all have been swallowed up by Rasputin's drinking bouts, especially since, as we shall see, he now caroused at the petitioners' expense. The officials were gripped by a strong suspicion regarding the remarkable and quite astonishing destination of the peasant's money.

'But In Time Of War All Becomes Different'

Vyrubova would afterwards justifiably explain to the investigators that she had not received a kopek from the royal family. At the same time, having barely recovered from her injury, the Friend would establish her own infirmary (following the Tsarina, who had her own hospital train). And she managed to support the infirmary at the wildly inflated prices of the war.

Nonetheless, as she would testify in the File:

> I got only four hundred roubles a month from my parents. I had to live and clothe myself on that money . . . It's hard to imagine how I got by (the dacha in Tsarskoe Selo alone cost me 2250 roubles a year) before I received . . . the 100,000 roubles from the railway company for my injury. Of that money I spent 20,000 roubles on the infirmary. And that was all my money and funds. And in the newspapers they said I had almost three million roubles. I of course had to pass on to the empress the petitions that were given to me by Rasputin, but it hardly needs to be said that I never received a kopek for doing so.

But the newspapers stubbornly continued to write about her millions, for they realized that an infirmary could not be supported on 20,000 wartime roubles. Vyrubova realized it, too. And she was obliged during her interrogation to disclose the other sources of her income. 'Individuals who wanted to ingratiate themselves with me and do something nice for me usually contributed something to the infirmary . . . The day that my infirmary was opened, Khvostov and Beletsky each sent me by courier a sealed package. In each of the packages was a thousand roubles . . . That money was entered in timely fashion as income by the infirmary's managing director, Nikolai Ivanovich Reshetnikov.'

The File, from Filippov's testimony: 'Reshetnikov was a point of contact for every kind of petitioning and special pleading, for which the petitioners also gave him money as if for the needs of the empress's institutions, although a significant part of it remained in Reshetnikov's and Vyrubova's hands . . . And a certain part . . . although not a very great one, was given to Rasputin himself.' The resourceful Reshetnikov had thus devised a distinctive tax on Rasputin's petitioners for the benefit of the infirmary. And from the apartment on Gorokhovaya Street to Anya's little house a river of money flowed.

But the money from Rasputin's clients was not only intended for Anya. And here something quite incredible follows.

'And once again [Nicholas] listened with approval to the warlike dreams of the Grand Duke Nikolai Nikolaevich. And felt with joy the popularity of his own mood. The young Russian bourgeoisie wanted war, and so did the old aristocracy. . . . the army's favourite, the six-and-a-half-foot tall Grand Duke Nikolai Nikolaevich.'

The Russian Council of Ministers in June 1915 at the tsar's headquarters at Baranovich Station. Front row, from right: State Controller P.A. Kharitonov, Grand Duke Nikolai Nikolaevich, Nicholas II, Chairman of the Council of Ministers L.I. Goremykin, Minister of the Imperial Court, General-Adjutant V.B. Fredericks; back row, from right: Minister of Internal Affairs Prince N.B. Shcherbatov, Minister of Information S.V. Rukhlov, Minister of Foreign Affairs S.D. Sazonov, Minister of Agriculture A.V. Krivoshein, Minister of Finance P.L. Bark; Head of Staff, Commander-in-Chief of the Infantry A.A. Polivanov; Minister of Trade and Industry Prince V.N. Shakhovskoy, unidentified.

The tsar, who has assumed the role of Commander-in-Chief, with Alexei at the front in 1916. 'Since [Nicholas] had started taking the heir to headquarters, loneliness and homesickness no longer tormented him so sharply. And [the tsarina] suddenly began to worry that the trips would disrupt the heir's studies. And it at once became clear that Our Friend no longer approved of the trips, either.'

Nicholas with his younger brother Mikhail (centre) and his cousin Dmitry. Mikhail shocked his family by marrying a divorcee and living abroad, but on the outbreak of war he returned to Russia and became a noted military commander. On Nicholas's abdication in 1917, Mikhail briefly succeeded him. 'Dmitry was the tsar's favourite. His letters to Nicholas have survived, the scoffing letters of a rake. A duelist and hard drinker, tall and well-built like most of the Romanovs, a favourite of the Guards – but Alix did not like him. For the youth did not hide his disdain for the peasant.'

Autumn 1914 and Russia is at war. Alix and her daughters Olga and Tatyana graduated from a nursing course and received their International Red Cross Certificates. 'The tsarina gave herself up to the cause of mercy with all the strength of her boundless energy. She organized her own hospital train and set up a hospital in Tsarskoe Selo in the great palace. She and the grand duchesses became sisters of mercy.'

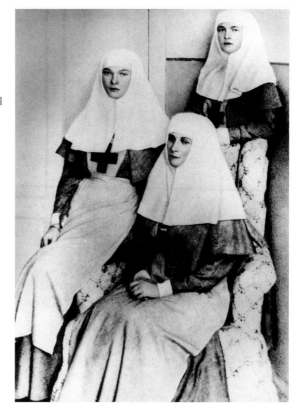

Anya Vyrubova followed the example of the tsarina and helped nurse the wounded. Here she is in an officers' carriage of a hospital train.

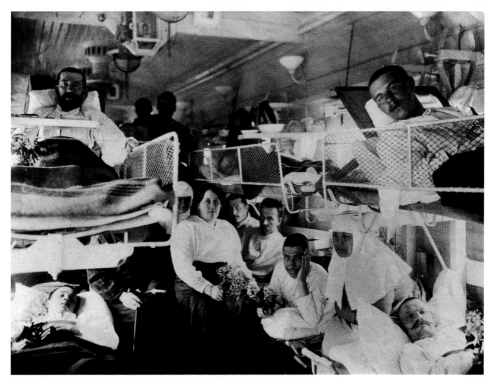

The tsar's niece Irina with her husband Felix Yusupov, a rake
and bi-sexual. Since relations between Felix's mother Zinaida
and the tsarina were 'strained, the wedding took place on what
was for Alix "enemy territory"– the Anichkov Palace of the
dowager empress. The couple were married in the palace
church. On 9 February 1914 Nicky entered in his diary,
"Everything went well. There were lots of people".'

The decision to kill Rasputin 'most likely originated with
Dmitry'– here seen with one of his cars for which he had an
enormous passion – 'that gallant guardsman, an athlete, and
a one-time participant in the Olympic games, who, as Felix
Yusupov correctly noted, "hated the elder".'

Felix Yusupov. The location is unknown. It could be in the Yusupov Palace, where the murder of Rasputin took place. The basement room had been 'turned into a charming dining room in old Russian style'. Yusupov later recalled that Rasputin took off his coat and 'started to study the furniture with interest. The chest with the maze particularly attracted his attention. Admiring it like a child, ... he opened and closed it and studied it inside and out. ... I offered him some tea and wine ... to my disappointment he declined. "Has something happened?" I wondered.'

The yard at the Yusupov Palace, with the doorway clearly visible on the left, across which Rasputin ran on a December night in 1916 while trying to save himself from his murderers. To the right, out of shot, is the Moika Canal.

Police photographs of Rasputin's corpse after it had been dragged from under the ice showing his mutilated face and his naked body with the bullet holes. 'Early on the morning of 19 December a corpse was found floating in the Malaya Nevka river near Great Petrovsky Bridge. It had surfaced in a frightening way. Its hands, which under the water had evidently been trying to untie the ropes, were raised. It was clear that this powerful man, though still breathing in the car, had concealed it, hoping to loosen his fetters in the water. But his human strength had failed him.'

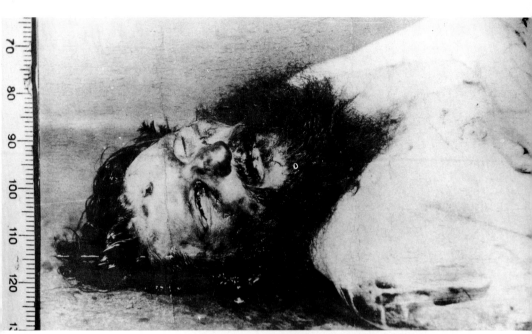
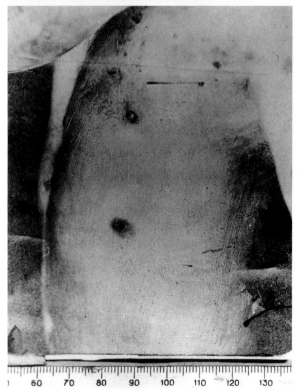

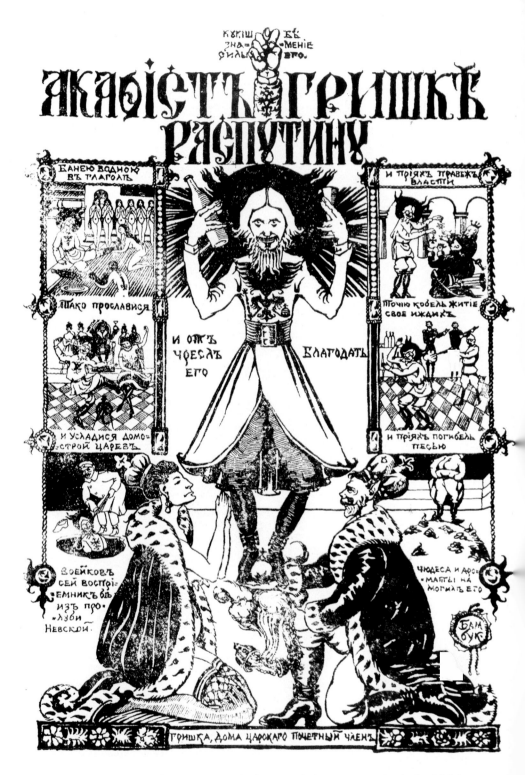

After the full story of Rasputin's murder began to leak out, cartoonists had a field day.

The File, from Filippov's testimony: 'The most odious thing about the recent time was that all the intermediaries [the 'secretaries'] who were openly offering to plead through Rasputin for definite advantages were maintaining that a part of the allocated funds would go to Madame Vyrubova and sometimes directly to the empress herself, as if for philanthropic causes.'

The very idea seems bizarre. It makes perfect sense in regard to Vyrubova. But the Empress of all Russia taking money from the peasant? Money that he had received for arranging high-ranking positions and for obtaining audiences with ministers? What rubbish! What nonsense!

But we shall let Alix speak for herself: '3 Nov. 1915 . . . One thing our Friend said, that if people offer great sums (so as to get a *decoration*), now one must accept, as money is needed & and one helps them doing good by giving in to their weaknesses, & 1000 profit by it – it's true, but again against all moral feelings. But in time of war all becomes different.'

The war had devoured both the annual allocation of funds from the treasury for the maintenance of the royal family and the family's own private resources. So in the name of helping the wounded, it had been necessary to take money in secret from Our Friend! 'In time of war all becomes different.' Which means that the peasant not only did not receive money from the tsarina, but that he himself may in some measure have become the provider for the tsarina and her Friend! And Alix had perforce to shut her eyes to the constant petitions that the peasant was generously bringing to the palace.

Khvostov and Beletsky's first test took place at that time. The tsarina demanded that the Duma be placated in order to avoid further resolutions of inquiry about Our Friend, which she regarded as tantamount to attacks against herself. But neither official knew how to do it. However, Rasputin proved a worthy partner. He suggested that they send the tsar to the Duma. As Khvostov testified, Rasputin 'said that he had already spoken to the tsar many times about the need to make peace with the Duma, about going to it and saying, "I am yours, and you are mine. What is there for us to quarrel about?"'

While the tsar was pondering the peasant's suggestion, Khvostov and Beletsky began to make preparations for that meeting of tsar and Duma. They both understood that the first thing was to butter up the Speaker of the Duma, Rodzyanko. But how were they to do that in view of the tsarina's hatred of him? Beletsky, who already grasped a great deal about the peasant, decided to consult him. And no sooner had Beletsky started talking about Rodzyanko's need for a sign of royal favour than Rasputin instantly reacted and 'said he would do everything to see that Rodzyanko got a decoration'.

And soon afterwards Alix wrote to Nicky, '3 Nov. . . . Khvostov finds he [Rodzyanko] ought to receive a decoration now, that wld. flatter him & he wld. sink in the eyes of the left party, for having accepted a reward from you. Our Friend says also that it would be a good thing to do. Certainly it's most unsympathetic, but, alas, times are such just now, that one is obliged out of wisdom sake to do many a thing one wld. rather not have.'

On 6 December the detested Rodzyanko received the decoration.

Fat Belly's Dreams

Meanwhile, Khvostov had set about bringing his own plans to fruition. 'At the time Khvostov had already sown the first seeds of doubt in Tsarskoe Selo about the rightness of Goremykin's Duma policy,' Beletsky testified. For 'Fat Belly' had had a clear goal from the very beginning: to take the old man Goremykin's place as prime minister.

And the cultivating of Rasputin now proceeded apace over dinners at the secret apartment. It was done candidly and openly. 'During . . . the dinners Khvostov . . . would try to convince Rasputin that he, Khvostov, would be the best chair for the Council of Ministers,' Komissarov testified. But Khvostov did not merely want power. He wanted unlimited power, the kind the great Stolypin had enjoyed. 'Khvostov tried to convince Rasputin that the post of prime minister should be combined with the internal affairs portfolio . . . for without that portfolio, the prime minister was nothing – a cat without his balls. As was his custom, Rasputin avoided giving a definite answer to any of this . . . being a shrewd person, he limited himself to monosyllabic replies.'

The peasant understood that the 'old man' Goremykin was finished. And he forewarned 'Mama'.

'6 Nov. 1915 . . . Well Lovy, He thinks I better now see the old Gentleman & gently tell it him, as if the Duma hisses him, what can one do . . . better he goes by yr. Wish than forced by a scandal.'

But whom to appoint? She had absolutely no idea. And once again it was time for Our Friend. No, he had no intention at all of appointing Khvostov. The latter was too tricky and stupid. A completely new person was required. One who would be acceptable to the Duma, yet who would agree to be 'ours'. The absence of Prince Andronikov, who knew everyone and everything, was telling. Rasputin was evidently obliged to discuss the candidacies for prime minister with his 'Brain Trust' – with Simanovich, Rubinstein, and Manasevich-Manuilov.

Meanwhile, the new Duma session was impending. And until a new prime minister could be found, it was necessary to rescue the old one. But to do that, the tsar first had to take a step towards reconciliation with the Duma. And the peasant proposed implementing the great move that he had suggested – that of the tsar appearing before the Duma. A move that appealed to Nicholas, although the proud tsarina regarded it coolly. But she too had learned to compromise. And on 13 November she surprised Nicky by writing, 'Of course if you could have turned up for a few words, quite unexpected at the Duma (as you had thought to) that might change everything & be a splendid deed & it wld. later be easier for the old man.'

But Rasputin understood that things would not continue that way for long. A new prime minister was needed. He and his 'Brain Trust' had to keep thinking.

The Salon And Its Last Days

While the search for a new prime minister was going on, Alix was forced to deal with the church again. Samarin's replacement, the portly, phlegmatic Baron Volzhin, had disappointed her. He was behaving independently. He had tried to bring about what the previous chief procurator had broken his neck on – the retirement of Varnava, a man hated by the Synod and already the subject of discussion in the Duma. But she would not hand 'ours' over: '10 Nov. . . . Volzhin will need a good deal of 'picking up' from you, he is weak & frightened . . . so when you see him, make him understand that he serves you first of all & the Church – & that it does not concern society nor Duma.'

It was then that the idea occurred to the 'Tsarskoe Selo cabinet' to make the notorious Pitirim metropolitan of Petrograd.

Alix put her usual pressure on Nicky.

'12 Nov. . . . Darling, I forgot to speak about Pitirim, the metropolitan of Georgia . . . he is a worthy man, and a great *Worshipper*, as our Friend says. He foresees Volzhin's fright . . . but begs you to be firm, as he is the only suitable man . . . it would be good you did it as soon as you come, to prevent talks & beggings fr. Ella etc.' One other idea completed Our Friend's bouquet of state proposals. 'Then Zh[e]vakhov he begs you straight to nominate as help to Volzhin . . . age means nothing & knows the Church affairs to perfection – it's your will & you are master.'

Prince Zhevakhov was the dark-haired young man shown standing at the back in the photograph of Rasputin's devotees. Nothing had been simple for him, either. He had been a minor official of the Council of State.

But Rasputin had noticed him at once. Rumour had it that Zhevakhov, too, was a person of non-traditional sexual proclivities, which could ruin a church career. But Rasputin started to promote him, and brought him to the palace. And soon afterwards, the modest official went to Belgorod at the empress's command to arrange a shrine for the relics of the Prelate Iosaf.

Volzhin refused to accept him as his deputy. A post of second deputy chief procurator was then created for Zhevakhov. After which the first deputy was driven out, leaving Zhevakhov alone.

At the end of 1915 it came to pass that Pitirim was appointed metropolitan of Petrograd and Ladoga. Thereby becoming one of the leading members of the church hierarchy and 'pre-eminent in the Synod'. He would take up residence in the metropolitan's chambers at the famous Alexander Nevsky Abbey, the chief monastery of the capital.

The refractory Volzhin was removed at the beginning of 1916. His place as chief procurator was taken over by the silent and submissive Nikolai Raev, the modest director of higher education courses for women.

The coup was over. Alix now had an obedient Synod. And later she would be able to write to the tsar: '21 Sept. 1916 . . . Fancy, the Synod wants to present me with a *Testimonial* & Image (because of my work with the wounded, I think) – you see poor me receiving them all? Since Catherine no Empress has personally received them alone, Gregory is delighted (I less so) – but strange, is it not, I, whom they feared & disapproved of always.'

She was entitled to the award. She and the peasant Grigory Rasputin had created a new Synod with obedient hierarchs.

'A Grand Duke? Higher!'

The year 1915 was drawing to an end. At the time, rumours of Rasputin's power over the 'tsars' had taken the shape of every conceivable myth. He had long since turned into a cult figure in the eyes of the capital's residents. It was then that the yearning rich woman Lydia Bazilevskaya turned up by his side. This tall brunette, the divorced twenty-eight-year-old daughter of a lieutenant general, immediately found her way into the agents' reports: 'He came home drunk at one in the morning . . . [with] an unknown officer and lad . . . And then Bazilevskaya arrived . . . They remained until 4:00 a.m.'

The singer Belling would afterwards recall:

It was in November 1915 at six in the evening. An acquaintance of mine,

L. P. B-aya [Lydia Platonovna Bazilevskaya] . . . of whom I knew only that she did 'charity work', although mostly for the sake of show . . . called me up on the phone: 'Sweetie, come over right away!'

'Why, what's the matter?' I asked, quite surprised by her request.

'I have a very important person here who is taken with your picture and demands that you come at once.' L. P. B-aya's voice was extremely urgent and agitated.

'Demands?' I repeated. 'Who is it, then? Some minister?'

'Higher!' I received in answer.

'What, a grand duke?'

'Higher,' I heard L. P. B-aya moan, obviously exasperated by my slowness. I was seized with indescribable curiosity. Just what sort of person was it? He 'demanded', and was higher than everything 'highly placed' as it then existed in our understanding . . . I went and, I must admit, urged the driver on from impatience. When I entered the vestibule, an agitated, flushed L. P. B-aya came out to me and herself quickly began helping me off with my fur coat and even my galoshes.

'Don't forget to kiss his hand. He likes that,' L. P. B-aya informed me in a whisper.

'What a nasty trick!' I thought, crestfallen. 'A priest!' L. P. B-aya pushed me into the next room, which turned out to be an elegant, bright bedroom with red mirrors, small chairs, and lace pillows. Several ladies and two or three men were sitting in it. I squirmed uncomfortably under the inquisitive stare of a pair of grey, deep-set, small, ugly eyes . . . Dishevelled, in a lovely lilac silk shirt, high boots, and an untidy beard, he seemed familiar to me, and subconsciously I realized it was Rasputin.

Thus did Alexandra Belling make Rasputin's acquaintance. And become a member of his salon.

The Salon On The Eve Of The End

While those political squabbles were taking place, the Rasputiniad continued, by then already smacking of madness. Zhukovskaya described the peasant's salon at the end of 1915 with its now familiar membership:

Sitting at the table by a boiling samovar that never ever seemed to go away was a now pudgy Akilina in her grey dress of a sister of mercy: she worked at the royal hospital. Taking refuge next to her was Munya, who was gazing in meek adoration at Rasputin, who had squeezed me into a corner of the sofa. The doorbell rang. Munya went to open it . . . The princess had arrived. Shakhovskaya, a tall, plump brunette with slow, lazy, alluring movements. She too was dressed a sister of mercy and worked in the Tsarskoe Selo hospital. 'I'm so tired, all I can think about is getting some sleep, but, as you see, I've come to you.'

'Well, let me have a look at you,' Rasputin said. 'You know how sweet you are. Oh, you are such a tasty dish,' he said, fondling her breasts and sticking his fingers inside her collar . . . And squeezing her knee, he added, squinting, 'Do you know . . . where the spirit is? You think it's here,' and he indicated his heart, 'but it's here,' and Rasputin rapidly and imperceptibly raised and lowered the hem of her dress . . . 'Oh, it's hard with you! Look at me, hypocrite,' he threatened her, 'or else . . . I'll strangle you. Here's the cross for you.'

'I'm going to go home now,' Shakhovskaya said, resting her head on his shoulder and snuggling up to him. 'I'll take a bath and sleep . . . Father, don't be cross now,' Shakhovskaya sweetly pleaded, presenting her face for a kiss. 'After all, you know, Father!'

'Come, come, my tasty one,' Rasputin benignly replied, squeezing her breast. 'She wanted to.'

This is what has always amazed me about Rasputin's strange manner. How is it that everything is possible and nothing shameful here? Or is it all different than it seems? To be sure, nowhere else will you see what took place there in that empty dining room. Where pampered aristocratic ladies waited for the caresses of a dirty middle-aged peasant, waited submissively for their turn without getting angry or jealous.

The Testimony Of Those Who Visited The Sofa

Yet all that time the police were describing his incessant search for *new* women. '3 November 1915. An unknown woman arrived to petition for her ensign husband . . . When she came out, she started telling the porter, "Rasputin barely listened to my request and started holding my face in his hands, and then my breasts, saying, 'Kiss me . . . I've fallen in love with you.' Then he wrote out some sort of note and started making advances again. He didn't give me the note, but said, 'Come back tomorrow.' " ' And she added, "To go to him, you have to make a down payment on what he wants, and I cannot do that." '

Now that the 'holy period' was over, what were all those endless women, so scrupulously recorded by the police agents, to him?

The ones who refused him are named in the agents' testimony. But the unhappy petitioners who agreed to 'make a down payment' unfortunately are not. As a rule they are identified by initial only – 'Madame K.' – or are referred to as 'a certain lady'. 'A certain lady,' Beletsky testified, 'in order to return her husband from exile, first gave Rasputin all her money, but he demanded more . . . She pleaded with him not to touch her.' But Rasputin 'gave her an ultimatum: either she did what he wanted and he would ask the sovereign about her husband, or she would never show herself again'. And 'taking advantage of her nervous state', he possessed her. And after that went to see her at her hotel several times. And then he 'broke off relations with her and gave orders not to admit her'.

Zhukovskaya tells similar stories about the obscure women from whom Rasputin extorted 'down payments'. All the stories have the same ending: he would sleep with the women and then drop them in disgust. But those unhappy women were all so fleeting, and thus unwilling to talk about their misfortunes, that the Extraordinary Commission was unable, except for Vishnyakova, to call a single one of them.

In trying to make sense of our hero, we shall want to remember his fastidious near-loathing of the unknown women who slept with him, and remember, too, their words: 'he took advantage of my nervous state,' as a 'certain lady' said to Beletsky; and 'after reducing me to hysterics, [he] deprived me of my virginity,' as the nurse Vishnyakova testified.

Yet the unknown fallen petitioners constituted a part of the round dance that might have astonished Casanova – all those flashing women's bodies passing through Rasputin's bed, or rather across the half-ruined sofa in his narrow little study, only to vanish at once from his life.

The tiny room and broken-down sofa have been described by Alexandra Belling, who visited the apartment. And they have been described in even greater detail by Zhukovskaya:

The sofa's leather was rubbed completely bare and its back was broken off and propped against it. 'Well, sit down, sit down.' Putting his arm around me and nudging and prodding me from behind, Rasputin leaned up against the sofa's back, and it fell off. After extricating myself, I said with a glance at the broken sofa, 'It isn't any good. You ought to at least call a carpenter.' He became flustered. 'Yes, it broke off from that itself,' he muttered, lifting up the heavy back with one hand and returning it to its place. 'It's all the sister from Simbirsk. As soon as she spends the night here, it will fall off for sure. It's goblinry.'

The bulky frame of the peasant woman who sometimes kept Rasputin busy at night had, in combination with the unfortunate sofa's numerous other tests both day and night, worn it out.

But who were they – the ones who passed over that oft-suffering couch?

From the words of his agents and his own conversations with Rasputin, Beletsky would generalize that besides the petitioners who were tormented by the requirement of having to 'make a down payment', the main clients of Rasputin's sofa were petitioners 'who took a light view of moral principles, [and] many of them were even proud of Rasputin's attentions to them and candid about their intimacy with him, however temporary it had been'.

Once again he does not provide their names. For the reason that as a rule they too disappeared with a strange swiftness from the apartment on Gorokhovaya after visiting the sofa. Only a few of them stayed on, in which case the external surveillance agents naturally established their names.

'Get Out Of Here!'

In 1917 the Extraordinary Commission required the ladies who had 'stayed on' to answer some disagreeable questions. Their testimony has survived in the File.

'Sheila Gershovna Lunts, twenty-five, a barrister's wife, of the Jewish faith, no criminal record.' This handsome woman had met Rasputin at a party given by Professor I. Kh. Ozerov, the friend of Rasputin's publisher, Filippov, whom Rasputin had once described to Filippov as 'a state nobody'. She testified:

> I had heard many nasty things about Rasputin before, especially about his attitude towards women, which is why when I came in, and this peasant in high boots and a Russian coat looked at me, I had an unpleasant feeling . . . Rasputin . . . made jokes, laughed, and read fortunes from the palms of those present, and his predictions took the form of barely comprehensible apothegms. To me, for example, he said, 'You are a sufferer, but the Lord Jesus will help you and your truth will win out!' He joked with the ladies, and tried to embrace first one and then another, but they wouldn't let him. He drank wine, although not very much.

Rasputin naturally took a liking to the curly-haired Sheila. And the familiar pursuit began.

'Once he called me in the evening from a certain Knirsha, whom I didn't know. He said to me over the phone, "Come on over. We're having a lot of fun here!"'

Knirsha's apartment was one of the main places Rasputin went for amusement from the end of 1915 to January 1916, his last year. It constantly flickers through the security agents' entries.

'21 January. Rasputin . . . went to Knirsha's.'

'30 January. Rasputin went to Knirsha's . . . He came home completely drunk at 4:30 a.m.'

Andrei Knirsha was an insurance company official, 'an Alphonse supported by women,' as a security agent said of him. And although Sheila's friends warned her that Knirsha 'was involved in shady deals', as she put it, she agreed to go to the suspicious apartment. At fault was the unlucky Jewish Pale of Settlement: 'I very much wanted my parents, who did not have the right of residence in the capital, to move to Petrograd,' she would testify. But knowing of Rasputin's 'nasty attitude towards women', she should not have had any doubt about the purpose of his call.

'I arrived at the apartment,' Lunts reported, 'with its chic furnishings, although it was the luxury of a parvenu, and found Knirsha himself there, young but very stout with broad cheekbones. His mistress was the wife of some old general.' She was amazed to find there too 'the well-known Duma member Protopopov, who at the time was still only the Deputy Speaker of the State Duma but with whom I was already acquainted at the time, having met him at Professor Ozerov's . . . Finding Protopopov in Rasputin's company gave me an awful start, and later in conversation I observed to him, "It does not befit you to be in such a place," to which Protopopov replied, "Yes, I agree!" and praised me for my frankness.'

She did not realize that she was present at an historic meeting. Protopopov, one of the leaders of the opposition, was in that haunt to establish good relations with Rasputin and the 'tsars'.

Hovering round the peasant

> at the soirée were several ladies, and Rasputin was provoking the jealousy of a tall blonde lady whose name was, I think, Yasinskaya, and with whom he was evidently on intimate terms. That lady didn't like me either, maybe because Rasputin had told everyone that he liked me very much, that my eyes knocked him out. A supper was served at Knirsha's with lots of wine. Rasputin drank his usual Madeira and then called for a Gypsy chorus . . . Rasputin danced . . . the party started to take on the character of an orgy . . . and I left.

Apparently without ever understanding why he had summoned her.

But whether it was the opportunity to help her parents or interest of

another kind that was very likely present in that sensual woman, Protopopov's future lover, she herself 'called Rasputin and told him [she] had
a matter to discuss with him'.

And so Sheila Lunts found herself in the room with the sofa.

'I heard voices coming from the dining room, but whom the voices
belonged to I had no idea. I related my request to him, and told him that
whenever my sister visited me and stayed on without official permission I
felt enormous anxiety, and I asked him to help me.'

But there were too many people in his dining room, and she was obliged
to leave.

And again she herself called Rasputin and told him:

'Remember the business I was asking about?' But it turned out he had
forgotten all about it, and he answered, 'I don't remember anything, come
on over!' I went over to his place. He wanted to hug and kiss, but I pushed
him away. When I repeated my request, he answered, 'Well, I'll come to
see you, meet your sister, and take care of everything!'

I called him, and he came to see me when there was nobody at home
except me and the maid. In the study he started pressing himself on me
terribly. I remarked to him, 'Leave off with that, don't, let's just be friends,
I have never deceived my husband.'

He asked, 'Is it true that you've never deceived him?'

'On my word of honour,' I replied.

'Well, I believe it then!' Rasputin said. 'But if you ever want to deceive
him, let me be the first!' Then Rasputin asked if I had any wine. I told him
I didn't have, but that there was some 180-proof spirits. Rasputin drank a
little glass of the spirits and took a bit of apple. Then indicating the chair
by the desk, Rasputin said, 'Sit!' I sat down. Then Rasputin . . . started
dictating some rubbish to me in Church Slavonic. I filled up a whole
page . . .

After he left, I was supposed to go to him again with my petition: it was
a tedious, endless fuss . . . I stopped going to see him.

And so, Sheila's testimony was that there had been nothing between her
and Rasputin. The easiest thing would be to suggest that she was lying. But
remembering Rasputin's peculiar visits to the prostitutes, I think that up to
a point she was telling the truth. And that is the reason why one senses
hidden astonishment in her testimony: he made advances to her, and after
receiving nothing more than the obligatory light rebuff, let her go with
something close to relief. And she continued to visit him. Although it must
have been quite clear to Rasputin that she was coming to 'make a down
payment'. And still he did not take it and continued his innocuous impor-

tuning, his 'fuss'. And then suddenly she herself, as she asserts, broke off those visits that were obviously a matter of concern to her. But why?

Just as suddenly broken off were Rasputin's meetings with another frivolous lady, Maria Gayer. Her own testimony is not in the File. But it does contain a characterization of her by her coachman, Yakov Kondratenko. 'She . . . had no occupation. She engaged in loose living. She was, one could say, simply a "woman of the streets". No sooner would she wink at some strange man, than you would have to drive them to a hotel . . . I know that she often went to see Rasputin, and that he would come to see her and drink until he was soused.'

The agents recorded constant encounters between Rasputin and Maria Gayer on the 15th, 17th, 19th, 23rd, 24th, 25th, and 28th. And then all of a sudden it came to an end. And she vanished from his life.

Disappearing from Rasputin's home no less suddenly was yet another extremely complaisant lady, the cocotte Tregubova, whom the agents had earlier described as 'exchanging deep kisses with Rasputin'. And in the File she tells a story very much like that told by Lunts. Tregubova herself went to see Rasputin frequently, during which the usual Rasputinian pestering went on. But she had only to resist slightly for Rasputin to give up.

'I went to see Rasputin about ten times, in view of the fact that he had promised to get me a place on the imperial stage, although with the condition that I consent to intimate relations with him. Which of course I did not.' It doesn't make any sense – the chasteness of this lady whom both the other witnesses in the File and the police agents are unanimous in calling a 'prostitute'. And why, given that chasteness, did she go to see Rasputin 'ten times' in spite of his 'pestering'?

According to Tregubova, their relationship ended in an ugly scene. After one of his periodic advances, 'He spat in my face and said, "To hell with you, then, you Yid." And he left.' Following which the vindictive Rasputin decided to drive her, as a Jew, out of Petrograd. On 17 January 1916, she received an order from Beletsky to 'leave Petrograd . . . by 10:00 p.m.' She then rushed to Rasputin, 'pleading to be allowed to stay in Petrograd'. Apparently, this time her visit satisfied the peasant, since he gave her a letter to Beletsky: 'Let her be, don't touch her, let her stay.' But as she would soon find out, Rasputin then called Beletsky and said, 'Don't let her stay, send her away.' According to the records of the Petrograd Address Bureau, 'the above-mentioned Tregubova departed from Petrograd for residence in Tiflis.'

What A Strange Story!

And there was another woman – Vera Varvarova. She was twenty-eight at the time. In the File she testified, 'I'm an artiste, I sing Gypsy romances . . . I sang in the presence of the tsar.'

On tour in Kiev she had insulted an official and been threatened with a jail term. She went to Rasputin. Soon afterwards she 'received a document from the Senate cancelling the punishment'. After which Rasputin 'called me and said, "Come sing for me as my guest." I went with Staff-Captain Ezersky, with whom I was living at the time. There were a great many guests at Rasputin's – ladies – and I sang and played the guitar, and his guests sang along and Rasputin danced . . . After that I often went to see him that year for soirées of that kind . . . He was completely correct with me, especially as I was constantly in the company of Ezersky,' she explained, insisting that she had never been in 'the room with the sofa'. And she described what she had seen happen before her eyes to the ladies who went with Rasputin to the little sofa.

'He would happen to be affectionate with some lady . . . and would go with her to the other room and then would chase her out: "Get out of here!"'

But Varvarova had no idea why that happened. And it may be that the sudden end of their relationship is evidence of that.

'I was tired of the situation, and the last year before Rasputin's death I did not go to see him even once,' she said, concluding her testimony.

And the agents' last entry about her does in fact relate to the end of 1915. But the entry is a very eloquent one: 'Rasputin came back at 9:15 a.m. along with Varvarova . . . He probably spent the night at Varvarova's.' After which the singer took her place among the throng of vanished petitioners, while leaving the same unanswered question behind, a very important one for understanding our hero: did she leave of her own accord? Or had Rasputin suddenly said to her after their night together, 'Get out of here!'

But there was still another category of sofa visitor. Beletsky defined them this way: 'Well provided for materially and having no requests to make of him. But out of a special interest in his personality they deliberately sought his acquaintance, knowing what they were getting into.' And among them, as Beletsky noted, 'was a princess from Moscow'.

And Stefania Dolgorukaya, the wife of a gentleman of the bedchamber of the highest court, really was a princess. That thirty-eight-year-old lady, with the abundant curves that were so in fashion at the beginning of the century, used to stay at the Astoria, the most expensive hotel in the capital.

'1 December. Rasputin and Princess Dolgorukaya arrived at the Hotel Astoria by motor at 3:30 a.m., and they remained together until morning,' the external surveillance agents reported. But it wasn't only passion that had brought Rasputin and the Moscow princess together. The princess had decided to get her husband transferred to Petrograd, and the peasant was helping her out by making appointments with the necessary people.

'17 December. Princess Dolgorukaya sent a motor for Rasputin, which took him to the Hotel Astoria . . . The former Petrograd mayor, General Kleigels, also arrived and they remained together until 2:00,' the agents reported.

And there were two other lady friends familiar to us who, although they did not belong to the highest aristocracy, were still quite 'well provided for materially'. On 8 December Rasputin 'took Dzhanumova and Filippova out to the Donon. After dinner he went to the Hotel Russia with them,' the agents reported.

Yet both Dolgorukaya and Dzhanumova would deny having been intimate with Rasputin. And Zhukovskaya would deny it, too. The latter's denial is especially implausible. The celebrated historian Sergei Melgunov, to whom she spoke about her relationship with Rasputin, transcribed her story in his diary, although not without scepticism: 'The elder liked Zhukovskaya very much . . . He would plead with her to spend the night with him. He did this openly in front of Munya Golovina . . . The elder would grab Zhukovskaya by the legs, kiss her stockings, stroke her neck and breasts . . . Zhukovskaya then proudly made the claim that the elder had never succeeded in kissing her lips.'

Prugavin, the man who had first sent Zhukovskaya to Rasputin, frankly explained to the investigator in the File, 'She was someone with strained nerves and very likely a propensity to eroticism, and one has to suppose that with her search for new experiences, she did not find Rasputin's own quest all that repugnant.' So indeed it was. Eroticism permeates her memoirs, and it tormented her.

And that bold and quite shameless woman, shameless both in her life and in her writings, would, in describing that microworld of carnality, insist in her book and in conversation with friends that for all the elder's onslaughts which she endlessly described, she never did yield to him!

But how interesting those onslaughts were. First came a lengthy sermon.

'It doesn't matter if you fornicate a little. This, you see, is how it ought to be: I have sinned and forgotten about it. But if, say, I should sin with you and afterwards can think of nothing but your . . . then the sin will go unrepented. Thoughts must be holy. And afterwards we'll go to church and pray side by side, and then you'll forget the sin and know happiness.'

'But if all the same you consider *that* a sin, then why do it?' I asked.

He squinted: 'Well, repentance and prayer are not given without sin, after all' . . . Bending ever lower, he laid his chest against me, and crumpling his body and twisting his arms, he reached a frenzy. It always seemed to me that at such moments he could feel nothing but that savage longing. You could stab him or cut him and he wouldn't even notice. Once I stuck a large needle in his palm . . . and he didn't even feel it . . . His brutal face drew near and turned almost flat, with his wet hair like matted like wool round his narrow, gleaming eyes that seemed through his hair to be made of glass. Silently pushing him away and freeing myself . . . I stepped back to the wall, thinking he would hurl himself at me again. But he slowly staggered towards me and said in a hoarse whisper, 'Let us pray!' And then he took me by the shoulder and pulled me over to the window where an icon of Saint Simeon of Verkhoturye stood. Thrusting a velvety lilac rosary into my hand, he threw me to my knees, while he himself collapsed behind me and started beating his head against the floor, at first silently, then intoning, 'Venerable Simeon of Verkhoturye, have mercy on me, a sinner!' . . . After several minutes, he dully asked, 'What's your name?' [he had forgotten it, since they were all 'Darling' to him], and when I answered, he began beating his head against the floor again, alternately mentioning himself and me. After repeating that . . . ten times or so, he stood up and turned towards me. He was pale, and the sweat ran in streams down his face, but his breath was perfectly calm, and his eyes gazed mutely and affectionately – the eyes of a grizzled Siberian wanderer. And then he kissed me with cold monastic exultation.

But in all her descriptions, one perceives the frantic curiosity and desire that drove Zhukovskaya to Rasputin's apartment. That lady–Satanist required force. And there wasn't any. Her strong resistance or rebuff, which Rasputin had seemingly been waiting for, had been enough for it all to end in exultation and prayer! And Zhukovskaya would keep coming to see him, and it would all be repeated. Alexandra Belling described her own encounters with Rasputin in the same way. Only unlike Zhukovskaya, who wanted Rasputin, Belling had come to exploit him, and he was repellent to her. And that is why there was no prayer after the onslaught, since there was nothing for him to pray about. She was not sinful. And for that reason was easily able to slip out of his embraces.

All this gradually creates the strange feeling that it is as if he craved that rebuff to his onslaughts, so as to let go. It is as if all his eroticism were contained in that constant attacking and rebuffing. In that obligatory rebuffing.

Once More About His
Erotic Secrets

'On my way home,' Zhukovskaya wrote, 'I wondered if he had acted the same way with Lokhtina – after driving her to ecstasy, did he set her to prayer? And maybe the tsarina, as well? I remembered the greedy, insatiable passion that burst through all of Lokhtina's frenzied caresses – such as could only be with a constantly heated yet never satisfied passion. But that isn't something you're ever likely to find out . . . It will, perhaps, only be learned much later, when they're all no longer alive.'

It's possible that it was all an extension of that same secret religious experience of his. The same constant summoning of lust and its suppression to the point of indifference, a process that served to 'refine his nerves' and that gave him his insights and his hypnotic power. That is why his 'romances' with the ladies who pushed him away, like Zhukovskaya, Dzhanumova, and Belling, were so drawn out. And why all those ladies who yielded to him, who satisfied his desires, disappeared without delay.

And the cocotte Tregubova, who obtained wealthy Jewish petitioners for him, visited him until she yielded. And that was why he had decided to send her away. For him, it was a fall. Sin had triumphed. As he had explained it to Zhukovskaya, 'he had started to think about Tregubova's.' And the field of his diabolical strength had been weakened. And for that reason he had begun to hate her. Here, presumably, is the true explanation as to why he tried to remove Tregubova and send her away from the capital. And when the simple Tregubova came to him and apparently yielded to him once again, certain it would help, he ordered her sent from the city without delay. And Lunts and Varvarova and Bazilevskaya and Gayer and the nameless victims of the 'down payment' evidently made the very same mistake. And immediately vanished from his apartment. And as soon as poor Khionia Berladskaya had yielded to him, he began to hate her, too. And to avoid her, and his admonitions ended. And the case of the royal nurse Vishnyakova is the same. She had given in to his fierce desire and had yielded in half-madness. And he had at once distanced himself from her. And the outraged nurse declared that he had raped her.

The only 'yielders' who remained with him were those who had been initiated into his experience, the true members of his sect, who were ready to put up with his disgust and continue to venerate him. Like the unhappy Lokhtina or the loyal Zinaida Manshtedt or the silent Baroness Kusova. And, ultimately, the sly Laptinskaya and the obedient Patushinskaya, who at their leader's command played the role of his 'celestial wives'. To meekly disappear from his bed at his order. Or the others who continued to torment him with unsatisfied desire and harmless 'fuss', such as Princess Shakhovskaya and Sana Pistolkors. And those ladies, too, were drawn into his incessant onslaughts, that endless sexual game ending in lofty repentance, exultation, and prayer. That is why there was no jealousy in any of them. And when they tried to persuade the 'new ones' Dzhanumova or Zhukovskaya to give themselves, they knew it would be the end of them. That the latest 'strangers' would then join the female army that had passed across the sofa and vanished. Vyrubova received her schooling there. It is where she discovered the appeal of the game of unrequited desire. The erotic game into which she had enticed the tsar and tsarina.

The Peasant Searches For A Prime Minister

Between his drinking bouts and 'nerve refinement' the peasant had all along been occupied with trying to find a future cabinet head. It was no accident that Sheila Lunts had run into the Duma deputy leader Protopopov at Knirsha's apartment. Our Friend was choosing the participants of his future political games. Taking place there were something like political auditions. That indeed was why he had brought along with him a certain Osipenko, the secretary (and more) of Metropolitan Pitirim. '20 December. Rasputin, along with Pitirim's secretary, Ivan Osipenko, went to see the hereditary nobleman citizen Knirsh[a] (twenty-eight, a bachelor). Delivered there as well were two baskets of wine from the restaurant the Villa Rhode . . . and a Gypsy chorus was invited,' the external surveillance agents reported.

The peasant's 'Brain Trust' had been considerably enlarged. Besides the Jews there were now hierarchs from the Alexander Nevsky Abbey. Rasputin had become a frequent guest in the chambers of his appointee, Metropolitan Pitirim. Twelve years before, Rasputin had arrived at the abbey a pitiful supplicant. Now he held sway there. Pitirim arranged banquets and luncheons in his honour. The guest list was unchanging: Bishop Varnava, Pitirim's secretary, Ivan Osipenko, the chief secretary of the Synod, Pyotr Mudrolyubov, and its treasurer, Nikolai Solovyov. Synod policy was decided at those luncheons.

Now at the end of 1915, however, they were feverishly discussing candidates for the future prime minister. It was not for nothing that Vyrubova, a member of the shadow cabinet, was also present.

'16 Dec. . . . Ania was yesterday at the Metropolitans, our Friend too – they spoke very well, and then he gave them luncheon – always the first place to Gregory,' Alix reported to Nicky, 'and the whole time wonderfully respectful to him and deeply impressed by all he said.'

'I Am A Devil, I Am A Demon'

Rasputin's last year had arrived. That examiner of prime ministers to whom the tsars deferred spent the entire month of January 1916 deep in drunkenness. The security agents' favourite entry was, 'There were guests till morning. They sang songs.'

On 10 January he celebrated his birthday. He had reached forty-seven. He would not see forty-eight. The festivities took place under the indefatigable watch of the agents. That morning of 10 January, Komissarov's men appeared at the peasant's apartment bearing gifts. Conveying presents, they offered to help take the coats of Rasputin's guests. After explaining that it was 'how gentlemen in good homes celebrated'. Finding such a quantity of servants flattering, the peasant agreed. Cunning yet simple, he was! The agents afterwards described the gifts received by Rasputin: 'a mass of valuable things in silver and gold, carpets, whole suites of furniture, paintings, money'. A congratulatory telegram from on high was also received and read out loud after Vyrubova and the other guests had arrived. The same Synod official Mudrolyubov gave a speech in which he emphasized Rasputin's 'significance for the state as a simple man who had brought the people's aspirations to the foot of the throne'. After Vyrubova's and Mudrolyubov's departure, the genuine merry-making began. The peasant drank a lot, read telegrams from all the ends of Russia, and by evening fell down drunk. They put him to bed. After a short nap, he was sober again. Evening arrived. By then a more intimate circle had gathered, ladies for the most part. And he began to drink, demanding the same of the ladies. He plied them all with drink. He demanded Gypsies. The Gypsies came to congratulate him. By then all were completely drunk, with the exception of the Gypsy chorus. The more sensible ladies hastened to leave. The peasant was turning into a beast. In endless dancing and intoxication, he had reached a kind of madness. As had the guests along with him. Everyone sang, danced, and shouted. As the agents reported, 'Those who remained were overcome by such mayhem that the Gypsy chorus hurried to leave.

By 2:00 a.m. only those remained in the apartment who had decided to spend the night. In the morning a noisy row commenced: the husbands of two of the ladies who had spent the night at Rasputin's burst into the apartment with firearms. The agents managed to escort the ladies out the back entrance.'

Before long Rasputin would himself go out the same back entrance to his death.

The husbands were taken round the apartment so that they could convince themselves that their wives were not there. After that, the agents immediately followed them in order to identify them, so that they too got into the police reports. The ladies, however, like their frivolous predecessors, did not turn up at the apartment again. And the peasant himself, frightened by the husbands, 'quieted down for several days and was afraid to leave the apartment'. But after a few days it started all over again.

'14 January. He returned home at 7:00 a.m. completely drunk in the company of Osipenko and an unknown man . . . He broke the large pane of glass in the front door of his building, and a swelling was visible by his nose – apparently he had fallen down somewhere.'

'17 January. An unknown lady came to see Rasputin after 11:00 and stayed until 3:00 a.m.' The lady did not turn up again, and the external surveillance agents failed to establish her name.

Three in the morning was in fact his usual time. The night was still young. And with the cry, 'Let's go see the Gypsies!' he would rouse his drunken company. And the half-asleep revellers would race off to a restaurant by carriage. And the utterly exhausted Gypsies would entertain their tireless guest till dawn. It was as if he sensed that he was seeing his last winter and was rushing to take pleasure in a wild debauch. Actually, the drinking bouts of rich Russian merchants at the time differed little then from the peasant's frenzies. The looming apocalypse was driving people mad.

In the File is the testimony of Isaac Bykhovsky, forty years old, a coal industrialist of Jewish faith from Kharkov. He came to Petrograd 'to arrange a profitable little deal'. And his business associates in Petrograd took him to see Rasputin. In appreciation for Rasputin's having given one of them 'a business card addressed to Shakhovskoy, the minister of trade and industry. On the card was written, "Receive him." Shakhovskoy did in fact receive him without his having to wait, although the meeting failed to yield any results.' The coal industrialists gave Rasputin no money and restricted themselves to a single banquet. Rasputin 'came at the height of the dinner and instantly buried his head in his bowl, ate only soup and fish, and drank Madeira . . . and then he made a telephone call, and a young Georgian appeared, who sat down by Rasputin, calling him "Father" and apparently ingratiating himself with him.'

(The Georgian was the officer Pankhadze, who, like the majority of Georgian noblemen, called himself 'prince' and was at the time betrothed to Rasputin's daughter Matryona. Thanks to Rasputin, he had avoided the front by doing his military service with the reserve battalions garrisoned in Petrograd. Vyrubova characterized him this way in the File: 'Pankhadze, a draft-dodger who did not wish to go into the army.')

During the dinner

> the Georgian kept pressing us to go see a Gypsy chorus in New Village, where, according to him, they were expecting Rasputin. We all drove off to see the chorus together, since when we came out an automobile was already waiting for Rasputin. A large group was waiting for Rasputin at the Gypsies. There Rasputin let himself go and danced the whole time and drank Madeira. I was impressed by his dancing. Sometimes he would whirl in place for half an hour, so that it was amazing to me that he didn't get dizzy. One of my colleagues didn't feel well, and around 2:00 I left the chorus [so he and the colleague slipped away without paying]. The rest of the company remained until 7:00 a.m. and kept ordering wine . . . for Brusilovsky [his other colleague] who ended up paying for everything.

And again they brought him home drunk before dawn, and again he tried to get into the apartment of a certain Katya in the same building, and again he was not allowed in, and, drunk, he tried to kiss the sleepy porter, but she lazily pushed him away. His apartment on Gorokhovaya Street had long since become a lair. As the investigator Simpson wrote in his summarizing 'Resolution':

> Living there for months on end in the intervals between the trips of her hospital train was the sister of mercy Laptinskaya, whose erotic exercises with Rasputin were, in the absence of blinds, observable from the street . . . [Other] guests were the beautiful Siberian Elena Patushinskaya, whose notary husband had through Rasputin's efforts been transferred to Odessa, where he shot himself . . . the beautiful baptized Jew Volynskaya, who had paid with herself and with cash for her husband's pardon through Rasputin's efforts; the Baroness Kusova who wanted to secure a better position for her husband, an officer attached to a Crimean regiment . . . the Gypsy singer Varvarova, who cost him too much money and who occupied him in every way . . . the lubricious . . . barrister's wife Sheila Lunts . . . the proprietor

of the restaurant the Villa Rhode, who put wine and women at Rasputin's disposal; the erotomaniac . . . Zhukovskaya . . . Prince Andronikov; Doctor Badmaev; the agent of numerous intelligence services, Manasevich-Manuilov; the inspector of public schools Dobrovolsky and his young wife; Molchanov, the son of the exarch of Georgia . . . who saw to his own and his father's affairs; the Jew Tregubova . . . the diamond dealer and gambling house impresario Simanovich; and the beautiful Princess Shakhovskaya.

And at the centre was the continually drunk peasant entangled in religious games that were ever more clearly turning into morbid lust, into a peculiar form of narcotic.

In the File his former close friend Sazonov related a remarkable scene to the investigator:

Rasputin was aware of his fall, and that consciousness made him suffer . . . I remember six months before his death he came to see me drunk and, bitterly sobbing, told me that he had spent the entire night carousing with Gypsies and had squandered two thousand, and that he had to be at the tsarina's at 6:00. I took him to my daughter's room, where between his sobs Rasputin said, 'I am a devil. I am a demon. I am sinful, whereas before I was holy. I am not worthy of staying in this pure room.' I saw that his sorrow was real.

'Bond' Captures The House On Gorokhovaya

At the end of 1915 Colonel Komissarov reported to his masters that Manasevich had suddenly acquired enormous influence in the apartment on Gorokhovaya Street. And, as the agents recorded, he ever more frequently accompanied the peasant in the official car to Tsarskoe Selo. Komissarov spoke with astonishment of the innovations that had appeared in Rasputin's home. Manasevich had brought in a typewriter and a typist. With the aid of that advanced technology Our Friend's thoughts were now being conveyed to Tsarskoe Selo in printed form without delay. At the bottom of them Rasputin put a cross and signed his name in a pompous scribble.

Rasputin's dealings with Tsarskoe Selo now proceeded without interruption.

At first Beletsky and Khvostov came to the conclusion that the clever adventurer had merely decided to use Father Grigory to make the mighty Friend's acquaintance. Only later would the two heads of the secret police realize that they had missed the point. For it was in fact then that Manasevich found a future prime minister for the country. And it was to discuss that most surprising candidacy with the Friend that the new close friends hurried off to Tsarskoe Selo.

The Ungrateful Lover

The only thing that Khvostov was able to establish through his agents was that the decision had indeed been made to let Prime Minister Goremykin go. And the stupid Khvostov decided that his own hour had finally arrived! He just did not understand Rasputin's attitude towards him. As Colonel Komissarov rightly put it, 'Rasputin continually felt his antipathy and could not, despite all of Khvostov's services, overcome his own.' Khvostov let loose a flurry of activity. He contrived to enlist Rasputin's new favourite among his advocates. And through Manasevich to bring Rasputin around in quick order.

That, it seemed, would be very easy to do. For Manasevich at the time had himself come to see Khvostov on a matter of some piquancy. Manasevich was in love with the actress Lerma-Orlova. This pretty half-French woman, a lady of the Petrograd demi-monde like Sheila Lunts, had completely turned the head of the amorous and uncommonly ugly Manasevich. But unfortunately the ill-fated 'Bond' had learned that while his lover was taking money from him, she had at absolutely no charge been making a gift of her charms to a young Swede, the riding master Petz, who was giving her lessons. And the actress was so absorbed in her study of riding that Manasevich had been quite unable to visit her longed-for bed. Khvostov delightedly agreed to help the unhappy Manasevich. As a result, poor Petz was charged with selling horses to the German army through Sweden. He was sent first to prison and then deported. And Manasevich again started seeing the frightened actress.

Khvostov thought he could now expect a reciprocal effort from the grateful lover. But the naive 'Fat Belly' had overlooked the fact that such people are never grateful.

For 'Bond' at the time was engaged in a great game of arranging clandestine meetings between Rasputin and the candidate that he – Manasevich – had found.

The Needed 'Old Chap'

Beletsky learned about those meetings from his agents in 1916 at the start of the new year. Both the identity of the candidate and the rather sinister setting of the meetings themselves astonished him. It turned out that Rasputin was being driven at night to the Peter and Paul Fortress – to the Russian Bastille. And there in the commandant's quarters the new candidate would be waiting, one whom Rasputin had already managed to nickname the 'Old Chap'. He was Boris Stürmer, a sixty-seven-year-old member of the Council of State.

Accompanying Stürmer was a youngish woman, a certain Nikitina, daughter of the fortress commandant. As Vyrubova has described her, that maid of honour of the empress 'enjoyed the reputation of being a frivolous person, and efforts were made to keep her out of the palace'. Even Stürmer's age was not 'proof against the rumours circulating about them'.

It was Nikitina who had arranged the secret meetings between Rasputin and Stürmer in her father's office at the fortress.

In 1917 in the same Peter and Paul Fortress where he and Rasputin had secretly met, Stürmer, now a prisoner there, would answer the investigators' questions.

On learning about Stürmer through his agents, Beletsky had at first been amazed. But on reflection he recognized that the choice was not at all bad. True, Stürmer had an awkward German name. But there were lots of German names at court. On the other hand, Stürmer 'was a man of tested loyalty to the throne who had a vast number of acquaintances in court circles'. In 1914 there had been a famous political salon at Stürmer's home. And in contrast to the usual unrestrained criticism of Rasputin, criticism of the constructive variety had held sway there – that is, how to save the drowning government without touching Rasputin. Beletsky himself had been a frequent guest at the salon.

'Stürmer's circle,' Beletsky testified, 'included the cream of the Russian aristocracy and the influential bureaucracy: members of the Council of State, senators, scions of the oldest Russian families ... governors, church hierarchs.'

So Alexandra Fyodorovna knew: the Stürmer circle had not called for the head of the favourite. But all the earlier attempts of the elderly statesman to return to active political life had been unavailing: his German name had got in the way. Now, however, his hour had come.

Beletsky easily figured out who had originated the idea of Stürmer. In the days of the mighty Minister of Internal Affairs Plehve, Stürmer had served as head of the Department of Police, where Manasevich had been an agent in special services. Grasping the situation, Beletsky summoned Manasevich to his office. 'I asked him, "Why did you betray Khvostov?" He apologized and expressively remarked, "It will go better for you under Stürmer."' And Beletsky, hoping to establish good relations with the future prime minister, decided to conceal the secret auditioning of Stürmer from Khvostov. 'I assured Stürmer through Manasevich of my favour and my readiness to pass on to him any intelligence known to me.'

Next, the tireless Manasevich arranged a meeting between Stürmer and Metropolitan Pitirim. Manasevich later testified that the churchman had asked him, 'Won't the replacement of Goremykin by someone with a foreign name raise questions?' Manasevich replied, 'What is important is the man not the name.' And he added, 'Stürmer is a new person as far as the Duma is concerned, and that is why the Duma members will be uncomfortable voting for him immediately.' And the cautious Pitirim, having behind him the tsarina and Rasputin, composed a favourable note to the Tsar about Stürmer's past activities.

Manasevich, who had once been expelled from special services and who had stained himself with numerous shady dealings, was promised the rank of official in charge of special commissions attached to the future prime minister. He was becoming an agent for Rasputin and the ladies' cabinet in the office of the prime minister. Everyone's dreams were realized: Stürmer had been appointed prime minister, Manasevich had joined the government, and the tsarina and Rasputin had found a new prime minister who would obey.

The time had come to inform Khvostov. Fearing the rage and vengeance of the stupid 'Fat Belly', Manasevich, who liked to operate on several fronts at once, decided to forestall events and go to see Khvostov on his own. He told him about Stürmer's future appointment as prime minister and explained that it had all been the work of Rasputin and Pitirim. Khvostov flew into a rage. And thirsted for revenge.

Meanwhile, events were following their course.

Stürmer was summoned by the tsar on 20 January 1916 at 3:00 p.m. and walked out as prime minister. Prime Minister Goremykin, who arrived at 5:00 with his scheduled report, left to his complete astonishment with a dismissal.

And soon afterwards Manasevich received the post of official for special commissions attached to the office of the prime minister.

In the days after Stürmer's appointment, a most important meeting took place. Despite all of Manasevich's reassurances and his conversations with the 'old fellow', Rasputin with his animal intuition sensed sullen hostility on the part of Stürmer.

And he decided to ask again for the necessary assurances.

From the external surveillance log: '21 January. Rasputin went with Gayer to Knirsha's, and from there he went alone to Orlova's, where Manuilov and B. V. Stürmer were waiting.' After the merry drinking bout at Knirsha's, the peasant went off to a meeting with the new prime minister.

This time, a romantic rather than a sinister place had been selected for the meeting. A love nest – the apartment of Manasevich's unfortunate Lerma-Orlova.

From Manasevich's interrogation by the Extraordinary Commission:

'You were present at the meeting?'

'No, I was in a different room.'

'And the person to whom the apartment belonged?'

'No, she wasn't there . . . As they [Rasputin and Stürmer] were saying goodbye, they exchanged kisses. I was in the dining room at the time.'

Those kisses seemed to confirm the results of the conversation. And Manasevich, continuing to play his favourite duplicitous role, went to Khvostov to tell him the details of the secret meeting. He was fond of setting people against each other.

From Khvostov's testimony: 'Manasevich arrived . . . and told me that the meeting had led to a good result, and that Rasputin was prepared to give him his support with the tsars . . . Stürmer promised, for his part, to consult with Rasputin on those matters having importance for the throne, and he asked to believe that Rasputin would regard him as a friend. After which they exchanged kisses.'

So the peasant tsar could then say, 'I hold Russia in the palm of my hand.'

A Comedy At The Abbey

Minister Khvostov began to take vengeance. He inflicted his first blow on Pitirim. He decided to bring into the open what the metropolitan had made such an effort to hide – his close friendship with Rasputin. To that end Khvostov contrived to play out a whole theatrical scene. He summoned Komissarov, and told him to dress in civilian clothes and to take Rasputin to see Pitirim. The colonel set off.

'In carrying out my instructions,' Komissarov testified, 'I discovered that

Rasputin was not at home but at Tsarskoe Selo. He arrived approximately an hour later accompanied by his family, Pitirim's secretary, Osipenko, and Akilina [Laptinskaya] . . . I discreetly informed Rasputin that Pitirim and Khvostov were expecting us at the abbey. After which Rasputin and I immediately left.' Sensing something untoward, 'Osipenko and Akilina started making a fuss about the fact that I was taking Rasputin away and . . . ran after our cab for a while, yelling to Rasputin, "Where are you going, he's leading you off somewhere!"'

Khvostov had by then already gone to the abbey and was sitting in Pitirim's quarters. He was quietly conversing with the metropolitan when the latter was privately informed of Rasputin's arrival.

From Komissarov's testimony: 'Pitirim, who had been keeping his close friendship with Rasputin a secret, told Khvostov that some Georgian had arrived whom he needed to speak to. And he came out to us. Pitirim and Rasputin kissed. After which Rasputin introduced me, identifying me as "Khvostov's general". You can imagine the hierarch's chagrin! Pitirim then sombrely asked, "Why aren't you in uniform?"' Komissarov answered that he only wore his uniform at the ministry. 'Pitirim had no choice but to invite us into the room where Khvostov was sitting.'

All Petrograd was talking about the practical joke. The metropolitan's prestige was destroyed. Vyrubova and the empress were seething with anger. As for Rasputin, he was pleased. He didn't like the fact that the metropolitan was ashamed of him; it was degrading to the peasant. On the other hand, he realized that Khvostov, whom he couldn't stand, was now finished! 'Mama' would never forgive him!

Having revenged himself on Pitirim, Khvostov decided to strike a blow against the peasant. The maddened minister planned to expel him from the palace. He believed that he would succeed where Stolypin himself had failed! And he devised another theatrical performance. He would 'draw Rasputin into a massive fist fight and carry it to the point of an immense scandal with a police report and publicity'. So that Tsarskoe Selo 'would be forced to agree to his removal'. And then Khvostov, even if driven from the post of minister, would be able to return to the Duma in triumph as the man who had toppled Rasputin.

The Minister's Theatre: 'Rasputin's Savage Beating'

To carry out his plan Khvostov decided to employ Manasevich! He had such trust in him! Manasevich was given money from Department of Police funds 'to arrange a merry soirée at the home of his friend, the reporter Mikhail Snarsky'. At the end of the soirée, Snarsky was supposed to delay Rasputin. And then, after the other guests had dispersed, to let him out onto the street alone. And then Department of Police agents in disguise were supposed to fall on Rasputin and take him away to a car. And savagely beat him. So that he would remember his place! And then they would announce that it had all been the result of a drunken fist fight provoked by Rasputin himself. Khvostov arrived incognito to watch the beating. The disguised agents were in place and waiting in a car by Snarsky's building. But for some reason the windows of Snarsky's apartment were strangely dark. While the incognito Khvostov impatiently walked about in the frost waiting for the peasant to appear, Rasputin himself was merrily carousing along with Manasevich and Snarsky in a private room in the Palace Theatre. They were drinking up the money received to arrange for Rasputin's beating! There was nothing Khvostov could say. He had been humiliated and made ridiculous. And that he could not forgive. It was then, according to Komissarov's testimony, that Khvostov said to him for the first time, 'Rasputin must be killed.'

The Minister's New Show: 'The Peasant's Murder'

Having accepted the idea of murder, Khvostov naturally talked things over with Beletsky. From Beletsky's testimony: 'He indicated that both of us were burdened by the meetings with Rasputin and the constant fear of having our closeness to him exposed as a result of tactlessness on Rasputin's part . . . And, finally, getting rid of Rasputin would clear the atmosphere around the throne and appease society and the Duma.' And, Khvostov supposed, killing Rasputin 'would not be hard'. And justifying why they had failed to keep track of him would be even easier 'by referring to the all the departures made by Rasputin that had been hidden from the agents'. And Beletsky said that he was in agreement. It was decided to entrust the murder to 'our colonel', that is, Komissarov.

Beletsky was of course lying when he said he agreed. As he later explained to the Extraordinary Commission, he 'had no faith in its success, having already been convinced of Rasputin's cunning and intuition and of Khvostov's incompetence in organizing secret police actions'. Moreover, 'after taking the sovereign's mystical personality into account, and remembering the many holy fools . . . before Rasputin', he asked himself what would happen after Rasputin's removal. And the answer was, 'the appearance in the palace of a strange new person in the spirit of Misha Kozelsky'. At least Rasputin was someone he knew how to work with.

Crucial, although he did not mention it in his testimony, was the fact that he had decided to dupe Khvostov, to let him organize the murder and then prevent it, and hand 'Fat Belly' over to the tsars. He hoped they would then understand in Tsarskoe Selo that they would find no better minister of internal affairs than himself.

A Private Fund For Murder

Beletsky initiated his friend Komissarov into the intrigue. And when Khvostov summoned the colonel and set out the assignment, Komissarov agreed to it, but only after portraying a certain hesitation for the sake of plausibility. And thereupon something astonishing happened. Seeing Komissarov's doubts, Khvostov immediately promised him money. More than that, he showed the money to him. And the sum was a truly large one. 'He promised me 100,000 and showed me two packets of 50,000 each,' Komissarov recalled. 'And then he increased the amount – to 200,000.' Komissarov was amazed, because Khvostov could not have taken such a sum from the ministry budget. Beletsky confirms this and adds that Khvostov had told him that he 'had for the affair a significant private allocation, so that one did not need stint on the money'. Beletsky understood that Khvostov's proposal to murder Rasputin was backed by very powerful forces.

Khvostov had meanwhile begun to propose plans for the murder. Beletsky's task for the time being was 'to criticize those plans, postponing their execution'. Or simply to demolish them. Finally, Khvostov suggested sending a case of poisoned Madeira as if from the banker Rubinstein. Beletsky immediately 'sent Komissarov . . . to get poisons'. Komissarov brought Khvostov a number of little bottles and explained how each one worked. For the sake of appearance, he experimented on one of Rasputin's cats. In fact, the bottles were medicine bottles and their contents harmless: Komissarov had merely copied out the names of different poisons from a pharmacology textbook.

But Beletsky sensed that even the inexperienced Khvostov was beginning to guess at his game.

A Provocation

The time had come to scuttle Khvostov and swim to the top. Beletsky devised a scene for the finale in the classic spirit of the Department of Police. After his flight from Russia, the monk Iliodor had moved to Norway, from which he was beginning to threaten publication of his book *A Holy Devil* and that it would include facsimiles of the letters from the tsarina and her daughters that were still in his possession. Naturally Khvostov was forced to conduct negotiations with the monk about purchasing the documents. Iliodor asked for an unconscionably large sum. And an exhausting effort had to be made to persuade him. It was then, apparently, that a new idea occurred to Khvostov. Under the pretext of buying Iliodor's book-in-progress about Rasputin, he would send an agent to Norway to see him. The agent would give Iliodor money and reach an agreement with him about organizing through his supporters in Russia what Iliodor had failed to achieve in 1914 – Rasputin's murder.

Beletsky immediately recommended to Khvostov one of his own people for the job, a certain Boris Rzhevsky.

The provocation began. The naive Khvostov gave Rzhevsky instructions and the documents. Rzhevsky then played everything out according to Beletsky's script. After he had got on the train and was on his way, he provoked a noisy row. When his passport was demanded, he threatened the officer, shouting about his closeness to Minister Khvostov. Rzhevsky was arrested. And in his very first interrogation he testified that he had been sent by Khvostov to negotiate with Iliodor about Rasputin's murder.

Simultaneously, Beletsky informed Iliodor through his agents that important people would be proposing Rasputin's murder to him, and that an agent was already on his way from Khvostov to see him. Beletsky had calculated precisely. Iliodor, who was in very difficult straits in Norway (he was employed as a factory worker), realized that an opportunity was at hand to be reconciled with Rasputin and to return to Russia.

He immediately sent warning telegrams to Vyrubova and Rasputin. From Vyrubova's testimony in the File:

> In the telegram received by Rasputin from Iliodor, it was said that lofty personages were readying an attempt on his life . . . and in the telegram received by me, he [Iliodor] informed me that his wife would be coming to see me and that she would have documents . . . that Khvostov was planning Rasputin's murder . . . A poor, modestly dressed woman then turned up, who began showing me . . . telegrams from Khvostov in which

he offered her husband 60,000 for the murder . . . I think the telegrams were signed. The Sovereign instructed Stürmer to investigate the matter.

Who Would Betray First?

Still not realizing who was behind the business with Rzhevsky, Khvostov rushed to Beletsky to discuss what he should do. Beletsky suggested to him a decisive step, or, more accurately, political suicide: to go to the tsar and show him the external surveillance log on Rasputin. And to lay out everything unambiguously. Khvostov agreed. With what impatience did Beletsky await his return!

According to Beletsky, when he came back, Khvostov said that the tsar took his report and went to the tsarina's chambers. Khvostov heard their conversation in excited tones. Then the tsar returned and, keeping the report, dryly bade him farewell. When after telling his story Khvostov stepped out of his office, Beletsky, as befitted the chief of the secret police, was not too fastidious to inspect the contents of Khvostov's briefcase. In it he found both copies of the report on Rasputin. And he understood what he had suspected all along: that Khvostov hadn't reported anything about Rasputin to the sovereign. In fact, Beletsky soon learned that instead of making a report on Rasputin, Khvostov had given the tsar one about Beletsky. After implicating Beletsky in the conspiracy to murder Rasputin, Khvostov had proposed sending him to the provinces as a governor-general. Thus each had betrayed the other. Beletsky struck another blow in reply. Simanovich gave a statement to the Department of Police that a certain engineer named Heine had come to him and declared that Rzhevsky, on Khvostov's orders, was organizing an attempt on Rasputin's life. Khvostov grasped it all, but it was too late.

From Vyrubova's testimony: 'A terribly agitated Khvostov came to see me. He wept and said that the whole story was a blackmail arranged by Beletsky to dislodge him from his post . . . that none of it was true, that it was a Yid provocation [a reference to Simanovich's statement], and he asked me to inform Their Majesties about it. I carried out his request but received in answer that even if he had not been at fault in the story, he was at fault for having had anything to do with a type like Rzhevsky.'

Such were the circumstances surrounding the opening of the Duma session that the tsar had come to visit! As the peasant had proposed he do! An investigator of the Extraordinary Commission would subsequently ask Prime Minister Stürmer, 'You recall, do you not, that the former emperor was present on 9 February 1916, for the prayer on the occasion of the opening of the Duma? Is it your knowledge that it was Rasputin who had insisted that the tsar go there, that it was he who had told the tsar to visit the Duma?' The idea was a brilliant one. Despite the scandal with Khvostov, the tsar's coming at such a time had calmed the Duma.

The Colonel's Departure

Stürmer's commission had already begun its investigation of the whole story of the assassination cabal and Khvostov's part in it, when Komissarov decided he would opt out of the game. The colonel withdrew in the most spectacular way.

From Komissarov's testimony: 'I went to his [Rasputin's] apartment and in front of Vyrubova and a large number of his devotees told Rasputin off, even using language of the street.' The colonel stood and swore at Rasputin for all his humiliations and mockery and errands, and couldn't stop himself. And thus unburdened his heart. After that he naturally 'didn't see Rasputin any more, and at the end of February 1916' he left Petrograd by his 'own choice and at the insistence of Tsarskoe Selo'. When Beletsky arrived to apologize for Komissarov, Rasputin, according to him, 'sighed and not without chagrin said, "He gave me a painfully hard cussing out, an awfully hard one."' The peasant respected the swearing ability of the true Russian gentleman.

An Anti-Rasputin Pogrom

The work of Stürmer's commission provoked yet another quite unexpected reaction. Realizing that he had been 'put at Stürmer's mercy', Khvostov made a desperate move. He had Simanovich arrested in the middle of the night.

He was taken right from his bed. After which Khvostov announced that he had reason to suspect Rasputin's secretaries of involvement in pro-German espionage! And shortly thereafter more arrests were made among the secretaries. And then Dobrovolsky's and Volynsky's apartments were searched. 'I managed to search them all,' Khvostov proudly testified later. And all were found to possess numerous memoranda attesting to 'Rasputin's patronage'. 'They were all the same, with a cross at the top and the following text: "My dear, sweet fellow, listen and help, Grigory." The subject and addressee weren't mentioned. The addressee could have been anyone you like on any question.' Khvostov threatened to broadcast all over Russia the trade in those memoranda, those peculiar indulgences. Steps were taken to banish Simanovich from Petrograd. Khvostov let loose the rumour that Rasputin's apartment was in line to be searched, as well.

Rasputin was rattled. The eternal fear of the defenceless Russian peasant instantly returned. Alexandra Belling saw Rasputin at the time. 'During tea at his home on Gorokhovaya, after grabbing his head, he shouted, "Villains! Why are you tormenting me? Stop it! Do you not know sorrow? Have you not experienced the wrath of God?" and quickly went off to his room,' she recalled.

Khvostov, in the meantime, circulated another rumour: Rasputin's apartment would be searched in the next few days. There was genuine alarm in Tsarskoe Selo.

From Vyrubova's testimony: 'I then immediately wrote Khvostov a letter . . . not to search Rasputin's apartment, adding, "Supposing it isn't just blackmail." I . . . wrote to Khvostov from the palace, in accordance with what I had been told.' Told, that is, by Alix.

This was more than enough! And at that time, in March 1916, Khvostov was sent into retirement. The infuriated tsar did not even summon him to inform him that he was being retired. The post of minister of internal affairs was free. But Beletsky was unable to take advantage of Khvostov's fall.

From Manasevich's testimony: 'Rasputin said, "Anushka asked me who to appoint minister. I myself do not know who. Beletsky wants it. But if he has not murdered me yet, he certainly will! And the Old Chap is in the chair. Let him sit and rule."'

And Stürmer received the long-awaited portfolio of the minister of internal affairs.

Compromising Material From Bygone Days

And so, the first ministerial appointment made on Andronikov's recommendation clearly had not worked out. With Khvostov's fall, they hurried to get rid of the suspicious 'deputy minister' as well. Beletsky would be sent away to the provinces as a governor-general. But here Beletsky made a blunder. He decided to explain the Rzhevsky matter in the pages of a newspaper – portraying his own innocence and Khvostov's guilt. Khvostov replied at once in the pages of another newspaper. And the details of the activities of the mighty minister who had secretly and ineptly arranged for the peasant's death, the squabbling and the intrigues of the secret police, the peasant's power and invincibility – all that compromising material poured out in waves of newsprint. As Milyukov summarized it in the Duma, after those mutual denunciations, 'the ministry's activities have all appeared before the country like a trashy novel . . . After this, we now understand that the government we have is not merely a bad one; it quite simply does not exist!' To which statement the hall replied with loud calls, 'What about Rasputin?'

That public washing of dirty laundry filled Stürmer, the tsar and the right with indignation. Beletsky was obliged to resign the post of governor-general as well. The tsar recommended that he 'leave Petrograd for a while'.

13

FAREWELL
TO THE TSARS

The Last Spring

Thus began Rasputin's last spring. After all the agitation connected with the searches, he wanted liberty. Work in the fields was starting, and he knew that the land needed the peasant. His son was now working as a medical orderly in the tsarina's infirmary far from their own land.

As always, he decided to stop at Verkhoturye on the way to pay his respects to his favourite saint, to atone by prayer for his carnal sins and to sweetly repent. And in repentance to acquire strength.

And at the beginning of March 1916 Rasputin left Petrograd, seen off as usual by Vyrubova, Munya Golovina, various other devotees and, of course, by Manasevich.

As they were saying their farewells on the platform, those around were horrified to see the mad general's wife, dressed in a shapeless white garment and carrying a basketful of squawking chickens. The File, from the testimony of Lokhtina:

> Father Grigory . . . did not want me to go with him [to Verkhoturye]. Without telling him or the others that I meant to go to Verkhoturye on the same train he was taking, I went to the station and had my things carried into the compartment. Including a basketful of chickens which I was taking to Father Makary . . . Father Grigory angrily ordered me to go several days later . . . Since the second bell had already rung, I quickly had to remove my things by myself. Manasevich, who was standing in the corridor and haughtily gazing at me, said in French, 'She's leaving, too!' I then ordered him in an imperious tone to take out the remaining basket with the chickens, which Manasevich did with a nervous glance around.

The Conspiracy Continues

But Our Friend soon afterwards returned to Petrograd. Alix had called him back, afraid again to let him go for too long, sensing that something was approaching. Many felt that way then.

The young poet Mayakovsky prophesied, '1916 is coming in a revolutionary crown of thorns.' Khvostov was gone, but those powerful people remained who had given Khvostov the large sum for the peasant's murder. And in 1917 Khvostov very carefully named them for the File. 'Dedicated to my intention of eliminating Rasputin were people of the highest society. For example, I talked about it with Princess Zinaida Yusupova, who gave me to understand that for that purpose I could count on unlimited funds. Princess Yusupova . . . as a spokeswoman for the views of the whole grand-ducal milieu, saw clearly that Rasputin was leading the dynasty to destruction.'

Yes, Zinaida Yusupova was a 'spokeswoman for the views of the *entire* grand-ducal milieu'. And the money that Khvostov had received for Rasputin's murder was a mere surface manifestation of the secret activity that by then was proceeding apace.

The Man In The Mask

Glimpsed from time to time in the countless agents' reports on those who visited Rasputin's apartment in 1915–16 is the name of Alexandra Belling.

'Alexandra Alexandrovna Belling, an ensign's wife', was seen by the agents at Rasputin's apartment on 13 February 1916, on 26 October and so on. The thirty-year-old singer, whom it was modish to invite to sing at the most fashionable musical evenings, had sung in Tsarskoe Selo at the tsarina's and in general, as she wrote of herself, 'enjoying favour "at the top" as an artist, I sang whenever and wherever I liked.' She was pretty, and since Rasputin was naturally by no means indifferent to her, she had to fend off his persistent courting. Then one day Alexandra Belling received a remarkable letter in the mail.

I found a manuscript excerpt of her recollections about that mysterious letter in the archive of Rasputin's murderer Felix Yusupov.

Belling recalled:

One morning, while I was going through my mail, I found an envelope in an unfamiliar hand. Opening it, I read the following: 'Believe that what I am about to say has been carefully thought over and places a great and serious responsibility on you. Tomorrow at 6:00 p.m. I shall call to find out where and when I may hope to meet with you. I suggest that you not come alone. The one with you may wear a mask, as I myself shall do.' What a joke, I thought.

But at 6:00 p.m. her telephone rang. 'I heard a low, beautiful, rather dry voice.' The voice suggested they meet. The singer decided to go along and told the stranger:

'Tomorrow I shall dine at the Donon. Since the only way you will show yourself is in a mask, which I find amusing, I shall have to dine in a private room. I've reserved No. 6. Make no mistake – I shall be waiting for you there at 7:00 p.m. sharp.' I then sent a wire to my friend K., asking him to be my escort. He was notable for his direct nature and clear mind. By 7:00 K. and I had already finished eating and were having coffee. Not five minutes had passed when a tall, dignified figure came in. And even though he did not take off his coat and his face was covered by a mask, it seemed to me that I had seen him before.

And the stranger began to speak.

'I ask that you hear me out in silence, without interrupting. We are aware of your views on everything that is taking place around us now, and we propose in all deliberation that you choose a way of eliminating Rasputin. We shall not tell you that we can shield you from revenge from "above". It's even likely that they will destroy you. But knowing that the purpose of your life is your daughter, we guarantee that she will be royally provided for the rest of her life.' He asked me to take my time before answering and to think about it, and then with a bow he left.

'For God's sake don't get mixed up in that business!' K. exclaimed. 'To hell with all their proposals! To hell with them! My poor friend, do you know what a type like that wants? He wants to prevent a revolution and save the dynasty. Who among them has the resolve to kill that vermin? They're worried about their own skins. Beware of them and don't touch him. Wait a bit, the time hasn't come yet. But it's getting closer. Another two or three strokes of the brush and Russia will be saved.'

Why did Rasputin's murderer preserve this document in his archive?

And why did Belling send the fragment to Felix in the first place?

I think because Felix was well acquainted with the man in the mask. A tall figure – but for the last tsar, all the Romanovs were very tall. And the hint that 'I had seen him before'. She, who had visited court gatherings, had recognized that man, despite his mask. And, of course, Yusupov had recognized the man in the mask and for that reason had held onto the manuscript. Most likely, the man was Felix's father-in-law, Grand Duke Alexander Mikhailovich (Sandro), who would soon plead with the tsar to get rid of Rasputin. So together with Felix's mother, who had contributed money for Rasputin's murder, men from the grand-ducal family were also active with their money. But their actions were unsuccessful. For the time being.

A Prophecy

But the noose round the peasant's neck was getting tighter and he felt it. And now he repeated ever more frequently a frightening prophecy: as long as I am alive, the dynasty shall live.

From Badmaev's testimony in the File: 'Visiting Rasputin and observing his security guard, I asked him, "Aren't you afraid?"

"No," he answered, "I am not afraid for myself, but I am afraid for the people and the royal family. Because when they kill me, things will go badly for the people. And there won't be any tsar."'

One can imagine what Alix felt when she heard that. And how worried she must have been about his life. What was it? The cunning of an intelligent peasant who had decided that that was a way to defend himself? Or was it in fact one of the visions that haunted that mysterious person?

And all that time Alix, who was helpless in such matters, had been trying to arrange for his security. The tsarina had naturally entrusted the organization of Rasputin's safety to Stürmer who, she knew, had worked for a long time in the ministry of internal affairs. As Stürmer testified, 'After Komissarov left, Rasputin was only guarded by the security department. Towards the end Rasputin started drinking a great deal, and the security people complained that it was impossible to keep an eye on him, since various motors would keep coming for him and taking him away who knows where.' Realizing that murder could not be avoided, the security department thus washed its hands of it ahead of time. And Stürmer washed his hands, too. The obligation of guarding Rasputin was dangerous and unpleasant to him. And so he found him a bodyguard. 'We needed someone who could more or less judge who might be dangerous and undesirable, which is something the lower-ranking agents could not do. That is where Manasevich-Manuilov proved useful. He was well received in the family.' Now the peasant's security, and with it all future responsibility, were lodged with Manasevich. With Alix's consent, although she had a poor grasp of such matters.

Rasputin was doomed. The agents followed him as before but security was lax. The peasant could tell by the scent that the wolf was circling. And drawing closer. And for that reason he decided to leave the capital for the summer – to abandon the 'tsars'.

A View Of Rasputin Through The Window

Preserved in the Extraordinary Commission archive is an amusing diary. It contains a description of Rasputin's life by a neighbour, a Synod official named Blagoveschensky: 'His kitchen was right across from my own, so I could see everything extremely well.' He could also hear extremely well, since Rasputin lived on the other side of the wall.

And he watched and listened and wrote it all down in his diary.

15 June. I'm writing at home in my study, and a bacchanalia of some sort has been taking place on the other side of the wall. A binge, evidently, before his return to his native region. Dancing, laughter. By 12:00 musicians arrived, a string orchestra from some amusement park. They played and sang operetta tunes accompanied by loud dancing . . . Georgian songs have been repeatedly sung by a baritone [presumably, Rasputin's daughter's fiancé Pankhadze]. The binge continued until early in the morning. By the end separate drunken voices could be heard and the dancing of one person. Apparently he himself had let go completely and was singing and dancing solo. They constantly came to the kitchen for snacks of fruit and bottles of wine, more and more ladies and young women, all animated, flushed, cheerful in a free-and-easy way. The ladies themselves washed all the dishes.

Farewell To Saint Simeon

As he was leaving Petrograd, Rasputin warned his devotees to value the time with him.

From Manasevich's testimony: 'At the end of 1916 in my and Vyrubova's presence, he assured his devotees that he had another five years left in the world [during which time, according to Vyrubova, he had promised that the heir would finally 'outgrow his illness']. And then he would withdraw from the world and all those close to him to a remote place known only to him, where he would be saved by following an ascetic way of life.' Manasevich didn't understand: Rasputin was again reminding them of the words of Jesus – 'I shall not always be with you'; he was reminding them of the *Khlyst* mystery – of the One who was supposed to be living in him.

But Alix soon afterwards called him back. And again he returned to the threatening capital, empty for the summer, eternally damp from its wet winds. Then at the end of the summer he broke free again to go to his peasant labours, the gathering of the harvest. And again he caroused before his departure, so that they would remember Grishka. A time of troubles was coming, and who knew if he would ever come back. And again his indignant neighbour wrote it all down in his diary.

'A binge continued all night. A Gypsy chorus of about forty people was invited. They sang and danced until 3:00 a.m. He has in fact been drinking heavily since 6 August and pressing himself on the servant girls in the courtyard and sneaking off with them to kiss. On 9 August he went back to his village, they say.'

He did not go by himself. As if he sensed that it was for the last time. He took the most loyal of his devotees to the Verkhoturye Monastery with him to make obeisance for the last time to the relics of Saint Simeon. The lame Vyrubova, accompanied by her maid Maria Belyaeva and the medical orderly Akim Zhuk, and Lili Dehn, Munya Golovina, and Rasputin's two daughters were all lodged at the monastery inn and resolutely endured the dirt and the swarms of bedbugs. Father Grigory himself stayed in a cell at the monastery. From the inn they drove to see the anchorite Makary at Verkhoturye, where in a small room built onto his cell the mad general's wife was also staying at the time. She carried firewood, cleaned, and washed his cell and prayed. From the testimony of the maid Belyaeva in the File: 'Lokhtina lived in a special cell . . . dressed all in white with little icons on her breast . . . Vyrubova and I spent the night with her. Dehn spent the night with us, too. The next day we went back to the monastery, where Saint Simeon's relics were kept.'

After paying his respects to Saint Simeon, Rasputin set off with his daughters for Pokrovskoe, while his devotees returned to the capital. They didn't know that it was their last parting with his monastery.

A Line For Conversations
With Berlin

But at the end of August Alix summoned him once again. And back in the capital he again felt doomed. At the time they were already saying on every corner and in every home that Rasputin was in the pay of German agents. And Rasputin, and the tsarina who deferred to him, and Vyrubova – the 'dark forces' – decided to lead Russia out of the war. 'Rasputin and treason weren't even talked about but simply referred to as self-evident,' wrote the celebrated man of letters Victor Shklovsky.

The 'dark forces', the danger of a separate peace with Germany, and getting rid of Rasputin were the ideas by which society lived at the time. Interspersed in the diary of Grand Duke Andrei Vladimirovich are lines like, 'Alix is remarkably unpopular'; 'O God, save Russia! Anything but that shameful peace'; 'Yesterday a sister of mercy from the Winter Palace reported that they have a secret phone line for conversations with Berlin.'

A main task of the Extraordinary Commission in 1917 was to establish as fact the tsarina's secret relations with her German relatives and their plans for a separate peace. However, the Commission could establish nothing of the sort. On the contrary, the facts confirmed the 'tsars'' innocence. When at the end of 1916 the German government approached the Entente with an offer of peace, Nicholas replied that 'the time for peace negotiations has not yet arrived, since the achievement by Russia of the goal of taking Constantinople and the Straits, as well as the creation of a free Poland from the three territories now partitioned, still has not been assured.' The British ambassador Sir George Buchanan made the same point in his memoirs by quoting a cable he had sent to the Foreign Office in February 1918: 'the one point on which we can count on his [the emperor's] remaining firm is the war, more especially as the empress, who virtually governs Russia, is herself sound on this question.' And Rasputin himself had declared several times that he was for fighting on until victory.

Her Secret . . . Her Tragedy

From Manasevich's testimony: 'Rasputin would say, "If I had been there at the beginning of the war, there would have been no war. But since they have already started it, it has to be carried through to the end. If there's an argument, then argue, but if it's a half-argument, it will still be an argument."' About her [the tsarina] he said, 'she is terribly in favour of continuing the war. But there have been moments when she has wept, thinking her brother had been wounded or killed.'

The master of the royal yacht *Standart*, Nikolai Sablin, who was very close to the 'tsars', said the same thing: 'The sovereign advocated carrying on the war to victory . . . and the empress viewed the war the same way.' No documents attesting to the contrary have been found.

The ashes found in Alix's fireplace after the February Revolution do indicate the burning of numerous documents, however. The question has naturally remained as to just what she burned. Something intimate? But then why have all the intimate letters about jealousy survived? And what could the tsarina, who was utterly devoted to her family, possibly have regarded as taboo? No, it's more likely that she burned something else, something dangerous to her.

In her correspondence with the tsar, there are references as early as September 1915 to letters from her brother Ernie, who so wanted that peace. Was it not his letters that had been turned to ashes in her fireplace? Actually, there's evidence enough in the documents that have remained:

'1 Nov. 1915 . . . Our Friend was always against this war, saying the Balkans were not worth the world to fight about.' But Nicky was silent. True to his ruinous obligations to his allies, he did not wish to understand her appeal. And she did not dare to continue. That topic was forbidden to her, whom the crowd called the 'German woman'.

But now in 1916, with a premonition of danger, she moved from calls to actions of a sort. In the last autumn of their reign, she wrote to her husband:

'18 Sept. . . . Put all my trust in God's mercy, only tell me when the attack is to begin, so as that He can particularly pray then; – it means too much & He realizes your suffering.'

The reference is to the offensive then being readied by General Brusilov. And then suddenly the attack did not take place. Nicholas called it off, to the great surprise of Headquarters. It turned out that Alix had pleaded with him not to go on with it, citing as always the predictions of Our Friend. And Our Friend naturally greeted Nicky's decision with joy.

'23 Sept. . . . Our friend says about the new orders you gave to Brussilov etc.: "Very satisfied with father's orders, all will be well." He won't mention it to a soul,' she wrote to her husband. But they had forgotten about the tsar's character. Those around him persuaded him to change his mind. And General Brusilov proceeded with his offensive.

'24 Sept. . . . Lovy, our Friend is much put out that Brussilov has not listened to yr. order to stop the advance – says you were inspired from above to give that order . . . & God wld. bless it. – Now he says again useless losses. Hopes you will still insist, as now all is not right.'

And the sovereign and commander-in-chief justified himself.

24 September. I have just received your telegram in which you report that our Friend is very upset. When I gave that order, I did not know that Gurko [who commanded an army] had decided to combine all the forces remaining at his command and prepare an attack jointly with the Guards and the neighbouring forces. That combination gives hope of success. These details are for you alone – I beg of you, dear one. Tell Him only that Papa has ordered that reasonable measures be taken!

He was concerned. He had heard about the spies in the elder's midst.

But she pleaded again. '25 Sept. . . . Oh, give your order again to Brussilov – stop this useless slaughter . . . Stick to it, you are head master & all will thank you on their knees – and our glorious guard! – Those boggs, impregnable – open spaces, impossible to hide, few woods, soon leaves will fall & no saving shelter for advance . . . Our generals don't count the 'lives' any – hardened to losses – & that is sin . . . God blesses yr. idea – have it executed – spare those lives.'

Those letters were the real expression of her thoughts, thoughts of which Buchanan was unaware: no advances whatsoever were needed; what was needed was to stop the war. Not long before, as the result of an unsuccessful offensive on the western front, 80,000 men had been lost over nine days. If the new offensive also miscarried, there would be terrible casualties, bringing closer an uprising among the people. But if the offensive should prove successful, that would a mean a continuation of the war and again produce the inevitable uprising, as Father Grigory had prophesied. For on his return from the village, Our Friend had been constantly telling Alix how much the peasants hated the war. And she was happy: the peasant had told her exactly what she wanted to hear – that the war must be ended at all costs.

The Clear Minds Of The 'Dark Forces'

The most amazing part is that at the time Alix and the peasant were the only ones who were right. Neither the great Romanov family, nor the court, nor the Russian bourgeoisie, nor the Progressive Bloc in the Duma had grasped that the war must stop. As not only the fate of the monarchy but also the downfall of the Provisional Government that came after it would eventually prove. It was the reason for the victory of the Bolsheviks, who understood and put into play the central idea of ending the war at all costs. Just as the Bolsheviks' predecessors, the 'dark forces', the last tsarina and Rasputin, had wanted to do. The 'dark forces' could have saved the empire.

Presumably, this was all reflected in her correspondence with her brother Ernie, and it was the letters from him that she burned.

And it was the reason behind a secret meeting that took place in Sweden, which the Provisional Government's Extraordinary Commission just could not figure out.

It's unlikely that anyone could have predicted then in the summer of

1916 that the Deputy Speaker of the Duma, Alexander Protopopov, that charmer and darling of the Duma opposition, that Lovelace and favourite of fortune, would in a matter of months become the most detested man in Russian political life.

In the summer of 1916 Protopopov was the head of a Duma delegation to Sweden.

In Stockholm he met a German named Warburg.

Warburg, the brother of a well-known German businessman, was attached to the German embassy in Stockholm. During his meeting with Protopopov, Warburg informed him of 'Uncle Willy's' wish to conclude a separate peace with his former friend Nicky and of the possible conditions for that peace. The peace that the German emperor was offering Russia was an honourable and advantageous one. On the delegation's return Protopopov made a report to Nicholas about his conversation. Nicholas, touchingly keeping his word to his allies, took a dim view of Protopopov's meeting and found the discussion of peace premature. With that the matter died. Protopopov was one of the leaders of the Duma opposition who had demanded war until victory, and it would never have occurred to anyone at the time to suspect him of dealings with the Germans.

The Favourite Of The Ladies
And The Deputies

Sheila Lunts's finding Protopopov boozing with Rasputin in Knirsha's disreputable apartment had been no accident. It turned out that the Duma's favourite had all along been in secret contact with Rasputin, the man most despised by the Duma.

Rasputin and Protopopov had been brought together by their mutual acquaintance Badmaev, the doctor of Tibetan medicine.

Alexander Protopopov was a typical figure of the end of the empire, a product of a decadent time. Brilliantly educated, he had been trained in a Jesuit college in Paris. He was charming in society, was an excellent pianist, and a friend of the famous Jules Massenet. But all these gifts had somehow been deformed and had become rotten in him. For that intelligent man was also quite mad! In both the literal and the figurative sense. Even during his service in the Horse Guards regiment he had been notorious for his participation in the most shameful orgies. He had reduced his extremely large fortune to disorder with his risky entertainment. As a result of his neglected venereal disease he had sought the acquaintance of Doctor

Badmaev, who undertook to treat what conventional medicine had given up on. Protopopov was suffering from the onset of progressive paralysis and attacks of severe depression. His only hope lay in Badmaev's mysterious Tibetan remedies.

At the end of 1915 Protopopov was again undergoing treatment at Badmaev's clinic. It was then that Badmaev learned from his friend Rasputin of the search for new ministers. And Badmaev, who had been trying his whole life to play a part in grand politics, this time did not let his chance slip away. Protopopov was the darling of the Duma. Here was the one the tsar needed. His patient would reconcile parliament and the government. Gentle and well brought up, he could not fail to be liked in Tsarskoe Selo. That ailing, weak-willed person would serve the tsarina uncomplainingly. And he would not forget his physician, either. An 'audition' took place – Protopopov's introduction to Rasputin.

From Protopopov's testimony before the Extraordinary Commission: 'Badmaev advised Rasputin to take me into the government . . . Badmaev wanted to make me Chairman of the Council of Ministers, and he had faith in the degree of Rasputin's influence over the tsar and tsarina. "If he wants it, he will obtain it."'

Protopopov's clandestine meetings with the peasant began after that. And it was then that their mutual friend, the pretty Sheila Lunts, first made her appearance. A woman who had visited Rasputin with very little success. But whom Protopopov started visiting with a great deal of it.

The File, from the testimony of Sheila Lunts: 'He impressed me as a gentle, intelligent, and enchanting person . . . At the time I was pining for my husband, and Protopopov would come by in the evenings to chat with me.'

And sometimes Rasputin would also come by 'to chat' with Protopopov.

The File, from the testimony of Filippov: 'Protopopov went to see her with exceptional frequency for meetings with her personally, and later on in the presence of Rasputin, who would be invited there . . . Protopopov started behaving in an extraordinarily secretive way once he had obtained Rasputin's promise to help him get the post of minister of internal affairs.'

Rasputinism

The road to power now ran through private restaurants and the apartments of tarts. The tsar, being at General Staff Headquarters, had ceded the disposition of power to the tsarina, the tsarina had entrusted it to the crafty peasant, and the peasant had entrusted it to crafty rascals. And the semi-feudal country's crafty financiers bought the power from the rascals. At the same time, all those crafty people were struggling and scheming against each other, drawing each other into cunning traps, and slinging mud. They all practised to perfection the art of mutual extermination, although without realizing that it was rocking the common boat, the very one they were in themselves. And which even so was just barely afloat. As is clear today in Russia at the beginning of a new millennium.

Only then it all ended in catastrophe.

Treated Affectionately By The Tsar

Let us return to June 1916 when Protopopov, after his return from Sweden and his discussions with Warburg, was first received by the sovereign.

Despite the tsar's dissatisfaction with his having met Warburg, Protopopov nevertheless 'was treated affectionately by the tsar'.

The File, from Vyrubova's testimony: 'This was typical of the sovereign, who would sometimes take an unaccountable liking to people on his first meeting with them.'

I think that the Friend was dissembling, as usual. Nicholas had been predisposed to like Protopopov. For the meeting with Warburg had been Protopopov's first commission for the tsarina. He, yesterday's fighter for war until victory, had brought back proposals for a separate peace. And it wasn't his fault that Nicholas had not dared to oppose those around him or the Duma and had remained loyal to his allies.

But during their meeting the tsar had understood: Rasputin was right, this favourite of the Duma was ready to carry out any commission for the 'tsars'. That is why Nicholas was so indulgent with the gentle Protopopov, who was so different from his previous loud-mouthed ministers. And at the end of the audience, he said something personal to him, something heartfelt. Protopopov recalled how through a door he 'had seen Alexei playing, and the sovereign suddenly remarked, "You cannot imagine what a comfort that boy is to me and how reluctant I am to let him go".'

Thus, a place was assumed near the throne by Protopopov, whom Rasputin would call 'Kalinin' or 'General Kalinin.'

From Badmaev's testimony: 'The nickname 'Kalinin' was given to Protopopov by Rasputin.'

And when Badmaev in surprise corrected Rasputin, the peasant said, 'It doesn't matter! Everybody at the sovereign's laughs when I call him Kalinin.'

Among the *Khlysty* nicknames were used to conceal real names. And the tsarina, who was fond of secrets and accustomed to hiding her inner life from the court, quickly made Rasputin's nicknames a part of the code used in her letters, which the court was so anxious to intercept. The railway minister was called 'Steely', Stürmer was referred to as the 'Old Chap', Khvostov was the 'Tail' and 'Fat Belly', Bishop Varnava was the 'Gopher', the tsar and tsarina were 'Papa and Mama', and so on.

The Warburg business was the beginning of Protopopov's advancement.

And as he himself testified, 'Rasputin told me I would not be chairman of the Council of Ministers at once but would first receive the post of minister of internal affairs.' He was supposed to become the second prime minister and the first minister of internal affairs to be advanced by the peasant. The long-awaited alliance of which Nicholas had dreamed at the beginning of his reign, that of the peasantry and the autocracy, had become a reality.

Why Had The 'Old Chap' Become So Bold?

Rasputin had by then already come to the realization that Stürmer had his own plans. More to the point, they were not the same ones that his predecessors Kokovtsev and Khvostov had had. They all kept to the same scheme: first use Rasputin, conclude an alliance with him, and then push him out of the way. The intelligent and intuitive Rasputin immediately sensed that the 'Old Chap' was playing his own game and avoiding meetings with him and 'Mama'. And avoiding them with Manasevich, too.

Manasevich was used to serving two masters; that is, he punctually sent Stürmer in envelopes marked 'secret' whatever information he had gleaned from Rasputin about what was happening in Tsarskoe Selo. Yet whenever they met, the prime minister would imperiously disregard him. And soon afterwards Stürmer simply reassigned him from his office to the command of the Department of Police. And Metropolitan Pitirim, according to Manasevich, 'was also disgruntled; he felt Stürmer was becoming more abrupt with him on the phone'.

Rasputin reacted to the prime minister's behaviour in his own way. As Manasevich testified, during his meetings with him the peasant would shout at the empire's highest official, 'Don't you dare go against Mama's wishes! Make sure I don't turn my back on you! Then you'll be done for!' When Manasevich would try to bring him to reason (thereby provoking him even more), Rasputin would distinctly explain, 'The Old Chap does not defer to Mama. He's started to hop about on his own and will soon break his neck. The wishes of Mama, the true prime minister, are law!'

By August the peasant realized that the prime minister had become dangerous. In August a powerful blow was struck against Rasputin: Manasevich was arrested.

Manasevich needed money. His constant card playing and his expensive mistress required a great deal of it. And in August 1916 the deputy director of the Moscow Union Bank informed the new director of the Department of Police, General E. Klimovich, that Manasevich had demanded 25,000 roubles from him, promising that with Rasputin's help his bank's transactions would not be audited.

And instead of informing Tsarskoe Selo, Klimovich at once set wheels in motion.

On Klimovich's advice, the banknote numbers were copied out, and Manasevich, the person closest to Rasputin, was arrested red-handed right on the street. The peasant realized that Klimovich would never have dared to do such a thing without Stürmer's support. And it was in fact learned in Tsarskoe Selo that Stürmer had said after Manasevich's arrest, 'Finally, that scoundrel and blackmailer is behind bars.'

Manasevich's bank accounts were sequestrated. It emerged that at the end of 1915 and the beginning of 1916 alone the enormous sum of 260,000 roubles had appeared in one of Manasevich's accounts at the Crédit Lyonnais. Rasputin hurried to 'Mama'. But there was nothing Alix could say. To speak out in defence of a Jew proven guilty of taking such bribes was not something she dared to do. Manasevich languished in jail.

Yet why had Stürmer suddenly become so bold, losing his fear of the dangerous peasant? Perhaps the old fox, having at his disposal the full extent of the information obtained by the secret police, knew that he would soon be free of Rasputin?

Rasputin's father had recently died, but Grigory did not go to his funeral. He sent his son to the requiem mass that was celebrated forty days after the burial, 'since he himself had to remain behind at the tsars' request'. According to the agents, Rasputin spoke of his father's death 'with appealing sorrow', although the agents recalled in their reports how mercilessly he had beaten his father. They were city people and did not understand: he beat his father just as his father had once beaten his grandfather.

But Rasputin loved his father, just as his father had once loved his grandfather.

Meanwhile, the offensive against Rasputin continued with another blow. The wife of the banker Rubinstein came to see Vyrubova in Tsarskoe Selo.

And fell on her knees before her. It turned out that Rubinstein, one of the wealthiest men in Russia, had been arrested at his home on the terrible charge of espionage. Rubinstein had bought up securities of the Anchor Insurance Company and had sold them at a profit to a Swedish insurance company. But among the securities, the plans of some 'Ukrainian sugar factories' insured by Anchor had been found. That was enough. A second member of Rasputin's 'Brain Trust' was behind bars. Alix and Our Friend knew that a new prime minister and a new minister of internal affairs needed to be found at once.

The Tsarina's Secret Banker?

Now in her letters to Nicky Alix constantly asked that Protopopov be appointed the new minister of internal affairs. Or, more accurately, it was not she who asked but Our Friend.

'7 Sept. 1916. My own sweetheart . . . Grigory begs you earnestly to name Protopopov there. You know him & had such a good impression of him – happens to be of the Duma . . . & so will know how to be with them . . . I don't know him, but I believe in our Friend's wisdom & guidance . . . His love for you & Russia is so intense & God has sent Him to be yr. help & guide & prays so hard for you.'

But Nicky was dubious. '9 September . . . I must think about that question . . . Our Friend's opinions about people are sometimes quite odd, as you yourself know. One should therefore be careful, especially where appointments to high positions are concerned.'

At the time Rubinstein was still in jail. He had been interrogated by the investigators of the Special Commission for Crimes on the home front. And soon afterwards rumours began circulating in society that Rubinstein was the tsarina's secret banker and had been introduced to her by Rasputin. And that through him she had covertly passed on money to her German relatives who had been impoverished in the war.

There are no documents to prove that. But unlike in the arrest of Manasevich, Alix did not remain neutral regarding that of the banker. And to her calls to the tsar for a new minister were added her demands concerning the ill-fated Rubinstein. It was not long before Nicholas gave in to her pressure. And on 18 September Protopopov was, to the utter astonishment of the Duma, appointed to the office of director of the ministry of internal affairs. And in anticipation of Nicky's meeting with his new minister, Alix sent her husband an outline for the conversation. In the name of Our Friend, naturally.

'27 Sept. . . . Keep my little list before you – our Friend begged for you to speak of all these things to Protopopov.'

And the second item in her list of speaking points was about Rubinstein. She wrote, 'Rubinstein to send away' (that is, to secure his release from jail and, more importantly, from investigation). She was very worried about the banker's fate.

An Apotheosis

It was with good reason that the singer Belling wrote about Rasputin's 'regal bearing'. No favourite had achieved such power since the times of the eighteenth-century Russian empresses. And the great Romanov family, the court and the ministers did everything on the sly, relying on conspiracy. They did not dare to proceed openly. General Klimovich, who had impudently arrested Manasevich, was immediately removed from his post. And Stürmer, who had presumed to oppose Rasputin – his days were numbered. 'Ours' – the shadow cabinet consisting of the tsarina, Anya, and Rasputin, together with the new minister of internal affairs and the secret police under his control – intended to rule Russia. As before, the symbol of loyalty for the tsarina was Our Friend. All enmity towards him was punished. In her letter of 15 September, the tsarina asked Nicky to replace the Petrograd governor Obolensky, who together with his sister, a maid of honour, had had the temerity to speak out against Rasputin. And who was at once accused of taking bribes.

The Petrograd governor, Prince Alexander Obolensky, a scion of one of the oldest Russian families and a major general in his Majesty's retinue, thereupon debased himself in the most direct sense – he wept before the peasant.

> 28 Sept. . . . Sweety, fancy only, Obolensky asked to see our Friend & sent a splendid motor for him . . . Received him very nervously at first & then spoke more & more till at the end of the hour began to cry – then Gr. went away as He saw it was the moment the Soul was completely touched . . . he will always ask our Friend's advice about everything . . . Then showed all the 20 letters our Friend had these years sent with petitions all tidily tied up – & said he had fulfilled when he could . . . I cld. not get over the idea that he, that proud man, had come around . . . Our Fr. says its very much in the <u>spiritual sense</u> that a man, a soul like [Obolensky] shld. have quite come to him.

The prince had wept. Somehow they forgot all about the bribes, and

Obolensky received an honourable assignment at the front as a brigade commander. How many of the proud had been forced to yield! Although one can imagine how in their humiliation they hated the mighty peasant.

Hold To The Centre, Mama!

And so, the new minister Protopopov had arrived. A new minister of internal affairs with incipient progressive paralysis. It was a symbol of authority.

Unlike his predecessors, Protopopov was prepared to deal with Rasputin. As Beletsky testified, 'In his relations with Rasputin, he was no novice like those who had been friendly with Rasputin, thinking him a simple man, and then got caught.' The Tsarskoe Selo 'cabinet' could be happy; it had found an obedient minister who at the same time was liked by the Duma. Rasputin told Manasevich, 'We made a mistake with Fat Belly, because he too was one of these rightist fools. I tell you that all the rightists are fools. This time we have chosen between the right and the left – Protopopov.' The peasant also spoke the best phrase about the members of the Russian parliament: 'Both our rightists and leftists are fools. You, Mama, hold to the centre.'

Yet what was the tsar's astonishment when the Duma greeted the appointment of yesterday's favourite with violent hatred. And merely because the tsarina and Rasputin had supported him. Not the senile Goremykin, nor Stürmer, nor any of the later prime ministers provoked such hatred as the Duma's former colleague.

From Guchkov's testimony: 'If Protopopov had been a confirmed enemy, I wouldn't have disdained having anything to do with him. But Protopopov made a volte-face not from conviction but out of career considerations helped along by the shady go-betweens Badmaev and Rasputin.'

Protopopov's peculiar meeting with the German Warburg was immediately recalled and linked to his appointment as minister. The unhappy 'tsars' had no idea what had happened. Nicholas even lost his temper for the first time!

From Vyrubova's testimony: 'When opposing voices were heard in the press and in society . . . the sovereign was surprised at how a person elected by the Duma to be its Deputy Speaker and then its representative abroad could in just a month become a scoundrel . . . After his report [to the tsar or tsarina] Protopopov would sometimes drop by to see me. He . . . impressed me as a very nervous person, and constantly complained of the fact that everyone was hounding him.'

Meanwhile, the new minister's oddities were becoming ever more apparent. And his severe attacks of neurasthenia — the result of his terrible disease — compelled him to seek the help of the celebrated psychiatrist Vladimir Bekhterev.

But he apparently concealed from the investigators one other doctor. Could Protopopov have failed to turn to Rasputin, who was regarded as a great healer? So Rasputin presumably also took part in easing the sufferings of the unhappy minister. That too would have been a source of his dependence on Rasputin.

The Lady Behind The Scenes

Protopopov at the time was very much alone. The good-looking Sheila had dropped him.

The File, from the testimony of Sheila Lunts: 'After returning home, my husband was displeased about my seeing Protopopov, and,' she ingenuously added, 'after Protopopov had arranged the right of residence for my father and sister in Petrograd, I stopped seeing him.'

And here, it seems that Rasputin was able to help. A lady of his circle rescued the minister from his loneliness. A lady, moreover, who had, according to the police reports been very close to Rasputin. And who at the time had a responsible role in the Tsarskoe Selo 'shadow cabinet'.

The File, from Vyrubova's testimony: 'But even more often than he came to see me, Protopopov would drop by to visit a nurse from my infirmary, Voskoboinikova, with whom he would sometimes also have dinner . . . I told him it was awkward, but he objected that he found the simple circumstances restful.'

The File, from the testimony of Feodosia Voino, Vyrubova's maid: 'Protopopov frequently came to see Vyrubova at the infirmary where Voskoboinikova worked. She was an intermediary between Vyrubova and Protopopov . . . The people who were closest to Vyrubova and the ones she trusted the most were Voskoboinikova and Laptinskaya.'

Voskoboinikova has remained behind the scenes in Rasputin's story. Even though she, like Laptinskaya, played a very serious part in it.

After the fall of the regime in 1917, Voskoboinikova was tracked down by the police and required to give the testimony preserved in the File.

At The Feeding Trough

Nadezhda Ivanovna Voskoboinikova, thirty years old, was the widow of a Cossack officer. After the death of her husband in 1911, she came from the provinces to Petrograd and took up with the family of Senator V. N. Mamontov, who was sixty-eight years old and deeply religious. According to Voskoboinikova, 'Mamontov's wife did not understand that friendship and even divorced him.' The police didn't understand it either, referring to her as 'Mamontov's lover' in their reports. It was in fact through Mamontov that Voskoboinikova acquired the most useful of her acquaintances when, 'on the grounds of religious inquiry', he invited Rasputin to his home.

Thus did Voskoboinikova begin her ascent to the palace.

'In 1915 . . . my nerves were in a shambles.' And although Mamontov did warn her that 'visiting Rasputin would be awkward in view of the rumours about him', she went to see the peasant. 'Rasputin encouraged me and said that God would help.'

After that, the investigator naturally asked her a very disagreeable question, to which she proudly replied, 'Not only did I not see Rasputin at night, I did not see any of my acquaintances then.' But the external agents' reports give information of a different kind, and that information was the reason for the investigator's question.

Although she had apparently visited 'the little room with the sofa', she, like many of her predecessors, was not invited back there again. And she could boldly declare: 'Rasputin did not permit himself to take any liberties with me.'

After Mamontov's death, which 'Rasputin had foretold', according to Voskoboinikova, Father Grigory did not forget her, and she found a position at Vyrubova's infirmary.

Rasputin was right to value her – she knew how to be useful. And soon afterwards she became a senior nurse and was introduced to the empress by the Friend. And the Empress, captivated by her devotion to Our Friend and the Friend, suggested that she 'take the infirmary more decisively into her hands'. Telegrams have survived from which it is apparent that the tsarina greatly confided in Voskoboinikova in those final months of power. 'It's terribly hard and difficult,' the tsarina complained to Voskoboinikova from Headquarters on 14 November 1916.

It was in the autumn of 1916 that through Rasputin, Voskoboinikova met the minister suffering from loneliness. Through her it would now be possible to address petitions to the Friend and obviously to Protopopov. She thus took her place at the feeding trough.

The File, from the testimony of Voino: 'She came to us completely destitute . . . But very rapidly she turned into a chic young lady with a mass of precious things made of gold and had her own apartment on Nevsky Avenue . . . She treated Protopopov . . . familiarly, as he did her. He was not shy about putting his arm around her waist in my presence.'

In 1916 she occupied the same position in relation to Vyrubova that Laptinskaya did in relation to Rasputin. We shall find Voskoboinikova's and Laptinskaya's names in the lobby register among those few people who were received by the tsarina. And in the 'shadow cabinet', Voskoboinikova and Laptinskaya linked the 'dark forces' – Rasputin, Vyrubova, the tsarina, and Protopopov – together in a single chain. It was through them that the latter sent each other their most secret and important messages. It was through Voskoboinikova that the peasant, the tsarina, and Anya controlled the ailing minister.

The Dance Of Death

Although he had achieved great power, the peasant lived in constant fear.

The threat of an attempt on his life haunted him. Belling tells how when Osipenko wanted to rouse the drunken Rasputin and take him away, it was enough for him to yell, 'What are you doing! They're readying an attempt against us here, and you're stuck in your chair!' And Rasputin would 'quickly put on his jacket and fur coat, pull his fur cap down over his head, and rush for the exit'.

With Komissarov's departure and Manasevich's arrest, he was only guarded by the security branch detail. And he realized that they could hand him over to his adversaries at any moment.

The File, from Filippov's testimony: 'Coming to see me now, he would try to get drunk as quickly as possible, demand Gypsies and entertainment, and if there was anything he was keen about, it was dancing.'

In drunkenness and dancing he sought to forget himself and recover a feeling of joy. He did not want to, but he sensed that a conspiracy was approaching. And it scared him.

Alix was already writing to Nicky, '21 Sept. 1916 . . . these brutes Rodzianko, Guchkov . . . & Co. are at the bottom of far more than one sees (I feel it) so as to force things out of the hands of the ministers. But you will see all soon & speak it over, & I'll ask our Fr.'s advice. – So often He has sound ideas others go by – God inspires Him.'

And the 'far more' occurred. The last act had begun – the fall of the empire.

Shortly thereafter, on 1 November the whole country was shaken by a speech given in the Duma by Pavel Milyukov, the leader of the most influential opposition party, the Constitutional Democrats: 'From border to border dark rumours have been spreading of betrayal and treason. The rumours have penetrated the highest circles and spared no one. The empress's name has been repeated ever more frequently along with those of the adventurers who surround her . . . Is it stupidity or is it treason?'

And the word 'treason', which fitted the mood of the badly wounded army, was immediately taken on faith and firmly rooted in the consciousness of millions.

Alix demanded that Stürmer take action. She was in a fury, and this time Stürmer was too frightened to refuse. He summoned Rodzyanko. The 'Old Chap' had at the time sprained his ankle and couldn't walk. The effect was comical. The helpless Stürmer, lying in bed with his leg elevated, tried to reprimand the enormous, powerful Rodzyanko, who towered over the prostrate prime minister.

From Rodzyanko's testimony: 'He said . . . he was asking me for a copy of Milyukov's speech with the object of instituting a criminal action against him. I answered that I would not be sending him any copies whatever, [and said] "What are you defending him [Rasputin] for? He's a first-class scoundrel – hanging him wouldn't be enough!"' And from his bed came the prime minister's feeble answer, 'It is what is desired on high.' Thus had he capitulated to the tsarina. Now enraged, the Speaker of the Duma continued to berate the old man: 'What kind of monarchist are you after this? You're a zealous republican who, by making allowances for Rasputin, is undermining the monarchist idea!'

No, they were all, with Rasputin's help, undermining that idea. From the tsarina to Rodzyanko himself.

Now the peasant was talking ever more frequently of death.

The File, from Molchanov's testimony:

In October 1916 I . . . visited him a couple of times or so. I noticed that he was in a rather melancholy mood. I noticed too that there was wine on the table, and that he had drunk a lot of it, as if to quiet a terrible foreboding. He kept repeating, 'The times are changing, everything will be changed.' On parting he was very affectionate and said that he appreciated my love and warm attitude. He remembered my late father with a kind word, and said that he would perhaps himself be killed and we would not see each other again . . . And then, as if suddenly regaining his senses, he said, 'No, no, we shall see each other again. You'll be coming to Petrograd.'

And every day on Gorokhovaya Street that mad, bewitching, drunken dancing went on, drowning out Rasputin's terror. His weak-minded son, who was now serving on the tsarina's hospital train, came to see him for several days and hid out from that madness in the remoter rooms. And if the apartment was quiet, it meant that the peasant was drinking in a restaurant or that a car had taken him to Tsarskoe Selo for a meeting of the 'Tsarskoe Selo cabinet'. On 16 October Alix wrote to Nicky, 'Had a nice evening at A.'s yesterday – our Friend, his son & the Bish. Issidor [the same Isidor Kolokolov who was accused of a liaison with a lay brother] . . . Gr. thinks it wld. be better to call in the younger men instead of those over 40, who are needed at home to keep all work going & to look after the houses.'

And that suggestion of the peasant's was a completely reasonable one.

Then November began, the next to the last month of his life.

The Burial Place Is Ready

On 5 November Alix informed Nicky, 'The laying of the foundation stone [of] Ania's church was nice, our Fr. was there, & nice Bishop Isidor.' Rasputin would soon be buried under the altar of the new church. And the 'nice bishop' would conduct the burial service.

A little celebration in honour of the laying of the foundation of 'Anya's church', the Serafimov Sanctuary, then took place at the infirmary, a celebration that would give rise to the next big scandal.

Shortly after the celebration, Rasputin's implacable enemy, the monarchist Purishkevich, stood surrounded by parliament members at the conclusion of the latest Duma meeting. He was passing out to whoever wanted one a highly amusing photograph. In it Rasputin was shown sitting at a table next to the 'nice Bishop Isidor', who was dressed in a cassock. There was wine on the table, and around the table there were balalaika players and sisters of mercy, laughing and obviously intoxicated. At a time when the Russian army was spilling its blood at the front and famine was looming over the country, how should the Duma members have reacted to the home-front jollity of that 'spy and rogue'?

The very next day one of the pictures was lying on Minister Protopopov's desk.

During his interrogation by the Extraordinary Commission, Protopopov testified that 'Purishkevich distributed 9000 copies of the photograph of

Rasputin – Rasputin surrounded by several people . . . A table, wine on the table, balalaika players, a priest.'

'How do you know that he distributed 9000 copies?'

'On the back of the photo sent to me from Tsarskoe Selo, probably at the orders of the empress through Vyrubova or Voskoboinikova, was written "9000 copies".'

The Last Picture Of The Living Rasputin

The story of that photograph – which, alas, I was not able to find – explains a great deal about the approaching denouement.

The news of the photograph was most likely brought to Protopopov by his pretty flame Voskoboinikova. And not only because she was at the time his lover, but also because she had a most direct relation to the picture. She herself was included in it as one of the gay sisters of mercy.

And she was required to give testimony for the File on the scandalous photograph.

'In the picture shown to me – Rasputin with Bishop Isidor – I am included in profile behind Isidor. The picture was suggested by Colonel Loman' (the builder and warden of the tsarina's favourite Feodor Cathedral).

It had happened after the 'official part was over' and Vyrubova and the other important guests had left the infirmary. Voskoboinikova testified:

After the guests had gone, Isidor and Rasputin stayed at the infirmary for a while. Loman had invited us to remain behind to have some coffee; although the 'upper crust' had left, he said, why shouldn't we labourers stay? Loman treated us to champagne and coffee and even to the singing of his choirboys . . . who artistically sang Russian songs . . . And then Loman suggested we have our picture taken. We were photographed by an employee of the Feodorov Cathedral. And Loman was among those to be photographed – he was standing behind Isidor. Later we asked for copies of the picture, but he said that they weren't ready yet . . . Why Loman wasn't included in the picture . . . I don't know. It's possible he sat down before the picture was taken. Besides the choirboys, included are Molchanova, a sister of mercy [the wife of Leonid Molchanov], my sister Bendina, and the sister of mercy Voino; seated are the sister Koscheeva, Rasputin, Bishop Isidor, and Maltsev [the builder of the Serafimov Sanctuary]. The sister Koscheeva is laughing in the picture and looks slightly tipsy.

Testimony about the scandalous photograph was also taken from Loman.

The File, from Loman's testimony: 'Shown in the picture is a luncheon
. . . on the occasion of the laying of the foundation of the Serafimov
Sanctuary, which was built at the orders of Vyrubova not by me but by
Maltsev. I did not intend to have my picture taken with the others, nor did
I pose with them. I was standing somewhere . . . far away from the table
and therefore did not show up in the photograph.'

No, it was no accident that Loman had not been included in the
picture. And it was no accident either that the intelligent Vyrubova, as
Voskoboinikova testified, 'had warned us of the need to be more careful
with Loman'. And it was no accident that Rasputin, according to Voskoboinikova, had said that 'Loman should not be trusted,' that he was an
'ambiguous' person.

The 'ambiguous Loman' was already serving two masters. And the
experienced courtier had at someone else's order devised the provocation.
He had decided to take a picture of Rasputin and the scandalous Bishop
Isidor in the merry company of inebriated sisters of mercy. He had decided
to take a picture of a 'Rasputin orgy'. And that is why they had 'made sister
Koscheeva laugh' as the picture was being taken, and why Loman had sat
down just before. The cunning Loman had already calculated the future
and was serving the conspiracy.

It was a signal. The denouement was approaching. The rats were already
fleeing the sinking ship. And Loman was making an effort and organizing
that photo of an 'orgy', which he then passed on to the Duma.

On The Eve

'Towards the end of 1916 the atmosphere in the building on Gorokhovaya
Street was becoming ever more intense,' Zhukovskaya remembered.

> On the outside it was the same bazaar . . . the constant phone calls . . . the
> women buzzing like hornets and crowding into the reception room, the
> dining room, and the bedroom, women both old and young, pale and in
> make-up, who came and went, bringing heaps of candy, flowers, and boxes
> of other things, all of which was strewn about . . . Rasputin himself, worn
> out and with a roving gaze, at times seemed like a hunted wolf, and for that
> reason, I think, one felt in his whole mode of life a certain haste and lack
> of confidence, and everything seemed accidental and precarious – the
> closeness of some blow, something looming over that dark, unwelcoming
> building.

And like many others in those times, Zhukovskaya remembered and recorded his whisper: ' "The ones over there are the enemies. They're all searching, and trying, and laying a trap. I see it all. You think I don't know it will soon all come to an end? Faith has been lost," he suddenly said . . . "there's no more faith in the people, that's what. Well, so long, my little bee! Kiss me goodbye."' She never saw him again.

'It Will Be A Revolution Of Rage And Revenge'

It had come to pass by the end of 1916. It was not the bullets of revolutionary terrorists, nor the shells of Germans at the front, but the existence of a single person that was threatening to destroy one of the greatest empires in the world. The opposition, society, the court had all struggled in vain against the illiterate peasant with the awful name from an unknown village.

In the days prior to Rasputin's murder, Vasily Maklakov, a Duma deputy of the most powerful opposition party, the Constitutional Democrats, came to Moscow to speak before the chief influential factory owners and merchants. A police agent among those present wrote down Maklakov's speech, and it has survived in the papers of the Department of Police. In the apartment of the millionaire Konovalov, his fellow party member, Maklakov spoke of the unavoidable revolution that Rasputin was bringing about.

'The dynasty is risking its very existence, and not by means of destructive forces from without. It is by means of terrible destructive work from within that it is shortening its potential existence by a good century.' And Maklakov then uttered some prophetic words: 'The horror of the coming revolution . . . It will not be a political revolution, which might follow a predictable course, but a revolution of rage and revenge of the ignorant lower classes, a revolution that cannot be anything but elemental, convulsive, and chaotic.'

And the sense of inevitable apocalypse that had once more appeared in society now became universal. It was then that the young Prince Zhevakhov told the tsarina of a vision that a certain Colonel O. had had. The colonel had been lifted onto a high mountain from which all of Russia was visible to him, a Russia flowing with blood from border to border.

Alone

They still didn't know that autumn in the Crimean grand-ducal palaces that their last year was ending. But they did sense that a terrible, inevitable time was ahead. And in that looming catastrophe the tsar was alone. As his cousin the historian Grand Duke Nikolai Mikhailovich afterwards recorded in his diary, 'Around Alexander III there had been a closed circle of a few trusted people . . . After the twenty-third year of Nicholas's reign he did not have a single friend left, neither among his relatives nor in high society.' More accurately, the lonely tsar had only one friend – Our Friend, the universally detested peasant who threatened the empire and the dynasty! Even his mother was opposed to her son, who was destroying the empire.

The File, from Vyrubova's testimony: 'The dowager empress was against the sovereign and the empress. They saw Marie Fyodorovna so rarely that in the twelve years I was with Alexandra Fyodorovna, I saw Marie Fyodorovna perhaps three times.'

Hatred of the tsarina was in universal fashion. The court and the Tsarskoe Selo nobility joined the grand dukes in expressing their *Fronde*-like discontent. Prince Zhevakhov recalled that the head of the church secondary school for girls in Tsarskoe Selo not only did not bow to the tsarina upon meeting her but conspicuously turned away from the ruler of all Russia. 'It is painful for me . . . not for myself but for my daughters,' Alix told the prince at the time. Shameful caricatures depicting the Tsarina of all Russia in indecent poses with a bearded peasant were circulated throughout the country. The Tsar of all Russia was now contemptuously called 'Nikolasha' in the war-torn, embittered villages. The tsar, who until recently had been for them a dreaded 'father', was now depicted in thousands of graffiti as a pathetic husband deceived by his wife and a dissolute peasant.

'I'm Terribly Busy With . . . Conspiracy'

How accurately did Maklakov observe, 'In the highest circles of the nobility and the court there is fear that the ruling authority on its way to ruin will pull them and all their privileges down with it.'

The legendary Yacht Club was the centre of aristocratic opposition at the time. It had been founded in 1840 during the reign of Nicholas I. Only the upper crust and the most well-born aristocrats – Russia's blue bloods – were allowed within its walls.

During the reign of Nicholas's father, Alexander III, the Yacht Club had in effect been a closed political assembly. From there the highest aristocracy conducted its struggle against nihilists and revolutionaries. The Yacht Club was surrounded by mystery and exclusivity.

The club was by tradition headed by the court minister – then Count Fredericks. But even there in that monarchist citadel, as Grand Duke

Nikolai Mikhailovich wrote in his diary, 'the empress's . . . conduct was openly criticized.' And that was a frightening symptom. Alix attempted through Count Fredericks to put a stop to the conversations. With the magnificent bearing of an old guardsman and his impeccable manners evoking the vanished grandees of the *ancien régime*, Fredericks made a splendid impression at balls, but as a minister he was helpless. Perishing authority has always been surrounded by pathetic people. Not only did the conversations about the tsarina continue, they turned provocative. Grand Duke Dmitry and Felix Yusupov were members of the Yacht Club at the time.

In Petrograd and Moscow, conspiracies were ripening in court circles, among the aristocracy, and in the magnificent apartments of the rich. But outside Petrograd in Tsarskoe Selo the lonely royal family continued to live its hopelessly isolated life. And as before, Alix, the head of the 'Tsarskoe Selo cabinet', worked untiringly, summoning the obedient but, alas, powerless ministers. Nicholas was far from the capital at Headquarters.

In the meantime, the last steps were being taken in the great Romanov family to appeal to Alix. It was then that Zinaida Yusupova asked for an audience. The fact that Khvostov revealed in 1917 – that she was involved in his own (unsuccessful) murder conspiracy, offering huge sums to fund it – was no coincidence. That beauty, who was endowed with many talents (she was a potentially brilliant actress with whom Stanislavsky had pleaded to join his theatre), was apparently also one of the principal figures in the great Romanov family conspiracy. And Zinaida Yusupova went to see Alix.

She was 'received coolly'. And no sooner had she begun to talk about Rasputin than she 'was asked to leave the palace'. But she declared that before she did so, she had to fulfil her duty before the empress and 'speak her piece'. Alix listened in silence and at the end of the monologue she said, 'I hope I shall never see you again.'

Zinaida was close to Alix's sister Ella. So it was no coincidence that Ella came to see Alix after Zinaida had been thrown out. Her once much-loved sister Ella. The empress listened to her sister in silence, too. And she saw her out to her carriage in silence. As Felix Yusupov wrote, 'Tears came to Ella's eyes. "She drove me out like a dog . . . Poor Nicky, poor Russia."' And Felix had not made it up.

I read in the archives a letter from Ella herself. She wrote it to Nicky after Rasputin was murdered. And in it she described her meeting with Alix: 'I have rushed to the two of you, whom I sincerely love, in order to warn you that all the classes from the lowest to the highest have reached their limit . . . She ordered me to say nothing . . . and I left wondering whether we would ever meet again . . . what tragedies might play themselves out, and what suffering was still in store for us.'

The grand dukes' conspiracy had apparently finally taken shape at the beginning of the dank, rainy Petrograd autumn. As Felix recalled, 'the grand dukes and a few aristocrats were engaged in a cabal to remove the empress from power and send her away to a convent. Rasputin was to be exiled to Siberia, the emperor deposed, and the tsarevich crowned.'

Not long before Rasputin's murder, Purishkevich was summoned to the palace of Grand Duke Kirill Vladimirovich. And the monarchist Purishkevich, one of those who would commit that murder, wrote in his diary, 'After our conversation, I took from the grand duke's palace a strong conviction that he was undertaking something impermissible in regard to the sovereign.'

In keeping with a favourite Russian tradition, however, the 'impermissible' was limited only to talk. None of them dared violate his oath and raise a hand against the tsar.

But if the grand dukes were going to act, they needed to hurry. For another conspiracy was already brewing at Headquarters. A dangerous conspiracy of generals and the Duma opposition.

'Among Konovalov [a Duma deputy], Krymov [a general], and Alexeev [the chief of command at Headquarters] some sort of cabal is brewing,' wrote General Brusilov. And how melancholy is the observation in his notebook of another the tsar's generals, General Lemke: 'I'm terribly busy with the matter of growing conspiracy.'

The Last Warning

Once again the grand dukes tried to resolve the situation 'within the family', as the 'dread uncle' had once suggested to the tsar. At the time a wedding was being planned, the last of the ruling Romanov dynasty.

It was the latest in a series of morganatic marriages. And by no means a joyful event for the dynasty's prestige. The tsar's sister Olga had divorced Pyotr Oldenburgsky. The sweet, gentle Pyotr, a scion of the ancient Oldenburgsky ducal family, was a homosexual, so Olga's decision was accepted with resignation. And now Nicholas's sister was marrying her ex-husband's adjutant, Nikolai Kulikovsky, the modest commander of a regiment of cuirassiers. And conferences took place within the great Romanov family to discuss the planned marriage. But the discussions weren't only about the marriage. The result was the next 'family embassy'.

Grand Duke Nikolai Mikhailovich arrived at Headquarters on 2 November. A well-known historian and, as Sandro's elder brother, nephew of Alexander II and thus the tsar's kinsman, he was reputed to be a brilliant conversationalist. And now that master of conversation was about to inform the tsar of the conclusions reached at the great Romanov family's conferences. After a long conversation, he handed Nicholas a letter that he had written beforehand. In it the grand duke said, 'I long hesitated to reveal the whole truth to you, but after your mother and sisters convinced me to, I have decided to proceed.' It was, as it were, a collective letter from the family.

The next day Nicky wrote to Alix, 'My precious . . . Nikolai Mikh. came here for one day – we had a long talk last evening wh. I will write to you about in my next letter – to-day I have no time . . . ever your old Nicky.'

He did not dare to tell her the content of that serious conversation, preferring instead to forward Nikolai Mikhailovich's letter to her.

Alix read:

> You have said to me more than once that you cannot trust anyone, that everyone deceives you. If that is true, then it is also happening with your wife, who passionately loves you, but who has been led astray by the sheer malicious deceit of those around her. You trust Alexandra Fyodorovna . . . That is understandable. But what comes from her mouth is the result of clever juggling and not the actual truth . . . If it isn't in your power to remove those influences from her, then at least protect yourself from the constant meddling and whispering of the spouse you love.

The grand duke went on to explain that he had decided on that mission of his 'in the hope . . . of rescuing you, your throne, and our dear country from the most terrible and irreparable consequences . . . You stand on the eve of a new era of unrest, I would even say, an era of assassination,' and he implored the tsar to provide 'ministers responsible to the Duma'.

The tsar had thus been warned for the last time that it was coming – the 'era of assassination'. And he had been warned on behalf of the entire Romanov Family.

Anger

Alix was enraged. '4 Nov. 1916 . . . I read Nikolai's [letter] & am utterly disgusted. Had you stopped him in the middle of his talk & told him that, if he only once more touched that subject or me, you will send him to Siberia – as it becomes next to high treason. He has always hated . . .

me . . . – but during war . . . to crawl behind yr. Mama and Sisters & not stick up bravely . . . for his Emperor's Wife – is loathsome and treachery . . . you my Love, far too good & kind & soft – such a man needs to be held in awe of you – He & Nikolasha are my greatest enemies in the family, not counting the black women . . . Wify is your staunch One & stands as a rock behind you.'

And a postscript: 'I dreamt I was being operated: th' my arm was cut off I felt utterly no pain. After a letter came from Nikolai.'

But her anger would not let her finish the letter. And she continued, as always relying on Our Friend's opinion. 'On reading Nikolai's letter He said, "Nowhere does Divine grace show through, not in a single feature of the letter, but only evil, like a brother of Milyukov, like all brothers of evil . . . The Lord has shown Mama that all that is worthless, asleep."'

The Last Wedding In The Family Of Tsars

They decided to get married in Kiev, where Olga's mother, the dowager empress, was living. And where the entire Romanov family decided to gather. And Alix, knowing that Nicholas would also be going to his sister's wedding, immediately started to worry. She understood what sort of conversations would come up. And she did not fail to condemn the coming celebration – in the words of Our Friend, naturally. '5 Nov. . . . Our Fr. is so angry, Olga married – as she did wrong towards you & that can bring her no luck.'

And then came the wedding that Olga described in her memoirs. A simple wedding, a dark little church, the bride in a Red Cross uniform. And when Olga saw her brother, she was shocked: Nicky had changed a lot, with hollow cheeks and bags under his eyes. After the sad wedding, Nicholas at once set off for Headquarters in order to avoid any further discussion of Rasputin.

The 'Era Of Assassination' Begins

Alix's dream had not been an idle one. For it was then, at the beginning of November, immediately after Nikolai Mikhailovich's unsuccessful visit that Felix Yusupov revived his acquaintance with Rasputin. And during the inquiry into Rasputin's murder, Yusupov told the investigator that 'after a long interval . . . I met Rasputin in November at Golovina's home.' This is confirmed by Maria Golovina in her own testimony: 'Prince Yusupov met Rasputin at my apartment in November 1916.'

This is how Felix tells it. 'M. G. [Maria Golovina] called me up. "Tomorrow Efim Grigorievich will be here, and he would very much like to see you." The path I had to take opened of its own accord . . . It is true that in taking that path I was compelled to deceive someone who was sincerely well disposed towards me.'

Felix is most likely not telling the truth here. It was simply that after Nikolai Mikhailovich's unsuccessful visit to Headquarters in November, the hunt for Rasputin had begun. And a plan for the hunt already existed in which the unhappy Munya was intended to play a fateful role in the death of the person she revered. Felix had, of course, called her up himself. 'Felix was complaining of chest pains,' Munya testified in the File. And complaining of an illness that the doctors were unable to cure, he easily drew from her a suggestion that she arrange a meeting with the great healer. For Felix knew that that had long been her wish – to unite the two people she loved so unselfishly. Thus, Felix and Rasputin met at Munya's apartment.

'Rasputin was much changed since the time I had first seen him. His face had grown puffy, and he had become quite flabby. He was dressed in a simple peasant's coat and a light blue silk shirt and wide peasant trousers made of velvet . . . He behaved in a highly familiar manner . . . He kissed me.' This time the prince did not try to avoid the kiss.

In conversation with Rasputin the day before, Munya had called Felix 'little' (little Felix Felixovich Yusupov in contrast to Felix Felixovich, his father). Rasputin, who adored nicknames, immediately took it up and began calling Felix the 'Little One'.

The Murderers Meet

After that encounter, Felix began, he says, to seek out comrades-in-arms for the murder. He afterwards recalled in Paris, 'Going over in my mind the friends whom I could trust with my secret, I stopped on two of them. They were Grand Duke Dmitry Pavlovich and Lieutenant Sukhotin . . . I was certain the grand duke would support me and agree to take part in executing my plan . . . I knew how much he hated the elder and suffered on the sovereign's and Russia's behalf.' And Felix requested a meeting with Dmitry. 'Finding him alone in his study, I quickly got to the point. The grand duke agreed at once and said that eliminating Rasputin would be the last and most effective attempt to save Russia.'

I think Felix is laying out a legend for us here – that Rasputin's murder was conceived by him alone, and that the grand duke had merely joined in.

Most likely, it was otherwise. The last unsuccessful warning – Nikolai Mikhailovich's visit to Headquarters – took place in November, after which the 'era of assassination' began. It was then that the Grand Duke Dmitry and Felix – those two very close friends – together decided to do what had received so much ineffectual discussion in the family – kill Rasputin. And the decision to kill him most likely originated with Dmitry, that gallant guardsman, who, as Felix correctly noted, 'hated the elder'. With the soldier Dmitry and not with the civilian Felix, about whom Ella, who knew him well, would write, 'Felix, who wouldn't hurt a fly . . . who didn't want to go into the military because he didn't want to shed anyone else's blood.' But Felix's hand was in the treachery of the plan. The ancient blood of the ruthless Tartar khans.

Dmitry and Felix were not, apparently, the only ones in the Romanov family who knew about their decision. It was no accident that Felix wrote of a 'conspiracy', or that the tsar would later write to the grand dukes: 'I know that the consciences of many are not clear, since Dmitry Pavlovich is not the only one involved in this.'

In any case, there is a strange coincidence: ten days before the murder, Grand Duchess Ella would abruptly leave Petrograd. And she would not only leave it. She would go off to pray in a monastery. And not merely a monastery. But the Sarov Monastery, the site of the relics of Saint Serafim, who was considered the royal family's patron saint. As if she knew that something important and terrifying for the family was about to happen. And she was going to pray to God and to Saint Serafim. She would subsequently write to the tsar, 'I went to Sarov and Diveev . . . for ten days to pray for you – for your army, the country, the ministers, for the weak of body and spirit, including that unfortunate one, that God might enlighten him.'

Ella prayed at the monastery for God to enlighten the 'unfortunate' Rasputin. In order to avoid the inevitable which was being readied and about which she was aware. She was also praying for those who had decided to spill blood. For they were her own protegés – Dmitry had lived with her family before her husband was killed, and Felix, whom she called 'my Felix', was someone in whose upbringing she had played a large part.

The Long-Suffering Job

But discussion of the murder plan was suspended for a short while. The grand duke had to return to Headquarters. But they knew that Dmitry would not be there long. For in Tsarskoe Selo 'he was not liked and his influence was feared.' And they proved to be right – as Alix's letters show.

The grand duke, Felix writes, told him that 'he had noticed something wasn't right with the sovereign. With each passing day he was becoming more and more indifferent to what was going on around him . . . in his opinion, it was all the result of a malicious plan: the sovereign was being given something that dulled his intellectual capacities.' There was a legend abroad at the time that Rasputin and the tsarina had done something to the Tsar's will with the aid of Tibetan drugs provided by Dr Badmaev.

Thus did the two of them egg each other on, assuring themselves of the need to carry out their mission quickly.

There was, incidentally, a real basis for the legend about the Tsar's growing apathy. On the eve of the Duma session, the right had proposed to the tsar its own way out of the situation, which was becoming ever more dangerous. Prince Rimsky-Korsakov, a member of the Council of State at whose home a small group of rightist aristocrats was accustomed to gathering, gave Stürmer a Memorandum for the tsar.

'Since there is now no doubt that the Duma has embarked on a clearly revolutionary course . . . the Duma must be prorogued at once without indicating when it will be reconvened. The military forces on hand in Petrograd are fully adequate to putting down any potential revolt.' But Stürmer was unwilling to risk giving the Memorandum to the Tsar. He too had noticed that strange aloofness in the sovereign. And so he merely informed the tsar of the current mood of the throne's defenders. The tsar heard him out in indifference. And ordered the Duma session to begin.

The tsar was indeed becoming more and more inactive, but it was because he had grasped the hopelessness of the situation. He had read the reports of the secret police and knew all about the growing general conspiracy. And he was tired of the endless struggle. He had decided to cede authority to them. He would withdraw into private life, so that his wife – who was going insane from her furious activity and terrible premonitions – would be left alone. And that peasant would also be left alone to help them survive by healing both her and their son. And for that reason he himself welcomed the inevitable, although for the time being he listlessly attempted to calm the seething Duma.

How many times had he hopelessly reshuffled the government. On 10 November he appointed Trepov prime minister in place of Stürmer, whom the Duma hated. Trepov was from a distinguished family of right-wing public servants. His father, Fyodor Trepov, had been a Petersburg mayor of notorious strictness. And his brother, Dmitry, had once headed the powerful ministry of internal affairs. But it was only with the greatest difficulty that poor Alexei succeeded in making his initial programmatic speech to the Duma. He was greeted by noisy heckling. The Duma no longer wanted sops from the authorities. It demanded ministers who would be responsible to the Duma. It was then that Nicholas decided to make his last concession – to hand over Protopopov. Rodzyanko had been able to tell him a great deal about the half-mad minister.

On 10 November the tsar wrote to Alix:

> You will have heard . . . about the changes wh. are absolutely necessary now. I am sorry about Prot. [opopov], a good honest man, but he jumped fr. One idea to another and could not stick to his opinion . . . People said he was not normal some years ago fr. a certain illness. It is risky leaving the ministry of Int.[ernal affairs] in such hands at such times! . . . Only please don't mix in our Friend. It is I who carry the responsibility [and] I want to be free to choose accordingly.

Thus did he plead with Alix not to invoke the peasant's words.

But she understood everything: he had decided to put an end to the 'Tsarskoe Selo cabinet' that was meant to save them. He had decided to turn once more to the odious people who dreamed of limiting the tsar's power. They would deceive him yet again! To 'be free to make his own choice' was not something she could allow. And the 'wise counsels of Our Friend' were at once brought to bear on the matter.

> 10 Nov. . . . Once more, remember that for your reign, Baby & us you need the strength prayers & advice of our Friend . . . Protopopov venerates our Friend & will be blessed – Sturmer got frightened & for months did not see him – so wrong & he lost his footing. Ah, Lovy, I pray so hard to God to make you feel & realise, that He is our caring, were He not here, I don't know what might not have happened. He saves us by His prayers & wise counsels . . . For me don't make any changes till I have come.

She came to Headquarters, and Nicky let Protopopov remain. Once again he yielded.

And once again he grasped the hopelessness of the situation. He was very tired.

Meanwhile, the new prime minister, Trepov, was starting out exactly like the recently fallen Khvostov. He had decided to calm the seething Duma by sending Rasputin away from Petrograd. Knowing about Rasputin from rumours, Trepov made the same mistake Khvostov had made. He thought he could buy Rasputin off. At his behest, Trepov's relative General Mosolov went to see Rasputin. The general thought he knew how to talk to peasants. And he therefore brought some wine with him. Rasputin drank the wine. After which Mosolov suggested to Rasputin on Trepov's behalf that he renounce all interference in the business of government and the appointment of ministers. And he offered him in the name of the generous prime minister 30,000 roubles a year. Or so Beletsky recounted in his testimony about the episode from Rasputin's own words. Beletsky also told how it ended: Rasputin rejected the offer and immediately 'informed the empress and the tsar of Trepov's offer to buy Rasputin's silence on everything that Rasputin considered not in the tsars' interest'.

Those pathetic fools were proposing that Rasputin trade the place of adviser to the 'tsars' for sums he would have regarded as insignificant! Sums he had squandered and flung to the winds! Trepov thus immediately forfeited the tsarina's confidence. And his fate was sealed. As Rasputin put it, 'The Trepovs should not be kept on; their last name [suggesting 'blather'] is unlucky.'

Meanwhile, an incredible thing had happened in the Duma. The monarchist Purishkevich, who was well known for his right-wing views – his bald head and pointed moustache were familiar throughout Russia from newspaper portraits – had given a speech that became famous at once.

'. . . Who Has Remained A German On The Russian Throne'

From the rostrum of the Duma, Purishkevich, large, heavily breathing, a fanatical monarchist notorious for his endless baiting of the opposition, on 19 November came down with a thundering voice upon the Empress of All Russia and the peasant behind the throne.

At two o'clock the next morning an infuriated Protopopov conveyed to Headquarters by telegraph the most dangerous excerpts from the speech. I found his telegram in the archives. These excerpts would be struck from the newspaper version by the censor. But the next day it was precisely those excerpts that were being repeated by all Petrograd. For numerous copies of the speech were already making their way around the city.

> Evil comes from those dark forces and influences that . . . have forced the accession to high posts of people unable to occupy them . . . From the influences that are headed by Grishka Rasputin (noise, voices, 'True!' 'A disgrace!') . . . I have not been able to sleep the last few nights – I give you my word . . . I have been lying with my eyes wide open imagining the

series of telegrams, notes, and reports that the illiterate peasant has written first to one minister and then to another . . . There have been instances where the non-fulfilment of his demands has resulted in those gentlemen, although strong and powerful, being removed from office . . . Over the two and a half years of the war I have assumed . . . that our domestic quarrels should be forgotten . . . Now I have violated that prohibition in order to place at the feet of the throne the thoughts of the Russian masses and the bitter taste of resentment of the Russian front that have been produced by the tsar's ministers who have been turned into marionettes, marionettes whose threads have been taken firmly in hand by Rasputin and the Empress Alexandra Fyodorovna – the evil genius of Russia and the tsar . . . who has remained a German on the Russian throne and alien to the country and its people.

There wasn't any further he could go!

One can imagine how the tsar read that speech. Now he definitely knew. They had left him just one choice: Alix or the throne. And he made his choice: her and private life. And he waited for the inevitable.

When Purishkevich's speech was read to Rasputin, he reacted just as Alix had expected him to; in Gospel fashion, he forgave. But he also understood that the 'tsars'' spirits needed to be kept up, and he sent a telegram to Headquarters. '19 November 1916. Purishkevich cursed impertinently but not painfully. My calm remains, it is not destroyed.' And in order to preserve their calm as well, he predicted that authority would remain with the 'tsars'. 'God will strengthen you. Yours is the victory and yours is the ship. No one else has the authority to board it.' Thus, he promised them a radiant future – a couple of months before the revolution. He reiterated the same thing to 'Mama', who at the time was with her hospital train. '22 November . . . Believe and do not be afraid of fear, give all that is yours to the Wee One [the tsarevich] intact. As the father has received it, so shall his son.'

In an unusually coherent note to Voiekov (the palace castellan), Rasputin wrote, 'If you aren't used to it, even kasha is bitter, let alone Purishkevich and his abusive mouth. Such wasps have multiplied now in the millions. We friends have to stand as one. Although a small circle, yet one of like-minded people. In them is malice, and in us the truth. Grigory Novy.' But Rasputin confirmed here the most terrible thing that Purishkevich had talked about: 'such wasps have multiplied in the millions.'

Felix Yusupov, who was in the gallery during Purishkevich's speech, had listened to it with the greatest interest.

The next day Purishkevich woke up even more famous. As he would describe in his – diary, 'The phone rang all day on 20 November with congratulations . . . Among the callers, one identifying himself as Prince Yusupov particularly interested me. He asked if he might visit me to clarify some matters relating to Rasputin's role that he preferred not to discuss over the phone. I asked him to come by at 9 a.m.'

'You Too Must Take Part In It'

The day that he went to see Purishkevich, Felix sent Irina a letter at their estate in the Crimea. Felix was then living in Petrograd, where he was receiving military training at the Corps des Pages. 'The young people's half' of the Yusupov palace on the Moika Canal was being remodelled, and Felix was staying at the palace of his father-in-law, Grand Duke Alexander Mikhailovich.

Warm rains were falling in the Crimea. The grand-ducal estates were deserted. Of all the brilliant society that had earlier sought refuge there from the dank Petrograd autumn, only Zinaida Yusupova and Irina had stayed on in the empty palace.

All that time the 'young people' – Irina and Felix – had been exchanging letters with constant assurances of love quite similar to those in the letters of Alix and Nicky. And even though their love did not at all resemble that of the 'tsars' (if only because of a few special old attachments of Felix's), it was the accepted style for letters of that kind. And they followed the style. Illnesses and melancholia, judging by their letters, did not abandon Irina, that delicate beauty. But Felix's most recent letter forced her to forget all about her ailments.

In that letter, instead of the customary words of love, Felix told her about the murder being planned. A murder that he had decided to take a passionate part in. (He had sent the letter with someone he trusted.)

'I'm terribly busy working on a plan to eliminate Rasputin. That is simply essential now, since otherwise everything will be finished. For that, I often see M[unya] Gol[ovina] and him [Rasputin]. They've grown quite fond of me and are forthcoming about everything with me.' And then he wrote the most surprising thing for her: 'You too must take part in it. Dm[itry] Pavl[ovich] knows all about it and is helping. It will all take place in the middle of December, when Dm. comes back . . . How much I want to see you before that. But it will be better if you do not come earlier, since the rooms won't be ready until 15 December, and not even all of them . . . and you won't have anywhere to stay . . . Not a word to anyone about what I've written.'

And in conclusion he said, 'Tell my mother to read my letter.'
For Zinaida Yusupova was very likely in on the conspiracy.

By 20 November, before Felix's meeting Purishkevich, the plan worked
out by Felix and Dmitry to assassinate Rasputin had been prepared and
already put into play.

Carnal Passion?

After Rasputin's death, his maid Katya Pechyorkina testified during her
interrogation that the first time that Felix came to Rasputin's apartment
was on '20 November, the day of the Feast of the Presentation of the Blessed
Virgin'. Since it was a church holiday, she remembered the date exactly.
And Felix had not come by himself but with Maria Golovina.

As Golovina testifies in the File, 'Felix . . . was complaining about chest
pains . . . I advised him to go and see Rasputin at his apartment . . . The
prince and I went together twice at the end of November and the beginning
of December. And he remained with [Rasputin] less than an hour.'

That is, Felix visited Rasputin's apartment the very same day that he
called Purishkevich. And that visit must have helped Felix carry out the
most important part of his plan – gaining Rasputin's complete confidence.

Felix very briefly described to the investigator in charge of the inquiry
concerning Rasputin's murder the mysterious process of treatment itself:
'At the end of November I went to Rasputin's apartment along with
Golovina. Rasputin made some hypnotic passes over me and it did seem to
me that there was a certain relief.'

He gave a much more detailed account after his emigration to Paris.

After tea Rasputin admitted me to his study, a little room with a leather
sofa, several chairs, and a large desk. The elder ordered me to lie down on
the sofa and gently moved his hands over my chest, neck, and head . . . and
then he got down on his knees and after placing his hands on my head,
started mumbling a prayer. His face was so close to mine that I saw only his
eyes. He remained in that position for a little while. Then he stood up in
an abrupt movement and began to make passes over me with his hands.
Rasputin's hypnotic power was enormous. I felt a strength enter me in a
warm flow and take hold of my entire being, my body grew numb, and I
tried to speak but my tongue would not obey me. Only Rasputin's eyes
shone before me – two phosphorescent beams. And then I felt awaken in
me the will to resist the hypnosis. I realized I had not let him subordinate
my will completely.

Surviving in the archive of the Russian Federation, however, is the diary of someone who knew Felix well. And who has expressed in it a number of interesting thoughts regarding Rasputin's 'healing'. That person is Grand Duke Nikolai Mikhailovich. After Rasputin's assassination he tried to get a little more out of Felix.

'Felix laid out the whole story for me. Grishka had taken a liking to him at once . . . and soon afterwards came to trust him – to trust him completely. They saw each other almost every day and talked about everything . . . and Rasputin even initiated him into his schemes, not being shy at all about such revelations.'

And reflecting on Rasputin's sudden faith in Felix who had the day before been a detractor, the grand duke raises an essential question: 'I cannot understand Rasputin's psyche. How, for example, is one to explain Rasputin's boundless trust in the young Yusupov – the trust of someone who trusted no one at all . . . afraid that he would be poisoned or killed?' Nikolai Mikhailovich was quite right to be astonished. Rasputin, as we know, was extremely afraid of assassination attempts.

The grand duke explains that trust this way:

> It remains to propose something rather incredible, and that is that [Rasputin] was infatuated with and had a carnal passion for Felix that darkened the strapping peasant and libertine and led him to his grave. Did they really just talk during their endless conversations? I'm convinced there were physical manifestations of friendship in the form of kisses, mutual touching, and, it may be, even something more cynical. Rasputin's sadism is not open to doubt. But just how great Felix's carnal perversions were is still little understood by me. Although before his marriage there were rumours in society about his lasciviousness.'

Thus, the grand duke is dubious about the 'healing' which in the language of the *Khlysty* and of Rasputin signified exorcising the demon of lechery. In this case, the demon of which the universal healer from the Siberian village had presumably undertaken to heal Felix was his lust for men. It's possible that the mysterious prehistory of their relationship, ending in a slap, had from the very beginning assured Felix of Rasputin's enthusiasm for the 'healing'. But, as the grand duke wrote, one thing at least is clear: it was after those encounters that 'Rasputin came to trust Felix completely'.

During those encounters, however, Felix was already preparing for the murder.

Arriving for his treatments, he went up to Rasputin's apartment by the back stairs, thereby avoiding the agents who were guarding the elder.

Explaining to Rasputin and Golovina why he wanted to come to see Rasputin only by the back stairway was easy: Felix's family were enemies of the elder, and he did not want conflicts in his family. Thus, he got Rasputin used to his secret arrivals at his apartment. As the maid noted during the same investigation, 'The "Little One" came by the back door.'

The Mystery Of Rasputin's Guard

The maid, Katya Pechyorkina, mentioned only two appearances by Felix, both of them with Maria Golovina. It's likely, however, that Felix came to the back door much more frequently, and that Rasputin tried to make sure that there were no witnesses to those visits for 'treatment'.

In any case, although Felix was evasive with the investigators about the number of his visits to Rasputin, he did talk about them in the plural: 'During my last visits to Rasputin'. And Lili Dehn would testify in the File that according to the peasant, 'the prince visited Rasputin often.' And the tsarina would write to Nicky on 17 December, 'Felix came often to him lately.'

Wishing to show the difficulties that they had overcome, the conspirators would afterwards refer to the fact that Rasputin 'was guarded by plain-clothes agents from three organizations: the empress, the Ministry of Internal Affairs, and spies from the banks'.

In fact, after Manasevich's arrest and Komissarov's departure, the only agents actually detailed to Rasputin were from the security branch. More-over, after visiting Rasputin secretly at night, Felix would note with surprise that after midnight Rasputin wasn't guarded by anyone.

That had been a secret order of Protopopov's. As Beletsky testified, the pitiful minister would, 'for especially important conversations, himself come to see Rasputin after 10 p.m.' And not wishing to have any witnesses to those meetings with Rasputin, Protopopov, according to Beletsky, had 'ordered the external surveillance agents removed after 10'. At the same time, he lied at Tsarskoe Selo and to Rasputin, assuring them that the security detail was still in place. But he said that after 10 p.m. 'it was stationed not by the gate but across the street out of sight.'

The agents stationed right next to the apartment also left the building by midnight. Thus Felix learned that 'after midnight Rasputin could be driven away without worrying about any agents at all.' And the plan to assassinate Rasputin at night was based on that fact.

The Royal Lure

And so on 21 November Felix met with Purishkevich. Purishkevich recorded in his diary that 'a young man in uniform [arrived] . . . I liked his appearance, in which an indescribable elegance and breeding and spiritual self-possession held sway. He was obviously a person of great will and restraint . . . qualities rarely characteristic of Russian people, especially those from the aristocratic milieu.'

Felix then set out the principal paradox to Purishkevich, who at the time was still intoxicated with his speech. 'Your speech will not achieve the results you expect. Rasputin's significance not only will not diminish, but on the contrary will grow stronger, thanks to his complete influence over Alexandra Fyodorovna, who effectively governs the entire state.'

Purishkevich was also sure of 'Rasputin's complete influence'. 'What is to be done?' he asked.

'Remove Rasputin,' said the tsar's kinsman.

Purishkevich readily agreed to take part in the murder. And Felix suggested that he meet the other two participants.

'On 22 November at 8 p.m. I was at the prince's,' Purishkevich recalled. There he met Lieutenant Sukhotin, a young officer of the Preobrazhensky regiment. And then 'into the room came a handsome, stately young man in whom I recognized Grand Duke Dmitry Pavlovich.' After that they introduced Purishkevich to the assassination plan.

Purishkevich described the plan in this way: 'It became clear that Rasputin had long been seeking an occasion to meet a certain Countess N., a young Petrograd beauty who frequented the Yusupov home. But she was in the Crimea. On his last visit to Rasputin, Yusupov had told him that in a few days the countess would be coming back to Petrograd, where she would be spending several days, and . . . that he could introduce him to her at his home.'

And so the Countess N., a certain beauty then living in the Crimea, was supposed to become the decoy that would draw Rasputin in. Purishkevich's memoir thus began with a necessary lie. For behind the identity 'countess' and 'beauty', he had decided to conceal Felix's wife Irina. Yusupov himself would later write that Rasputin 'had long wanted to meet my wife. Thinking that she was in Petrograd and my parents were in the Crimea, he agreed to come to my home.' But the tsarina's friend Lili Dehn gave an even more interesting account of the story of the 'lure'.

The File, from the testimony of Lili Dehn: 'In the last year of Rasputin's life, the prince often visited Rasputin . . . and according to Rasputin told him some astonishing, much too intimate things about his wife. What kind of things Rasputin didn't say, but Rasputin was supposed to visit the prince in order to cure his wife.'

To cure 'intimate things', that is, to exorcise the demon of lechery. Presumably, by the usual Rasputinian method. But Purishkevich simply could not write that they had decided to employ the tsar's niece as a sexual lure to trap the debauched peasant. His monarchist convictions required him to conceal a part of the truth. That will have to be kept in mind in the reconstruction of that Petrograd night, the night of the murder. And if Nikolai Mikhailovich's conjectures about Rasputin's and Felix's relationship are correct, then Rasputin had been fraudulently promised more 'healing' at the Yusupov palace. After casting lechery out of the prince, he was supposed to cast it out of his wife, too. The niece's body had been promised to the peasant that night. It made him lose his head. The cunning peasant was turned into a black grouse singing his mating call. Primeval forest (paganism) and lechery had overcome his reason.

Towards the end of November, however, the conspirators were faced with complications. Felix received Irina's reply written in Alix's own peremptory style. Irina called the plan 'savage' and a 'dirty business'.

> 25 November 1916 . . . Thanks for your insane letter. I didn't understand half of it. I see that you're planning to do something wild. Please, be careful and don't stick your nose into all that dirty business. The dirtiest thing is that you have decided to do it all without me. I don't see how I can take part in it now, since it's all arranged. Who is 'M. Gol.'? I just realized what that means and who they are while writing this! In a word, be careful. I see from your letter that you're in a state of wild enthusiasm and ready to climb a wall . . . I'll be in Petrograd on the 12th or 13th, so don't dare do anything without me, or else I won't come at all. Love and kisses. May the Lord protect you.

But the main thing was unclear: had she agreed to participate?
On 27 November Felix wrote back to her:

> What happiness your long letter was. You simply don't realize how much I need you, especially now when my whole head is exploding into pieces from all my thoughts and plans, etc. I so want to tell you all about it. Your presence by the middle of December is essential. The plan I'm writing to you about has been worked out in detail and is three quarters done, and only the finale is left, and for that your arrival is awaited. It [the murder] is the only way of saving a situation that is almost hopeless . . . You will serve as the lure . . . Of course, not a word to anyone.

At the end of the letter (presumably to persuade her) he added the enigmatic phrase, 'Malanya's also taking part.'

And so, in addition to Irina, a certain Malanya was also supposed to participate in the murder.

'At Midnight A Friend Will Come To See Him'

So Irina was supposed to arrive in Petrograd in the middle of December. And the murder was planned for that time. Meanwhile, Felix informed Rasputin that Irina was on her way. As he recalled, Rasputin 'agreed to the suggestion that he come and meet my wife . . . he did so on the condition that I pick him up myself and bring him back home. At the same time he asked me to use the back stairs. I noted with surprise and horror how simply Rasputin agreed to it all . . . removing all the obstacles himself.'

I think that Felix is dissembling here. He himself proposed coming by the back entrance after explaining the ticklishness of the situation. And Rasputin agreed. He thought that the agents guarding his building would still see them as they left the courtyard. And would follow them. And if something did happen, he thought it would be possible to flee the building the same way that he had fled the soirée at Belling's. And the agents would protect him. He didn't realize that he was no longer being guarded after 10 p.m.

The 'rehearsals' had ended, as Felix put it in his letter to Irina about the preparations for the murder. The Yusupov palace had been selected as the murder scene. But the palace was on the Moika Canal. And it was across from a police station, and that, as Purishkevich wrote, 'excluded a pistol shot'. For that reason they decided 'to finish Rasputin off with poison'.

At first they thought that it would just be the four of them – the grand duke, Purishkevich, Lieutenant Sukhotin, and Felix. But Purishkevich properly asked for a fifth, since a driver would be needed to take away the corpse. Purishkevich suggested for this a certain Dr Lazavert, a physician whom he knew well from the hospital train that he himself was in charge of.

The murder was planned for the night of 16–17 December. As Purishkevich wrote, 'We settled on that day, since Dmitry Pavlovich was busy every evening until the 16th.' Doing the murder on the night of 16–17 December also suited Purishkevich very well. His hospital train was supposed to leave for the front on the 17th, so that after the murder he could disappear from the capital.

The Poison

On 24 November one of the conspirators' last meetings took place in Purishkevich's car on the hospital train. Yusupov came with the grand duke, and Purishkevich introduced them to Dr Lazavert. Yusupov showed the others the potassium cyanide that he had obtained from Maklakov, the Constitutional Democratic leader who had given the speech about the horror of 'Rasputinism'. The poison was both in crystalline form and dissolved in liquid in a small vial. It was decided to use it to poison the pastries and wine for Rasputin. Not wishing to be party to a murder, Maklakov afterwards informed them that he had given the others a harmless powder. But Dr Lazavert knew how to tell potassium cyanide from mere powder. No, Maklakov became a humanist much later. At the time he took a great deal of trouble to see Rasputin killed. Maklakov even provided Felix with a rubber-coated dumb-bell handle, in case it should be necessary to finish the peasant off. But he himself didn't take part in the murder, pleading a trip to Moscow. He had decided to skip it. It was murder, after all.

It was then on the train that they agreed on the final plan. They would gather at midnight. And by twelve-thirty prepare for the murder by sprinkling the poison in the pastries and the wine. At twelve-thirty (as Felix had agreed with Rasputin) Felix and Dr Lazavert, disguised as a chauffeur, would set out to collect the peasant and bring him back to the Yusupov palace. Not to the front entrance, however, but a doorway off the yard. So that the silhouettes of those getting out of the car would not be visible through the cast-iron grating of the gate. And through the little door from the courtyard they would take the peasant inside.

That door opened onto a narrow winding staircase by which Rasputin would be led down to the basement. By 16 December, the basement would be turned into a charming dining room, old-Russian style. Once in the basement, Felix would explain to Rasputin that he would have to wait a little while to make his desired acquaintance with Irina. For there were unexpected guests upstairs who would soon be leaving. And in the meantime Felix would treat Rasputin in that basement dining room to the poisoned pastries and the poisoned wine.

And the other four would await the denouement on the stairway leading down to the basement. To be ready 'to burst in and render assistance' in case anything happened.

A Mystic Rehearsal

On 28 November Purishkevich arrived to look over the murder scene. 'I passed through to Felix's study with anxiety upon viewing the array of servants crowding the entryway with a blackamoor in livery at their head. Felix reassured me, explaining that all the servants would be off duty, with only two people on duty at the main entrance.'

The dining room they were going to set up in the basement for the reception of their dear guest had, Purishkevich wrote, 'a dishevelled look, since a complete remodelling was in progress and they were installing electrical wiring'. But the room seemed extremely suitable to Purishkevich for what they had in mind: the walls were thick, and the two little windows looking out onto the courtyard were small and at pavement level. So that it would even be possible to shoot.

At the time Felix himself was staying with his father-in-law, Grand Duke Alexander Mikhailovich. But more and more frequently he would drop in at the Yusupov palace to supervise the furnishing of the murder scene. An arch divided the vaulted basement into two parts, one meant as a small dining room, the other as a tiny living room.

Felix recalled:

> Three vases of Chinese porcelain already adorned niches in the walls . . .
> Old chairs of carved wood upholstered in leather had been brought from
> the storerooms . . . along with precious chalices made of ivory . . . There
> was a cabinet of the period of Catherine the Great of inlaid ebony with a
> whole maze of cut glass and bronze columns behind which drawers were
> concealed. Placed on the cabinet was a crucifix of sixteenth-century Italian
> work made of rock crystal and chased with silver . . . The large fireplace
> was decorated with gilt bowls, majolica earthenware, and a sculpture group
> of ivory. Spread on the floor was a Persian carpet, and in front of the cabinet
> lay an enormous polar bear skin . . . Positioned in the centre of the room
> was the table at which Rasputin was supposed to drink his final cup of tea.

The basement was joined to Felix's rooms by a winding staircase. And halfway down that staircase was the little door through which they were to bring Rasputin.

The murderers spent the entire morning of 26 November searching the outskirts of Petrograd by car for the best location to dispose of the future corpse through a hole in the ice. They found a suitable, poorly lit place on the Malaya Nevka river well out of town.

As I was reading Yusupov's and Purishkevich's memoirs about the prep-arations for the murder, it seemed to me that I was already familiar with it. How in anticipation of the murder they carefully searched for a place to take the corpse. For one way or another, the killing wasn't the hard part. The important thing was concealing the corpse well. And how they talked about where to do the killing and then decided to do it in the basement, so that any pistol shots wouldn't be heard. Yes, and the basement itself – small, divided in two, with its small windows at pavement level. The preparations for the murder of the royal family in a very similar basement in the Ipatiev House would closely resemble the preparations for Rasputin's murder. As if the night that their beloved peasant was killed was a dress rehearsal for the future murder of the royal family. As if the Yusupov night was a rehearsal for the Ipatiev night.

'Don't Drag Me To Petrograd'

And so that night Rasputin was simply supposed to disappear. Felix would take him from his home while everyone there was asleep and the security branch men had left. And Rasputin had promised to tell no one where he was going that night. But if he did tell anyone, then the murderers had devised the following ruse, as Felix remembered: 'Since Rasputin liked to drink at the restaurant Villa Rhode, Lieutenant Sukhotin would after the murder call the . . . Villa Rhode and ask, "What room is Rasputin in?" And after getting a negative answer, he would say, "Ah, so he isn't there yet? Well, he should be soon."' And then they would be able to say that he had been at the palace but had gone afterwards to the Villa Rhode. And the authorities would hear from the restaurant management that he really intended to go there. So that if he disappeared along the way, then it was the fault of whatever dubious character he had last associated with. And even if the authorities didn't believe them, well, let them try to prove it. They had decided to lie to the end and deny the murder.

But just before the attempt itself, a blow was struck against them. And what a blow! And who had struck it! A messenger from the Crimea brought a letter from Irina.

> 3 December . . . I know that if I come [to Petrograd], I shall certainly get sick . . . You don't know how things are with me. I want to cry all the time. My mood is terrible. I've never had one like it before. I didn't want to write all this, so as not to worry you. But I can't go on any more! I don't

know myself what's happening to me. Don't drag me to Petrograd. Come down here instead. Forgive me, my dear one, for writing such things to you. But I can't go on any more, I don't know what's the matter with me. Neurasthenia, I think. Don't be angry with me, please don't be angry. I love you terribly. I can't live without you. May the Lord protect you.

It was a strange hysteria. Terror of some sort had taken hold of her. Evidently, she too believed in the peasant-devil. She understood what a shock her letter would be for Felix, but she couldn't do anything with herself. And she not merely refused to come to Petrograd but implored him to leave: 'Come down here instead.' On the eve of the murder Felix's wife had left them without their main character – without their lure.

Irina Without Irina

But there is a gap here in Felix's account and in Purishkevich's. How did they react? What did they contrive to do instead? For they were forced to contrive a whole theatrical performance, as we shall come to realize.

Essentially, however, the plan remained unchanged. It was to announce to Rasputin that Irina had arrived in Petrograd. And to proceed as arranged: to bring Rasputin to Felix's rooms at the palace for a meeting with Irina. And to tell him the same thing – that Irina was having a little soirée which should be over soon – it had dragged on a bit. And to ask Rasputin to wait in the charming dining room down in the basement. Where the table would be laid. As if Irina's guests, scared off by Rasputin's arrival, had abruptly abandoned it. And were continuing the soirée upstairs. And to stage that soirée with music from the gramophone and, naturally, with noise and voices. And while Rasputin was waiting for a quick end to the soirée in anticipation of his meeting with Irina, Felix would poison him downstairs with the wine and pastries.

And so everything was ready. It remained only to wait for 16 December. And early on the morning of the 17th the murder would take place.

On The Eve Of The 'Reign Of Will And Power'

At the time, 'Rasputin was growing ever more infatuated with Yusupov,' Grand Duke Nikolai Mikhailovich wrote, 'and frankly recounted his incredible plans for the future. It was decided to sign a separate peace with

Germany by the end of December. That provoked in Yusupov a desire and firm resolve to remove him at any cost.'

Yusupov would say the same thing in his memoirs. Was it merely the repetition of a widespread rumour in order to provide further justification for the murder? Or were my suppositions right after all that Alix had decided that Russia should get out of the war before the decisive new offensive then being prepared (and which could end in catastrophe with all the blame laid on the commander-in-chief)? It may well be that that decision was a source of the sovereign's devastation and sadness, since he understood how essential a separate peace was and yet how shameful! For it would mean violating his word.

But it would be possible to withdraw from the war only if he took the measure that the monarchists had so often called on him to take – to dissolve the Duma.

In the days of the final 'rehearsals' for the peasant's murder, the tsar left Tsarskoe Selo to return to Headquarters. His latest brief visit home had ended. On 2 December two days before his departure Nicholas saw Rasputin for the last time. And bade him farewell. Rasputin had had another dream that promised success and prosperity. The dream of the man of God cheered Alix. As always, the dream had been timely. For she had sensed a despondency in Nicky. And in order to keep his spirits up, she had allowed him to take the tsarevich with him to Headquarters.

On 4 December the tsar left for Headquarters with the heir. And Alix's letter was already waiting for him on the train. And there are traces in that letter of the very serious decisions then being contemplated.

> 4 Dec. 1916 . . . just a little more patience & deepest faith in the prayers & help of our Friend – then all will go well. I am fully convinced that great & beautiful times are coming for yr. reign & Russia. Only keep up your spirits . . . Show to all, that you are the Master . . . – the time of great indulgence & gentleness is over – now comes your reign of will & power . . . – obedience they must be taught . . . you have spoilt them by yr. kindness & all forgivingness . . . All is turning to the good – our Friends dream means so much. Sweety, go to the Moghilev Virgin & find peace & strength there . . . Let the people see you are a christian sovereign.

All the time that they were preparing his death, Rasputin was equable and cheerful.

Apparently he too was waiting for certain serious decisions from the tsar that had been discussed by the 'Tsarskoe Selo cabinet'. Soon, soon the Duma would be gone and with it those malicious chatterers.

And Alix wrote to Nicky, '6 Dec. . . . Yesterday we spent the evening cosily, calmly in the little house. Dear big Lili [Dehn] came too later & Munia Golovina. He was in good, cheery spirits – one sees how lives & thinks for you the whole time & that all shld. be well . . . be the master; listen to your staunch Wify & our Friend.'

Out Of The Mouths Of Babes

Felix had by then resigned himself to Irina's decision and sent her a letter. Now all he asked her for was a telegram. '8 December 1916 . . . I'm leaving on the 16th or 17th. What happiness it will be to be together with you. You don't know how much I love you . . . The rehearsals have been going well . . . Send a telegram on the 16th that you are sick and ask me to come to the Crimea, that it's imperative I do so.'

Like Purishkevich, Felix planned to leave the capital immediately after the murder. And he needed the telegram about her illness so that it wouldn't seem as if he was running away.

But Irina's nervousness had not passed. Nor could it have. She understood that the 'rehearsals' would soon end in the bloody première. And as before she was out of her mind with fear of Felix's meeting with the dangerous peasant, who had other-worldly powers at his command. And that nervousness had ended in illness.

9 December . . . Dear Felix . . . Did you receive my raving? Don't think I made it all up – such has been my mood these days. This morning my temperature's normal, but I'm still lying down. For some reason I've got terribly thin . . . Forgive me my last letter. It was terribly unpleasant. I wanted to save it all until your arrival, but as it turned out I wasn't able to and had to pour my heart out. Something unbelievable's been going on with Baby. A couple of nights ago she didn't sleep very well and kept repeating, 'War, nanny, war!' The next day she was asked, 'War or peace?' And Baby answered, 'War!' The next day I said, 'Say, "peace."' And she looked right at me and answered, 'War!' It's very strange. Kisses and looking forward to seeing you terribly.

War, blood, and death. She was afraid that 'out of the mouths of babes'. . .

'In Those Days There Were So
Many Strange Things'

Our Friend maintained his mellow state with wine. In order to forget that death was gaining on him. Now he was constantly drunk.

The File, from the testimony of Maria Golovina: 'Towards the end he drank heavily and that made me pity him. The drunkenness was not reflected in his intellectual capacities. He spoke even more interestingly.'

Now the unhappy Protopopov was obliged to visit him during his drinking bouts. It was a way of checking on the minister's submissiveness, which the latter found unbearable.

The File, from Golovina's testimony:

> Protopopov complained in conversation with me that he was very tired, that he was in pain, and that only God could help him. And that he would go away to a small cloister somewhere, if only he could, but that he wasn't able to out of love for 'them' – the sovereign and empress, as I understood him . . . If you think about it, then of course it was strange that the minister of internal affairs was having such a conversation with me, but in those days there were so many strange things!

But as before, Rasputin would be transformed whenever he was called to Tsarskoe Selo. As Komissarov testified in the File, 'On that day he wouldn't drink . . . but would go to the baths and light a candle . . . he always did that whenever he was going to see the tsar personally. Then he would spend the whole day getting ready. And on the way he would concentrate and focus his will.'

And even when he was taken to the 'tsars' after the merry laying of the foundation of Anya's church, he was, as the tsarina noted in her letter, sober. He knew how to sober up, as Komissarov observed with astonishment on more than one occasion. And the 'tsars' never saw him other than sober.

An Icon For His Grave

On 11 December, only a few days before Rasputin's murder, Alix visited Novgorod with the grand duchesses and of course the Friend.

In Novgorod a mass was celebrated in the ancient Saint Sophia cathedral. And at the Novgorod Desyatina Convent, they visited a prophetess. '12 Dec. . . . She lay in bed in a small dark room, so they brought a candle for us to see each other. She is 107, wears <u>irons</u> (now they lay near her).'

In the flickering light of the candle, the tsarina made out her 'young, shining eyes'.

And the old nun, who had lived in the time of the great Romanovs Nicholas I, Alexander II, and Alexander III, started to speak out of the darkness. She said to the tsarina, '"and you the beautiful one – don't fear the heavy cross" (several times),' Alix wrote to Nicky.

Thus ended her last journey as empress. The next time that she set out from Tsarskoe Selo, it would be as a dethroned prisoner bound for exile. She and the Friend had brought back from Novgorod a little icon as a gift for Our Friend.

The same one that would later be found in his grave.

The Last Days

On 13 December Yusupov called Purishkevich and said, 'Vanya has arrived.' It was Felix's way of confirming that everything was ready for 16 December.

Rasputin continued to be in the mellowest of moods. Everything was turning out in the best way possible. By 'Mama's' order, the case against Manasevich-Manuilov had been dropped.

Manasevich-Manuilov would be quite candid in his testimony before the Extraordinary Commission in 1917: 'Rasputin told me, "Your case cannot be examined – it would make too much noise."' And he told the tsarina to write herself to the minister of justice. He was afraid of a newspaper campaign . . . was afraid his name would come up. Rasputin called immediately: 'I've just heard from the palace: "Mama" got a telegram from her husband that the case has been dropped.'

It actually did happen that way. Literally. On 10 December Alix wrote to Nicky, 'On Manuilov's paper I beg you to write "discontinue the case" & send it to Minister of Justice . . . Otherwise . . . there can be very disagreeable talks . . . Well, please at once without delay send Manuilov's paper to Makarov [the minister of justice] otherwise too late.' And a few days later Manasevich was at liberty. Rasputin's favourite secretary once more appeared at the apartment on Gorokhovaya Street. And turned up at his club, too. And gambled for high stakes. He took a drive around Petrograd. He was sniffing about to make sure everything was calm. And apparently he was satisfied. For Rasputin, who until then had been afraid to go out into the street, even decided to take a walk around the city.

On 15 December 1916, the day before the murder Alix wrote to her husband:

Thanks so much (& fr. A. too) for Manuilov . . . Our Fr. . . . never goes out since ages, except to come here, but yesterday he walked in the streets with Munia, to the Kazan and St. Isaacs (Cathedrals) & not one disagreeable look, people all quiet. Says in 3 or 4 days things will go better in Roumania & all will go better . . . Please, tell Trepov Duma on leave till beginning of Feb. . . . believe our Friend's advice. Even the Children notice how things don't come out well if we do not listen to Him & the contrary – good when listen.

It was the last time Our Friend would advise what she so wanted. And the night before the last day of Rasputin's life, the tsar signed a ukase proroguing the Duma's work until 19 February. Thus began Rasputin's last day. Death on the eve of victory.

14

THE YUSUPOV NIGHT (THE MYSTERY OF THE MURDER)

The Last Evening

Everything passed as usual that day. First the touching Munya appeared and spent the whole day with Rasputin. 'I arrived before 12:00 and stayed until 10:00 p.m. ... he was excited and said, "Today I'm going," although he didn't say where,' Golovina testified in the File.

Badmaev's testimony before the Extraordinary Commission was different: 'Golovina confessed to her grief. She had known the day before that Rasputin intended to drink at Prince Yusupov's.'

Vyrubova also dropped by. Beletsky testified that Vyrubova had been at Rasputin's at 8:00 p.m., and that Rasputin had told her he was supposed to be going with young Prince Yusupov to treat his wife.

Vyrubova didn't know that the prince's wife wasn't in Petrograd, but she advised Rasputin to turn down the invitation. She said it was degrading to him that they were ashamed to receive him openly in the daytime and chose night instead. And he gave her his promise he wouldn't go.

So, having promised Felix to keep the trip a secret, the cunning peasant had not taken any chances and had told all his close friends where he was going. He believed that the agents would be accompanying him. But he was wrong about that, thanks to Protopopov's lie. So even though he trusted Felix completely, he had still taken security measures.

Golovina left him at ten. After that a caller came by. From among those transitory women who made their appearances in the 'little room with the sofa' and then disappeared. As the building porter later testified, 'A lady of about twenty-five was with him from 10:00 p.m. until 11:00.' That was confirmed by his niece Anna, who at the time was staying at his apartment. 'Around 10 p.m. a plump blonde arrived who was called "Sister Maria", although she was no sister of mercy. For she helped him to remove the tension that apparently took hold of him against his will.' And to 'refine his nerves' before the night that promised him so much. His daughters returned around eleven.

The next day they both gave their accounts to the investigators.

Varvara: 'Matryona and I had been visiting someone and went to bed at 11:00, and I did not see how, where, or with whom he left. Father didn't say anything to me . . . about planning to go anywhere.' But, on the other hand, her older sister Matryona testified, 'After I got back and was going off to bed, Father told me that he was going to visit the Little One.'

And to complete the night, Protopopov arrived around midnight.

'I stopped by to see Rasputin the night he was murdered . . . around 12 after seeing Voskoboinikova off at the station,' Protopopov testified before the Extraordinary Commission. (He supposedly arrived at that time because he knew that the agents directly guarding the apartment would have left the building around 11:30.) 'I . . . saw him for about ten minutes and saw only him, since he opened the door himself. He didn't say anything to me about intending to go out.' Rasputin, who was expecting Yusupov, hastened to curtail his conversation with the minister.

It was after twelve when Rasputin started to get dressed. As his maid testified, he put on a light blue shirt embroidered with cornflowers, but 'he couldn't button the collar and I buttoned it for him.' He continued to be agitated. After dressing, he lay down on his bed to wait for Felix. His daughters were already asleep. But his niece and his maid, Katya Pech-yorkina, still hadn't gone to bed. The niece told the investigator, 'Uncle lay down on his bed just after twelve in his clothing,' and in reply to her and Pechyorkina's puzzled questions, he said, '"I'm going . . . to visit the Little One tonight." The "Little One" was what Uncle called Yusupov.'

After that the niece went to bed in the daughters' room, and Pechyorkina went into the kitchen and lay down behind the partition set aside for the maid. Apparently her master's suspicious preparations had aroused her curiosity, and she did not sleep but waited to see who would be coming for him. Finally, 'the bell rang at the back door.' And parting the curtains that shielded her bed, she saw Rasputin with the person who had rung. It was the 'Little One' – Prince Yusupov.

A Chronicle Of The Morning

At 8:00 a.m. on 17 December, Rasputin's niece, Anna, telephoned Munya Golovina and said her uncle had left the night before with the Little One but still hadn't returned.

Early the same morning Protopopov was awakened by a phone call. The mayor of Petrograd, Alexander Balk, informed him in a very worried voice that a constable standing on the Moika Canal had heard shots coming from the Yusupov palace. After which the constable had been called into the building and told by the Duma member Purishkevich, who was there, that Rasputin had been killed. Protopopov immediately called the building on Gorokhovaya Street and ascertained that Rasputin hadn't spent the night there and still wasn't back.

Maria Golovina arrived at Gorokhovaya Street around eleven. She told Rasputin's daughters that she had called the prince, but 'they were still asleep there.' Afterwards Munya testified that at the time she wasn't concerned, since 'Rasputin had asked the prince in my presence to take him to the Gypsies, and so knowing he had gone with him, I didn't worry.' Finally, around noon, Felix himself called her. And she reassured the daughters by telling them that Felix had given his word that he had not seen their father. What was her horror when the maid Katya swore to her that this was a lie! That Felix had come by for Rasputin during the night, and that she herself had seen him in the apartment.

Golovina immediately called Vyrubova at her little house in Tsarskoe Selo.

The File, from the testimony of the medical orderly Zhuk: 'They called around 12:00 p.m. and said that Rasputin had left and not come back. Vyrubova immediately informed the palace, and there was a great deal of anxiety and constant discussion with Petrograd.'

Protopopov was in continuous contact with Tsarskoe Selo at the time. He passed on to the empress and Vyrubova the information given to him by the constable about the events at the Yusupov palace. Then on the morning of 17 December Protopopov summoned General Popov and ordered him to open an investigation at once. So under the number 573 an order was issued to General Popov 'to conduct an inquiry into the matter of the disappearance of Grigory Efimovich Rasputin', and to do so, moreover, in absolute secret.

The Impatient Visitors

Early that same morning visitors appeared at Rasputin's apartment, visitors who were very interested in the papers left behind by their vanished owner.

From the interrogation of Manasevich by the Extraordinary Commission:

'Were you at Rasputin's apartment the night he disappeared?'

'I was there in the morning . . . I arrived . . . and there was a commotion. Simanovich had arrived with Bishop Isidor and said they had been to the police chief, where everything had taken place.'

'Did you go through his papers?'

'They weren't my concern,' Manasevich naturally testified.

'Did Protopopov visit Rasputin's apartment while you were there?'

'Not while I was there.'

(Protopopov had evidently been there before Manasevich and the others.)

From Protopopov's interrogation:

'There is a rumour that you were at his apartment immediately after the murder.'

'Never . . . after all, the police were there.'

But the minister of internal affairs, taking into account Rasputin's relations with him and the 'tsars', had simply had no choice but to get there ahead of the police and everyone else. As soon as he had learned of Rasputin's disappearance. So that after the visits to the apartment of all those inquisitive guests, no important papers whatever could have remained to be found.

Events had meanwhile taken a turn. At 2:00 p.m. General Popov received information that there were bloodstains on Great Petrovsky Bridge over the Malaya Nevka river, and that a brown boot had been found lodged in a wall of the bridge's foundation. At 3:00 p.m. the same afternoon, the boot was shown to Rasputin's daughters, and they 'recognized it as belonging to their father'.

'I Cannot And Won't Believe He
Has Been Killed'

By then rumours had already begun to spread through the city. The presumed death of the favourite excited all of high society. Grand dukes, ambassadors, ministers, the royal family at Tsarskoe Selo – all were passionately discussing the rumours of the death of the semi-literate peasant from the Siberian village.

From the diary of the Grand Duke Nikolai Mikhailovich:

17 December . . . At 5:30, two phone calls – one from Princess Trubetskaya, the other from the British ambassador Buchanan . . . They told me that Grigory Rasputin was killed last night. The unexpected news stunned me, and I rushed by automobile to my brother Alexander's home on the Moika Canal in order to find out what was going on [so evidently he had been told not only about the murder, but also about the fact that Felix, who was living at his brother Alexander's at the time, was suspected of it]. A servant informed me that Felix would be coming back late.

But the grand duke knew where to get information. He went to the seditious Yacht Club. That day the club was packed. Numerous carriages and automobiles were waiting by the entrance. And that whole aristocratic anthill was anxiously buzzing.

'I went to dine at the club, where the only thing being talked about was Grishka's disappearance,' he recorded.

'Towards the end of dinner, Dmitry Pavlovich came in, pale as death, although I didn't talk to him, since he sat down at another table . . . [Prime Minister] Trepov was arguing for everyone to hear that it was all nonsense . . . But Dmitry Pavlovich declared to others that, in his opinion, Rasputin had either gone off somewhere or been killed . . . We sat down to cards, while Dmitry Pavlovich went to the French-language Mikhailov Theatre.' So everyone got the required information. For somehow they all knew that Dmitry was somehow involved.

At the time the Friend had moved to the palace at the tsarina's demand.

From Zhuk's testimony in the File: 'Vyrubova started staying overnight at the palace at the empress's orders. They were afraid she too might be killed, since she . . . had begun receiving threatening letters a year before Rasputin's murder . . . They were especially . . . afraid of the young grand dukes. I was ordered not to admit any of the grand dukes . . . The inside shutters in Vyrubova's apartment were changed.'

Alix suspected that it was only the beginning of a reprisal against 'ours' by the Romanov youth. And on the afternoon of the 17th, she wrote to the tsar:

We are sitting together – can imagine our feelings – thoughts – our Friend has disappeared. Yesterday A[nya] saw him & he said Felix asked him to come in the night, a motor wld. fetch him to see Irina . . .

This night big scandal at Yusupov's house – big meeting, Dmitri, Purishkevitch etc. all drunk, Police heard shots, Purishkevitch ran out screaming to the Police that our Friend was killed.

Police searching . . .

Felix wished to leave to-night for Crimea, begged Kalinin [Protopopov] to stop him. . . .

Felix pretends He never came to the house & never asked him. Seems like quite a paw [a trap]. I still trust in God's mercy that one has only driven Him off somewhere . . .

I cannot & won't believe He has been killed. God have mercy . . .

. . . come quickly – nobody will dare to touch her [Anya] or do anything when you are here.

Felix came often to him lately . . .

From her telegram of 17 December 1916: 'We still hope in God's mercy. Felix and Dmitri implicated.'

Tsarskoe Selo knew by evening that both men were implicated.

From the memoirs of Princess Olga, Dmitry's stepmother:

On Saturday evening, December 17/30, a concert was given in Tsarskoe Selo . . . Around eight o'clock the phone rang. An instant later Vladimir [her son from her marriage to the grand duke] ran into my room: 'It's the end of the elder. They just called me. Lord, now we can breathe easier. The details still aren't known. He did in any case disappear twenty-four hours ago. It may be we'll find out something at the concert' . . . I shall never forget that evening. No one listened either to the concert or to the performers. During the intermission, I noticed that the gazes directed at us were especially intent. But at the time I still hadn't guessed why.

Finally, one of her friends told her. ' "It appears those responsible for the affair are from the highest aristocracy. Felix Yusupov, Purishkevich, and the grand duke have been named." My heart stopped. By evening's end Dmitry's name was on everyone's lips.'

The Case Of The Missing Peasant
Grigory Rasputin

The morning of the 18th came and Rasputin still had not been found. Felix was unable to leave for the Crimea that day. He had been invited to give testimony in the case of 'the missing peasant Rasputin' under General Popov's charge. For three days beginning on 17 December General Popov conducted continuous interrogations along with Colonel Popel. Among the interrogated were the two constables who had been standing that night near the Yusupov palace, Rasputin's two daughters, the maid, Rasputin's niece, and Maria Golovina.

And Felix himself was interrogated on 18 December by Minister of

Justice Makarov. Felix's testimony is especially interesting, since it was given while the trail was still warm – the day after.

But on 19 December, the third day of the inquiry, Protopopov suddenly issued an order immediately terminating the case and he appropriated all the depositions. After the fall of the Romanovs, the case file lay in the archive, and then it vanished. In 1928 a certain Vasiliev died in Paris in great poverty. He had been the last director of the Department of Police. Surviving him and published soon afterwards was the manuscript of a book he had written about the tsarist secret police. And in the book he quoted (with errors) certain documents from the missing file. The documents (together with the errors) from his book thereafter made their way into many of the works about Rasputin.

It turns out, however, that the case file itself was published. Immediately after the February Revolution, the magazine *Times Past* printed the file in an issue devoted to the most sensational documents of the fallen regime.

We shall compare the testimony in the case file with the story of the murder created by the murderers Purishkevich and Yusupov. A story that has generally been accepted.

And that case file, along with other documents, will help us to establish a true picture of the mysterious Yusupov night.

The Police Account

According to the case file, when Felix was personally interrogated by Minister of Justice Makarov, the inquiry already had at its disposal the most interesting testimony of the two constables. The testimony of both men is contained in the case file.

The forty-eight-year-old constable, Stepan Vlasyuk, who was on duty not far from the Yusupov palace, reported: 'Around three or four in the morning I heard three or four shots quickly following one another.' Vlasyuk went up to the constable Efimov, who was on duty nearby on the other side of the Moika canal.

[In answer] 'To my question as to where the shooting had been, Efimov indicated the Yusupov palace.' Vlasyuk set off for the palace. Next to it he met the building custodian. But the latter said he hadn't heard any shots. 'At the time,' Vlasyuk testified, 'I saw crossing the courtyard in the direction of the gate two men in military jackets but no hats, in whom I recognized Prince Yusupov and his butler Buzhinsky. I asked the latter what the shooting had been. He replied that he hadn't heard any shots.' After which Vlasyuk, his mind now set at ease, went back to his post. 'I didn't inform anyone about what had happened, because I had heard such sounds before from bursting automobile tyres. But after fifteen or twenty minutes, Buzhinsky came over to me and said that Prince Yusupov was asking for me. No sooner had I crossed the threshold of Prince Yusupov's study than he came to meet me with someone I didn't know with a reddish beard and moustache . . . and a khaki military jacket.'

Vlasyuk then related a remarkable conversation.

> The person asked me, 'Have you ever heard of Purishkevich?'
> 'I have.'
> 'I am Purishkevich. And have you ever heard of Rasputin? Well, Rasputin is dead. And if you love our mother Russia, you'll keep quiet about it.'
> 'Yes, sir.'
> 'You can go now.'
> 'About twenty minutes later, Kalyadin, the district police officer, came to me and I reported everything to him.'

A Woman's Cry And A
Mysterious Automobile

The second constable, Fyodor Efimov, across the canal from the Yusupov palace, was fifty-nine years old – an old, experienced policeman. He reported:

'At 2:30 a.m. I heard a shot, and three or four seconds later, I heard the sound of three or four more shots in quick succession. After the first shot, I heard a not loud cry, as if from a woman.'

In reply to the investigator's question about an automobile arriving at or leaving the palace after the shots were fired, Efimov reported, 'For twenty or thirty minutes no automobile or horse cab passed along the Moika. It was only a half hour later . . . that an automobile drove past, although it didn't stop anywhere.'

We shall remember that both policemen watching the building testified about having heard three or four shots at the Yusupov palace. And that Efimov, the one who was closer, also heard 'a not loud cry, as if from a woman'. And one other important detail – that no automobile went to the palace after the shots. The only automobile seen was one that drove from the direction of the palace half an hour after the shots.

The inquiry had this testimony to hand when Felix Felixovich – Prince Yusupov and Count Sumarokov-Elston – was interrogated on 18 December.

After telling the story of his acquaintance with Rasputin, Felix turned to 'that evening'.

'It Was The Grand Duke Who Had Killed The Dog'

At the time I was redoing . . . a room in my house on the Moika . . . and the Grand Duke Dmitry Pavlovich suggested I have a house-warming party. It was decided to invite to it Vladimir Mitrofanovich Purishkevich and several officers and society ladies. The party was planned for 16 December . . . For reasons you can readily understand, I don't want to give the names of the officers and ladies; it could damage them and give rise to false rumours. In order not to hamper my guests, I ordered the servants to lay out everything for tea and supper . . . and then not come in. The majority of the guests were supposed to come not by the front door . . . but by the side entrance . . . to which I had my own key. Those who gathered drank tea and danced. Around 12:30 Rasputin called from somewhere . . . inviting us to go to the Gypsies. To which the guests responded with jokes and wisecracks . . . Rasputin wouldn't tell me where he was calling from. But voices could be heard over the phone, as well as a woman's squeal.

Makarov could have tripped Felix up here with the testimony of Rasputin's household. But the minister did not dare impugn a kinsman of the tsar with the testimony of a servant and a peasant's daughters. And the prince continued:

Around 2–2:30 a.m. the . . . ladies were ready to go home, and Grand Duke Dmitry Pavlovich went with them . . . After they had left, I heard shots in the courtyard. I went into the courtyard and saw a dog lying dead by the gate. His imperial highness subsequently informed me that it was he who had killed the dog . . . After that I called in the constable from the street and told him that if anyone should ask about the shots, to say that a friend of mine had killed a dog.

A question apparently then followed about Purishkevich's words to the constable. The prince's answer is amusing.

After that Purishkevich, who was in my study, started speaking. I didn't catch everything he said . . . In regard to the constable's testimony that Purishkevich allegedly told him in my study that Rasputin had been killed, Purishkevich was drunk, and I don't recall what he said . . . I wasn't at Rasputin's on the 16th either in the afternoon or in the evening, as my guests and servants can corroborate. Some people have given serious thought to a murder plan and have linked it to me and the party in my home.

A Sensation At The Station

Felix had sent similar testimony to the tsarina the day before. Afterwards, on the evening of 18 December, he finally got ready to take the train to the Crimea. But . . .

From the diary of Grand Duke Nikolai Mikhailovich for 18 December:

The next day, still not having seen Yusupov, I learned that Felix . . . and my nephews were leaving for the Crimea. But the rumours continued unabated all day, and A. F. Trepov informed me on the 18th by telephone that very probably Rasputin really had been killed, and that Dmitry Pavlovich, Felix Yusupov, and Purishkevich had been persistently named as involved in the murder . . . I breathed more easily and quietly sat down to play cards, glad that scoundrel would be causing no more harm, but afraid Trepov's information might be false.

At 9:00 p.m. I visited my nephews and bade them farewell . . . What was my surprise when at 10:30 Felix called me up and said that he had been detained by a gendarme officer at Nikolaev Station, and that he very much asked that I drop by to see him. Felix was already in bed. I spent half an hour with him listening to his confidences.

Felix repeated verbatim to Nikolai Mikhailovich the story that he had told Minister of Justice Makarov. But the grand duke already knew about the rumours.

'I listened to his narrative in silence and then told him the following: his fiction wouldn't stand up to any criticism, and that . . . he was the murderer.'

The next morning all Petrograd was abuzz with the sensational news that Prince Yusupov had been detained the night before at the Nikolaev Station. That the train to the Crimea had left without him.

'I Greet You, Gentlemen Murderers!'

Felix had not merely been detained; he had been placed under house arrest. The tsarina had demanded that the inquiry get the truth. Grand Duke Dmitry had been placed under house arrest, too. But the arrest was a highly peculiar one. Felix moved to Dmitry's house the next day, which gave them the opportunity to work out a common story in anticipation of the investigator's summons. But they wouldn't be summoned by the investigator

any more. The tsar was fond of history. And he remembered the events of
the French revolution. The public examination of the case implicating
Marie Antoinette in the theft of the queen's necklace had been the prologue
of the end of Louis XVI. That is why when Rasputin's corpse came to the
river's surface on 19 December, General Popov was ordered to end the
inquiry.

By then the police had already intercepted the first congratulatory telegrams sent to Dmitry and Felix. Those from the God-fearing Ella must
have especially stunned Nicholas II. She, the meek intercessor, had written
to Dmitry: '18 December, 9:30 a.m. . . . I just returned late last night after
spending the whole week in Sarov and Diveev praying for all you dear ones.
I ask you to send me a letter with the details of the events. May God give
Felix strength after the patriotic act performed by him.' And she sent
another telegram to the Crimea to Zinaida Yusupova: 'All my ardent and
profound prayers surround all of you for the patriotic act of your dear son.'
So Ella, having only just returned from Diveev on 18 December, already
knew all about the murder and the murderers. And she blessed the murder.
She lacked only the details that Felix would tell Grand Duke Nikolai
Mikhailovich the day after after the murder.

From the diary of Grand Duke Nikolai Mikhailovich: 'The next day, the
19th, after Felix had moved to the apartment of Dmitry Pavlovich, I blurted
out upon entering the room, "I greet you, gentlemen murderers!"' And
seeing that resistance was 'pointless', Felix began his story.

The Story Of The Murder As
Told By The Murderers

Afterwards in Paris Felix Yusupov would publish his memoirs of the murder
in a variety of editions. In them he would basically repeat what he had told
Nikolai Mikhailovich on that evening in Petrograd.

At the same time, however, there is another story about everything that
happened at the Yusupov palace, written down by another participant in
the murder.

Unlike Felix, the Duma member Purishkevich had succeeded in getting
out of the city. His hospital train safely left for the front the day after
the murder. Purishkevich wrote continuously in his car, describing what
happened. 'I am surrounded by the deep of night and utter silence, while
my train, gently swaying, carries me off into the distance . . . I cannot sleep

. . . the events of the last forty-eight hours whirl through my mind . . . Rasputin is no more, he has been killed . . . It has pleased fate for him to fall at my hand . . . Thank goodness that the hand of Grand Duke Dmitry Pavlovich has not been stained with that dirty blood.' And he explains: 'The royal youth must not be guilty of . . . any matter connected to the spilling of blood. Even if it is the blood of Rasputin.' We shall remember that: 'the royal youth must not be guilty.' And then Purishkevich proceeds to his narrative.

It is in fact on the basis of those two sources – Yusupov's and Purishkevich's memoirs – that the story of Rasputin's murder has been repeated from book to book. It is a story that, as Grand Duke Nikolai Mikhailovich wrote in his diary, is 'reminiscent . . . of murder in medieval Italy'. Or, more accurately, of the thriller so popular in Rasputin's time and our own, in which a terrible demon is killed by human heroes. Sensing that element of trashy fiction, Leon Trotsky would call the story 'tasteless'. Its resemblance to 'literature' already puts you very much on your guard. And the more carefully you read about it, the more suspect it seems.

Let us first permit the two murderers to speak for themselves, however.

'An Evening Of Unforgettable Nightmare'

Purishkevich: 'I shall try to recount with photographic accuracy the whole course of the historically significant drama that unfolded. On that night . . . the weather was a mild two to three degrees above freezing and wet snow was falling.'

And in that wet snow a military automobile rare for those times appeared at the Yusupov Palace. The automobile stood for a while, then departed, then came back again. And then, finally, it drove up to the palace's main entrance.

In the automobile, as Purishkevich writes, were himself and Dr Lazavert, who was sitting in for the driver. According to the agreement, they were supposed to drive into the courtyard up to the side entrance so as to enter the building unnoticed. But the courtyard gate was closed. Purishkevich realized the silly Felix had forgotten all about their compact.

Purishkevich: 'After circling a couple of times we drove up to the main entrance.' And from there they passed into Yusupov's study, where the others had already gathered (the grand duke, Felix, and Lieutenant Sukhotin). Felix greeted Purishkevich and Lazavert as if nothing was the matter. But they were in no mood for explanations. They all quickly went downstairs to the basement, where Purishkevich, delighted by its transformation 'into an elegant *bonbonnière* in the style of the ancient Russian palaces', forgot his anger.

'That charming room,' Purishkevich wrote, 'was divided into two parts: the front one nearer the fireplace was a sort of miniature dining room . . . A fire was cosily burning in the fireplace, on the mantle stood a magnificent ivory crucifix, and under the window there was a small table with bottles – sherry, port, madeira, and marsala. The rear part of the room was a sitting room with a polar bear skin on the floor . . . in front of a settee.'

They sat down at the table in the 'dining room', and Yusupov suggested they sample the pastries prepared for Rasputin before stuffing them with the poison. The pastries were well matched to the dining room – 'little pink and brown petits fours chosen to complement the colour of the wall'. They drank tea and nervously 'waited for 11:30 when the spies would abandon Rasputin's apartment'. Felix knew that the external surveillance would be lifted then, as well. After finishing their tea, they 'tried to make it look like a whole group had been scared off by the arrival of an unexpected guest'. They poured a little tea in the cups and scattered wrinkled napkins on the table. Then Dr Lazavert put on gloves and began to chip the poison – pellets of potassium cyanide – onto a plate for inserting into the little pastries with the pink cream filling. The chocolate pastries were left unpoisoned (for Felix). Lazavert 'thickly sprinkled the poison inside the pastries'. After completing that rather awful task, Lazavert tossed the gloves into the fireplace, which 'started smoking, so that the room had to be aired out'. Then he changed into a chauffeur's uniform. Felix threw a fur coat over his shoulders and 'pulled his fur cap down over his ears so that his face was completely hidden'. And shortly after, those remaining behind heard the sound an automobile pulling away.

They drove up to the house on Gorokhovaya Street. The building custodian testified during the inquiry that 'A motor drove up to the locked gates of the building after midnight. And an unknown man, after getting out of the motor, went directly to the door. In answer to the question where he was going, he said, "To Rasputin's."' He was 'beardless . . . with a black moustache . . . dressed in a long fur coat . . . and on his head he had a black fur cap'. The custodian pointed him to the front door, but instead of using it, the stranger went to the 'back door. It was clear from everything that he was someone familiar with how the building was arranged,' the custodian testified.

'I went up the back stairway,' Felix recalled. 'It was unlit, and I felt my way along, finding the door to the elder's apartment with great difficulty.'

The chain jangled, the bolt squeaked, Rasputin opened the door, and Felix stepped into the kitchen.

'It was dark, and it seemed to me that there was someone watching me from the next room. I instinctively pulled my cap down over my eyes.'

It was not for nothing that Felix had sensed someone's gaze. We recall here that he had been watched as he entered the kitchen by Katya Pech-yorkina, who slept in the kitchen behind a curtain.

And she testified when, 'both passed by me in the kitchen to the other rooms', parting the curtain, she saw 'that it was the Little One who came'.

'We went into the bedroom, whose only illumination was an icon lamp,' Felix wrote.

> Rasputin lit a candle. I noticed that the bed was mussed. It's possible he had been resting. His fur coat and beaver cap were ready by the bed. Rasputin was wearing . . . a silk shirt embroidered with cornflowers and girded with a thick crimson cord with two large tassels on the ends, wide black velveteen pants, and high boots . . . I was suddenly overwhelmed with infinite pity for that person. I was ashamed of the dirty, monstrous lie I was resorting to. At that moment I despised myself. I asked myself how I could have conceived such a base crime . . . I looked with horror on my trusting victim.

But Rasputin did not sense Felix's disturbed state at all. And for that reason Felix asks the questions that we ourselves should like to ask. 'What of his clairvoyance? What good was his gift of foresight if he did not see the trap that had set for him? But my pangs of conscience yielded to a firm resolve to carry out the business. We went out into the dark stairwell and Rasputin locked the door after him. I felt his fingers roughly take hold of my arm. "Better let me guide you," he said, leading me down the dark stairway.' Thus, they went down arm in arm. And even while holding his arm, Rasputin did not sense anything. For even with all his intuitive powers, he trusted Felix completely and blindly. They got in the car and set off for the Yusupov palace.

Back at the palace, as Purishkevich recounts, they 'were checking the gramophone' that was supposed to create the impression of a soirée in progress, and 'were busy with a vial of dissolved potassium cyanide', which they added to two of the four wine glasses, as had been agreed with Felix. Then, they 'waited, silent pacing, since there was no interest in talk'. Purishkevich 'took out the heavy Sauvage revolver that was weighing down his pocket' and placed it on the table in Yusupov's study. A revolver that would, according to him, play a central role in the tragedy. Finally, they heard the sound of the car entering into the yard. 'And then the lieutenant turned on the gramophone and started playing the American march "Yankee Doodle",' a march that Purishkevich would remember for the rest of his life. Then they heard the voice of Rasputin saying, 'Where be you, dear one?'

Yusupov: 'Entering the house . . . I heard the voices of my friends . . . the gramophone was merrily playing an American tune . . . Rasputin listened and said, "What's going on there, a spree?"

"No, my wife's got company. They'll be leaving soon. In the meantime, let's have some tea in the dining room."' And Rasputin and Felix went downstairs to that basement turned into 'a charming dining room'.

Meanwhile, Dr Lazavert, after doffing his chauffeur's uniform, had gone upstairs to the study to join the other murderers. And they all came out of the room and stood by the railing of the stairway leading to the basement. And started their vigil. Halfway down the stairs below them was the door from the courtyard through which Rasputin and Felix had come in. Crowding against the railing, they waited. 'I with a knuckleduster in my hand, behind me the grand duke, behind him Lieutenant Sukhotin, and Dr Lazavert in the rear,' Purishkevich recalled. Thus they stood 'listening to every rustle coming from below'. They heard the echoes of speech and the strains of 'Yankee Doodle' but not the crucial sound – the sound of bottles being uncorked. They were talking downstairs, but 'they weren't drinking or eating anything.'

'Rasputin took off his coat and started to study the furniture with interest,' Felix recalled.

> The chest with the maze particularly attracted his attention. Admiring it like a child . . . he opened and closed it and studied it inside and out . . . I offered him some tea and wine . . . to my disappointment he declined. 'Has something happened?' I wondered. We sat down at the table and chatted, going through our mutual acquaintances. Exhausting that topic, Rasputin asked for some tea. I offered him a plate of pastries. For some reason I offered him the ones that hadn't been poisoned. A moment later, I passed him the plate with the poisoned pastries. At first he refused. 'I don't want any; they're too sweet.'

And that is a moment we shall remember – Rasputin refusing to eat the pastries after explaining, 'I don't want any; they're too sweet.'

But afterwards, Felix declares, 'he took first one and then another. I looked at him in horror.' But between those two events another event took place that Felix does not mention. Alhough it is described by Purishkevich.

When Rasputin refused to eat the 'sweet' pastries, Felix, as it turns out, panicked and went upstairs. And Purishkevich describes in detail how, as they stood by the stairway, they heard the sound of a door opening downstairs in the basement, and how they 'all soundlessly hurried back on tiptoe to Yusupov's study. Yusupov came in. And said, "Imagine, gentlemen, the animal will not eat or drink."'

'What's his mood?' Purishkevich asked.

'Not good. It's as if he's had a premonition.'

And Felix went back downstairs to Rasputin.

And it was then that Rasputin for some reason changed his mind and started to drink and partake of the pastries. And that circumstance is one that we shall also remember. Purishkevich: 'Soon afterwards the sound of bottles being uncorked was heard. "They are drinking," the grand duke whispered. "We won't have to wait much longer, now." But half an hour passed and nothing.'

'The potassium cyanide should have had an immediate effect,' Felix recalled, 'but Rasputin . . . continued to chat with me as if nothing was the matter.' Felix poured a second glass and Rasputin drank it, but 'the poison did not manifest its strength'. A third glass remained, the last. Felix himself had then 'in desperation started drinking to force the peasant to drink the last glass'.

> We sat in front of each other and silently drank. He looked at me, and his eyes cunningly smiled: 'so you see, however hard you try, you can't do anything to me.' Then . . . an expression of hatred suddenly took the place of that craftily saccharine smile. Never had I seen him so frightening. He looked at me with diabolical eyes . . . I was overcome by a kind of strange immobility and my head began to spin . . . Coming to, I saw Rasputin on the settee, his head down, hiding his eyes from view. 'Pour me a cup, I'm very thirsty,' he said in a feeble voice. While I was pouring him a cup, he got up and walked across the room. His eye fell on a guitar that I had accidentally forgotten in the dining room.
>
> 'Play something merry, my friend. I like it when you sing.'

And Felix began to sing. 'When I finished singing, he . . . looked at me with a sad, quiet expression. "Sing some more, I really like the music, you have much soul in you." I started singing again . . . And the time passed – the clock showed 2:30. The nightmare had lasted over two hours.'

Two legitimate questions arise here. The fact is that because of his delight in Felix's singing, Rasputin completely forgot why he had come – he forgot all about Irina. The 'several friends' he had been promised 'would soon be leaving' had been sitting upstairs for two and a half hours! And he hadn't objected! For two whole hours and more he'd been drinking and listening to songs and forgetting the purpose of his visit. Furthermore, during that two and a half hours he hadn't sensed anything peculiar in Felix's behaviour – the sensitive, nervous, and, as we shall see, highly susceptible Felix. Could Felix, obviously no professional murderer, really not have revealed anything of his agitation during that two and a half hours? It's highly unlikely! And there is a third question that will perplex everyone and provoke numerous other questions. And that would become the basis of the legend about Rasputin's superhuman capacities. Why hadn't the poison taken him?

However, let us leave these questions unanswered for the time being and continue our narration of the murder.

And so the poison had not taken Rasputin. Felix was naturally shaken by the situation. 'Upstairs, their patience had apparently run out,' Felix recalled. 'The noise coming from up there grew louder and louder. "What's all that noise?" Rasputin asked.

"The guests are probably leaving. I'll take a look."'

Purishkevich:

A wan Yusupov came upstairs. 'It's not possible! He drank two glasses with poison and ate several of the pink pastries and nothing. It's beyond me what we'll do now, all the more since he's started worrying why it's taking the countess so long to come to him [note that he has already 'started worrying' after more than two hours]. I managed to explain that it would be hard for her to absent herself without being noticed . . . as there aren't many guests upstairs, but that in all likelihood she'll be down in ten minutes or so . . . He's sitting gloomily . . . the poison's effect is apparent only in the fact that he keeps belching and there seems to be an increase in saliva. Gentlemen, what do you advise me to do?

And the gentlemen decided that if the poison did not take effect within the next five minutes, Felix should come back upstairs to them and they would decide how to do away with the peasant.

It was then that Lazavert began to feel ill. Although he had worked many times under fire at the front, the doctor sat exhausted and apoplectically red in a chair and whispered, 'I don't think I can bear it.' And then Yusupov came upstairs again and told them that the poison still wasn't working. At that point he asked, 'Do you mind if I shoot him?' And, as he recalled, he 'took a pistol from Dmitry [we shall remember that, too] and went back down to the basement'.

'How did he not notice with his perceptive eyes that I was clutching a pistol behind my back?' (And here we may share Felix's wonder.)

And Felix was also stunned (as are we) that Rasputin, who sensed and guessed at everything, 'was then far from any awareness of his own death'.

The scene next described by Felix definitely seems like an episode from a novel of the period about a noble avenger.

Felix went over to the rock crystal crucifix.

'I like this Cross very much.'

'I kind of like the cabinet, it's more interesting.' And Rasputin opened the cabinet with the maze again.

'Grigory Efimovich, you would do better to look at the Crucifix and pray to It.' Rasputin glanced at me in surprise and almost in fear. You might say that he read in my eyes something he had not expected.

And then something quite strange happened. Rasputin, who would soon be struggling furiously for his life, was unaccountably submissive – like a sleepwalker. He waited patiently to be killed.

'I raised the pistol in a slow, deliberate motion. Rasputin stood in front of me without moving . . . his eyes fixed on the Cross . . . I . . . shot. Rasputin began to howl in a savage, bestial voice and fell back heavily onto the bearskin.'

Purishkevich: 'A few minutes later after two abrupt sentences, the sound of a shot, followed by a protracted "a-ah". And the sound of a body falling heavily to the floor.' They all rushed headlong downstairs, although on entering the room they tripped on on an electrical wire and the lights went out. But they felt around, found the wire, plugged it back in, and saw: 'The dying Rasputin lay in front of the settee with Yusupov calmly standing over him, a pistol in his hand. "We need to get him off the rug immediately, lest the blood seep out and stain the bearskin," the grand duke started to say.'

And Felix and Purishkevich carried Rasputin over onto a bare slab.

Purishkevich: 'I stood over Rasputin. He was still alive and breathing and in agony. With his right hand he covered his eyes and half his nose, long and spongy . . . and his body jerked convulsively.'

'There wasn't any doubt. Rasputin was dead. We turned off the light, locked the dining-room door, and went upstairs to the study. Everyone was elated,' Felix recalled.

And then comes another inexplicable part. According to Purishkevich's and Felix's memoirs, Grand Duke Dmitry and the doctor set off in the automobile to Purishkevich's hospital train to burn Rasputin's clothing – his fur coat and boots. But it would later turn out that Rasputin's fur coat and boots were not burned. And Purishkevich gives a surprising explanation for that: it seems that Purishkevich's wife, who had been anxiously waiting to see how it would all end, was a lazy, capricious woman. And since 'the fur coat wouldn't fit in the stove, she found it impossible to busy herself with tearing it up and burning it piecemeal. She even clashed with Dmitry,' Purishkevich writes. In short, the brazen woman refused to carry out her husband's instructions and sent the grand duke back with the fur coat and boots like a little boy. If you consider that Purishkevich was no less a tyrant at home than in the Duma, then his wife's behaviour is very strange.

But while the grand duke was away, something extraordinary occurred.

'I felt an irresistible desire to look at Rasputin,' Yusupov recalled. And he went down to the basement.

> The dead Rasputin lay by the table where we had left him. He wasn't moving, but after touching him I was convinced he was still warm. Then bending over, I started taking his pulse but couldn't feel any. Blood was seeping from his wound in little drops. For some reason I suddenly grabbed hold of him and shook him – his body fell back to its original position. After standing over him for a little while, I was about to leave, when my attention was attracted to a slight movement of his left eyelid. His face shuddered convulsively – ever more strongly. Suddenly his left eye started to open . . . his right eyelid twitched, and both his eyes were fixed on me in an expression of diabolical wickedness.

And then a scene right out of the thrillers of those days (and of our own) entitled, 'The devil revived.'

> An incredible thing happened. With an abrupt, furious movement, Rasputin sprang to his feet. He was foaming at the mouth. He was horrifying. The room resounded with a savage roar, and I saw the flash of his convulsively clenched fingers. Then, like red-hot iron, they sank into my shoulder and reached for my neck . . . The revived Rasputin repeated my name in a hoarse whisper. Seized by a terror like no other, I tried to break free, but an iron vice held me with unbelievable strength. In that poisoned and bullet-pierced body there was, raised up by dark powers to avenge his death, something terrible and monstrous . . . I pulled away and with a last incredible effort broke free. Rasputin, gasping for breath, fell onto his back, holding in his hand my epaulette, which he had torn off. I rushed upstairs to Purishkevich. 'Quick . . . the pistol! Shoot! He's still alive!'

Rasputin was crawling on all fours up the stairs.

Purishkevich had at the time just returned from a smoke and 'was upstairs slowly walking around the study', when some inner force suddenly impelled him to the table where his Sauvage was lying. He put the pistol in his trouser pocket. Then 'under the pressure of the unknown force', he went out of the room to the stairway. And he heard 'Felix's inhuman cry, "Purishkevich, shoot! He's still alive! He's getting away!"'

And then he saw Yusupov. 'His face was literally gone, his handsome . . . eyes had come out of their sockets . . . [and] in a semi-conscious state . . . almost without seeing me, he rushed past with a crazed look . . . to his parents' half [of the palace]. I heard the sound of someone's . . . heavy footsteps making their way to the courtyard door.' And Purishkevich drew his Sauvage and ran downstairs. Grigory Rasputin, whose last gasp he had contemplated half an hour before, 'was running in a stagger along the fence over the sloppy snow of the yard'.

Purishkevich 'could not believe' his eyes, and then he heard a loud yell. It was the fleeing Rasputin: 'Felix, Felix, I'll tell everything to the tsarina.' And he 'ran after him in pursuit and fired . . . and in the darkness of the night an extraordinarily loud noise rang out'.

He missed. 'Rasputin increased his pace.' And Purishkevich 'shot a second time on the run and missed again'. Rasputin had already reached the gate. Then Purishkevich 'bit his hand' to make himself concentrate. And with the third shot he 'hit him in the back. He came to a stop.' And then Purishkevich fired a fourth time and 'hit him in the head', and he 'fell like a stone . . . in the snow and started jerking his head back and forth'. He lay with his arms stretched out, clawing at the snow. And then in a fury Purishkevich 'kicked him in the temple'.

But during all that Purishkevich for some reason had neither heard nor seen Yusupov running into the yard and shouting to him in the still of the night.

'Two shots rang out,' Felix recalled.

Leaping down the front steps, I ran along the Moika in order to cut Rasputin off in case Purishkevich missed. I myself was unarmed, since I'd given my pistol to the grand duke. There were three gates, but only the middle one was unlocked. I saw through the fence that it was in fact that gate to which Rasputin's animal instinct had drawn him. A third shot rang out, then a fourth one. I saw Rasputin sway and then fall down by a snowdrift. Purishkevich ran towards him and came to a halt by the body. I shouted to him, but he did not hear me.

After that Purishkevich went back to the house. When he reached the main entrance he told the soldiers there that he had killed 'Grishka, Russia's enemy and the tsar's', and after hearing their joyful endorsement, he ordered the body immediately dragged away from the fence.

It was then that Felix saw in the courtyard 'a constable walking from the gate towards where the body was lying'.

'I stopped the constable . . . As I was talking to him, I purposely faced the snow drift, so that the constable was obliged to stand with his back to where Rasputin was lying.

"Your highness, there were shots. Did something happen?"

"Nothing serious. I had a soirée this evening. A comrade of mine drank too much and started shooting."' And the constable left.

There's another description of what happened. And, as we have already seen, it belongs to the constable himself. Constable Vlasyuk testified, 'At the time I saw crossing the courtyard in the direction of the gate two men in military jackets but no hats, in whom I recognized Prince Yusupov and his butler Buzhinsky. I asked the latter what the shooting had been. He replied that he hadn't heard any shots . . . I think the prince also said he hadn't heard anything.' And Vlasyuk left.

After that, according to Felix, two soldiers dragged Rasputin into the house. And carried him down to the stairway landing by the basement where he had just been feasting with his host. Felix saw Rasputin lying motionless in the stairway. 'He was bleeding profusely from his many wounds. The fixture above cast its light on his head, and you could see every little detail of his bruised and mutilated face.' But something threatening and morbid apparently still connected the peasant to the prince. 'I was drawn irresistibly to that bloodied corpse. I no longer had the strength to struggle against myself. Rage and malice suffocated me. I was overwhelmed by a state I cannot explain. I flew at the corpse and began to beat it with the rubber-coated dumb-bell handle [given him by Maklakov]. I struck indiscriminately in my rage and fury, flouting every divine and human law.'

Purishkevich ordered the soldiers to pull Felix off. And they 'sat him down, splattered all over with blood, on the sofa in his study . . . It was awful to look at him with his vacant gaze and twitching face as he mindlessly repeated, "Felix, Felix".' And Purishkevich would never be able to forget Felix flailing at the peasant with the two-pound dumb-bell handle. The most amazing thing, Purishkevich would write, was that Rasputin was still alive. 'He gasped for breath and the pupil of his right eye rolled and gazed emptily and horribly at me . . . I see that eye before me to this day.'

After that Purishkevich ordered the body wrapped up as quickly as possible. But Buzhinsky apparently then told him about the constable who had inquired about the shots.

Afraid that the constable would tell his superiors that there had been shooting, Purishkevich came up with a preposterous plan. He decided to summon the constable.

And Constable Vlasyuk came back to the palace. And a conversation took place that in its general features was identically described by them all – Purishkevich, the constable, and Felix.

'Answer me according to your conscience. Do you love our father the tsar and our mother Russia, and do you want victory for Russian arms over the German?' Purishkevich asked.

'Yes, sir, Your Excellency.'

'And do you know who the most wicked enemy of the tsar and Russia is, the one who is preventing us from fighting, who has saddled us with the various Stürmers and other Germans in positions of authority, and who has taken the tsarina into his hands and through her has been making short work of Russia?'

'Yes, sir. I know. Grishka Rasputin.'

'Well, brother, he is no more. We have killed him and were shooting at him now. Will you be able to say if they ask you, "I don't know and am unaware"? Will you be able to keep silent?'

But the constable's answer was a dangerous one: 'So if they don't ask me under oath, then I won't say anything. But if they put me under oath, then there's nothing I can do – I'll tell them the whole truth, as it would be a sin to lie.' And the constable left to report at once to his superiors on the entire conversation with Purishkevich.

Finally, it was all done; wrapped in heavy cloth and bound with rope, the corpse lay by the dining room. By then, as both Felix and Purishkevich noted, Grand Duke Dmitry Pavlovich had returned in his automobile from his strangely unsuccessful errand. And they got ready to take the corpse away. Dawn was approaching. So they were in a hurry. They decided to leave Felix behind, 'putting him in the care of his servants with a request to help him clean up and change his clothes'.

They drove through the Petrograd darkness. The illumination was scarce, the 'road was deplorable . . . and the body kept jumping around, despite the soldier sitting on top of it. Finally, it came into view – the bridge where we were supposed to drop Rasputin's body through an ice hole. It was outside of town, and Dmitry Pavlovich [who was sitting in for the driver] slowed down and stopped by the railing . . . and for a moment the sentry-box at the other end of the bridge lit up. The motor continued to rumble.' (It was all as it would be when the Romanovs were executed: the blood and the secretly transported corpses, and the regicide Yurovsky's memory of the sound of the engine running.) Wordlessly, the four of them — the soldier, the lieutenant, Lazavert, and Purishkevich — 'after swinging the corpse back and forth, threw it hard into the hole in the ice, though forgetting to attach weights to it by chain'. Meanwhile, as Purishkevich writes, Dmitry Pavlovich 'stood look-out' in front of the car. 'The royal youth's hand must not touch the criminal body.' Searching through the car, they found one of Rasputin's boots and tossed it off the bridge, as well. Then they retraced their route. 'On the way back . . . the engine kept stalling, and Dr Lazavert would jump down and fiddle with one of the spark plugs. The last little repair was in front of the Peter and Paul Fortress.'

In 1919 Dmitry Pavlovich's father, Grand Duke Pavel, would be executed in that fortress.

Finally, they reached Grand Duchess Elizaveta Fyodorovna's palace, where the grand duke was residing at the time (the grand duchess herself, we shall remember, had just before the murder gone to pray at the monastery in Sarov). After that, the other three — Lieutenant Sukhotin, Lazavert, and Purishkevich — grabbed a horse-drawn cab (more reliable than the grand duke's automobile) and set off to the Warsaw Station, where Purishkevich's hospital train was waiting. It was after 5:00 a.m. Later that day Purishkevich sent Maklakov in Moscow a telegram: 'When are you coming?' which meant that Rasputin had been killed.

The stir began the following afternoon. At 5:00 p.m. Lieutenant Sukhotin came to see Purishkevich at the hospital train with the request that he visit Grand Duke Dmitry at the palace at once. At the palace Purishkevich found Yusupov and the grand duke. Both 'were nervously drinking cognac and cup after cup of black coffee'. They reported that 'Alexandra Fyodorovna has already been told of the disappearance and even death of Rasputin and had named us as the guilty parties in the murder.' 'Because of that reptile,' Yusupov said, 'I had to shoot one of my best dogs and lay her out on the blood-stained snow.'

It was then at the palace that Yusupov and the grand duke composed Yusupov's letter to the empress, in which he assured Alix that neither he nor the grand duke had had anything to do with Rasputin's death. After setting down their lie, they felt 'awkward with each other'. But it was necessary to go on.

After making up the story for the empress, they were obliged to make up another one for society, in the event that they should have to confess.

But having decided to avoid a new lie as much as possible, they made promises to each other as to how much they would remain silent about. (Just as the royal family's murderers later promised each other to keep silent.) And they immediately violated those oaths. (As did the others, in fact.)

At 8:00 p.m. on 17 December Purishkevich's train pulled out of Petrograd. And Purishkevich wrote all night, describing the murder 'for posterity'. Yusupov did the same thing, but in several works and only after he had emigrated.

In 1997 in Paris, Marina Grey, the daughter of the White leader General Denikin, gave me several newspaper clippings that she found in her mother's archive. They were of an interview with Grand Duke Dmitry regarding the publication of Felix Yusupov's book. In the interview, which was printed in the 19 July 1928 issue of the newspaper *Matin*, the grand duke said, 'The murder was carried out by us in a paroxysm of patriotic madness . . . We pledged never to speak of that event . . . Yusupov acted quite improperly in publishing his book. I did everything possible to keep him from carrying out that intention but was unsuccessful. That circumstance put an end to our friendship. We have not seen each other in five years.' Another clipping from a Russian newspaper published in Paris: 'Not a single person, including the members of my own family, has heard from me about the events of that terrible night . . . The same force that impelled me to the crime has prevented me and now prevents me from lifting the curtain on that affair.' It was hateful to the grand duke to maintain the lie that they had apparently agreed on. And that Purishkevich and Yusupov had piously adhered to in their memoirs.

For in my view those accounts were nothing more than a tale fabricated by the participants. A tale with a very definite purpose.

15

THE TRUTH ABOUT THE 'NIGHTMARE EVENING'

Cherchez La Femme

The fabrications were introduced, we shall recall, at the very beginning of the murderers' version. From noble considerations. Purishkevich decided to hide the identity of Felix's wife Irina behind the name 'Countess N.' (it wasn't fitting for the tsar's niece to serve as a lure for a peasant). But the noble considerations went further. Both Purishkevich and Yusupov claimed that there had been no women among those gathered at the Yusupov palace on the night of the murder.

In fact, however, the presence of women was simply essential. When Irina refused to take part, it had been necessary to stage her presence in the house. And that was accomplished very convincingly. Everything had been thought of to create the impression of a soirée at which Irina was enjoying herself with guests who had arrived all of a sudden – from the gramophone to the pastries that her guests, scared away, had abandoned. Yet for some reason, the most important thing seems to have been forgotten – her voice. The woman's voice that was supposed to be heard coming from upstairs. They had evidently failed to invite a woman to play the role of Irina. But, really, there had to be a woman's voice coming from upstairs. Because 'distant voices from upstairs' had been heard downstairs – by Yusupov and by Rasputin. 'On entering the house with Rasputin,' Felix recalled, 'I heard the voices of my friends.' And later on, when they were sitting in the 'dining room', 'the noise from upstairs grew louder and louder,' Felix wrote. 'What's all that noise?' Rasputin asked him. The alert Rasputin, who heard the 'noise of voices', would certainly have suspected something, had there been no woman's voice in all that noise. And he didn't suspect anything. And he didn't do so for more than two hours. And that is possible only if he did hear a woman's voice coming from upstairs.

'Malanya's Also Taking Part'

The murderers could not, of course, have failed to arrange for the participation of women. It was not for nothing that when the preparations for the murder were being made, Felix had written to Irina, 'Malanya's also taking part.' It was not for nothing, either, that the police had information about the presence of women that night. And that Tsarskoe Selo had the information, too. And that in society they were talking about the same thing. The actress Vera Leonidovna Yureneva spoke of a certain ballerina, who was Grand Duke Dmitry Pavlovich's lover. As we've already noted, Coco Chanel's future boyfriend was liberal in love.

I easily found the ballerina's name in the Department of Police case file. There are several whole reports about Vera Karalli, whom the police suspected of taking part in the murder night. 'Vera Karalli, a performer with the ballet company of the Imperial Theatres, twenty-seven years old. During her stays in the capital, she was visited by Grand Duke Dmitry Pavlovich,' an agent reported. Vera Karalli's presence at the Yusupov palace on the night of the murder was also claimed by Simanovich, who went to the police station on the Moika canal on 17 December with Bishop Isidor. After looking into it, however, the security branch agents reported that 'there was no note of her being absent [from her hotel].' 'There was no note of her being absent.' But that was the very reason for the cunning 'rehearsals': the sly substitution of another woman at the hotel for Vera Karalli on the night of the murder in order to give the latter an 'alibi' – not a complicated thing.

But Vera Karalli was apparently not the only woman at the Yusupov palace that night. They knew in Tsarskoe Selo of the participation of another lady, a much more important one. Vyrubova names her straight out: Marianna Derfelden, née Pistolkors, daughter of Grand Duke Pavel's wife Olga by her first marriage and sister of Alexander Pistolkors. But if her brother and his wife were among the most dazzling of Rasputin's devotees, Marianna had taken Dmitry's side. And she hated the peasant for the servile devotion of her weak-willed brother and for the disgrace of her brother's wife, about whose relations with Rasputin the most shameful rumours had been circulating. The police evidence against Marianna was so serious that she, the stepdaughter of a grand duke, was arrested!

But into what did her arrest turn! As her mother recalled, 'When we arrived at 8 Theatre Square, where Marianna lived, we were stopped by two soldiers who let us through only after taking down our names. All the highest society was at Marianna's! Some ladies she barely knew arrived in order to express their sympathy with her. Officers came up to kiss her hand.' It was then that the brakes were put on the murder case. The tsar did not want all those public displays of affection for the perpetrators. Moreover, Grand Duke Pavel was taking his son's involvement very hard. So the tsar did not want to finish off his ailing uncle by prolonging the arrest of the stepdaughter.

She was called Marianna, but her sarcastic friends had mockingly twisted that French name into the simple peasant name 'Malanya'. There had been women there. But to protect them from the police and to preserve their honour, the participants had not identified them.

Were The Pastries Poisoned?

Purishkevich and Yusupov's account of what took place was dictated by noble considerations in other ways, as well. And here's the most interesting and mysterious part: just what did in fact happen between Felix and Rasputin in the charming basement 'dining room'?

And, above all, what about the mysterious story of the poisoning?

'Protopopov passed on to me,' Beletsky testified, 'that Rasputin was still alive when they threw his body into the hole in the ice. That was shown by the autopsy.'

First they poisoned him, but he was still alive. And then they shot him, but he was still alive. A story of the devil. And Felix stresses this in a number of ways: 'his diabolical malice', 'he was foaming at the mouth' — all that is repeated in Yusupov's memoirs.

But Grand Duke Nikolai Mikhailovich, that 'Voltairean' who did not put much stock in demons, would write in his diary, 'The fact that the potassium cyanide had no effect I explain very simply . . . having often resorted to it in the past to poison insects. The solution was too weak.' He may well be right about that: in their haste and anxiety, they made too weak a solution for the wine glasses. But there was still the poison that they had 'chipped into the pastries' — enough to kill an ox. Does this mean Rasputin really was a superman? But then how was it that he behaved like a very ordinary person, when he was seriously injured and almost died after the inexperienced Guseva stabbed him just once with a knife in 1914 with her weak woman's hand? And when a surgeon was dispatched from Petrograd to save him? Why is that? His daughter Matryona raises the same question in her memoirs. And she offers an explanation.

Rasputin could not have eaten any of the poisoned pastries. He followed a special diet. His daughter reports that 'Father never ate sweets, meat, or pastries.' This is confirmed by the many various descriptions of him.

Simanovich writes that Rasputin did not eat sweets. And Beletsky and Khvostov report in their testimony that Rasputin kept to a strict diet. Rasputin, as his friend Filippov explained, linked that diet to his abilities as a healer. Fish and the avoidance of sweets. And he did not break that diet even when drunk. Although his devotees gave him boxes of candies, he himself never ate them. Konstantin Chikhachev, deputy chief of the Saratov Judicial Chamber, spoke about that in the File, as we shall recall: 'In the compartment lay boxes of candy, which he shared but did not touch, expressing himself vulgarly that he didn't eat that "scum"!' 'Scum' was what he called sweets. And Felix himself wrote about it: 'A moment later, I passed him the plate with the poisoned pastries. At first he refused. "I don't want any; they're too sweet."'

But then, Felix declares, he ate them. How could he agree to do what he had never done? And why would he? No, he could not have eaten the pastries. Rasputin's daughter was right: it was another lie. He only drank the poison dissolved in the wine. Which, it may be, was too weak a solution. Felix made up the story about the pastries later as part of his fable about a devil whom ordinary people had heroically destroyed.

And so, Rasputin never did eat the pastries. And he evidently didn't drink much, either. What then did take place in the room where Rasputin, according to Felix's own account, spent more than two hours? Or, as the meticulous historian Grand Duke Nikolai Mikhailovich would write in his diary, 'around three hours'? And why did he forget the reason for his visit? Or, more accurately, forget all about it, since only that way can we explain the normally nervous and impatient Rasputin waiting almost three hours for Irina to show up. Felix could hardly with ballads alone have caused Rasputin to forget all about the reason for his visit. And, essentially, have put his intuition completely to sleep.

An Erotic Version

It may be that Felix – that exquisitely corrupt child of the century – was aroused by the sense of danger and imminent bloodshed. And that in the dining room there took place an encounter of the kind that so exercised Grand Duke Nikolai Mikhailovich's imagination. Which is why Rasputin had been willing to wait, and as long as you like, for Irina's appearance, which promised him a continuation of a remarkable interlude that had captivated Felix, too. And it was only 'when they started to express their impatience upstairs' that Felix had been forced to act. And then he went upstairs and informed his confederates that Rasputin was taking neither pastries nor wine. And after obtaining the grand duke's pistol, he went back downstairs to the dining room. And it is why, given all that had just passed between them, Rasputin failed to notice the pistol in Felix's hand. And why his intuition was fast asleep. And why Felix succeeded in shooting him. But Felix was no murderer. He, who hated military service, was naturally not the best of shots. And he was agitated besides! So all he could do was gravely wound Rasputin. The record of the autopsy on Rasputin's body unfortunately disappeared after the revolution. But one thing is indisputable: Felix did not kill him then. Rasputin was simply unconscious. Although the murderers did bring on a death agony in him and an apparent cessation of his pulse. (The regicides would establish the death of the entire royal family in the Ipatiev basement in exactly the same way – by pulse. After which the grand duchesses would begin to revive.) But Rasputin revived! Or, more accurately, he merely regained consciousness.

As Nikolai Mikhailovich would later write, using Felix's own words, after coming to, Rasputin 'tore his epaulette off'. For Felix was not worthy of an officer's epaulettes! Felix, the Little One, who had deceived him with love! That is why, reproaching him, the duped peasant had familiarly cried, 'Felix, Felix!' And it is why Felix would not be able to forget that cry or forgive those words. And why the disgraceful scene would take place in which Felix suddenly started flailing at the dying Rasputin with the dumb-bell handle. Repeating during it, 'Felix, Felix,' the words with which the humble peasant had dared denounce him, a nobleman! The peasant who had torn off his epaulette.

A Realistic Version

The most plausible version of what happened is much more boring, however. Most likely, it all took place very quickly. When Rasputin declined to eat the pastries and drink the wine, Felix left as if to find out when the guests upstairs would be leaving. And after conferring with the other murderers, he proposed shooting the peasant. And then Felix returned with the pistol. And shot Rasputin at once. After that, the others ran downstairs. After deciding that Rasputin was dead, they then went back upstairs to celebrate their successful deliverance from the dangerous peasant. All the notions about the poison and the wine that had not affected Rasputin were invented after the fact as proof of what Felix would write: 'It should be remembered that we were dealing with an extraordinary person.' The man-devil they had defeated!

And then they had something to drink upstairs while they waited for the

city to go to sleep and the streets to empty completely. So the corpse could
be taken away without witnesses. During that time Rasputin recovered his
strength and regained consciousness. And as he had done once before when
Guseva stabbed him, the peasant attempted to save himself by fleeing. But,
as Felix and Purishkevich claim, he was shot right next to the gate by
Purishkevich.

That claim is the third and biggest of the fabrications.

Who Killed Him?

While filming my television programme at the Yusupov palace, I followed
the path of the injured Rasputin up the steep staircase. And emerged outside
by the same door through which he had tried to escape.

Looking around, I could still imagine Rasputin fleeing across this small
unfenced area next to the house. And Purishkevich running after the gravely
wounded Rasputin and missing him at an effective distance of two or three
paces. Which is entirely understandable, since Purishkevich was a civilian,
a historian and philologist by training, who had worked in the executive
office of the Ministry of Internal Affairs. When he wishes to prove in his
memoirs that he was a good shot, the only thing he can say is that he 'shot
well at – '!

And it will have to be proved. For after the first wild shots at Rasputin,
who was after all not very far from the gunman (Purishkevich explains the
misses as nervousness), two masterful shots followed when Rasputin was
already quite far away – by the gate. One 'in the back', as Purishkevich
writes. And the second, precisely aimed, in the head. No, nervousness had
nothing to do with it. It was simply that the second two shots were of
another class, as if belonging to a completely different marksman. An
excellent and cold-blooded one. So, who among the accomplices fits the
role of that kind of marksman? Grand Duke Dmitry Pavlovich above all. A
brilliant Guards officer, an athlete, and a one-time participant in the
Olympic Games. It was he who gave Felix the pistol with which he shot
Rasputin. And it was no coincidence that Dmitry had come with a revolver.
For if anyone had personal reasons to do the peasant in, Dmitry did. It was
Rasputin who had wrecked his betrothal; it was Rasputin who had told the
scurrilous tales about him and his fiancée; it was Rasputin who had disgraced
the royal family in which Dmitry had been raised; and it was Rasputin who
had caused the schism in the great Romanov family, not to mention in his
father's immediate family. And it was no accident that the woman who did
not become his wife, the tsar's daughter, Grand Duchess Olga, had thought

of that at once. And had written it down in her diary in advance of all the official inquiries: '18 December . . . we have learned that Father Grigory has definitely been killed, it must have been by Dmitry.'

The Grand Duke And The Murder

But, as Yusupov and Purishkevich claimed, the grand duke was not in the Yusupov palace at the time of the murder. He had gone off on that strange, abortive errand of incinerating Rasputin's fur coat. And he had returned by automobile only after Rasputin had been killed.

So they claimed. But both were lying. And it is easy to prove it.

According to the testimony of the two constables, Vlasyuk and Efimov, who after the shots were fired began to watch the Yusupov palace, they did not see any automobile *go up* to the house after the shots. Although not to see such a rare thing as an automobile on an absolutely empty street would have been impossible.

They only thing they noticed was an automobile *leaving* the house after the shots (the one in which Rasputin's corpse was carried away). And we will find the same incident (based on the constables' words) described in numerous memoirs. As General Globachyov, the chief of the security branch, wrote in a coded telegram of 18 December, 'several shots rang out, a human cry was heard, and later a car drove away.'

And so, after the murder no automobile whatever came to the palace. That means that the grand duke could not have returned to the house. But nevertheless he was there.

How so? Because he had never left. He had been in the palace the whole time. And he was there at the moment Rasputin was murdered. And he left along with the rest of them only after the murder.

And so, the grand duke was in the palace at the time of the murder. And it was for that reason that Purishkevich and Yusupov were obliged to make up the ludicrous story about Dmitry and the burning of the fur coat.

So what actually did happen?

The Instant Of Murder (A Reconstruction)

The vestiges of truth, in my view, are to be found in Felix's first testimony given immediately after the murder. After Felix shot Rasputin with Dmitry's pistol, the grand duke, Felix says, took back the gun. After leaving the 'dead

Rasputin' in the basement, they celebrated the event upstairs, waiting for the depths of night when they could take the body away. But first it was necessary to get the two women who were in the house out of it. And as Felix truthfully stated to Minister of Justice Makarov, 'Around 2–2:30 a.m. the two ladies were ready to go home, and Grand Duke Dmitry Pavlovich left with them.'

The grand duke had apparently been about to take them home in his automobile when the monstrous scene of Rasputin's 'resuscitation' took place after Felix had gone down to the basement. Mad with fear, Felix had rushed upstairs shouting, 'Shoot! He's getting away!'

Purishkevich was by himself in the study. He grabbed his heavy Sauvage revolver and ran after Rasputin. Bounding into the courtyard, Purishkevich shot twice and missed. But Dmitry was already in the courtyard with the ladies. The grand duke shot twice with his Browning. The first shot brought Rasputin to a halt; the second one, in the back of the head, laid him out on the wet snow. And one of the ladies cried out in terror. Hence the woman's cry heard by Constable Efimov. The ladies' departure naturally had to be postponed, and Rasputin's body was quickly dragged out of the courtyard. Hearing the shots, Felix had then got a grip on himself and summoned the butler to go with him into the courtyard, since he realized that the shots would alarm the constables. And it would be necessary to explain. And he wanted the butler to do that. It was in fact then that Constable Vlasyuk appeared at the palace. Felix's calm deceived the constable. But Felix paid a steep price for that calm. And the ugly scene of Felix beating the dying peasant took place right after Vlasyuk left. But it began to seem to the murderers that the constable had suspected something. And they presumably conferred. One must keep in mind that they were drunk. And then the crazy idea occurred to Purishkevich, the chief expert among those present on the national mood, to tell the whole truth to the constable. Purishkevich was convinced that he, like the rest of the country, would have to hate Rasputin! That truth was the undoing of the whole business.

After giving explanations to the constable, they quickly took Rasputin's body away. Or, more accurately, they took the still-alive Rasputin away. They had never tried to kill a defenceless person before. So they had not shot him again 'to make sure'. And Rasputin was still breathing. The women presumably left the palace later that morning.

But why had it been necessary for Purishkevich (and then Yusupov) to make up the story that it was Purishkevich who had killed Rasputin? The answer is, in order to have the right to say (and to say so several times, so that willy-nilly it looked suspicious) that 'the hands of the royal youth' had not been 'stained with . . . blood'. And the point here was not just that it was not fitting for a grand duke to be a murderer. There was also a political factor. For in the event of a coup, Dmitry, a young military man, a favourite of the Guards, and an organizer of the deliverance from the Rasputin ignominy (but not the murderer himself) would be a realistic pretender to the throne. But as the peasant's murderer, he would have a much harder time becoming tsar. And so that it would be easier for the grand duke to lie, they made him swear to repeat their story – 'there is no blood on my hands.' Those words, if taken literally, were of course the truth. The blood was only on the hands of those who had actually dealt with the peasant's bloody corpse.

By dawn on 18 December, Purishkevich's train was already a good distance from Petrograd. And having stayed awake all night, he wrote, 'It is still dark, but I sense that daylight is coming. I cannot sleep. I am thinking of the future . . . of that great land . . . I call Motherland.'

A little over two months remained until the revolution.

On 18 December the inquiry continued in anticipation of the tsar's arrival in Petrograd.

Alix's telegram to Nicky on 18 December: 'In your name I order Dmitry forbidden to leave his house till yr. return. Dmitry wanted to see me today, but I refused. Mainly he is implicated. The body still not found.'

Nicky's telegram to Alix of 18 December: 'I have only just read your letter. Am horrified and shaken. In prayers and thoughts I am with you. Am arriving to-morrow at 5 o'clock.'

However, Olga, Grand Duke Pavel Alexandrovich's wife, recorded the account of her husband who had just returned from Headquarters: 'He drank tea with the sovereign and was struck by the expression of serenity and bliss on his face. For the first time in a long time, the tsar was in an animated state . . . Loving his wife too much to go against her wishes, the sovereign was happy that fate had delivered him from the necessity of taking action on his own.' No, Nicky, as always, had merely been reticent about his feelings. 'Horrified and shaken' – that was his true attitude. 'Monsters' is what he would call the murderers in his diary.

Finding The Corpse

Early on the morning of 19 December a corpse was found floating in the Malaya Nevka river near Great Petrovsky Bridge. It had surfaced in a frightening way: its hands, which under the water had evidently been trying to untie the ropes, were raised. It was clear that this powerful man, although still breathing in the car, had concealed the fact, hoping to loosen his fetters in the water. But his human strength had failed him. A photograph has survived; the corpse has just been pulled out and loaded onto a sledge. And all around is the white expanse of the frozen river.

His corpse was taken by automobile to the Academy of Military Medicine. He rode through the capital with stiffened, upraised hands, threatening it. In the evening, before the autopsy was done, the tsarina and Rasputin's daughters came to see the body. When Alix saw those menacingly raised hands, she was overwhelmed by a feeling of inevitable catastrophe.

She collapsed in a swoon. The 'Tsarskoe Selo cabinet' had ceased to exist. She would no longer be able to rely on his counsels and predictions.

On the night of 20 December Professor Kosorotov of the department of forensic medicine of the Academy of Military Medicine performed an autopsy and an embalming of the remains. The heart was removed and placed in a special vessel. The record of the autopsy was kept for a long time at the Academy of Military Medicine. But in the 1930s it vanished. All that remained were the police photographs of the naked body with its bullet holes.

After the autopsy, Bishop Isidor was permitted to celebrate a requiem mass. Then Rasputin's corpse was transported by truck with an escort of plain-clothes policemen to the Feodorov Cathedral in Tsarskoe Selo. The funeral took place on 21 December.

The Truth About The Secret Burial

That secret funeral (like the secret burial of the royal family after it) is tangled with rumours and legends.

The File contains the only immediate descriptions of the funeral by several eyewitnesses.

From the testimony of the medical orderly A. Zhuk:

Vyrubova told me to come to her in the morning at half past eight . . . Vyrubova went by carriage to the new church she was building. On the way she told me that Father Grigory was going to be burried there. I had heard about it the day before from the architect Yakovlev, who told me the tsarina herself had chosen the place . . . When we drove up to the place, we found a grave already dug and a coffin in it. The place was in the centre of the church in the left side of the nave. There we came upon their

Majesties' confessor, Father Alexander Vasiliev, the infirmary's own priest, the architect Yakovlev, a sexton, and Colonel Maltsev, who was in charge of the construction [of the Serafimov Sanctuary], and Laptinskaya. Laptinskaya told how Rasputin was lying and what he was wearing, and said she had brought the coffin at night by automobile. Vyrubova asked, 'Can the coffin be opened?' But Laptinskaya and Yakovlev said that it could not be done. Around ten minutes after our arrival at the grave, a motor drove up with the tsar, the tsarina, and the children. By nine the burial service was over. The grave was covered up by security branch agents, who until then had been stationed in the woods.

Naturally, the tsarina's Second Friend also came to see Our Friend off on his last journey. As Vyrubova's maid Feodosia Voino testified, 'Dehn rode with me.'

The File, from the testimony of Yulia Dehn: 'Upon learning of Rasputin's death, I went to Tsarskoe Selo, spent the night there, and was present when Rasputin's body was committed to the earth . . . I arrived along with the royal family . . . Colonel Loman was watching us from behind the bushes. They didn't open the coffin . . . The sovereign and empress were stunned by what had happened. But the empress had so much strength of will that she supported Vyrubova, who wept a lot.'

The one who 'was watching from behind the bushes' also described the funeral.

The File, from Loman's testimony:

The burial service itself was conducted by the confessor Father Alexander Vasiliev and an ordained monk from Vyrubova's infirmary. There were no choristers; Ischenko, the assistant deacon of the Feodorov Cathedral, sang. The day before, Father Vasiliev had informed me that he had been given orders to carry out the committing of Rasputin's body to the ground, for which he would come from Petrograd to spend the night in Tsarskoe Selo . . . and in the morning drop by for the assistant deacon and his chasuble and other vestments, so that I should give the corresponding orders. The next day Father Vasiliev dropped by the cathedral, where I was waiting for him, and together we went to the Serafimov Sanctuary, that is, to the site where the church was to be erected. Instead of driving all the way to the site itself, Father Vasiliev walked to the burial place (the coffin was already in the hole), while I remained off to the side. So although I was unseen, I could see everything . . . Before the royal family arrived, I approached the grave and saw a metal coffin. There was no opening in the coffin of any kind.

(Vyrubova's testimony is the same. None of the eyewitnesses speaks of an opening, in fact. But the myth of an opening in the coffin's cover, supposedly made at the tsarina's command so that whenever visiting Rasputin in his crypt, she could see his face after death, has appeared in numerous memoirs and writings.)

'The coffin was immediately covered up with earth, and there was no crypt under construction,' Loman testified.

From the tsar's diary for December 21: 'At nine o'clock we went to . . . the field where we were present at a sad scene: the coffin with the body of the unforgettable Grigory, killed on the night of the 17th by monsters in the Yusupov house, already stood in the grave. Father A. Vasiliev conducted the service, after which we returned home.'

Punishment Of The Princes

After that the reprisals started. Grand Duke Dmitry asked to be tried before a court-martial. He understood that after such a trial he would become a hero for all Russia. And it was also needed for the future, in order to give public voice to the story they had concocted, that the peasant's blood was not on Dmitry's hands. The tsar understood that, too. And so no trial took place.

In the meantime, the peasant's murderers had been under house arrest, waiting for their fates to be decided. And during that time, the details of the murder had been seeping out of the palace, and a rumour had taken shape: that it wasn't Dmitry but Yusupov and Purishkevich who had done the killing. And Grand Duchess Elizaveta Fyodorovna wrote to Nicky, asking him to pardon Felix:

'When I got back here I learned he had been killed by Felix . . . who didn't want to go into the military because he didn't want to shed anyone else's blood. I pictured what he must have gone through before he decided to do it; I imagined how, moved by love of the Fatherland, he had decided to rescue the sovereign and the country from a person who had made everyone suffer. The crime may be considered an act of patriotism.'

Nicholas didn't answer her letter. And then measures were taken. Felix was treated remarkably leniently. 'The chief culprit, Felix Yusupov,' Dmitry's stepmother Olga said in bewilderment, 'got off with exile to the country. Whereas Grand Duke Dmitry was ordered to leave for Persia.' He was sent into combat, to a field army in a terrible climate ruinous to the health. Evidently, it wasn't the murderers' story that Nicholas believed but the secret reports of his policemen. Obviously, he knew who had shot Rasputin. The whole numerous imperial family was outraged at the tsar's decision. 'I myself composed the text of the petition,' recalled Dmitry's stepmother. 'The exile seemed to us the limit of cruelty. The petition was signed by all the members of the imperial family.'

That petition has survived in the archive. With the tsar's appended response: 'No one has the right to commit murder. I know that the consciences of many are not clear, since Dmitry Pavlovich is not the only one involved in this. I am amazed that you have appealed to me.' And the grand duke, his favourite, was sent to Persia, despite all the pleas.

I held it in my hand, that letter from the Romanov family with its numerous signatures. So many of those who signed that document would perish, caught unawares by the revolution. But Dmitry, thanks to the cruel exile from which they had so pleaded he be delivered, would survive intact.

Once in Persia Dmitry did not forget his beloved friend. 'My dear, much-loved, true friend,' he wrote to Felix. 'I can say, without fear of going to extremes, my dearest friend!'

And Felix honourably and faithfully continued to hold to the story they had agreed.

But shortly after the new year, the dangerous Felix wrote a letter to his mother-in-law, Nicholas's sister Xenia – an odd letter that sounds like a letter about Dmitry:

2 January . . . I'm much tormented by the idea that the Empress Marie Fyodorovna and you will regard the person who did it as a murderer and a criminal. However you view the rightness of that action and the reasons that prompted its doing, there will be a feeling deep in your heart that he is still a murderer. Knowing everything that person did before, during, and after, I can say with complete certainty that he is not a murderer but merely an instrument of Providence, which helped him to carry out his duty before his motherland and tsar by destroying an evil, diabolical force that had disgraced Russia.

'An End Must Without Fail Be Put To . . . Alexandra Fyodorovna'

Hiding out in Tsarskoe Selo, the tsarina and Vyrubova waited for a continuation of the bloodshed – the further revenge of the grand dukes. Were they groundless fears? The diary of Grand Duke Nikolai Mikhailovich contains an answer:

Everything they [Rasputin's murderers] have done is without question a half-measure, since an end must without fail be put to both Alexandra

Fyodorovna and Protopopov. So you see, murder plans have occurred to me again, still vague but logically necessary, as otherwise it may be worse than it was ... [enough] to make your head spin. The Countess Bobrinskaya, Misha Shakhovskoy [Prince Mikhail Shakhovskoy], and I have been scared into taking action, and prodded, and pleaded with, but how? With whom? To act alone would be pointless! Meanwhile, the time passes, and with their departure and Purishkevich's, I see hardly any others capable of action. But really and truly I'm not of the breed of aesthetes and even less of murderers. I need to get out into the fresh air, best of all on a hunting trip in the forest, for here, living in a state of excitement, I'll talk and do such nonsense.

So it was 'logically necessary' to kill the Tsarina of All Russia. This was written by a grand duke! Who regretted seeing no 'others capable of action' after the exile of Rasputin's murderers, who regretted not knowing 'how and with whom' to achieve it!

So thoughts about a continuation of the bloodshed, about a new conspiracy, were fermenting in highly placed minds. It was no coincidence that Nikolai Mikhailovich was exiled to the 'fresh air' of his estate just before the new year. And it was with good reason that Alix begged the tsar to return, telling him that she had found a safe place for the Friend in her palace.

As he was departing for exile around the new year, Nikolai Mikhailovich met on the train (and surely not by accident) two prominent members of the Duma opposition, the monarchist Shulgin (who would subsequently accept Nicholas's abdication) and the manufacturer Tereschenko (who would become a minister in the Provisional Government after the February Revolution). And Nikolai Mikhailovich wrote, 'Tereschenko's certain everything will come apart in a month's time and I'll return from exile. God grant that it be so! But what malice there was in those two men. Both spoke in one voice of the possibility of regicide! What times we live in, what a curse has befallen Russia.' Such was their thinking: the grand duke about murdering the tsarina, the Duma leaders about a possible assassination of the tsar. It was in the air.

Blood was in the offing. And the tsar was warned of it.

On 10 February before his departure for Headquarters, the tsar received Nikolai Mikhailovich's brother, the Grand Duke Alexander Mikhailovich (Sandro), a friend of his childhood and youth. And Sandro said, 'Events have shown that your advisers are bent on leading Russia and, it follows, you to inevitable destruction and death.'

On 22 February the emperor left his beloved Tsarskoe Selo for the last time.

'Always Together, Never Alone'

As usual, there was a letter from Alix waiting for Nicky on the train: '22 Feb. 1917 . . . such terrible times for us now! – and even harder apart, I can't stroke you so tired & worried.' As before, she lived by her meetings with Our Friend, only now they were meetings at his grave: 'I can do nothing but pray & pray & Our dear Friend does so in yonder world for you – there is yet nearer to us – Tho' one longs to hear his voice of comfort and encouragement . . . Holy angels guard you, Christ be near you & the sweet Virgin never fail you – Our Friend left us to [join] her.'

Now they often went to his grave – the Tsarina, the Friend, and the grand duchesses. And the church's newly constructed walls shielded them from the eyes of strangers.

'26 Feb. 1917 . . . Went to our Friend's grave. Now the church [being built over Rasputin's burial place] is so high that I could kneel & pray there calmly for you all without being seen by the orderly.' And in her letter of 22 February: 'Feel my arms hold you, feel my lips press tenderly upon yours – always together, never alone.'

The revolution had already begun in Petrograd. Just as Our Friend had prophesied in his 'serious' 1914 telegram to the tsar.

And on 2 March 1917, when Petrograd was already full of raging mobs, when the tsarina's palace was already surrounded by mutinous soldiers, when the train with the helpless tsar was already blocked at the station in Dno and all the army commanders were demanding his abdication, and when Guchkov, whom Alix hated so much, and Shulgin had already left the Duma to receive that abdication, she sent Nicky a letter from Tsarskoe Selo with an important postscript: 'Wear his cross, even if it is uncomfortable, for my peace of mind.'

EPILOGUE

An Excursion To The Murder Scene

Another world had begun. After their house arrest, the tsar and tsarina continued to live in Tsarskoe Selo, where 'Citizen Romanov' conscientiously cleared his garden, went for walks in the park, read books out loud to his family in the evenings, and was perhaps for the first time secretly happy. Alix, however, was exhausted by the humiliation. She would subsequently write in a letter how she had withered and turned grey. The Friend was taken away to Petrograd to the Peter and Paul Fortress.

As Tereschenko had predicted to Grand Duke Nikolai Mikhailovich, everything rapidly 'came apart', and the grand duke returned from exile. By then the grand dukes' automobiles had been appropriated. And in the middle of March, Nikolai Mikhailovich went by horse cab to the Yusupov palace on the Moika canal. The historian had decided to take a look at the murder scene that the young Yusupov had told him so much about. Felix and Irina had also recently returned from exile. And Rasputin's murderer took pleasure in the general attention. Nikolai Mikhailovich wrote in his diary: '16 March 1917 . . . Irina and Felix are in enthusiastic spirits . . . I visited them, [and] examined the place of drama in detail. It's incredible, but they calmly have their dinner in the same dining room.' In the end, nothing special had happened – a nobleman had merely shot an insolent peasant. How many others had been flogged to death in the stable at the orders of his ancestors in the Yusupov family history.

Missing Money And People

By then the hunt for Rasputin's wealth was starting to heat up. Simanovich added fuel to the fire. Beletsky testified that Simanovich told him in secret 'that the deceased had left very good resources . . . up to 300,000 roubles'.

The 'best of Jews' knew where to send them to look for the funds. And the Extraordinary Commission conscientiously searched the banks for Rasputin's money. Preserved in the File are the Commission's endless inquiries to all the great banks – the Union of Provincial Commercial Banks, the Bank of the Caucasus, the Petrograd Municipal Credit Association, the Russian-Asiatic Bank, the Moscow Merchants Bank, and so on. But the replies of the numerous banks surviving in the File are all the same: 'The bank has the honour of informing the Extraordinary Commission that there are no deposits, securities, or safety deposit boxes in the bank in the name of Grigory Efimovich Rasputin-Novy, his wife, Praskovia Fyodorovna Rasputina-Novaya, his children, Varvara, Matryona, and Dmitry Rasputin, or his niece, Anna Nikolaevna Rasputina.' Rasputin's wealth had vanished and evaporated. For no wealth at all survived him. Grand Duchess Olga had been right when she wrote in her memoirs, 'He left nothing behind, and the empress gave his orphans money.' The hundreds of thousands of roubles that had passed through Rasputin's hands were left in the restaurants where he drank to suppress his fear of death; they were left with the Gypsy choruses and in the hands of the endless petitioners and, more often, beggars to whom he gave countless sums. Sums that he treated with contempt. And, of course, some of the money was left in the hospital train and in Vyrubova's and the tsarina's infirmaries. But mainly, as Filippov accurately testified, it wound up in the hands of his secretaries, above all Simanovich's. And, of course, in those of the elusive Akilina Laptinskaya. Not only did she lay out Rasputin for his final journey, but, it would appear, had the remaining money in the house under her disposal.

Yet no sooner had the February Revolution begun than Akilina, who knew all that mysterious person's secrets and who had followed him all the way from the chapel under the stable to the empress's palace, vanished from Petrograd, slipping away into the chaos of the new life. And 'Voskoboinikova, as soon as she heard about the abdication, immediately left Tsarskoe Selo', as Vyrubova's maid, Feodosia Voino, testified. 'Voskoboinikova left the infirmary on 3 March and never returned.'

Rasputin's family met the revolution in Petrograd. His wife, Praskovia, went back to Pokrovskoe to claim their right to his legacy. The writ of distraint inventorying Rasputin's property and executed in her presence has survived. And the inventory is a pitiful one. Dmitry would return from the war to Pokrovskoe after the Bolshevik coup. And then all of them – Praskovia, Dmitry, and the daughter Varvara – would be sent north by the Bolsheviks to the town of Salekhard. Praskovia would die there, as would Dmitry – of scurvy. Varvara would return to Pokrovskoe, where all trace of her would be lost for a long time. And then she would re-emerge in Leningrad, only to die in obscurity at the beginning of the 1960s.

But, to make up for all that, Matryona, Grigory's elder daughter and his favourite, would prove worthy of him. She too would play a fateful role in the destiny of the royal family.

Life After Death

After her arrest in Tsarskoe Selo, Alix was no longer able to visit his grave. But Our Friend could now visit her in her dreams. One of them was terrifying.

She was standing in the Malachite Room at the Winter Palace. And he appeared by the window. His body was covered with terrible wounds. 'They will burn you at the stake,' he cried, and the whole room burst into flames. He beckoned to her to run, and she rushed towards him. But it was too late – the whole room was on fire. And she woke up, stifling a scream.

Now she waited in terror for the inevitable. And it came. Captain Klimov and his detachment of soldiers stationed in Tsarskoe Selo succeeded in opening Our Friend's grave. And all the papers wrote about the grave discovered beneath the altar of the chapel under construction. The soldiers, who were looking for jewels, immediately tore off the coffin's cover. There were no jewels to be found, but they did turn up a little wooden icon without a frame. On the back of it the tsarina, her daughters, and the Friend had signed their names in indelible ink. How many sneers and maledictions there were in the papers! To put an icon in a grave, and especially that of a profligate! They wrote of sacrilege. In fact, as the File makes clear, it had not been the tsarina's doing at all. The tsarina's friend Yulia Dehn testified that 'The icon with the signatures that was written about so much was given to Rasputin while he was still alive, and Laptinskaya, who bathed and dressed Rasputin's body, herself, on her own initiative, put the icon in Rasputin's coffin.'

The little icon was sent to the Petrograd Soviet. That year the magazine *A Small Light* published a picture of it: 'On the image's obverse side is an icon of "The Sign of the Mother of God". On its reverse are the signatures of Alexandra, Olga, Tatyana, Maria, and Anastasia. One under the other. In the corner beneath them is an inscription by Vyrubova: "11 December 1916. Novgorod. Anna."'

The coffin was pulled from the grave. Covered with make-up, Rasputin's disfigured face gazed at the sky. The soldiers, crowding around, examined the shaggy beard sticking out. And the large bump on his forehead resembling a budding horn that during his lifetime he had carefully concealed with his hair, as his daughter Matryona wrote. Then, as called for by the revolutionary times, a political meeting was held alongside the coffin. And those present decided to remove the corpse from Tsarskoe Selo. At which point Alix, overcoming her contempt for Kerensky, asked him through Colonel Kobylinsky, the commander of the security guard, to protect the body from further outrages. And Kerensky gave orders for the corpse to be secretly taken away and buried.

And the body's wanderings began. First the corpse was hauled by truck to Petrograd, where it stood in the garage of the former court chancery alongside the royal marriage coaches. Then it was taken at night to the Vyborg highway in order to bury it secretly off the side of the road in an unpopulated place. But on the Vyborg highway the car with the coffin unexpectedly got stuck. And those accompanying it decided 'to burn the corpse right there on the spot'. They immediately built an immense bonfire and, after pouring gasoline over the corpse, set fire to it. The report of the incineration remains to this day in the former Lenin Museum in Petersburg. Rasputin did not, during the burning, disappoint the expectations of the onlookers: through the action of the fire, the corpse seemed to levitate and only afterwards did it disappear in the flames. They scattered the ashes to the wind. Thus did Rasputin pass through all the elements: water, earth, fire, and air.

But even after his incineration, Rasputin remained with the royal family. He continued to be with them during their whole sad confinement. Hermogen stood at the head of the Tobolsk eparchy, having earlier been exiled there by the tsars for his denunciation of Our Friend. That stern pastor's power and authority were still unquestioned in Tobolsk. Hermogen wanted to help them escape and could have done so. But Alix could not forget that Hermogen had been Grigory's enemy. And she did not trust him.

But there was someone else she was willing to trust. This was Boris Solovyov, the son of Nikolai Solovyov, who had been Rasputin's admirer and the treasurer of the Most Holy Synod. The rascal son had grasped the situation and had married Rasputin's daughter Matryona. That was enough. Alix believed: he had been sent to them by Our Friend. And she gave him the royal jewels to organize their escape. Solovyov took everything. And after the Bolsheviks seized power, he conscientiously turned over to them the unlucky officers who had come to the Ekaterinburg to plan the royal family's liberation. Thus the peasant continued to be their undoing from beyond the grave.

The jewels, however, did not bring Solovyov riches. Everything would disappear during the civil war. The semi-indigent Solovyov would find work in Paris in an automobile factory and he died there in 1916 from tuberculosis. Matryona Rasputina-Solovyova got herself a position as a governess and lived with her two little daughters in a tiny Parisian apartment. After the appearance of Yusupov's memoirs, she noisily brought her father's murderer to trial. And then that native of a Siberian village turned up in America, where she found work as a lion tamer! She died in the 1970s.

Blessed Unto Death

The former tsarina wrote to Anya all about the dead man of God. She connected the blood and horrors of the civil war to God's punishment for the death of Our Friend. On 17 December 1917, the anniversary of his death, she wrote to the Friend, 'We are experiencing it together again . . . I remember . . . the terrible 17th. Russia too suffers for this, all must suffer for this, what they have done, but no one understands.'

On 9 January 1918, she wrote, 'Yet I firmly believe that He will save everything. He alone can.' Who's the subject? Grigory? God? Sometimes it isn't clear any more in her letters.

Then came their last journey. And the almighty Our Friend was again at their side. The tsar, the tsarina, and their daughter Maria were taken to Ekaterinburg, the city where they would be killed, via Pokrovskoe. The road, the highway from Tobolsk to Tyumen, exists to this day. It passes the houses of the village of Pokrovskoe. And it passed Grigory's house. Thus, the dream that she had not dared to realize as tsarina, she realized as a prisoner. She saw his river, his trees, and his house – the places where his mysterious transfiguration had taken place, the one he had spoken of so often. The former tsars stopped for a while in front of his house, two steps away from the windows of Our Friend. As Alix wrote in her diary, 'About 12, got to Pokrovskoe . . . stood long before our Friend's house, saw his family & friends looking out of the window' (14 April 1918).

Thus, a year and a half after his own murder, he had led them also to a harrowing death. Had his prophecy come true?

Had There Been A Prophecy?

Simanovich published in his book about Rasputin a famous prediction of his that has been repeated in numerous books about him. 'Russian Tsar! I have a presentiment that I shall leave this world before the first of January. If I am killed by hired assassins, then you, tsar, will have no one to fear. Remain on your throne and rule. But if the murder is carried out by your kinsmen, then not one [member] of your family will survive more than two years . . . I shall be killed, I am no longer among the living . . . Pray, be strong, and take care of your chosen clan.' This text, allegedly composed by Rasputin not long before his death, was supposedly given to the tsarina by Simanovich.

Although this 'prophecy' may perhaps sound all right in translation, it does not in Russian withstand any criticism at all. There is not a single word in it from Rasputin's uneducated but highly poetic lexicon. Beginning with the salutation 'Russian Tsar!' Not only could Rasputin not address the tsar that way; no Russian could. It's Simanovich's own language. This 'prophecy', like numerous other 'prophecies' of the kind, was published after the execution of the royal family, and it was undoubtedly written by Simanovich himself. It is one of the many myths that fill his memoir of Rasputin.

Nonetheless, Rasputin's predictions of the death of the royal family in the event of his own murder have been attested by many witnesses. Rasputin's friend, the Asian doctor Badmaev, spoke of them, as did his daughter Matryona, his publisher Filippov, and so forth. To a certain degree, those predictions could have been a means of self-defence for the peasant, who, knowing how much his powerful enemies hated him, had decided by that means to make the 'tsars' more vigilant in his defence! But only to a certain degree. For one did not need to be a prophet to predict the death of the 'tsars' at that time. Thoughts about the fall of the regime and the death of the royal family were in the air. The bloody first revolution of 1905 had already thundered. And the possible spilling of royal blood had been predicted then not merely by Russian revolutionaries but also by the tsar's own Prime Minister Witte. The grand dukes and the Speaker of the State Duma also constantly spoke of the need to 'save ourselves'. So Rasputin's predictions were merely part of a general sense of looming apocalypse.

But Rasputin unquestionably did have visions and make prophecies. And they were part of the mysterious dark strength that he possessed. On 24 February 1917, well after Rasputin's death, G. Shavelsky, the archpresbyter of the Russian army and navy and a man who hated Rasputin, wrote down

a conversation he had had with Professor Fyodorov, the physician responsible
for treating the heir.

'What's new with you in Tsarskoe Selo? How are you managing without
the "elder"?' Shavelsky mockingly asked.

'You should not laugh,' Fyodorov seriously replied.

> Everyone laughed here in regard to Grigory's prophesy that after his death
> the heir would become ill on such and such a day. On the morning of the
> day in question I'm hurrying to the palace. Thank goodness, the heir is
> completely healthy. The court scoffers had already begun to make fun of
> me, but . . . in the evening I got a sudden call: 'The heir is ill!' I rushed to
> the palace. It was terrible! The boy was haemorrhaging, and I just barely
> managed to stop it. That's the elder for you. Laugh at the miracles all you
> want.

So among the visions that that mysterious seer was visited by, must be
included the threatening spectre of future regicide and the death of the
unfortunate boy. As, of course, must his own inescapable death.

The Heavy Hand

And, of course, that mystical person could not have failed to sense his own
'heavy hand'. He could not have failed to observe in his own life the sorry
fate of those who were connected to him. This brings to mind the words
in the File of Leonid Molchanov, the son of the exarch of Georgia, who in
a meditation on the death of his father, observed: 'reviewing the past of all
the people who had linked their destinies to Rasputin – Iliodor, Hermogen,
[and] Damansky, who through Rasputin had made a brilliant career and
then had fallen ill with an incurable disease – I came to the perhaps
superstitious conviction that Rasputin's hand was a heavy one.' Beletsky
would use virtually the same words to tell his investigator that he 'saw the
sad end of all the people who had sought support from Rasputin . . . the
fatal disgrace that inevitably was their lot'. The highly placed official
Beletsky was considering here the ends of the careers of people who had
been connected to Rasputin. He still didn't realize that he should have
been considering the ends of their lives, as Molchanov had done regarding
his dead father and Damansky.

For the February Revolution was merely the first step in the bloodshed.

Soon October came crashing down. And replenished the cells of the
Peter and Paul Fortress. Now to the tsarist ministers sent there by the
February Revolution were added the begetters of that revolution. Amusing

conversations took place. The same Tereschenko, who had talked of regicide with Grand Duke Nikolai Mikhailovich, and who had reportedly invested five million roubles in the February Revolution, encountered the tsarist minister Scheglovitov. And Scheglovitov happily greeted Tereschenko, 'So, it is you, Mikhail Ivanovich! Really, you didn't have to give the February Revolution five million roubles to get in here. Had you hinted to me before, I'd have sheltered you here for nothing!'

And, on his Gorokhovaya Street, as a symbol, as a recollection of Rasputin's threatening, upraised hands, the most terrifying establishment in Petrograd was opened – the Bolshevik Extraordinary Commission or Cheka, so unlike the Provisional Government's idyllic Extraordinary Commission of the same name. And from the Cheka's new building on Gorokhovaya, many of Rasputin's friends would follow each other to the firing-squad wall.

What a desperate cemetery there is of people tied to Rasputin who died violently. The dangerous gossip Prince Andronikov, who was so close to the elder, was shot in 1919. And the whole honest company of people pushed ahead by Rasputin would lie down in unknown graves with a bullet in the heart – Protopopov, Alexei Khvostov, and Beletsky. With the capital's removal to Moscow, the former dignitaries were transferred to Butyrki Prison, which survives in Moscow to this day.

The lawyer S. Kobyakov, who served as a defence attorney before revolutionary tribunals, recalled: 'On 5 September . . . in the days of the Red Terror . . . they were informed that they would be shot. The former archpriest Vostorgov [yet another friend of Rasputin's] exhibited greatness of spirit before his death: he heard everyone's confession and absolved them of their sins before they died.'

All of them were shot in Petrovsky Park next to the Yar restaurant, where Rasputin so liked to drink. The executions were public. Several minutes before he was shot Beletsky made a run for it, but they drove him into a circle with sticks. Varnava and Isidor would perish, too. Nor was Rasputin's enemy Bishop Hermogen spared an agonizing death. Pavel Khokhryakov, the head of the Tobolsk Bolsheviks, told how he took the bishop out to the middle of the river, draped andirons around the pastor's neck, and shoved him into the water. And when the powerful Hermogen tried to stay afloat, they beat him with boat hooks, and pushed him under water. So Rasputin's arch-enemy perished, as had Rasputin, in the water. And like Rasputin, he sank to the bottom alive. Rasputin's admirer, the journalist Menshikov, and the royal priest Father Alexander Vasiliev were also killed – it would take a long time to exhaust the martyrology of Rasputin's friends who died from Bolshevik bullets. And, of course, Manasevich-Manuilov, who skilfully exploited the October Revolution to get out of jail. He managed to reach the Finnish border before he was identified there by a sailor. 'Are you by any chance Manasevich-Manuilov?' Manasevich hastily denied it. And was about to leave bloodied Russia for ever, but he had forgotten about Rasputin's 'heavy hand'. At that moment his old actress-lover, who was also going to Finland, walked into the room. Upon seeing Manasevich, she delightedly cried, 'Vanichka!' They executed Manasevich right there at the border.

The grand dukes Nikolai Mikhailovich and Pavel would also perish in 1919, men whose relatives had taken such a large part in the Rasputin story.

'On the night of 16 January . . . I suddenly awoke and distinctly heard my husband's voice: "I've been killed"' (from the memoirs of Pavel's wife, Olga). Beside the tombs of their ancestors, the great Russian tsars, they took the Bolshevik bullet. That bullet didn't forget Dzhunkovsky, either. He managed to survive the revolutionary period, but then the Stalinist terror came. The former gendarme chief, with his martial moustache, was at the time living in quiet poverty as a churchwarden. But the Stalinist broom swept cleanly. In 1938 Rasputin's enemy was taken to the Lubyanka Prison and the firing-squad wall.

The Survivors

The rascal Simanovich successfully got out of Russia and took his family with him. The elder's 'heavy hand' did not hinder him. It may be that Simanovich was protected by the gratitude of the dozens of Jews whom he had saved with Rasputin's help from punishment and the front, as well as that of the hundreds of other Jews for whom he had obtained, through Rasputin, permission to live normal lives in Petrograd. Whether for money, as the police claimed, or disinterestedly, as he himself maintained, he did help the disenfranchised. Iliodor also survived. Although it is unclear which was better: the bullet or the torments that were his portion. In America, to which he emigrated, he was a victim of the stock market crash of 1929, a terrible ruin that consumed all the money he received from his book on Rasputin. Then came the death of his son and divorce from his wife. He took monastic vows and entered a monastery in Melville, and was later seen in New York. He died in 1952, destitute and completely alone.

Vladimir Sabler, the former chief procurator of the Holy Synod who had been exiled to Tver, also survived the Red Terror. Although not for long. He lived by alms and died of starvation.

The Golovins continued to live quietly in Petrograd. After the death of

Father Grigory, they waited, like the tsarina, for universal punishment. And they were not surprised when the Bolsheviks came to power in October. Zhukovskaya recalled:

> I found Munya just as quiet and affectionate, with her usual twinkling gaze and even her invariable knitted cardigan, when I went to see her on the Moika, after accidentally finding myself in Petrograd immediately after the October Revolution. Nothing in the house had changed; even the little servant boy dozing in the vestibule and the vicious poodle, Cockroach, were in their places. I was taken to Munya's little room, and everything there was as of old, even Lokhtina's bed behind the screen and her staff with its little ribbons, although since Rasputin's death, she herself had been living continuously in Verkhoturye.

Here Zhukovskaya is mistaken. After the February Revolution, Lokhtina was detained. And contained in the File are documents pertaining to her arrest: 'On 8 March at the Oktai Cloister Rasputin's well-known follower . . . Olga Vladimirovna Lokhtina was arrested.' She was lodged in the Peter and Paul Fortress. But the Bolshevik coup freed her. And she set off again for Verkhoturye. But the Bolsheviks had obliterated the monastery. In 1923 she was seen in Petrograd at a train station. The former general's wife – an old woman in a torn and filthy shapeless dress but holding a tall staff – was aggressively begging for alms.

Zhukovskaya suffered misfortune, too. Mainly the death of her passionately loved husband. And in 1924, although still young, she left the city for good and took up residence in the village of Orekhovo in the Vladimir province. And there in the backwoods she lived the rest of her life as a voluntary recluse, as if atoning for some sin.

Vyrubova also lived as a recluse, in Finland. Having taken religious vows in secret, she lived by herself, almost never going out. She died in a Helsinki hospital in 1964 in absolute loneliness.

Despite the revolution and the terror, all of Rasputin's murderers escaped. None of them died from the bullet nor shared the fates of so many of his friends. Purishkevich died in his bed of typhoid fever during the civil war, and Grand Duke Dmitry also died in his bed in 1942 – one of the few Romanovs to survive the revolution intact. Prince Yusupov and Dr Lazavert passed comfortably away in Paris.

But memories of the peasant followed them to their graves. Marina Grey, General Denikin's daughter, told me a story about Dr Lazavert. The doctor had purchased an apartment in France. And he lived quietly in it, trying to

wipe out of his memory the nightmare of that evening. One summer he
went away on vacation. When he came back he saw that a new restaurant
had opened in his building. The restaurant was called 'Rasputin'.

The peasant continued to play a mystical role even in the lives of their
children. Felix Yusupov's granddaughter Xenia Nikolaevna told of a trip to
Greece her mother had taken after her marriage in 1946. Travelling under
her husband's name, she met the wife of the Dutch ambassador to Greece,
a charming Russian woman. They became inseparable friends. When the
time came time to part, the ambassador's wife told Yusupov's granddaughter,
'I want to reveal a bitter truth to you that it is possible may displease you.
The fact is, my grandfather was Grigory Rasputin' (she was one of Matryona
and Solovyov's daughters). 'My truth,' her friend replied, 'may perhaps
displease you even more. The fact is, my father murdered your grandfather.'

'Always Together, Never Alone'?

In death and after it Our Friend remained with the family.

The royal family would meet their deaths in a very similar basement to
that in the Yusupov palace. And in exactly the same way their bodies would,
after the bullets, know water (their corpses were first thrown into a flooded
mineshaft). And only later, like the peasant's remains, would they be
committed to the earth. Also like the corpse of Our Friend, the corpses of
the royal family would after the execution wander from place to place. And
during the search for a secret burial site, the truck carrying the royal family's
corpses would also suddenly get stuck, and a bonfire would be built to burn
their remains. As their murderer Yurovsky would write in his diary, 'Around
4:30 a.m. the vehicle got completely stuck . . . and it was left to bury or
burn them. We wanted to burn Alexei and Alexandra Fyodorovna, but
instead of the latter . . . we burned Demidova by mistake.'

Thus, the body of the heir, for whose sake the peasant had been called
to the palace, would also, like the corpse of his dangerous healer, know fire.
Bullets, water, earth, and fire. And as a symbol of Our Friend's presence,
Yurovsky saw amulets with the elder's face and his prayer on the grand
duchesses' unclad bodies. Amulets attached to their naked bodies like snares.

So, as a member all those years of the Government Commission for the
Funeral of the Royal Family, I often thought during the incomprehensible,
agonizing, many-yeared history of the non-interment of their remains:
might it be that he still hasn't left the royal family? That, as before, his heavy
hand remains stretched out over them?

The Precursor

Just who was that man, who appeared in the fire of the first revolution and perished on the eve of the second? He was undoubtedly a deeply religious person. And at the same time a great sinner. With the simplicity of a century of uneducated, ignorant Russian peasantry, he tried to combine the mysterious passions of the body with the teachings of Christ. And he ended up a sectarian, a *Khlyst*, a profligate, yet at the same time remaining a deeply religious person.

He was the epitome of the Russian's staggering ability to live upright within while enveloped in unceasing sin. Alexander Blok, who was employed by the Extraordinary Commission, wrote a celebrated 1914 poem about that blend of sin and religiosity.

> To sin shamelessly, endlessly,
> To lose count of the nights and days,
> And with a head unruly from drunkenness
> To pass sideways into the temple of God.
>
> Three times to bow down to the ground,
> Seven times to make the sign of the cross,
> To bow one's burning brow in secret
> Upon the bespittled floor.
>
> To put in the plate a copper coin,
> Three or even seven times in a row
> To kiss the hundred-year-old, poor
> Much kissed icon frame.

Happy suffering from the repentance of sin. And the scope of that suffering (and happiness) corresponds to the scope of the sin. Christ had abandoned Rasputin long before. But the peasant continued to pray, not realizing that for a long time he had been serving the Antichrist. And for that reason it was given to him to destroy the very legend of Holy Rus by disgracing the church and the power of the tsar who had been consecrated by it, and by joining his sinful name to that of God's anointed sovereign.

Rasputin is a key to understanding both the soul and the brutality of the Russia that came after him. He was a precursor of the millions of peasants who, with religious consciousness in their souls, would nevertheless tear down churches, and who, with a dream of the reign of Love and Justice, would murder, rape, and flood the country with blood, in the end destroying themselves.

AFTERWORD

In the city to which at the end of the twentieth century the name Saint Petersburg has been restored, I waited for the return of the last tsars. They were coming back in coffins from Ekaterinburg, the city that had executed them, to their own spectral city, the former capital of their drowned Atlantis.

And once again everything was as it had been in the peasant's day: the Romanov family divided, discord among the people, and the church hierarchs who were inexplicably opposed to the funeral.

And then the airport. A guard of honour stood in ranks, and the wind tore at the banner held by the standard bearer. And later, closer to the plane that had just arrived from Ekaterinburg, the Romanovs formed up, the great rulers' descendants who had survived the storm. As a member of the Government Commission for the Funeral of the Royal Family, I too was standing at the airport, and I was witnessing a remarkable thing for a writer: the funeral of his own characters.

Those who had flown in with the coffins from Ekaterinburg told how the coffins of the 'tsars' had been carried out of the cathedral, and how the heavens had suddenly opened with a pelting rain, a sheet of water over the church. And we who were meeting the coffins replied that in Petersburg, where the day before it had been rainy, the sun had been shining brilliantly all morning.

Everyone wanted miracles.

Then the funeral march burst forth. The cortege of buses with the royal coffins began to move. And the miracle was extended. The quarrels all vanished. And the entire city came out to meet them. People stood in an unbroken line, extending for many kilometres, from the airport all the way to the Peter and Paul Fortress. And there were people in the open windows of the buildings. And others were waiting on their knees. And the President, who the day before had refused to attend the funeral, had that day suddenly flown to Petersburg to repent before their coffins for all our evil deeds in the departing century.

They found their resting places in the Peter and Paul Cathedral – across the Neva river from their palace and among the tombs of their ancestors. And all Russia buried them that day. And in the country there was a long forgotten sense of joyful union, of a moved, happy ease. As if a stone had fallen away from the soul. As if some terrible spirit had at last released the 'tsars' and flown away from Russia for good.

Or was it only for a moment? And an illusion, after all?

Documentary Sources

The File

Purchased at a Sotheby's auction in 1995. Bound in hard cover. The cover is inscribed, 'Extraordinary Commission of Inquiry for the Investigation of Illegal Acts by Ministers and Other Responsible Persons of the Tsarist Regime. Investigative Section.'

All the interrogation records in the File are written on forms of the Extraordinary Commission and signed both by those interrogated and by the investigators. If an interrogation took place at a remote site, and the record was forwarded to the Extraordinary Commission, then it bears an Extraordinary Commission stamp and a document registration number.

The File consists of 426 numbered folios of double-sided interrogation records, so there are in fact 852 pages of documents.

The following interrogation records have been used in this book:

Feofan, Bishop of Poltava and Pereyaslavl (folios 7–20). The interrogation was conducted in the city of Poltava by V. V. Likhopoy, Senior Investigator for the Poltava Judicial District. Supplementary interrogations of Bishop Feofan were conducted in Petrograd by T. D. Rudnev, an investigator for the Extraordinary Commission (folios 219–20, 317–20). Handwritten text.

Ruschya Georgievich Mollov, former deputy minister of internal affairs (folios 22–5). The interrogation in the city of Poltava was conducted by V. V. Likhopoy, Senior Investigator for the Poltava Judicial District. Handwritten text.

Maria Timofeevna Belyaeva, Vyrubova's maid (folios 29–30, 48–9). The interrogation was conducted by I. V. Brykin, an investigator for the Extraordinary Commission. Handwritten text.

Akim Ivanovich Zhuk, a medical orderly who worked for Vyrubova (folios 31–6). The interrogation was conducted by I. V. Brykin, an investigator for the Extraordinary Commission. Handwritten text.

August Ventselovich Berchik, Vyrubova's servant (folios 37–40). The interrogation was conducted by I. V. Brykin, an investigator for the Extraordinary Commission. Handwritten text.

Maria Ivanovna Vishnyakova, who was employed as the nurse of the royal children (folios 43–5). The interrogation was conducted by T. D. Rudnev, an investigator for the Extraordinary Commission. Typed copy.

Zinaida Timofeevna Ivanova, Vyrubova's maid (folios 47–8). The interrogation was conducted by T. D. Rudnev. Handwritten text.

Feodosia Stepanovna Voino, a doctor's assistant who worked for Vyrubova (folios 50–2). The interrogation was conducted by I. V. Brykin. Handwritten text.

Alexander Mikhailovich Omerg, who worked as a footman in the Alexander Palace (folios 57–8). The interrogation was conducted by P. A. Korovichenko, commandant of the Alexander Palace. Handwritten text.

Andrei Andreevich Zeyer [Zeer], in charge of dispatching the royal family's carriages (folio 61). The interrogation was conducted by P. A. Korovichenko, commandant of the Alexander Palace.

Anna Alexandrovna Vyrubova, a maid of honour and a close friend of the tsarina's (folios 78–81). The interrogation was conducted by G. P. Girchich, an investigator for the Extraordinary Commission. Typed copy.

Iakov Pavlovich Kondratenko, who worked as a coachman for Rasputin's devotee Maria Andreevna Gayer [Gaer] (folios 84–5). The interrogation was conducted by G. P. Girchich. Handwritten text.

Konstantin Iakovlevich Chikhachev, a former deputy chief of the Saratov Judicial Chamber (folios 86–92). The interrogation was conducted by S. Filonenko-Borodin, Investigator for the Second Judicial District of the city of Orel.

Olga Vladimirovna Lokhtina, the wife of an actual state councillor and a devotee of Rasputin's (folios 100–4, 109–12). The interrogation was conducted by the investigator T. D. Rudnev. Typed copy.

Maria Evgenieva Golovina, a chamberlain's daughter and a devotee of Rasputin's (folios 113–22). The interrogation was conducted by the investigator T. D. Rudnev. Handwritten text.

Olga Vladimirovna Lokhtina (folios 130–4, 140–2). The interrogation was conducted by the investigator T. D. Rudnev. Handwritten text.

Baroness Vera Illarionovna Kusova, the wife of a cavalry captain and a devotee of Rasputin's (folios 135–8). The interrogation was conducted by T. D. Rudnev. Handwritten text.

Nadezhda Ivanovna Voskoboinikova, a Cossack officer's widow who worked in Vyrubova's infirmary (folios 154–62). The interrogation was conducted by T. D. Rudnev. Typed copy.

Vladimir Fyodorovich Dzhunkovsky, a former Deputy Minister of Internal Affairs (folios 164–5). The interrogation was conducted by the investigator T. D. Rudnev. Handwritten text.

Dmitry Nikolaevich Loman, a colonel assigned to court administration and the warden of the Feodorov Cathedral (folios 174–81). The interrogation was conducted by the investigator T. D. Rudnev. Typed copy.

Ioann Aronovich Simanovich, the son of Rasputin's secretary (folios 182–3). The interrogation was conducted by V. M. Rudnev. Handwritten text.

Ivan Fydorovich Manasevich-Manuilov, a former official of special commissions for the prime minister (folios 191–4). The interrogation was conducted by the investigator G. P. Girchich. Typed copy.

Ksenofont, Archimandrite of the Nikolaev-Verkhoturye Monastery (folios 210–13, 215–16). The interrogation was conducted by A. Pokrovsky, Judicial Investigator for the Ekaterinburg Regional Court. Handwritten text.

Sophia Ivanovna Tyutcheva, a maid of honour responsible for the royal daughters (folios 223–5). The interrogation was conducted by the investigator F. P. Simpson. Typed copy.

Alexander Pavlovich Martynov, a former head of the Moscow security branch. The interrogation was conducted by the prosecutor Yastrebov at the Moscow Correctional Prison. Handwritten text.

Vera Iovlevna Tregubova, a friend of Rasputin's (folios 246–51). The interrogation was conducted by A. I. Tsitovich, Judicial Investigator for the Tiflis Regional Court. Typed copy.

Alexandra Georgievna Guschina [Gushchina], a doctor's widow and a devotee of Rasputin's (folio 263). The interrogation was conducted by the investigator F. P. Simpson. Typed copy.

Leonid Alexeevich Molchanov, the son of the exarch of Georgia and a devotee of Rasputin's (folios 264–73). The interrogation was conducted by the investigator F. P. Simpson. Typed copy.

Pyotr Alexandrovich Badmaev, a doctor (folios 274–82). The interrogation was conducted by the investigator F. P. Simpson. Typed copy.

Mikhail Stepanovich Komissarov, a gendarme officer in charge of Rasputin's security (folios 286–96). The interrogation was conducted by the investigator V. V. Likhopoy. Typed copy.

Lydia Ivanovna Kondyreva, the widow of an actual state councillor (folios 297, 311). The interrogation was conducted by the investigator F. P. Simpson. Typed copy.

Grigory Petrovich Sazonov, an economist and publicist and a devotee of Rasputin's (folios 298–300). The interrogation was conducted by the investigator F. P. Simpson. Typed copy.

Alexei Nikolaevich Khvostov, a former minister of internal affairs (folios 302–10). The interrogation was conducted by the investigator F. P. Simpson. Typed copy.

Alexey Frolovich Filippov, a publisher and a devotee of Rasputin's (folios 327–42). The interrogation was conducted by the investigator F. P. Simpson. Typed copy.

Vera Karlovna Varvarova, a performer of Gypsy ballads and a friend of Rasputin's (folios 343–4). The interrogation was conducted by the investigator F. P. Simpson. Typed copy.

Anna Alexandrovna Vyrubova (folios 347–63). The interrogation was conducted by the investigator F. P. Simpson. Typed copy.

Yulia Alexandrovna Dehn [Den], a senior captain's wife, a friend of the tsarina's, and a devotee of Rasputin's (folios 364–7). The interrogation was conducted by the investigator F. P. Simpson. Typed copy.

Sheila Gershevna Lunts, a barrister's wife and a friend of Rasputin's (folios 375–7). The interrogation was conducted by the investigator F. P. Simpson. Typed copy.

Isaak Viktorovich Bykhovsky, a barrister (folio 378). The interrogation was conducted by the investigator F. P. Simpson. Typed copy.

Alexander Stepanovich Prugavin, an ethnographer and publicist and an expert on Russian sectarianism (folios 389–90). The interrogation was conducted by the investigator F. P. Simpson. Typed copy.

Victor Ivanovich Yatskevich, a former director of the chancery of the chief procurator of the Most Holy Synod (folios 391–7). The interrogation was conducted by the investigator F. P. Simpson. Typed copy.

Nikolai Pavlovich Sablin, a senior captain and the master of the royal yacht *Standart* (folios 419–21). The interrogation was conducted by the investigator F. P. Simpson. Typed copy.

Olga Apollonovna Popova, clergyman's wife (folios 424–6). The interrogation was conducted by Rybalsky, an investigator for the Simferopol Regional Court. Typed copy.

Record of the inspection by the investigator G. N. Girchich of the documents seized from Vyruvbova's apartment (folio 42). Typed copy.

Record of the inspection on 21 March 1917, of the rooms occupied by Vyrubova by Lt. Colonel Korovichenko, commandant of the Alexander Palace in Tsarskoe Selo (folios 55–6). Handwritten text.

Inventory of the letters and other materials confiscated from O. V. Lokhtina upon her arrest (folio 72). Typed copy.

Memorandum from Baron Budberg of 23 December 1906, granting G. E. Rasputin the right henceforth to call himself Rasputin-Novy (folio 128). Typed copy.

Copies of the documents pertaining to the row produced by Rasputin at the restaurant, Yar. Typed.

Archival Documents By Repository And File Number

STATE ARCHIVE OF THE RUSSIAN FEDERATION (GARF)

601 Nicholas II
640 Empress Alexandra Fyodorovna
673 Grand Duchess Olga Nikolaevna
613 Princess Olga Valerianovna Paley [Palei]
645 Grand Duke Alexander Mikhailovich
662 Grand Duchess Xenia Alexandrovna
656 Grand Duchess Elizaveta Fyodorovna
660 Grand Duke Konstantin Konstantinovich (KR)
670 Grand Duke Nikolai Mikhailovich

612 Grigory Rasputin
623 A. A. Vyrubova
102 Department of Police
111 Petersburg (Petrograd) security branch
1467 Extraordinary Commission of the Provisional Government

TOBOLSK BRANCH OF THE STATE ARCHIVE OF THE PROVINCE OF TYUMEN (TFGATO)

164 Investigation file of the assassination attempt on Grigory Rasputin in 1914
154 Inventory of Grigory Rasputin's property after his death
156 File of the Tobolsk Ecclesiastical Consistory in regard to the charge against G. E. Rasputin of 'spreading false teachings similar to those of the *Khlysty*'

STATE ARCHIVE OF THE PROVINCE OF TYUMEN (GATO)

205 Birth register with Rasputin's birth date
239 Reports of the external surveillance agents on Grigory Rasputin's visits to the village of Pokrovskoe

STATE HISTORICAL MUSEUM

411 Correspondence of Nikolai and Felix Yusupov with Marina Heiden [Geiden]
411 Correspondence of Felix Yusupov with Marina Golovina
411 Letters of Felix Yusupov to his wife, Irina, pertaining to the murder of G. E. Rasputin

RUSSIAN STATE ARCHIVE FOR OLD DOCUMENTS

1290 Irina's letters to Felix Yusupov

RUSSIAN STATE HISTORICAL ARCHIVE

1101 Rasputin's diary

Bibliography

English-Language Sources

Alexander, Grand Duke of Russia. *Once a Grand Duke*. London, 1932.

Alexandrov, V. *The End of the Romanovs*. Boston, 1967.

Benkendorff, P. *The Last Days of Tsarskoe Selo*. London, 1927.

Botkin, G. *The Real Romanovs*. New York, 1931.

Buchanan, G. *My Mission to Moscow*. London, 1923.

Chachavadze, D. *The Grand Dukes*. New York, 1990.

Cyril, Grand Duke. *My Life in Russia's Service*. London, 1939

Dehn, Lili. *The Real Tsaritsa*. London, 1992.

De Jonge, Alex. *The Life and Times of Grigorii Rasputin*. New York, 1982.

Fuhrmann, Joseph T. *Rasputin: A Life*. New York and London, 1990.

Gilliard, Pierre. *Thirteen Years at the Russian Court*. New York, 1921.

Kerensky, Alexander. *The Crucifixion of Liberty*. New York, 1934.

King, Greg. *The Man Who Killed Rasputin: Prince Felix Youssoupov and the Murder That Helped Bring Down the Russian Empire*. Secaucus, N. J., 1995.

Le Queux, William. *The Rascal Monk*. London, 1919.

Marie, Grand Duchess of Russia (Marie Pavlovna Romanova). *Education of a Princess: A Memoir*. New York, 1931.

Massie, Robert K. *Nicholas and Alexandra*. New York, 1967.

Maylunas, A., and S. Mironenko. *A Lifelong Passion: Nicholas and Alexandra*. London, 1996.

Minney, R. J. *Rasputin*. London, 1972.

Moynahan, Brian. *Rasputin: The Saint Who Sinned*. New York, 1997.

Nicholas II. *The Secret Letters of the Last Tsar: The Confidential Correspondence between Nicholas and His Mother*. New York, 1938.

Paley, Princess Olga. *Memories of Russia*. London, 1924.

Pipes, Richard. *Russia under the Old Regime*. New York, 1974.

Radziwill, Catherine. *Nicholas II: The Last of the Tsars*. London, 1931.

Rasputin, Maria. *My Father*. London, 1934.

—, and Patte Barham. *Rasputin: The Man behind the Myth: A Personal Memoir*. Englewood Cliffs, 1977.

Richards, G. *The Hunt for the Czar*. New York, 1970.

Vassilyev, A. T. *The Ochrana: The Russian Secret Police*. Philadelphia, 1930.

Wilson, Colon. *Rasputin and the Fall of the Romanovs*. New York, 1964.

Yusupov, Prince Felix. *Rasputin: His Malignant Influence and Assassination*. New York, 1927.

—. *Lost Splendour*. London, 1953.

Russian-Language Sources

Al'bionov. *Zhitie nepodobnogo startsa Grigoriia Rasputina*. Petrograd, 1917.

Aleksin, S. A. *Sviatoi chert (Blagodat' Grishki Rasputina): Zhitie v 1–m deistvii*. Moscow, 1917.

Alfer'ev, E. E. *Pis'ma tsarskoi cem'i iz zatochen'ia*. Jordanville, N.Y., 1984.

Almazov, B. *Rasputin i Rossiia: Istoricheskaia spravka*. St Petersburg, 1990.

Azadovskii, K. *Nikolai Kliuev*. Leningrad, 1990.

Bashilov, B. *Istoriia russkogo masonstva*. Moscow, 1992.

Beletskii, S. P. *Grigorii Rasputin (Iz zapisok)*. Moscow, 1923.

—. 'Vospominaniia.' In *Arkhiv Russkoi Revoliutsii*, vol. 12. Berlin, 1923.

Belling, A. *Iz nedavnego proshlogo (Vospominaniia)*. Moscow, 1993.

Berberova, N. *Liudi i lozhi. Russkie masony XX veka*. New York, 1986.

Betskii, K., and P. Pavlov. *Russkii Rokombol' (I. F. Manasevich–Manuilov)*. Leningrad, 1927.

Blok, A. A. *Zapisnye knizhki*. Moscow, 1965.

Bogdanovich, A. V. *Tri poslednikh samoderzhtsa: Dnevnik A. V. Bogdanovich*. Moscow and Leningrad, 1924.

Bok (Stolypina), M. P. *P. A. Stolypin. Vospominaniia o moem ottse*. Moscow, 1922.

Bonch-Bruevich, V. D. 'O Rasputine,' *Den'* [Petrograd], 1 July 1914.

Borisov, D., *Vlastiteli i chudotvortsy (Iliodor, Germogen i Rasputin)*. Saratov, 1926.

Bostunich, G. V. *Otchego Rasputin dolzhen byl poiavit'sa: obosnobaniia psikhologicheskoi neizbezhnosti*. Petrograd, 1917.

—. *Masonstvo i russkaia revoliutsiia. Pravda misticheskaia i pravda real'naia*. Moscow, 1993.

Budberg, A. *Dnevnik belogvardeitsa*. Leningrad, 1929.

Bunin, I. A. *Sobranie sochinenii*. Moscow, 1988.

Chernyshov, A. V. *Grigorii Rasputin v vospominaniiakh sovremennikov*. Moscow and Tyumen, 1990.

—. 'Zhitie nepodobnovo startsa.' *Tiumen' literaturnaia* 2, 3 (1990).

Danilov, IU. N. *Na puti k krusheniiu*. Moscow, 1992.

'Delo ob ischeznovenii krest'ianina Grigoriia Efimova Rasputina.' *Byloe* 1 (1917).

Diterikhs, M. K. *Ubiistvo tsarskoi sem'i i chlenov Doma Romanovykh na Urale*. Part 1. Vladivostok, 1922.

Durnovo, N. N. 'Kto etot krest'ianin Grigorii Rasputin?' *Otkliki na zhizn'* [Moscow], 11–12 (September–October 1914).

Dzhanumova, E. F. *Moi vstrechi s Rasputinym*. Moscow, 1990.

Dzhunkovskii, V. F. *Vospominaniia*. 2 vols. Moscow, 1997.

Epanchin, N. A. *Na sluzhbe trekh imperatorov*. Moscow, 1996.

'Episkop Varnava.' *Vechernii kur'er* [Moscow] 348 (1915).

Etkind, A. *Khlyst*. Moscow, 1998.

Evreinov, N. N. *Taina Rasputina*. Moscow, 1989.

Faleev, V. 'Za chto ubili Grigoriia?' In *Dorogami tysiacheletii*. Vyp. 4. Moscow, 1991.

Fiulop-Miller, Rene. *Sviatoi d'iavol: Rasputin i zhenshchiny*. St Petersburg, 1994.

Gariazin, A. L. 'V. M. Skvortsovu. Otkrytoe pis'mo.' *Dym Otechestva* [Petrograd], 13 July 1913.

Gavrilov, A. K. 'Predmet vserossiiskoi spletni.' *Dym Otechestva*, 26 July 1914.

Grigorii Rasputin i misticheskoe rasputstvo: sbornik statei. Preface by M. A. Novoselov. Moscow, 1912.

Grigorii Rasputin. Sbornik istoricheskikh materialov. 4 vols. Moscow, 1997.

Grigorii Rasputin v vospominaniiakh sovremennikov. Sbornik. Moscow, 1990.

Grigorii Rasputin v vospominaniiakh uchastnikov i ochevidtsev: iz materialov Chrezvychai–noi komissii Vremennogo pravitel'stva. Moscow, 1990.

Gurko V. I. *Tsar' i tsaritsa*. Paris, 1927.

Iasenetskii, G. *Za kulisami velikoi katastrofy*. San Francisco, no date.

Iliodor (S. M. Trufanov). 'Sviatoi chert.' *Golos minuvshego* (1917).

Iusupov, F. *Konets Rasputina. Vospominaniia*. Moscow, 1990.

Kak khoronili Rasputina. Kiev, 1917.

'Kazn' Grishki Rasputina.' In *Al'manakh 'Svoboda'*, vyp. 1. Petrograd, 1917.

Kerenskii, A. F. *Rossiia na istoricheskom povorote. Memuary*. Moscow, 1993.

Khersonskii. *Akafist Grishke Rasputinu*. Petrograd, 1917.

Kokovtsev, V. N. *Iz moego proshlogo. Vospominaniia*. 2 vols. Moscow, 1992.

Kovalevskii, P. *Grishka Rasputin*. Moscow, 1922.

Kovyl'-Bobyl', I. *Tsaritsa i Rasputin*. Petrograd, 1917.

—. *Vsia pravda o Rasputine*. Petrograd, 1917.

Kozlov, N. *Drug tsarei*. 1994.

Krivorotov, V. *Pridvornyi iuvelir (Strashnoe igo): Rasputiniada i ee sekretar'*. Madrid, 1975.

Kurlov, P. G. *Konets russkogo tsarizma: Vospominaniia byvshego komandira korpusa zhandarmov*. Moscow and Leningrad, 1923.

Lamzdorf, V. N. *Dnevnik*. Moscow, 1934.

Lemke, M. K. *250 dnei v tsarkoi stavke*. Petrograd, 1920.

Leontovich, V. V. *Istoriia liberalizma v Rossii*. Moscow, 1995.

Likhachev, D., et al. *Smekh v Drevnei Rusi*. Leningrad, 1984.

Markov, S. V. *Pokinutaia tsarskaia sem'ia*. Vienna, 1928.

Materialy k zhitiiu prepodobnoi velikomuchenitsy Elizavety Fedorovny. Pis'ma, dnevniki, vospominaniia. Moscow, 1996.

Mech (Mendelevich), R. A. *Golos s togo sveta, ili Grishka Rasputin v gostiakh u satany*. Moscow, 1917.

Mel'gunov, S. P. *Na putiakh k dvortsovomu perevorotu (zagovory pered revoliutsiei 1917 goda)*. Paris, 1931.

—. *Nikolai II. Materialy dlia kharakteristiki lichnosti i tsarstvovaniia*. Moscow, 1917.

Mel'gunov, S. P., and N. P. Sidorov, eds. *Masonstvo v ego proshlom i nastoiashchem.* Moscow, 1914.

Mel'nik (Botkina), T. E. *Vospominaniia o tsarskoi sem'e i ee zhizni do i posle revoliutsii.* Belgrade, 1921.

Miliukov, P. N. *Istoriia vtoroi russkoi revoliutsii.* Sofia, 1921–4.

——. *Vospominaniia.* Moscow, 1993.

Mosolov, A. A. *Pri dvore imperatora.* Moscow, 1992.

Nabokov, V. D., trans. *Pis'ma imperatritsy Aleksandry Fedorovny k imperatoru Nikolaiu II.* 2 vols. Berlin, 1922.

Nilus, S. A. *Dukhovnye ochi. Iz besed so startsami.* Sergiev Posad, 1906.

——. *Na beregu Bozh'ei reki.* 2 vols. Moscow, 1969–75.

——. *Protokoly Sionskikh mudretsov.* Berlin, 1922.

——. *Sila Bozhiia i nemosh' chelovecheskaia (Optinskii starets Feodosii).* Sergiev Posad, 1908.

——. *Velikoe v malom, i Antikhrist, kak blizkaia politicheskaia vozmozhnost'.* Tsarskoe Selo, 1905.

Novaia knizhka o 'sviatom cherte' Grishke, ob Nikolae bezgolovom, glupom i bestolkovom, ob Alise–nemke, chto snimala s russkikh penki, o ministrakh–predateliakh i vsekh pridvor–nykh obitataliakh. Moscow, 1917.

Ol'denburg, S. S. *Tsarstvovanie imperatora Nikolaia 2.* Moscow, 1992.

Ostretsov, V. *Chernaia sotnia i krasnaia sotnia.* Moscow, 1991.

Padenie tsarskogo rezhima. Stenograficheskie otchety doprosov i pokazanii, dannykh v 1917 gody Chrezvychainoi sledstvennoi komissii Vremennogo pravitel'stva. 7 vols. Moscow and Leningrad, 1924–7.

Paleolog, M. *Rasputin. Vospominaniia.* Moscow, 1990.

——. *Tsarskaia Rossiia nakanune mirovoi voiny.* Moscow, 1923.

Perepiska Nikolaia 2 i Alexandry Romanovykh. Vols. 3–5. Moscow and Leningrad, 1923–7.

'Perepiska Nikolaia 2 i Marii Fedorovny.' *Krasnyi Arkhiv* (1927).

'Perepiska Nikolaia 2 i P. A. Stolypina.' *Krasnyi Arkhiv* 5 (1924).

'Pis'ma kniagini O. V. Palei.' *Istochnik* 6 (1994).

Platonov, O. A. *Ternovyi venets Rossii.* Moscow, 1995.

——. *Zhizn' za tsar: Pravda o Grigorii Rasputine.* St Petersburg, 1996.

'Poezdka v Sarov.' *Golos minuvshego* 4/6 (1918).

Poslednie dni Rasputina. Arkhangel'sk, 1917.

Poslednii samoderzhets. Berlin, no date.

'Postanovlenie sledovatelia ChSK F. Simpsona o deiatel'nosti Rasputina i ego priblizhennykh lits i vliianii ikh na Nikolaia 2 v oblasti upraveleniia gosudarstvom.' *Voprosy istorii* 10, 12 (1964) and 1, 3 (1965).

Prugavin, A. S. *Leontii Egorovich i ego poklonnitsy.* Moscow, 1916.

——. *Starets Grigorii Rasputin i ego poklonnitsy.* Samara, 1993.

P. Sh. *Grigorii Rasputin: ego zhizn', rol' pri dvore imperatora Nikolaia Vtorovo i vliianie na sud'bu Rossii.* Moscow, 1917.

Purishkevich, V. M. *Dnevnik.* Moscow, 1990.

Ramazanov, V. V. *Nochnye orgii Rasputina (Tsarskii chudotvorets): Byl' v odnom deistvii.* Petrograd, 1917.

Rasputin, G. E. *Blagochestivye razmyshleniia.* St Petersburg, 1912.

—. *Dukhovnoe nasledie: Izbrannye stat'i, besedy, mysli i izrecheniia.* 1994.

—. *Moi mysli i razmyshleniia. Kratkoe opisanie puteshestviia po sviatym mestam.* Petrograd, 1915.

—. *Velikie torzhestva v Kieve! Poseshchenie Vysochaishei Sem'i! Angel'skii privet!* St Petersburg, 1911.

—. *Zhitie opytnogo strannika.* 1907.

Rodzianko, N. *Krushenie imperii.* Leningrad, 1927.

Romanov A. V. 'Dnevnik velikogo kniazia Nikolaia Mikhailovicha.' *Krasnyi Arkhiv* 4, 6, 9 (1931).

Rom-Lebedev, I. I. 'Zapiski moskovskovo tsygana.' *Teatr* 3, 4, 6–8 (1985).

Rudnev, V. M. 'Pravda o tsarskoi sem'e.' *Russkaia letopis'* 2 (1922).

Semennikov, V. P. *Romanovy i germanskie vliianiia vo vremia mirovoi voiny.* Leningrad, 1929.

—. *Monarkhiia pered krusheniem.* Leningrad, 1931.

Shavel'skii, G. *Vospominaniia poslednego protopresvitera russkoi armii i flota.* New York, 1954.

Shchegolev, P. E. *Poslednii reis Nikolaia II.* Moscow and Leningrad, 1928.

Shulenberg, V. E. *Vospominaniia ob imperatritse Alexandre Fedorovne.* Paris, 1928.

Shul'gin, V. V. *Dni. 1920.* Moscow, 1989.

Simanovich, A. *Rasputin i evrei: Vospominaniia byvshego sekretaria Grigoriia Rasputina.* Riga, 1928.

Smertel'naia iazva russkogo samoderzhaviia (Grigorii Rasputin). Kazan, 1917.

Sokolov, N. A. *Ubiistvo tsarskoi sem'i.* Berlin, 1925.

Stolypin, P. A. *Nam nuzhna velikaia Rossiia. Polnoe sobranie rechei v Gosudarstvennoi Dume i Gosudarstvennom Sovete.* Moscow, 1991.

Struve, P. B. *Razmyshleniia o russkoi revoliutsii.* Sofia, 1931.

Sukhomlinov, V. A. *Vospominaniia.* Berlin, 1924.

Shaika shpinov Rossii i gnusnye dela Grishki Rasputina. Moscow, 1917.

'Sviatoi chert': Rasputin, Grishka, zloi genii Doma Romanovykh. Moscow, 1917.

Sviatoi chert. Taina Grigoriia Rasputina. Vospominaniia. Dokumenty. Materialy sledstvennoi komissii. Moscow, 1991.

Taina Doma Romanovykh ili Pokhozhdeniia Grigoriia Rasputina. Kiev, 1917.

Taina vliianiia Grishki Rasputina: Grishka i zhenshchiny. Petrograd, 1917.

'Tainy Doma Romanovykh.' In *Al'manakh 'Svoboda',* vyp. 2. Petrograd, 1917

Tainy tsarskogo dvortsa i Grishka Rasputin. Moscow, 1917.

Teffi, Nadezhda (N. A. Buchinskaia). *Zhit'e–byt'e.* Moscow, 1991.

Temnye sily starogo rezhima. Grigorii Rasputin. Feodosia, 1917.

Temnye sily. Tainy rasputinogo dvora. Rasputin. Petrograd, 1917.

Tikhmenev, N. *Vospominaniia o polednikh dniakh prebyvaniia Nikolaia II v stavke.* Nice, 1925.

Tiutcheva, A. F. *Pri dvore dvykh imperatorov.* Moscow, 1990.

Tolstoi, A. N., and P. E. Shchegolev. *Zagovor imperatritsy. P'esa.* Moscow, 1926.

Trotskii, L. D. *Russkaia revoliutsiia.* New York, 1932.

Ubiistvo Stolypina. Svidel'stva i dokumenty. Riga, 1990.

'U Grigoriia Rasputina.' *Novoe vremia* 12/90 (1912).

Uspenskii, K. N. 'Ocherk tsarstvovaniia Nikolaia II.' *Golos minuvshego* 4 (1917).

Vasilevskii, M. *Grigorii Rasputin.* Moscow, 1917.

Vin'erg, F. A. *Krestnyi put'. Chast' 1—Korni zla.* 2nd ed. Munich, 1922.

Vitte, S. IU. *Vospominaniia.* 2 vols. Moscow, 1960.

Voeikov, V. N. *S tsarem i bez tsaria.* Helsingfors, 1936.

Vonliarokii, V. *Moi vospominaniia. 1852–1939 gg.* Berlin.

'Vospominaniia sovremennikov ob ubiistve Rasputina.' Istochnik 3 (1993).

Vyrubova, A. A. *Stranitsy iz moei zhizni.* Berlin, 1923.

Za kulisami tsarizma (Arkhiv tibetskogo vracha Badmaeva). Leningrad, 1925.

Zhdanov, L. G. *Nikolai Romanov—poslednii tsar'.* Petrograd, 1917.

Zhevakhov, N. D. *S. A. Nilus: Kratkii ocherk zhizni i deiatel'nosti.* Novi Sad, 1936.

Zhevakhov, N. D. *Vospominaniia Tovarishcha Ober–Prokurora Sviashchennogo Sinoda kniazia Zhevakhova.* Vol. 1. Munich, 1923.

Zhil'iar, P. *Imperator Nikolai 2 i ego sem'ia.* Moscow, 1992.

—. *Tragicheskaia syd'ba russkoi imperatorskoi familii.* Tallinn, 1921.

'Zhitie i chudesa pravednogo Simeona Verkhoturskogo—chudotvortsa.' *Zhitia sviatykh na russkom iazyke, izlozhennye po rukovodstvu Chet'ikh–Minei Sviatogo Dmitriia Rostovskogo, Sentiabr'.* Moscow, 1902.

'Zhitie Simeona, Khrista radi iurodivogo, i Ioanna, spostnika ego.' *Zhitiia sviatykh na russkom iazyke, izlozhennye po rukovodstvu Chet'ikh–Minei Sviatogo Dimitriia Rostovskogo.* Moscow, 1904.

Zhizn' i pokhozhdeniia Grigoriia Rasputina. Kiev, 1917.

Zhukovskaia, V. A. *Moi vospominaniia o Grigorii Efimoviche Rasputine. 1914–1916.*

Index